DAIDALIKON

STUDIES IN MEMORY

of

RAYMOND V. SCHODER, S.J.

Raymond V. Schoder, S.J. 1916–1987

DAIDALIKON

STUDIES IN MEMORY
of
RAYMOND V. SCHODER, S.J.

Edited By
ROBERT F. SUTTON, JR.

BOLCHAZY-CARDUCCI PUBLISHERS
Wauconda, Illinois

Paperback Cover by Thom Kapheim

BOLCHAZY-CARDUCCI PUBLISHERS
1000 Brown Street, Unit 101
Wauconda, Illinois 60084

Printed in the United States of America

International Standard Book Number:

Hardbound 0-86516-200-X
Softbound 0-86516-201-8

Library of Congress Catalog Number:
88-62693

Library of Congress Cataloging-in-Publication Data

Daidalikon : Studies in memory of Raymond V. Schoder, S.J. / edited by Robert F. Sutton, Jr.
p. cm.
Consists chiefly of papers presented at Schoderfest, held at Loyola University of Chicago on April 11-12, 1986.
Includes bibliographical references.
ISBN 0-86516-200-X : $49.00. — ISBN 0-86516-201-8 (pbk.) : $29.00
1. Civilization, Classical—Congresses. 2. Schoder, Raymond V., 1916-1987—Congresses. I. Schoder, Raymond V., 1916-1987. II. Sutton, Robert F. (Robert Franklin) III. Schoderfest (1986 : Loyola University of Chicago)
DE59.D35 1989
938—dc20 88-62693
CIP

CONTENTS

PREFACE

This volume represents the tangible result of Schoderfest, a celebration held at Loyola University of Chicago on April 11–12, 1986 in honor of the seventieth birthday of Father Raymond V. Schoder, S.J., Professor Emeritus in the Department of Classical Studies. Most of the papers included here were delivered before an audience of several hundred former students, colleagues, and friends, who came from as far as Tokyo and Rome to participate. It unfortunately proved impossible to print here the presentations of Brunilde S. Ridgway on the bronze statuary from the Porticello wreck and Kevin Glowacki on "Marsyas, Dionysos, and Dithyramb." That loss is offset, however, by the inclusion of Father Schoder's bibliography together with papers that could not be delivered in person, those by J.A. Brinkman, J. DeVoto, S. Dow, J. Kilgallen, B. Lavelle, A. MacGregor, G. Nagy, P. Properzio, and the undersigned.

A sad final addition is the eulogy of Father Schoder by the Reverend Robert Wild, S.J., Provincial of the Chicago Province of the Society of Jesus. None of us involved in Schoderfest could foresee that within little more than a year the honoree would be gone, and that our honorary volume would become his posthumous memorial. Although he would not see this volume in print, Father Schoder knew that it was imminent and was able to read all but one of the scholarly contributions himself.

When this project began, I little suspected the full range of Father Schoder's activity it would reveal. His own bibliography and the reflection of its range through the papers of this volume provide ample testimony both to his many-faceted intellect and his ability to inspire others to follow him in such diverse directions. Though his contributions to scholarship are scarcely negligible, they easily pale in comparison to his role in tirelessly spreading the word—not only in the classroom, but also to the public at large through his books, articles, over a thousand public lectures, and service to any number of professional organizations. The successive editions and translations of his works tax the bibliographer and testify to the global audience he has reached in several fields.

It is not easy to capture a man's life briefly. In recalling Father Schoder one is reminded first of πολύτροπος Odysseus created by his beloved Homer, and also of Daedalus to whom he compared himself in suggesting the title of this volume. Both figures of myth share Father's facile intellect, his wide travel, and even his favored modes of transportation. Yet, another, historical figure of philosophy also suggests himself for comparison—Chairephon as described by Socrates in Plato's *Apology*: καὶ ἴστε δὴ οἷος ἦν . . . , ὡς σφοδρὸς ἐφ' ὅ τι ὁρμήσειεν, "you know what sort of man he was, how energetic about whatever he undertook." Father Schoder was indeed σφοδρός, and it was this energetic, almost fanatical enthusiasm that fired his many labors and inspired so many of us working in several fields. He will be missed.

An undertaking as complex as this volume and the celebration it commemorates could not have succeeded without considerable assistance. Thanks go first to the authors for their participation, promptness, and patience; I have sought to allow them their own voices, even at some cost in editorial uniformity. Next, special gratitude is expressed to those providing the necessary funds: Loyola University of Chicago, particularly Dr. Alice B. Hayes, Associate Academic Vice President, who always found a way, Dr. Thomas Bennett, Director of Research Services, and Fr. Lawrence Biondi, S.J., former Dean of the College of Arts and Sciences; and the Chicago Providence of the Society of Jesus, and its Provincial, the Very Reverend Robert A. Wild, S. J. At Loyola University the Department of Classical Studies and its members deserve special mention, especially the Chair, Dr. Edwin Menes, and the secretary, Mrs. Mari O'Brien, as well as Dr. James Keenan, Dr. John Makowski, Dr. Brian Lavelle, Dr. JoAnn Sweeney, Fr. John Murphy, Mr. Joseph Orth, Ms. Christina Thurston, and Mr. Mark McIntyre. I am grateful to the Office of Research Services, directed by Dr. Thomas Bennett and Dr. Timothy Austin, for typing the manuscripts onto computer disk to ease typesetting, and especially to Ms. Sheila Honda, who oversaw the process. Thanks also to Dr. Victor Edmonds and Ms. Patti Schor of the Center for Instructional Design for advice and help with illustration. Photographic copy work was performed by Ms. Marcy Paul, and keylining by Mr. Michael Cabonce. We are also grateful for the kindness of those who permitted us to reproduce illustrations; individual credit is provided *ad loc*. Dr. Alexander MacGregor has provided kind advice on all matters. Special thanks are owed to the Publications Office of the American School of Classical Studies at Athens for preparing camera-ready copy. I am particularly indebted to two of the staff: Mr. Mark Rose, who provided editorial assistance and saw the articles into galleys, and Dr. Sarah George Figueira, who carried the work to completion after his departure for *Archaeology*; I would have been lost without their help. Finally, Dr. Ladislaus Bolchazy and Bolchazy-Carducci Publishers deserve great praise for undertaking to issue this volume, whose only certain reward is intangible.

ROBERT F. SUTTON, JR.

Ὡς τὰ γενέθλια σοῦ, πάτερ, ὑμνοῦμεν διὰ αὐλάς
μνῆμά τέ σοι ἀρετῆς, σοί τε χάριν φιλίων·
ὃς νῦν, ὡς Ὀδυσεύς, πλάγχθης διὰ ἄστεα καὶ γῆν
ἀνδρῶν ἀλλοτρίων—Χριστῷ πειθόμενος—
ταῦθ' ἵνα δὴ ἡμᾶς νεαροὺς ἐρααν καλὸν αἰεί
παιδεύσαις προφέρων, καὶ ἀγαθὸν φιλέειν.
ὦ πάτερ ἐσθλ' ἡμῶν, τόδε τοι κρήηνον ἐέλδωρ·
ἑπτάδα περ δέκ' ἐτῶν ζῇς ὡς ἑπταφαής.

Composed for Father Schoder's fortieth birthday by R. Mackowski, S.J. and F.T. Gignac, S.J.; adapted for Schoderfest by E.P. Menes.

LIST OF ABBREVIATIONS

AA = *Archäologischer Anzeiger.*

AbhBerl = *Abhandlungen der Deutschen Akademie der Wissenschaften zu Berlin.*

AbhLeip = *Abhandlungen der Sächsischen Akademie der Wissenschaften zu Leipzig, Philologisch-historische Klasse.*

ABV = J.D. Beazley, *Attic Black-figure Vase-painters* (Oxford: Clarendon 1956).

ActaAbo = *Acta Academiae Aboensis, Ser. A. Humaniora.*

AfO = *Archiv für Orientforschung.*

Agora = *The Athenian Agora. Results of Excavations Conducted by the American School of Classical Studies at Athens.*

AHR = *American Historical Review.*

AJA = *American Journal of Archaeology.*

AJP = *American Journal of Philology.*

AJSemL = *American Journal of Semitic Languages and Literatures.*

AM = *Mitteilengen des Deutschen Archäologischen Instituts, Athenische Abteilung.*

AmEcclRev = *American Ecclesiastical Review*

AMIran = *Archäologische Mitteilungen aus Iran.*

AnatSt = *Anatolian Studies. Journal of the British Institute of Archaeology at Ankara.*

AncW = *The Ancient World.*

ANRW = H. Temporini ed., *Aufstieg und Niedergang der römischen Welt* (Berlin: de Gruyter 1972–).

AntCl = *L'Antiquité classique*

AntK = *Antike Kunst.*

ArchEph = Αρχαιολογική Εφημερίς.

ArchNews = *Archaeological News.*

ArchRW = *Archiv für Religionswissenschaft.*

ArtB = *The Art Bulletin.*

ARV[2] = J. D. Beazley, *Attic Red-figure Vase-painters*, 2nd ed. (Oxford: Clarendon 1963).

BaBesch = *Bulletin Antieke Beschaving. Annual Papers on Classical Archaeology.*

BaM = *Baghdader Mitteilungen.*

BCH = *Bulletin de correspondance hellénique.*

Beazley Addenda = L. Burn and R. Glynn, *Beazley Addenda. Additional References to* ABV, ARV[2] *and* Paralipomena (Oxford: Oxford University Press for the British Academy: 1982)

BEFAR = *Bibliothèque des Écoles Française d'Athènes et de Rome.*

BICS = *Bulletin of the Institute of Classical Studies of the University of London.*
BonnJbb = *Bonner Jahrbücher des Rheinischen Landesmuseums in Bonn und des Vereins von Altertumsfreunden im Rheinlande.*
BPW = *Berliner philologische Wochenschrift.*
BSA = *The Anuual of the British School at Athens.*
CAH = *Cambridge Ancient History.*
CathW = *Catholic World.*
CB = *Classical Bulletin.*
CIA = *Corpus Inscriptionum Atticarum.*
CIG = *Corpus Inscriptionum Graecarum.*
CJ = *Classical Journal.*
ClMed = *Classica et mediaevalia. Revue danoise de philologie et d'histoire.*
CQ = *Classical Quarterly.*
CR = *Classical Review.*
CSCA = *California Studies in Classical Antiquity.*
CVA = *Corpus Vasorum Antiquorum.*
CW = *Classical Weekly*; later *The Classical World.*
DarSag = C. Daremberg and E. Saglio, *Dictionnaire des antiquités grecques et romaines* (Paris: Hachette 1875–1919).
Délos = *Exploration archéologique de Délos faite par l'École Française d'Athènes.*
EAA = *Enciclopedia dell'arte antica, classica e orientale* (Rome: Istituto della Enciclopedia Italiana 1958–1966).
FdD = *Fouilles de Delphes, École Française d'Athènes.*
FGrHist = F. Jacoby, *Fragmente der griechischen Historiker* (Berlin: Weidmann 1926–1958).
G&R = *Greece and Rome.*
GRBM = *Greek, Roman and Byzantine Monographs.*
GRBS = *Greek, Roman and Byantine Studies.*
HistB = *Historical Bulletin*
HSCP = *Harvard Studies in Classical Philology.*
HZ = *Historische Zeitschrift*
ICr = *Inscritiones Creticae.*
ICS = *Illinois Classical Studies*
IG = *Inscriptiones Graecae.*
IJNA = *International Journal of Nautical Archaeology and Underwater Exploration.*
ILS = Dessau, *Inscriptiones Latinae Selectae.*
IrAnt = *Iranica antiqua.*
JAOS = *Journal of the American Oriental Society.*

JBL = *Journal of Biblical Literature.*
JCS = *Journal of Cuneiform Studies.*
JdI = *Jahbuch des Deutschen Archäologischen Instituts.*
JEQ = *Jesuit Educational Quarterly*
JHS = *Journal of Hellenic Studies.*
JP = *Journal of Philology.*
JRS = *The Journal of Roman Studies.*
JThS = *Journal of Theological Studies.*
JWalt = *Journal of the Walters Art Gallery.*
LavThéolPhil = *Laval théologique et philologique.*
LCM = *Liverpool Classical Monthly*
LIMC = *Lexicon Iconographicum Mythologiae Classicae* (Zurich and Munich: Artemis 1974–).
LSJ = H.G. Liddell, R. Scott, H. Stuart Jones, *Greek-English Lexicon*, 9th ed. (Oxford: Clarendon 1940).
MÉFRA = *Melanges de l'École Française de Rome, Antiquité.*
MemLinc = *Memorie. Atti della Accademia Nazionale dei Lincei, Classe di scienze morali, storiche e filologiche.*
ModSch = *Modern Schoolman*
MonInst = *Monumenti inediti pubblicati dall'Instituto di Corrispondenza Archeologica.*
MVAG = *Mitteilungen der Vorderasiatisch-Aegyptischen Gesellschaft.*
Nash = E. Nash, *Pictorial Dictionary of Ancient Rome*, 2nd ed. (New York: Praeger 1968).
NC = *Numismatic Chronicle.*
NTS = *New Testament Studies*
OA = *Oriens antiquus.*
OCD[2] = *Oxford Classical Dictionary*, 2nd ed. (Oxford: Clarendon 1970).
OGIS = *Orientis Graeci Inscriptiones Selctae.*
ÖJh = *Jahreshefte des Österreichischen Archäologischen Instituts in Wien.*
ÖJhBeibl = *Jahreshefte des Österreichischen Archäologischen Instituts in Wien. Beiblatt.*
OlForsch = *Olympische Forschungen.*
Paralipomena = J. D. Beazley, *Paralipomena. Additions to* Attic Black-figure Vase-painters *and to* Attic Red-figure Vase-painters *(second edition)* (Oxford: Clarendon 1971).
PCPS = *Proceedings of the Cambridge Philological Society.*
PECS = R. Stillwell et al. eds., *Princeton Encyclopedia of Classical Sites* (Princeton: University Press 1976).
PP = *La parola del passato.*
ProcBritAc = *Proceedings of the British Academy.*

ProcPhilSoc = *Proceedings of the American Philosophical Society.*
QU = *Quaderni urbinati di cultura classica*
RBibl = *Revue biblique.*
RE = Pauly-Wissowa, *Real-Encyclopädie der klassischen Altertumswissenschaft.*
REA = *Revue des études anciennes.*
RhM = *Rheinisches Museum für Philologie.*
RIC = *The Roman Imperial Coinage* (London 1923–).
RivFil = *Rivista di filologia e d'istruzione classica.*
RM = *Mitteilungen des Deutschen Archäologischen Instituts, Römische Abteilung.*
SBMünch = *Sitzungsberichte, Bayerische Akademie der Wissenschaften, München, Philosophisch-historische Klasse.*
SBWien = *Sitzungberichte der Akademie der Wissenschaften in Wien.*
SEG = *Supplementum Epigraphicum Graecum.*
SIG = Dittenberger, *Sylloge Inscriptionum Graecarum.*
SIMA = *Studies in Mediterranean Archaeology.*
TAPA = *Transactions of the American Philological Association.*
TAPS = *Transactions of the American Philosophical Society.*
ThSt = *Theological Studies.*
Travlos = J. Travlos, *Pictorial Dictionary of Ancient Athens* (New York: Praeger 1971).
WS = *Wiener Studien.*
WVDOG = *Wissenschaftliche Veröffentlichungen der Deutschen Orient-Gesellschaft.*
YCS = *Yale Classical Studies.*
ZA = *Zeitschrift für Assyriologie und vorderasiatische Archäologie.*
ZDMG = *Zeitschrift der Deutschen Morgenländischen Gesellschaft.*
ZNTW = *Zeitschrift für die neutestamentliche Wissenschaft.*
ZPE = *Zeitschrift für Papyrologie und Epigraphik.*

BIBLIOGRAPHY OF RAYMOND V. SCHODER, S.J.

COMPILED BY
ROBERT F. SUTTON, JR., and MATTHEW CREIGHTON, S.J.*

This select listing, based on Father Schoder's records, includes formal academic publications together with other items that attest to his diverse professional and pastoral activity. A more complete record is preserved in the Archives of Loyola University of Chicago.

Books

1. With Vincent C. Horrigan, S. J. *A Reading Course in Homeric Greek*. Revised edition. 2 volumes. Ann Arbor, Mich.: Edwards Brothers 1945–46.[1]

1a. *Teachers Key, Teachers Manual, Transition to Attic Greek*. Chicago: Loyola University Press 1947.[2]

1b. 2nd revised edition. 2 volumes, with *Teachers Manual and Key*. Chicago: Loyola University Press 1985–86. *Transition to Attic* Greek incorporated in volume II; with flashcards and tests for Book I.

1c. *Curso para leer Griego Homerico*. Translated by Victor M. Contreras, S. J. Còrdoba: R. Argentina Instituto de Literatura y Humanidades Classicas 1956.

1d. *Homerus lezen*. Revised translation by W.J. Schmidt. Haags Montessori Lyceum [1954] and 1956.

2. Assisted Norman T. Weyand, S.J., editor. *Immortal Diamond. Studies in Gerard Manley Hopkins*. Introduction by John Pick. New York: Sheed and Ward 1949.

3. *Masterpieces of Greek Art*. Greenwich, Conn.: New York Graphic Society 1960 and London: Studio Books 1960.

3a. 2nd revised edition. Greenwich, Conn.: New York Graphic Society 1965.

3b. 3rd revised edition. Chicago: Ares 1975.

3c. *Capolavori di arte greca*. Translated by Fluffy Mello Mazzucato. Milan: Electa 1960.

3d. *Chefs-d'oeuvre de l'art grec*. Translated by Luce Botté. Paris and Brussels: Éditions Sequoia 1961.

3e. 2nd revised edition. Paris and Brussels: Éditions Sequoia 1965.

3f. *Graesk Kunst*. Translated by H. C. Huus. Copenhagen: Samlerens 1961.

3g. *Mästerverk i grekisk Konst*. Translated by Kerstin Karling. Stockholm: Natur och Kultur 1961.

3h. *Meesterwerken der griekse Kunst*. Translated by C. Isings. Amsterdam and Brussels: Elsevier 1961.

3i. *Meisterwerke griechischer Kunst*. Translated by Hildegard and Wolf D. von Barloewen. Zurich and Stuttgart: Artemis 1961.

3j. *Obras maestras del arte griego*. Translated by José Milicua. Barcelona: Editorial Rauter [1962].

3k. *Mistrovská díla řeckého umění*. Adapted translation by Jiří Frel. Prague: Státní nakladatelství krásné literatury a umění 1963.

4. *Wings Over Hellas. Ancient Greece from the Air*. New York: Oxford 1974.

4a. *Ancient Greece from the Air*. London: Thames and Hudson 1974.

* We are grateful for the assistance of John Murphy, S.J. and Christina Thurston.

[1] This revised edition is distinguished from the initial version tested in the classroom during 1945–1946, mentioned in no. 80 infra, vol. 8, p. 35. In 1946 the publisher is listed as Chicago: Loyola University Bookstore, subsequently as Chicago: Loyola University Press. A Portuguese translation was planned but apparently never appeared.

[2] Tests, exercises, and flashcards subsequently became available.

4b. *Hellas in Vogelvlucht. Het oude Griekenland vanuit de Lucht gezien*. Translated by Titia Jelgersma. Utrecht and Antwerp: Het Spectrum 1974.

4c. *Das antike Griechenland aus der Luft*. Translated by Joachim Rehork. Bergisch Gladbach: Gustav Lübbe 1975.

4d. Revised edition. Bergisch Gladbach: Gustav Lübbe 1976.

4e. *La Grèce antique vue du ciel*. translated by Marie-Hélène Fraïssé and Francis Ledoux. Paris: Éditions Seghers 1975.
Cf. also no. 169 infra.

5. With Peter Milward, S.J. *Landscape and Inscape. Vision and inspiration in Hopkins's poetry*. London: Elek and Grand Rapids, Mich.: Eerdmans 1975. Recipient of the Religious Book Award, Best Illustrated Book in 1975, from the Catholic Press Association and the Associated Church Press.

5b. Photocopy reprint. Ann Arbor, Mich.: University Microfilms 1980.

6. With Peter Milward, S.J. *Readings of* The Wreck. *Essays in commemoration of the centenary of G.M. Hopkins'* The Wreck of the Deutschland. Chicago: Loyola University Press 1976.

7. *Paul Wrote from the Heart. Philippians, Galatians in straightforward English*. Oak Park, Ill.: Bolchazy-Carducci 1987. Revision of no. 17 infra.

8. *The Art and Challenge of Translation*. Oak Park, Ill.: Bolchazy-Carducci 1987. Nos. 14, 16, 17 (revised) infra with the original texts.

Verse and Translation

9. "Multiple Reflection." *Athenaeum* (Xavier University), Summer 1937, 28.

10. "Libro Amico." *Athenaeum*, October 1938, 33.

11. "A Poet's Land of Dreams. (Horace, *Odes* 2.6)." *CB* 15 (1938) 4.

12. "Bernard's Praise of Mary. Dante, *Paradiso:* 33.1–21." *America*, June 1940, 300.

13. "Reproof for Tears." *The Fleur de Lis* (Xavier University) 31 (1942) 4.

13a. Subtitled "A meditation for evil days." *Alter Christus*, September 1949, 43–44.

14. "Echoes of Sappho." *Classical Outlook* 20 (1943) 47.

14a. No. 8 supra, 85–92.

15. "In Diem Octavam Decembris." *CB* 21 (1944) 19.

16. *The Inaugural Address of John Fitzgerald Kennedy in the Language of Marcus Tullius Cicero*. Chicago: Office of the Dean of Admissions, Loyola University [1964].

16a. *Classical Folia* 18 (1964) 49–53.

16b. *CJ* 60 (1964) 13–15.

16c. No. 8 supra, 93–107.

17. St. Paul, *Epistles to the Galatians and Philippians* in *The New American Bible*. Paterson, N.J.: St. Anthony Guild 1970. *New Testament*, pp. 221–227, 233–237.

17a. No. 7 supra.

17b. No. 8 supra, 1–83.

18. "Verbum Caro" *In Memoriam Vandick L. da Nóbrega. Omnia* (Rio de Janeiro: SEPE 1985).

Articles, Chapters of Books, and Pamphlets

Classical Studies

19. "Vergil Looks at the Stars." *CB* 14 (1938) 31–32.

20. "Vergil—Or His Commentators?" *CB* 14 (1938) 47–48.

21. "Moses and Muses: Why Catholics Cherish the Classics." *America*, August 19, 1939, 451–52.

22. "Homer—Chief Humanist." *CB* 16 (1940) 70–71.

23. "Plato's Concept of the Philosophic Life." *ModSch* 19 (1941) 2–7.

24. "Herodotus: Historian and Humorist." *HistB* 20 (1942) 53–54, 66–67.

25. "The Uniqueness of Vergil." *CB* 19 (1942) 59.

26. "Found: A Portrait of Vergil?" *CB* 19 (1942) 1–2.

27. "Vergil's Love of the Stars." *CW* 36 (1942) 94–95.

28. "The Artistry of the First Pythian Ode." *CJ* 38 (1943) 401–12.

29. "Horace's Satiric Use of Fable." *CW* 37 (1944) 112–14.

30. "Homer's Artistry of Plot." *CB* 24 (1948) 25–28.

31. "The Common People of Homer's World." *CW* 41 (1948) 184–87.

32. "More Memories of John A. Scott." *CB* 24 (1948) 65.

33. "Vergil in the Divine Comedy." *CJ* 44 (1949) 413–22.

34. "John Bull on Helicon. The state of the Classics in England." *CJ* 44 (1949) 332–34.

35. "Lucretius' Poetic Problem." *CJ* 45 (1949–50) 128–35, 177–82.

36. "Ancient Cumae." *Scientific American* 209.6 (December 1963) 108–21, 178–80.

37. *The Catholic Encyclopedia for School and Home*. New York: McGraw Hill 1965:

37a. "Greece, Ancient. Religion." G 692–95.

37b. "Greek Gods." G 704–707.

37c. "Hades." H 60–61.

38. "Greek Art and Architecture." *Book of Knowledge. The Children's Encyclopedia* (New York: Grolier 1967) G 340–48.

39. "The Theater at Epidauros as a Work of Art." *Greek Drama. A collection of festival papers.* Grace L. Beede, ed. *Festival Papers* 2 (Vermillion: University of South Dakota Press 1967) 13–39.

40. "On Two Portraits of Vergil." *Vergilius* 13 (1967) 8–15.

41. *The New Catholic Encyclopedia* (New York: McGraw-Hill 1967):

41a. "Agnostos Theos." I 209.

41b. "Decapolis." IV 699–700.

41c. "Gadara." VI 237.

41d. "Gerasa." VI 380–81.

41e. "Perea." XI 118.

42. "Preface to the American Edition" and "Supplementary Bibliography 1897–1966." Reprint of *The Elder Pliny's Chapters on the History of Art*, translated by K. Jex-Blake with Commentary and Historical Introduction by E. Sellars. Chicago: Argonaut 1968, pp. A–Y.

42a. With "Preface to the Second American Edition" and "Further Bibliography 1960–1975." Chicago: Ares 1976, [pp. 4].

43. "Literary Sources Cited by Aristotle in the *Poetics*." *CJ* 65 (1969) 75.

43a. Revised *CJ* 66 (1970) 359.

44. "Vergil's Poetic Use of the Cumae Area." *Romanitas* (Rio de Janeiro) 11 (1970) 187–98.

44a. Revised *CJ* 67 (1971) 97–109.

45. "Conversion Charts for Equivalents of Length Between the English-American and Metric Systems." *AJA* 77 (1973) 340–42.

46. "Graeco-Roman Antipolis on the French Riviera." *Antipolis. Journal of Mediterranean Archaeology* 1 (1974) 1–8.

47. "The Roman Theater at Antipolis in Southern France." *Antipolis* 1 (1975) 97–106.

48. *The Princeton Encyclopedia of Classical Sites*. Princeton: University Press 1976:

48a. "Aenaria (Ischia)." 14.

48b. "Antipolis (Antibes)." 64–65.

48c. "Asisium (Assisi)." 101.

48d. "Clitumnus." 227.

48e. "Misenum." 585.

48f. "Tarracina (Terracina)." 881–82.

48g. "Veleia (Velleia)." 960–61.

49. "Adventures in Aerial Photography of Archaeological Sites in Greece." *Aerial Archaeology* 2 (1978) 29–33.

50. "Vergil's Humane Message." *Thought* 55 (1980) 65–80.

51. "Alexander's Son and Roxane in the Boscoreale Murals." *AncW* 5 (1982) 27–32.

52. "Ancient Antipolis in Southern France." *AncW* 7 (1983) 89–98.

53. "Vergil's Vision of Life." *Journal of Ultimate Reality and Meaning* 6 (1983) 205–20.

54. "Theodoros of Samos: an ancient Greek artistic genius." in *Apophoreta. Latin and Greek Studies in Honor of Grace L. Beede*, Jeremiah Reedy, ed. (Chicago: Bolchazy-Carducci 1985) 247–57.

55. "Fable as Satire in Horace." *In Memoriam Vandick L. Nóbrega. Omnia* (Rio de Janeiro: SEPE 1985) 303–306.

56. With Eleanor Guralnick. *Art Museums of the World.* Virginia Jackson, editor in chief. New York: Greenwood Press 1987:

56a. "Archaeological Museum of Delphi." I 438–44.

56b. "Archaeological Museum of Olympia." I 453–59.

57. "Odysseus' Route." *CJ* 82 (1987) 319–24.

Theological, Philosophical and Ecclesiastical Studies

58. "Putting the Scalpel to the Soul." *CathW* 153 (1941) 54–62.

59. "Suarez on the Temporal Power of the Pope." *Studies* (Dublin) 30 (1941) 425–38.

60. "St. Chrysostom and the Date of Christ's Nativity." *ThSt* 3 (1942) 140–44.

61. "A Section-Correlation of St. Thomas' *In Ethica Aristotelis* with the Bekker-pages of the Greek text." *ModSch* 21 (1943) 47–48.

62. "The Need for Jesuit Writers. Points for meditation." *JEQ* 8 (1946) 164–67.

63. "The Significance of St. Augustine." *AmEcclRev* 115 (1946) 260–70.

64. "The Rebirth of Scriptural Theology." *AmEcclRev* 117 (1947) 81–101.

65. "Introduction" to W.I. Young, S.J., translator, *St. Ignatius' Own Story* (Chicago: Regnery 1956) v–ix.

66. *Celibacy. A glory of the priesthood.* St. Louis: Missouri Knights of Columbus, Religious Information Bureau [1971].

Post-Classical Languages and Literature

67. "Dante, the Crown of a Catholic Education." *JEQ* 3 (1940) 97–100.

68. *"Spelt from Sibyl's Leaves." Thought* 19 (1944) 633–48.

69. "An Interpretative Glossary of Difficult Words in Hopkins' Poems." No. 2 supra, 192–221.

70. "What Does *The Windhover* Mean?" No. 2 supra, 275–306.

70a. Excerpted in John Pick, *Gerard Manley Hopkins*, The Windhover. Columbus, Ohio: Merrill (1969) 30–44.

71. "'The Carrier-Witted Heart.' The Ignatian quality of *The Wreck*." No. 6 supra, 52–67.

Pedagogy

72. "Learning Latin Words. Points for High School students." *CB* 16 (1940) 29–30.

73. "Pity the Greekless. The sad story of an unenlightened collegian." *CathW* 153 (1941) 574–80.

73a. Revised as *Pity the Greekless. The sad story of Egbert, an unalert sophomore.* [Chicago 1942].

74. "Psychological Efficiency in Teaching the Classical Languages." *JEQ* 5 (1942) 132–40.

75. "Against Overworking Translation." *CW* 37 (1943) 5–6.

76. "Why the Latin Teacher Needs to Know Greek." *CW* 37 (1943) 58–59.

77. "Straight Shooting in Latin Defense." *CB* 20 (1943) 6–8, 14–16.

78. "Proverbs as Spice for our Latin Courses." *CB* 21 (1944) 17–18.

79. "Interesting Latin Proverbs." *CB* 21 (1945) 32, 48, 71; vol. 22 (1946) 40.

80. "Starting them off with Homer. Communique on a new strategy in High School Greek." *JEQ* 7 (1944–45) 210–221; vol. 8 (1945–46) 25–37.

80a. Translated by Duclos, *L'Entre-Aide* (Montreal) 28 (1946) 1–7, 35–43, 117–122.

81. "Read All About It." *Practice* 3 (1946) 37–38.

82. "Revitalizing Beginners' Greek through Homer." *CJ* 41 (1946) 254–65.

83. "Giving Greek a New Chance." *CB* 22 (1946) 57–59.

84. *Classical Books for High School Needs.* St. Louis: *CB* 1947.

85. "Homer to the Rescue. A new method in beginners' Greek." *G&R* 18 (1950) 10–18.

86. "Unhexing the Hexameter." *CB* 30 (1953) 9–10.

87. "Foreword." B. Fuerst, O. S. B., *Reading Course in Greek, Book I.* St. Meinrad, Ind.: Grail 1953.

88. "Vergilian Society of America: Classical Summer School at Cumae. Readings on the sites visited." *CW* 49 (1956) 166 and 171.

89. *Italian Is Easy if you know Latin and use these charts.* Oxford, Ohio: American Classical League [1960]; with corrections [1970].

90. "Pronunciations, Mediaeval and Italianized." *CB* 43 (1966) 30.

91. "What Catholic Colleges Are For." *AmEcclRev* 163 (1970) 154–65.

92. "The Genesis and Goals of Cardinal Newman College." *Homiletic and Pastoral Review* 78.5 (February 1978) 59–62.

Abstracts

93. "Poetic Imagination vs. Didacticism in Lucretius." *Proceedings of the American Philological Association* 76 (1945) xxxix.

94. "The Roman Impress on North Africa." *AJA* 60 (1956) 183.

95. "Djemila: A North African Pompeii." *AJA* 62 (1958) 226.

96. "Some Major Greek Sites from the Air." *AJA* 69 (1965) 175.

97. "Major Mycenaean Sites from the Air." *Atti e memorie del 1º Congresso Internazionale di Micenologia, Roma 27 Settembre–3 Ottobre 1967*. Rome: Edizioni dell' Ateneo, 1968: 169.

98. "A Problem Treasure: A Unique Gold Fibula in Winnetka." *AJA* 74 (1970) 203.

99. With Al. N. Oikonomides, "Antipolis in Southern France: Pre-Excavation Investigations, 1973." *AJA* 78 (1974) 177–78.

Reviews

100. C.H. Reinhardt, S.J., *An Outline of Roman History: Constitutional, Economic, Social. JEQ* 2 (1939) 158.

101. D.W. Thompson, *Science and the Classics*. "In Love with Science and the Classics." *CB* 17 (1940) 21–22.

102. K. von Fritz, *Pythagorean Politics in Southern Italy. HistB* 19 (1941) 68.

103. A. Efron, *Sacred Tree Script. ModSch* 19 (1941) 19–20.

104. *Greece and Rome* May 1941. "Greece and Rome." *CB* 18 (1941) 20–21.

105. H.E. Cory, *The Emancipation of a Freethinker. ModSch* 19 (1942) 59–60

106. R. Robinson, *Plato's Earlier Dialectic. ModSch* 19 (1942) 77–78.

107. F. Solmsen, *Plato's Theology. ModSch* 20 (1942) 49–50.

108. *The Republic of Plato*, trans. F. M. Cornford. *ModSch* 20 (1942) 57.

109. C.E. Smith, *Tiberius and the Roman Empire. HistB* 21 (1943) 46.

110a. J.H. Finley, *Thucydides. HistB* 21 (1943) 67.

110b. *CJ* 40 (1945) 432–35.

111. E.K. Rand, *The Building of Eternal Rome. HistB* 22 (1943) 20–21.

112. J.C. Plumpe, *Mater Ecclesia, An Inquiry into the Concept of the Church as Mother in Early Christianity. HistB* 23 (1945) 93.

113. W. Jaeger, *Paideia: The Ideals of Greek Culture, Vol. II. ModSch* 22 (1945) 235–36.

114. J.Sánchez Villaseñor, S.J., *Pensamiento y trayectoria de José Ortega y Gasset. Thought* 22 (1947) 538–41.

115. J. Ortega y Gasset, *The Dehumanization of Art and Notes on the Novel. Thought* 23 (1948) 694–96.

116. W.R. Agard, *Classical Myths in Sculpture. CB* 28 (1951) 11–12.

117. *Tertullian: Apologetical Works. Minucius Felix: Octavius. The Fathers of the Church, X*, translated by R. Arbesmann, O.S.A, E.J. Daly, C.S.J., and E. A. Quain, S.J. *ThSt* 12 (1951) 579–80.

118. C. Kerényi, *The Gods of the Greeks. CB* 28 (1952) 59–60.

119. C. Pharr, *The Theodosian Code and Novels, and the Syrmondian Constitutions: A Translation with Commentary, Glossary, and Bibliography. The Catholic Biblical Quarterly* 14 (1952) 396–97.

120. E.B. Smith, *The Dome: A Study in the History of Ideas. AJA* 57 (1953) 46–47.

121. J. Bérard, H. Goube, and R. Langumier, *Homère, Odyssée: Chants I, V–VII, IX–XII, XIV, XXI–XXIII. CW* 46 (1953) 181.

122. A. Lesky, *Die Homerforschung in der Gegenwart. CB* 29 (1953) 70.

123a. M.E. Reesor, *The Political Theory of the Old and Middle Stoa. CB* 29 (1953) 70.

123b. "Stoic Thinkers," *Review of Politics* 15 (1953) 400.

124. P.Agostino Augustinović, O.F.M., *Gerico e dintorni. AJA* 57 (1953) 130.

125. R.M. Grant, *Miracle and Natural Law in Graeco-Roman and Early Christian Thought. ThSt* 14 (1953) 474–77.

126. J. Pick, *A Hopkins Reader. Thought* 28 (1953) 619–21.

127. W. Lowrie, *Action in the Liturgy: Essential and Unessential. AJA* 58 (1954) 351.

128. *The Acts of the Pagan Martyrs: Acta Alexandrinorun*, edited with commentary by H.A. Musurillo, S.J. *ThSt* 16 (1955) 285–86.

129. M.L.B. Shepard (trans.), *Life in the Imperial and Loyal City of Mexico in New Spain, and the Royal and Pontifical University of Mexico: Dialogues by Francisco Cervantes de Salazar*. *CB* 32 (1956) 58.

130. M.I. Finley, *The World of Odysseus*. *Archaeology* 9 (1956) 294.

131. A. da Costa Ramalho, *Dipla onomata no estillo de Aristopfanes*; E. Brunius-Nilsson, *Δαιμόνιε: An Inquiry into a Mode of Apostrophe in Old Greek Literature*; and E. Mikkola, *Isokrates: Seine Anschauung im Lichte seiner Schriften*. *CB* 33 (1957) 59.

132. M. van der Mijnsbrugge, ed., *P. Cornelius Tacitus. Uitgelezen Teksten*. *CB* 34 (1958) 57.

133. J. and G. Roux, *Greece*. *CJ* 54 (1959) 278–79.

134. G.M.A. Richter, *A Handbook of Greek Art*. *CW* 53 (1959) 12–13.

135. Fr. Rolfe (Frederick Baron Corvo), *Nicholas Crabbe*. *Renascence* 12 (1960) 203–204.

136. W. Zschietzschmann, *Hellas and Rome: The Classical World in Pictures*. *CW* 54 (1960) 60

137. V.F. Lenzen, *The Triumph of Dionysos on Textiles of Late Antique Egypt*. *CW* 54 (1961) 264.

138. A. Giuliano, *Il commercio dei sarcofagi attici*. *CW* 56 (1963) 137.

139. A.G. McKay, *Naples and Campania: Texts and Illustrations*. *CB* 39 (1963) 80.

140. R. Beny, *A Time of Gods: A Photographer in the Wake of Odysseus*. *CW* 57 (1963) 134–35.

141. R.L. Scranton, *Greek Architecture* and F.E. Brown, *Roman Architecture*. *CB* 40 (1964) 95.

142. E.H. Richardson, *The Etruscans: Their Art and Civilization*. *CB* 41 (1964) 15.

143a. R.L. Scranton, *Aesthetic Aspects of Ancient Art*. *CB* 41 (1965) 64.

143b. *CW* 58 (1965) 239.

144. E. Vermeule, *Greece in the Bronze Age*. *CB* 42 (1966) 48.

145. T.S. Brown, ed., *Ancient Greece* and W.G. Sinnigen, *Rome*. *CB* 42 (1966) 92.

146. J.J. Pollitt, *The Art of Greece: 1400–31 B.C. Sources and Documents in the History of Art*. *CB* 42 (1966) 93.

147. M. Bieber, *Alexander the Great in Greek and Roman Art*. *CB* 43 (1966) 15.

148. G.M. Stratton, *Theophrastus and the Greek Physiological Psychology before Aristotle*. *CB* 43 (1967) 63.

149. J.J. Pollitt, *The Art of Rome: 753 B.C.–337 A.D. Sources and Documents in the History of Art*. *CB* 43 (1967) 95.

150. L.A. Richards, ed., *Ancient Greek Literature in Translation—an Anthology*. *CB* 43 (1967) 95–96.

151. G. Mylonas, *Mycenae and the Mycenaean Age*. *Manuscripta* (St. Louis University) 11 (1967) 166.

152. P. Whelun and H.J. Bellars, *Historical Numismatic Atlas of the Roman Empire*. *CB* 44 (1968) 63.

153. G. Becker, *Isidori Hispalensis, De Natura Rerum Liber*. *CB* 44 (1968) 64.

154. M. Zerwick, S.J., *Biblical Greek*. *CB* 44 (1968) 64.

155. P. LaBaume, *Romans on the Rhine*. *CB* 44 (1968) 78.

156. A.W. Gomme, *The Population of Athens in the Fifth and Fourth Centuries B.C.* *CB* 44 (1968) 78–79.

157. P. Milward, *A Commentary on G. M. Hopkins' "The Wreck of the Deutschland"*. *Thought* (1969) 469–70.

158. *Greece and Rome. Builders of Our World*, ed. M. Severy et al. *CJ* 66 (1971) 163.

159. B. Schweitzer, *Greek Geometric Art*. *CW* 65 (1972) 236.

160. N. Platon, *Zakros. The discovery of a lost palace of ancient Crete*. *CW* 66 (1973) 374–75.

161. E. Gareau, ed., *Classical Values and the Modern World*. *Vergilius* 19 (1973) 41–42.

162. P. Merlan, *A Syllabus in the Humanities*. *ModSch* 52 (1975) 332.

163. A. Burford, *The Greek Temple Builders at Epidauros: A social and economic study of building in the Asklepian sanctuary during the fourth and early third centuries B.C.* *CJ* 68 (1973) 385–86.

164. J. Hawkes, ed., *Atlas of Ancient Archaeology.* CW 71 (1977) 92.

165. E.S. Ramage, ed., *Atlantis: Fact or Fiction?* CW 73 (1979) 44–45.

166. A. Ničev, *La catharsis tragique d'Aristote.* CW 77 (1984) 330.

Photographs

167. Sets of color slides (20 slides each) with commentary. West Baden, Ind.: Photo Service Department, West Baden College 1956:

A. Greece I. Athens, Central & Northern Greece

B. Greece II. Peloponnesus & Islands.

C. Rome.

D. Rome's Empire.

E. Classic Italy.

F. Vergil's World

167a. New York: Slide Archives of the Archaeological Institute of America 1968 and 1970.

168. Slides available individually and in sets. New York: Slide Archives of the Archaeological Institute of America 1968 and 1970. The sets include Egypt I, II; Samothrace I, II; Tiryns; Mycenae; Delphi I, II; Athens: The Acropolis I, II; Perge; Assos; Southwest Turkey; Didyma; Miletos; Kenchreai; Ephesos; Pergamon; Rome: Monuments I, II, Palatine, Forum Romanum; Herculaneum; Leptis Magna; Sabratha and Sbeitla; Peru.

169. "Ancient Greece From the Air. Wings Over Hellas". 70 slides in 2 sets. Oak Park, Ill.: Bolchazy-Carducci 1986. Views from no. 4 supra.

170. Photographs in more than 200 books of professional and popular interest.

IN MEMORIAM RAYMOND V. SCHODER, S.J.

A homily delivered at the Funeral Mass of Father Schoder, May 5, 1987

Robert A. Wild, S.J.

It is an honor for me, an honor for all of us to gather here to celebrate the life of Father Raymond Schoder. We come together as his family, as his brother Jesuits, as his colleagues, as his students, and as his friends to remember Ray with respect and affection. He did amazing things in his lifetime, he was a great man, he was certainly a great Jesuit.

Raymond Schoder brought vigorous effort, enthusiasm, and energy, especially energy, to whatever he set his hand to. At the beginning of his scholarly life when he did his doctoral program at St. Louis University—it was during World War II—he completed everything in four years. During the last of these years, the year when he was writing his doctoral dissertation, he was assigned as a full-time teacher at our high school in Detroit. Now anyone who has done a doctoral thesis and who also knows the intense work required in full-time high school teaching will tell you what an amazing feat the combination of those two things was! And at the end of his life, whenever I talked with him, I found Ray still full of new scholarly projects and ideas. His enthusiasm and energy never left him even when cancer pressed upon him.

Our Gospel this evening [Luke 12:35–40] tells us that the Lord's true servants will be always alert for his coming. All his life Ray was certainly "ready for action." His belt was always fastened, his lamp alight. It is impossible to think of Ray Schoder asleep or inactive at the coming of his Master. He loved the Lord; he gave himself unstintingly to the work of teaching, lecturing, and writing, the work that he had as the Lord's servant.

When we look at just the bare statistics of Ray Schoder's life work, we cannot help but be amazed. In his lifetime he published eight books, ninety-four articles, sixty-five book reviews, and even four poems, the creative efforts of his youthful days. He was also very proud of the fact that he had given no fewer than fifteen hundred public lectures. He even founded a college, Cardinal Newman College in St. Louis. It was not, as he himself would admit, his most successful venture, but, as in everything else, he gave himself heart and soul to that enterprise as long as it lasted. He left us a collection of some seventeen thousand photographic slides, slides that he had taken of the archeological remains and art objects of the classical Greek and Roman world. This collection is perhaps his greatest legacy. His photographs appear in countless publications, and they are of amazing taste and quality.

There are countless stories about Ray Schoder and his activities, and I am sure that each of us has a favorite. The newspaper obituaries recorded one of the best known, how he strapped himself in the open doorway of a Greek Air Force bomber and took pictures of various classical sites in Greece from the air for a book that he later produced. When I was a scholastic, I remember how we used to recount that particular story and how we always improved it a bit in the telling. We had this image, you see, of Ray suspended from an airplane on a fifteen foot rope and searching out just one more careful camera shot! But let me tell you my own special favorite among all of the stories that I can recall. When I was a Jesuit novice thirty years ago, I remember Ray Schoder coming to the novitiate and giving us a slide lecture on the glories of the late Roman mosaics at Ravenna in Italy. It was an amazingly interesting lecture, one which I vividly remembered when I finally managed myself to get to Ravenna many years later. But at one point during it he said in his characteristic manner (which has inspired much affectionate imitation over the years), "Now here we have a close-up of the right eyeball of the Emperor Justinian. Note the amazing workmanship and the texture of the mosaic *tesserae*." Then he went on to tell us how he got that particular close-up. He had managed to hide in the Basilica of San Apollinare Nuovo, the church in which there are in the nave two amazingly beautiful mosaics depicting processions of saints and of the royal household of the Emperor Justinian. He then proceeded to climb up on a thirty- or forty-foot scaffolding left by workers who were cleaning these mosaics in order to photograph the figures up close. I had always thought that he had himself been locked in the church overnight, but he assured me about a month ago that it was only during the four-hour afternoon siesta period when the workers had gone for their main meal. There can be no doubt about it: when Ray Schoder set his mind to do something, he generally achieved his purpose.

But, we must ask, what was the driving force that kept Ray so busy and so active? Part of it, to be sure, was his own need for fame and recognition. He wanted his accomplishments known, and he himself very lovingly kept the statistics that I listed above. I suspect that he perhaps was a little bit afraid that if he himself did not remind us of the things that he had done, we might think that he was not contributing all that much. No chance of that! If Ray Schoder never had spoken a word, his many works would speak for themselves.

A much more profound driving force was his own vision of Christian humanism. He loved humanity and the creative energy and work of humanity. Both through his classical training and scholarship and his very Catholic and Jesuit view of things he was convinced of the fundamental goodness of all of creation. I chose the first reading [Rom 8:14–23], a text from Ray's favorite New Testament author, the Apostle Paul, to reflect this fundamental aspect of his own vision and sense of purpose. That text speaks not only of the salvation and deliverance of humanity but also of the hoped-for salvation for all of creation. Ray Schoder knew that creation as we experience it is indeed "groaning" and "in frustration" because of evil and sin. Yet he also saw this created universe and the creative efforts of humanity as coming from God and therefore as good. Consequently, both nature and the creative achievements of the human family reflect and image the goodness of God. If Ray Schoder had any Jesuit hero, it was probably the English nineteenth century Jesuit poet Gerard Manley Hopkins. Hopkins again and again in his writings returns to the theme, a theme dear to the hearts of Jesuits everywhere, that "the world is charged with the grandeur of God." It is this vision that Ray Schoder sought to convey in his writings, to teach in his classes, and to hand on to his younger brethren in the Society of Jesus.

I have spoken of Ray's work and effort and energy. These were constants with him and, as someone remarked to me a day or so ago, if will power were the fundamental factor, Ray would have been able to surmount any difficulty. As Ray's major superior, I have had the privilege of sharing some of his most intimate feelings as he faced the progress of cancer and the onset of his own death. Whenever I talked with him in these last months, I found him brimming with new projects and ideas. He was determined to keep active as long as he could, and this led him even in the last few months to give a series of public lectures in different parts of the country. Yet at the same time, he was fully informed about his health, he knew that he was failing, he knew that he could not accomplish all that he hoped. More and more he felt himself in the Lord's hands, more and more with the sense that it was the Lord and not he himself who would have to achieve the good that he dreamed of. Human effort, he recognized, is not the final story. Rather, it is the Lord's power, the Lord's grace that achieves the victory.

I mentioned Father Schoder's special love for Gerard Manley Hopkins. In his lifetime he published two books on Hopkins, a book of photographs and a collection of essays which he edited under the short title of *Immortal Diamond*. It is appropriate therefore to offer to you a section of a poem of Hopkins, "That Nature Is a Heraclitean Fire and of the Comfort of the Resurrection," a text which, I think, reflects Ray's own growing spiritual experience in the last months and weeks of his life:

Man, how fast his firedint, his mark on mind, is gone!
Both are in an unfathomable, all is in an enormous dark
Drowned. O pity and indignation! Manshape, that shone
Sheer off, disseveral, a star, death blots black out; nor mark
    Is any of him at all so stark
But vastness blurs and time beats level. Enough! the Resurrection,
A heart's-clarion! Away grief's gasping, joyless days, dejection.
    Across my foundering deck shone
A beacon, an eternal beam. Flesh fade, and mortal trash
Fall to the residuary worm; world's wildfire, leave but ash:
    In a flash, at a trumpet crash,
I am all at once what Christ is, since he was what I am, and
This Jack, joke, poor potsherd, patch, matchwood, immortal diamond,
    Is immortal diamond.

Let us therefore commend our brother, Father Raymond Schoder, to the Lord. We pray for him, we ask the Lord to take him to Himself. May Ray share in the victory of the Risen Lord and share in His peace forever and ever.

FATHER SCHODER

AND *ANCIENT GREECE FROM THE AIR*

STERLING DOW

For most Classical and for other Humane scholars, scholarship is not physically hazardous. No crude life-threatening menace disturbs the Humane scholar. He sits in a tranquil place, in a "study" or "office" (in the eighteenth century it would be called a "closet") (cf. Frontispiece). He is safe. He rarely needs to go out, riskily or otherwise, collecting material. His needs are few. Some scholars do not even need books. The "model" for the principal habitat of many scholars (nowadays every generalized entity seems to need a "model") might well be the study of the famous philosopher L. Wittgenstein, in Trinity College Cambridge. Wittgenstein's study was furnished with a table, a chair, a pad of paper, and a pencil. Otherwise the room was completely bare. Two deckchairs could be brought out for visitors (Sir Alfred Ayer, *Wittgenstein* [New York: Random House 1985] 11).

Scholars Who Took Risks

In this context, a conspicuous part of Father Schoder's work has been exceptional. To make the photographs for *Ancient Greece from the Air*, he took formidable risks day after day. Thinking about him and his achievement, it is natural to think also of other Classical scholars who have done heroic things for scholarship. To honor Father Schoder, who in some ways is surely the greatest of the company, and to give *Ancient Greece from the Air* a deserved setting, it occurred to me that these other valiant members of our profession might be gathered—I think for the first time. My effort to do so can include only the ones I remember or happen to have heard about. As mere chance will have it, they are all Americans. Their number is limited: let others write on more persons, and more worthily.

On Land

First mention undoubtedly belongs to a graduate student from Cornell. **Eugene Andrews** dangled in a bosun's seat below the eastern pediment of the Parthenon. The seat hung from one rope. Some sixty feet below were the marble steps of the Parthenon. Andrews was making squeezes of the cuttings for great bronze letters—the only non-structural inscription ever carved in the Classical Parthenon. He was making the squeezes in winter, when the Akropolis can be windy and chilly, but Andrews was athletic, and he had determined, *not* to read the inscription, because only attachment-holes remained, so that there was just a lot of big dot-like gouges, and apparently it was hopeless to read; his only hope was merely to record the holes. One afternoon at tea some ladies in the American School of Classical Studies joked him annoyingly about what he was doing. He was thus goaded into trying to make sense of the pattern of attachment-holes. Meantime the rope from which the bosun's seat hung had almost worn through. No one had noticed it, but Wilhelm Dörpfeld, the famous head of the German School, happened to offer him a better rope, and when the old one was pulled down, it was found to be worn nearly through. Another day or two of fraying against the marble edge, and that would have been the end. Andrews completed the decipherment of most of the text; it honors the Emperor Nero.

Andrew's feat was in 1896, at the time of the first modern Olympic Games. Later, back at Cornell and rewarded with an instructor's appointment, Andrews settled down to the happy life of a congenial and valued member of the community. He had been trained as a philologist and he had no desire to work on Nero and Neronian Athens. He wrote nothing, not even on the Parthenon inscription.

Long after, as a mere devotee, I found that the squeezes were at Cornell. There I was able to complete the text by reading the last few words, and I gave the whole to Kevin K. Carroll, who solved the historical problems and produced a handsome publication (*The Parthenon Inscription. GRBM* 9 [1982]). It is pleasant to add that a little over a year ago, when scaffolding had been set up for renovation of the east facade of the Parthenon, Carroll was able to ascend and to examine the cuttings. Andrews' squeezes had recorded them accurately.

After WW I, **Francis P. Farquhar**, already becoming one of America's most skilled and daring mountaineers, determined on a grand ascent of Mt. Olympos. The Home of the Gods had been visited once or twice before the War, but this time it was to be the site of the first radio broadcast from any peak in Greece. A young Greek scholar, Aristeides Phoutrides, made the ascent with Farquhar, and for protection against the brigands of those days, the Greek Army dispatched as guards an entire company of soldiers.

The brigands did not show themselves, even for a distant pot- shot, and the broadcast from the summit was a success.

Oppositely, underground Korinthos offered a formidable challenge. Ever since Archaic Greek times, the main water supply of Korinthos had been Peirene. A fountain-house was ultimately developed in fine style, with ample numbers of fonts, a splendid facade, and an open court. What was underground, behind the fonts, was unknown. **Bert Hodge Hill**, the Director of the American School, and founder of modern excavating techniques, was always attracted to any good problem. He determined to explore Peirene. Behind the façade, long storage cisterns were found to terminate in tunnels that went far back into the forward base of the 1000-foot Akrokorinthos. Lights of course had to be carried; it was dank and cold, and slippery. Every step had to be cautious: a fall, a broken limb, might make an awkward predicament. Hill did it all, measuring and mapping. Few scholars have ever carried out such a task (Bert Hodge Hill, *Corinth*, I, vi, *The Springs: Peirene, Sacred Spring, Glauke* [Princeton: American School of Classical Studies 1965]).

Prentice Duell, an architect who among other interests was head of the University of Chicago expedition to Sakkara in Egypt, urged **Lucy T. Shoe [Meritt]**, who was then in Greece as a graduate student from Bryn Mawr, to collect profiles of Greek architectural moldings. Mostly alone, and faced with all the problems of finding and identifying the scattered blocks at scores of Greek sites, of handling a template (not a light one, either), of getting the profiles on paper with the necessary data, she traveled everywhere undeterred and worked diligently.

Her book, now unprocurable, is the monument of this courageous and arduous work (Lucy T. Shoe, *Profiles of Greek Mouldings*, 2 vols. [Cambridge, Mass.: American School of Classical Studies 1936]).

Another Director of the School, **Rhys Carpenter**, also a skillful and daring mountaineer, without ladders or ropes, ascended by sheer climbing skill to the pediments of the Parthenon. Standing on those narrow shelves, he determined the locations of the various pedimental statues by studying the weathering of the blocks on which they had stood. Most of the statues themselves are in the British Museum, but Carpenter, with his unequalled eye for sculptural style, had identified another of the statues standing unrecognized by the very door of the Akropolis Museum (Rhys Carpenter, "New Material for the West Pediment of the Parthenon," *Hesperia* 1 [1932] 1–30, and "The Lost Statues of the East Pediment," *Hesperia* 2 [1933] 1–88).

A deep well is also dangerous. To be lowered into a deep well requires implicit faith in the gear itself and implicit faith in the men working the cranks. There must be the utmost caution to prevent any rock from being dislodged and dropping. In the American excavations, both at Korinthos and in the Athenian Agora, a great many wells have been found. (Can one not say, the American School is the great Well School?) Wells cannot be excavated, or even properly explored, by any mechanical means: *men* have to go down. Every well discovered has been fully explored. Thus far, in many decades now, there has been no injury. Most of the work at the bottom is pick-men's work, but staff members of the excavation have also gone down. All praise to all who have made these descents. Perhaps the deepest at Korinthos was by **Henry S. Robinson**, Director (yet another one) of the American School of Classical Studies. The well was part of an elaborate hydraulic system, and it went down over 100 feet.

William Bell Dinsmoor, Sr. was not a mountaineer, but his studies of Greek architecture are supreme because he went to the blocks, and measured them with care, and got the measurements to tell the story. So he had ample experience clambering around among blocks. He wanted measurements of blocks at the highest levels of the Parthenon. To help with the tapes and the records, he needed an assistant, and he selected **Theodore Leslie Shear, Jr.**, who was then in his teens, and (aided by being young?—I think not) was fearless. They did the job.

In the region of the Laureion mines, while exploring Attike for inscriptions, J. Kirchner and I had made some real acquaintance with modern studies, mostly Italian, of the Classical silver mines. We had been in some of the underground passages, but only in the large spacious passages. Later, following these preliminary visits, students from the American School really probed the depths. The spacious passages were only certain ones high up. Most of the silver was mined from the rich "second contact," deep down. Both high (comparatively) and low, the real mining was done from narrow passages—burrowings—in which you have to go on hands and knees (you cannot stand up), with a light on your hat. There is hardly room to turn around. The supply of air soon gives out; the vents to supply air are few and barely adequate. No setting—not even the inside of the Great Pyramid—is so claustrophobic.

The darkest aspect of the whole Athenian community, which was also the darkest aspect of Greek slavery, was the toil of the pick-men in the Laureion silver mines. To explore those wretched tunnels, stamina, courage, self-possession of a high order were needed. A Ph.D. student of mine, taller and perhaps less athletic than the eventual explorers, tried going in, but he reappeared after no long time, in such muscular pain that he could hardly bear to pause for a photograph as he emerged. It was **James R. McCredie**, yet another Director of the American School of Classical Studies, who carried out the exploration of certain ones of these tunnels. It could not be done alone. McCredie enlisted **Martin Jones**, who did the map of Koroni, and **Arthur R. Steinberg**. The explorations were made at intervals over some weeks. They carried compasses and made measurements. For lights they had ordinary flash-lights. Breathing proved to be no problem; of course they did not linger in one spot—it was not as if they were miners. They found no silver, nor any object of note except, oddly, one Christian graffito. This extraordinary feat of exploration has never before been mentioned in print.

Under Water

So much for the heroes on land. Diving—the underwater exploration of wrecks and their cargoes—must certainly be included. Leave out for the moment the dominating fact that underwater exploration is a large part of the future of archaeology. Take it one wreck at a time: every bit of scholarly knowledge gained from wrecks stands for a defiance of death. Archaeological diving calls for elaborate planning, athletic personnel, careful training, fancy equipment, fancy expenditures—and, hardest of all, adequate publication. Not to mention courage, and faith in the crew: a single careless mistake, by the diver or by the crew, can be serious.

And so, as a counterpart to the airborne scholar and his fellows on or under land, mention ought to be made of diving. Alas, even if I could write it all out, to name all the names, to say anything much about depths and durations of time under water would make a catalogue of disproportionate size. To **George F. Bass**, more than to any other one person, underwater exploration owes most. He has written *Archaeology under Water* (London: Thmes and Hudson 1966), and his close associate, another pioneer, **Peter Throckmorton**, also has a readable account, *Shipwrecks and Archaeology* (Boston: Little Brown 1970).

World War II

For all his progeny, Poseidon was a god apart. So was Ares. Naturally in WW II it was mostly archaeologists, women as well as men, who, knowing Greece, served the good cause. None more than **Rodney S. Young**, who survived wounds in the early ambulance-driving stage, and later virtually created the Greek Intelligence unit of OSS. Other Americans, but none of greater achievement, could be named; among our allies, most of all **Capt. Nicholas G.L. Hammond**; among our adversaries, **Capt. Gunther Klaffenbach**.

Schoder's Photographing

Air Surveys and Perspectives before Schoder

Paintings that have as their subject whole cities date from late in the Renaissance; details, if available, would not help here. In the nineteenth century there were brilliant surmises of what might be done from the air. By WW I, air photography had made more than a beginning. Presently various governments carried out air surveys on a large scale. Sheets covering admirably, in some detail, all sections of the USA became obtainable from our government. By the early 1930's the Greek government was producing, in eight large sheets, a survey of Athens. Later an air survey in great detail of Messenia (scores of sheets) was obtained by **W.A. McDonald** for the University of Minnesota Messenia Expedition.

In 1922 **O.G.S. Crawford** made a discovery of revolutionary importance. From air photographs of County Wessex, he discovered that archaeological remains not discernible on the ground could be made out, often with startling clarity, from the air—all over the countryside, and often abundant: the lower courses of buildings, walls for fortification, boundaries, roads, irrigation works, and much else. A new book about the past was opened. The British went on to successes worthy of the beginning.

To round off this aspect of air photography, viz. discoveries made by direct observation and mostly by survey (vertical) photographs, add that in WW II, lenses almost fantastically keen (actually multiple lenses) were perfected for air photography. In photographs taken 700 feet up, you could see a string lying on a lawn. Interpretation of air views became an important function of air forces in the field. Among Classical scholars, **Lt. W.K. Pritchett** became the most proficient and experienced, though in scenes far from the Classical.

For two of the grand volumes which follow (made known to me by the Roman architecture historian William F. MacDonald), no such elaborate equipment (so far as I know) was required; for the first it was not available:

Père A. Poidebard, S.J., *La trace de Rome dans le desert de Syrie. Le limes . . . recherches aériennes (1925–1932).* Two vols. (Paris: Geuthner 1934).

R. Mouterde et Père A. Poidebard, S. J., *Le limes de Chalcis, Organisation de la steppe en haute Syrie romaine. Documents aériens et épigraphiques . . .* Two vols. (Paris: Guethner 1945).

Col. J. Baradez, *Fossatum Africae. Recherches aériennes sur l'organisation des confins sahariens à l'époque romaine* (Paris: Arts et Métiers Graphiques 1949).

But to go back. Before 1930, aerial explorations aiming at results of the same type had been tried in Greece. For Greece they did not work. As Rhys Carpenter explained to us, Greek customs and laws of inheritance had led to subdivision of the land generally into plots, with stone or shrubbery boundaries, so small that the features visible in England, with its larger fields, could not be discerned in Greece.

The "popular" (really substantial however) book on aerial exploration and photography is L. Deuel, *Flights into Yesterday* (New York: St. Martin's 1969). It is interesting that for Greece, of any period, he has nothing to report. So likewise there is nothing in two other notable works: John (S.P.) Bradford, *Ancient Landscapes in Europe and Asia* (London: Bell 1957) and J. Dassié, *Manuel d'archéologie aérienne* (Paris: Éditions Technic 1978).

It may be useful to add that two great monumemts of ancient Greece might some day be clarified by air surveys. One is Xerxes' Canal, for which Schoder's *Greece from the Air* (pages 236–237) is little help. The other is the Diolkos at Korinthos.

For the Greek and Roman world as a whole, the first ambitious use of large air views—not surveys but oblique views—was in A.A.M. Van Der Heyden and H.H. Scullard, *Atlas of the Classical World* (London: Nelson 1957). In this remarkable volume, the maps, which have much delicate color, seem almost crowded out by an abundance of black and white photographs, including plenty of ground views of archaeological significance; even particular objects are shown. Far more than an atlas, it is a rich volume. Only the maps, however, are inclusive. The photographs give a selection of typical and famous areas and scenes, not inclusive coverage.

The air photographs were made by the Greek Air Force, evidently using their own large cameras, manipulated by skilled military personnel, on flights made to obtain one view, or a few views, each. In these views, most of which are made from a great height, large areas are included. The Attic coast is shown (photograph no. 5), from Sounion, nearest, at the bottom, to Peiraieus, and, vaguely, beyond. (Where else is there a photograph of Attike so complete?) In these quarto-size pictures, archaeological sites are tiny.

Changes Projected by Schoder

Sketchy though it has to be, the foregoing account of air photography as it relates to Greece, which so far as I know is not duplicated anywhere, is the prelude to Father Schoder's work. Before him, only a few of the air views were exclusively of individual sites, such as, inevitably, the Akropolis. Father Schoder made changes. He conceived the idea of doing *all* the important sites, each one to be photographed not as part of a panorama, but for itself. The setting, in Father Schoder's conception, would be included, but it would be included, not for itself, but in order to make a complete visual presentation of the archaeological remains. Another major Schoder contribution was to be color. Not very long ago, a color plate in a book cost a thousand dollars, and was likely to be imperfect. That had changed. The difference which color made cannot easily be put in words: it is visual, not verbal. Suffice it to say that after Schoder's book, every book on Greek sites intended for a general class of readers will be in color.

Schoder Photographing

Father Schoder's idea, in getting the Greek Air Force to make flights available, may have been suggested by what Van Der Heyden and Scullard had accomplished for *Atlas of the Classical World*. But the differences Father Schoder contemplated called, not for a relatively few, set, semi-conventional semi-cartographic gray pictures, but rather for color photographs each of which should be a low-altitude portrait of an ancient city. Whole series of low-altitude flights would be needed, criss-crossing the whole area of today's Greece.

Father Schoder had the imagination, the boldness, and the tact to bring this about. Not just in one year. The beginning was modest. In 1950 the pilot of a United Nations plane which patrolled the Bulgarian border took Father Schoder along, and he made his first photographs of Mount Olympos. Seeking to expand the work, he next went to the U.S. Information Service, which sent him to the Chief-of-Staff, General Antonakas.

The interview was a success. "By the time I was through with him, he was completely sold on the idea. I convinced him that I was a friend of Greece and also a top-rate photographer. Then I persuaded him that I was working for him, not for me, that what I was doing would be for the benefit of the Greeks" (*National Jesuit News*, December 1974). The Air Force was so heartily won over to the project that they were willing to do it in three more years after the first year.

The plane which the Greek Air Force provided was a DC-3, the old reliable workhorse plane used everywhere in those days. It was big enough not to be much buffeted by freak breezes, and likewise it was stable enough for good pictures to be taken. It could fly at 1000 feet or lower with reasonable safety. And it did not mind if one door were taken off and left on the ground; the plane flew just as well. But it was the Greek Air Force that flew it. The pilots were trainees, but evidently well advanced. They knew what to do and how to do it. The book, dedicated to "the Officers and Pilots of the Hellenic Air Force" is a tribute to Greek skill, generosity, and love of learning.

In this connection note that one of the reviewers paid Father Schoder and the Greek Air Force an extraordinary, though unintended, compliment. The pictures are so good, he declared, that Father Schoder must have been untruthful. Contrary to what is stated with some fulness on pages 11–13, some of the pictures must have been taken, not from an aeroplane moving fast, but from a helicopter, poised stationary for each picture. The name of this reviewer need not be given here. Doubtless it is fully recorded by the computers with which, surely, the Nether Region is now equipped.

Disregard the rude interruption. The doorway was in the rear of the plane, 40 feet from the pilot; communication was by notes. For his position at the door opening, Father Schoder was held by a single strap (Pl. 1). Whether the plane ever lunged sideways with enough force really to test that strap and its attachment, we shall never know. The strength of the outward air suction is however considerable. Despite the buffetings, and often chilled, Father Schoder stayed on board, and the four lenses laid out in front of him for quick changing also survived. He used a Leica (35 mm.), holding it in his hands. The film was Kodachrome-X, then new. Unless airplane pictures are taken with some care, a wing of the plane is likely to show. In Schoder's volume only the slight blur of part of the plane is ever visible (pages 102, 183).

Snapping the picture however was only the last act in a long series. Every flight had to be planned. There had to be consideration of what lighting was best suited to each site. The atmosphere itself had to be taken into account: contrary to what nearly everyone believes, the Greek atmosphere is rarely clear. Most days, even in summer, Greece is not bathed in really pellucid sunlight. Perfectly clear days are so rare that when there is one, all the photographers leap for their cameras. Father Schoder had to cancel a dozen flights, on days when plane and crew were ready, but the air wasn't. Salamis, for instance, always so difficult to photograph, and probably off bounds even then, is partly lost in haze (pages 185 and 186).

The Flights and Their End

A few photographs (we are not told which ones) in *Ancient Greece from the Air* were made on flights in commercial planes; and there are also two views of Delphi taken from the cliffs (J.M. Cook noted these) and one shot taken on the ground (infra). The rest are from the Greek Air Force plane. One flight was in August 1962, the rest of the 13 flights, each of 5–7 hours, were in August 1967 and June 1968. Lykosoura and Kekyra City had not been photographed, and by 1972 there had been important new digs at Messene and Zakros. Father Schoder wished to add these. The excavators were willing and eager to have the new excavations included. The Greek Air Force was ready and eager. In October and November 1972 the atmosphere was "beautifully clear." But the military authorities forbade (pages 11B, 13B). The time had passed, they evidently decided, when the country could be exposed to what for safety considerations was virtually promiscuous photographing, exposing, it may be, vital military installations. On the

PLATE 1

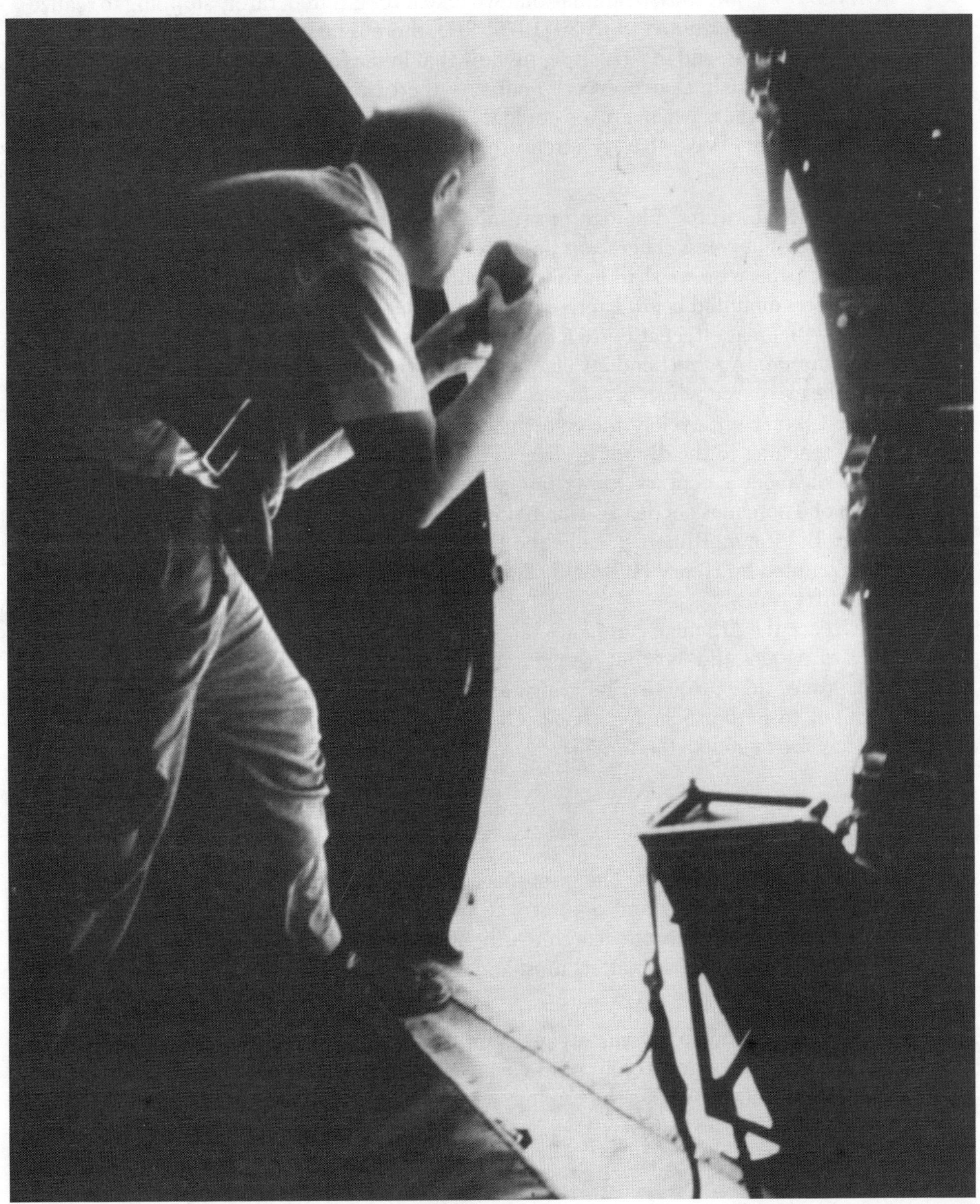

PLATE 1. Father Schoder photographing Greece from the air.

ground, Father Schoder took the wide-angle photograph of the excavated square at Messene (page 144) but that was all.

Greece from the Air is so familiar that we take it for granted, rarely stopping to realize that, as R.L. Pounder noted (*AJA* 80 [1976] 431), there is no book like it. But such photographing came to an end in 1972. It seems now that in the foreseeable future there will not be another book like it. Does everyone realize?—there can't be. The Schoder pictures were made in the last years when a plane could fly freely over Greece and photograph what it chose. The Schoder book, already a treasure, has become a rare treasure.

Substitutes

Are there substitutes? Photographs from commercial flights, when not forbidden, are limited but not hopeless. There can be more views than have been made from hills and mountains. Otherwise we shall have to be content, in the main, with photographs taken from cameras mounted below captive balloons, in the fashion pioneered by J. Whittlesey, and used with great effect at Porto Kheli. These can be excellent: see now J. McK. Camp, II, *The Athenian Agora* (London: Thames and Hudson 1986).

Another resource which is comparatively new is three-dimensional scale models. In Widener Library are cycloramic color models of Harvard and the entire setting, all its features, reaching to the distant horizon. There are three of these, showing the place at intervals of about a century (some say, showing the desecration of a fine scene—the tradition of Thoreau is not dead). The making of such models was perfected by my friend Theodore B. Pitman: Rupert B. Lillie did the research; the background (rivers, bays, sea, sky) was painted by Henry H. Brooks. This was financed by an intelligent alumnus (each tree cost fifty cents).

In Greece the Athenian Agora has taken the lead. Visitors can stand by the models in the Stoa of Attalos and look out over the whole Agora. The new volume by John Camp (supra) proves that for actual buildings and monuments, models are the best possible supplement to Father Schoder's book. Of course, they can tell only part of the story, unless they are to be like the three Harvard models, including all features of the terrain.

The Book: Editorial and Other Decisions

Efforts for perfection, heroic or (like most of ours most of the time) unglamorous, usually end when publication begins. The publishers of *Greeece from the Air*, who have done a great deal for archaeology and done it well, probably would agree that in the book as published some things needed changing—though *not* the quality of the reproductions of photographs: they are what matters most and they are fine.

The Limits of the Book

These were of course beyond anyone's control. No fewer than 70 places are included. All had to be what the Air Force could cover, scil. within the boundaries of present-day Greece. Omitted are of course the Euxine, Asia Minor (would that we had a few Schoder views of Troy!), Kypros, Egypt, Libya, and all the European coast west beyond Kerkyra.

Toponyms

The sites (i.e. the photographs, plans, articles) are all in alphabetical order. To make the volume usable for speakers of various languages, all the place-names are given, in the Contents (pages 7–10), on the Map (pages 14–15; the Map is not listed in the Contents), and in the text, first in *Modern Greek*, transliterated. Thus we have Avdira, Fili, Heronia, Olimbos. Bauron is not under B but under V (Vravron). (In the present article, except for quotations from the Map, I have avoided these, and also all Latinizations, in favor of direct transliteration.)

Apportionment of Photographs

For the 70 places included, the total number of photographs is 139 (plus the cover of the paperback edition, which repeats page 69). Of the 70 places, 46 are given one photograph each: 24 of the rest have 2 each, but a few have more, and Athenai has 8.

Layout

The layout of the (9½ × 7 inch) pages was an awkward problem. For any one site, article, plan, and (one) photograph usually take a page and a half; Aigina, for instance (pages 16–17): the essay for Aigosthena, on page 17, is directly below the photograph of Aigina. The photograph and plan of Aigosthena, on page 18, are opposite the essay on Hagia Triadha, on page 19. And so on. Not seldom a reader unacquainted with a site might be confused. All the bibliographies on all the places are printed together (without notice except in the Contents) way at the back, pages 243–254. In the next edition, which we all look forward to, article, bibliography, photograph(s) and plan must be comfortably together, on a larger page.[1]

Plans

Nearly all the photographs are accompanied by a small pen-and-ink plan which is intended to identify the buildings, etc. shown in the photograph by means of numbers and a numbered list. This feature is not Schoder's work and evidently was not under his control. A devotee of the elaborate feeling for proportions (or numerical mysticism) shown in the Theater at Epidauros, he can hardly have been pleased at the distorted diagram provided (on page 67). The reviewers' criticisms of the drawings are justified in the main. Some few are good, e.g. the Aphaia Temple (page 16): the draughtswoman was evidently given access to a published plan. Compass directions are always given; scales never.

[1] Not primarily archaeological, B. Wolman, *Above the Holy Land: Israel from the Air* (San Francisco: Chronicle Books), just published (1987), is a handsome presentation of the country today. It shows advances, some of which these 25 years have prompted: the photographer in his own plane and obviously with the most advanced cameras (makes not specified); a book of large pages (10 inches tall, 12½ wide), with identifications and descriptions close at hand—they could be brief, however, since they did not need to include much scholarly detail.

Much the same can be said of another fine new volume, F. Quilici, *Italy from the Air* (London: Weidenfeld 1987).

Apparatus

The Map (pages 14–15) has flaws (makers of small maps usually err): Festos and Aghia Triadha are put on the coast; so is Korinthos, which is put northeast of Kenchree; Pilos (Blegen's is intended) is below Sfaktiria.

At the end of the volume, after the last of the photographs and articles, are four sets of apparatus. Perfectionists who want to make their copies perfect may want to note the following.

"Mediterranean Chronology" (page 241) mentions four (very good) authorities, warns about controversies, prudently uses "c." and "?". Thus the Trojan War is not Blegen's earlier date but "c. 1210–1200," as if the "epic" duration were to be respected.

"Glossary" (pages 242–243): add Postern and (for pages 228–229) Stibadeion.

The Bibliography is preceded by a short List of Abbreviations (page 243) in which there is an error oddly not caught in London: for *Journal of Hellenistic Studies* read *Journal of Hellenic Studies*. There is a short bibliography for every site, no small labor (pages 243–254, double-columned). There being few items in each bibliography, the order of the items should not be alphabetical, but should be chronological, to show the progress of excavations and study. The (limited) entries seem to be good ones, and errors few—mostly erroneous and omitted initials. Homer A. Thompson is the author, not the editor, of all but the first chapter of the *Guide to the Athenian Agora* (3rd ed.; page 244B), and W.B. Dinsmoor, Sr., *The Architecture of Ancient Greece*, should appear, as 2nd ed. (1950), not once (Megalopolis) but many times.

The Index (pages 255–256), it should say, is limited to men and women, including a few who are mythical (e.g. Amphiaraos, Bellerophon) and some who are semi-divine (Asclepius). Add Amasis, page 187.

The Book: Articles and Photographs

Reviews: General Remarks

There were nine reviews. The first was in *The Times Literary Supplement* (*TLS*), the rest in Classical journals, except for the one in *The Journal of the Society of Architectural Historians* (*JSAH*). The *TLS* reviewer, J.M. Cook, who had had more field experience than any of the others, alone showed full appreciation of the many kinds of effort involved. The book, he says, is "well balanced." Schoder "has thought out what he wants to do and has done it conscientiously."

The review in *JSAH* was by J. Tyrwhitt, a specialist in the relations of architecture to the environment ("ektistics"; and she lives in Greece). She found it "helpful to architects," who are "accustomed to [the limitations of] working from plans." She calls it "a magnificent job, a beautiful and useful book."

D.R. Wilson (*CR* 1977, 310–11), a member of the Committee for Aerial Photography, Cambridge, found that the book, the aim of which was to provide a new experience and perspective, is "splendidly successful"; it is "breath-taking and informative."

All of the reviews are short. None attempts to find from study of the book any positive addition to knowledge of Ancient Greece. Nevertheless all the reviewers really did work, and they criticize. What follows herein is intended to touch on all the criticisms.

The Articles

For each site, Father Schoder himself provides a short article intended to give the general reader what he might like to know—history, archaeology, all the rest; and also a bibliography. This is a tall order! calling for the essence of knowledge about the 70 principal places of Ancient Greece, including the Bronze and Dark Ages.

None of the reviewers comments at length on the articles. Father Schoder—it hardly needs saying—is not one who would make a half-hearted job of this. He tackled it head on, studying problems, providing measurements and other precise facts and figures. Not everyone would refrain, as he does, from dwelling on the values of the pictures, values which are by no means all obvious. The articles do not, so to speak, get in the way. But more than that: for anyone needing to get a quick first sampling of knowledge about any one of the 70 places, the Schoder articles (with their bibliographies, and even apart from the photographs) are just about the easiest first port of call. Even apart from the pictures, the reviewers should have said, it is a useful book.

Beyond these general comments is the small multitude of details, mostly unimportant for the "tourist." For the amusement of colleagues, should something be said about each of the articles in a sample lot?—say the first nine, all of them places in A— ? Some, but only some, of the notes that follow here might have been in the book.

Aigina, "eye-sore of the Peiraieus" (emphasize that it was a world beset by fly-borne eye disease): how remarkably wealthy, paying Athenai an annual tribute, T(alents) 30, far larger than any other member of the Athenian Empire.

Aigosthena: infra.

Hagia Triadha: still strange is its relation to Phaistos: it was surely no "summer palace," because it is hardly cooler. Allude to its great paintings, and add a phrase on what all of us have considered the most important monument of Minoan religion, the Sarcophagus (C.R. Long, *The Ayia Triadha Sarcophagus*, *SIMA* XLI [Göteborg: Åström 1974]).

Amphiareion: for recent excavations, see *Archaeological Reports for 1986–1987*, page 108. It was a rationally located place of healing. Like the not far distant slopes of Pentele, where many infirmaries were built a century ago, it is a healthy-seeming place, and despite there being in Attike several healing cults, the Amphiareion was closely related to the city. Two strange items: its water-clock was a twin of the one in the Agora (Camp, supra, 157); and certain women members of Epikouros' School (the Kepos) made dedications in the Amphiareion, of course for health, as they did also in the big Athenian sanctuary of Asklepios—hardly actions which Epikouros would approve. Though not the first or only philosopher to admit women to his School (Platon admitted one or two), he was the most liberal, and their acts of dedicating may have surprised him. For the history of women in Greece, this must have been a crisis (C.J. Castner, "Epicurean Hetairai as Dedicants to Healing Deities?" *GRBS* 23 [1982] 51–57).

Amphipolis: reviewers find the photograph dim and uninformative. It *is* dim, but it shows the river and the city's situation quite clearly, from inland to the sea, whereas the excavations would not make much of a picture. The article is very good, and the bibliography contains the Lion, reconstructed by O. Broneer.

Argos, as one end of a sort of Korinthos-Argos axis, has come more into its own, now that the remarkable synthesis is published of the history of the northeast Peloponnesos by Katherine Adshead (*Politics of the Archaic Peloponnese: The Transition from Archaic to Classical Politics* [Avebury Monograph, Aldershot, Eng.: Gower Co. 1986]).

Athenai, not "the Greece of Greece" but "the Hellas of Hellas" (somehow there is a real difference). Not to forget Sir Alfred E. Zimmern's *The Greek Commonwealth* (5th ed., Oxford: University Press 1931). Various recent attempts to deny, or to modify, the primacy of Athenai, out of jealousy or mere rebelliousness, are merely tiresome. On the other hand, they, and Sir Alfred, and practically everyone, have made no real answer to the fact that a short three decades after the Funeral Oration and a very few years after Thoukydides ceased to write, leaving the Funeral Oration as we now have it, the Athenaioi executed Sokrates. So there is more to be said; including the Thirty Tyrants.

Abdera: some day further excavations may help us to understand better how the tribute can have been as much as T15.

Aulis: here for once we miss the Schoder readiness with figures, but this is rational: the preposterous number of ships listed in the Catalogue cannot possibly have been accommodated at Aulis. The myth had to give *some* point of departure. Iphigeneia had to be sacrificed *some*where. The place had to be plausibly situated. The myth named no major city, no dynast who could have the credit.

The Photographs

The reviewers all found some of the photographs to be really awesome, but several reviewers found various photographs faulty. Of the faults, not a few were attributed to a failure to conceive an exact purpose for the book. It is best to distinguish two aspects: archaeological remains, and settings.

Archaeological Remains

These of course are mostly buildings. Exceptions begin at once. The Khaironeia Lion is the only archaeology on page 96—but how admirably centered, how pleasing the two live animals and the man, how well-judged the low altitude! Marathon, the Mound, almost lost on page 139. Aigina, the Aphaia Temple, page 17, has a limited jumble of other remains. But who would leave these out?

The great majority of the sites are shown in photographs which include buildings. These vary extremely, from Delos, pages 57, 59, with scores of buildings in tiny size, to Hagia Triadha, page 21, with nearly every room distinct. One reviewer finds, correctly it seems to me, that no photograph in the book provides as clear an image as the architect's drawings in the regular publication of the site (Pounder, supra, 431). Photographs made by captive balloons are also likely to be superior (supra p. 22). Grant all that. One distinctive value of *Greece from the Air* consists, as the author claims (page 11), in showing how the buildings really look when seen together in their setting.

The Settings

These also should be considered in logical divisions. Some of the sites are shown solely in photographs which have no distinct archaeological remains at all: Amphipolis (page 24), Aulis (44), Ithake (101, 102), Kerkyra (114), Khalkis (91), Mount Olympos (163, 164),

Salamis (185, 186), Sphakteria (194, 194), Thermopylai (214), Xerxes' Canal (237). Together, these make up one-seventh of the book. Most of these are first-rate pictures.

One of the most valuable features of the book is the separate, more distant photograph which provides a setting for every major site. The decision to provide these settings must have been made early on. It usually involved also a decision to take the setting from a different direction. One can only say, How admirable.

Admirable for archaeology, but also for what is shown of the Greek lands today: Greece as it now is, painted as it were in full colors on 139 canvasses. No other book—is it not true to say?—has has so much of Greece in it.

Among the photographs, taking them as a whole, every user of the book will have his favorites; everyone, or at least nearly every reviewer, finds some pictures disappointing. Certainly there is much variation in quality, there was bound to be. Making a list of my own favorites, I find I have 31 of them. My list of the disappointers would be much shorter. If, despite the subjective factors in picking favorites, some favorites have to be named, I venture to say that nearly anyone can turn again, without fear of disappointment, to some of the less obvious prizes: Akropolis (both views on page 32); the Stadion (you can see the curvature in the rows of seats, 39); Khalkis, setting (91); Knossos, setting (116); Bassai, setting, how extraordinary (232). Gla (79) is phenomenal.

Let's not forget teaching. In years past, giving a full-year three-times-a-week course in Greek History, I tried near the beginning to lecture on soils and surfaces (with small Geology to help); on seasons, rainfall; flora, crops; the sky and the sea. Much of such lecturing may still today be necessary—I think it is—but now I see that almost at once *Greece from the Air* should be laid before the students. The pictures are worth hours of words.

We come to the several reviewers, who, doing their duty, asked, For what class of readers was the book intended? As nearly always, the fact that the question is asked implies that the reviewer's answer will be pejorative. The answer is sure to be: The question was not properly considered; or, Wrongly answered. In the present instance, it does not seem to me that the question leads to any profitable answer. It might, however, lead to a narrower but more important question, viz. Can anything new be learned by study of the photographs? Perhaps not; but hoping for corrections by scholars more fully informed, I add here notes on two sites.

Aigosthena: why does it seem to have amounted to so little? The fortifications, as E.F. Benson noted, were the finest preserved in Greece (they have stood for all the centuries, but a recent earthquake is said to have damaged them severely). The quarrying of the limestone and the actual constructing must have taken a large force and ample funds. Once it was constructed, a garrison to hold so commodious a fort must have been much larger than local resources could support. The photographs record, what a visit instills: very limited farmland, only a mountainous rocky hinterland extending inland for miles. Timber was no doubt abundant, but there was seemingly nothing else except fishing, tolls (but it was an arduous march north), and guard duty. Aigosthena needs explaining, but at least the photographs help to raise the question. Whatever it proves, the Emperor Hadrian, as Father Schoder notes, went there.

Ithake: at least for one who has never explored it, also looks barren in the pictures. Father Schoder's article shows that he has given much attention to the Odyssean problem. Schliemann was among the first to search for Odysseus' palace. Even now, year after year, hopeful young archaeologists go to Ithake. Allow for ca. 3000 years of change: do not the pictures suggest that Ithake could not create, and could not support, a Mykenaian palace? A Mykenaian palace was above all a place of wealth. It was created by large resources and it was maintained by large resources. It seems more than possible that, like Homer's other great hero, Akhilleus, Odysseus had a palace only in never-never land.

Publishng History

So there were many aspects, many labors, spread over ten years, on which Father Schoder toiled. Naturally the greatest of Heroes, Herakles, comes to mind. Perhaps wrongly: somehow it seems unlikely that Herakles, for all his power and versatility and usefulness, would have made a good photographer.

Publication

The publication by Thames and Hudson, London, had been arranged for some years before, and they had planned American, Dutch, French, and German translations and editions. All of these were issued, also one in Switzerland. The London edition, *Ancient Greek Sites from the Air*, was published in 1974, export being forbidden, at £4.95 (paperback £2.95); and the others soon followed. The plates (photographs, all in color) are the same in all. The American edition was issued by the Oxford University Press, New York, with the title *Wings over Hellas, Ancient Greek Sites from the Air*, at $17.50.

Sales

The foreign language editions were published, as planned, in 1974, the same year as the English (the translation of the Dutch, however, was faulty: see W.J. Verdenius, *Mnemosyne*, 1978, 337–38). Review copies either were not sent out to France, Germany, and Italy, or not acted on, or the reviews somehow escaped *L'Année philologique*. But the sales were large: in Germany, 12,000 in the first eight months, the second printing was of 18,000 copies; the English edition, not vigorously backed, had early sales of only (!) 8000. For the subsequent paperback edition, figures are lacking.

L'Envoi: Plataiai

Now leave these matters, so as to end with a glance at Plataiai. Surely no Greek polis had a history of more ardent patriotism, of more strenuous effort, of more bitter suffering, and, as I think we are about to see, of more rousing and masterful action. But how calm it looks on page 179!—a carpeting of green and tan fields, modern roads ambling off into the distance, not a hint of that Boiotian winter mud. In the midst of so many exciting views, it is good to have this image of placidity.

IMPERIUM ROMANUM, DEUTSCHES REICH:
The Evocation of Antique Symbolism

HERBERT W. BENARIO

The nationalist uprisings of 1848 in Europe proved immediately unsuccessful in Germany and Italy.[1] Yet, within slightly more than a score of years, there was a unified monarchy in Italy and a new empire in Germany. The German Empire, with Bismarck as Chancellor, was much the stronger and more important of the two, but in one significant respect Italy was more fortunate: she had an illustrious ancestry reaching back to antiquity upon which she could call for emotional and national support.

Not so in the case of Germany. That land's antiquity was exemplified by Tacitus' *Germania*; it was a land "gloomy with forests or unwholesome with swamps" (5.1). Its earliest known history was inextricably linked with Rome, from the invasions of the Cimbri and Teutones, late in the second century B.C., into the warm lands of the south, to Caesar's "hoisting of the flag" on Germanic territory, and on to the great struggles of the decades around the beginning of the Christian era, when Roman invasion was countered by German defense.

During the first three-quarters of the nineteenth century, there was a yearning through much of Germany for a national monument. The Wars of Liberation against Napoleon gave particular impetus, above all in Bavaria where Ludwig I had built a German Hall of Fame in a replica of the Parthenon high above the Danube east of Regensburg, called Walhalla, and upon its completion began a monument to celebrate German victories over the French emperor at Kelheim, southwest of Regensburg, the model of which, at least for the interior, was the Pantheon.

But neither proved to be representative of Germany as a whole. The decade of the seventies, however, saw two monuments which represented the aspirations of the German people and the German empire, one defiant, the other arrogant, one the culmination of an individual's dream, the other the expression of a people's pride. Both are essentially "Roman" monuments, in appearance as well as inspiration; I suggest that the borrowing of Roman panoply was a conscious attempt to borrow as well some of the glory of antiquity's greatest empire. The two monuments are the Hermannsdenkmal in the Teutoburg Forest near Detmold, and the statue of Germania, the Niederwalddenkmal, above the Rhine near Rüdesheim. As a Roman antecedent, an example of the type rather than a direct model (since in the nineteenth century the remains were merely a battered hulk), we may consider the Tropaeum Augusti at La Turbie, above Monaco in southern France. I shall discuss this first.

[1] The following abbreviation will be used:
EJ = V. Ehrenberg and A.H.M. Jones, *Documents Illustrating the Reigns of Augustus and Tiberius* (Oxford: Clarendon 1955[2]).

Although the Romans possessed Spanish provinces after 197 B.C. and established a province in the south of France in 121, they did not undertake to secure the narrow land route through Liguria which led from Italy to these western provinces. Appian, writing much later, expressed surprise at this omission:

> It was considered astonishing that the great Roman armies marching against the Gauls and Iberians, passing many times through the Alps, had for so long neglected the Alpine tribes. I believe, however, that the Romans preferred to march straight to their goal, thrusting their way through these hostile people and that Caesar, occupied in Gaul and elsewhere and also with his quarrel with Pompey, put off a settlement until a later period. (*Ill.* 15)

For Caesar that "later period" never came. As with so much else, it was left to Augustus to rectify the situation. In four campaigns over a period of eleven years, in 25, 16, 15, and 14 B.C., the hazards of movement over the entire Alpine belt were removed.[2] The first is the best recorded; it involved the defeat and virtual annihilation of the Salassi and the establishment of a colony for the veterans of the Praetorian Guard, Augusta Praetoria, the modern Aosta.[3] The site was a road junction for passage of the Great and Little St. Bernard Passes.[4] An immediate result of the pacification of the western Alps was construction of the Via Julia Augusta in 13–12 B.C.; the highway continued the Via Aurelia from its termination in Liguria.[5] A second was an agreement with King Cottius, who was designated a prefect and ruled over several tribes; this settlement was commemorated by an arch at Susa, dated 9–8 B.C.[6] And two years later was dedicated a much more impressive monument of Roman supremacy, recording the submission of forty-four tribes, the Tropaeum Augusti at La Turbie (Pl. 2a). Placed high on the cliff above Monaco, it was visible from well out at sea, and from both directions along the coast; its magnificence was emphasized by its gleaming exterior of white Carrara marble.[7]

The Tropaeum consisted of three parts, the lowest a large square base, on one side of which was inscribed the text, stretching more than eight meters in length. It reads (*CIL* V 7817 = EJ 40):[8]

> imp. Caesari divi filio Aug. pont. max. imp. XIIII tr. pot. XVII s.p.q.R., quod eius ductu auspiciisque gentes Alpinae omnes quae a mari supero ad inferum pertinebant sub imperium p. R. sunt redactae. gentes Alpinae devictae Triumpilini Camunni Venostes

[2] See P. Casimir, *Le trophée d'Auguste à la Turbie* (Marseille: Tacussel 1932) 23–45: "Les guerres alpines d'Auguste."

[3] Strabo 4.206; Dio. 53.25; *ILS* 6753.

[4] On Aosta see *Archeologia in valle d'Aosta* (Aosta: Assessorato del Turismo Urbanistica e Beni Culturali 1982).

[5] See V.W. von Hagen, *The Roads That Led to Rome* (Cleveland & New York: World Publishing 1967) 192–98; G. Radke, "Viae Publicae Romanae," *RE Supp.* 13 (1971) 267–68; R. Chevallier, *Roman Roads* (Berkeley & Los Angeles: California 1976) 137; N.H.H. Sitwell, *Roman Roads of Europe* (London: Cassell 1981) 73.

[6] *ILS* 94 = EJ 166.

[7] Casimir (supra n. 2); P. MacKendrick, *Roman France* (London: Bell 1971) 86–89.

[8] The same tribes are recorded by Pliny, *NH* 3.136–38; see A. Stein, *Römische Inschriften in der antiken Literatur* (Prague: Taussig & Taussig 1931) 34.

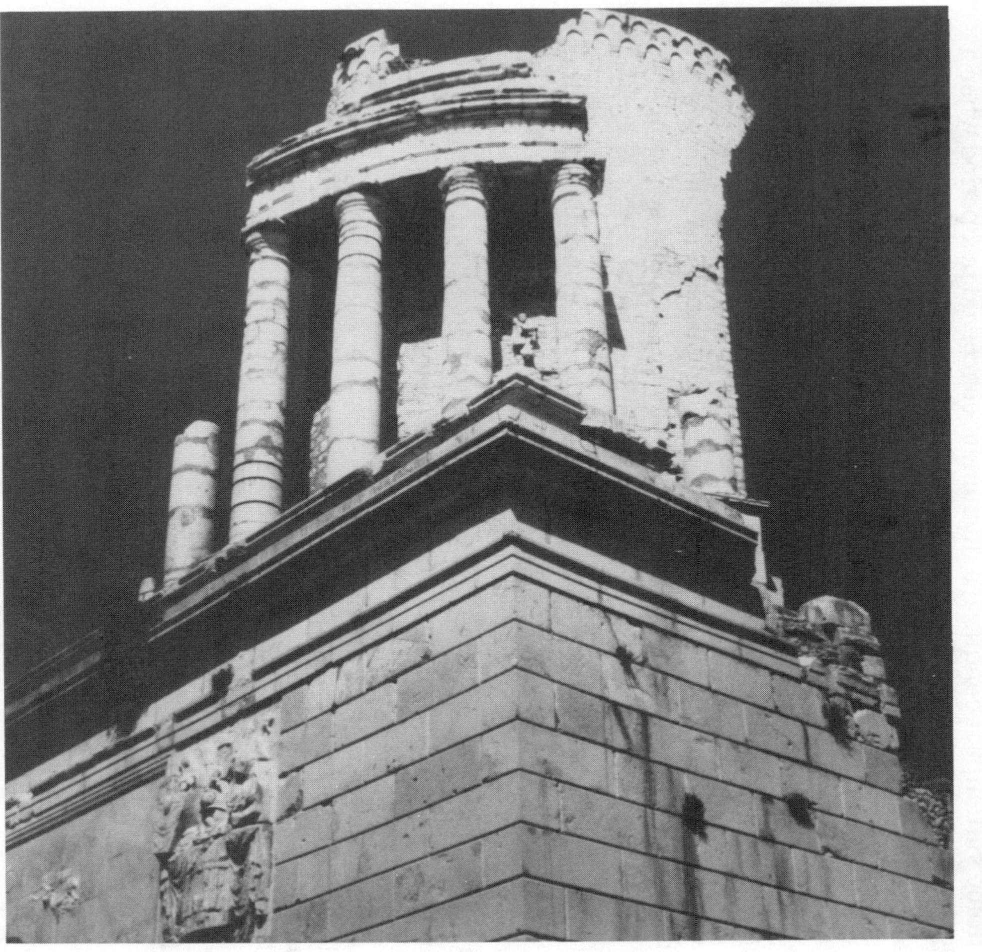

PLATE 2a. The Tropaeum Augusti at La Turbie. Photo author.

2b. The Hermannsdenkmal in the Teutoberg Forest near Detmold. Photo author.

> Vennonetes Isarci Breuni Genaunes Focunates Vindelicorum gentes quattuor Consuanetes Rucinates Licates Catenates Ambisontes Rugusci Suanetes Calucones Brixenetes Leponti Uberi Nantuates Seduni Varagri Salassi Acitavones Medulli Ucenni Caturiges Brigiani Sogiontii Bodiontii Nemaloni Edenates Vesubiani Veamini Galli taetri Ulatti Ecdini Vergunni Egui Turi Nematuri Oratelli Nerusi Velauni Suetri

In the *Res Gestae*, Augustus later claimed (26.3) *Alpes a regione ea quae proxima est Hadriano mari ad Tuscum pacificavi nulli genti bello per iniuriam inlato.* One may wonder whether all forty-four tribes here recorded would have agreed that Rome's warfare was in every instance marked by an absence of *iniuria*. Above the base was a circular drum, smaller in diameter, surrounded by columns. Topping the whole was a statue of the emperor with two trophies of weapons at his feet.

The entire monument, in its praise of Augustus, in its seemingly endless roster of the subjugated, in its domineering location, in its handsome and sumptuous appearance, was a clear statement of Rome's supremacy. It was by no means unique; it is only one of many by which Rome made its superiority tangibly visible: one may recall the temple of Jupiter Anxur at Terracina, the huge arch at Richborough in Britain, the Tropaeum Traiani at Adamklissi in Dacia, and the arches trumpeting triumph throughout the empire. Rome had been destined to rule the world—*tu regere imperio populos, Romane, memento*[9]—and the world was compelled to gaze upon symbols of that rule.

This was, I suggest, the background of the two modern German monuments to which we now turn.[10] The first, the Hermannsdenkmal (Pl. 2b), commemorates ancient German resistance to Rome's attempt at conquest, a monument conceived in a period when a larger Germany had not yet come into existence. The second, the statue of Germania (Pls. 3, 5), no longer spoke of the pride of resistance but rather of the arrogance of conquest, gazing in the direction of the France which the German Empire had humbled and humiliated at Sedan, not many years before its conception.

Arminius was one of the major figures in Tacitus' narrative of the principate of Tiberius. The Cheruscan chieftain received one of the historian's most splendid obituaries:

> liberator haud dubie Germaniae et qui non primordia populi Romani, sicut alii reges ducesque, sed florentissimum imperium lacessierit, proeliis ambiguus, bello non victus (*Ann.* 2.88.2).

About a century and a half ago, the endeavor began to erect a monument to the memory of Arminius (the German Hermann) on the approximate site of the great disaster which the Romans suffered at Arminius' hands, in A.D. 9, in the Teutoburg Forest. The monument (Pl. 2b), the work and lifelong dream of the sculptor Ernst von Bandel, was dedicated by Kaiser Wilhelm I on August 16, 1875. The place chosen is atop a rather

[9] Verg., *Aen.* 6.851.

[10] See T. Nipperdey, "Nationalidee und Nationaldenkmal im 19. Jahrhundert," *HZ* 206 (1968) 529–85 = *Gesellschaft, Kultur, Theorie. Gesammelte Aufsätze zur neueren Geschichte* (Göttingen: Vandenhoeck & Ruprecht 1976) 133–73, 432–39.

PLATE 3. Germania, The Niederwalddenkmal above the Rhine near Rüdesheim. Photo author.

steep hill some four miles from Detmold, a small town about thirty miles north of Paderborn. Here one is presented with a superb view, overlooking the thick forest, and it then becomes all too clear how Varus could have been waylaid. The approach to the Hermannsdenkmal, once the top of the hill has been negotiated, is by a gently sloping path which brings the visitor to the rear of the statue. It is a most imposing complex, some fifty meters high including the base; Arminius himself wears a winged helmet and holds his right arm aloft. His right arm grasps a sword, raised on high, on the blade of which, on the two sides, are the inscriptions, *Deutsche Einigkeit meine Stärke* and *Meine Stärke Deutschlands Macht*, "German unity is my strength, my strength is Germany's might."

Little could Arminius, who was unable to unify his own tribe and who died by the treachery of relatives, have realized that the unity here invoked was not to be attained for more than 1800 years. Unity, indeed, was not a concept which the ancient Germans understood or pursued. Tribal supremacy was paramount, and warfare both within and between tribes was common. One people would eagerly extirpate another, if opportunity offered, as Tacitus reports:

> pulsis Bructeris ac penitus excisis vicinarum consensu nationum, seu superbiae odio seu praedae dulcedine seu favore quodam erga nos deorum; nam ne spectaculo quidem proelii invidere. (*Germ.* 33.1)

It was for this reason that Tiberius believed that Germanicus could be recalled from his German command, *posse et Cheruscos ceterasque rebellium gentis . . . internis discordiis relinqui* (*Ann.* 2.26.3). The blatant nationalism expressed on the statue's sword is rather a statement of the pride of the German Empire and a warning to other European nations.[11] It is a precise expression of the mood of Bismarck's Germany.

As Augustus had trophies of defeated peoples at his feet on the monument at La Turbie, so does Arminius here, although not as near. In front of the monument is a porch with a hemicycle, at the two ends of which were placed representations of trophies, with weapons and armor, this time Roman, not barbarian, hanging in disarray. The Arminius statue is thus symbolic, evoking Germany's first "national" hero, a man who, with the passage of centuries, had assumed epic characteristics. The sculptor's achievement is not, perhaps, artistically significant; it gains whatever merit and renown it possesses from its subject.[12]

[11] See also R. Kuehnemund, *Arminius or the Rise of a National Symbol in Literature* (Chapel Hill: North Carolina 1953) and W. Laqueur, *Germany Today. A Personal Report* (London: Weidenfeld & Nicolson 1985) chap. 6, "Arminius or Patriotism Rediscovered."

[12] P. Clemen, *Der Denkmalbegriff und seine Symbolik* (Bonn: Scheur 1933) 19: "Nicht der absolute und nicht der relative Kunstwert ist hier das Bestimmende, sondern der symbolische Gehalt . . . . Gilt das nicht auch von Ernst Bandels Hermannsdenkmal im Teutoburger Wald, das in der Geschichte der deutschen Denkmalplastik vielleicht nur einen bescheidenen Platz beansprucht, das aber nicht wie der grosse Herkules von Wilhelmshöhe uns nur als ein bergbekrönendes dekoratives Kunstwerk erscheint, sondern als Träger einer hohen nie zu vergessenden Symbolik und uns deshalb etwas unendlich Ehrwürdiges ist."

The same can be said, in even stronger terms, of the "National Monument" in the Niederwald (Pl. 3).[13] The statue of Germania was the winner of a competition to commemorate a contemporary event, the founding of the empire. The intent was that this statue would symbolize, to German and foreigner alike, the power of the new state. The monument was an attempt to represent national identity in a visible, tangible figure.

The heroic Germania evokes the Roman symbolic goddesses Italia (as shown e.g. on the Ara Pacis, Pl. 4a) and Roma, representative of the state which produced antiquity's greatest empire.[14] There were, to be sure, other antecedents, not so complimentary. The first personifications of Germania, as *capta*, appear on coins of Domitian, dated from 85 on (Pl. 4b). The most outstanding, however, were surely Hadrian's denarii, dated 134–138. On the reverse is a frontal view of the standing Germania, head turned either to right or left, holding a spear in her right hand and resting her left on a shield.[15] These coins are part of a series which displays the typical personifications of the Roman provinces. Similar in conception and message is the series of splendid reliefs of the provinces which, it may be, decorated the podium of the Hadrianeum, the Temple of the Deified Hadrian, in Rome.[16] The modern German Empire did not, at least at that time, have aspirations to match Rome's achievements; it was content to have reduced France and to have rendered moot, at the battle of Sedan, France's traditional claim that the Rhine River should be the boundary of the two states.[17] That is why Germania gazes westward; that is why such a prominent place on the base of the monument is given to the words of the poem *Die Wacht am Rhein*, which, set to music, became a national hymn during the Franco-Prussian War (Fig. 1). The Rhine is German and will so remain! The refrain has place of honor, writ large: *Lieb Vaterland, magst ruhig sein: fest steht und treu die Wacht am Rhein.*

The foundation stone was laid on September 16, 1877; the inauguration, attended by the Kaiser, occurred on September 28, 1883. Built on a rectangular substructure of sandstone and quartzite stone, the monument features Germania, who symbolizes the union of all German tribes, as earlier, in Munich, the statue of Bavaria had represented the unity of that kingdom.[18] In her uplifted right hand Germania holds the German Imperial Crown of old and in her left hand the sword of the Reich. The central space of the monument is occupied by a bronze relief 10.80 m. long and 2.60. m. high (Pl. 5). Some two

[13] Clemen (supra n. 12) 7: "der Germania auf dem Niederwald, in der eine grosse Aufgabe einen Künstler leider nur mittleren Formats gefunden . . . ."

[14] See, *inter multa*, the splendid figures on the Ara Pacis Augustae and the base of the Column of Antoninus Pius, easily accessible in Nash I 68 and 272, and the Cancelleria reliefs, for which see P. MacKendrick, *The Mute Stones Speak* (New York: St. Martin's 1960) 238.

[15] *RIC* Domitian 69, 252, Hadrian 302, 303.

[16] See J.M.C. Toynbee, *The Hadrianic School* (Cambridge: University Press 1934) 86–97 for discussion of the coinage, 152–59 for the "Hadrianeum" provinces. For the latter, see also Nash I 559–67.

[17] Recall Danton's statement, in 1793, that France's frontiers have been fixed by nature on the Rhine: "it is there that our boundaries are fated to be placed, and no power on earth shall keep us from our goal."

[18] Nipperdey (supra n. 10) 158.

PLATE 4

Plate 4a. Italia, panel from the Ara Pacis Augustae. Photo Schoder.

4b. *Germania Capta* on an aureus of Domitian issued in 88. Munich, Staatliche Münzsammlung; photo courtesy Bernhard Overbeck.

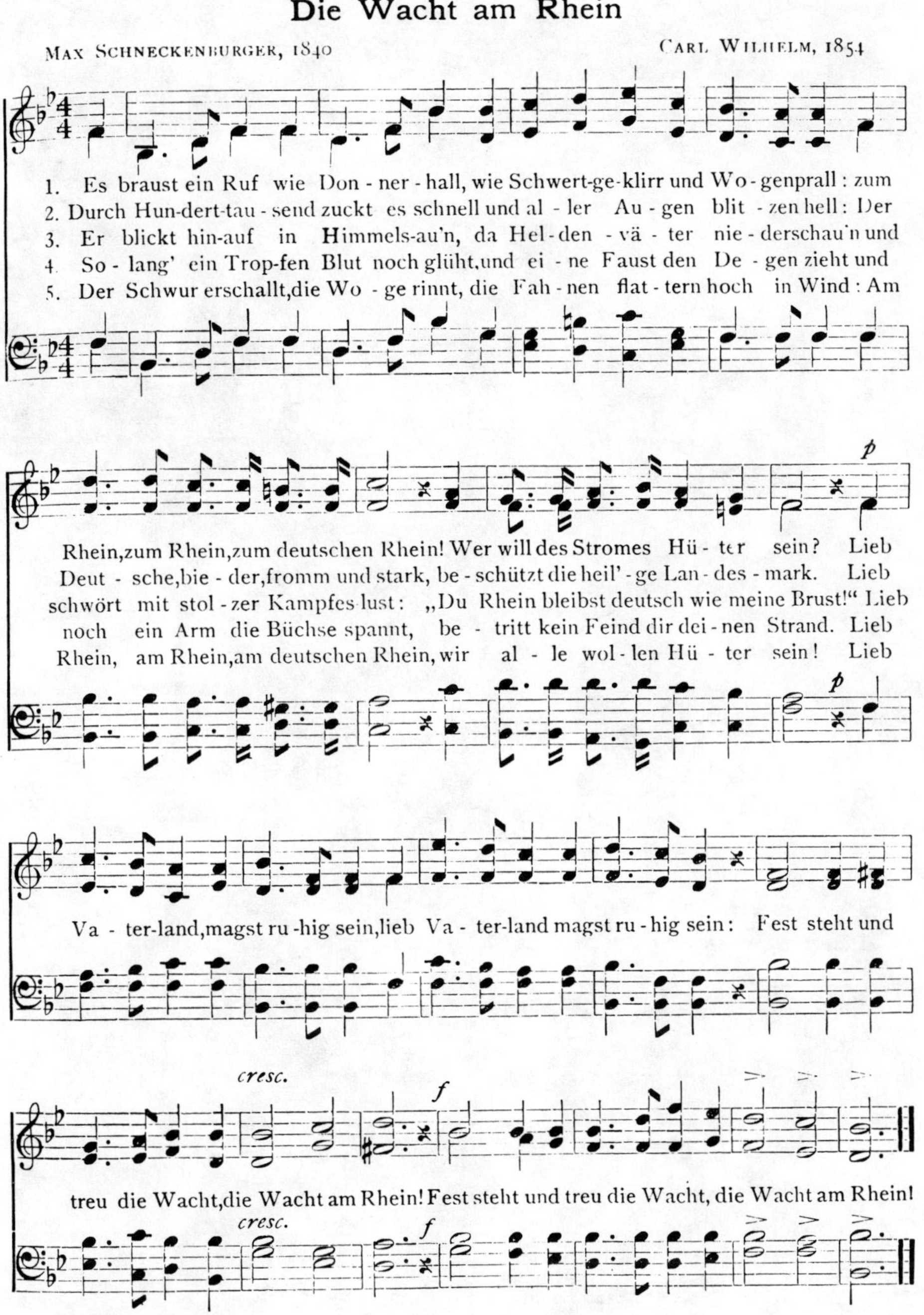

Fig. 1. Die Wacht am Rhein. *Deutsche Lieder*, P. Scherer and L. Dirks, eds. (New York: American Book Co. 1913) p. 31. Courtesy Giles Hoyt.

PLATE 5. The bronze relief of the Niederwalddenkmal; detail, pl. 3. Photo author.

hundred individuals are depicted life-size; in the center is Kaiser Wilhelm I on horseback; assembled around him are the Chancellor, Bismarck, all the reigning German princes, their commanders-in-chief, and soldiers of all arms. The relief is flanked by the allegoric figures "War" and "Peace," each 6.80 m. high. The group on the lower part of the pedestal depicts the meeting of old Father Rhine with the young daughter Moselle. This group is 3.45 m. high and 6.15 m. wide. Finally, on the sides of the Monument there are two reliefs showing the farewell of soldiers marching to battle and their happy return.

The overall height of the monument is 37.60 m., the statue itself 12.38 m. The substructure is 21 m. wide and 14.10 m. deep. Like the trophy of Augustus at La Turbie, the monument was meant to be seen from a great distance, from the Rhine below as it curves from west to north through the Bingen Gap and from the land in all directions save the north. But the Augustus monument was simpler in its statement: a majestic inscription to record history, some relief sculpture, the emperor himself surmounting all, on what is essentially an architectural monument. The Niederwalddenkmal, on the other hand, incorporates numerous features of Roman imperial monuments, particularly sculptural, and some viewers may find the whole too blatant, too rich if not banal in its conception. The relief with the Kaiser reminds one of the procession of the Ara Pacis of Augustus (Pl. 36b), the juxtaposition of the statues of War and Peace the tension exemplified by the location of the Ara Pacis in the Campus Martius, the river divinities evoke a Roman commonplace, and the side reliefs the important themes of *profectio* and *adventus*.

The "German National Monument" or "Deutsches Nationaldenkmal," was the result of collaboration between an architect, Karl Weisbach, and a sculptor, Johannes Schilling.[19] They had been aware of the enormous enthusiasm which had greeted the dedication of the Hermmannsdenkmal only a year before the beginning of their own monument. Hermann had represented the bravado and valor of the young German people, fighting for *libertas* against an imperial power. In the newer monument, Germany had become that imperial power; as for so long the German states had been at the heart of the Holy Roman Empire, so now the new German Reich was the new Rome of Europe. Her ruler bore the title "Caesar," and much of her symbolism, such as the great eagle, "der Adler," recalled Rome. The National Monument was an overwhelming statement, of pride, of power, of ambition. Augustus and Trajan would have understood it well. *Superbia, imperium, ambitio* were, after all, also Roman qualities.

[19] On the Niederwalddenkmal, see *Brockhaus Enzyclopädie* XIII (Wiesbaden: F.A. Brockhaus 1971) 450, and *Meyers Enzyklopädisches Lexikon* XVII (Mannheim/Wien/Zürich: Bibliographisches Institut 1976) 246–47; on Germania see *Brockhaus* VII (1969) 166, and *Meyer* X (1974) 147–48.

RECENT ACQUISITIONS IN THE CLASSICAL COLLECTION AT THE ART INSTITUTE OF CHICAGO

Louise Berge

Father Schoder and his work belong to and encompass wider spheres of heaven and earth than those which oversee and bound our city. On an unashamedly chauvinistic note, however, Chicago can claim him for over a third of his seventy years, and it is a great honor and pleasure to wish him a happy birthday on behalf of The Art Institute of Chicago, and in his honor to make public several recent additions to the Classical Collection of its Department of Oriental and Classical Art.

Classical antiquities form the historical nucleus of the Art Institute's collections.[1] Although the Insitute's first concern was to provide casts of ancient sculpture for its art students, in 1889 Charles T. Hutchinson, the President of the Art Institute's Board of Trustees, and its first active Director, William M.R. French, set off for Europe to buy original works of art. Spending only $154 over the $1,000 budget authorized them, they brought back some hundred ancient objects. These included several Roman marble heads, a number of terracotta lamps and over forty Greek vases, one of which, twenty years later, Sir John Beazley was to designate the name-piece of the Chicago Painter.[2] Mr. French spent $1.94 of his own money to buy for the Institute two sections of Roman lead pipe. These are now, unfortunately, nowhere to be found.

Something else of interest and relevance to both the Art Institute and Schoderfest happened here in 1889. The Chicago Society of the Archaeological Institute of America, of which Father Schoder has been an active officer and mainstay, was founded then. The meeting to organize it was held at the home of its first Life Member and President, Charles T. Hutchinson, who was also, you will recall, President of the Art Institute's Board of Trustees. Other members of that first Executive Committee were intimately connected with the young Art Institute. The Secretary, Professor Alfred E. Emerson, would be named Curator of Classical Antiquities at the Art Institute in the following year, and Vice-presidents Martin A. Ryerson and George Armour were Governing Members of the Art Institute. The story of those early years and the interrelationship between these two organizations is a fascinating one, which involves also the University of Chicago and its Oriental Institute. We cannot linger on it now but to say that Mr. Hutchinson and his colleagues would certainly be gratified to see the Art Institute join in honoring

[1] The following historical information is taken from an unpublished history of the collection brought together for the department in 1983 by Mrs. Karen Alexander.

[2] J.D. Beazley, *Attic Red-Figured Vases in American Museums* (Cambridge: Harvard University Press 1918) 155, there called "Painter of the Chicago Stamnos"; *ARV*[2] 628 no. 4; W. Moon and L. Berge, *Greek Vase Painting in Midwestern Collections* (Chicago: Art Institute 1979) no. 111.

another well-traveled President of The Chicago Society of the Archaeological Institute of America, one especially who has devoted so much of his time and energy to that organization which they founded.

From its early beginnings the Classical Collection of the Art Institute grew to its present size in fits and starts as interest in antiquity over the years grew and waned. In earlier periods of diminished interest parts of the collection were loaned, or given to other organizations, or, sadly, in the case of many of the casts, destroyed. The growth of the collection has now, however, assumed a steady pace, and it is once again taking its proper and necessary place, not only with respect to its role in the history of the museum, but with respect to its role in the history of western art.

The collection includes some three thousand Greek and Roman coins, fifteen hundred Egyptian objects, five hundred pieces of ancient glass, one hundred Greek vases, forty stone and larger terracotta sculptures, two hundred terracotta figurines, seven late Roman mosaics, nine bronzes, and twenty-five pieces of jewelry and goldwork.

We cannot hope in this day and age to fill all lacunae in the present collection, nor to see all categories of material and object, or all periods and places of classical antiquity represented. As an integral part of a museum of art, we must try by gift or purchase to acquire objects which have great esthetic value as well as historical interest. I think that the objects which we have acquired recently satisfy both these criteria in addition to remedying conspicuous lacks in the collection.

One of these is a small rectangular Roman marble sarcophagus, which awaits cleaning and repair before it can be displayed (Pls. 6–7).[3] It is a particularly welcome addition to an area of the collection which otherwise includes only two Roman cinerary urns of the first century and one fine allegorical relief of the second and third century from Roman Syria which is variously taken to be part of an Attic sarcophagus or from an architectural complex.[4]

The back of this small sarcophagus has been broken away, but enough remains to show that the relief decoration covered only the front and sides. This is characteristic of sarchophagi from the Roman west which were placed with a frontal orientation in niches or tombs.[5] The lid is lacking.

On the front, a naked bearded hero downs a centaur for whom reinforcement is coming up on the right, while at the left another centaur carries off an unwilling woman over a fallen wine jar (volute-krater). A tree stump which borders the action at right is carried around the edge to border also the right side of the sarchophagus, where there remain the hind part of a centaur in flight and a panther skin flying out behind him. On the left side of the sarcophagus is a moving representation of a dead or dying centaur

[3] 1984.1338, gift of Mr. and Mrs. A. N. Barozzi. Height: 31.6 cm., length: 85.2 cm., depth: 41.3 cm. The shape inside is rectangular with rounded edges. The marble is grayish-white with large crystals.

[4] Cineraria: 1923.969, gift of Mrs. George A. Thorne; 1926.621, gift of Mrs. E. C. Chadbourne. Relief: 1983.584, gift of The Alsdorf Foundation.

[5] A. M. McCann, *Roman Sarcophagi in The Metropolitan Museum of Art* (New York: Metropolitan Museum of Art 1978) 20.

PLATE 6

PLATE 6. Roman marble sarcophagus, Art Institute of Chicago 1984.1338, gift of Mr. and Mrs. A.N. Barozzi. Front. Courtesy of The Art Institute of Chicago; negative E9650.

a. Left side; negative E9649.

b. Right side; negative E9888.

PLATE 7. Roman sarcophagus (Pl. 6). Courtesy of The Art Institute of Chicago.

flanked by tree stumps, the living limbs of which, decked in pine cones and needles, curve protectively about him. All the centaurs are saddled with garlands.

The story which comes to mind immediately of course is Theseus fighting in the midst of the Battle of Lapiths and Centaurs, the centaur Eurytion carrying off Pirithous' bride Hippodamia. But certainly the central figure conforms to the normal iconography of Herakles with his short curly hair and beard and compact muscular body. Herakles was said to have fought alongside Theseus at Pirithous' wedding, but he is not normally featured in representations of that event. Indeed, in general, Herakles battling centaurs is not a common subject on Roman sarcophagi.[6]

There are other occasions when Herakles crossed clubs, arrows, or fists with centaurs, hints of which might be seen here as well. The dead or dying centaur on the left side, together with the fallen wine jar on the front recalls the story of Herakles and the hospitable centaur Pholos. This, however, involved a poisoned arrow, as did the accidental wounding of the centaur Chiron by Herakles, and neither episode had to do with the carrying off of a woman. The centaur Nessus did carry off Herakles' wife Deianira, but he was not accompanied by a group of garlanded comrades. The scenes on front and left are featured on the cover of a recent issue of the periodical *The Ancient World*.[7] They are there described as showing Herakles, in one of the minor episodes (*parerga*) of his legend, killing the centaur Dexamenos, while the centaur Eurytion carries off Dexamenos' daughter Deianeira, the fallen wine bowl and the garlands of the centaurs indicating that Herakles has arrived while the wedding of Eurytion and Deianeira is in progress.

This interpretation accommodates what is certainly Herakles battling centaurs in the midst of a festival, the carrying off of a woman, and a dying centaur. It is based however on a literary tradition which is rather complicated and relatively obscure, and, for Herakles killing the centaur Dexamenos, depends on an inscribed fifth century B.C. Attic red-figure vase painting.[8] It is ingenious and attractive, but it involves identifications of and relationships among the main characters which are not so frequently recognized in art and literature. I would therefore suggest that what we are seeing here might be an amalgam of Herakles-Centaur stories, meant to recall Herakles' trips of rescue to the world of the dead. Mixed myths are not uncommon on sarcophagi.

This sarcophagus has been placed in the second quarter of the third century, around A.D. 230.[9] The composition of the scene and the shape of the container, however, speak for a date perhaps some fifty years earlier, in the later Antonine period, a time also when violent mythological scences on sarcophagi were popular.[10]

[6] G. Koch and H. Sichtermann, *Römische Sarkophage* (Munich: Beck 1982) 149.

[7] *AncW* 13, nos. 1 and 2 (1986) cover and inside cover.

[8] "Dexamenos" in W. H. Roscher, *Ausführlisches Lexikon der griechischen und römischen Mythologie*, (Leipzig: Teubner 1884–1886) I.1, cols. 998–1001, including a drawing of the vase in question, a stamnos, Naples 3089, by an undetermined painter of The Group of Polygnotos (*ARV*[2] 1050, no. 4). I am grateful to Prof. Al. N. Oikonomides for this reference.

[9] Dr. Jiri Frel, in a personal communication to the donor.

[10] McCann (supra n. 5) 21 and 60.

An Italo-geometric terracotta standed lebes which was purchased in 1984 certainly satisfies our criteria for acquisitions (Pls. 8–11a).[11] It has esthetic merit, historical interest, and is of a period represented by only two other objects in the collection, a bronze fibula discussed below (p. 52), and an Attic Geometric horse-pyxis.[12] The Institute's Greek vase collection is centered mainly on fifth-century B.C. Attic red-figure ware.

Though there is much restoration, it has not been disguised and does not detract from the visual pleasure in this vase. It is especially fortunate that the conical lid has been preserved. Its handle is made up of four crossing rolled straps, of which enough of each exists to reconstruct the criss-crossing with reasonable accuracy.[13]

The vase itself is composed of an open bowl with double-arched horizontal handles. This is joined by a narrow, sloping band to a stand of two parts, a bulbous upper section above a high conical pedestal with spreading base. The entire stand is hollow up to the bowl, which was pierced by a hole. The proportions of the articulated whole, the vase, lid and handles, are exceptionally pleasing.

The taut design of the decoration is also pleasing. The clay is fired to an orangish-brown, the paint to a uniform orange-red. Inside the bowl, a painted circle decorates the bottom, and wide bands of paint alternating with narrower reserved bands decorate the walls. Outside, bands of cross-hatched triangles ring the vase and lid above and below larger patterned and figured bands, and decorate the upper surface of the vase rim. Those surrounding the top of the vase rim and the edge of the lid complement each other, the triangles pointing outward and downward respectively; all other triangles point upward.

The principle decoration, a metope frieze of whip-bearing horsemen, is set at the greatest circumference of the bowl, spanning the handle zones on both sides of the vase.[14] Broadly speaking, it is anchored to the vase by the bands of decoration on lid, bowl and stand which border it above and below in a syncopated fashion.

A metope frieze of waterbirds surrounding the lid is echoed by a smaller one (punctuated by one quatrefoil metope) surrounding the bulbous section of the stand,[15] while a

[11] 1985.627, Costa A. Pandaleon Fund. Height with lid: 56.0 cm., height of vase: 39.3 cm., outside diameter of mouth: 38.2 cm., diameter of base: 20.5 cm. (all measurements "as restored").

[12] Fibula: see note 18 infra; pyxis: 1976.2, Costa A. Pandaleon Fund.

[13] The resting surface of the lid is painted ("paint" here designating the coloring medium of clay). Turning marks on the inside of the lid are quite pronounced. The lid rests directly on the bowl, with no specific fitting device such as a flange or groove. This, together with the decoration of the bowl rim, brings into question the interesting possibility that vase and lid were not originally made for each other. The harmony of dimensions, proportions, shape and decoration, however, weighs against this. Both lid and vase are much broken and pieced, with large sections missing and restored, notably the greater part of each of the straps which form the lid handle, and almost three quarters of one side of the bowl (thus, "reverse") with much of the handle to its left, which is restored on the model of the preserved handle. The paint is much worn in places. In several areas on the lid where the decoration is quite worn away it looks as if it had been laid over a light wash. On the lid there is repainting of the stripes on the handle-straps, the diagonal cross-hatching between handle-roots, and parts of some triangles, but none on the waterbird and maeander friezes. On the vase, there is much repainting of the triangles and cross-hatching on the stand, but none of significance on the main friezes of the stand and bowl.

[14] There were four metopes on each side. Three of those on the reverse are lacking.

[15] Consisting of twelve and eleven metopes respectively.

a. Side A; negative E9820.

b. Side A-B; negative E9821.

Plate 8. Italo-geometric lebes. The Art Institute of Chicago 1985.627, Costa A. Pandaleon Fund. Courtesy of The Art Institute of Chicago.

a. Side B; negative E9823.

b. Side B-A; negative E9822.

PLATE 9. Italo-geometric lebes (Pl. 8). Courtesy of The Art Institute of Chicago.

PLATE 10

a. Detail, side A; negative E9828.

b. Side A, showing interior; negative E9825.

PLATE 10. Italo-geometric lebes (Pl. 8). Courtesy of The Art Institute of Chicago.

narrow band of hatched maeander ("running dog") under the waterbird frieze of the lid, in its nature and position, parallels a metope frieze of geometic motifs, lozenges in hatched frames alternating with hatched quatrefoils, below the main decorative frieze of the vase.[16]

Wide checkerboard patterns alternate with vertical lozenge chains to separate the horsemen of the main frieze, while the same lozenge chains alone separate the geometic metopes of the frieze below it. All these patterned panels are set between single hatched bars which echo the hatched-bar "triglyphs" separating the metopes of the waterbird friezes. All the patterned bands and friezes on lid, bowl and stand are separated by triple bordering lines.

Handles of both lid and vase are striped, and the cross-hatched triangular areas of the lid between handle-roots pick up the cross-hatching of the broader surfaces of the vase handles and the triangles which fill the open spaces on the vase between the handle-roots.

The ornament filling the friezes follows a similar rhythm. Bodies of men and birds are cross-hatched, eyes of men, horses and birds are, for the most part, reserved in the silhouette heads, while muzzles of horses are done in outline. The two hatched leaves above each horse's rump are paralleled in the two hatched leaves above the body of each bird on the lid. A diagonal zigzag below the head of each lid bird echoes a horizontal zigzag above the body of each bird on the stand. The upright cross-hatched triangle below the tail of each lid bird, repeated below the tail of each bird on the stand, is mirrored in a dependent one above the crook of each horseman's right arm. Below each horse's muzzle is an inverted triangle in outline and below each horse's body, betweeen its forelegs and the horseman's legs is an angular object, different in each metope: of those preserved, a hatched right triangle, a crossed square, a hatched ⊓, a cross-hatched square. In the geometric frieze below the horsemen, the lozenges include one with an X in the center, two with quartered centers, and two narrower ones with empty centers.

This vase was probably made in Etruria in the early part of the seventh century B.C., under the influence of, or indeed in, a workshop established in the previous century by Euboean settlers. Stylistic elements such as the birds and hatched leaves (which may reflect earlier bird and lozenge motifs), and the cross-hatched bodies of the horsemen derive from Euboean motifs. The shape of the stand, however, is of eastern origin and occurs in Etruscan metalwork influenced by objects imported from Urartu and other areas of the Near East by traders, possibly Euboeans themselves.[17]

In this vase we have, so to speak, a potted history, exemplifying the transition between the Geometric and the Orientalizing styles of art during a vigorous and exciting period of recovery, discovery, and development of trade and colonization.

[16] Ten metopes of this geometric frieze remain, five of each, with two rather narrow metopes under the handle at left of obverse succeeding each other without an intervening quatrefoil.

[17] The conclusions summarized here are based on J. N. Coldstream, *Geometric Greece* (London: Methuen 1977) 192–195 and 232–233.

PLATE 11

11b, c. Bronze Spectacle Fibula, The Art Institute of Chicago 1986.973, gift of The Professional Museum Association of The Art Institute of Chicago. Courtesy of The Art Institute of Chicago; negatives E10334, E 10335.

Plate 11a. Italo-geometric lebes (Pl. 8). Courtesy of The Art Institute of Chicago. Lid.

The most recent addition to the collection is a particularly beautiful example of an important type of bronze object from the same period, an elegant fibula, or garment fastener, of the so-called "spectacle" type (Pl. 11b, c).[18] It is formed with the pin from one length of wire into two spirals linked by two small twisted loops. The wire is rectangular in section. The bronze has a superb green patina.

This fibula conforms to John Alexander's type Ib in his study of southern European spectacle fibulae, from which the following historical summary and dating are derived.[19] Most of the spiral-decorated fibulae found in tenth to fifth century B.C. contexts in Europe come from the Balkans. The distribution of spectacle fibulae from sites south of the Danube suggests that the type of the Institute's fibula was carried from central and northeastern Europe through Macedonia to central and southern Greece, and thence, probably by trade, reached the south and west coasts of Italy, where it was in use from the eighth to the sixth centuries B.C. It is possible that this fibula came from South Italy, in which case it may be dated within that period. This acquisition is important for us because the collection is weak in bronzes and in early pieces, and it is particularly dear to us because it was chosen in competition with other curatorial presentations and donated by our friends and colleagues on the museum staff.

Only a very few objects from the Classical Collection are on exhibit now while new galleries are being constructed. Of the pieces we have discussed, the Geometric lebes and the fibula were exhibited from April to October, 1986 over a special label which read:

> Displayed in Conjunction with
> Celebrations at Loyola University
> to Honor Rev. Raymond V. Schoder, S.J.,
> Classicist and Archaeologist, on his
> Seventieth Birthday, April 11, 1986

[18] 1986. 973, gift of The Professional Museum Association of the Art Institute of Chicago. Length: 10.1 cm., length of pin: 6.5 cm.

[19] J. Alexander, "The Spectacle Fibulae of Southern Europe", *AJA* 69 (1965) 7–11. Cf. especially M. Comstock and C. Vermeule, *Greek, Etruscan and Roman Bronzes in the Museum of Fine Arts Boston* (Boston: Museum of Fine Arts 1971) 206, no. 267.

THE AKKADIAN WORDS FOR "IONIA" AND "IONIAN"*

J. A. Brinkman

ἦλθες ἐκ περάτων γᾶς ἐλεφαντίναν
λάβαν τὼ ξίφεος χρυσοδέταν ἔχων
τὸν ἀδελφὸν 'Αντιμενίδαν . . . φησιν 'Αλκαῖος Βαβυλωνίοις συμμαχοῦντα τελέσαι
ἄεθλον μέγαν, εὐρύσαο δ' ἐκ πόνων
κτένναις ἄνδρα μαχάταν βασιλη<ί>ων
παλάσταν ἀπυλείποντα μόναν ἴαν
παχέων ἀπὺ πέμπων.

Alcaeus (E.-M. Voigt, *Sappho et Alcaeus: Fragmenta* [Amsterdam: Athenaeum—Polak & Van Gennep 1971] no. 350)

Introduction

Akkadian is a generic name for the East Semitic language used in ancient Mesopotamia (roughly coextensive in area with modern Iraq) from at least 2600 B.C. to A.D. 75. Akkadian had two major dialects: Babylonian, used in the south of the country, and Assyrian, used in the north. Documents in both dialects were written in the cuneiform script. In the first millennium B.C., Akkadian texts recorded Mesopotamian contacts with eastern Greeks or Ionians. The Akkadian terms for Ionia (*Yawan*) and Ionian (*Yawnaya*, *Yawanaya*) on occasion seem also to have been used to designate Greeks in general as well as non-Hellenic inhabitants of western Asia Minor.

There are at present less than forty known attestations of the words *Yawan*, *Yawnaya*, and *Yawanaya* in Akkadian, spread over slightly more than half a millennium from about the year 735 to perhaps the middle of the second century B.C. In this article, I would like to enumerate these attestations, to give a translation and brief commentary for them, and to draw a few conclusions about the form of the pertinent words in Akkadian and their general semantic range. The emphasis in the discussion will be philological, with broader historical and cultural ramifications deferred for future consideration.

* Supplementary abbreviations:

AHw	W. von Soden, *Akkadisches Handwörterbuch*
AOAT	*Alter Orient und Altes Testament*
API	E. Herzfeld, *Altpersische Inschriften*
BM	British Museum (siglum of cuneiform tablet collection)
CAD	*The Assyrian Dictionary of the Oriental Institute of the University of Chicago*
CII	*Corpus inscriptionum iranicarum*
MDP	*Mémoires de la Mission Archéologique en Perse*
Mélanges Dussaud	*Mélanges syriens offerts à Monsieur René Dussaud*
PTS	Princeton Theological Seminary (siglum of cuneiform tablet collection)
rev.	reverse
RGTC	*Répertoire géographique des textes cunéiformes*
TCL	*Musée du Louvre, Départment des Antiquités Orientales: Textes cunéiformes*
TCS	*Texts from Cuneiform Sources*
YOS	*Yale Oriental Series, Babylonian Texts*

This article will present the occurrences of *Yawan*, *Yawnaya*, and *Yawanaya* in Akkadian in chronological order:

1) Neo-Assyrian references (735–669 B.C.)
2) Neo-Babylonian references (601–539 B.C.)
3) Achaemenid references (521–359 B.C.)
4) Hellenistic references (*c.* 330–160 B.C.)

These will be followed by a section containing general conclusions, observations on the present state of inquiry into Mesopotamian-Greek relations, and prospects for future research.

In the translations below, "Ionia" and "Ionian(s)" will be enclosed in quotation marks as a reminder that, in context, these English renderings may not always match the modern geographic and gentilic range of the terms. The exact form of the Akkadian word for "Ionia" or "Ionian" in each passage will be given in transliteration following the appropriate part of the translation. It will suffice for present purposes to note that Akkadian distinguishes between:

1) a noun form *Yawan* (for "Ionia"), usually written with historical—but no longer pronounced—case endings as *Yawanu*, *Yawani*, *Yawana* (without regard for actual case); and
2) an adjectival form *Yawnaya* or *Yawanaya*, which can be either singular or plural ("Ionian" or "Ionians").

In the cuneiform writing system, proper names in both nominal and adjectival forms are usually preceded by signs called determinatives, which indicate the class to which the following name belongs. The determinatives used before *Yawan*, *Yawnaya*, and *Yawanaya* are most commonly KUR ("land," used before the names of countries and their inhabitants) and LÚ ("man/men," used before the names of peoples and occupations). In the first millennium B.C., intervocalic *w* was written as *m* in cuneiform; *w* before a consonant could be written as *m* or, less commonly *u*. Thus what was pronounced as *Yawan*, *Yawnaya*, or *Yawanaya* will appear in the script as *Yaman*, *Yamnaya*/*Yaunaya*, or *Yamanaya*, respectively.

In the transliteration of cuneiform texts, the following symbols are used:

[ ]	to enclose restorations
[( )]	to enclose possible/optional restorations[1]
⌜ ⌝	to enclose damaged signs
< >	to enclose alleged scribal omissions in the text
x	to indicate an illegible sign

1. Neo-Assyrian References (735–669 B.C.)

The earliest known attestations of the Akkadian words for "Ionia" and "Ionian" occur in the late Neo-Assyrian period in official letters written in the reign of Tiglath-pileser III (744–727 B.C.) and in royal inscriptions from the reigns of Sargon II (721–705) and Esarhaddon (680–669). As might be expected from the nature of the documentation, these

[1] This indicates theoretically available, though not necessarily filled, space.

passages have a military or political context, referring either to hostile contacts between "Ionians" and Assyrians (including Assyrian subjects) or to tribute paid by "Ionia" to the Assyrian king.

The first of these references is in a letter written by Qurdi-Aššur-lāmur, an Assyrian official in Syria,[2] to Tiglath-pileser III. This letter may be dated to the latter part of Tiglath-pileser's reign, probably between 735 and 727 B.C. Qurdi-Aššur-lāmur reported to the king that "Ionians" were harassing the Phoenician coast.

[1.1] "The 'Ionians' (KUR *ia-⌈ú⌉-na-⌈a⌉-a*) have come. They have fought in the cities of Sams[imuruna], Ḫariṣū, and [. . .]."

—Nimrud Letter 69:3–6[3]

Another possible mention of "Ionians" in this archive has been adduced by Simo Parpola, who suggested that lines 41 and 44 of Nimrud Letter 12, also written by Qurdi-Aššur-lāmur to Tiglath-pileser, contain references to [KUR *i]a-ú-na-a-a* and KUR *ia-[ú]-na-a-a* respectively.[4] These emendations make sense in the context of Syro-Palestinian geography,[5] but they do not fit the traces on the cuneiform tablet as published by Saggs.[6] The original tablet in the Iraq Museum, Baghdad should be collated to check whether Parpola's readings are possible; in the meantime, it is preferable to defer judgment.

Most Neo-Assyrian references come from the royal inscriptions of Sargon II (721–705), whose forces campaigned on Cyprus.[7] Sargon's texts allude on several occasions to "Ionians" as people connected with the Mediterranean whom the monarch claims to have caught like fish.

[1.2] "(Sargon) . . . who caught 'Ionians' (KUR *ia-am-na-a-a*)[8] of the midst of the Sea like fish."

—H. Winckler, *Die Keilschrifttexte Sargons* (Leipzig: Pfeiffer 1889) I 148: 34–35; II pl. 38, no. IV (text: III!)

[1.3] "I (Sargon) . . . caught 'Ionians' (KUR *ia-am-na-a-a*) of the midst of the Sea of the Setting Sun like fish and [dep]orted(?)[9] them."

—F. Weissbach, "Die Prunkinschrift des Saales XIV.," *ZDMG* 72 (1918) 178:15–16

[2] Qurdi-Aššur-lāmur is known primarily as the author of Nimrud Letters 12, 13, and 69 (published by H.W.F. Saggs, *Iraq* 17 [1955] 127–31, pls. XXX–XXXI and *Iraq* 25 [1963] 76–78, pl. XIII). These reports covered the areas of Tyre, Sidon, Kašpuna, and "Mt. Lebanon."

[3] Primary edition by Saggs, *Iraq* 25 (1963) 76–77 and pl. XIII. The forms of the city names follow the readings in Parpola *AOAT* 6 (1970) 152, 303. A later section of the letter (line 11) mentions "in his ships"; but it is not clear what relation, if any, this phrase has to the "Ionians."

[4] *AOAT* 6 (1970) 186–87.

[5] Yawnaya (known from Nimrud Letter 69 to be active in this area) is more likely to have been mentioned than Yasubaya (connected with the land of Yasubi in eastern Mesopotamia).

[6] The traces read [(x)]⌈x⌉ *ia-na-a-a* in the first instance (line 41), i.e., without an *-ú-*, and KUR *ia-⌈su-ba(?)⌉-a-a* in the second (line 44); see the cuneiform copy in *Iraq* 17 (1955) pl. XXX.

[7] Assyrian *Yadnana*.

[8] A textual variant (in D.G. Lyon, *Keilschrifttexte Sargon's Königs von Assyrien* [Leipzig: Hinrichs 1883] 14:25) reads URU for KUR, as though the referent "Ionia" were a city rather than a country.

[9] The verb [*as-s*]*uḫ* is usually restored in line 16.

[1.4] "(Sargon) . . . who in the midst of the Sea caught 'Ionians' (KUR *ia-am-na-a-a*) as a *fowler* (does)."

—C.J. Gadd, "Inscribed Prisms of Sargon II from Nimrud," *Iraq* 16 (1954) 199 and Pl. LI, line 19[10]

[1.5] "(Sargon) . . . who in the midst of the Sea caught 'Ionians' (KUR *ia-am-na-a-a*) as a *fowler* (does) fish."

—D.G. Lyon, *Keilschrifttexte Sargon's Königs von Assyrien* (Leipzig: Hinrichs 1883) p. 4:21[11]

These stock passages invariably associate the "Ionians" with the Mediterranean,[12] either by calling them "Ionians of the midst of the Sea" or by stating that they were caught like fish "in the midst of the Sea." The passages generally occur in sections where Sargon summarizes his far-flung conquests.[13] No detailed campaign narrative concerning a battle or battles of Sargon against the "Ionians" has survived; and it has yet to be proven that Sargon's forces reached far western Asia Minor either by land or by sea. Contact with Ionians is probably therefore to be set in another context, possibly in an Assyrian campaign against Cyprus or Cilicia, with attendant naval maneuvers.[14]

The latest known Neo-Assyrian reference to "Ionians" occurs in a royal inscription of Esarhaddon (680–669 B.C.).[15]

[10] For the adverb *sandâniš* or *sandânišu*, derived from *us/šandû*, "fowler," see A. Salonen, *Vögel und Vogelfang im alten Mesopotamien, Annales Academiae Scientiarum Fennicae* 180 (1973) 26–27. Cf. *AHw* 1022 and *CAD* S (1984) 146a.

[11] Text: (*ša*) . . . *sandâniš kīma nūni ibarru*.

[12] Which is usually termed the "Sea" (*tâmtu*) or sometimes more fully the "Sea of the Setting Sun" (*tâmtu ša ereb šamši*), i.e. the "Western Sea." See also infra n. 46.

[13] The historical context of the Sargon II passages is discussed more fully by J. Elayi and A. Cavigneaux, "Sargon II et les Ioniens," *OA* 18 (1979) 59–75.

[14] A ruler of Ashdod in the time of Sargon II was named Yamani (generally written ᵐ*ia-ma-ni*); and several men mentioned in the eighth- and seventh-century Nineveh economic archives bore names such as ᵐ*ia-man-ia-a*, ᵐ*ia-a-ma-ni*, ᵐ*ia-man-ni*, ᵐ*ia-man-nu-u*, [ᵐ]*a-a-i-man-ni* (C.W.H. Johns, *An Assyrian Doomsday Book* [Leipzig: Hinrichs 1901] pl. XI, no. 7 ii 4′ = F.M. Fales, *Censimenti e catasti di epoca neo-assira* ["Studi economici e tecnologici" 2; Rome: Centro per le Antichità e la Storia dell' Arte del Vicino Oriente 1973] no. 22 ii 4′; C.H.W. Johns, *Assyrian Deeds and Documents*, vols. 1–2 [Cambridge: Deighton Bell 1898–1901] nos. 76 rev. 4, 214:4.10, 233 rev. 12.15, 801 rev. 14). There have been suggestions, e.g., by T.F.R.G. Braun (*CAH* 3/3, 2nd ed., pp. 16–17 and 21) and T.J. Dunbabin (*The Greeks and Their Eastern Neighbours* [Westport, CT: Greenwood Press, 1979, reprint of 1957 edition] 31), that one or more of these names may mean "Greek" (or "Ionian") and imply Hellenic connections. This is incorrect. There is marked dissimilarity between these personal names (*Yāmani* or *Yamani*) and the Assyrian word for "Ionian" (*Yamnaya*, pronounced *Yawnaya*) which has no vowel written between *m* and *n* and ends with the gentilic suffix *-aya*.

[15] The reference to "Ionian sailors" in the annals of Sennacherib (705–681 B.C.) cited by T.F.R.G. Braun in *CAH* 3/3, 2nd ed., 19 is inaccurate. The text in question reads KUR *ia-ad-na-na-a-a*, "Cypriot" (D.D. Luckenbill, *The Annals of Sennacherib* ["Oriental Institute Publications" 2; Chicago: University Press 1924] 73, line 60). Cf. the older, largely superseded discussions by L.W. King, *JHS* 30 (1910) 327–35 and

[1.6] "All kings of the midst of the Sea, from the land of Cyprus (and) the land of 'Ionia' (KUR *ia-man*) to the land of Tarsisi, bowed down at my feet. I received [their] heavy tribute."

—R. Borger, *Die Inschriften Asarhaddons Königs von Assyrien* (*AfO* Beiheft 9 [1956] p. 86 AsBbE:10–11

This citation comes from a passage summarizing Esarhaddon's relations with foreign countries, including offerings received from tributaries and lands conquered. Among the places mentioned are Tyre, Egypt, Nubia, and Tilmun (modern Bahrein). In the passage cited above, Yadnana is the name used for Cyprus; and Tarsisi has sometimes been interpreted as referring to Tartessus on the Iberian peninsula.[16] "Ionia" is mentioned briefly among the tributary areas, again without indication of Assyrian military action.

These Neo-Assyrian references give little specific information except to indicate that "Ionia" was a foreign land, that the earliest contacts with the "Ionians" were hostile and probably either maritime or in areas of the Levant near the seacoast. Only in the latest text was "Ionia" said to be submissive and offering tribute to Assyria. Assyrian claims of political or military dominance were not always firmly grounded in reality.

It is also of interest that the earliest Akkadian forms of the words *Yawan* and *Yawnaya* apparently show a short *a* vowel in the initial syllable. This can be deduced from syllabic loss through contraction in the expected gentilic **Yawanaya*, where the second of two consecutive short stem vowels is dropped.

2. *Neo-Babylonian References (601–539 B.C.)*

In contrast to the political or military context of the Neo-Assyrian references, Neo-Babylonian passages mentioning "Ionia" and "Ionians" occur in economic and administrative texts from the reigns of Nebuchadnezzar II (604–562) and Nabonidus (555–539).

The earliest of these texts is an account concerning weavers dated on the second day of the month Ayaru in the fourth year of Nebuchadnezzar II (= April 29, 601 B.C., according to the Julian calendar).[17]

[2.1] "Four and one-half minas of purple wool of 'Ionia' (KUR *ia-a-ma-nu*) for . . . ,[18] at the disposal of Kudurru son of Bēl-nāṣir and Nanaya-iddin son of Nabû-ušallim, the weavers."

—*YOS* 17 253:1–6

D.D. Luckenbill, *ZA* 28 (1914) 92–99. A tale of Sennacherib fighting against Ionians (or Greeks) is, however, preserved in the Berossos and Abydenos traditions (*FGrHist* 3/C/1 680 F 7, 685 F 5).

[16] Note the commentary by Braun (*CAH* 3/3, 2nd ed., 20), who argues for a location in the Guadalquivir valley; see also G.L. Huxley, *The Early Ionians* (New York: Humanities Press 1966) 71–72. The location is still under discussion.

[17] Julian dates here follow the tables of Richard A. Parker and Waldo H. Dubberstein, *Babylonian Chronology 626* B.C.–*A.D. 75*, Brown University Studies 19 (1956).

[18] Line 3 of the text is damaged. The traces favor a translation like "for making (x) garment(s)." Compare lines 7–8 of the same text: "ten shekels of purple wool for (making) a *lamaḫuššû* garment."

Next in time is an archive of administrative texts, also to be assigned to the time of Nebuchadnezzar II,[19] which were excavated early in this century by Robert Koldewey in a palace area of Babylon (Südburg) immediately southwest of the Ishtar Gate.[20] These documents deal with oil, barley, date, and spice rations issued to captives or exiles of high rank in residence at the royal court; and four of them have been discussed and published at least in part by Ernst Weidner.[21] These texts have been studied primarily because they provide cuneiform references to Jehoiachin, a king of Judah known from the Bible, and other prominent Jews in exile. But the same texts list other guests or detainees at court, including Phoenicians (from Tyre, Sidon, and Byblos), Philistines, Elamites, Medes, Persians, Egyptians, and "Ionians." Among the "Ionians" are included:

[2.2] "Eight 'I[onian]' carpenters" (LÚ.NAGAR.MEŠ LÚ *i[a-man-na- a-a])*[22]
—E.F. Weidner, *Mélanges Dussaud*, vol. 2, 923–35 pl. I, text A:19

[2.3] "LABBunu,[23] the . . . [24] of the land of the 'Ionians'" (KUR *ia-man-na-a-a*)
—ibid., pl. II text A rev. 12

[2.4] "Kunzumpiya the . . . [25] of the land of 'Ionia'" (KUR *ia-man-na*)
—ibid., pl. II text A rev. 16

[2.5] "Eight 'I<o>nian' carpenters" (LÚ.NAGAR.MEŠ LÚ *ia-<man>*[26] *-na-a-a*)
—ibid., pl. II, text A rev. 21

[2.6] "Aziyak the 'Ionian' carpenter" (LÚ.NAGAR LÚ *ia-man-na-a-a*)
—ibid., pl. II, text A rev. 27

[2.7] "Eight of the same [i.e., carpenters], 'Ionians'" (8 KI.MIN LÚ *ia-a-man-a-[a]*)
—ibid., p. 933, text B ii 43

[19] The archive as a whole includes tablets dated between the tenth (595/4) and thirty-fifth (570/69) years of Nebuchadnezzar II (Weidner, *Mélanges Dussaud*, vol. 2, 924).

[20] The exact findspot of these tablets, in the staircase room between the Vaulted Building and the palace, is described in R. Koldewey, *Die Königsburgen von Babylon*, 1: *Die Südburg*, *WVDOG* 54 (1931) 49, with appropriate maps and illustrations on pls. I, V, and VIII. Cf. R. Koldewey, *Das wieder erstehende Babylon* (Leipzig: Hinrichs 1925) 99.

[21] E.F. Weidner, *Mélanges Dussaud*, vol. 2, 923–35. Among these four, only Text B bears a date (year 13 of Nebuchadnezzar II = 592/1 B.C.).

[22] Restored on the basis of other references to Ionian carpenters in [2.6–9] below.

[23] Because of the ambiguities of the cuneiform writing system, LABBunu can be read as Labbunu, Lappunu, Libbunu, Lippunu, Ribbunu, Rippunu, Kalbunu, or Kalpunu—to mention some of the more obvious alternatives. It is also possible that the vertical wedge preceding LAB represents the end of a sign other than a masculine personal determinative.

[24] We do not know either the reading or the meaning of the title or occupation name LÚ.EDIN-*ú*, which occurs in the text here. Emendation to the slightly similar signs SIMUG ("smith") or BÁḪAR ("potter") would still pose problems because of the unexpected phonetic complement.

[25] The same title LÚ.EDIN-⌈*u*⌉ is given in the text here (see preceding note). Kunzumpiya also occurs in line 15 of this text (without gentilic).

[26] The textual emendation seems likely because of the "Ionian" carpenters in [2.6–9] below. The vertical wedge before A may be the end of the preceding sign rather than the masculine personal determinative.

[2.8] "Seven of the same [i.e., carpenters], 'Ionians'" (7 LÚ.KI.MIN *ia-man-a-a*)
—ibid., pl. IV, text C rev. ii 15

[2.9] "[x] 'Ionian' carpenters" ([x LÚ].⌜NAGAR.MEŠ LÚ *ia*⌝*-a-man-a-a*)
—ibid., pl. V text D:18

These texts are particularly interesting because they preserve the names of at least three "Ionians": Aziyak, Kunzumpiya, and LABBunu.[27] None of these names has been demonstrated to have Greek connections; but Kunzumpiya has been compared to Isaurian (/Lycian/Luwian) Κονζαπεας or Κοναυζαπ[ε]ας.[28] These names have generally been interpreted as referring to non-Hellenic inhabitants of western Asia Minor or to Ionians from Cilicia.[29]

In slightly later times, the land of the "Ionians" is mentioned on several occasions as the source of bronze and iron in Babylonian private commercial inventory texts from the reign of Nabonidus (555–539 B.C.). These texts, discussed in detail by Leo Oppenheim,[30] list metals, lapis lazuli, chemicals (principally dyes and alum), resin, foodstuffs (wine, honey, spices), and fine cloth (linen, wool) imported by overland trade into Uruk in southern Babylonia from such faraway lands as Lebanon, Egypt, and "Ionia."

[2.10] "four talents fifty-five minas of bronze of 'Ionia' (KUR *ia-a-ma-na*)"
—*TCL* 12 84:1–2[31]

[2.11] "two talents ten minas of iron of 'Ionia' (KUR *ia-a-ma-nu*)"
—ibid., line 7[32]

[2.12] "ten talents of bronze of 'Ionia' (KUR *ia-a-ma-na*)"
—*YOS* 6 168:1[33]

[2.13] "four talents fifty-five minas of bronze of 'Ionia' (KUR *ia-a-ma-na*)"
—ibid., line 7

[27] To these might be added the name Patam (ᵐ*Pa-ta-am*), which is associated with a Kunzumpiya in *Mélanges Dussaud*, vol. 2, 923–35 pl. I, text A:15 (although neither of the names has a preserved ethnic designation in this passage).

[28] The discussion by Weidner in *Mélanges Dussaud*, vol. 2, 933 may now be augmented by other, more recent studies on the onomastics of non-Hellenic Asia Minor: a) Philo H. J. Houwink ten Cate, *The Luwian Population Groups of Lycia and Cilicia Aspera during the Hellenistic Period, Documenta et monumenta orientis antiqui* 10 (1965) 138–139, 191–92; b) Louis Robert, *Noms indigènes dans l'Asie-Mineure gréco-romaine*, 1, *Bibliothèque archéologique et historique de l'Institut Français d'Archéologie d'Istanbul* 13 (1963) 427; c) Ladislav Zgusta, *Kleinasiatische Personennamen* (Prague: Czechoslovakian Academy of Sciences 1964) 238 §§647-4 and 647-5.

[29] Following Weidner, *Mélanges Dussaud*, vol. 2, 933. It might also be considered whether such names could have been borne by the offspring of marriages between Ionian Greeks and non- Greeks; note, for example, Herodotus' legend of the original male settlers of Ionia marrying Carian women (1.146).

[30] "Essay on Overland Trade in the First Millennium B.C.," *JCS* 21 (1967) 236–54.

[31] The text is dated on the fifth day of the month Tashritu, year 5 of Nabonidus (= Oct. 14, 551 B.C.). The amount is equivalent to approximately 142 kilograms.

[32] The amount is about 62 kilograms.

[33] The text is dated on the seventh day of the month Tashritu, year 6 of Nabonidus (= Oct. 5, 550 B.C.). The amount is about 288 kilograms.

[2.14] "two talents ten minas of iron of 'Ionia' (KUR *ia-a-ma-na*)"
—ibid., line 15

[2.15] "two talents ten minas of iron of 'Ionia' (KUR *ia-a-ma-na*)"
—PTS 2098 rev. 11[34]

A further oblique reference may occur in a damaged text apparently dealing with a Babylonian invasion of Egypt in 568/7 B.C. There a local city bears the name Pūṭu-Yaman (written URU *pu-ṭu-ia-a-man*[(- . . .)], which could be translated "Libya of the Ionians."[35]

Neo-Babylonian economic and administrative documents thus provide several references to "Ionia" and "Ionians" in the context of trade and foreign skilled workers resident in Babylon. The allusion to purple wool coming from "Ionia" is atypical, since in Mesopotamia imported dyed materials of this sort more commonly came from Phoenicia or greater Syria. The origin of metals in Anatolia or western Asia Minor is well attested, and it is noteworthy that iron from "Ionia" fetched a higher price than iron from "Lebanon."[36] The carpenters from "Ionia" adumbrate the skilled workmen from the same region who were to labor on Achaemenid royal buildings at Susa later in the sixth century.[37]

The Neo-Babylonian forms for the words "Ionia" and "Ionian(s)" are also worthy of comment.[38] The name of the land uniformly exhibits an historical case ending: written

[34] Published in transliteration by Oppenheim, *JCS* 21 (1967) 236 n. 1. Since PTS 2098 is a virtual duplicate of *YOS* 6 168, line 1 in the former text could be partially restored to read: "talents of bronze of ['Ionia'] (K[UR *ia-a-ma-na*]), "restored by comparison with [2.12] above. It is also possible that the "four talents fifty-five minas of bronze" mentioned in PTS 2098 rev. 1 (without identifying place of origin) could be understood to be from "Ionia," since the line is otherwise parallel in the text to *YOS* 6 168:7, i.e., [2.13] above. The date of PTS 2098 is not preserved.

[35] J.N. Strassmaier, S.J., *Inschriften von Nabuchodonosor, König von Babylon* (Leipzig: Pfeiffer 1889) no. 329 rev. 2; republished in cuneiform copy by D.J. Wiseman, *Chronicles of Chaldaean Kings (626–556 B.C.) in the British Museum* (London: British Museum 1956) pls. XX–XXI. Note that the geographical name here occurs at the end of the preserved portion of the line and could be damaged at the end (where an ending such as *-nu*, *-ni*, *-na*, or *-na-a-a* could have been present originally). See also Zadok, *RGTC* 8, 252. The translation of this tablet cited by Braun, *CAH* 3/3, 2nd ed., 23 is misleading because it does not indicate the textual gap between "Putu-Yaman" and "distant regions"; there is no indication that the latter phrase is in apposition to the former.

[36] According to information in *YOS* 6 168, one shekel of silver could purchase only four minas of iron from "Ionia," but approximately six minas of iron from Lebanon. For a sketch map indicating the location of ancient iron deposits in Anatolia, see K.R. Maxwell-Hyslop, "Assyrian Sources of Iron," *Iraq* 36 (1974) 141.

[37] See the passage [3.3] below.

[38] Zadok, *RGTC* 8, 187–88, calls attention to two Neo-Babylonian personal names perhaps related to Yawan, Yawanaya. The first of these is a farmer named Imanaya or Iwanaya (written ^{m}*i-ma-na-a-a*; T.G. Pinches, *Neo-Babylonian and Achaemenid Economic Texts, Cuneiform Texts from Babylonian Tablets in the British Museum* 56 (1982) no. 506:1 (economic text of undetermined date from the Neo-Babylonian or Achaemenid period). But this name lacks the *ā* of the initial syllable in Neo-Babylonian *Yāmanaya*; so it is unlikely that the two are to be equated, since long vowels do not usually vanish without a trace. The second name (ibid., no. 813 rev. i′5′) is that of a woman who is identified as ^{f}*ia-man-na*[(- . . .)]. The preserved beginning of this name shares a common writing with attested Neo-Babylonian orthographies of the gentilic; and one could complete the form as *Yamanaitu*, to yield a feminine. This interpretation, therefore, seems possible.

Yāmanu (nom.) or *Yāmana* (acc.), but presumably pronounced *Yāwan* in each instance by this time.[39] The gentilic form *Yāmanaya*, pronounced *Yāwanaya* or *Yāwanay*, presumably had a long *a* in the initial syllable, since the short second syllable does not drop and the first syllable is frequently given plene writing (*ia-a-*).[40] In these respects, the Neo-Babylonian forms differ from the Neo-Assyrian.[41]

3. Achaemenid References (521–359 B.C.)

The Akkadian references from this time come principally from royal inscriptions of Darius I (521–486), Xerxes I (485–465), and Artaxerxes II (404–359), which have parallel versions written in Elamite and Old Persian. There is, in addition, an isolated reference in a legal text from the reign of Darius I.

The following passages are from the royal inscriptions of Darius I:

[3.1] "The cedar which was used here (for building) men from Eber-nāri[42] brought from a mountain called [Labnānu] to [Babylon]. From Babylon the Carians and 'Ionians' (KUR *ia-ma-na-a-a*) [brought (it)] to Susa."

—foundation tablet from Susa; principal edition: Herzfeld, *API* 15 no. 5:21–24. Cf. Scheil, *MDP* 21 no. 1; König, *MVAG* 35/1 (1930) 43–44 §6; Herzfeld, *AMIran* 3 (1931) pl. VI.

[3.2] "The material for the [palace] reliefs was brought [fr]om 'Io[nia]' (⌈KUR *ia-x*⌉[. . .])."

—ibid., line 29

[3.3] "The [stonecutters who] worked [the stone] were 'Ionians' (LÚ [*ia*]-*ma-na-a-a*) and [men from Lydia]"[43]

—ibid., lines [32]–33

[3.4] "King Darius states: 'These are the lands that obey me. Under the protection of Ahura Mazda I became their king. Persia, Elam, Babylonia, Assyria, Arabia, Egypt, (those) on the sea, Lydia, 'Ionia' (KUR *ia-a-ma-nu*), Media, Urartu, Cappadocia, Parthia,

[39] Cf. James Philip Hyatt, *The Treatment of Final Vowels in Early Neo-Babylonian, Yale Oriental Series, Researches* 23 (1941).

[40] Plene, i.e. fuller, vowel writings by themselves do not necessarily indicate vowel length.

[41] Determining the origin of these differences could pose intriguing problems. Did knowledge of the "Ionians" come to Babylonia and Assyria at different times and/or through different intermediaries?

The writing with two *n*'s (e.g., KUR *ia-man-na-a-a*) in Neo Babylonian is not significant since the first *n* is always part of a CVC (i.e., consonant-vowel-consonant) sign; and a consonantal cluster formed in part by the end of such signs does not reliably indicate a doubled consonant.

[42] Eber-nāri, literally "Across the River," is a generic name for Syria-Palestine used as early as the Neo-Assyrian period (*CAD* E [1958] 8; Zadok, *RGTC* 8, 129).

[43] Restorations based on the Elamite and Old Persian versions. The work of Greek artisans in Persia is discussed, inter alios, by Carl Nylander, *Ionians in Pasargadae* (*Boreas* 1; Uppsala 1970); Ann Farkas, *Achaemenid Sculpture, Uitgaven van het Nederlands Historisch-Archaeologisch Instituut te Istanbul* 33 (1974) 83–119; David Stronach, *Pasargadae: A Report on the Excavations Conducted by the British Institute of Persian Studies from 1961 to 1963* (Oxford: Clarendon 1978).

Drangiana, Aria, Chorasmia, Bactria, Sogdiana, Paruparaesanna, Scythia, Sattagydia, Arachosia, Maka—a total of 23 lands.'"

—Elizabeth N. von Voigtlander, *The Bisitun Inscription of Darius the Great: Babylonian Version*, *CII*, Part I, Vol. 2, Texts 1 (1978), p. 12, lines 4–7[44]

[3.5] "These are the countries which have brought me the materials for this house [i.e., palace]: Persia, Elam, Media, Babylonia, Assyria, Arabia, Egypt, the lands which are on the Sea, Lydia, 'Ionia' (KUR *ia-a-ma-ni*), Urartu, Cappadocia, Parthia, Drangiana, Aria, Chorasmia, Bactria, Sogdiana, Gandara, Scythia, Sattagydia, Arachosia, Maka."

—foundation tablet from Susa, published in *Bastan Chenasi va Honar-e Iran* 6 (1971) 8 (Persian section): pl. 13: 18–31[45]

The following reference is from an inscription of Xerxes I.

[3.6] "Darius the king speaks: 'Under the protection of Ahura Mazda, these are the countries, in addition to Persia, over which I am king. I rule over them; they bring me tribute. What I command them, they do. My laws they observe. Media, Elam, Arachosia, Urartu, Drangiana, Parthia, Aria, Bactria, Sogdiana, Chorasmia, Babylonia, Assyria, Sattagydia, Lydia, Egypt, 'Ionians' (KUR *ia-a-man-na*) who live in/on the Sea and who live on the far shore of the Sea,[46] Maka, Arabia, Gandara, India, Cappadocia, Dahia, the land of the hauma-drinking Scythians, the land of the Scythians with pointed hats, Skudria,[47] Akaufaka, Lybia, Caria,[48] Ethiopia."

—*API* 30 and pl. XII–XIII no. 14:9–23

The next two references are legends above reliefs of thronebearers carved on the tomb of Artaxerxes II (404–359 B.C.) at Naqsh-i-Rustam:

[3.7] "[These are the 'I]onians' ([LÚ *ia*]-*ma-na-a-a*)"

—Schmidt, *Persepolis*, vol. 3, *Oriental Institute Publications* 70 (1970) p. 109:23; *API* 47: no. 24:23[49]

[44] For a study of the various lists of lands in Achaemenid royal inscriptions and comparable literature, see P. Calmeyer, "Die 'Statistische Landcharte des Perserreiches,'" *AMIran* 15 (1982) 105–87, 16 (1983) 141–222.

[45] An Elamite version of this inscription was found by the excavators, but not apparently a corresponding Old Persian text.

[46] Text: *ša ina* (ÍD) *marrat ašbū u ša aḫu ullû ša* (ÍD) *marrat ašbū*. This could be taken as differentiating "Ionians" in Asia Minor (and/or on the Aegean islands) from "Ionians" in mainland Greece. There is no clear evidence that the Akkadian generic designation "Sea" (*marratu* in the Achaemenid period, *tâmtu* in Neo-Assyrian times) could not have included the Aegean as well as the Mediterranean.

[47] Text: KUR *is-ku-du-<ru>*. Possibly Thrace and Macedonia; see Zadok, *RGTC* 8, 182, with literature.

[48] On the various terms for "Carian," see W. Eilers, "Kleinasiatisches," *ZDMG* 94 (1940) 225–26; cf. Zadok, *RGTC* 8, 64–65.

[49] Reliefs depicting these "Ionians" may be found in Schmidt, *Persepolis*, vol. 3, fig. 47 no. 23.

[3.8] "These are the other 'Ionians' (LÚ *ia-ma-na-a-a*) who wear *maginàta* on their heads."
—Schmidt, *Persepolis*, vol. 3, *Oriental Institute Publications* 70 (1970) p. 109:26; *API* 47 no. 24:26[50]

The sole non-royal text is a badly damaged legal document from Sippar dated on the 18th day of Ayaru in year 35 of Darius I (= May 15, 487 B.C.). A broken line just before the main verb *inaddin* ("he shall pay") has the isolated word:

[3.9] "(. . .) 'Ionian(s)' (LÚ *ia-ma-na-a-a*) (. . .)"
—George A. Barton, *AJSemL* 16 (1899–1900) 74 no. 17:11

In the royal inscriptions, Akkadian *Yāwanu/i*, *Yāwanaya* is paralleled by Old Persian *Yauna* (nom. masc. sg.; nom. masc. pl.: Yaunā)[51] and Elamite *Yauna* (animate pl.: *Yaunap*).[52] The Akkadian forms are essentially the same as in Neo-Babylonian times.

4. Hellenistic References (c. 330–160 B.C.)

The references from this periods are in badly damaged passages in Babylonian chronicles and in two astronomical diaries, one of the year 331/0 and the other for the years 36–38 of the Seleucid Era (= 276/5–274/3 B.C.). The Babylonian chronicle references are:

[4.1] "[. . .]uṭṭudâ, the 'Ionian' (LÚ *e-man-na-a*⌜*(-a)*⌝)" (in broken context)
—*TCS* 5 120, Chronicle 11 rev. 2′[53]

[4.2] "the 'Ionian(s)' (LÚ *ia-a-ma-na-a-[a]*)" (in broken context)
—*TCS* 5 121, Chronicle 12:5′ (referring to events in the month Simanu of year 30 of the Seleucid era [= June 10—July 9, 282 B.C.])

[50] Reliefs portraying this group of "Ionians" may be seen ibid., fig. 48 no. 26. The translation of *maginàta* (pl.) has been debated over the years. *CAD* M/1 (1977) 44b has identified the object (reconstructed singular: *maginnu*) as a type of headgear, probably the petasos (πέτασος), a felt hat with a wide brim (as pictured on the corresponding relief). This was first suggested by F.H. Weissbach, *Die Keilinschriften der Achämeniden*, *Vorderasiatische Bibliothek* 3 (1911) 88–89 note p. Wolfram von Soden in *AHw* 576b has identified the *maginàta* as shields and compared the word with Hebrew *māgēn*/Aramaic *mgn*'. The verb in the sentence, *našû*, can mean either "to bear" or "to wear," depending on context.

For further commentary on the reliefs, see W. Hinz, *Altiranische Funde und Forschungen* (Berlin: De Gruyter 1969) 98, 104; cf. G. Walser, *Die Völkerschaften auf den Reliefs von Persepolis*, *Teheraner Forschungen* 2 (1966) 86–88.

[51] R.G. Kent, *Old Persian: Grammar, Texts, Lexicon*, *American Oriental Series* 33, 2nd ed. (1953) 204; W. Brandenstein and M. Mayrhofer, *Handbuch des Altpersischen* (Wiesbaden: Harrassowitz 1964) 156.

[52] R.T. Hallock, *Persepolis Fortification Tablets*, *Oriental Institute Publications* 92 (1969) 772; cf. M. Mayrhofer, *Onomastica persepolitana*, *Veröffentlichungen der Iranischen Kommission* 1 (1973) 252, no. 8.1804. Note also the Neo-Elamite masculine personal name *Yaunā*.

[53] *uṭṭudâ* may stand for the end of a masculine personal name. The year dates in this chronicle are broken away; but Antiochus the prince (^{m}*an-ti-ʾ-uk/ku-su mār šarri*) is mentioned in lines 3′, rev. 3′, ⌜6′⌝, ⌜11′⌝.

[4.3] "the 'Io[nian(s)]' (LÚ *ia-a-ma*[*-na-a-a*])" (in broken context)

—*TCS* 5 122, Chronicle 12 rev. 6′ (from the same chronicle as the preceding passage, perhaps alluding to events in the following year)

[4.4] "[. . .]a, the 'Ionian' (LÚ *e-man-n*[*a*]-⌜*a-a*⌝)" (in broken context)

—*TCS* 5 124, Chronicle 13a rev. (?) 5′[54]

Next is a damaged passage in an astronomical diary for 331/0.

[4.5] "Fifteenth day: the 'Ionian(s)' (LÚ *ia-ma-na-a-a*). . . . "

—BM 36761 rev. 9′, published by D.J. Wiseman, *Nebuchadrezzar and Babylon* ([London]: British Academy 1985) pp. 120–21

The name of the month for this reference is not preserved, but astronomical observations earlier in the text place the occurrence in the month Tashritu (VII). The fifteenth day of Tashritu in the fifth year of Darius III would correspond to October 22, 331 B.C., exactly three weeks after Alexander's defeat of Darius's forces at Gaugamela.[55] According to the diary entry (rev. 9′), this would be just before Alexander (m⌜*a*⌝*-lik-sa-an-dar-ri-is*) entered Babylon (rev. 11′).[56]

The following references are from an astronomical diary for years 36–38 of the Seleucid era.

[4.6] "In that year, merchandise in Babylon and (the other) cities was bought with copper coins of 'Ionia' (KUR *ia-man-nu*)."

—BM 36710 + 92688 + 92689 rev. 33 (Babylonian astronomical diary, here referring to year 38 of the Seleucid era [= 274/3 B.C.])[57]

[54] The fragment at the beginning may be the end of a masculine personal name. The reference is to an undetermined date, but the "troops of m*an-ti-*'-[ ]" in rev. (?) 10′ may refer to forces of either Antigonus or an Antiochus.

[55] Wiseman, who recently published the first edition of this diary (*Nebuchadrezzar and Babylon*, 116–21), has misunderstood the chronology of the text. A.J.Sachs, *Late Babylonian Astronomical and Related Texts* (Providence: Brown 1955) xiii, dated the astronomical phenomena to the year "–330/29" (astronomical notation for 331/0 B.C.). Wiseman (*Nebuchadrezzar and Babylon*, 117–18) misconstrued Sachs's conclusions as referring to 330/29 B.C. and attempted to date the battle of Gaugamela and the other events mentioned in the diary a year later than they should be.

[56] The verb in the passage, however, is destroyed. All that is preserved is Alexander, his royal title, and the words "to/into Babylon" (*ana* E.KI).

[57] Significant publications dealing with this text are: a) Joseph Epping and J.N. Strassmaier, "Neue babylonischen Planeten-Tafeln, III," ZA 6 (1891) 217–44; b) eidem, "Babylonische Mondbeobachtungen aus den Jahren 38 und 79 der Seleuciden-Aera," *ZA* 7 (1892) 220–54; c) Sidney Smith, *Babylonian Historical Texts Relating to the Capture and Downfall of Babylon* (London: Methuen 1924) 150–59 and pl. XVIII (note that Smith, rev. lines 10–23 = rev. 29–42 in the numbering system followed here); d) Sachs (supra n. 55) xiv; e) R. J. van der Spek, *Grondbezit in het seleucidische Rijk* (Amsterdam: Vu Uitgeverij 1986) 211–13. I wish to express my gratitude to C.B.F. Walker of the Department of Western Asiatic Antiquities, British Museum for additional information on dating this text and for textual collations.

[4.7] "In that year . . . [merchandise] in Babylon and (the other) cities was bought with well-made copper coins of 'Ionia' (KUR *ia-man-nu*)."

—ibid., u.e. 2 (apparently referring to year 38 of the Seleucid era = [274/3 B.C.])[58]

Few suggestions have been made for the interpretation of these cryptic references to copper coins, which should have been significant to merit mention in the historical section of an astronomical diary. Sidney Smith, drawing a parallel with the terms of the decree of Gortyn, suggested that "the introduction of a copper coinage was always considered a hardship."[59] This is possible, but one may envisage a broader scenario. There are other indications in the same astronomical diary that particularly difficult times had befallen northern Babylonia in this year: conditions of famine and disease are recorded.[60] Since the text refers also to a noteworthy removal of inhabitants of Babylon to Seleucia,[61] I would propose that the overall picture involved the Seleucid decision to downgrade the old imperial capital at Babylon and to transfer part of its population to Seleucia, the new capital on the Tigris. If we look for a significant analogue in the coinage of Mesopotamia about this time, it could be found in the history of the lion staters of Babylon. The twice-repeated reference in the diary to purchases being made in "copper coins of 'Ionia'" could simply mark the prevalence of the new Seleucid forms of coinage in everyday commerce in Babylon (and other southern Mesopotamian cities) and the concomitant cessation of traditional minting privileges in Babylon, which had been allowed to continue the production of the lion staters into the early Seleucid era. Newell in his classic study of the coinage of the eastern Seleucid mints sought for a date about this time for the termination of the Babylon lion series.[62] We might consider the possibility that the enigmatic diary passages record the initial phases of the supersession of the old coinage by the new Hellenistic types.

It is of further interest that, in the chronicles, *Yāwanaya* twice appears as *Ēwanaya*, perhaps indicating contemporary pronunciation.[63]

[58] What is the significance of the addition of "well-made" (Akkadian *epšu*) in the second reference? Would it imply that the earlier coins [4.6] were of lesser quality? The inference is far from clear.

[59] *Babylonian Historical Texts* 158. The text of the decree of Gortyn is published in *ICr* IV 222–25, no. 162; a recent translation of the decree may be found in M.M. Austin, *The Hellenistic World from Alexander to the Roman Conquest* (Cambridge: University Press 1981) 185, no. 105. Note that *καυχός* (the Cretan dialect form for *χαλκός*) can mean either "copper" or "bronze."

[60] BM 36710 + 92688 + 92689 rev. 20.

[61] Ibid., rev. 16–17.

[62] Edward T. Newell, *The Coinage of the Eastern Seleucid Mints from Seleucus I to Antiochus III* (rev. by Otto Mørkholm) *NS* 1 (1978) 99–106 (especially 104–105). For illustrations of the lion staters, see ibid., pl. XXI, and G.F. Hill, *Catalogue of the Greek Coins of Arabia, Mesopotamia and Persia* (London: British Museum 1922) pls. XX–XXII. Note the late Babylonian word °*ištatirru*, a loanword from Greek "stater" used in the time of Alexander and the Seleucids (*CAD* I/J [1960] 204b).

[63] The suggestion of A.K. Grayson apud Gilbert J. P. McEwan, *Priest and Temple in Hellenistic Babylonia, Freiburger altorientalische Studien* 4 (1981) 151 and n. 349 that Late Babylonian *ina im-man-na-a-tú* means "in Greek" has generally been rejected. As *CAD* M/1 (1977) 208a pointed out, this is rather to be read IM *man-na-a-tú*, "account tablet." See the comments by M. Stolper, *JAOS* 105 (1985) 142, and Zadok, *RGTC* 8, 188. There is no evidence that *Yāmanaya*/*Yāwanaya* was ever written with doubled *m*.

Conclusions and Prospects

The conclusions that may be drawn from the passages cited above will inevitably be skewed by the non-random distribution of the source types in which they occur. Over the six centuries under consideration, each of the four major periods exhibits substantially different textual materials with differing perspectives. The Neo-Assyrian sources, royal inscriptions and official correspondence, show the "Ionians" on the periphery of the main sphere of Assyrian politico-military activity: raiders attacking coastal towns in Syria, denizens of the Sea who were caught like fish, and inhabitants of one of the western lands paying heavy tribute. There is no recorded intimate involvement or prolonged contact between Assyrians and "Ionians," and we are afforded only fleeting glimpses of a vaguely limned entity hovering on the western extremity of the known world. In the Neo-Babylonian period, the sources, both royal administrative lists and private inventories, are concerned with economic matters: trade and apportioning rations for foreigners in residence at the royal court. "Ionia" furnished purple wool, bronze, and iron through trade; and artisans, specifically carpenters, worked at the royal court. In the time of the Achaemenid empire, the overwhelming majority of sources once again are official royal inscriptions. "Ionia" was a subject land, paying tribute to the Persian emperor and providing building materials and laborers (artisans, transport workers) for the construction of royal edifices. Two Achaemenid inscriptions differentiate two types of "Ionians"; but their criteria for these distinctions differ:

1) geography: "Ionians" living in/on the Sea vs. "Ionians" dwelling on the far shore of the Sea;
   and
2) raiment: ordinary "Ionians" vs. "Ionians" who wear *maginãta* (petasos).

In the Hellenistic period, source types again change, this time to chronicles and astronomical diaries. The only notable information gleaned from these is that copper coins of "Ionia" were used as common currency in Babylonian cities by the year 275 B.C.[64] In summary, these texts depict "Ionia" and "Ionians" in a pattern of conflict with and then loose subordination to the Late Assyrian Empire and later in full subjection to the Achaemenid Empire, in economic relations with the Neo-Babylonian Empire under Nebuchadnezzar II and Nabonidus, and providing artisans for the Neo-Babylonians and Persians. Where one would expect maximum evidence for contact, namely in Hellenistic times when Mesopotamia was ruled by Greek or Macedonian overlords, there is little mention of "Ionia" and "Ionians," perhaps because these were no longer a novelty.[65]

The exact location of "Yawan" is unspecified in these texts. It is mentioned together with Cyprus and Tarsisi and is said to be either in (the midst of) the Sea, on the Sea, or

[64] One expects that the many astronomical diaries currently being prepared for publication by Hermann Hunger may also yield further references to *Yaman* and *Yamanaya*.

[65] Another term in use to designate Greek-dominated areas is *ḫanî* (sic; the putative nominative °*ḫanû* is not yet attested); but it has been suggested that this is just a general designation for regions west of Babylonia, and there are at present insufficient attestations either to prove or disprove that assertion. See Zadok, *RGTC* 8, 151, with citation of earlier literature.

reached by the Sea. In one instance, "Ionians" are said to be dwelling on the opposite shore of the Sea.[66] But even this is not particularly helpful, since we are by no means sure that the "Sea" (*tâmtu* in the Assyrian texts, *marratu* in the Achaemenid) designated the Mediterranean to the exclusion of the Aegean. If it were not for the obvious similarity between *Yawan*, *Yawanaya*, etc., and ʼΙάϝονες and cognates in other ancient Near Eastern languages (particularly in the Old Persian–Elamite–Babylonian trilinguals), we would be hard-pressed to assert, from Akkadian cuneiform evidence alone, that Akkadian *Yawanaya* designated eastern Greeks—especially since the only personal names attested for the Yawanaya are non-Greek.

The evolution and dialectal differentiation of the Akkadian name forms for "Ionia" and "Ionians(s)" have not, to my knowledge, been previously observed. We can construct the following table:

	NEO-ASSYRIAN	NEO-BABYLONIAN	ACHAEMENID	HELLENISTIC
"IONIA"	Yawan	Yāwan(u/a)	Yāwan(u/i)	Yāwan(u)
"IONIAN"	Yawnaya	Yāwanaya	Yāwanaya	Yāwanaya/Ēwanaya

The distribution of historical, but unpronounced case endings (nom./acc. in Neo-Babylonian, nom./gen. in Achaemenid, nom. only in Hellenistic) may be random, since this has not as yet been observed for comparable geographical names in Babylonian. The short/long alternation in Assyrian vs. Babylonian is also of interest, as is the shift from *Yā-* to *Ē-* (or perhaps alternation between *Yā-* and *Ē-*) in Hellenistic times. As yet, the phonology of Hellenistic Babylonian, which was essentially a written rather than a spoken language, remains imperfectly understood.

It is plain that, even within the narrow confines of the present topic dealing with Yawan, Yawnaya, and Yawanaya, there is much work to be done. In this article, we have made a few preliminary observations; but we may perhaps sketch examples of pertinent research yet to be undertaken. There needs to be systematic investigation of archaeological materials and supplementary documentation to determine more closely the patterns of the metals trade in the greater eastern Mediterranean region (including the Aegean and Western Asia) in the first millennium B.C., especially for bronze (including copper/tin sources) and iron.[67] This would include research on mine locations, smelting technology, trade mechanisms, and trade routes. One should also examine in more detail the broader context of the sources from which passages have been excerpted here. Are there, for instance, detectable variations in the context of the "Ionian" references in Sargon's building inscriptions that would yield clues as to the date and location of the Assyrian encounters with the "Ionians" and other western groups?[68] One should moreover

[66] [3.6] above.

[67] See, as general background, Theodore A. Wertime and James D. Muhly eds., *The Coming of the Age of Iron* (New Haven: Yale 1980) and the proceedings of the June 1986 London Bronze symposium now published in John E. Curtis ed., *Bronze-Working Centres of Western Asia in the Early Iron Age, 1000–539 B.C.* (London: Kegan Paul 1988).

[68] This has already been begun by J. Elayi and A. Cavigneaux, "Sargon et les Ioniens," *OA* 18 (1979) 59–75, who have suggested that Sargon's contacts with the Ionians probably took place in 715 in Cilicia

undertake for Neo-Assyrian and Neo-Babylonian architectural and art forms a detailed investigation similar to that which has been done for Greek influence on Achaemenid building techniques and art motifs.[69] But here one would have to reckon with the possibility of influence either from east to west or from west to east. A detailed, comparative philological study—with due attention to diachronic and synchronic variation—between Greek Ἰάϝονες, Ἴωνες, etc. and their apparent cognates in Hebrew (*Yāwān*), Aramaic (*Ywn*), Egyptian (Demotic *Wjnn*, Coptic *weyenīn*), Assyrian (*Yawan*, *Yawnaya*), Babylonian (*Yāwan*, *Yāwanaya*), Elamite (*Yauna*), Old Persian (*Yauna*), and other pertinent languages might indicate dates, trends, and intermediaries for onomastic borrowing that would shed light on general cultural contacts between the Greeks and their eastern neighbors and on the process whereby "Ionian" became the generic term for Greek in most eastern lands.

Finally we may consider the broader spectrum of Greek-Mesopotamian relations, which in turn form part of general Hellenic-West Asiatic interchanges. The first great cycle of European-Asiatic contacts in historical times took place from the Late Bronze Age (1600–1200 B.C.) until the rending of the Seleucid empire between the expansionist forces of Parthia and Rome (141–64 B.C.). Over this period of slightly more than a millennium, there were myriad political, military, economic, and cultural contacts between East and West. The archaeological and documentary sources are abundant and varied. Historical studies dealing with areas affected by European-Asiatic relations have tended to be uneven both in control of the broad source material and in perspective. The era that has perhaps fared the best is the time of the Achaemenid Empire in the East and of the classical Greek city-states in the West, where a growing number of historians have attempted to acquaint themselves with the rich epigraphic and anepigraphic materials on both sides and are gradually achieving more balanced appraisals of the international cultural scene.[70]

Pedias, the plain between the Taurus and Amanus ranges. Note that the supposed reference (*CAH* 3/3, 2nd ed., 19) in an Assyrian geographical text to Cilicia (KUR *ḫi-lak-ku*) and "Ionia" (KUR *ia-x-na*) is uncertain because of the damage to the second name; the text is published in H.C. Rawlinson ed., *A Selection from the Miscellaneous Inscriptions of Assyria* ("The Cuneiform Inscriptions of Western Asia," 2; London: Bowler 1866) pl. 53, no. 1 ii 8.

[69] Compare, for instance, the detailed studies of Greek influence on Achaemenid art and architecture by Carl Nylander and Ann Farkas (supra n. 43). Note also the interesting examples of Greek graffiti at Persepolis cited by Margaret Root, *The King and Kingship in Achaemenid Art*, Acta Iranica, Troisième Série 9 (1979) 10. Chester Starr has called attention to "A Sixth-Century Athenian Tetradrachm Used to Seal a Clay Tablet from Persepolis," *NC*, 7th series 16 (1976) 219–22 and has commented on "Greeks and Persians in the Fourth Century B.C.: A Study in Cultural Contacts before Alexander," *IrAnt* 11 (1975) 39–99, 12 (1977) 49–115.

There has been little detailed study of Neo-Assyrian or Neo-Babylonian artistic connections with Greece. One can note in passing Babylonian-style bronzes found in seventh-century context on Samos (Ulf Jantzen, *Ägyptische und orientalische Bronzen aus dem Heraion von Samos*, *Samos* 8 [1972] 70–71; cf. P. Calmeyer, *ZA* 63 [1973] 128–29; H. Kyrieleis, "Babylonische Bronzen im Heraion von Samos," *JdI* 94 [1979] 32–48) and also the columned Assyrian *bīt-ḫilāni* architecture, which has stylistic analogues in Syria as well as Greece.

[70] See supra nn. 43 and 69. Note also J.M. Cook, *The Persian Empire* (London: Dent 1983) and revised sections of *CAH* 4–6 currently under preparation.

Still at a preliminary stage of study, but recently arousing more interest is the evidence from the Late Bronze Age, the time of the Minoan and Mycenaean syllabic scripts and the appearance of the Ahhiyawa (ʼΑχαιοί) in western Asia Minor. In the past few years, renewed debate on the significance in Hittite documents of Attarissiyas the "man of Aḫḫiyā" (Atreus the ruler of the ʼΑχαιοί?), Aleksandus of Wilusa (Alexandros of (W)Ilios?), and Milawata (Miletos?) has led to the reopening of broader questions of relations between Asia Minor and mainland Greece, on both linguistic and archaeological grounds.[71] The possibility of at least mediate contact between Mesopotamia and Greece has been raised by new archaeological evidence: the hoard of cylinder seals, including some with Babylonian cuneiform inscriptions, excavated at Boeotian Thebes[72] and the Mycenaean-style oxhide ingot unearthed in the Kassite palace at Tell el-Abyad (Dur-Kurigalzu) in northern Babylonia.[73] Nautical archaeology has brought to light wrecks of Bronze Age vessels which carried on trade between the Levant, Cyprus, Crete, and possibly the Aegean.[74] Additional evidence for a wide range of interconnections through the broader Eastern Mediterranean world should further illuminate the picture.

The early phases of the Iron Age (1200–550)[75] are at present poorly documented. This was clearly the time of major developments such as burgeoning Phoenician commercial activity around the Mediterranean, Greek settlements in Cilicia, Syria, and Egypt (as well as in the western Mediterranean), the origin of the Greek alphabetic script from an essentially consonantal West Semitic prototype (perhaps Phoenician), an orientalizing period in Greek art, and incidental similarities in architectural style between

[71] See the recent summation of the *status quaestionis* by Hans G. Güterbock, "The Ahhiyawa Problem Reconsidered," *AJA* 87 (1983) 133–38; and note the archaeological comments by Machteld Mellink and E. Vermeule, ibid., 138–43. Cf. Güterbock, "Hittites and Akhaeans: A New Look," *ProcPhilSoc* 128 (1984) 114–22 and "Troy in Hittite Texts? *Wilusa, Ahhiyawa*, and Hittite History," in Machteld J. Mellink ed., *Troy and the Trojan War* (Bryn Mawr: Bryn Mawr College 1986) 33–44. Also pertinent to the discussion are H.A. Hoffner, Jr., "The Milawata Letter Augmented and Reinterpreted" in H. Hirsch and H. Hunger eds., *Vorträge gehalten auf der 28. Rencontre Assyriologique Internationale in Wien, 6.–10. Juli 1981* (*AfO* Beiheft 19; Horn, Austria: Berger 1982) 130–37 and T.R. Bryce, "A Reinterpretation of the Milawata Letter in the Light of the New Join Piece," *AnatSt* 35 (1985) 13–23.

[72] Published in a series of articles by E. Porada, H.G. Güterbock, and J.A. Brinkman in *AfO* 28 (1981–82) 1–78.

[73] J.A. Brinkman, "Twenty Minas of Copper," in Francesca Rochberg-Halton ed., *Language, Literature, and History: Philological and Historical Studies Presented to Erica Reiner, American Oriental Series* 67 (1987) 33–36.

[74] Especially the wrecks from Cape Gelidonya and Ulu Burun. See George F. Bass, *Cape Gelidonya: A Bronze Age Shipwreck, TAPS* 57/8 (1967); Cemal Pulak and Donald A. Frey, "The Search for a Bronze Age Shipwreck," *Archaeology* 38/4 (1985) 18–24; George F. Bass et al., "A Late Bronze Age Shipwreck at Kaş, Turkey," *IJNA* 13 (1984) 271–79; George F. Bass, "A Bronze Age Shipwreck at Ulu Burun (Kaş)," *AJA* 90 (1986) 269–96.

[75] For the purposes of this article, the traditional approximate date of 1200 B.C. has been accepted for the shift from the Late Bronze Age to the Early Iron Age in Western Asia. There is an increasing body of evidence that this date varied in different lands and that in a considerable portion of Western Asia a date in the tenth century might be more appropriate. See inter alia, Jane C. Waldbaum, *From Bronze to Iron: The Transition from the Bronze Age to the Iron Age in the Eastern Mediterranean, SIMA* 54 (1978); Wertime and Muhly (supra n. 67); J.A. Brinkman, "Textual Evidence for Bronze in Babylonia in the Early Iron Age, 1000–539 B.C.," in Curtis (supra n. 67).

Assyria, Syria, and Greece. The amount of concrete evidence here has been slim, but is steadily growing; and we anticipate further elucidation of the broadening range of commercial and political contacts hinted at in the Neo-Assyrian and Neo-Babylonian written materials.[76]

In many ways, the era of Mesopotamian-Greek contacts that has fared worst to date is that which is best documented, namely the time of the Seleucid empire. Many Hellenistic historians, including some writing for the recent revision of the *Cambridge Ancient History*,[77] seem almost totally unaware of the abundant cuneiform sources and pertinent archaeological materials coming from Seleucid Mesopotamia.[78] On the other hand, Mesopotamian historians and philologists have tended to underestimate the relevance of Greek sources; and Mesopotamian archaeologists have made only the sketchiest of comparisons with Greek architecture and art. This is perhaps the field ripest for development as Hellenists and Orientalists gradually become better acquainted with the full range of materials available in Greek, Babylonian, and other eastern languages and begin to appreciate the integrated and segregated aspects of political, socio-economic, and cultural life in Seleucid Mesopotamia. We can begin to see the full panorama of urban centers founded by the Greeks, ancient cities and temples cherished by the natives, rich literary and scientific traditions in cuneiform carried on by the old scribal families,[79] the flourishing realms of commerce and agriculture, the splendors of ancient architecture and of the new Greek theatre at Babylon, the fresh Greek coinage and the traditional lion staters, the changing hierarchy of urban settlements with their extensive lifeline of canals, and demographic shifts to the Tigris axis and Seleucia in northern Babylonia. It is surely significant that Alexander the Great at the climax of his career selected Babylon to be his imperial capital—as a symbol of political and cultural unity over a broad expanse of

[76] One hopes for further research on subjects as diverse as the eastern background of early Greek mathematics and astronomy (adumbrated in Otto Neugebauer, *The Exact Sciences in Antiquity*, 2nd ed. [Providence: Brown 1957]) as well as the art of divination (cf. Dunbabin [supra n. 14] 57).

[77] Vol.7, part 1, 2nd ed. (1984).

[78] This is especially difficult to understand in view of the statement made concerning the Seleucid empire in *CAH* 7/1, 2nd ed., 181: "This was the compact economic, strategic and political nucleus: Mesopotamia, Syria and Cilicia." Note also the misleading comment by M.M. Austin (supra n. 59) 1: "The oriental evidence from Mesopotamia, abundant in previous Near Eastern History, is relatively scanty in the Hellenistic period."

[79] In addition to temple rituals and copies of older Babylonian literature, this includes Graeco-Babylonian bilingual sources and both unilingual Babylonian and Sumerian-Babylonian written phonetically in Greek characters. The Graeco-Babyloniaca has been published and discussed by T.G. Pinches, "Greek Transcriptions of Babylonian Tablets," *Proceedings of the Society of Biblical Archaeology* 24 (1902) 108–19; A.H. Sayce, "The Greeks in Babylonia: Graeco-Cuneiform Texts," ibid. 120–25; Woldemar G. Schileico, "Ein babylonischer Weihtext in griechischer Schrift," *AfO* 5 (1928–29) 11–13 and pl. VIII; E. Sollberger, "Graeco-Babyloniaca," *Iraq* 24 (1962) 63–72; M.J. Geller, "More Graeco-Babyloniaca," *ZA* 73 (1983) 114–20. Greek names written in cuneiform and Babylonians bearing both Greek and Babylonian names have been discussed by Raymond A. Bowman, "Anu-uballiṭ—Kefalon," *AJSemL* 56 (1939) 231–43; W. Röllig, "Griechische Eigennamen in Texten der babylonischen Spätzeit," *Orientalia* 29 (1960) 376–91. Note also the presence of local compositions in Greek such as the Βαβυλωνιακά, a history of Babylonia *ab initio* compiled by the Babylonian priest Berossus.

territory from India to Greece. This is one of the most fertile areas for present-day research, and the renaissance on the Mesopotamian side is already under way.[80] Seleucid Mesopotamia deserves and will repay closer study by both Hellenists and Orientalists.[81]

This article is dedicated with affection to Father Raymond Schoder, πολύτροπος, a philologist by training and an archaeologist by avocation, who first taught me the values of a multi-cultural approach to the wonders and beauties of the ancient world.

[80] In the past two decades, there has been a series of studies and text editions, including: a) Douglas A. Kennedy, *Late-Babylonian Economic Texts, Cuneiform Texts from Babylonian Tablets in the British Museum* 49 (1969); b) Joachim Oelsner, *Materialien zur babylonischen Gesellschaft und Kultur in hellenisticher Zeit* (Budapest: Eötvös University 1986; rev. ed. of diss., Jena 1970); c) Ursula Lewenton, "Studien zur keilschriftlichen Rechtspraxis Babyloniens in hellenistischer Zeit" (unpub. diss., Münster 1970); d) Hermann Hunger and E. von Weiher, *Spätbabylonische Texte aus Uruk*, 1–3 (Berlin: Mann 1976–1988); e) L.T. Doty, "Cuneiform Archives from Hellenistic Uruk" (unpub. diss., Yale 1977); f) Jan van Dijk and Werner Mayer, *Texte aus dem Reš-Heiligtum in Uruk-Warka, BaM* Beiheft 2 (1980); g) Gilbert J.P. McEwan, *Priest and Temple in Hellenistic Babylonia, Freiburger altorientalische Studien* 4 (1981); (note also the reviews of this book in *JCS* 35 [1983] 229–43 and *JAOS* 105 [1985] 141–42); h) Gilbert J.P. McEwan, *Texts from Hellenistic Babylonia in the Ashmolean Museum, Oxford Editions of Cuneiform Texts* 9 (1982); i) Bernd Funck, *Uruk zur Seleukidenzeit, Schriften zur Geschichte und Kultur des Alten Orients* 16 (1984); j) van der Spek (supra n. 57). For archaeology, see inter alia: k) the reports on the Italian excavations at Seleucia and Ctesiphon by G. Gullini et al. appearing in *Mesopotamia* 1 (1966) through 8/9 (1973–74); l) Robert McC.Adams, *Heartland of Cities: Surveys of Ancient Settlement and Land Use on the Central Floodplain of the Euphrates* (Chicago: University Press 1981; note that the total settled hectarage for the Seleucid-Parthian period, listed as "3,210" ibid. 178, must be corrected to "2,955" [in line with the computation ibid., table 15] and the average settlement size correspondingly reduced from 7.71 to 7.12 hectares); m) Uruk surface surveys reported on by U. Finkbeiner et al. in *BaM* 15 (1984) and 16 (1985).

[81] I wish to express my gratitude to Klaus Baer, W. Randall Garr, and Matthew Stolper, who kindly provided information for or comments on various parts of this paper.

CONTRASTING BEHAVIOR PATTERNS IN PLAUTUS

Gilda S. de Brito

At the very beginning of the *Amphitruo*, one of the best known plays written by Plautus (ca. 254–184 B.C.), staged on an uncertain date, the god Mercury addresses the audience as follows:

> Vt uos in uostris uoltis mercimoniis
> Emundis uendundisque me laetum lucris
> Adficere atque adiuuare in rebus omnibus,
> Et ut res rationesque uostrorum omnium
> Bene expedire uultis peregrique et domi,
> Bonoque atque amplo auctare perpetuo lucro
> Quasque incepistis res quasque inceptabitis,
> Et uti bonis uos uostrosque omnis nuntiis
> Me adficere uultis, ea adferam, ea ut(i) nuntiem,
> Quae maxime in rem uostram communem sient—
> Nam uos quidem id iam scitis concessum et datum
> Mihi esse ab dis aliis, nuntiis praesim et lucro—
> Haec ut me uultis adprobare, adnitier,
> Lucrum ut perenne uobis semper subpetat,
> Ita huic facietis fabulae silentium
> Itaque aequi et iusti hic eritis omnes arbitri.
>
> (vv. 1–16)[1]

> (All people here that would have me prosper their affairs and bring
> them gain in the buying and selling of merchandise or any other business—
> You that would wish me to forward your interests and undertakings
> at home or abroad, and bless with everlasting profit your present
> and future enterprises wheresoever and whatsoever—
> You that expect me to bring to you and all your friends nothing but
> good news; to announce, report and convey such information as will be
> to your greatest advantage [reports and profits being, as you are
> aware, the department specially entrusted to me by the company of the gods]—
> You that desire all these benefits and services from me—have
> the goodness to listen to this play attentively, one and all, and
> judge it with fair and open minds.)[2]

According to this *Prologue* it seems clear that Mercury tries to "bribe" his audience in order to keep it quiet and attentive during the performance which was about to take

[1] All Latin quotations from Plautus are from the text established and translated by Alfred Ernout, published by the *Société d'Édition "Les Belles Lettres"*, in 5 vols., sponsored by the *Association Guillaume Budé*, Paris, 1932.

[2] Plautus, *The Rope and Other Plays*, translated by E.F. Watling (London: Penguin 1964) 228.

place. What kind of audience was this, that had to be bought off with divine promises to sit still and maintain a civilized behavior at the staging of a play in a Roman theater in the second century B.C.?

We are all aware that theatrical performances, and comedies in particular, at that time were basically meant to amuse and distract the common people, and that those that did not could not expect a successful season on a Roman stage. Terence himself, at least initially, tested this handicap. In spite of being so closely linked to the Greek type of New Comedy which, in Athens, aimed at a more sensitive and intelligent audience, Roman comedies were supposed to show some degree of originality, at least as far as *humor* was concerned. There can be no doubt that, in this sense, Plautus achieved perfection in transplanting Menander's humor to the less refined taste of a Roman audience. That probably accounts for the enormous popularity of his plays for so many years and centuries after his death, and justifies Aullus Gellius's (born ca. A.D. 130) statement that Plautus excelled in Roman letters.[3] The *Amphitruo*, for one, was still staged in Rome during the reign of Diocletian (A.D. 284–305), and is easily detected in Shakespeare's *Comedy of Errors*, Molière's *Amphitryon*, Rotrou's *Les Sosies*, Dryden's *Amphitryon*, Giraudoux's *Amphitryon 38*, and in *Um deus dormiu lá em casa* (A God Slept at my Place) by the Brazilian playwright Guilherme de Figueiredo.

It seems to be a commonplace among certain critics to consider Plautus an immoral and pornographic writer. Nothing could be more unfair. Cicero himself states that Plautus's jests are clever and witty, not rude or indecent.[4] John Hough, in his *Miscellanea Plautina*, published in the *Transactions of the American Philological Association* (1940) discussing the matter, entirely agrees with Cicero. The distinguished French Romanist Pierre Grimal, of the Institut de France and the Sorbonne, in a lecture delivered at the University of Pisa in 1972 in honor of Marino Barchiesi,[5] points out the fact that Terence, Plautus's counterpart in Roman comedy, frequently in his plays raises such moral problems as the education of young people, the relationship between parents and children, the involvement of young men in the life of the *Vrbs*, and the sentiment of love. Most of these ethical items are discussed according to the philosophical principles of Aristotle, just as they were found in the authors whom Terence used as his models. But, asks Grimal, what about Plautus, who had also adapted his plays from Athenian comedies whose authors were immersed in the same spiritual world as those imitated by Terence? Was Plautus as original in approaching philosophical and moral subjects as he was typically Roman in transplanting Menander's humor? Or did he just ignore the nature of these subjects altogether? These are not easy questions to answer.[6]

[3] Gell. 6 (7). 17. 4: Plautus . . . homo linguae atque elegantiae in verbis Latinae princeps.

[4] Cf. *De Off.*, I, 29, 104: Duplex omnino est iocandi genus: unum illiberale, petulans, flagitiosum, obscenum, alterum elegans, urbanum, ingeniosum, facetum; quo genere non modo Plautus noster et Atticorum antiqua comoedia, sed etiam philosophorum Socraticorum libri referti sunt . . .

[5] Grimal, P., "Existe-t-il une 'morale' de Plaute?," in *Lettres d'Humanité* 34 (1975) 485.

[6] Ibid.

Although Plautus's main goal was to entertain his audience and not to preach morality or show a deep knowledge of human nature, one still is able to find in his humor a certain sensibility concerning the serious aspects of life. Despite the burlesque quality of his plots, some ethical principles can be found in them. It is true that a number of shameful acts and a rather exaggeratedly liberal behavior in matters of sex are dealt with tolerantly by Plautus, but on the other hand in many instances vices are made repulsive and virtues valued highly. As Duff judiciously points out in his *Literary History of Rome*, the Plautine theater is no carnival of unredeemed profligacy; self-sacrifice is rewarded in the *Captiui*, perfidy overthrown in the *Rudens*, avarice defeated in the *Aulularia*, and loyalty justified in the *Trinummus*.[7] Indeed, the passage in the *Persa* showing the young girl, the *Virgo*, feeling offended when her own father is willing to sell her as a slave, is an example of dignity:

VI. Amabo, mi pater,
Quamquam lubenter escis alienis studes,
Tuin uentris causa filiam uendas tuam?
SA. Mirium quin regis Philippi caussa aut Attali
Te potius uendam quam mea, quae sis mea.
VI. Vtrum pro ancilla me habes an pro filia?
SA. Vtrum hercle magis in uentris rem uidebitur.
Meum, opinor, imperium in te, non in me tibist.
VI. Tua istaec potestas est, pater. Verum tamen,
Quamquam res nostrae sunt, pater, pauperculae,
Modice et modeste meliust uitam uiuere.
Nam ad paupertatum si admigrant infamiae,
Grauior paupertas fit, fides sublestior.

(vv. 336–348)

(*Daugh.* But, oh, father dear, no matter how eager you are to enjoy other people's food, would you really sell your own daughter for the sake of your stomach?
Sat. (gruffly) A likely thing I should sell you for the sake of King Philip or Attalus, rather than for my own sake, when you're mine.
Daugh. Which do you consider me, father, your maidservant, or your daughter?
Sat. Whichsoever seems more serviceable to my stomach, by Jove! I have authority over you, I take it, not you over me.
Daugh. Yes, father, you have the right to do it. Just the same, even if we are nothing but poor people, it's better to live modestly and as our means allow; for if on top of poverty comes dishonor, one's poverty becomes a heavier burden and one's good name a byword.)[8]

Again in the *Persa* the words of the *Virgo* to Toxilus and Sagaristio condemning sinful actions and praising the fruits of virtue are highly commendable:

[7] Duff, J. Wight and A.M. Duff, *A Literary History of Rome from the Origins to the Close of the Golden Age* (New York: Barnes & Noble 1963) 139.
[8] *Plautus III* (Loeb Classical Library), translated by Paul Nixon (Cambridge, Mass.: Harvard 1950) 463.

SA. Quid id quod uidisti? ut munitum muro tibi uisu oppidumst?
VI. Si incolae bene sunt morati, id pulchre munitum arbitror
Perfidia et Peculatus ex urbe et Auaritia si exula
Quarta Inuidia, quinta Ambitio, sexta Obtrectatio,
Septimum Periurium . . .
TO. Eugae!
VI. Octava Indiligentia,
Nona Iniuria, decimum, quod pessimum adgressust, Scelus
Haec unde aberunt, ea urbs moenita muro sat erit simplici;
Ubi ea aderunt, centumplex murus rebus seruandis parumst.

(vv. 554–559)

(*Sag.* How about what you have observed? The wall—what do you think of that as a fortification for the town?

Daugh. If the citizens are of sound character, I consider the town splendidly fortified. If perfidy and peculation and greed are banished from this city, yes, and envy, for a fourth, and fifth, place hunting, sixth, vilification, seventh, perjury—

Tox. (*aside to Dordalus, with a dig in the ribs*) Hear! Hear!

Daugh. —and eighth, indifference, ninth, injustice, and tenth and worst in its assaults, crime—the city from which these vices are absent will be walled well enough with a single wall. But where they are present, a hundred-fold wall is not enough to preserve the property within it.)[9]

As we know, love was the leit-motif of most of the *palliatae*, and in Plautus the characters of his comedies differ in their attitudes concerning their emotional approach towards sentimental values. In the plays, love, in the "romantic" and poetic sense of the word, is frequently found in unmarried couples, but almost never in those bound by matrimony. But the so-called free-love between young men and women is regarded as improper and immoral, as we can see from the words of young Philolaches in the *Mostellaria*:

Nam ego illud frugi usque et probus fui,
In fabrorum potestate dum fui.
Postea, quom immigravi ingenium in meum.
Perdidi operam fabrorum ilico oppido.
Venit ignauia. Ea mi tempestas fuit;
Mi adventu suo grandinem imbremque attulit.
Haec uerecundiam mi et virtutis modum
Deturbavit texit detextitque a me ilico.
Postilla optigere me neglegens fui;
Continuo pro imbre amor aduenit in cor meum.
Is usque in pectus permanauit, permadefecit cor meum
Nunc simul res, fides, fama, uirtus, decusque
Deseruerunt; ego sum in usu factus nimio nequior.

(vv. 133–145)

[9] Ibid. 485.

(Just look at me. I was a lad
Of modest manners, blameless life,
While they were building me.
Left to my own devices—well,
It didn't take me very long
To undo all the builder's work
And make the house a ruin!

Idleness was the rainy weather
That sapped my timbers; showers of sloth,
Hailstorms of carelessness, attacked me,
Shook my foundations of respect,
Twisted my lines of rectitude,
And rapidly unroofed me—
Which damage I did nothing to repair.

Then love—ah, love was the next wet season.
It poured like anything!—into my heart,
Into my soul. I was flooded out!
Good-bye to fortune, faith, good name,
Honour, and virtue. Wear and tear
Just left me fit for nothing.)[10]

Yet, for Palestrion, in the *Miles Gloriosus*, free-love is not only tolerated but also morally acceptable, as we can see from his speech:

Erat erus Athenis mihi adulescens optumus.
Is amabat meretricem matre Athenis Atticis
Et illa illum contra; qui est amor cultu optumus.

(vv. 99–101)

(My master at Athens was a young man of excellent character.
He loved an Athenian woman, and she loved him;
Which is love as it should be.)[11]

As for female characters in Plautus, they are developed in a very limited universe, since they are usually bound by strict social conventions. In view of the oriental type of feminine seclusion and arranged socially "convenient" marriages, it would be impossible for a young girl of free birth to get involved in a romantic type of relationship or affair, as so frequently happens nowadays. Out of wedlock, sex had to be searched for elsewhere. Still, even those who look for spurious "liaisons" with less virtuous free women cannot expect in Plautus a consistent behavior in the *meretrix* or in the courtesan: we can detect a great difference in attitudes concerning human values in the courtesan Philamatium of the *Mostellaria* and in the Acroteleutin of the *Miles Gloriosus*.

[10] Trans. Watling (supra n. 2) 31.
[11] Plautus, *The Pot of Gold and Other Plays*, translated by E.F. Watling (London: Penguin 1965) 156.

The widowed sister in the *Aulularia*, Eunomia, shows respect for the family type relationship when she says:

Velim te arbitrari med haec uerba, frater,
Meai fidei tuaique rei (haec)
Causa facere, ut aequum est germanam sororem.
Quamquam haud falsa sum nos odiosas haberi:
Nam multum loquaces merito omnes habemur
Nec mutam profecto repertam ullam esse
Hodie dicunt mulierem ullo in saeculo.
Verum hoc, frater, unum tamen cogitato,
Tibi proximam me mihique esse item te;
Ita aequum est quod in rem esse utrique arbitremur
Et mihi te et tibi (me) consulere et monere,
Neque occultum id haberi neque per metum mussari,
Quin participem pariter ego te et tu me (ut) facias,
Eo nunc ego secreto te huc foras seduxi,
Vt tuam rem ego tecum hic loquerer familiarem.

(vv. 120–134)

(I hope you understand that I am only speaking to you as a sister has a right to speak, in your own interest and as my conscience bids me. Oh, I know no man loves a sister: we talk too much, they say; they are right, we do; there was never a woman born, in this age or any other, who could keep her thoughts to herself. But I *am* your nearest relative, don't forget, and you're mine. It's only natural that we should discuss things together and give each other what advice seems best; not keep each other in the dark, or be afraid to speak frankly. I want to have no secrets from you, and I hope you have none from me. That's why I've brought you out here away from your household, to give you a little private talk about your affairs.)[12]

Further on, she sets forth her feminine self-criticism:

Decet te equidem uera proloqui.
Nam optuma nulla potest eligi:
Alia alia peior, frater, est.

(vv. 138–140)

(You shouldn't tell such fibs, my dear brother. No woman can be the best woman you know. Each one is worse than another in some way.)[13]

But still, she tries to convince her brother Megadorus of the necessity of engaging in matrimony:

Id quod in rem tuam optumum esse arbitor, te id monitu aduento.
....

[12] Ibid. 16.
[13] Ibid.

Factum uolo.
....
Quod tibi sempiternum
Salutare sit, liberis procreandis...
....
Volo te uxorem
Domum ducere.

(vv. 145–148)

(I have been thinking about what you ought to do, in your own best interest, and that is what I have come to advise you about.
....
For your own advantage, in this world and the next, and in the hope of your fathering a family—
....
I should like to see you married.)[14]

In the *Menaechmi*, Plautus shows us the hurt feelings of a betrayed wife:

Egone hic me patiar frustra in matrimonio,
Vbi uir compilet clanculum quicquid domist
Atque ea ad amicam deferat?

(vv. 559–561)

(How much longer am I expected to put up with this kind of marriage, I'd like to know, with my husband quietly robbing me of all I possess to make presents to his mistress?)[15]

He also demonstrates how strong and determined the reactions of the wife can be:

. . .
Nam domum numquam introibis, nisi feres pallam simul.

(v. 662)

(. . . You're not coming into this house again until you bring the gown with you.)[16]

But no less determined and strong is the reaction of the *Meretrix*:

Nec te ultro oraui ut dares;
Tute ultro ad me detulisti. Dedisti eam dono mihi;
Eandem nunc reposcis, patiar: tibi habe, aufer, utere
Vel tu uel tua uxor, uel etiam in loculos conpingite.
Tu huc post hunc diem pedem intro non feres, ne frustra sis;
Quando tu me bene merentem tibi habes despicatui,
Nisi feres argentum, frustra ('s): me ductare non potes
Aliam posthac inuenito, quam habeas frustratui.

(vv. 689–696)

[14] Ibid. 17.
[15] Ibid. 122.
[16] Ibid. 127.

(And I never asked for it in the first place, did I? It was your idea to bring it to me; you said it was a present for me; now you want it back. It's all the same to me; You can keep it, take it back, wear it yourself, let your wife wear it, or lock it up in a cupboard for all I care. If that's all you think of me, after all I've done for you, you're not coming into this house anymore, I give you my word—not without ready money in your hand. You can't muck about with me like that, young man. You can go and find someone else to make a fool of.)[17]

In the *Casina*, the important roles of three female characters, Cleostrata, Pardalisca and Myrrhina, disclose a carefully woven scheme against the weak male characters in the play, showing women capable of plotting and acting in a conspiratorial manner, which was not usual within the traditional context in those days.

In the *Mercator*, the speech of the old woman-servant Syra concerning the differences between men and women as far as infidelity in marriage is concerned takes us back to the eternal problem of the behavior of husband and wife:

Ecastor lege dura uiuont mulieres
Multoque iniquiore miserae quam uiri.
Nam si uir scortum duxit clam uxorem suam,
Id si resciuit uxor, inpunest uiro.
Vxor uirum si clam domo egressa est foras,
Viro fit causa, exigitur matrumonio.
Vtinam lex esset eadem quae uxori est uiro!
Nam uxor contenta est quae bona est, uno uiro;
Qui minus uir una uxore contentus siet?
Ecaster faxim, si itidem plectantur uiri.
Siquis clam uxorem duxerit scortum suam.
Vt illae exiguntur quae in se culpam commerant,
Plures uiri sint uidui quam nunc mulieres.

(vv. 817–829)

(My, my! Women do live under hard conditions, so much more unfair, poor things, than the men's. Why, if a husband has brought home some strumpet, unbeknown to his wife, and she finds it out, the husband goes scot free. But once a wife steps out of the house unbeknown to her husband, he has his grounds and she's divorced. Oh, I wish there was the same rule for the husband as for the wife! Now a wife, a good wife, is content with just her husband; why should a husband be less content with just his wife? Mercy me, if husbands, too, were taken to task for wenching on the sly, the same way as wanton wives are divorced, I warrant there'd be more lone men about than there now are women.)[18]

In the *Asinaria*, while the attitude of the *meretrix* Philenia, when caught by the wife of Deaenetus, is the one expected of a woman of her sort, the matron Artemona behaves in an unconventional way, planning revenge and making threats:

[17] Ibid. 128.
[18] Trans. Nixon (supra n. 8) 92.

Ain tandem? edepol ne tu istuc cum malo magno tuo
Dixisti in me. Sine: (re) uenias modo domum; faxo ut scias
Quid pericli sit dotatae uxori uitium dicere.

(vv. 901–903)

(So? You would, would you? Good gracious, sir, that fling at me will cost you dear. Very well! just you come back home, sir! I'll show you the danger of vilifying a wife with money.)[19]

And a few lines further:

Ego pol uiuam; et tu istaec hodie cum tuo magno malo
Inuocasti.

(vv. 909)

(My heavens, sir, I will live, and you shall pay dear for that petition of yours just now!)[20]

And the panderess Cleaereta gives us a perfect portrait of a woman in her profession:

Non tu scis? quae amanti parcet, eadem sibi parcet parum.
Quasi piscis itidemst amator lenae: nequam est nisi recens
Is habet sucum, is suauitatem; eum quouis pacto condias,
Vel patinarium, uel assum; uerses quo pacto lubet.
Is dare uolt, is se aliquod posci; nam ibi de pleno promitur,
Neque ille scit quid det, quid damni faciat; illi rei studet:
Volt placere sese amicae, uolt mihi, uolt pedisequae,
Volt famulis, uolt etiam ancillis, et quoque catulo meo
Subblanditur nouos amator, se ut quom uideat gaudeat.
Vera dico; ad suum quemque hominem quaestum esse aequomst callidum.

(vv. 177–187)

(You miss the point? The lady that spares her lover spares herself too little. Lovers are the same as fish to us—no good unless they're fresh. Your fresh ones are juicy and sweet; you can season them to taste in a stew, bake them and turn them every way. Your fresh one wants to give you a full cupboard, you scc; and he has no idea what he's giving, what it costs him. This is his only thought: he wants to please, please his girl, please me, please the waiting-woman, please the men servants, please the maid servants, too; yes, the new lover makes up to my little dog, even, so that he may be glad to see him. This is the plain truth: every one ought to keep a sharp eye for the main chance.)[21]

Before the *lex Hortensia* of 287 B.C., which enhanced equal rights for patricians and plebeians and transformed the concept of the individual as a human being, the traditional Roman morality used to make a neat distinction between the principles that were to rule the public conduct of the citizen (*ciuis*) and those which concerned the private behavior of the individual. The former were strict and demanding, the latter were more

[19] *Plautus I* (Loeb Classical Library), translated by Paul Nixon (Cambridge, Mass.: Harvard 1950) 92.
[20] Ibid. 223.
[21] Ibid. 143.

tolerant and permissive. The tolerant and permissive type of moral standard is the one found in the *palliatae* for the ethical behavior involving domestic relationship among people, inspired by Greek New Comedy. Such is the morality of the dramatic context of Plautus's plays, with the exception of the *Amphitruo*, the only one that cannot be labeled as typically bourgeois.

We are not sure about what Greek original Plautus used in writing his *Amphitruo*. Casaubon, for instance, indicates *The Long Night* by a certain Plato, a comic playwright, probably from Athens, of the V/IV century B.C., while Dietze suggests *The Night* by Philemon, a contemporary of Menander (IV/III century B.C.). Yet, according to Ernout,[22] neither of them presents conclusive evidence.

The main fact is, though, that the *Amphitruo* is really quite different from all the other Plautus plays. To begin with, the gods in the plot are not mere accessories as in the *Miles Gloriosus* or the *Aulularia*, for example, but prominent characters playing important parts. No doubt some of the scenes in the *Amphitruo* remind us of the bourgeois type of drama, but in the last act especially we find heroic, almost epic passages.[23] It seems, though, that the uniqueness of the Amphitruo in the whole of Plautus's theater lies in the approach given to subjects involving typical Roman morality, the Catonian type of *uirtus*— bravery, honor, patriotism, self-sacrifice, religious sentiment, and fidelity.[24] The traditional Roman virtue in the play is not to be found in the actions of Jupiter or Mercury, nor in the attitudes of the triumphant general, the *imperator* Amphitruo, but in the extraordinary role of a woman, the matron Alcmena. The immaculate character of Alcmena, her love for virtue, her irreproachable honor, and her qualities as an exemplary wife contrast with the various burlesque situations found in the play, and are largely responsible for the fact that Mercury himself, in the Prologue, gives the *Amphitruo* the status of a tragicomedy.

The *uirtus* of the Roman woman, as Grimal reminds us, is directly dependent on her obligations towards the family which she would become a part of by the bonds of matrimony. If she were not destined to perpetuate a legitimate lineage, a *prolis*, her personal behavior would be subject to the less strict rules of the "domestic" *uirtus*, the *uirtus* of the individual, a sort of *mores*. Otherwise she was supposed to act according to the rigid and demanding principles of the civic type of *uirtus*, the "public" *uirtus*. We find such *uirtus* in the strong character of Alcmena , and Jupiter himself appears to be ethically inferior to her, for even Mercury finds it necessary to apologize for the moral attitude of the *pater deorum*:

Erroris ambo ego illos et dementiae
Complebo atque omnem Amphitruonis familiam.
Adeo usque satietatum dum capiet pater
Illius quam amat: igitur demum omnes scient
Quae facta. Denique Alcumenam Iuppiter
Rediget antiquam coniugi in concordiam,

[22] Ernout (supra n. 1) I, 4.
[23] Ibid. 6.
[24] Cf. Grimal (supra n. 5) 491.

Nam Amphitruo actutum uxori turbas conciet
Atque insimulabit eam probri. Tum meus pater
Eam seditionem illi in tranquillum conferet.

(vv. 470–479)

(That's it—I'll have them both and all the family
So muddled up they won't know where they are!
And then—when father's finished what he's doing
In there—we'll let them all into the secret.
Jupiter of course will see that husband and wife
Kiss and forgive each other, and no harm done.
To begin with, naturally, Amphitryo
Will give his wife a devil of a talking-to
And call her all sorts of names. But in the end
Jupiter will sort it out and quell the riot.)[25]

The character of Alcmena has always been highly praised as the perfect picture of the model wife, serious and dignified beyond reproach. Loving and virtuous, she finds in her noble feelings the way to her moral rectitude, her *uirtus*:

Satin parua res est uoluptatum in uita atque in aetate agunda,
Praequam quod molestum est? ita cuique comparatum est in aetate hominum;
Ita diuis est placitum, uoluptatem ut maeror comes consequatur;
Quin incommodi plus malique ilico adsit, boni si optigit quid.
Nam ego id nunc experior domo atque ipsa de me scio, cui uoluptas
Parumper datast, dum uiri mei mihi potestas uidendi fuit
Noctem unam modo; atque is repente abilit a me hinc ante lucem.
Sola hic mihi nunc uideor, quia ille hinc abest, quem ego amo praetor omnis.
Plus aegri ex abitu uiri quam ex aduentu uoluptatis cepi. Sed hoc me meat
Saltem, quom perduellis uicit et domum laudis compos reuenit. Id solacio est.
Absit dum modo laude parta domum recipiat se: feram et perferam usque
Abitum eius animo forti atque offirmato, id modo si mercedis
Datur mihi, ut meus uictor uir belli clueat: satis
Mihi esse ducam. Virtus praemium est optimum,
Virtus omnibus rebus anteit profecto.
Libertas, salus, uita, res et parentes, patria et prognati
Tutantur, seruantur.
Virtus omnia in sese habet, omnia adsunt bona quem penest uirtus.

(vv. 633–653)

(For every pleasure in the path of life
How many pains we suffer! Such is our lot,
Poor mortals as we are. There is no joy
Without its sorrows, heaven has so decreed,
And still, the more the joy, the more the sorrow.

[25] Trans. Watling (supra n. 2) 246.

I know; now it comes home to me; I know;
A few brief hours of happiness with my husband—
One night—less than a night—dawn not yet come;
And he must go. And I am here alone,
Without the one whom most of all I love
In all the world. My joy at his return
Was great, but how much greater was the pain
Of parting from him . . .

Still there is comfort—
This is the joy—
He has come home
A hero! Conqueror! Praised by all his people!

To let him go is not so hard, I see,
If he comes back with glory. I can be brave.
I can endure his going, I can endure it,
If this is my reward—to see my husband
Hailed victor, crowned with laurels, borne in triumph.
It is enough. There is no greater gift
Than valour, Valour is all. Valour protects
Our life, our liberty, our health, our wealth,
Our home, our kith and kin. Valour is all,
And he hath all that hath it!)[26]

In another remarkable passage, complaining about the vexation imposed upon her, Alcmena proclaims her ideal of a perfect Roman matron and wife:

Non ego illam mihi dotem duco esse, quae dos dicitur,
Sed pudicitiam et pudorem et sedatum cupidinem,
Deum metum, parentum amorem et cognatum concordiam,
Tibi morigera atque ut munifica sim bonis, prosim probis.

(vv. 839–842)

(And what is my dowry? Not that treasure which the world calls dowry. What is it if not honour and purity and temperance, fear of the gods, love of my parents, the happiness of my family, and the will to love and obey you, to be good to all good friends and helpful to all honest men.)[27]

Again, further on, addressing Jupiter, she resents Amphitruo's suspicious behavior and is willing to go to extremes to defend her honor:

Durare nequeo in aedibus. Ita me probri,
Stupri, dedecoris a uiro argutam meo!
Ea quae sunt facta infectare est at clamitat;

[26] Ibid. 254.
[27] Ibid. 264.

Quae neque sunt facta neque ego in me admisi, arguit,
Atque id me susque deque esse habituram putat.
Non edepol faciam neque me perpetiar probri
Falso insimulatam, quin ego illum aut deseram
Aut satis faciat mihi ille atque adiuret insuper
Nolle esse dicta quae in me insontem protulit.

(vv. 882–890)

(I cannot stand this house a minute longer. To be accused by my husband of such vile, disgraceful, filthy counduct! Insisting that what never happened did happen, and declaring I did something I never did, and could never think of doing! If he imagines I can laugh that off, he's mistaken. I certainly can't, and don't intend to. I'm not going to sit down under such wicked and injust insinuations. Either he apologizes, or I've finished with him. He'll have to swear that he withdraws all the accusations he has made against his innocent wife.)[28]

Where do all these few samples, reflections and comparisons lead us? It seems to imply that the exhausting process of Romanization of the Greek new Comedy carried out by Plautus is not restricted to the adjustment of Athenian humor to Roman comic taste, as we have already pointed out, but also includes the reconciliation of Greek moral concepts with Roman ethical principles in a much higher degree of originality than is found in Terence. Although it seems also justified to infer that it is extremely difficult to reach a definite critical judgement concerning the moral standards of the Plautine theater, Pierre Grimal, in a remarkable book on Rome in the days of the Scipios, is absolutely right when he emphasizes the fact that Plautus's "morality" basically expresses the superiority of the Roman *mos maiorum* over foreign innovations.[29] It also remains clear that in the reading of Plautus we find a great deal of inconsistency in the paradoxical and contrasting behavior of his characters as far as moral issues are concerned, and a great instability in his judgment of ethical values.

[28] Ibid. 266.

[29] Grimal, P., *Le siècle des Scipions. Rome et l'hellénisme au temps des guerres puniques* (Paris: Aubier, Éditions Montaigne 1975) 162.

DEATH IN VENICE: ITS THEME REEXAMINED

Emily Joseph Daly, C.S.J.

In the light of the many perceptive analyses of Thomas Mann's *Death in Venice* it may appear presumptuous to suggest that few, if any, of the critics have really heard what Mann was saying. Isadore Traschen's thesis is accepted by most readers: "Mann . . . gave us a marvelously complex expression of what is probably the central concern of our time . . . the problem of realizing our irrational drives within the framework of a rational society."[1] Aschenbach, for Traschen as for others, is not a tragic hero. Confronted by his irrational drives he does not transcend them but travels down the path of ignominy and debauchery to final destruction. Such an analysis may, however, be insufficient. The following questions are here raised: Does Mann's *novella* end with Aschenbach's destruction or does Mann imply something more? Was the author subtly telling his readers that in life, as in a story, *finis coronat opus*? What is Mann's theme and how does he develop it?

Traschen's study analyzes Mann's successful development of his theme by ironic treatment of Campbell's monomythic hero[2] and parodistic handling of the Apollonian-Dionysian mythology.[3] Others, too, have admired the artistry with which Mann draws upon the mythical element to transform a story, told with simple realism, into a penetrating psychological study. André von Gronicka, in particular, points out how Mann, in this story, adopts the technique of blending myth and psychology to raise his narrative to a new level of significance.[4] Gronicka, however, for whatever reason, refrains from identifying any but a few of the allusions which abound in *Death in Venice*. These allusions are extraordinarily subtle and may be easily overlooked. Yet, recognizing the punctilious attention Mann paid to each detail in his story, one recognizes, too, the danger of failing to understand the whole if one fails to recognize the significance of the parts. Careful examination, then, of many of the allusions will reveal a Hermes-motif pervading the story which, in turn, supports the thesis that Mann was proposing something other than a life-death theme (about which there is no subtlety), namely, a theme of life-death-life.

Aschenbach's story can be quickly told. Impelled by a trivial incident, he decides to relax his literary efforts and take a vacation in Venice. Settled into the Hotel des Bains on the Lido, Aschenbach, a man well past fifty, is captivated by the extraordinary beauty of a fourteen-year-old Polish boy. As the days pass, Aschenbach's thoughts, activities, *horarium* come to have a single focus—the youth, Tadzio. The latter becomes for the artist

[1] Isadore Traschen, "The Uses of Myth in 'Death in Venice,'" *Modern Fiction Studies* 11 (Summer 1963) 179.

[2] Joseph Campbell, *The Hero with a Thousand Faces* (New York: Pantheon Books 1949).

[3] Friedrich Nietzsche, *The Birth of Tragedy*, trans. Francis Goldfing (Garden City, N.Y.: Anchor-Doubleday 1956).

[4] André von Gronicka, "Myth Plus Psychology: A Stylistic Analysis of *Death in Venice*," in *Thomas Mann*, ed. Henry Hatfield (Englewood Cliffs, N.J.: Prentice-Hall 1964) 46–61.

the embodiment of "an almost exaggerated sense of beauty, a lofty purity, symmetry, and simplicity" (13)[5] —characteristics which mark Aschenbach's literary style. Tadzio becomes the god of Aschenbach's life, but the devotee's worship is offered wordlessly and only from a distance. Gradually but likewise wordlessly the lad acknowledges the worship, and furtive glances forge a bond between the two in the wake of which Aschenbach loses all rationality, dignity, self-esteem.

Meanwhile cholera infects Venice. Aschenbach first suspects, then uncovers all the fearsome details of the plague which the city officials try to conceal lest their economy suffer if the tourists take flight. A morbid delight in the thought that his dear god Tadzio appears too delicate to withstand an attack of plague reveals the depths of the degradation to which Aschenbach has sunk. Suddenly the "lover" himself is attacked by the dread disease. He collapses and dies in his customary watch-post—the beach chair from which he feeds his passion by gazing at young Tadzio at play upon the seashore.

A note from Mann's biography is not without significance for the identification of the Hermes-motif in *Death in Venice*. Around 1909 Mann began work on a novel which would have a dual aspect. Its hero, Felix Krull, would be a rogue, a swindler—a *Hochstapler*—and the story would take the form of a "confession," somewhat of a transposition to the criminal sphere of the "aristocratic" confession of Goethe's *Dichtung und Wahrheit*— "a parody of an artist's life and an artist's style."[6] In 1911 Mann interrupted work on the Krull novel for, as he recounts in his autobiography, a trip to the Lido in Venice furnished him with raw material for a *novella*: " . . . the 'pilgrim' at the North Cemetery, the dreary Pola boat, the gray-haired rake, the sinister gondolier, Tadzio and his family, the journey interrupted by a mistake about the luggage, the cholera, the upright clerk in the travel bureau, the rascally ballad-singer . . . they were all there."[7] Breathing his own creative spirit into this material, Mann produced a "small novel . . . written with consummate skill. There are no extraneous or accidental elements."[8] The result was an achievement that proves the truth of Mann's own words: "Whether he [the creative artist] fills an inherited tale or fills a piece of living reality with his breath and his being, it is the bringing to life, the penetrating and filling the material with the artist's own personality which make it his own."[9] What Mann brought to life was *Death in Venice*, and the spirit breathed into the *novella* was the spirit of Hermes.

That the Hermes-motif is interwoven in *The Confessions of Felix Krull* has been competently demonstrated in a study by Donald Nelson.[10] As Mann interrupted his work on the Krull novel yet remained caught up in the Hermes-motif, the role of this god must have appeared singularly appropriate to him. However, with something of the Hermes-

[5] Thomas Mann, *Death in Venice*, trans. H.T. Lowe-Porter (New York: Vintage 1954). All subsequent references to this work appear in the text.

[6] Ignace Feuerlicht, *Thomas Mann* (Boston: Twayne 1968) 92.

[7] Thomas Mann, *A Sketch of My Life*, trans. H.T. Lowe-Porter (New York: Alfred A. Knopf, 1960) 46.

[8] Feuerlicht (supra n. 6) 120.

[9] Quoted by Gronicka (supra n. 4) 49.

[10] Donald Nelson, *Portrait of the Artist as Hermes* (Chapel Hill: North Carolina 1971).

like playfulness of T.S. Eliot, who delighted in tantalizing his readers by offering merely a provocative hint in the form of a classical allusion that would enrich the meaning of his work, Mann offers only one allusion (but that, an unmistakable one) to reveal the presence of Hermes in this *novella*. At the moment of death, as Aschenbach's head sinks upon his chest while he sits watching Tadzio wading on the beach, " . . . it seemed to him the pale and lovely Summoner out there smiled at him and beckoned; as though, with the hand he lifted from his hip, he pointed outward as he hovered on before into an immensity of richest expectation" (75). The Summoner (*Psychagog*)—Hermes Psychopompos—had for once given up his traditional role of deceiver; Tadzio did not merely possess a godlike beauty; Tadzio was the god.

With the finesse his readers have come to expect, Mann established an artistic unity between the opening and closing scenes of the *novella*. As Hermes is present at the end of the story as conductor of souls to Hades, so is he present (in his relationship to the dead) as the story opens. Aschenbach's walk through Munich brings him to the North Cemetery, to "the Stonemason's yard, where crosses, monuments, and commemorative tablets made a supernumerary and untenanted graveyard opposite the real one" (4). Thus does Mann introduce the Hermes-motif with a veiled allusion to the hermae standing at the entrance of each home in ancient Greece, stone slabs having the form not of statues but of square pillars, though they were characteristic monuments honoring Hermes.

As Aschenbach pauses to read the inscription the sudden appearance of a stranger, "obviously not Bavarian" (4), attracts his attention. Simultaneously he feels a longing to travel—something which he has until now regarded as a "necessary evil" (6). He reflects upon the tedium of the work to which he relentlessly, scrupulously devotes every ounce of energy—work from which he get no joy—"not though a nation paid it homage" (7). His resolve forms: "He would go a journey" (8). He becomes a wayfarer—and the wayfarer's guardian deity was Hermes.

Who was this stranger with a "pilgrim air" who had "something not quite usual" in his appearance? Mann's description offers some significant clues: "He was of medium height, thin, beardless, and strikingly snub-nosed; he belonged to the red-haired type and possessed its milky, freckled skin . . . and the broad, straight-brimmed straw hat he had on even made him look distinctly exotic. True, he had the indigenous rucksack buckled on his back, wore a belted suit . . . and carried a grey mackintosh cape across his left forearm, which was propped against his waist. In his right hand, slantwise to the ground, he held an ironshod stick, and braced himself against its crook, with his legs crossed" (4). At least four details in this description allude to Hermes: the broad, straight-brimmed straw hat, so like the famed *petasus* or broad-brimmed cap of Hermes, gift of Zeus for whom he served as messenger; the rucksack and garb, symbolic of Hermes, god of travelers; the iron-shod stick, equivalent of the caduceus which had originally the form of a walking stick or shepherd's staff, symbol of Hermes as herald as well as god of shepherds: the mackintosh cape draped across his left forearm. This last item associates him assuredly with the famed statue of Hermes by Praxiteles who arranged on the sculpted youth's left forearm a carelessly draped cloak.[11]

What further association would Mann suggest by creating,in the stranger's appearance, a similarity to the masterpiece of Greek sculpture? The sculptured Hermes held in his arm the infant Dionysus on his way to deliver him to the nymphs who would bring him up. Mann thus introduces a second motif—the Dionysus-motif —which, as the plot develops, is seen to be of prime importance for appreciation of *Death in Venice*. For at the heart of Aschenbach's story is the bitter conflict waged in the soul of one who, while patterning his life along Apollonian lines —rational, disciplined, restrained, harmonious —has been woefully neglectful of the great god Dionysus—a god whom, as Euripides long ago dramatized in the *Bacchae*, one ignores to his own peril.

As a glance is exchanged between the stranger and Aschenbach, the latter "felt the most surprising consciousness of a widening of inward barriers, a kind of vaulting unrest, a youthfully ardent thirst for distant shores" (5). The longing to travel comes upon him "with such suddenness and passion as to resemble a seizure, almost a hallucination" (5). The marvelous vision which sweeps him up carries him to a land—India?—of "tropical marshland, beneath a reeking sky, steaming, monstrous, rank" with trees "mis-shapen as a dream . . . ." And in the vision "among the knotted joints of a bamboo thicket the eyes of a crouching tiger gleamed—and he felt his heart throb with terror, yet with a longing inexplicable" (5f.). With a firm act of will Aschenbach forced the sudden impulse to travel to conform "to the pattern of self-discipline he had followed from his youth up" (6f.). The influence of Nietzsche upon Mann is unmistakable in this passage. In *The Birth of Tragedy*, Nietzsche dwells at length upon the conflict between the moral and aesthetic approaches to life—a discussion which he presents in terms of the "two prime agencies,"[12] the Apollonian power and the Dionysiac magic, a "marvelous combination which at once heats the blood and induces meditation."[13]

On ominous chord is struck as Aschenbach's reverie ends: "He would go a journey. Not far—not all the way to the tigers" (8). And the same chord recurs as Aschenbach, several weeks later in Venice, learns the truth about the cholera-infected city. For several years past, a travel bureau clerk in the Piazza San Marco informs him, Asiatic cholera has shown a tendency to spread. Originating in the hot, moist swamps of the delta of the Ganges, breeding in the mephitic air of that primeval island-jungle, "among whose bamboo thickets the tiger crouches" (63), it has advanced across Asia and Europe until finally, in May, it claimed its first victims in Venice. Thanking the clerk for the information,

[11] For this statue, discovered by German archaeologists at Olympia in 1877, see G.M.A, Richter, *Sculpture and Sculptors of the Greeks*, ed. 4 (New Haven: Yale 1970) 199f. For the present argument, it matters little if the statue is by Praxiteles or, as seems to be the case, a later work; on the controversy see now K.D. Morrow, *Greek Footwear and the Dating of Sculpture* (Madison: Wisconsin 1985) 83–84. [Ed.]

[12] Nietzsche (supra n. 3) 145. See also p. 124: "Indeed, my friends, believe with me in this Dionysiac life . . . crown your heads with ivy, seize the thyrsus, and do not be surprised if tiger and panther lie down and caress your feet! . . . It has fallen to your lot to lead the Dionysiac procession out of India into Greece. Gird yourselves for a severe conflict . . . "

[13] Ibid., 125.

Aschenbach "strode up and down the spacious flags, feverishly excited, triumphant in possession of the truth at last, but with a sickening taste in his mouth and a fantastic horror at his heart" (65). Caught in the grip of his infatuation for Tadzio he cannot bring himself, though he realizes it is the "one, decent, expiatory course . . . open to him," to return home, return "to reason, self-mastery, and ordered existence, to the old life of effort" (65f.).

Within Aschenbach's soul there rages the Nietzschean "battle between the two hostile principles"[14] showing "the effects . . . that passion works in a well-ordered human life."[15] Briefly the aging artist considers approaching Tadzio's mother to advise her to leave the plague-ridden city with her family. "Then might he lay his hand in farewell upon the head of that instrument of a mocking deity, and thereafter himself flee from the accursed morass. . . . It would restore him, would give him back himself once more; but he who is beside himself revolts at the idea of self-possession" (66). And even as he vacillates, he suddenly recalls "the strange pilgrim apparition that had awakened in the aging man a lust for strange countries and fresh sights"(66).

Who is this "mocking deity"? Dionysus? Assuredly. Yet Hermes, too, the playful one, is close at hand as god of dreams. "That night he [Aschenbach] had a fearful dream" (66), to the description of which Mann devotes two pages. The sights, the sounds, the locale, even the smells transport the reader to a scene of Dionysiac revelry and abandon, strongly reminiscent of the orgy Euripides presents in the *Bacchae*. And lest there be a mistake, a voice heralds, even as the dream begins, "The stranger god!" (67).[16] With horrifying, revolting frenzy the orgy proceeds, and Aschenbach "trembled . . . shrank, his will . . . steadfast to preserve and uphold his own god against this stranger who was sworn enemy to dignity and self-control" (68). Yet resistance is useless; caught up in a " . . . whirling lust . . . the dreamer was in them and of them, the stranger god was his own . . . and now began the rites in honor of the god, an orgy of promiscuous embraces—and in his very soul he tasted the bestial degradation of his fall" (68). He wakes from the dream "shattered, unhinged, powerless in the demon's grip" (68), obsessed with his love for Tadzio, whom "lost to shame, he would follow . . . through the city's narrow streets where horrid death stalked too" (69). Like another Pentheus, he has been destroyed by the "stranger god." He has gone "all the way to the tigers."

In the *Bacchae*, Pentheus' degradation begins when he allows Dionysus, in disguise, to persuade him to dress up like a Maenad in order to go to see for himself what the god's

[14] Ibid., 36.

[15] The words of Mann in his acceptance speech on being awarded the Nobel Prize in 1929. See *Nobel Prize Library* (New York: Helvetica 1971) 226.

[16] In "Thomas Mann's Early Interest in Myth and Erwin Rohde's *Psyche*," *Publications of the Modern Language Association* 79 (1964) 297–304, Herbert Lehnert examines Rohde's work as a source for some of the mythological material in *Death in Venice*. Lehnert refers also to a handbook of Greek and Roman mythology by Friedrich Nösselt which was obviously another source used by Mann. No mention is made by Lehnert of Mann's familiarity with Greek tragedy, yet his interest in Nietzsche's *Birth of Tragedy* would presuppose this. The *Bacchae* certainly provides a source for "the stranger god," a phrase which Lehnert says "neither Rohde nor Nösselt emphasizes."

votaries are doing. Thus he puts himself in the god's power and suddenly, shamelessly, fatuously he struts and preens with narcissistic self-approval in the female garb, a deplorable caricature of a king. Mann thrusts his "lover" into an almost identical situation. Casting all self-respect aside, Aschenbach takes any and every measure to conceal signs of age, submits to every trick of the barber which will restore the signs of youth, and goes off as in a dream, "in his red neck-tie and broad straw hat with its gay striped band" (70).

Once this tangent point with Euripidean drama has been observed, one comes to recognize a somewhat startling bond of similarity between the Greek tragedian and the author of *Death in Venice*. Both develop their plots relying upon the element of chance—chance meetings, mishaps, the totally unplanned event. Luck (*Tyche*) is the omnipotent ruler of the Euripidean universe. For Mann it is Hermes, son of Zeus and Maia—goddess of rain clouds—who dominates the course of events. Hermes was originally a wind god. And because the wind, without apparent reason, arbitrarily changes, Hermes is the god of changing, unstable fortune and chance. Control, reason, and calculated design gave pattern, stability, and direction to Aschenbach's life until that morning—it happened to be in May!—when the writer, "overwrought by a morning of hard, nerve-taxing work" (3), goes for a walk. He *just happens* to stop by the North Cemetery. There he *chances* to see a stranger and, within moments, has made an *unpremeditated* decision to take a trip. "He chose an island in the Adriatic . . . .But there was rain and heavy air . . . an inner impulse made him wretched, urging him on he knew not whither . . . then *all at once* his goal stood plain before his eyes" (15f.) He sets out for Venice.

What better place for chance meetings than a hotel? Gathered at the table next to the traveler is a group of young people, among them a "long-haired boy of about fourteen. Aschenbach noticed with astonishment the lad's perfect beauty. His face recalled the noblest moment of Greek sculpture" (25). "Ah!" reflects the reader, "The moment of Praxiteles' Hermes!" Yet, previously it was the stranger in the cemetery who bore a resemblance to the Hermes statue. Does Mann intend this coupling? The answer seems to be a resounding "Yes!" Moreover, as the novelist has created a stranger-Hermes and a Tadzio-Hermes, he also introduced the Hermes-motif into the role of several other characters who cross Aschenbach's path in the interval between his encounter at the cemetery and his final moments on the beach. These characters, in the order of their appearance in the story, are the ticket agent in Pola, the disgusting old fop on the boat sailing to Venice, the gondolier who ferries Aschenbach from the city to the Lido, the guitarist who entertains the hotel guests, and the barber who panders to the artist's desire to regain his youthful appearance. Add to them the stranger in the cemetery and Tadzio and they number seven— a number which had a strange fascination for Mann.[17]

To Tadzio alone does Mann give a name, yet in each case he provides so detailed a description of their physical features and clothes that each stands out vividly on the page. In his subtle handling of the Hermes-motif in relation to these characters the skill of

[17] Feuerlicht (supra n.6) 29f. points out the extraordinary prominence of the number seven in the *Magic Mountain* and observes that "Mann had an almost superstitious belief in the significance of certain numbers."

Mann is superbly illustrated. A comment by one of his critics offers a key to this: "Thomas Mann is passionately concerned with the meaning of words, and the musical quality of his prose does not lie so much in their rhythmical arrangement, as in the repetition of certain phrases in different contexts, phrases which call up a whole world of associations as a snatch of song might do. This is the leitmotif technique which he adopted from Richard Wagner . . . The reason for the effectiveness of the verbal leitmotif is that we remember not only in images, but also emotionally."[18] A remarkable illustration of the leitmotif is found in the reaction of Aschenbach to the fop on the boat. The artist shudders when he first notices him, feeling "not quite canny, as though the world were suffering a dream-like distortion of perspective" (17f.). An hour later, as the boat approaches Venice, his attention is drawn to the young-old man; his "brow darkened. . . . and there came over him once more a dazed sense, as though things about him were just slightly losing their ordinary perspective, beginning to show a distortion that might merge into the grotesque" (19).

Thus skillfully availing himself of this leitmotif technique, Mann suffuses his *novella* with an aura of mystery. What significance have the repeated details that are associated with each of the characters mentioned above? Are these characters essential to the story, or are they incidental? The answer depends on the extent to which the Hermes-motif dominates the story and the degree to which each contributes to this motif.

As Aschenbach studies the stranger in the cemetery he recognizes that he is "not Bavarian." The offensive gondolier is "of non-Italian stock." The guitarist is a "foreigner in Venice." The old fop on the boat appears definitely out of place among the pleasure-bound, lively youths off for a holiday in Italy. To the Polish youth, Tadzio, his English sailor suit "lent the slight figure something 'rich and strange'" (26).

Three of the characters—the stranger, the gondolier, the performer—are described as snub-nosed; each is slight in build and each carries something appropriate to his role: the stranger, a traveler, carries an iron-shod walking stick; the gondolier plies his oar; the entertainer twangs his guitar. The stranger and the performer, both of whom are red-haired and thin, are alike in another physical trait: the stranger's "chin was up, so that the Adam's apple looked very bald in the lean neck rising from the loose shirt" (4). The performer "wore a white sport shirt . . . and a strikingly large and naked-looking Adam's apple rose out of the open collar" (60). The leitmotif varies slightly for Tadzio. His light sailor suit has "a simple white standing collar round the neck—a not very elegant effect—yet above this collar the head was poised like a flower, in incomparable loveliness" (29). The stranger and the guitarist share one more similarity: their brows are marked by two pronounced perpendicular furrows.

The leitmotif occurs most strikingly in three further details. The stranger wears a broad, straight-brimmed straw hat and a belted suit. The fop is dressed in a "dandified, buff suit, a rakish panama with a coloured scarf, and a red cravat" (17). The gondolier "wore blue clothes like a sailor's, with a yellow sash; a shapeless straw hat with the braid

[18] E.M. Wilkinson, "Tonio Kröger: An Interpretation," in Hatfield (supra n. 4) 31.

torn at the brim perched rakishly on his head" (22). As for the guitarist, "his shabby felt hat rested on the back of his neck" (59). Tadzio appears in different, yet always similar outfits. At one time he wears a striped sailor suit, blue and white, belted. On another occasion he dresses in white with a gay-colored sash. Once he has on a dark blue reefer jacket with a red silk breast-knot.

The man in the cemetery, with the bold, domineering, even ruthless air, has lips that seem to curl back to lay bare "the long, white, glistening teeth to the gums" (5). In almost identical terms the gondolier is described: now and then his exertion "curled back his lips and bared his white teeth to the gums" (22). The fawning guitarist glided between the guests' tables, "showing his strong white teeth in a servile smile" (60). In the elevator Aschenbach notes that Tadzio's teeth are imperfect, rather jagged and bluish, without a healthy glaze. The fact gives Aschenbach a pleasure he cannot explain.

Mann adds another link in the chain of likenesses among his characters. Tadzio falls into a fit of unprovoked temper. "His brow darkened, his lips curled, one corner of the mouth was drawn down in a harsh line that marred the curve of the cheek" (31). The fop, swaying on the deck of the boat, disgustingly intoxicated, accosts anyone who comes near: "He stuttered, he giggled, he leered . . . his tongue kept seeking the corner of his mouth in a suggestive motion ugly to behold" (19). The guitarist accompanies his song "with leers and winks and the loose play of the tongue in the corner of his mouth" (60). Of all the characters (except Tadzio) that Aschenbach encounters, it is only the fop that he meets twice. Both times the leitmotif occurs. As the fop appears on the boat from Pola the reader is told that "his turned-up moustaches and the small imperial were dyed" (17). Later, as the boat docks, "the ghastly young-old man" importunes the traveler from Munich and bids him a pleasant sojourn. "He drooled, he blinked, he licked the corner of his mouth, the little imperial bristled on his elderly chin" (20). It is notable that, whereas Praxiteles' Hermes is a beautiful youth, patron of athletes, Hermes Psychopompos, the Olympian deity, is represented almost invariably on Greek vase paintings wearing the type of neatly trimmed beard called "imperial"—a goatee.

Only a brief description is given of the ticket agent in Pola, but the details are significant and fit into the leitmotif just mentioned. He sits below deck in a "cavernous, lamplit cabin . . . a man with a beard like a goat's; he had his hat on the back of his head" (16). He addresses Aschenbach as "*signore mio*" whom he declares himself "delighted to serve."

By this leitmotif technique Mann achieves a twofold identification. In some mysterious way the stranger, the ticket agent, the fop, the gondolier, the entertainer, the barber, and Tadzio merge into one character.[19] And it is Hermes, in one or other of his multifarious mythological roles whom each character represents. The meetings are all by chance, yet a certain element of inevitability is associated with the presence of each as he advances Aschenbach's progress toward his final moments on the beach in Venice.

[19] In Benjamin Britten's opera these seven characters are sung by the same bass-baritone. In this way and by use of a recurring musical motif the identification of these minor characters is recognized and preserved.

An element of ambiguity, too, attends this identification, an ambiguity which is stamped upon every page of Mann's *novella*. Venice is the locale—"ambiguous Venice," as she is hailed in Britten's opera. Venice, were stone is wedded to water. Venice with its "mild soft brilliance and ease . . . uniting the charms of a luxurious bathing-resort with the immediate nearness of a unique and marvelous city" (41). Venice, a vacation spot for lively, adventure-seeking tourists who pursue their pleasures in coffin-like gondolas. Venice, the plague-infected city that lures Aschenbach to his death.

Gustave von Aschenbach himself is the embodiment of ambiguity. Throughout his life he has given his "rigid, cold, and passionate service" (7) to "his god," Apollo. Suddenly he finds himself yielding to Dionysus who inspires in the artist "another yearning, opposed to his art and perhaps for that very reason a lure, for the unorganized, the immeasurable, the eternal—in short, for nothingness" (31).

Ambiguity marks, too, his feelings toward Venice, the site he has chosen for his vacation. At first he feels threatened by a repetition of foul weather which on an earlier occasion had forced him to flee from the city. Next he is physically overcome by the "hateful sultriness in the narrow streets" (35), makes a sudden decision to leave, boards the boat to the station, "but the tale of his journey across the lagoon was a tale of woe, a passage through the very valley of regrets" (37). At this point the ambiguity is heightened by the introduction of the element of chance. Hearing, at the station, that his luggage has been misdirected, he demands to be taken back to the hotel to await its return. "A reckless joy, a deep incredible mirthfulness shook him almost as with a spasm," (38) and when he reached his room "he felt rejoiced to be back, yet displeased with his vacillating moods, his ignorance of his own real desires" (40).

Four weeks pass. From various quarters come indications that the outbreak of cholera has forced many tourists to return to their homes. "[Aschenbach] felt in his heart a curious elation at the events impending in the world about him . . . .The city's evil secret mingled with the one in the depths of his heart—and he would have staked all he possessed to keep it, since in his infatuation he cared for nothing but to keep Tadzio here, and owned to himself, not without horror, that he could not exist were the lad to pass from his sight" (53f). Here again lies ambiguity: Will the cholera or Aschenbach's passionate love for Tadzio result in death in Venice?

The relationship between the elderly artist and the young Polish boy is strangely ambiguous. Between Aschenbach, with his "unerring gift of words and their power to charm" (34), and the "pampered darling" whom he sees almost constantly for several weeks no words are ever exchanged. The narrator makes comment: "There can be no relation more strange, more critical, than that between two beings who know each other only with their eyes, who meet daily, yes, even hourly, eye each other with a fixed regard, and yet by some whim or freak of convention feel constrained to act like strangers. Uneasiness rules between them, unslaked curiosity, a hysterical desire to give rein to their suppressed impulse to recognize and address each other; even, actually, a sort of strained but mutual regard. For one human being instinctively feels respect and love for another human being so long as he does not know him well enough to judge him; and that he does not, the craving he feels is evidence" (50).

The ambiguity at the heart of *Death in Venice* is dramatized in an episode that occurs at mid-point in the narrative. Inspired, enraptured by Tadzio's beauty, Aschenbach sits on the beach and feels a sudden desire to write; for "a certain problem had been raised, the intellectual world challenged for its opinion on a great and burning question of art and taste. By nature and experience the theme was his own" (46). With "his idol full in his view . . . he fashioned . . . a page and a half of choicest prose, so chaste, so lofty, so poignant with feeling," as to be "the wonder and admiration of the multitude" (46). Yet, the aftermath is unexpected: " . . . strangely fruitful intercourse this, between one body and another mind! When Aschenbach put aside his work and left the beach he felt exhausted, he felt broken—conscience reproached him as it were after a debauch" (47).

Such contrasts abound in *Death in Venice*: youth versus age; disease versus health; discipline versus disorder; spirit versus nature; Apollo versus Dionysus. And these contrasts are embodied in Aschenbach of whom "a nice observer once said . . . 'You see, Aschenbach has always lived like this'—here the speaker closed the fingers of his left hand to a fist—'never like this'—and he let his open hand hang relaxed from the back of the chair" (9).

Pervading the story is the life-death contrast. Initially there is the scene in the cemetery. There is the selection of Venice as a vacation spot, a city infected with death-bringing cholera; Aschenbach rides in a gondola "black as nothing else on earth except a coffin" (21) which calls up "visions of death itself, the bier and solemn rites and last soundless voyage" (21). Even Aschenbach's name, the first part of which means ashes, suggests death; so, too, the dregs of pomegranate juice in his glass, bringing to mind Persephone, bride of Hades. The figure of death marches through the pages.

Yet, this very pomegranate was to the ancients a symbol of fertility—of life. And Hermes was a fertility god. Is the prominent role of Hermes in the story Mann's way of providing a clue to the reader that death is not the final word in *Death in Venice*? Was Mann, in writing this *novella*, indulging in what one critic calls "intellectual playfulness"?[20] Why has he incorporated into one story every possible item of mythological lore that concerns Hermes? One could almost call it a celebration of Hermes, son of Maia, playful brother of Apollo, a wind god and guardian of travelers, the Olympian escort of souls to Hades, the god of dreams and of chance and one closely associated with Dionysus—all these aspects and functions of Hermes are represented, making him practically omnipresent in the *novella*.

Then, too there is a final contrast—the contrast between chance and choice, a contrast over which Hermes most appropriately presides. From the moment at the cemetery when the Hermes-motif is introduced, fortuitous happenings seem to snatch from the artist control of his destiny. Yet, strangely, he seems at every point to be making a deliberate choice. The stranger happens to appear; Aschenbach decides to take a vacation.

[20] Feuerlicht (supra n. 6) 46.

Though he chose an island in the Adriatic, the rain and heavy air make him choose to go to Venice. Once there he is uncomfortable, cannot endure the weather, and makes "a quick decision" to seek a more agreeable resort site. A day later he is irresolute, regretting his decision. About to board the boat he learns that his baggage has been accidentally sent off in the wrong direction. Indignantly he at once chooses to return to the hotel to await its return. The contrarieties in his nature shine forth: "Things could not, he told himself, have fallen out more luckily . . . all would be well once more, a mischance prevented . . . . And did the boat's swift motion deceive him, or was the wind now coming from the sea?" (39). Back the traveler goes, back to the enervating air of the plague-stricken city where the hotel manager welcomes him and the elevator boy smilingly assures him, "*Pas de chance, monsieur*" (40).

Indeed, not by chance but under the supervision and design of some power that seems to be controlling his life is Aschenbach thrust into a milieu that challenges every principle upon which he has doggedly built a life and achieved his goal—fame. Suddenly, as the godlike Tadzio enters his life and enraptures his spirit, he is metamorphosed from an aging, solitary, disciplined artist into a "fond fool," rationalizing his abandonment of Apollo. His very soul becomes the reveling ground for Dionysiac forces. Forgotten is his favorite motto, "Hold fast!", and a delirium born of his erotic passion and aggravated by cholera-fever sends him wildly pursuing "his charmer deep into the stricken city's huddled heart" (70). He is beguiled, he is obsessed, "and it seemed at times . . . that death and fear together might clear the island of all other souls and leave him there alone with him he coveted" (69).

At the height of his literary achievement Aschenbach had produced *The Abject*, a novel in which, as author, he takes the stance of one who " . . . with rage . . . rejects the rejected . . . and the measure of his fury is the measure of his condemnation of all moral shilly-shallying. Explicitly he renounces sympathy with the abyss, explicitly he refutes the flabby humanitarianism of the phrase '*Tout comprendre c'est tout pardonner*'" (13). Now, after weeks of exposure to the plague, in the grip of fever, exhausted from his mad pursuit of his beloved of whom he has momentarily lost sight, quite unnerved, he sits on the steps of a well in a deserted Venetian street. "There he sat, the master; this was he who . . . had written *The Abject*, and in a style of classic purity renounced bohemianism and all its works, all sympathy with the abyss and the troubled depths of the outcast human soul" (71).

Once again the leitmotif evokes the emotional response. Should one scorn and rebuke this outcast, demanding of him, "Why did you not 'hold fast'?" Or does the heart respond with understanding, with a willingness to pardon, asking, "Who shall unriddle the puzzle of the artist's nature? Who understands that mingling of discipline and license in which it stands so deeply rooted? For not to be able to want sobriety is licentious folly" (47). And what was Aschenbach's folly? Mann spells it out in an exquisite passage modeled on Plato's *Phaedrus* in which Aschenbach imagines Socrates discoursing to the handsome youth on the nature of virtue and desire, telling him " . . . of the shuddering and unwonted heat that come upon him whose heart is open, when his eye beholds an image of eternal beauty . . . .'For beauty, my Phaedrus, beauty alone, is lovely and visible at once. For, mark you, it is the sole aspect of the spiritual which we can perceive through our senses, or bear so to perceive. Else what should become of us, if the divine, if reason and virtue and truth were to speak to us through the senses? . . . .So beauty, then, is the beauty-lover's way to the spirit—but only the way, only the means, my little Phaedrus'" (45).

Alas, for Aschenbach the beauty he beholds in Tadzio becomes more than the means; it becomes the end. Gone is all striving for that "heroism born of weakness" extolled in the writings of his youth when he was "poet-spokesman of all those who labour at the edge of exhaustion; of the overburdened, of those who are already worn out but still hold themselves upright . . . whom he justified, he exalted . . . [and] sang their praise" (12). Rather, as he sits in utter weariness, confused, solitary, his "rouged and flabby mouth uttered single words of the sentences shaped in his disordered brain by the fantastic logic that governs our dreams" (72). Again he addresses an imaginary Phaedrus, parodying Socrates and speaking of beauty as the artist's way to the spirit—"a path of perilous sweetness, a way of transgression [that] must surely lead him who walks in it astray" (72). Ultimately, he reflects, the struggle is between sensual delight and form disciplined by knowledge. But this way lies ambiguity! The chaotic rambling, the irrationality, all that lies suppressed in his unconscious, spills out as he continues: "And by beauty we mean simplicity, largeness, and renewed severity of discipline; we mean a return to detachment and to form. But detachment, Phaedrus, and preoccupation with form lead to intoxication and desire, they may lead the noblest among us to frightful excesses, which his own stern cult of the beautiful would make him the first to condemn. So they too, they too, lead to the bottomless pit. Yes, they lead us thither, I say, us who are poets—who by our nature are prone not to excellence but to excess" (73). The Apollonian/Dionysiac note has been struck again.

Euripides' Pentheus is inhumanly destroyed, and the meaninglessness of his sufferings has prompted some to classify Euripides as a forerunner of the absurdist school. "Such is the fate," the Greek tragedian would seem to say, "of one who defies the 'stranger god.'" Pentheus is annihilated. The audience is horrified, terror-stricken, but feels little, if any, pity for the stricken king. Not so in the case of Aschenbach. If a vengeful Dionysus sets out to claim his share of worship, the playful Hermes intervenes to restrain the mode of the revenge. Guardian of wayfarers, Hermes accompanies Aschenbach "all the way to the tigers." But here the god of chance exerts his power: the cholera claims its victim, but its onslaught is gentle. Aschenbach is among the plague stricken of whom the travel bureau agent has observed, "He is fortunate indeed, if, as sometimes happens, the disease, after a slight *malaise*, takes the form of a profound unconsciousness, from which the sufferer seldom or never rouses" (64). As the elderly man sits in his customary position watching his idol playing on the beach, the lad, "stepped into the shallow water . . . a remote and isolated figure, with floating locks, out there in the sea and wind, against the misty inane" (74). As always, Aschenbach is mesmerized by the godlike perfection of Tadzio—mesmerized, too, by the sea which possesses, for him, a peculiar fascination, responding to his "yearning for the unorganized, the immeasurable, the eternal—in short, for nothingness. He whose preoccupation is with excellence longs fervently to find rest in perfection; and is not nothingness a form of perfection?" (31).

Weeks of torture have preceded this moment of bliss. Forces had entered the life of Apollo's devotee to transform it into one of disorder, dissolution, derangement—utter degradation. The artist is no more; he has been annihilated by the "stranger god," Dionysus, whom throughout his life he has ignored. The transformation is an excruciatingly painful one, yet the suffering possesses, in some mysterious way, purifying, redemptive powers. Aschenbach does not lose all. Surprisingly, his transformation is wrought in secret. For, even as the city officials conceal the plague-ridden city's evil secret, so the solitary lover, slyly pursuing his beloved and nurturing his guilty secret in his wildly surrendered heart, conceals the turmoil within behind a façade of conventionality. Though outwardly ravaged by the disease, he is still the writer who had "adjusted himself to the burdens and obligations of fame; whose renown had been officially recognized and his name ennobled, whose style was set for a model in the schools" (72).

The final moment comes: "He rested his head against the chair-back and followed the movements of the figure out there, then lifted it, as it were in answer to Tadzio's gaze. It sank on his breast, the eyes looked out beneath their lids, while his whole face took on the relaxed and brooding expression of deep slumber. It seemed to him the pale and lovely Summoner out there smiled at him and beckoned; as though, with the hand he lifted from his hip, he pointed outward as he hovered on before into an immensity of richest expectation. And, as so often before, he rose to follow" (74f.) Acceptance, serenity, fulfillment. The stranger-Hermes, Tadzio-Hermes escorts the wayfarer from life in Munich to death in Venice, then on "into an immensity of richest expectation." Gustave von Aschenbach, the "abject," is not rejected: " . . . before nightfall a shocked and respectful world received the news of his decease" (75).

Adopting the Hermes-motif, associating with it the Apollo-Dionysus dichotomy, Mann has enriched his *novella* and established the life-death-life theme. He reflects upon the ambivalent nature of an artist's energies. He speculates upon the perplexing, enigmatic meaning of those elemental forces in man to which the Greeks gave names such as Eros, Apollo, Dionysus. He dramatizes the hidden tortures the soul endures when opposing forces war within it—tortures of which the world, even when close by, is oblivious. With consummate skill he probes "the troubled depths of the outcast human soul" (71), stirring his reader to the compassionate response, "*Tout comprendre c'est tout pardonner*" (13).

THE LIBERATION OF THEBES IN 379/8 B.C.

James DeVoto

Shortly after the December solstice in 379 B.C. a startling turn of events took place in Boiotia. A resolute band of exiles, aided by sympathizers from Athens and within Thebes, secretly gained entrance to their native *polis* and assassinated the leaders of the pro-Spartan government. Subsequently they negotiated the departure of the Spartan garrison as a prelude to the creation of Boiotia's first true democracy. Although no ancient writer who discussed the coup failed to grasp its political significance, the modern researcher who would venture a reconstruction faces a seemingly insoluble problem.[1] The difficulty arises from the widely divergent accounts of the five authors who describe the coup. There are even striking differences in two versions written by the same author.[2] The purpose of this paper will be to propose a reconstruction based on literary, topographical, and historical considerations.

Background to the Events of December 379/8 B.C.

Tension between Sparta and Thebes dating from the aftermath of the fall of Athens eventually flared into open hostility as the two *poleis* found themselves on opposite side for eight years in the Korinthian War.[3] When the war finally ended in 386 B.C. with the defeat of Thebes and her allies, Agesilaos, Spartan king and Greece's leading political figure, forced the dismemberment of the Boiotian League.[4] The emergent pattern of Spartan policy, ever based on a narrow, self-serving interpretation of "autonomy" as specified in the King's Peace, revealed itself no less clearly in the Peloponnesos than it had in Boiotia.[5] Chafing at the Mantineians' lack of enthusiasm during the war, the Spartans first intimidated and later invested that small *polis* and dissolved it into its original four or five villages.[6] A similar fate befell Phleious which Agesilaos personally forced to

[1] Plutarch gives the most eloquent survey of the coup's long-term impact on Greek politics and popular imagination (*Pelop.* 13.3–4). E. Fabricius, "Die Befreiung Thebens," *RhM* 48 (1893) 455 and E. Delébècque, *Essai sur la vie de Xenophon* (Paris: Klincksieck 1957) 289, note that with his introduction to the liberation of the Kadmeia (*Hell.* 5.4.1), Xenophon introduces a major shift in tone which permeates the rest of his work.

[2] Plut. *Pelop.* 7–13 and *De genio* 595a–f.

[3] The discordance began when the Thebans, the strongest force at Dekeleia, simply seized their share: see Xen. *Hell.* 2.3.8, 3.5.5; *Hell. Oxy.* 17.4–5; Justin 5.10.12. Later the Thebans refused to surrender the Athenian exiles to Lysander's Thirty and actually aided Thrasyboulos in overthrowing them: see Lys. fr. 120; *Hell. Oxy.* 17; Xen. *Hell.* 2.4.2; Diod. 14.6.1–3; Plut. *Lys.* 2.7.2; Justin 5.9.8. C. Hamilton, *Sparta's Bitter Victories* (Ithaca: Cornell 1979) 326–27, discusses the effects of Spartan high-handedness after 404 B.C. and the resultant Theban antagonism. The Korinthian War, born of wide-spread resentment of Sparta, broke out in the autumn of 395 B.C. with the formation of an anti-Spartan coalition: see H. Bengtson, *Staatsverträge des Altertums*, vol. 2 (Munich: Beck 1965) 171–72; M. Tod, *A Selection of Greek Historical Inscriptions* (Oxford: University Press 1968) no. 102; and Hamilton (supra) 207.

[4] Xen. *Hell.* 5.1.32–33; Plut. *Ages.* 23.3; Diod. 14.110.3–4.

[5] See esp. Bengtson (supra n. 3) 188–92.

[6] Xen. *Hell.* 5.2.2–7; Diod. 15.5.12.

surrender while another Spartan army was concluding a campaign against Olynthos in the northern Aegean.[7]

This campaign had resulted from a joint Makedonian and Chalkidic legation to Sparta in 383. Arkanthian and Apollonian legates appealed to Sparta for aid against the Chalkidic League whose leading *polis* was Olynthos.[8] Kleigenes the Akanthian made the following argument against the League to the Spartan assembly. First, he asserted, the Olynthians had overrun much of Makedonia at the expense of Amyntas, who had earlier attached himself to Olynthos by treaty.[9] Second the Olynthians were developing cordial relations with Thrakian tribesmen and, third, they had contracted and alliance with Athens. Finally Kleigenes accused the Olynthians of trying to force Akanthos and Apollonia to join their league, which would have been a contravention of "autonomy" as spelled out in the King's Peace.[10] Because the Spartans perceived both a threat to their interests[11] and an opportunity to aid an ally Amyntas, while expanding their influence in the north, they voted to go to war.[12] In the fall of 383 the ephors sent Eudamidas on a preliminary expedition which the Thebans pointedly refused to join. He proceeded nonetheless to Poteideia which he detached from the Chalkidic League and made a base of operations.

Eudamidas, however, had requested that his brother Phoibidas follow him with a comparable force somewhat later. Thus in 382 Phoibidas set out, ostensibly en route to Poteideia. After crossing into Boiotia, he bivouacked outside the walls of neutral Thebes. Here the leading Theban Lakonizer, Leontiades, induced the young Spartan officer to effect a *coup d'état*. With the aid of other Theban Lakonizers, who were embroiled in bitter factional strife with pro-Athenian Thebans, Phoibidas feigned a departure. Later from only a short distance, Lakonizers led the Spartans back to the city. As it was a summer day during the women's festival of the Thesmophoria, the Kadmeia was deserted and the Council was meeting elsewhere. Leontiades and his supporters now directed the Peloponnesians through the empty streets to the akropolis. There he convened an Assembly in which he alerted the citizens to changed circumstances and introduced them to their new masters.[13]

[7] Xen. *Hell.* 5.2.8–10, 5.3.21–24: see also R. Legon, "Phliasian Politics and Policy in the Early Fourth Century B.C.," *Historia* 16 (1967) 324–37.

[8] Xen. *Hell.* 5.2.12; Diod. 15.19.3. Akanthos (mod. Ierissos) lies just north of Xerxes' canal: see Pietchman, "Akanthos," *RE* 1.1 (1893) 1147 and Miller, "Akanthos," *PECS* 23. Apollonia lay 17 km. NE of Olynthos: see Hirschfeld, "Apollonia," *RE* 2.1 (1895) 114.

[9] Isok. *Archidam.* 46; Diod. 14.92.2–4; Aelian, *VH* 4.8.3: see also Bengtson (supra n. 3) 178–80 and Tod (supra n. 3) no. 119. The pact dates to 383 B.C.

[10] Bengston (supra n. 3) 118–92. Though Kleigenes does not refer explicitly to the treaty of 386, the pretext for intervention was clear.

[11] An alliance between Athens and Olynthos later joined by Thebes could have been a source of anxiety to Sparta because of the rich sources of Thrakian ore and timber. T. T. B. Ryder, *Koine Eirene* (Oxford: University Press 1965) 47, however, believes that the Olynthian threat to Sparta was exaggerated.

[12] See Bengtson (supra n. 3) 198–99.

[13] Xen. *Hell.* 5.2.12–30.

The markedly pro-Spartan Xenophon rather disingenuously ascribes this act of war to Theban factional rivalry and Phoibidas' defective judgment.[14] Plutarch, though noting Phoibidas' rashness, advances the more plausible view that Agesilaos and his partisans were behind the coup.[15] Diodoros in his Ephoran mode[16] explicitly attributes the coup to secret orders from the Spartan authorities.

The leader of the pro-Athenian faction, Ismenias, was arrested and later executed in Sparta after conviction on trumped up charges. Androkleidas and 300 Attikizers, however, escaped into exile at Athens.[17] Although many Greeks, and not a few Spartans, were outraged at this unprovoked aggression against a nominally allied and certainly peaceful *polis*, Phoibidas received nothing more than loss of command and a small fine. Thus for three and a half years not only did the Boiotian League remain dissolved, but with aid of traitors a foreign garrison had occupied its premier city.

Modern Opinion and the Ancient Sources

Although the scholar will note some slight discrepancies in the various accounts of the background to the coup, the major traditions' striking incongruence only becomes clear in the descriptions of the operations itself. The best approach to the problem raised by these discrepancies is to divide the extant versions into two groups, one thorough and the other summary. After noting where the latter and former differ, one can begin the analysis of the major accounts from which nearly all of our information derives.

Briefly stated, the problems is as follows. What was the exiles' plan for their return? What precisely was the route they took to cross from Attika into Boiotia? How did they conceal their purpose and identities in transit? What arrangements had they made with sympathizers in Thebes? How did they plan to kill the pro-Spartan magistrates? How many magistrates died and in what manner? How many conspirators were there and who were their leaders? Finally, did Athenians participate or assist in any way? The ancient testimony on all these points leaves perplexity and doubt. Hence a brief survey of each author's methods and purpose for describing the coup is in order.

Altogether the researcher has six versions of the liberation upon which to base a reconstruction. The group of lengthier accounts includes Xenophon's *Hellenika*, Plutarch's essay on Sokrates' *δαιμόνιον* (*De genio*) and his biography of Pelopidas. The second group comprises the shorter versions found in Diodoros, C. Nepos's sketch of Pelopidas' life and two notices in Polyainos' *Stratagemata*.

[14] Xen. *Hell.* 5.2.25–28: regarding this trait, see E. Meyer, *Geschichte des Altertums*[6] vol. 4.1 (Stuttgart: Gotta 1958) 260–61; A. Lesky, *Geschichte der Griechischen Literatur* (Munich: Beck 1971) 694; T. Brown, *The Greek Historians* (Lexington, Mass.: Heath 1973) 95. Delébècque (supra n. 1) p. 275, thinks that Xenophon's bias is not so much pro-Spartan as it is *pro Agesilao.*

[15] Plut. *Pelop.* 5.2–6.1 and *Ages.* 23.7–24.1.

[16] See E. Schwartz, "Ephoros," *RE* 6.1 (1907) 15–16; G. Barber, *The Historian Ephoros* (Cambridge: University Press 1935) 105; Brown (supra n. 14) 114–15; also supra nn. 3–6.

[17] Xen. *Hell.* 5.2.31, 33–36; Diod. 15.20.2; Plut. *Pelop.* 5.3; *De genio* 576a.

As one might except, Diodoros' version of the tyrannicide (15.25.1–3) is summary and curt.[18] He writes that the pro-Spartan leaders were killed at home in their sleep, omitting the clash in the *polemarcheion* and misconstruing the deaths of Leontiades and Hypates, who indeed died near home but were quite awake at time. Although he records the flight of 1500 people to the Kadmeia after the polemarchs' demise, he neglects the release of political prisoners and confuses Athenian aid to the Thebans after Sphodrias' failed raid into Attika with the earlier, unofficial help for the conspirators.[19] This type of error, which often mars Diodoros' work, is caused by his carelessness and his overcompression of sources.[20]

Another synopsis of the coup appears in Nepos' life of Pelopidas (2.1–4.1). While Nepos is more expansive than Diodoros, his treatment of the liberation reveals no new information. His version is shorter than Xenophon's which is the most compact of the lengthier accounts. What Nepos writes parallels Plutarch's discussions so that, according to Accame, Nepos, like Diodoros, must have based his account on Ephoros.[21] Though Nepos seems to have exercised better judgment than Diodoros in this case, his sketches are generally more anecdotal than analytical. He traces only the barest outline of his subjects' lives, and in recounting the coup at Thebes he omits much detail. Though he was essentially a popularizer, his work is not entirely without value to the modern historian.[22]

Indeed, both Diodoros and Nepos are positively helpful in comparison to the garbled and ridiculous notices in Polyainos' *Stratagemata* (2.3.1 and 2.4.3). Polyainos tells only of the struggle at the *polemarcheion* where, he asserts, the victims, were not the polemarchs, but the Spartan harmost! Polyainos' defects as a compiler exceed at times even those of Diodoros. Like the latter, he apparently exercised little or no judgment in selection of material, perhaps because of his lack of military experience and preoccupation with rhetoric. The coup eventually produced numerous oral versions whose distortions, embellishments and misapprehensions led to Polyainos' absurd retelling.[23]

Since the lesser sources present compressed versions of the coup which, despite misapprehensions in Diodoros and Polyainos, offer no new insights, any reconstruction must rest on analysis of the three longer narratives. Many scholars have noted the divergent and often contradictory testimony preserved by Xenophon (*Hell.* 5.4.2–13) and Plutarch (*Pelop.* 7–13 and *De genio* 594b–98f).

[18] Diodoros abridged the much longer work of Ephoros of Kyme for the period in question. C. A. Volquardsen, *Untersuchungen über die Quellen der griechischen und sizilischen Geschichte bei Diodor XI–XVI* (Kiel: Schwers 1868) esp. 58–66. See also S. Accame, "L'attentato di Pelopida contro i polemarchi," *RivFil* 64 (1936) 340–42 and F. Jacoby, *FGrHist* vol. 1A.1 (1961) 70 and vol. 2A.2 (1961) 22–27.

[19] Plut. *Pelop.* 11.6 and *De genio* 597f.

[20] E.Schwarz, "Diodoros," *RE* 5.1 (1903) 663; H. J. Rose, *A Handbook of Greek Literature* (New York: Dutton 1960) 412; J. Hornblower, *Hieronymus of Cardia* (Oxford: University Press 1981) 19 and 28–29.

[21] Accame (supra n. 18) 340–42.

[22] See H. J. Rose, *A Handbook of Latin Literature* (New York: Dutton 1960) 208–209 and J. Bayet, *Literature Latine* (Paris: Armand Colin 1965) 177–78.

[23] E. von Stern, *Geschichte der spartanischen und thebanischen Hegemonie* (Dorpat: University 1884) 56. P. L. Stadter, *Plutarch's Historical Methods* (Cambridge, Mass: Harvard 1965) 125–26 and 137–40 shows that Polyainos relied in part on Plutarch's *Moralia*, but showed little of his source's good sense and judgment.

The purpose and methods of Xenophon, our only primary source for the coup, are easier to discern than those of Plutarch. There has been much speculation over the years about Xenophon's sources for these events. One theory is that he consulted the polemarch's secretary Phyllidas and spoke to Leontiades' widow about her husband's death. Another has it that he drew on official Spartan records, while yet another suggestion is that such records and numerous eyewitnesses were available to him. One scholar thinks that Xenophon's moralism and bias against Thebes reflect a desire to reconcile Spartan and Athenian interests—a point of view not unanimously accepted. Others think that Xenophon intended to highlight divine retribution against the Spartans for the seizure of the Kadmeia, but to suppress the roles of all conspirators except Melon and Phyllidas. Such an approach would sustain the reputation of Agesilaos, Xenophon's benefactor and hero.[24] In any case, Xenophon's rather summary retelling has found more favor than the longer versions of Plutarch, probably because he was a contemporary of the events he describes.[25] Finally, many modern historians consider the two traditions to be irreconcilable.[26] As I plan to show, however, there are good reasons for re-examining both of these assumptions.

As a secondary source nearly four hundred years removed from the events, Plutarch clearly presents a different sort of problem. Historians have expended considerable energy and ink both in *Quellenforschung* and in efforts to lay bare Plutarch's motives for recounting the coup. The question of his reliability is further complicated in that there are significant variants, not only from Xenophon's version, but also in his own two accounts. Hence a brief review of scholarly thought on his sources and purpose should prove helpful.

Plutarch's *De genio* is highlighted by epic and novelistic touches, embellishments, inventions, and the author's own personality. This is not surprising since, as we have seen, even Polyainos' distortions attest to the coup's inherent interest. Kallisthenes' *Hellenika* (ca. 350 B.C.) has been suggested as Plutarch's source for details of the coup.[27] At the same time it seems certain that the *Pelopidas* preceded *De genio*, which dates from Plutarch's later career.[28] The close correspondence between both Nepos' and Plutarch's lives of

[24] Von Stern (supra n. 18) 57 and A. Schäfer, *Die Berichte Xenophons, Plutarchs und Diodors über die Besetzung und Befreiung Thebens, 382–379 v. Chr.* (Diss. Munich 1930) 19–22, 68, 71, 73, 77 consider the omission of any reference to Epameinondas or Pelopidas as clear proof of Xenophon's anti-Theban bias. Nevertheless, Jacoby, *FGrHist* 2B.2 420–32 and L. Pearson, *The Lost Histories of Alexander* (New York: APA Monographs 1960) 32 object to some of Schäfer's analysis. See also Delébècque (supra n. 1) 275, 285, 283 and Accame (supra n. 18) 339.

[25] G. Grote, *A History of Greece*, vol. 8 (London: J. Murray 1888) 77–83 prefers Xenophon, but thinks that one might add credible details from Plutarch. See also Accame (supra n. 18) 337. J. Buckler, *The Theban Hegemony* (Cambridge, Mass.: Harvard 1979) 36–40, clearly favors Xenophon over Plutarch in most cases.

[26] See for example von Stern (supra n. 18) 53; Fabricius (supra n. 1) 449–55; K. J. Beloch, *Griechische Geschichte*[2] vol. 3.2 (Berlin: De Gruyter 1927) 234–35; Accame (supra n. 18) 339 and P. Lacey and B. Einarson, *Plutarch's Moralia*, Vol. 7 (Cambridge, Mass.: Harvard 1959) 362–64.

[27] See von Stern (supra n. 23) 55–56.

[28] K. Ziegler, "Plutarchos," *RE* 21.1 (1951) 842. See also C. Jones, "Towards a Chronology of Plutarch's Work," *JRS* 56 (1966) 61–74 for a general survey of Plutarch's works.

Pelopidas led to the view that Ephoros was the common source for both, but that Plutarch probably also had Kallisthenes' *Hellenika* to work from.[29] Although he lamented Chaironeia's lack of a good library, it is clear that in using Ephoros or Kallisthenes, Plutarch rejected the Xenophontic tradition.

Plutarch's purpose in writing the *Pelopidas*, as in the *Alexander* (1.2–3), is not to write history, but to reveal the subject's character, τὰ τῆς ψυχῆς σημεῖα, by describing his education and then his conduct at major junctures of his life. In the case of the liberation, it is reasonable to suppose that Plutarch the Boiotian hoped to offset the negative image that his countrymen were dull of wit in comparison with the Athenians. He makes it clear that the exiles drew not only the inspiration for their eventual democratic government, but also moral encouragement from their Athenian hosts to stage the coup. Moreover, he shows that the philosophical Epameinondas, who remained behind throughout the Spartan occupation, constantly strove to imbue Theban youths with the physical and intellectual stamina to resist the Spartan occupiers and the traitorous despots of their city. Finally, he stresses the analogy to earlier Theban aid for Athenians under Thrasyboulos who from exile overthrew the Thirty Tyrants in 403 B.C.[30]

His motives for writing *De genio* are similar to those for the *Pelopidas*, but more complex. In *De genio* Plutarch emphasizes Theban religious and philosophic affinities with Athens as well as political matters common to both *poleis*. The dialogue occurs in a Pythagorean club in Athens whose members have met with some Theban friends to discuss dramatic recent developments. The essay is thematically flawed, however, by the insertion of a mythical visit to the Lebadeian oracle, which clearly disrupts the narrative's chief focus, the liberation of Thebes.[31]

It seems that Plutarch relied on memory and that his technique is more that of the storyteller than the historian. He would invent small details from time to time for narrative embellishment. Often he would use more than one variant of an incident, adapting details from each to suit his own purposes. In fact, *De genio* appears to be more historical fiction than history, though it is clearly based on the same sources as the *Pelopidas*.[32] All

[29] Accame (supra n. 18) 350–52. H. D. Westlake, "The Sources of Plutarch's *Pelopidas*," *CQ* 33 (1939) 11–12, believes that the "unphilosophical" Pelopidas would have been much less attractive to biographers than Epameinondas. Hence he reasons that Plutarch would have relied on lengthy historical narratives for his life of the Theban hero. G. Shrimpton, *The Epameinondas Tradition* (diss. Stanford, publ. Ann Arbor: University Microfilms 1970) 53–54, 63–65 contends that for his lost biography of Epameinondas, Plutarch used Ephoros, while Kallisthenes' *Hellenika* served for the *Pelopidas*.

[30] Plut. *Pelop.* 6.2–7.2; Ziegler (supra n. 28) 84 stresses Plutarch's Boiotian patriotism, while Stadter (supra n. 23) 137–40 emphasizes his wide reading in major historical works and lively antiquarian interests.

[31] Y. Vernière, *Mythes et symboles dans la pensée de Plutarque* (Paris: Les Belles Lettres 1977) 93–95 admits the disjointed effect of the myth, but tries to justify its inclusion by claiming that it shows that intellect yields to revelation, even in a political coup where reason and courage should predominate. Vernière (89, 99–100) and F. Brenk, *In Mist Apparelled* (Leiden: Brill 1977) 39–40, 139–40 discuss the effect of neo-Platonism and religious conviction in Plutarch's later writings.

[32] Stadter (supra n. 23) 140. In a recent study, P. Desideri, "Il *De genio Socratis*: un esempio di storiografia tragica?" *Athenaeum* 62 (1984) 569–85, strives to show that Plutarch used "tragic historiography" with its omens, dreams and dramatic emphasis on chance to highlight the triumph of ἀρετή over τύχη and to celebrate individual freedom: see esp. 576–85 and Westlake (supra n. 29) 21.

this may have stemmed from his greater preoccupation with philosophical and literary matters than historical precision, so that *De genio* is actually *eine eigentümliche Mischung aus einer historischen Novelle und einem philosophischen Dialog*.[33]

Although there is clearly a complex mixture of fact and fiction in the *De genio*, its outline is historically correct.[34] Even the description of Trophonios' oracle at Lebadeia corresponds closely to Pausanias' (9.39–42).[35] Further, oral versions of the coup could well explain the differences between Plutarch and Xenophon. Eyewitness testimony would vary, while later partisanship would affect detail and emphasis; thus Xenophon is not necessarily preferable where discrepancies occur. In short, Plutarch's versions have considerable merit since he had a great curiosity about monuments, places, festivals, and even artifacts which recalled the past. Although he was not primarily an historian, he was well read in major historical works and was not a mere compiler as Diodoros and Polyainos seem to have been.[36]

The task of the modern historian who would venture a reconstruction of the coup thus requires a careful sifting of the evidence in the three major accounts which have come down to us. As the terrain between the two *poleis*, the authors' literary styles and historical methods are all one has to work with, the task is complicated, and many conclusions must remain tentative. The archaeological remains of classical Thebes are scanty, and no epigraphical material bearing on the coup has survived. While a series of coins stamped HIΣME or ANΔP, which date to the period from 378 to 336 B.C., probably commemorate the two martyrs to Theban sovereignty, Ismenias and Androkleides, they provide no specifics about the coup.[37] With the evidence we do have, however, how might we restore a plausible sequence of events? The following discussion seeks to answer this question.

The Exiles Plot to Regain Their Homeland

Vexation at Athens with the Spartans since the King's Peace provided fertile soil for a Theban counterinsurgency. After Phoibidas' coup, 300 Theban Attikizers had found a favorable reception in Athens.[38] The exiles could expect aid and comfort since the memory of Theban assistance to Thrasyboulos in 404/3 was still vivid.[39]

Two circumstances now combined to create the climate for a conspiracy. First, the more perceptive exiles realized that Athenian hospitality would eventually blunt rather than pique the urge for vengeance against the traitors. Second, Leontiades, Archias, and

[33] Accame (supra n. 18) 348 and Ziegler (supra n. 28) 841.

[34] Vernière, (supra n. 31) 51, 100, 105–106.

[35] Westlake (supra n. 29) 21–22.

[36] H. Hack, *The Rise of Thebes: A Study of Theban Politics and Diplomacy* (diss. Yale, publ. Ann Arbor: University Microfilms 1975) 57–58 and Stadter (supra n. 23) 137–40.

[37] See C. Seltman, *Greek Coins*² (London: Methuen 1965) 159 and C. Kraay, *Archaic and Classical Greek Coins* (Berkeley: California 1976) 113–14.

[38] See W. Judeich, "Athen und Theben vom Königsfrieden bis zur Schlacht bei Leuktra," *RhM* 76 (1927) 175–80 and D. Rice, "Xenophon, Diodoros and the Year 379/78 B.C.," *YCS* 24 (1975) 97–98, n. 9.

[39] Xen. *Hell.* 2.4.2–23; Plut. *Pelop.* 6.2–4.

other Lakonizers had ordered the murder of Androkleidas and other exiles in Athens, though only Androkleidas actually fell.[40] Pelopidas gradually restored the exiles' damaged confidence and moved them to think of retaking their city when the initial shock of this blow had worn off.

At last an opportunity arose when Phyllidas, a friend of the exile Melon, visited Athens. Though secretary to the polemarchs, he had grown disgusted with their despotism and was delighted to find that the exiles shared his feelings.

Plutarch tells us in the *Pelopidas* that Phyllidas became *γραμματεύς* after meeting with Melon, but it is more likely, as he writes in *De genio* and as Xenophon affirms, that he was already in the polemarchs' trust when he visited Athens. Plans were now laid for a conspiracy to coincide with the Theban *Aphrodisia* when the polemarchs left their annual office. At approximately the winter solstice a chosen few would leave Athens at dawn, while others under Pherenikos with some Athenian volunteers would remain in the Thriasian plain.[41] This much larger group would enter Thebes upon word of the polemarchs' death. After learning that the first group was actually on Kithairon, Charon (the name is grimly appropriate) offered his house in Thebes as a base for all conspirators exiled or resident.[42]

The Exiles' Path

From the outset the coup was to proceed in two distinct phases. First, a band chosen from the youngest and fittest exiles set out for Thebes. Pherenikos' group would remain at the border with the Athenians to await word of the first group's success.[43] According to Plutarch (*Pelop.* 8.1), as Pherenikos was to gather in the Thriasian plain, his path would be the west central pass over Kithairon, the usual road to Thebes leading west of Athens.[44] Though an easier road led through the plain east of Mt. Parnes and Tanagra to Thebes, the west-central pass over Kithairon was preferred at ca. 50 km. to the longer easterly path (ca. 100 km.).[45] Since the westerly route through the Thriasian plain past the outposts of Eleutherai and Erythrai was the most travelled to Boiotia, it would have also been the most watched. Spartan garrisons at Thespiai and especially at Plataiai may well have had orders to monitor all travelers entering Boiotia, since before Androkleidas' murder rumors had abounded of exiles secretly plotting to reenter Thebes.[46] Although Pherenikos' men and the Athenian volunteers would have little to fear after the coup, the

[40] Plut. *Pelop.* 6.2.

[41] Xen. *Hell.* 5.4.3, 9; Plut. *Pelop.* 8.1, *De genio* 577b and Deinarchos, *Contra Demosth.* 38–39: see von Stern (supra n. 18) 45.

[42] Xen. *Hell.* 5.4.2; Plut. *Pelop.* 7.3 and *De genio* 576d.

[43] Xen. *Hell.* 5.4.3, 9; Plut. *Pelop.* 8.1–2.

[44] See O. Maull, "Kithairon," *RE* Suppl. 4 (1924) 904–905; A. Philippson, *Die Griechische Landschaften*, vol. 1 (Frankfurt: Klöstermann 1951) 522–29 and Buckler (supra n. 25) 11. The pass is 585 m. above sea level.

[45] See Philippson, (supra n. 44) vol. 1, p. 522 and Buckler (supra n. 25) 9. Today the best highway between the two cities is, in fact, the longer route, although the shorter, more westerly route is also marked.

[46] Plut. *De genio* 596b.

few chosen to carry out the assassination likely entered Boiotia by a less conspicuous path. There is no doubt that these men were at pains not to attract attention and had been chosen at least in part for their physical toughness.[47]

Thus, after sending a messenger to Phyllidas, these men probably crossed Kithairon, not at the usual west central pass, but rather through a more easterly one close to Mt. Parnes and the outpost of Phyle. Accordingly, they would have descended into Boiotia just west of the modern village of Skourta. Despite Xenophon's assertion that the assassins were armed *only* with daggers (*Hell.* 5.4.3), Plutarch's description of a double disguise, first as hunters on Kithairon (who would have likely had spears or bows) and then as peasants outside Thebes, is inherently plausible. Suspicions of possible reprisals by the exiles and latent sympathy for them within the city ever since Phoibidas' act of war perhaps had induced the Lakonizers to murder Androkleidas before he could set in motion a similar strike against them. Thus there could well have been need for more than ordinary precautions on both sides, a sense missing in Xenophon's version, but at least implied by Plutarch.[48] If this were the route taken by the plotters, though of approximately the same length as the westerly one, it was perhaps more difficult, since it was also less travelled. (One might also note that this had been Thrasyboulos' path from Boiotia to Attica twenty-five years earlier [Xen. *Hell.* 3.4.2–6]). Because of the assassins' great caution in concealing their true purpose, even to the inclusion of dogs to complete the hunters' disguise, the Phyle-Skourta path would appear to have been the most secure and least obvious crossing.[49]

The Exiles Arrive in Thebes

As noted earlier, the testimony for events of the next two or three days grows quite confused and is in places contradictory. Nonetheless, the leading insurgents, accompanied by their dogs, set forth at dawn towards Phyle. Here Plutarch is preferable to Xenophon, since men armed only with daggers, should someone spy them on Kithairon's slopes, would raise suspicion more easily than a party of hunters with their ὅπλα and hounds.[50]

Xenophon's and Plutarch's testimonies also differ as to numbers. The former tells us that six men under Melon set out for Boiotia, while the latter puts their strength at twelve. We have seen that Xenophon, probably to downplay the sweeping triumph of the great Theban leaders over Sparta at the time he wrote his account, resolutely ignores the role of Pelopidas and Epameinondas in the liberation. Thus despite the artistic symmetry with the number of Thebes' gates and the title of Aischylos' famous drama, Plutarch's number

[47] Plutarch (*Pelop.* 7.2.3 and *De genio* 576c) implies that the plotters in Thebes kept themselves physically fit, as did the exiles in Athens.

[48] Plut. *Pelop.* 8.2 and *De genio* 576d.

[49] See Maull (supra n. 44) 904–905 and Philippson (supra n. 44) vol. 1, p. 522. Nepos (*Pelop.* 2.5) corroborates Plutarch's testimony about the hunting disguise and the use of dogs. For a recent topographical survey of the Skourta plain, see M. Munn, "Agesilaos' Boiotian Campaigns and the Theban Stockade of 378–377 B.C.," *CSCA* 20 (1987) 111–17.

[50] Plut. *Pelop.* 8.2 and *De genio* 576d.

is likely correct. If Kallisthenes was Plutarch's source, as Ephoros was for Nepos, who also has the plotters at twelve, there is independent corroboration from two contemporaries of the event.[51]

When the exiles' messenger had alerted the conspirators at home that the assassins were *en route*, Hipposthenidas, one of those privy to the plot at Thebes, had second thoughts. He told a friend named Chlidon to have Pelopidas and Melon with their ten followers turn back to Athens. Plutarch's testimony in *De genio*, however, ascribing this decision to Amphitheos' impending execution, can hardly be correct. It is unlikely that the polemarchs would have kept a follower of Ismenias in prison for three and a half years only to condemn him to death on the very day of the exiles' return. A more plausible reason would be that Hipposthenidas simply lost his nerve. In any case, Chlidon, failing to locate his bridle, had a row with his wife and never left Thebes. Accame, viewing the whole incident as mere invention by Plutarch to contrast Charon's constancy with Hipposthenidas' hesitation, has overhastily dismissed it as unhistorical.[52] Yet Hipposthenidas appears elsewhere in the narrative, and there is nothing inherently impossible in the incident as Plutarch relates it. Thus as darkness fell the day on which they set out from Athens, the exiles under Pelopidas and Melon at last regained their native city.[53]

The *Aphrodisia* and Death of the Polemarchs

The exiles, now disguised as peasants, slipped through the city's sundry gates and assembled at Charon's house. As with the artistically effective, but fanciful reason offered for Hipposthenidas' second thoughts, one must doubt Plutarch's suggestion (*De genio* 576d) that Charon only volunteered his house when the plotters' messenger arrived with the news that the twelve were already on Kithairon. Although this interpretation may heighten dramatic tension, the testimony of the *Pelopidas* (7.3) is more likely correct. It seems scarcely credible that the twelve would steal into the city without a place of concealment secured in advance. Plutarch, again perhaps fancifully, reports (*De genio* 596a) that some of the twelve, as they moved through the streets, saw lightning without thunder which they took as a favorable omen.

The next day was the festival of Aphrodite which coincided with the polemarchs' leave-taking of office. Xenophon (*Hell.* 5.4.4) and Polyainos (2.4.3) specify that the tyrannicide occurred during the Theban *Aphrodisia*. That the city's women celebrated the feast at the outset of winter emerges indirectly from the *Pelopidas* (9.1) and *De genio* (594d–e), although Plutarch makes no reference to the *Aphrodisia*, perhaps from religious scruple.[54]

[51] Plut. *Pelop.* 8.2 and *De genio* 586b, 587f–88a and Nepos *Pelop.* 2.5. For date of composition of this part of Xenophon's work, see supra n. 24.

[52] Accame (supra n. 18) 349; Buckler (supra n. 25) 38, rightly rejects the notion of Amphitheos' impending death as a motive for the plotters' decision.

[53] Xen. *Hell.* 5.4.3; Plut. *Pelop.* 9.1, *De genio* 594d–e; Diod. 15.25.1; Nepos *Pelop.* 2.5.

[54] For particulars of dating, see F. Schober, "Thebai," *RE* 5A.2 (1934) 1438, 1505.

The conspirators passed the following day at Charon's house where they were joined by thirty-six others from the city. Here Xenophon's chronology is more realistic than Plutarch's which states that the coup occurred on the same night as the exiles' arrival. At sunset the plotters were donning breastplates and swords when two servants of the polemarch Archias arrived with a summons for Charon. Fearing for his friends' safety and his own honor, Charon offered his son as hostage to the others in proof of innocence of any betrayal. His friends, however, rejected the gesture, urging him instead to respond calmly to Archias' summons.[55]

Upon arriving at the *polemarcheion* where Phyllidas had arranged the evening's entertainment for the officials, Charon found Archias and Philippos already incapacitated by drink. Archias nonetheless informed Charon of a report that exiles had been seen in the city. Perhaps the arrival of the exiles's messenger the day before, unfamiliar faces in the streets at yesterday's sunset, or unusual activity at Charon's house during the day had alerted someone. Charon, though taken aback, dismissed the report as hearsay of the kind that occasionally surfaced before the murder of Androkleidas in Athens. He then suggested an invitation to which Phyllidas conspiratorially assented as he led the befuddled Archias back to the carousal. Greatly relieved, Charon returned home to allay the anxieties of his friends.[56]

The plotters now split into two groups. One under Pelopidas, Damokleidas, and Kephisodoros went to attack Leontiades, ex-polemarch and author of the Spartan occupation, and Hypates, a third polemarch who lived near Leontiades but had not come to the revel. Both of these men were to die at home. According to *De genio* (577c), Archias, expecting a woman of high standing to join the revelry, out of shame did not want Leontiades present. More plausibly, however, Leontiades did not attend simply because, though he was still leader of the Lakonizing faction, he was no longer polemarch.

The second group under Melon and Charon went to the *polemarcheion* to kill Archias and Philippos. Though not aware of it at the time, the conspirators now faced a second, more serious threat of exposure when a letter arrived from Archias' friend and namesake, an Athenian hierophant. The letter contained a detailed description of the plot and a dire warning to the polemarch. Accame, again citing literary motives, believed that Plutarch altered the Athenian's name from Archinos (as recorded in Nepos) to enhance the irony of the polemarch's response. Angry at the interruption, Archias said that weighty matters could wait until morning and placed the letter under his pillow. Since there is independent evidence, however, that an Athenian hierophant named Archias lived at this time, Plutarch's testimony should again take precedence. In any case, Archias' ill considered response became proverbial in the light of subsequent developments.[57]

[55] Plut. *Pelop.* 10.1–2, *De genio* 594e–95f. In the *Pelopidas* only one messenger came. In *De genio*, one of the 48 was taking omens when Archias' men arrived.

[56] Plut. *Pelop.* 10.1–2, *De genio* 596a–c. In the *Pelopidas*, Charon concealed the real reason for Archias' summons from his friends, but in *De genio* he told them the truth.

[57] Plut. *Pelop.* 10.1–2, *De genio* 596e–f, *Moral.* 619d–e; Nepos *Pelop.* 3.2–3: see also Accame (supra n. 18) 350. The independent reference to Archias the hierophant appears in Demosth. 59.116.

Disguised as women and komasts (only as women in the *Pelopidas*), the conspirators chosen for the assassination set out for the revel. A wind had arisen, while snow fell mixed with a thin drizzle. Phyllidas, who had nervously watched for the plotters from the *polemarcheion*, escorted the assassins to the officials. With garlands hiding their faces, the plotters made their way to the delighted polemarchs who believed that the "stately and beautiful" women Phyllidas promised had come at last from the *Aphrodisia*. Melon, however, suddenly rushed the drunken Archias who quickly succumbed to the assault. Philippos, though struck in the neck by Charon, managed to defend himself for a time, but eventually fell to Lysitheos. The other plotters easily dispatched a few drunken guests and servants who resisted, while they locked those who submitted into the room as a precaution until the outcome of Pelopidas' mission was learned. In *De genio*, a religious official chosen by lot recognized Melon. The conspirators tried to win him over, but in his confused and drunken state, the priest berated them until an exasperated Theopompos killed him as the tyrants' lackey despite his sacred office. Such is the story as told by Plutarch.[58]

A slightly different version emerges from Xenophon's account (*Hell.* 5.4.4–7). Here Phyllidas has the polemarchs and their guests leave the main area for the anteroom of the treasury. Phyllidas explained this by saying that the courtesans refused to entertain them unless the servants were absent. The plotters then sat themselves next to each man whereupon they easily dispatched their victims with the knives hidden in their clothes. Xenophon mentions *en passant* the more plausible tradition repeated by Plutarch (*De genio* 596) in which the plotters arrived disguised as both women and komasts. This scheme would be much less likely to arouse suspicion since it did not entail a sudden and artificial separation of the revellers and servants into two groups. Also it seems unlikely that women, even ἑταῖραι, would wander the streets after dark on a snowy evening in winter.

The Demise of Leontiades and Hypates

While events took their course at the *polemarcheion*, Pelopidas' group arrived at Leontiades' house. Although the ex-polemarch had retired to his bedroom, the conspirators persuaded a servant that a message had come from Kallistratos of Aphidna (Plut. *De genio* 597d).[59] According to Xenophon, however, Leontiades had just finished dinner and was with his wife, who was carding wool, when the plotters arrived. In Plutarch's *Pelopidas* (11.3) the household was already asleep so that the plotters had to awaken a servant whom they simply overpowered. Since we have three quite distinct versions of what Leontiades was doing when the conspirators assaulted his home, it is almost impossible to decide which, if any, is the true one. Von Stern preferred Xenophon since he believed that Leontiades' widow was one of his sources for the coup.[60]

Once past the bewildered doorman, the plotters reached the bedroom where a now alert Leontiades was awaiting their attack. He had forgotten to extinguish the lamps, but with a knife-thrust to the ribs he killed Kephisodoros, the first to enter the chamber.

[58] Plut. *Pelop.* 11.1–3, *De genio* 596f–97d.
[59] Kallistratos' group tended to favor Spartan, not Theban interests at this time: see supra n. 38.
[60] See supra n. 24.

Although he called to his servants, the plotters checked and overawed them while Pelopidas engaged the tyrant in personal combat. Despite inflicting a minor headwound on his assailant, the author of the Spartan occupation eventually fell to the superior skill and weaponry of the younger man.[61] In *De genio* Kephisodoros lived to see himself and the city avenged and to give a final salute to Pelopidas. As this is almost certainly a romantic fiction, the version of the *Pelopidas* in which Kephisodoros dies almost at once should take precedence.

The second group now attended to the last of the three polemarchs, Hypates, who had not been at the revel. They gained entrance to his house by a ruse similar to the one used against Leontiades' servant, but perhaps as he had heard the uproar nearby, Hypates had taken flight across the roof to a neighbor. The conspirators nonetheless trapped and dispatched him with little difficulty in his place of refuge.[62]

In his much shorter version, Xenophon makes no mention of a second group of plotters, probably because Pelopidas was the leader. Rather he has Phyllidas take three men from the *polemarcheion* to Leontiades' house and is silent about Hypates except for a reference out of context to his fate at *Hell.* 7.3.7. The existence of two distinct groups would make better sense tactically in that it would help keep the revellers' fate secret from the other intended victims.[63] Although Nepos (*Pelop.* 3.3) ascribes the polemarchs' death to Pelopidas, by an error of overcompression, he also represents the operation as unitary.

It seems likely, however, that there were three polemarchs, not two, and since Kallisthenes or Ephoros, younger contemporaries of these events, were probably his sources, Plutarch here is preferable to Xenophon and Nepos.

Release of the Political Prisoners and the Assault on the Kadmeia

Pelopidas' group now joined those with Phyllidas and Melon at a *stoa* from which they set out for the prison. According to Xenophon (*Hell.* 5.4.8), the prison lay near the temple of the Dioskouroi (τὸ Ἀνάκειον). Here Phyllidas in his capacity as γραμματεύς accompanied by Melon and Pelopidas told the guard that they had a prisoner sent by Archias and Philippos. When the suspicious guard asked for proof, however, Phyllidas responded by running him through with a lance. That many Thebans loathed the man became clear the next day when numerous women trampled and spat upon his corpse. Here Xenophon is preferable in that the plotters pretend to have a prisoner. Plutarch instead has them asking for Amphitheos, which is inherently implausible.[64]

The plotters and freed prisoners, who had received weapons from the *stoa*, now assembled at the temple of Athena where Epameinondas, Gorgidas and others joined

[61] Plut. *Pelop.* 11.3–6 and *De genio* 597d–f.

[62] Plut. *Pelop.* 11.6 and *De genio* 597f.

[63] See Grote (supra n. 25) vol. 8, pp. 77–83; Beloch (supra n. 26) vol. 3.2, pp. 234–45; Meyer (supra n. 14) vol. 5, p. 365, no. 1; supra nn. 29 and 30. Von Stern (supra n. 18) 48–49 follows Plutarch.

[64] Xen. *Hell.* 5.4.8; Plut. *De genio* 598a–b: see von Stern (supra n. 18) 48 and supra n. 52. Plutarch makes no mention of this incident in the *Pelopidas*.

them. The liberators proclaimed the tyrants' death and urged the citizens to arm themselves and defend the *polis*. Although some Thebans stirred as news of the coup spread, most remained indoors until dawn out of fear.

The liberators meanwhile had sent a rider to Pherenikos and the Athenians in the Thriasian plain, urging them to hasten to the city. At the same time, growing jubilation in Thebes had driven the Spartan garrison and many Lakonizers to take refuge on the Kadmeia. Before withdrawing to the akropolis, however, one of the harmosts present had sent riders to the Spartan garrisons at Plataiai and Thespiai to plead for assistance. In the *Pelopidas*, Plutarch writes that many viewed the retreat to the Kadmeia as a serious tactical blunder since the Spartans had over 1500 soldiers and armed supporters in the city. Yet he makes no mention of the harmosts' request for aid nor of the patriots' repulse of a cavalry detachment from Plataiai during the night.[65]

At dawn the exiles under Pherenikos and the Athenian volunteers arrived. Epameinondas and Gorgidas, who had not been in exile, now convened an Assembly and introduced the people to their liberators. In keeping with his portrait of Epameinondas as philosopher, Plutarch (*De genio* 594b–c) tells us that the great Theban general refused to take a fellow citizen's life without a trial. He also suggests that it was good for the new government to have at least a few men in power who were not guilty of the bloodletting, a point also made by Nepos (*Epam.* 10.3).

The full citizen body with the Athenians' help now laid siege to the akropolis. Their aim was to compel the surrender of the 1500 before any large relief force could arrive. Prizes were offered to the first men to breach the Spartans' defenses. Faced with their assailants' vigor, the failure of the Plataian cavalry and dwindling supplies, the 1500 surrendered about two weeks later.

The new government agreed to safe conduct out of Boiotia for the 1500 and allowed them to keep their weapons. Nevertheless, Xenophon tells us that the Athenians had to intervene to cut short a massacre of the Lakonizers by the enraged Theban patriots. Since Plutarch nowhere refers to Athenian aid in the coup and passes over in silence the incipient slaughter of Spartan sympathizers, it seems reasonable to assume a causal relation between the two omissions. The behavior of some of his compatriots after Epameinondas had promised safe conduct to the 1500 would do little to enhance the Boiotians' reputation for civility. As bitter factional strife in Greece going back nearly 50 years indicates, however, such incidents are unfortunately all too believable. A final point should be made here: the ancient sources make it clear that the patriots had good reason to press for the dislodging of the 1500, while their anxiety to avoid a large Spartan relief army contradicts Fabricius' hypothesis that the Lakedaimonians were still engaged at Phleious and Olynthos at the time of the liberation.[66]

H. Hack has suggested that Xenophon's chronology, which allows two or three weeks for the full Spartan response under Kleombrotos, implies a swift surrender by the 1500.

[65] Xen. *Hell.* 5.4.9–10; Plut. *Pelop.* 12.1–3 and *De genio* 598d–f.

[66] Xen. *Hell.* 5.4.10–12; Plut. *Pelop.* 13.1–2, *De genio* 598e–f; Nepos *Pelop.* 3.3; Diod. 15.27.2; Polyainos 2.3.1 and 2.4.3. See also Fabricius (supra n. 1) 462–64.

He thinks that the third harmost, who was in Haliartos at the time of the coup, decided not to move after the repulse of the Plataian horsemen. It is more likely, nonetheless, that all three harmosts were lamely awaiting a move from Lakedaimon. Thus the 1500 would have only surrendered when their provisions were exhausted. If this were not the case, Lysanoridas, who received a fine, probably for inaction, would have suffered the death penalty as Herippidas and Arkissos did for the actual surrender.[67]

Aftermath and Conclusion

In less than three weeks after leaving Athens, the exiles and their supporters in Thebes had killed the polemarchs, repelled a Plataian cavalry attack, and driven out the Spartan garrison with the remnants of the Lakonizing faction. Word of the coup, nonetheless, had reached Sparta, probably from Thespiai or Plataiai. The newly elected Melon, Pelopidas, and Charon (who after this all resumed the title Boiotarch) sent a conciliatory legation to Sparta. Accame believes that the Thebans offered alliance to the Spartans without insisting on the resurrection of the Boiotian League, asking only that the Peloponnesians refrain from attacking their city.[68] Agesilaos and the ephors insisted, however, on restoration of the exiled Lakonizers. As this was the one condition which they could not accept, the Theban legates departed.

The ephors decided to send a punitive expedition against the Thebans, even though Agesilaos declined command, citing his service of over forty years. Command thus devolved on the young and inexperienced Kleombrotos.[69] The Peloponnesians upon reaching either Korinth or Megara executed Herippidas and Arkissos, the two harmosts who had surrendered the Kadmeia. Though Xenophon (*Hell.* 5.4.13) mentions only one harmost's execution, Plutarch (*Pelop.* 13.2 and *De genio* 598f) and Diodoros (15.27.3) make it clear that two men died and a third suffered exile after a ruinous fine had reduced him in status to ὑπομείων or "inferior." There is no way to decide whether the executions took place in Korinth or Megara as Plutarch's versions, the only two to specify these details, contradict each other.

After a sixteen-day march, Kleombrotos withdrew from Boiotia without any lasting achievement. Nevertheless his incursion and the earlier Theban legation to Sparta had serious consequences for the new government. The Athenians voted to execute the two *strategoi* who had aided the conspirators in deposing the pro-Spartan regime. Thus the Thebans found themselves isolated and threatened by a much larger invasion in the spring.[70] The danger of isolation evaporated, however, after Sphodrias, an officer

[67] See Hack (supra n. 36) 63–65.

[68] Plut. *Pelop.* 13.1; S. Accame, *La lega ateniese del secolo IV A.C.* (Rome: Signorelli 1941) 21–22, 26–28 believes that the Thebans did elect *Boiotarchs*, not polemarchs, after Kleombrotos' incursion, despite Beloch's contention that Plutarch's report was an error ([supra n. 26] vol. 3.1, p. 145, n. 2).

[69] Xenophon (*Hell.* 5.4.13–14) reveals the real reason for Agesilaos' polite refusal, namely his reluctance to incur odium as a supporter of tyrants, to say nothing of possible overt dissension in the ranks, if he were to command: see also Plut. *Ages.* 24.1–2, *Pelop.* 13.2 and Diod. 15.27.3.

[70] Xen. *Hell.* 5.4.19; Plut. *Pelop.* 14.1 and Isok. *Plat.* 29. For a discussion of the impact of both factors in Athens, see Judeich (supra n. 38) 176; Accame (supra n. 68) 21–23; Rice (supra n. 38) 97, n. 1 and p. 104.

appointed harmost of Thespiai by Kleombrotos, attempted to seize the Peiraieus, but obtained acquittal in Sparta.[71] Indignation at this flagrant double affront provoked a *volte-face* in the Athenian assembly which now voted an official levy to assist the Thebans in their resistance to Agesilaos' invasions of 378 and 377 B.C. Since the Spartans could not reassert domination in Boiotia, the ultimate success of the exiles' coup was assured.[72]

The vigorous new government in Thebes slowly expanded its authority throughout Boiotia, expelling the sundry Spartan garrisons and reconstituting the Boiotian League, this time on a democratic basis. As Buckler observes, most of those participating in the liberation, whether from exile or from within Thebes, were instrumental in creating the democracy after the Athenian model.[73]

A discussion of the new league's rise to power, even in outline, would be beyond the scope of this paper. The Theban patriots, nevertheless, had ushered in a new era in the struggle for supremacy in Hellas. A serious rent had now appeared in the fabric of Spartan control beyond the Isthmos. Only a few months before, all opposition in European Greece to Agesilaos' hegemony had been silenced or crushed. It seems quite fitting, therefore, that the first major fissure in that hegemony should have been effected by the king's most enduring and tenacious foes, the exiles of Thebes.

[71] Xen. *Hell.* 5.4.14–18; Plut. *Pelop.* 14.2 and *Ages.* 24.3.

[72] Sphodrias' failed assault and its consequences are discussed in Xen. *Hell.* 5.4.20–58; Plut. *Pelop.* 14–16, *Ages.* 24.3–27.2 and Diod. 15.29.5–7, 31.2–34.2.

[73] Buckler (supra n. 25) 36, 132.

THE GREAT WANDERINGS OF ODYSSEUS: THEME AND STRUCTURE

Daniel H. Garrison

Father Schoder and I met fourteen years ago at a Homeric symposium on the island of Chios; it seems appropriate that my tribute to his achievement should take the form of observations about the travels of Odysseus, a hero with whom Father Schoder shares qualities which everyone who knows him will appreciate.

The storytelling center of the *Odyssey* was known by the scholars of antiquity as the Ἀπόλογοι, or Apologue.[1] Odysseus' account of his wanderings prior to his arrival on Phaeacia is less a self-defence or apologia than a complex self-revelation through narrative. Rhetorically, it is an amplification of his response to King Alcinous's question at the end of Book Eight: "Tell me the name by which your mother and father called you . . . ".[2]

Odysseus' reply to his host pointedly avoids his adventures at Troy, and it includes only a short account of his misadventure with the Thracian Kikones; the bulk of what he tells his host has to do with encounters of a supernatural kind, isolated from the ordinary world by the occurrence of strong winds or a storm of unusual intensity. What happens in this wonder-world is based on folklorish tales, arranged and modified to suit the themes of the *Odyssey*.

Unlike the self-serving Lying Tales concocted in Ithaca for Athene, Eumaeus, the Suitors, Penelope, and Laertes, the stories told to Alcinous are authentic: though fantastic, they are presented as what really happened to the real Odysseus. What makes them interesting is not the consistency of the hero's behavior, but rather an inconsistency which fits his errant and complex nature. The impression these stories give is of a chaotic miscellany, a farrago of adventures and misadventures unlike the orderly routine of everyday life in Greece and the islands.

In spite of their supernatural character—or perhaps because of it—readers of the *Odyssey* from antiquity onward have enjoyed speculating about the exact whereabouts of Odysseus' adventures abroad. But the physical locations of the Lotus-Eaters, the Cyclopes, Circe, and the rest are misleading because the real action of the Great Wanderings takes place in another dimension, one that is thematic rather than geographic. The map which will help us through the Wanderings is topological rather than topographical because its order consists of thematic rather than spatial *topoi*.

We must therefore lay aside our ordinary maps to chart the thematic *topoi* of Homeric narrative, and look for landmarks of repetition, rather than place, to learn how this part

[1] "Apologue" is a somewhat misleading term, however, as it implies an allegorical narrative. Theagenes of Rhegium began the practice of allegorizing Homer in the late sixth century B.C.; there is little reason to believe that Homer was knowingly an allegorist, either in The Great Wanderings or anywhere else.

[2] On the name of Odysseus, which Homer (by a folk etymology) connected with odium and trouble, see G. Dimock, Jr., "The Name of Odysseus," in *Essays on the Odyssey* (Bloomington: Indiana 1963) 54–72.

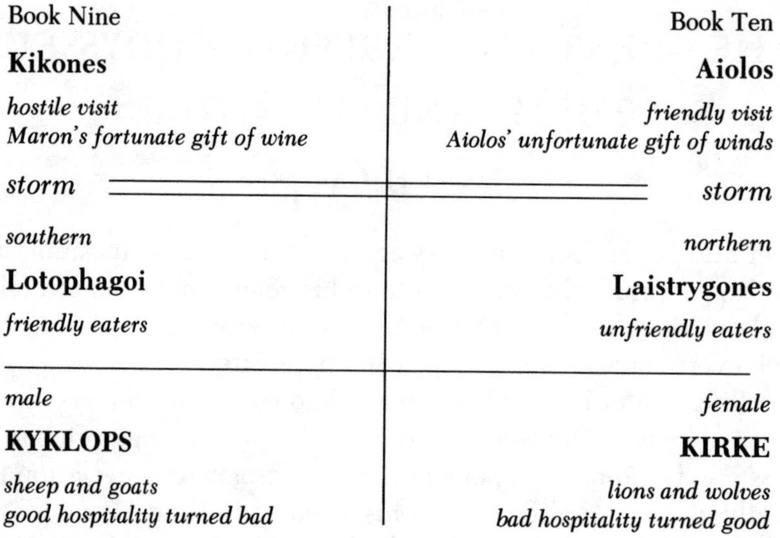

Book Nine	Book Ten
Kikones	**Aiolos**
hostile visit	*friendly visit*
Maron's fortunate gift of wine	*Aiolos' unfortunate gift of winds*
storm	*storm*
southern	*northern*
Lotophagoi	**Laistrygones**
friendly eaters	*unfriendly eaters*
male	*female*
KYKLOPS	**KIRKE**
sheep and goats	*lions and wolves*
good hospitality turned bad	*bad hospitality turned good*

FIG. 1. Parallel structure in Books Nine and Ten

of the *Odyssey* works. The first repetition to be seen is a very simple one: Books Nine and Ten each take us through two short adventures and a long one. In Book Nine, we get the Kikones of Ismaros, the Lotus-Eaters, and the long Cyclops tale; in Book Ten, there are the short Aeolus and Lestrygonian episodes followed by the long Circe narrative (see Fig. 1). In each Book, the first episode is followed by a storm which blows Odysseus out of the real world into the wonder-world. The use of the storm as a sort of boundary-marker is first emphasized by verbal repetition of a specific formula. The storm that marks the crossing from Calypso's magical isle "in the navel of the sea" to the half-real land of the Phaeacians[3] (5.293f.) is described by words identical to those describing the storm that drives Odysseus' ships from the Thracian Kikones towards the unlocated Lotus-Eaters (9.68f.):

> Zeus hid earth and sea alike
> beneath the clouds, and night came from heaven.

When we get a third storm, the one that blows up after the companions of Odysseus open the bag of winds (the θύελλα of 10.48), the sign is purely thematic rather than verbal.

The pattern of two short stories and a longer tale is a useful coincidence, strengthened by the repetition of that stormy crossing into the world of magic. Another coincidence—a phonetic one which we will see again in this section of the *Odyssey*—is the naming of the second and the third episodes: the "Lambda" set for the Lotophagoi/Laistrygones, and the "Kappa" set for the Kyklops/Kirke narratives.

[3] Phaeacia appears to be related to φαιός, "gray," suggesting that its inhabitants are neither divine nor mortal: "We live apart . . . the farthest off, and no one else of mortals mixes with us" (6.204f.); "We are close to [the gods], like the Cyclopes and the savage tribes of the Giants" (7.205f.). See Niles (infra n. 7) 56.

That this patterning is something more than idle coincidence becomes clear when you notice that each adventure is the opposite of its counterpart in the adjacent Book in some important way, each having to do with themes of hospitality and hostility. The encounter with the Kikones is a hostile visit on the part of Odysseus and his ships, but there is a friendly gift from Maron, priest of Apollo, whose gift of magical wine, carried in a goatskin bag (9.196, 212), later tames Polyphemus. The corresponding visit with Aeolus is friendly, but this time the guest-gift, an oxhide bag of winds (10.19), turns out badly when it is opened prematurely just as Odysseus' ship is in view of Ithaca.

The corresponsion of opposites is clear also in the "Lambda" episodes: the Lotophagoi are friendly and gentle eaters, the Lestrygonians hostile and violent: they eat too, but their diet is human. The pairing of these episodes is flagged by the verbatim repetition of a three-line "exploration" theme (9.88–90 = 10.100–102). The Lotus-Eaters are vaguely located somewhere south of Greece (Odysseus is driven there from the sea off Cythera by Boreas, which would blow him southward, 9.90). The Lestrygonians are put with equal vagueness somewhere in the north, where the (summer) days are extra long and "the paths of night and day are close" (10.86) because of the short nights in the season when traders from the Mediterranean were most likely to visit northern Europe. The narcotized torpor of the southern Lotus-Eaters contrasts perfectly with the rugged savagery of the nordic Lestrygonians, who trap the ships from Ithaca in a waveless harbor that could easily be taken for a fjord (10.87–94).

Reverse the order of events in the "Kappa" episodes for the repellent, masculine Kyklops versus the attractive, feminine Kirke. Each of these has a special relation with animals: Polyphemus shares his cave with goats and sheep, Circe's house is surrounded by lions and wolves. Each is the child of a god of nature who later does great harm to Odysseus. Polyphemus is the son of Poseidon, who answers his blinded son's prayer for vengeance; Circe the daughter of Helios, whose cattle slain on Thrinakia are avenged near the end of Book Twelve. Circe's grandfather, Okeanos, suggests a kinship of sorts with Poseidon's son, the Cyclops. The sight of smoke leads Odysseus to Circe (10.149, 197) as it did to Polyphemus (9.167). The same "interval of rest" formulas which bracket the Cyclops adventure (9.168–172, 556–561) are repeated verbatim at the beginning and end of the visit on Circe's isle (10.185–188, 476–478, 12.29–31). These parallels of theme and language invite us to pair the Cyclops with Circe.

These are the two adventures which Odysseus' companions beg him to avoid (9.224–227, 10.198–202, 266–269). Here, themes of hospitality and captivity are intertwined, friendliness and danger treacherously mingled. The good hospitality of Polyphemus quickly turns to a deadly captivity, while the bad hospitality of Circe, which imprisons some twenty-two[4] companions in the form of pigs, is soon turned into a blessing. In the former adventure Odysseus is saved by his wit; in the latter he is saved by divine

[4] Is there something to the numbers with which the Odyssey is so crowded? This number, for example, recurs only in the Cyclops episode, where the stone that seals the cave of Polyphemus is larger than twenty-two wagons could carry (9.241–244).

intervention in the form of a magical talisman of *moly* provided by Hermes. The olive beam with which Odysseus blinds Polyphemus has its counterpart in the sword with which he neutralizes Circe.

This symmetrical pattern of opposites organizes the adventures which precede the *Nekuia*. Odysseus' greatest adventure, in which he meets the spirits of the dead, is a kind of centerpiece and turning point for the epic as a whole as well as the wanderings of Odysseus. The things Odysseus sees and hears there cap off, in a manner of speaking, his life as an adventurer by making him aware of the limitations of the heroic life and reminding him of his home. His mother Anticleia tells him about his family, Teiresias about his unwarlike and unheroic death "in the ebbing time of a sleek old age"; Agamemnon reflects upon his own unhappy *nostos*; and Achilles avers that he would prefer life as a slave rather than high rank among the "perished dead." Here, Odysseus propitiates the spirits of the dead and learns of his obligations to the living. For the first time in the Great Wanderings, we see Odysseus in the underworld as a passive figure, listening and learning instead of acting and speaking. It is significant how little Odysseus talks in this book, whose main ingredient is talk. His longest speech is to tell the ghost of Achilles what a fine hero Neoptolemos has grown up to be—a speech calculated to give comfort to the sad spirit of the greatest of the Achaeans. But the chief burden of the trip to Hades, as he tells his mother Anticleia, is his χρείω, his need to consult Teiresias. Little of what he sees or hears gives him cheer, and he departs in fear of the spirits which crowd around him. Needy, frightened, regretful of the prize he had won from Ajax, perhaps oppressed by the spectacle of failed heroes with which the visit ends,[5] Odysseus exits the underworld with a new detachment regarding his past. He does not completely renounce his past swashbuckling identity as Odysseus πτολιπόρθιος, sacker of cities,[6] but his recent experience has left him without the appetite for plunder and conquest which flavored his earlier ventures.

The episodes which follow the *Nekuia* are combined in Book Twelve. Their number corresponds with the number of episodes prior to the *Nekuia* if we omit the raid on Ismaros which precedes Odysseus' entry into the world of magic. These post-*Nekuia* events are different in several ways: they are shorter in the telling, and they show Odysseus in a somewhat different role, avoiding confrontations rather than seeking them out. The post-*Nekuia* Odysseus is doing his best to get home, and though he still has his old curiosity (as in his scheme to hear the Sirens' song) and his old combativeness (as seen when he arms himself to fight Scylla against the instructions of Circe), he slips through without catastrophe—save only on the island of Thrinakia, where his companions' uncontrolled hunger brings on their doom. The quality which Odysseus displays to best advantage in this set of events is his fabled prudence. Here we see a different Odysseus;

[5] Are lines 568–627 authentic? They were excised an antiquity by Aristarchus, and they precede by generations any suggestion in Greek that Hades is a place of punishment. At the same time, they tend to complement one theme of the *Nekuia*, which might be called the vanity of heroic ambition.

[6] An epithet he shared with Achilles in the *Iliad*: 8.372, 15.77, 21.550, 24.108.

but rather than a change of character, he has gone through a re-orientation. He is less the piratical hero of Troy and more the seeker of his home and his domestic identity.

Another difference worth noticing in these later episodes is the comparative prominence of female encounters: with the exception of the central episode on Thrinakia where the (unseen) opposite is Helios the Sun God, all his encounters are now with female figures: the Sirens, Scylla, Charybdis, and Calypso. The opposite was the rule before the *Nekuia*: the masculine dominated, and even in the single exception, the sojourn with Circe, Odysseus plays a dominating and masculine role, shouting at Circe, threatening her with his sword, and making her swear an oath not to castrate him when he is naked.

Circe does not castrate Odysseus, but after going to bed with her, he undergoes a sort of sea-change. He spends a year feasting and sleeping with his hostess, until it is his companions' turn to remind their captain of home. Now, instead of being supplicated by Circe (as he was when he threatened her with his sword in line 323), Odysseus is the suppliant (481), asking her for help in finding his way home. She now becomes the guide, directing him to consult with the soul of Teiresias and, after he carries out that mission, how to cope with the trials that await him on his journey back to Ithaca.

Circe's liminal role begins the removal of Odysseus from the masculine field of violence, deception, and leadership to a subtler and in some ways more feminine field where he is less the captain, fighter, and leader of men, and more a figure who must endure and survive. He becomes increasingly dependent on a series of female figures who take care of him: Calypso, Ino, Nausicaa, Arete, Athene, and finally Penelope herself. The Lestrygonians have stripped him of his ships, and in a final debacle his men defy his orders and slaughter the cattle of Helios, resulting in their doom and Odysseus' helpless isolation in the waters of an unknown sea. An important function, therefore, of the Great Wanderings is the stripping-away of the hero's heroic paraphernalia and his consignment to the womblike hollowed caves of Calypso "in the navel of the waters."

This process takes place within an elaborate double structure, consisting in the first place of the matched triads of Books Nine and Ten, and in the second place of the elaborate ring structure shown in Figure 2.[7] This second ring-structure works on two axes or

[7] The pattern in this diagram was first called to my attention by a student of mine, Caroll Robertson, who discovered it independently three years after its first publication in Italy by A.B. Lord. The literature concerning patterns of narrative in *Odyssey* 9–12 includes the following:

N. Austin, *Archery at the Dark of the Moon* (Berkeley: California 1975) 132ff.

J.S. Clay, "Aeolia, or Under the Sign of the Circle," *CJ* 80 (1985) 289–291.

———„ *The Wrath of Athena* (Princeton: University Press 1983) 125–132.

E. Delebecque, *Construction de l'Odyssée* (Paris: Les Belles Lettres 1980).

G. Germain, *Genèse de l'Odyssée* (Paris: Presses Universitaires de France 1954) 333.

A.B. Lord, "Tradition and the Oral Poet," *La poesia epica e la sua formazione* (Rome: Accademia Nazionale dei Lincei 1970) 13–28.

M. Nagler, "Dread Goddess Endowed with Speech," *ArchNews* 6 (1977) 77–85.

J.D. Niles, "Patterning in the Wanderings of Odysseus," *Ramus* 7 (1978) 46–60.

D. Page, *Folktales in Homer's Odyssey* (Cambridge, Mass.: Harvard 1973).

L. Radermacher, "Die Erzählungen der Odyssee," *SBWien, phil.-hist. Klasse* 178 (1916) 18–21.

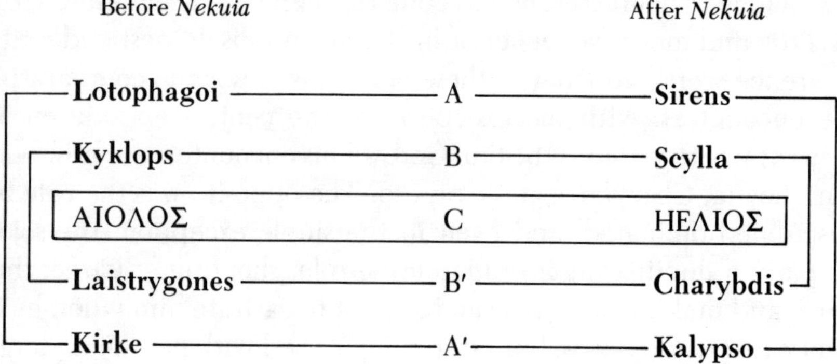

FIG. 2. Ring structure in Books Nine, Ten, and Twelve

centers. The first is Book Eleven, the *Nekuia*, which provides the vertical axis dividing the ten episodes which bracket it. The second, horizontal axis consists of encounters with nature-gods which frustrate the return home because of the disobedience and folly of the men. The gods themselves are sound-alikes: Αἴολος and ’Ηέλιος. These are emphasized because of their position in the ring-structure, and because Homer repeatedly mentions the crime against the cattle of the Sun, which from the opening lines of the *Odyssey* is emblematic of self-destructive folly.

Two or three other clues mark the pairing of the Aeolus and Helios episodes. In each, Odysseus is undone because he falls asleep.[8] The oxhide backstay with which Odysseus lashes together the mast and keel of his wrecked ship after the storm off Thrinakia (12.423) may be an echo of the oxhide bag of winds in 10.19. The storm which punishes the companions' misbehavior, symbolic of chaos unleashed by folly, is the chief signal that these misadventures are a pair.

The second element in the pattern, marked "B" in Figure 2, consists of paired male and female monstrosities. The Lestrygonians are variants of the Cyclopes in very much the same way as Charybdis is paired with Scylla. In this circle of the ring-structure, men are eaten or in danger of being devoured. The Lestrygonian woman "big as a mountain peak" (10.113) reminds us of Polyphemus, "like a wooded peak of high mountains"

K. Reinhardt, "Die Abenteuer der Odyssee" in *Tradition und Geist* (Göttingen: Vandenhoeck & Ruprecht 1960).

J. de Romilly, "A propos d'Ogres," *Mélanges Eduard Delebecque* (Marseilles: Laffitte 1983) 331–340.

S. Scully, "Doubling in the Tale of Odysseus," *CW* 80 (1987) 401–417. This appeared after the composition of my paper.

C. Whitman, *Homer and the Heroic Tradition* (Cambridge, Mass.: Harvard 1958) 288.

W.J. Woodhouse, *The Composition of Homer's Odyssey* (Oxford: Clarendon 1930) 33–34.

[8] Throughout the *Odyssey*, it is food and not sleep which symbolizes human frailty (e.g. 7.215ff., 15.344f., 17.286ff., 473f., 18.53f.). But as early as the Gilgamesh epic where the hero is denied everlasting life because he cannot stay awake for six days and seven nights, the need for sleep has a similar meaning.

(9.191f.) Horizontal affinities continue to be as important in this set of events as they were in the central pair consisting of Aeolus and Helios. The Cyclops, a "monstrous" (πελώριον, 9.190—he is a πέλωρ in 428) figure eats six of Odysseus' men: the monster (πέλωρ, 12.87) Scylla devours the same number. The Lestrygonians prepare one victim for eating; Charybdis likewise has one victim to devour—Odysseus himself—but he escapes by clinging to a fig tree. The monsters of circle "B" are repellent and rocky: Polyphemus and the Lestrygonians throw rocks after the escaping Greeks, Scylla lives in a cave in a rock cliff, and Charybdis is just below a rocky cliff.

Those of the outer ring (marked "A" in the diagram), are not rocky monsters who repel or devour but soft enchanters who attract and delay. Magical rather than violent, they are associated with eating rather than being eaten; their character is gentle and generally feminine. The danger is forgetfulness of the way home, particularly before the *Nekuia* (9.97, 10.236). Circe, Calypso, and the Sirens are enchanters in the most literal sense in that they are singers.[9] To overcome the irresistible attraction of the Lotus-Eaters, Odysseus must bind his men (9.99) to their rowing benches; he himself must be bound to the mast to overcome the lure of the Sirens. Circe and Calypso are doubles in many ways, each detaining Odysseus for a long time, each an islander, each luxurious, and each willing, in the end, to surrender her lover and graciously assist his departure. Homer poses them similarly in his description, singing in a lovely voice as they work their loom (5.61f., 10.221f.). He places Calypso in a lovely bower populated by nocturnal and predatory birds (5.63–74), while Circe, whose name is a feminine variant of κίρκος, "hawk" or "falcon," lives in a forest glen populated by lions and wolves.

The *Odyssey* as a whole organizes its material in six bundles of four Books each, with a structure that is more obvious than anything found in the *Iliad*.[10] The center section, Books Nine through Twelve, is a remarkable example of this poem's instinct for structure. In the Great Wanderings, Homer has used the traditional ring structure to compose a sonata-like composition of theme and variation where he transforms Odysseus from a traditional raider captain to a survivor in a largely female world.

The purpose of such patterning is immediately to delight but ultimately to instruct, by exploring "in various combinations and permutations the elements of the superhuman and the subhuman, of civilization and barbarism, [in a way] which finally moves toward a definition of the properly human."[11] Homer's arrangement of elements to show the evolution of Odysseus away from the violent and amoral bravado of the primitive raider toward the less combative, more purposeful ways of *homo civilis*, *homo faber*, and *homo domesticus* shows an underlying ethical dimension of a kind that Father Schoder has always insisted gives Homer a special place in literature.

[9] Nagler (supra n. 7) calls attention to the repetition of the formula δεινὴ θεὸς αὐδήεσσα—"dread goddess endowed with speech" at the boundaries between episodes of similar thematic import: 10.136, 11.8, 12.150 (Circe), and 12.449 (Calypso).

[10] Notwithstanding the pervasive ring structures found by Whitman (supra n. 7) chap. xi.

[11] Clay (supra n. 7) 289.

ST. JOHN'S JESUS, SIGN-SEEKERS, AND GNOSTICS: A READING OF JOHN 6:22–71

CHARLES HOMER GIBLIN, S.J.

Debate about Jesus' "Bread of Life" discourse in John 6:22–71 has focused on sources and redactional composition.[1] Allied discussions about the situations faced by the Johannine community have certainly not been wanting. Fortunately, in the course of such discussions, the key concern for the inner, *theological* unity and coherence of the discourse has emerged—or has re-emerged.[2] To further this salient concern, I offer the following modest contribution.

A brief survey of the text is in order: The introductory portion (vv. 26–31) of the discourse consists of a dialogue in which Jesus rebukes those who have not perceived the meaning of his signs and challenges them to produce a concrete work, namely faith in the one whom God has sent. His hearers require a further sign, such as providing manna in the desert. Jesus' discourse proper begins (v. 32) with revelatory statements which highlight his own transcendence and counter the earth-bound, materialistic interests of the sign-seekers. He responds to progressively more serious misunderstandings (vv. 31, 41–42) by speaking of himself as God's own gift from heaven and of faith, too, as a gift from the Father, who enables Jesus to give life now and risen life to come. In verses 47–58, his discourse takes a new turn.[3] He insists on eating the bread which is his flesh (given) for the life of the world. When his hearers' misunderstanding bursts out into open argumentation among themselves (v. 52), he proceeds to use almost crassly materialistic language (not simply "eat", vv. 51, 53, but "dine on, chew", vv. 54, 56, 57, 58: *τρώγειν*).[4] After he concludes his discourse with the Jews (v. 59), many of his own disciples express revulsion at his language and leave him (v. 60). Jesus then pointedly relates these scandalous words to the greater mystery of his going to the Father (though his passion, death, and resurrection-ascension; vv. 61–62) and comments on all his own words, even the apparently crass ones he has uttered, as not being on the level of "flesh" (merely human

[1] Among the more relevant bibliographical surveys are: H. Thyen, "Aus der Literatur zum Johannesevangelium," *Theologische Rundschau* 43 (1978) 328–59, 338–59 and 44 (1979) 97–134; M. Roberge, "Le discours sur le pain de vie (Jean 6,22–59). Problèmes d'interprétation," *LavThéolPhil* 38 (1982) 265–99, and "La composition de Jean 6, 22–59 dans l'exégèse récente," *LavThéolPhil* 40 (1984) 91–123.

[2] Cf. U.C. von Wahlde, "*Wiederaufnahme* as a Marker of Redaction in Jn 6, 51–58," *Biblica* 64 (1983) 542–49, and especially H. Weder, "Die Meschwerdung Gottes. Überlegungen zur Auslegungsproblematik des Johannesevangeliums am Beispiel von Joh 6," *Zeitschrift für Theologie und Kirche* 82 (1985) 325–60; Ludger Schenke, "Die literarische Vorgeschichte von Joh 6, 26–58," *Biblische Zeitschrift* 29 (1985) 68–89.

[3] Simon Légasse, "Le pain de la vie," *Bulletin de Littérature Ecclésiastique* 83 (1982) 243–61, 256–57, points out that it is impossible not to think of the Eucharist in v. 51 because of the mention of "eating"; the phrasing "give . . . on behalf of" also recalls the words of institution (Luke 22:19–20).

[4] C. Spicq, "ΤΡΩΓΕΙΝ: Est-il synonyme de ΦΑΓΕΙΝ et d'ΕΣΘΙΕΙΝ dans le Nouveau Testament?" *NTS* 26 (1980) 414–19, shows that the words are not really synonyms, and that John stresses realism as well as the superior quality of the Eucharistic food.

DAIDALIKON: Studies in Memory of Raymond V. Schoder, S.J.

understanding)[5] but as "spirit and life" (v. 63). That is, they are to be understood on the level of a concrete but supra-human mode of revelation which effects life. On this basis, as acknowledged by Peter, he is accepted by faithful disciples (vv. 66–71).

Not a few exegetes think that the sacramental imagery in the closing portion of Jesus' discourse to the Jews comes from an ecclesial redactor who did not fully share the mind of the Evangelist.[6] Peder Borgen[7] has provided a partial corrective to their view by arguing for a midrashic development from the text quoted by the Jews (v. 31): "He gave them bread from heaven to eat" (Ps 78:24; Exod 16:4–15). Jesus first corrects the understanding of "He gave them bread from heaven", and then clarifies the meaning of "to eat". Thus, up to verse 51, at least, the passage is unified and coherent.[8] Nevertheless, the harsh or "unpleasant" language (cf. σκληρός, v. 60) of verses 52–58 and the quite negative reaction of many of Jesus' disciples (vv. 60–61, 66) are not thereby explained. Nor does one thereby find an intrinsic continuum of theological understanding for the whole of verses 22–71 which is grounded thoroughly in the tradition of John the Evangelist.

In the spirit of our honoree, who directed my M.A. thesis on the Odyssey (Telemachus) over three decades ago, I offer some thoughts to support the unity of this text and the tradition underlying it as a whole. These reflections concern analogous lines of thought elsewhere in John's Gospel. For Father Schoder helped teach me that a well-composed text serves as a reliable commentary on itself.

John's Prologue (1:1–18) serves as an introduction to the whole Gospel narrative. As I have shown elsewhere,[9] the Prologue has two complementary structures, each reflecting one of the last two stages of its composition, namely, its final (or present) stage, and the immediately previous, earlier (or penultimate) stage. The elements added to create the final stage (viz., those dealing with John the Baptist, vv. 6–8 and 15, but also v. 13) build upon the earlier structure, take it over, and reaffirm it even as they make it into an introduction to the narrative (which begins with 1:19). Interestingly, however, it is in the earlier stage, that which immediately preceded the final organization of the Fourth Gospel as we have it and which is therefore unquestionably fundamental to the Johannine tradition, where we find a line of thought similar to that in John 6:32–58. For the same

[5] Or, with R. Schackenburg, *Johannesevangelium* II (Freiburg: Herder 1971) 105–106, one can read v. 63a in the light of what only the Son of Man's death, resurrection, and ascension will make possible.

[6] In one way or another, this position derives from that of R. Bultmann, *The Gospel of John. A Commentary*, trans. G.R. Beasley-Murray from the 1964 German ed. and 1966 Supplement (Oxford: Basil Blackwell 1971) 219–20.

[7] P. Borgen, *Bread from Heaven. An Exegetical Study of the Concept of Manna in the Gospel of John and the Writings of Philo* (Leiden: Brill 1965).

[8] Borgen's view has been sharply criticized by Thyen 1978 (supra n. 1) 350 and by G. Richter, "Zum Formgeschichte und literarischen Einheit von Joh 6, 31–58," *ZNTW* 60 (1969) 21–55. More perspicaciously, Barnabas Lindars (*The Gospel of John* [London: Oliphants 1972] 251–53, 259–60) looks to the homily form as John has adapted it, and finds the Eucharistic interpretation latent beneath the sapiential section (6:35–50) and the sapiential aspect continuing without diminution in the Eucharistic section (vv. 51–58). The most satisfactory, albeit complicated, defense of the unity of the discourse (including close analysis of its compositional development) has quite recently been provided by Schenke (supra n. 2).

[9] Charles H. Giblin, "Two Complementary Literary Structures in John 1:1–18," *JBL* 104 (1985) 87–103.

event, the incarnation, is presented successively in two complementary ways. In the first portion (vv. 1–5, 9–12) of the earlier stage of the Prologue, the incarnation is presented (from v. 3c onwards) largely under the image of light come into the world, and as intended for third persons. In the second portion (vv. 14, 16–18), the Word is presented more concretely and personally, as *enfleshed* (Καὶ ὁ Λόγος σὰρξ ἐγένετο), and as seen by first persons ("we/us" members of the Johannine community).

This earlier, penultimate stage of John's Prologue initially uses imagery (light) that might be attractive to a gnostic-oriented mentality yet be alien, perhaps, to those who would look for a quite physical specification of the theophany. With verse 14, however, John drives home the reality of the Word's incarnation by restating his position concretely. He does not say, "The Word became man", or " . . . appeared as man", or "existed in flesh", for a gnostic or docetist might cope with such sayings.[10] He says what no gnostic or docetist could stomach, saying: "The Word *became* flesh," and proceeds to tie in with that attested event the manifestation of his glory. The Word is truly human, but in language intolerable to gnostic or docetist alike. At the same time, John proceeds to contrast in climactic parallelism the law given through Moses and the new creation, a directly personal relationship with God, through Jesus Christ.[11]

Comparison between this earlier (penultimate) stage of the the Prologue and John 6:32–58 requires reservations. First, the Bread of Life discourse moves from the incarnate Jesus himself as the heaven-sent gift to his abiding sacramental presence in the Eucharist.[12] Nonetheless, the line of thought also moves from a kind of "spiritual", highly metaphorical language to speech which is arrestingly concrete. Furthermore, the personal relevance of the strong language emerges perceptibly in each passage. The Prologue moves from third persons (as the objects of the communication) to first persons (plural). John

[10] Cf. the gnostic expressions: " . . . he came by means of fleshly appearance," *Gospel of Truth*, I, *3*, 31.4–5, and " . . . existed in flesh," *Treatise on Resurrection* (= *Letter to Rheginos*) I, *4*, 44.14–15; *The Nag Hammadi Library in English*, ed. J.M. Robinson (San Francisco: Harper and Row 1977) 43, 51. For the gnostic, the fleshly appearance is at best transitory (infra n. 16).

The relationship between docetism and gnosticism is not easy to determine. It seems that docetism, which denies the incarnation of Jesus and so also the reality of his death, does not necessarily presuppose gnosticism; cf. William R. Schoedel, *Ignatius of Antioch* (Hermeneia; Philadelphia: Fortress 1985) 55. Anti-docetism in John's Gospel has long been recognized; cf. J.H. Bernard, *The Gospel According to St. John* I (International Critical Commentary; Edinburgh: T. and T. Clark 1928) 210. It seems likely that the Fourth Evangelist dissociated himself from any line of thought which compromised the reality of the incarnation and its consequences (infra nn. 16, 17).

[11] Cf. Giblin (supra n. 9) 89, n. 7.

[12] Cf. Légasse (supra n. 3) who points out that entrance into the mystery of Christ by faith is the basis for the Eucharistic sharing described in John 6:52(51b)–58. Cf. also R. Schnackenburg, *Johannesevangelium* IV (Freiburg: Herder 1984) 212, who cites appreciatively Ulrich Wilckens, "Der eucharistische Abschnitt der johanneischen Rede vom Lebensbrot (Joh 6, 51c–58)" in *Neues Testament und Kirche* (Freiburg: Herder 1974) 220–48, 247: "'Der Evangelist hat eine eucharistiche Tradition aufgenommen und in seinem Sinn interpretiert . . . ' nämlich, 'daß der reale Genuss des Fleisches und Blutes Jesu als des Menschensohnes eine wesenhafte personale Verbindung mit ihm bewirkt wie, weil Jesus de Ewig-Lebendige ist, dem Christen ewiges Leben schafft.' Darum komme er einerseits auf den Glauben an Jesus, den von Gott gesandten Heilsmittler, an, anderseits darauf, dass die Glaubenden bei ihm 'bleiben.' 'Die Eucharistie ist der konkrete Vollzug solchen Bleibens.'"

6:32 ff. oscillates between references to second persons and third persons, but becomes quite emphatic regarding second persons in the passages where Jesus refers to eating his flesh and drinking his blood, both in his speaking to the Jews and in his addressing the disciples: "Unless you eat . . ." (v. 53), "Does this scandalize you? . . ." (v. 61).

Second, the Prologue distinguishes recipients of the communication, but more simply. The first portion speaks of mankind in general (or, vaguely, of "his own" in particular); the second portion looks only to believers ("us / we"). In John 6:32 ff., however, the audience becomes more complicated. In the first (synagogue) discourse (to v. 59) one finds the Jews, who become divided; in the second discourse (vv. 60–71), one finds the disciples, who also become divided. "The Jews" in the first discourse, as often elsewhere in John, represent the world at large.[13] They are confronted both with the spiritual, metaphorical imagery of "bread from heaven" and with the arrestingly concrete imagery of "eating his flesh". One and the same audience, the world at large, are sign-seekers, bound to a materialistic view of divine manifestations, or incipient gnostics, unable to take Jesus' message about himself, both incarnational and sacramental.[14] "They fought with one another" (v. 52). Neither seems to have accepted Jesus, at least not when confronted with the Eucharistic or sacramental portion of his discourse:[15] his incarnate self (his flesh) to eat (sacramentally). Those most scandalized, however, prove to be many of Jesus' own disciples. In context, they seem to represent those "Christians" of John's acquaintance who would accept Jesus' discourse about being "bread from heaven" insofar as he was God's revelatory gift to them and their way to being "taught by God". They cannot, however, accept the sacramental realism of John's community, which must serve as a test of their acceptance of a genuine incarnation. Not only that, but they seem as well unable or most unlikely to accept the climactic mystery to which the Eucharist itself attests, Jesus' going to the Father, sc., in his death-resurrection-ascension (cf. vv. 61–62).[16] They

[13] Cf. Giblin (supra n. 9) 95, n. 25. The "typing" of "the Jews" as "the world (sc., as of this world, 'below')" is especially relevant here in view of repeated references to the one "who has come down from heaven"; cf. 8:23.

[14] According to the context, the audience does not change at all before the conclusion to the synagogue-discourse in John 6:59.

[15] Instead of the distinction between sapiential and Eucharistic sections, M. Gourges proposes one between (interconnected) Christological and Eucharistic sections, "Section christologique et section eucharistique en Jean VI. Une proposition," *RBibl* 88 (1981) 515–31, 526; cf. Lindars (supra n. 8). This strikes me as being a mainly terminological, perhaps nominalistic refinement. The most tightly reasoned and promising analysis to date has been offered by L. Schenke (supra nn. 2 and 8), which, unfortunately, I cannot develop in this short paper. I trust, however, that my own mode of analysis will help support Schenke's position.

[16] One may bear in mind that, according to the *Gospel of Philip*, a gnostic work, "The eucharist anticipates the union of the gnostic with his 'angel image' . . . the 'flesh' and 'blood' of Christ as they are presented in the Last Supper are for the gnostic 'word' (*logos*) and 'Holy Spirit,' understood as a celestial pair of aeons." Kurt Rudolph, *Gnosis. The Nature and History of Gnosticism* (trans. ed. McLachlan Wilson from the 1977 German ed.; San Francisco: Harper and Row 1983) 241.

seem to exemplify already the docetist view to which Ignatius of Antioch refers repeatedly, most clearly in his letter to the Smyrnaeans.[17] The disciples who remain faithful accept Jesus' "words of everlasting life" (v. 68), which must include "all his words" in 6:26–58, if only because that was their obvious scope: life now and to come.

Space may allow brief treatment of another analogy, namely, John's account of Jesus' discourse with Nicodemus (3:1–21). This discourse correlates three major points which appear in John 6:22–71: the Son's coming into this world, a sacrament presented in "earthly terms", and the Son's going back to the Father. Nicodemus acknowledged Jesus as a teacher come from God (3:2), on the grounds of his signs. Jesus went on to speak of the need for rebirth (ἄνωθεν = both "again" and "from on high") by water and the spirit (3:3,7). Baptismal imagery proved to be too difficult for Nicodemus. How was such rebirth possible? It seemed crass to him (v. 4). He had acknowledged Jesus' signs (v. 2), but still desired to see how this rebirth "worked". Jesus continued to insist on its necessity as a spiritual reality (vv. 5–6), and coaxed his listener with a parabolic comparison (vv. 7–8) which illustrated the lack of human comprehension and, therefore, of human control. Nicodemus remained preoccupied with the issue of how sacramental rebirth was possible (v. 9). In reply, after a mild rebuke (v. 10) to the effect that his own tradition should enable him to rise to the proper level of understanding, Jesus proceeds to insist on the need to accept testimony (v. 11) which deals not only with "earthly things" (sc., the teaching about Baptism, which Nicodemus did not believe) but "heavenly things" as well. These , in effect, are things more difficult to understand (v. 12).[18] Reiterating his appeal to testimony, Jesus then points out that the only one who has had access to heavenly mysteries is himself, the incarnate Son of Man (v. 13). He then presents the "heavenly mystery": the death of the Son of Man on the cross as the ultimate source of life for believers and the proof of God's love for the world in sending his Son (to give life as the alternative to judgment; vv. 14–21).

[17] W. R. Schoedel (supra n. 10) 242: "For part of even the most elementary docetism is an emphasis on spirit that brings readier dissatisfaction with the 'cruder' elements of the religious tradition. The history of Gnosticism where docetism and elitism went hand in hand provides relevant commentary on this point." The basic text in Ignatius of Antioch is *Smyrnaeans* 7.1. Schoedel admits this text; he seems almost unnecessarily guarded about the others: *Trallians* 8.1; *Romans*, 7.3; *Philadelphians* 5.1; even *Ephesians* 20.2. After all, these letters were written within a rather short time by the same person, who had a rather clearly focused, intensely affirmed, and, as is obvious to any reader, repeated, almost repetitious message. One text suffices; others surely help at least to undergird it and need not be "explained away."

[18] The language is reminiscent of apocalyptic literature, in which one mystery leads to another which may be even more mind-boggling but is the answer to or fulfillment of the prior one; on the other hand, understanding the second mystery in a *Visionsreihe* depends on somehow grasping the first. A passage perhaps particularly relevant (*mutatis mutandis*) is the thought-pattern in 2 Baruch 55:4–8 (cf. *The Old Testament Pseudepigrapha*, I, *Apocalyptic Literature and Testaments*, ed. J.H. Charlesworth [Garden City: Doubleday 1983] 640.) For an exegetical and theological examination of a related, apocalyptic method, cf. C.H. Giblin, "Revelation 11. 1–13: Its Form, Function, and Contextual Integration," *NTS* 30 (1984) 433–59.

According to John 3:1–21, the Son is sent into the world to prove God's love for the world by giving life. The sacrament (in this case, Baptism) effects the very beginning of that life, and Jesus' teaching about it forms an integral part of his mission as being sent by God. The ultimate attestation of the sacrament, however, lies in Jesus' "glorification" as the Son of Man, which is here focused on his death as the cause of life (3:14–15; cf. Num 21:4–9; Wis 16:5–7). John's line of thought in 6:32–63 is not dissimilar. The teacher come down from heaven testifies to the Father's gift of life through himself and offers sacramentally communicated life. The sacrament itself is not understood by one who looks to miraculous signs alone (even, in Nicodemus's case, with some minimal perception). Admittedly, Nicodemus is not a "sign-seeker" precisely on the same level as those in John 6:26–30. Nor is he a "gnostic" type in any sense. As a "leader of the Jews", he is a Pharisee, not, therefore, a "representative of the world at large". Lastly, unlike many of Jesus' disciples, he does not become disaffected and leave him, and his very conversion remains questionable.[19] Nevertheless, allowing for the difference of audiences between John 3:1–21 and 6:22–71, the line of Johannine thought is stikingly similar. Jesus' coming as a teacher and, indeed, as a unique revealer of the way to life entails his incarnation (being sent into the world), his teaching on sacramental life, and the further ordering of this sacrament to the climactic revelatory act of his life-giving death.

CONCLUSION

The theological coherence of the Bread of Life discourse is secured by coordinated lines of thought which are basic to the Johannine tradition. One must think both "spiritually" and quite concretely about the Son's incarnation, negating what seems attractive to the mind-set either of a kind of sign-seeker, intent on physical phenomena, or of the very opposite, a gnostic rationalizer. This disciplined mode of thought can be discerned by reading John 6:22–71 in the light of the Prologue (1:1–18), notably its earlier (penultimate) state, already well-rooted in the Johannine tradition and not the work of an ecclesial redactor. Although the "redactor's" (or, I would suggest, the younger "co-author's") work in John 6:22–71 is not to be denied, the discourse as we have it remains true to an underlying Johannine tradition, and even develops it. The same line of thought should also be discerned in the light of John 3:1–21. Furthermore, as the sacramental "sign" becomes more a test of faith than the physical "signs" (miracles) which Jesus worked, this test finds its grounds in Jesus' insistent word, particularly in speaking of the mystery of his death and resurrection as the proof of the Father's sending him to give life to the world. Incarnation, sacramental reality, death and resurrection are intrinsically linked in John's view of the Son's revelatory communication of life for the world.

[19] Cf. R.E. Brown, *The Gospel According to John XIII–XXI* (Garden City: Doubleday, 1970) 940, 959–60, who does not even pose the question, but gives data relevant to one's informed opinion. The Fourth Evangelist (19:38–40) seems more concerned with Nicodemus's profound personal respect for Jesus and his public profession of it rather than specifically with his "conversion to Christianity". The Evangelist does not try to determine the issue.

THE DEVELOPMENT OF GREEK PHONOLOGY: THE FIFTEENTH CENTURY B.C. TO THE TWENTIETH CENTURY AFTER CHRIST

FRANCIS T. GIGNAC, S.J.

It is a great honor for me to present this paper to Father Schoder today on his seventieth birthday because I regard him as the best teacher I ever had. After learning my first Greek in high school from his textbook, *A Reading Course in Homeric Greek*,[1] I had the privilege of doing my master's work in classical languages and literature under his tutelage at old West Baden College. It was he who introduced me not only to some of the world's greatest literature, art, and architecture but also to the exciting field of historical Greek grammar and comparative linguistics. Under his direction I wrote my master's thesis in 1957 on the recently deciphered Linear B script and the Mycenaean dialect it preserves.[2] This work in turn led me to Oxford and a doctorate in Greek philology, where I concentrated on the language of the nonliterary papyri of Roman and Byzantine times.[3] Since then I have been working mainly in the area of biblical Greek. I chose the development of Greek phonology as the topic of my paper because it is representative of the various areas of Greek into which Father Schoder led me, and above all because it allows me to demonstrate one great lesson that he taught me, namely, the paramount value of a sound historical approach and the necessity of always studying changing phenomena, whether linguistic or other, in their proper historical perspective.

I have chosen to isolate seven significant stages in the historical development of Greek phonology ranging from the earliest evidence we have of this language in the Linear B syllabary to contemporary Modern Greek. I have illustrated these seven stages in the Table (p. 132 below) by presenting the phonemic structure of the language at each stage. As you well know, in dealing with any ancient language, where the bulk of our evidence consists of written documents, neither the original sounds nor the transitional sounds can be assigned precise phonetic values. But phonemic oppositions can be established, that is, a given sound can be distinguished from other sounds that are significant in

[1] With Vincent C. Horrigan, S.J., 5 vols. (Chicago: Loyola University Press 1947; new revised edition 1984).

The following will be referred to only by the author's last name: E. Schwyzer, *Griechische Grammatik*. Handbuch der Altertumswissenschaft. I: *Allgemeiner Teil, Lautlehre, Wortbildung, Flexion* (Munich: Beck'sche 1953) and M. Lejeune, *Phonétique historique du mycénien et du grec ancien* (Paris: Klincksieck 1972).

[2] "The Decipherment of Mycenaean Greek in the Linear B Script and Its Consequences in the Field of Homeric Scholarship," unpublished; see summaries in F. T. Gignac, "Some Ramifications of Linear B," *CB* (1957) 37–44; Idem, "The Decoding of Linear B," *Thought* 33 (1958) 255–71.

[3] A revision and expansion of my D.Phil. thesis is published as *A Grammar of the Greek Papyri of the Roman and Byzantine Periods*. Testi e Documenti per lo Studio dell' Antichità 55. I: *Phonology* (Milan: Cisalpino-La Goliardica 1976); II: *Morphology* (1981); III: *Syntax* (in preparation).

Table

1. The phonemic system of Mycenaean Greek:
/ p t k b d g p^h t^h k^h k^w g^w k^{wh} t^s s m n l r h j w; i e a o u ai ei oi ui au eu ou; length; pitch /

2. The phonemic system of Attic Greek of the late fifth century B.C.:
/ p t k b d g p^h t^h k^h s m n l r h; i ɛ a ɔ o y ai ei oi au eu ou; length; 3 syllabic pitches /

3. The phonemic system of New Testament Greek prescinding from Semitic interference:
/ p t k β d g p^h t^h k^h s z m n l r h; i e ɛ a ɔ o u y ai oi au eu ɛu; stress /

4. The phonemic system of Greek papyri of the second-third centuries after Christ with no evidence of bilingual interference from Coptic:
/ p t k β δ γ p^h t^h k^h (f) s z m n l r h j; i e ɛ a o u y au eu ɛu; stress /

5. The phonemic system of Greek papyri of the second–third centuries after Christ with maximum evidence of bilingual interference from Coptic:
/ p t k (t^j) (k^j) β (f) s (ʃ) m n l h j w; i e ɛ a u (or i e a o u); stress /

6. The phonemic system of Greek papyri of the sixth–seventh centuries after Christ with no evidence of bilingual interference:
/ p t k β δ γ f θ x s z m n l r j; i e a o u y; stress /

7. The phonemic system of Modern Greek:
/ p t k b d g v δ γ f θ x s z m n l r j; i e a o u; stress /

the language of a particular time and place, and relative phonetic values for these sounds can be drawn up. For most languages, and Greek is an outstanding example, the original values can be reconstructed by comparative studies of cognate sounds in related languages, in this case the languages of the entire Indo-European family, to within certain definite positions of articulation. With the original sound system thus determined, and the current state of development easily ascertainable from the modern spoken form of the language, the general framework of the sounds of the language over transitional periods is quite clear.

To begin with Mycenaean Greek (stage no. 1 in the Table), you will observe that the Indo-European vowel system, including the original Indo-European diphthongs, has in large measure been preserved in this earliest stage of the Greek language of which we have evidence.[4] The suprasegmental phonemes of quantity and pitch allow for vowel gradation and constitute distinctive features strikingly characteristic of all classical Greek dialects.[5] In consonants, the three series of voiceless, voiced, and voiceless aspirated stops (the first nine phonemes) are indicated (the Indo-European voiced aspirated stops[6]

[4] For Indo-European phonology in relation to subsequent developments within Greek, see Schwyzer and Lejeune at the treatment of individual sounds. C. D. Buck's *Comparative Grammar of Greek and Latin* (Chicago: University Press 1933) is still useful.

[5] See especially Schwyzer I 371–76; Lejeune §§191, 322, 336–50.

[6] The I-E voiced aspirated stops /bh dh gh/ are reflected in Greek in, e.g., the initial sounds of φέρω, θύρα, and χήν respectively.

having already been eliminated), although the syllabary, adapted only imperfectly to Greek, represents the three labial stops by a single symbol, the velar stops by another, and the dental stops by two more.[7] There is no reason to think that the syllabary here reflects the spoken language accurately, for the original Indo-European oppositions among these orders of stops have remained constant right into Modern Greek, even though the voiced stops have uniformly shifted to voiced fricatives and the aspirated stops to voiceless fricatives. Most significant of all in Mycenaean Greek is the presence of the Indo-European labiovelars /k^w g^w k^{wh}/ in words in which their original use was postulated on grounds of comparative grammar.[8] The resolution of these labiovelars into stops of other orders, varying according to dialect and phonetic conditions,[9] took place between the cessation of the Linear B documents and our earliest records of alphabetic Greek writing several centuries later. The labiovelars are followed by an affricate /t^s/, transcribed conventionally from the syllabary by *z*.[10] In standard Mycenaean this phoneme had a voiced allophone [dz], corresponding to a ζ in many Greek words; in substandard Mycenaean it seems to have remained a palatalized velar /k^j/.[11] Both liquids were present in Mycenaean speech, though represented by one set of symbols in writing, which could be equally well transcribed by *l* as by *r*.[12] There is no evidence for psilosis in Mycenaean; although the /h/ is not represented in the syllabary, its presence is postulated in words in which the prehistoric shift of intervocalic /s/ to /h/ is still attested in later dialects, as Laconian.[13] Especially significant is the representation in writing of the semivowels /j/ and /w/, used both in initial position and as vowel glides.[14]

The phonemic system of Attic Greek of the end of the fifth century B.C. (stage no. 2 in the Table) contains the same three orders of voiceless, voiced, and aspirated stops. These last remained occlusives,[15] pronounced like the initial sounds of the English *pin*, *tin*, *kin* respectively and not like fricatives, as in the academic pronunciation of Greek commonly used in Europe and America. Note that there is only the voiceless sibilant /s/; the several sounds that came to be represented by ζ were still double consonants or consonant clusters.[16] The simple vowels were distinguished by quality as well as by quantity; contrary to our traditional academic pronunciation, /ω/ represented a long open /ɔ/ and was not used to represent the long closed /o/ arising from the contraction of two omicrons or

[7] The Linear B syllabary, originally designed for pre-Hellenic languages, possessed a *d* series as well as a *t* series by way of exception; in general, it did not mark oppositions between voiced and voiceless (Lejeune §21).

[8] E.g., Mycenaean *qe-to-ro-* = Homeric πίσυρες = Attic τέτταρες = Latin *quattuor*.

[9] See especially Lejeune, "Elimination des labiovélaires," §§30–41.

[10] E.g., *to-pe-za* = τόρπεζα, *me-zo* = μείζων.

[11] This is indicated by an occasional interchange of symbols of the *z* series with those of the *k* series, e.g., standard *a-ke-ti-ri-ja*, substandard *a-ze-ti-ri-ja* ἀκέστριαι.

[12] E.g., *re-u-ko* = λευκός; *e-re-ta* = ἐρέται.

[13] E.g., *pe-i* = σφέhι; cf. Laconian νικάhāς, etc.

[14] E.g., *ra-wa-ke-si-jo* = λāϝāγέσιος; *wa-na-ka-te-ro* = ϝανάκτερος; *i-ja-te* = ἰατήρ.

[15] Schwyzer I 204–205; Lejeune §22.

[16] Schwyzer I 329–32; Lejeune §§102–108. See further W.K. Mathews, "The Pronunciation of the Attic Greek ζ in the Sixth and Fifth Centuries B.C.," *Lingua* 4 (1954) 63–80; L. Lupaş, *Phonologie du grec attique*. Janua Linguarum. Series Practica, 164 (The Hague & Paris: Mouton 1972) 26–28.

from compensative lengthening. Similarly, η (representing the Attic-Ionic shift of original long α and perhaps pronounced [æ] at this time) was never used to represent the long closed /e/ arising from the contraction of two epsilons or from compensative lengthening. Rather, the digraphs ει and ου were adopted, indicating in turn that these original diphthongs had been reduced to simple long closed vowels, respectively /e/ and /o/, not /u/ as in our academic pronunciation.[17] Upsilon in Attic represented the short or long closed high front vowel /y/.[18] Accent consisted of length and pitch, with quantity dominant and determining poetic meter; stress was subphonemic. Pitch was used in such fashion that each syllable had a rising intonation regardless of quantity or origin, and the main word accent had an intonation rising to about a musical fifth above the ordinary level of the other syllables.[19]

Early in the Koine, a fundamental change took place in Greek accentuation, as Greek came to be spoken by non-native speakers who tended to retain their own accentual patterns, in which stress was dominant over both quantity and pitch, causing in Greek the loss of length as a phoneme. This may be seen in stage no. 3 in the Table, where I present the phonemic system of New Testament Greek. In doing so, I prescind from questions of Semitic interference in the phonology of biblical Greek; although undoubtedly extensive and of considerable importance for New Testament textual criticism, it is difficult to control because of the vagaries of the manuscript tradition. Among the stop consonants, you will notice that the bilabial voiced stop represented by /b/ in stages no. 1 and no. 2 has now shifted to a voiced bilabial fricative /β/, as Spanish intervocalic *b*. Evidence for this shift appears as early as the fifth century B.C. in inscriptions from Laconia and the Argolid and in the next century from Crete; the shift seems to be universal by the beginning of the first century after Christ.[20] The aspirated stops are still occlusives and have not yet shifted to fricatives.[21] There is the addition of a voiced sibilant /z/, as elsewhere in the Koine, with the reduction of the consonant cluster /dz/ or /zd/ to simple /z/, which now frequently interchanges with /s/ before voiced consonants.[22] In the simple vowels, with all loss of quantitative distinction, /i/ is now represented not only by ι but also by ει; /e/ is represented by η, /ϵ/ by ϵ, /ɔ/ by ω, /o/ by ο, /u/ by the former diphthong ου, and /y/ by υ and the former diphthong υι.

In the next stage isolated in the Table (no. 4), reflecting the language of the second and third centuries after Christ in documentary papyri from Egypt containing no evidence of bilingual interference from Coptic, the identification of the two [o] sounds into one /o/ phoneme, represented by either ο or ω without distinction of quantity or quality, may be observed.[23] In this stage also, the diphthongs in /-i/ are eliminated. There has been an identification of the former /ai/ diphthong with the vowel /ϵ/, and of the /oi/

[17] Schwyzer I 191–94; Lejeune §§234, 240–41.
[18] Schwyzer I 181–84; Lejeune §252.
[19] Schwyzer I 180, "Zusatz"; 371–76, 391–95; Lejeune §§191, 322, 336–49, 383.
[20] Schwyzer I 207–208; Lejeune §44.
[21] Gignac, *Grammar* (supra n. 3) I 98–101.
[22] Ibid. 120–24.
[23] Ibid. 275–77.

diphthong with the vowel /y/. This is shown in the papyri by a general confusion of *αι* with *ε* and of *οι* with *υ*.[24] In the consonant system (still no. 4 in the Table), I have chosen to represent the former voiced stop phonemes by voiced fricatives, in accordance with the pronunciation increasingly evidenced by the papyri for these phonemes in positions other than after a nasal,[25] although the stop allophone may still be basic in at least the dental series.[26] The phonemic oppositions among these voiced fricatives and the voiceless and aspirated stops remain intact. It is also now necessary to add a /j/ phoneme, as in Mycenaean Greek, for while there are no longer the diphthongs in /-i/, a consonantal /j/ is now attested by the recognizable shift of paroxytones with an accented penult in /i/ followed by a single vowel to oxytones, as [karðjá] from *καρδία*, or the genitive [kyrjú] *κυρίου*, frequently written *κυροῦ*, as opposed to the nominative [kýris], frequently written *κῦρις*.[27] A borrowed phoneme /f/ should probably also be postulated to account for the pronunciation of the [f] sound of Latin loanwords represented by *φ*, although a spelling pronunciation as an aspirated labial stop is attested sporadically.[28]

In stage no. 5 in the Table, reflecting Greek in Egypt in the second and third centuries after Christ in nonliterary papyri showing the maximum evidence of bilingual interference from Coptic, one can observe a great difference between this phonemic system and the contemporary one represented in no. 4. These two systems of course represent extremes that admit of many intermediate systems in evidence in the documents, omitted for simplification and heightened contrast. In documents showing the maximum divergence from the common phonemic system, there is an absence in consonant phonemes alone of six of the traditional stop, fricative, and sibilant phonemes, and one liquid phoneme /r/, plus an addition of a /w/ phoneme and perhaps also of the parenthesized palatalized dental and velar stop phonemes and a grooved alveopalatal fricative, for which the evidence is either sporadic or indirect.[29] This phonemic system, shown in no. 5 of the Table, is indicated by such documentary evidence as the following. There is widespread confusion of the symbols for both the voiced stops and the aspirated stops with those for the voiceless stops, indicating a plosive quality for all the sounds so represented, and pointing to an identification of these three orders of stops.[30] Similar confusion is found in the interchange of *σ* and *ζ* for the sibilants[31] and of *λ* and *ρ* for the liquids.[32] In vowels, there is a frequent interchange of *α* with *ε* or *ο*,[33] and of *η* not only with *ι* and *ει*, but also with *ε* and especially with *υ*.[34] These identifications appear quite foreign to Greek, but a phonemic analysis of Coptic reveals at once that the most striking anomalies

[24] Ibid. 191–202.
[25] Ibid. 68–76.
[26] Ibid. 75–76.
[27] Ibid. 302–303.
[28] Ibid. 99–100.
[29] See especially the Summary of Consonants, ibid. 178–79.
[30] Ibid. 76–98.
[31] Ibid. 120–24.
[32] Ibid. 102–107.
[33] Ibid. 278–89.
[34] Ibid. 235–49.

in the papyri have their simplest and most adequate explanation through a hypothesis of bilingual interference. There was no phonemic distinction between voiced and voiceless stops in any dialect of Coptic. Aspirated stops were phonemic only in the Bohairic dialect of the Delta, from which area relatively few papyri come. There was no phonemic distinction between voiced and voiceless sibilants, nor between liquids in at least the Fayumic dialect. The Coptic letter ⲏ represented at least two different sounds, and in no dialect of Coptic were there more than two phonemes corresponding to the three Greek phonemes represented by α, ϵ, and ο.[35]

Stage no. 6 in the Table shows a later phonemic structure of the language unaffected by phenomena of bilingual interference in the sixth and seventh centuries after Christ in the early Byzantine period. Again, another phonetic shift is indicated in the consonants. There is evidence that the aspirated stops were now replaced by voiceless fricatives,[36] although the phonemic oppositions remained intact. The /h/ phoneme, which occurred only initially or after a prefix in composition, as in ἀνίστημι, has also been lost.[37] Among the vowels, there has been an identification of the closed /e/ phoneme of earlier stages, represented by η, with the /i/ phoneme,[38] leaving a symmetrical three-height vowel system. The diphthongs in /-u/ are eliminated as unit phonemes because the second element has shifted to a bilabial fricative identical with the phoneme /β/ that corresponds in its oppositions to the original voiced bilabial stop.[39]

Finally, stage no. 7 in the Table shows a phonemic analysis of Modern Greek. The voiced stop phonemes are not part of the inherited phonemic opposition but are modern borrowings with which post-nasal allophones resulting from primary splits from the ancient orders have coincided.[40] There has also been a merger of the /y/ phoneme still preserved in the seventh century with the /i/ phoneme, through unrounding, about the tenth century after Christ.[41] Modern Greek accent, coinciding with the historical pitch marks, is at once musical, quantitative, and intensive; it consists generally of a musical elevation ranging from a third to a fifth, immediately achieved, not ascendant, accompanied by a degree of lengthening and of intensity that is not considerable.[42] The word accent is dominant and forms the metric ictus in poetry.

[35] See especially J. Vergote, *Grammaire copte.* I: *Introduction, phonétique et phonologie* (Louvain: Peeters 1973) 1–59.

[36] Gignac, *Grammar* (supra n. 3) I 98 and n. 2.

[37] Ibid. 133–38.

[38] Ibid. 235–42.

[39] Ibid. 226–34.

[40] See especially A. Thumb, *Handbook of the Modern Greek Vernacular* (Chicago: Argonaut 1964) §15; A. Mirambel, *Grammaire du grec moderne* (Paris: Klincksieck 1949) 21–22.

[41] Schwyzer I 183–84; Lejeune §252.

[42] Mirambel, *La Langue grecque moderne: description et analyse* (Paris: Klincksieck 1959) 27–28; Idem, *Grammaire* (supra n. 40) 18.

Greek is often referred to as a dead language. I think this is a misnomer. The task of the student of language is always to analyze the secondary phenomenon of writing in order to grasp the living reality of speech that lies behind it and which it represents only imperfectly. In applying this principle to Greek, I feel I am being faithful to the spirit of Father Schoder, who always took the greatest care to make the printed texts of Homer and Sappho, Euripides and Thucycides, Demosthenes and Aristotle, come alive for his students.

EXPLORING MEXICAN ARCHAEOLOGY

FRANCIS X. GROLLIG, S.J.

We were honored when the Latin American Studies Committee was invited to participate in Schoderfest. Another section of the field of archaeology, and another area of the world, Mexico, are here to pay homage to the memory of Father Schoder, S.J.

XOCHIMILCO

The waterways of Xochimilco flow among the *chinampas*, the man-made islands. Used in Aztec times to grow food, these islands now provide flowers for the local markets. Each beautifully decorated passenger boat has its own name.

TULA

One Pyramid Temple is at Tula in the State of Hidalgo. The day of the Toltecs, who built Tula, was but a brief time from about A.D. 900 to 1200, when they virtually dominated the central Valley of Mexico. Some think that the Aztecs or their predecessors (perhaps the Chichimecs) were the conquerors of the mighty Toltecs, though no one knows for sure. Toltec influence after the fall of Tula, however, is quite visible when we see their Chacmool (or Chac-Mool), Quetzalcoatl, and ball courts appearing as far away as Yucatan.

Caso gives a picture of a ball game as it is represented in the *Codex Magliabecchiano*, and comments that it "appears very early in the history of Mexico and Central America for we find it being played in the cities of the classical age of the Maya and among the old cultures of Oaxaca. Undoubtedly the Aztecs inherited this game from their predecessors" (Caso, *The Aztecs*, 1958, 78–79). Incidentally, the same *Codex* (from c. 1566) gives us the details for an ancient game, Patolli, that probably came from the Valley of Mexico, and which is now manufactured and sold as a popular table-game, "Patolli" (*Los Codices*, 1979, 108–109). Maybe it also started with the Toltecs at Tula.

The Atlantids at Tula have flat tops. This indicates that these pillars (about 30 feet tall) were used to support the roof of the temple. These colossal Telamon warriors, as they are sometimes called, date back to between A.D. 900 and 1250. They are made of basalt stone and apparently were painted red (Ragghianti, *National Museum*, 1970, 123).

TEOTIHUACAN

Teotihuacan, a true and tremendous city, at its height had about 150,000 inhabitants. With about "2,600 major structures, including markets and apartment compounds" (Meyer, *Teotihuacan*, 1973, 11), it was the greatest urban development in North America. For many, the Pyramid of the Sun at Teotihuacan *is* Mexican archaeology. The tremendous pyramid covers some 12 acres and is about 20 stories high. Since 1967, this has been one of the favorite places in Teotihuacan's justly famous Light and Sound production. It seems that nearly everybody who goes to Mexico City takes a trip to Teotihuacan.

DAIDALIKON: Studies in Memory of Raymond V. Schoder, S.J.

It is quite impossible to give adequate treatment to an archaeological zone like Teotihuacan in a short paper like this. Once, spending a whole day there, I walked 21 miles, but that is nothing compared to the whole decade that Rene Millon used to direct the extensive excavations at this zone (Pfeiffer, *Horizon*, Winter, 1975, 84).

The remains of this magnificent city that covered some ten square miles were first discovered by the Aztecs. With dim beginnings, maybe as early as 300 B.C., it rose to tremendous metropolitan power around A.D. 300 to 600, then collapsed around A.D. 650. About 650 years later the Aztecs found it. They were no archaeologists, and they thought the great mounds over the collapsed buildings were tombs. Who but the gods (they asked themselves), would have tombs that big? So they called their discovery: "Teo-Tihuacan", the City of the Gods (Pfeiffer, *Horizon*, Winter, 1975, 84).

One can examine just a small part of the Temple of Quetzalcoatl, the façade which is adorned with numerous heads of the god (Fernandez, *Mexican Art*, 1967, 22). There, in an oft repeated theme, Tloloc, the Rain God, in the center of the panels has eyes that look like little (or big?) lifesavers. He "was widely venerated by the Teotihuacan peoples. He received the most worthy of the dead in his heaven" (Ragghianti, *National Museum*, 1970, 60). Tlolocan, this heaven of Tloloc, is presented in the "fascinating 'paradise' mural from Tepantitla" (Adams, *Prehistoric Mesoamerica*, 1977, 197). Tloloc is "very probably the most ancient of the gods worshiped by man in Mexico and Central America" (Caso, *The Aztecs*, 1958, 41). The frequently associated god, Quetzalcoatl, the Feathered Serpent, undulates across the bottom of the panel. After the destruction of Teotihuacan in about A.D. 650, the people "scattered in all directions, carrying with them their dominant consuming religion and its focus on the rain deities: Tlaloc in combination with the Feathered Snake" (Stone, *Pre-Columbian Man*, 1972, 130).

The Temple of Quetzalmariposa, the Feathered Butterfly, is at the north end of the Avenue of the Dead. Along here are the giant jaguars in the monumental style of murals developed at Teotihuacan (Adams, *Prehistoric Mesoamerica*, 1977, 198). Much of this temple is reconstructed with the beautiful obsidian disks glowing like eyes in the stone temple walls.

Extensive additions could be made here to comment on the palace residences. For example, there are those uncovered in the early 1930's by Sigvald Linne who unearthed the first one "which turned out to be larger than anyone had expected. At one complex Linne uncovered a conglomeration of 175 rooms built around a network of corridors and encompassing a total of 4,000 square yards" (Meyer, *Teotihuacan*, 1973, 133).

Xochicalco

About 75 miles to the south of Mexico City beyond Cuernavaca is Xochicalco with its splendid Temple of Quetzalcoatl. A fine publication by the Mexican Ministry of Tourism tells us the unique Xochicalco "was a crossroads of Aztec, Toltec, Zapotec, Maya civilizations, all of which are reflected in the decorative details of the main temple. No other site in Mexico documents so many styles of expression" (*Mexico: Major Archeological Sites* in *Archeology: Mexico to Go*, Brochure. 1984).

The Temple of Quetzalcoatl at Xochicalco shows the Toltec Feathered Serpent as it wends its way all around the four sides of the Temple. There are many fabulous representations on the sides of this temple. Among them is a Maya priest-figure in a cross-legged sitting position with words coming out of his mouth. Why do we say "Maya"? We examine carefully the profile of the forehead and the headdress. Here is an example of the easily recognized Maya artificial head-deformation. This was produced by tightly wrapping the head of the infant. We see the resulting high slope of the frontal bone. Barbachano Ponce (*Los Mayos*, 58) notes that "this was thought to be fashionable." Some say deformation was a sign of Maya nobility but others say artificially deformed heads "were so necessary to orthodox Maya ritual" (Stone, *Pre-Columbian Man*, 1972, 136).

Mexico City

The National Museum of Anthropology

Officially inaugurated in 1964, the National Museum of Anthropology in Chapultepec Park is acclaimed by many as the finest anthropology museum in the whole world: it is certainly the finest I have seen. There are many spectacular pieces from virtually each of the major archaeological zones in Mexico. Here are some of my favorites.

The Skull in Disk, for example, was found near the Plaza of the Pyramid of the Sun. It is the first piece pictured in Stuart's *The Mighty Aztecs* (1981, 1). Bernal comments that this "stone disk from Teotihuacan may foreshadow Aztec portrayals of a Lord of the Dead, Mictlantecutli, as a skull with lolling tongue and pleated paper crown," and he adds that the recognition of this symbol as the God of Death was originally made in a 1580 document, *Relacion de Teotihuacan* (Bernal, *100 Masterpieces*, II). It probably was associated with a temple to the same god that stood at Teotihuacan.

Guacamaya de Xochicalco is the classic Head of a Bird. "The guacamaya or macaw is a rare bird associated with the cult of the sun, and was often represented in the markers set into the walls of" the ball courts (Ragghianti, *National Museum*, 1970, 118). One finds it fascinating to note tiny details like the completely carved tongue of the bird. This neat artifact dates back to the 8th or 9th century after Christ and was found in the excavation of the ball court at Xochicalco (Cervantes, *Los Tesoros*, 1978, 31).

Chacmool, associated with human sacrifices, is recumbent and usually has "the tray in her hands on which the still warm hearts of victims were placed" (Wiesenthal, *Yucatan*, 1978, 54). "Chacmool" translates "Red Jaguar." The name was given erroneously but has been kept for this reclining figure (Ivanoff, *Monuments*, 1973, 104).

The Toltec Dancing Jaguar comes from Tula. The jaguar, whose pelt represents the stars in the night sky, is identified with the underworld. This motif, which probably came from between A.D. 900 and 1200, was copied at Chichen Itza when the Toltecs became influential there (Bernal, *100 Masterpieces*, III).

The Aged God of Fire is Olmec. The statue in the Museum was found in the area of Cerro de las Mesas, Veracruz, and is identified as Huehueteotl, the God of Fire, from the final phase of Totonac art (Ragghianti, *National Museum*, 1970, 118–119). There are crosses in the bowl on the top of the head that was for fire. Tongue, beard, and ear spools are elegantly detailed. The piece was quite broken when it was found in 1941. Ignacio Bernal comments (*100 Masterpieces*, XIII) that the figure of this old man with a beard is quite deformed by age.

It might be noted that in the selection of the artifacts included in the volume, *100 Masterpieces of the Mexican National Museum of Anthropology*, the author is careful to point out that in any selection like this "the choice necessarily becomes subjective" (Bernal, *100 Masterpieces*, 17). He is not attempting to define the 100 best pieces in the Museum's collection. I do like some fine pieces, even though Bernal did not place them among his choice 100 masterpieces.

Tenochtitlan

In the very heart of Mexico City, just one block from the Cathedral and the National Presidential Palace are the ruins of the ancient Aztec capital, Tenochtitlan. "Tenochtitlan" is a kind of magical word. It takes us across modern Mexico to ancient Mexico. Tenochtitlan was founded by the Aztecs in A.D. 1325. As you probably know, its site, according to legend, was dictated by the gods who gave the sign: the city would be founded at the place where the Indians would see an eagle holding a snake in its beak and sitting on a cactus. So proud are the Mexicans of this legend that they use this symbolism in their national seal.

It was known for about 60 years that remains of the ancient Tenochtitlan were just across the "Avenida Republica de Argentina", from the cathedral (and one block from the National Palace). It is interesting to see a picture of this tiny little ruin (Wiesenthal, *Mexico City*, 1978, 8) just before a whole city block was torn down to excavate the *Templo Mayor* in the center of Tenochtitlan. The discovery of a third figure of Quetzalcoatl, a figure that did not match the two already found, was a clue to the archaeologists that they were about to find the main temple of the Mexicas, the Aztecs. A typical Aztec temple had a double staircase, surmounted by a double temple. A bit of excavating to the left of this third visible head showed that there was, indeed, another staircase and thus it was the *Templo Mayor*. The real search started with a discovery of Coyolxhaqui that is briefly related: "On February 24, 1978 some Light and Power Company workers happened upon the lower part of a carved stone. Four days later it was unearthed by the archaeologists from the Recovery and Preservation Department of the National Institute of Anthropology and History. Before them was an admirable work of art: the Coyolxauqui" (Cantu, *Art, Great Temple*, 1981, 9). The stone was not buried very deeply by the four centuries since the conquest. And, the author continues: "there, some few centimeters beneath such footsteps, outstretched in her sacred place, lay the dead goddess, the woman warrior abused by fire, cast down headlong, unmoving in the impossible, ill-starred dance of her body violated by destruction, she, mirror and guardian of the final remains of the divine perfection that gave her eternity and death" (Ibid., 16). In passing, we can consider some of the materials recovered here. Scholarly work is necessary to identify the 7,000 artifacts, including temples and complete statues, that appeared among these ruins of Tenochtitlan.

Since 1978, there have been extensive excavations at the very center of Tenochtitlan, the place of the Major Temple. One facet, the Altar of the Skulls, is a stone altar decorated with rows of stone skulls on all four sides. Here were placed the heads of the victims of the Aztecs' human sacrifices. Commenting on this aspect of Aztec life, we find: "Human sacrifice was not performed for the purpose of harming the sacrificed, nor was cruelty or vengeance its objective . . . The victim was considered a messenger to the gods . . . (It) was nothing more than one of many such aberrations which assume a religious guise in the history of mankind" (Caso, *The Aztecs*, 72).

In a country that has developed archaeology to such a vast extent and uses it for a tourist attraction, it is easy to find other archaeological zones close to Tenochtitlan. They may be so simple as the little Shrine to Ehecatl in the Pino Suarez subway station, or they may be so tremendous as the old Aztec market place, Tlatelolco (Wiesenthal, *Mexico City*, 1978, 7–8). Tlatelolco is also known as the "Plaza of the Three Cultures" for here you have the temples, the Church (where Juan Diego, the Indian who received the vision of Guadalupe, was baptized), and the modern high-rise apartment and office complexes: the Aztec, the Spanish, and the Mestizo cultures.

Tenayuca and Santa Cecilia

A few miles to the north of Mexico City we find two more archaeological zones, Tenayuca and Santa Cecilia. There is a fine little Aztec temple at Santa Cecilia. Unique? Yes, this site is unique because here is the only Aztec temple that has been restored completely. But only one (of the two) temples has been restored "with the peculiar Mesoamerican Korbel Arch" (Bloomgarden, *Mexico City*, 1976, 5). It would have been necessary to tear down the Church of Santa Cecilia to restore the other tiny temple because many of the fine stones from the Aztec pyramidal structure were used in the church's walls. About one kilometer away are the better known ruins of Tenayuca. Here, too, there are evidences of the dual temple of the Aztecs. But what makes this zone unique are the cordons of Quetzalcoatls around the base of the dual temple pyramid.

Cholula

In Aztec times the market around the Cholula pyramid, the largest pyramid in the world, "was renowned for jewelry, precious stones, and fine feather work" (Adams, *Prehistoric Mesoamerica*, 1977, 30). Now you can walk one-half of a mile in the passageways that the archaeologists have cleared by excavations inside of this pyramid. Nearly all of the excavating on the outside of the pyramid has been done since I first visited Cholula in 1956. Not much excavating has been done inside the pyramid of Cholula since then, but now there are better lights (and no bare wires) in the tunnels.

Oaxaca

In Mexico, besides numerous site museums, there are also regional museums. On the second floor of the Regional Museum of Oaxaca in the city of Oaxaca is the fabulous Treasure of Tomb no. 7. As you walk past the sign, you walk into a vault that encloses three large rooms. Tomb no. 7, discovered by Alfonso Caso and his crew in 1932 at Monte

Albán, is the richest tomb ever found in North America. Tomb no. 7 had a fabulous wealth of art objects including "over five hundred objects of gold, silver, turquoise, jade, pearls, rock crystal, and so forth" (Covarrubias, *Indian Art*, 1957, 144). A good educated guess seems to indicate that perhaps the Mixtecs were being attacked by the Zapotecs, and hid all of their jewelry in this tomb before they fled. They hoped to recover it when they returned: they never came back.

A crystal cup is just one of the treasures from Tomb no. 7 of Monte Albán that caught my attention. When I first saw this collection in 1956, it was estimated that these displayed items had a market value of about one million dollars. Photographic tripods, of course, are forbidden in this Museum. But Father Schoder taught me how to use just a string, suspended from the camera, to get pictures of artifacts like the crystal cup where the use of a flash is also forbidden.

THE OLMECS

One of the fabulous things about Mexican archaeology is the incredible number of distinctly different cultures that flourished in this area. First, there were the Olmecs. "Their name means 'dweller in the land of rubber,' and this suggests an origin in tropical country associated with rubber trees. Their generally accepted homeland is southern Veracruz, Mexico, where as early as 1200 B.C. they had attained such a superior standard of living that they can be considered the cultural forbearers of Meso-America" (Stone, *Pre-Columbian Man*, 1972, 39). This is the culture that produced the Olmec Heads.

About 18 colossal Olmec heads, weighing up to nearly 25 tons each, have been found in the area around the Isthmus of Tehuantepec and the Gulf of Mexico's coastal region. Some consider these to represent *jefes*, leaders, of the villages which were given a certain importance just by the presence of the great stone heads (Cervantes, *Los Tesoros*, 1978, 17). I have seen at least four of them. One Olmec Head is located in the park at the center of Villahermosa. Another stands out in the Archaeological Park outside of Villahermosa. This one, we are told, "represents a chieftain wearing a leather helmet, the symbol of authority" (Fernandez, *Mexican Art*, 1967, 9 and 30). Two more are in Mexico City's National Museum of Anthropology. Of course, there are copies of these Olmec Heads in many places like the campus of Universidad Iberoamericana and the Sunken Garden Park on "Avenida Insurgentes Sur."

The heads "were originally set on low bases having the form of a truncated pyramid" as is the one outside of the Anthropology Museum (Ragghianti, *National Museum*, 1970, 32–33). It is easy to compare them. "Two characteristics of these sculptures are immediately evident: in the first place, they are not more or less mythical beings, endowed with feline features or wearing masks, but realistic statues, and secondly, these heads are at one and the same time very much alike and highly individualized. Their similarities are quite obvious . . . the same broad faces with full cheeks, the same fleshy protuberance just above the bridge of the nose, the same almond shaped eyes. The nose is large, the lips are full, the mouth generally bow-shaped with down-turned corners" (Soustelle, *The Olmecs*, 1984, 44.) The influence of the Olmecs, generally associated with sites like La

Venta, actually extended from Veracruz and Tabasco all the way up to Monte Albán, near Oaxaca, and Tlatilco, next to Mexico City in the Federal District.

THE MAYA

To move into an entirely different culture, a most fascinating component of Mexican archaeology, we can go to the Yucatan and the land of the Maya. "There are more than 50,000 archeological centres in Yucatan preserving the traces of Maya history. The immense temple-cities of the Mayas were at the same time religious and civic centers. Legions of specialized workmen toiled in the construction of these enormous buildings" (Wiesenthal, *Yucatan*, 1978, 48).

Edzna

In one of the Mexican National Tourist Bureau's fine publications, we find that Edzna (or Etzna) is "a very old Maya city first inhabited in 600 B.C. In the Maya world, it was known by the rather disconcerting name of 'House of Grimaces.' Well worth exploring is the 100 foot tall Temple of the Five Stories, constructed in A.D. 650. Edzna is a Classic Maya site, and there are many outlying ruins in its three square mile area, some still overgrown" (*Mexico: Major Archeological Sites. Mexico: Archeology*, Ministry of Tourism, 1985. Brochure). Sometimes we do not attribute city planning to the Maya, but Edzna certainly deserves credit for this because it is "beautifully planned with large squares and open spaces" (Wiesenthal, *Yucatan*, 1978, 74). A few of the temples have been manicured by the archaeologists.

Chichen Itza

Looking through the arch of the doorway of the Hotel Mayaland, one can see the Observatory at Chichen Itza. I looked through that doorway for the first time in 1958. Twenty-four years later, I had the same view again! It is unforgettable to see ancient and modern Mexico in such a single glance.

One unique item in the Maya world is the Caracol, the "Snail," the Maya Observatory at Chichen Itza. Unique? Yes, this is the only round building in all of Mayaland. It is considered to be a Toltec building (Ivanoff, *Monuments*, 1973, 114), and elsewhere we read that the "windows operating out of the dome from the interior spiral stair were used for astronomical sightings" (Henderson, *Ancient Maya*, 1981, 216). Finally, an even more specific analysis of Maya astronomy tells us that the Carocol was "a tower destined for use in the observations of the heavens. By means of openings in the upper part, certain points of astronomical observation could be fixed; one of the windows looked to the geographic South, and the sunset could be observed through the others during the vernal and autumnal equinoxes, also the setting of the moon on the same dates" (Wiesenthal, *Yucatan*, 1978, 54).

An intriguing sight at Chichen Itza is the Cenote, the Well of Sacrifice, of the Maya Indians. Ivanoff (*Monuments*, 1973, 113), notes: "This circular, natural well seems manmade. It has a diameter of two hundred feet and its walls rise sixty-five feet above the greenish water . . . The vestiges of a steam bath on its edge testify that sacrifices were probably accompanied by purification rites." Wiesenthal (*Yucatan*, 1978, 56) adds: "Archeological exploration has revealed that it was used for human sacrifice." Some 40 skeletons (men, women, and children) were brought out of the well by Edward Thompson in his (1904–1907) excavations and dredgings. Of course these skeletons were accompanied with objects of gold, jade, copper, flint and other stones. The nearby High Priest Temple is a splendid (or horrible) example of early and unprofessional endeavors in Maya archaeology. To get into the solid and impregnable wall, dynamite was used.

A Toltec-Maya Jaguar is in the Temple of the Jaguar at Chichen Itza. The Temple is just outside of the Ball Court and the Jaguar was an altar. Perhaps it was to this altar that the hearts of the victims were brought. The human sacrifice factor is vividly portrayed in bas-relief on the walls on both sides of the ball court. We do not know for sure if it was the winning or the loosing captain who was decapitated after a ball game. But, after his heart was given to the Jaguar, his head was impaled on top of the nearby Altar of the Skulls (Ivanoff, *Monuments*, 1973, 107–112).

Uxmal

One carved Maya cross lay quite unnoticed in the courtyard of the Hotel Nututun near the ruins of Uxmal. Incidentally, evidence like this makes it easy to say: Yes, as a geometric form, the cross is certainly pre-Columbian, though it did not have Western civilization's religious signification. Many pieces like this have been removed from the archaeological zones. Some are seen just lying around; many more have been incorporated into "lesser" buildings than those for which they were originally carved by the Maya artists.

One of the first books that I ever had on Mexican archaeology, given to me in Mexico City in 1961, came from the Petroleos Mexicanos, and had the simple title, *Archeology in Mexico Today*. In it (page 63) I saw a picture of "The House of the Doves, Uxmal." I never dreamed that 23 years later I would get to the Yucatan to take a slide of this very same archaeological monument. There are some 40 portals in the wall of the Maya House of the Doves. Obviously, it is just one wall of a large building that has collapsed. But it still has a beautiful roof-comb. From one vantage point you can look at the inside of the front wall of this part of the structure and see one-half of the fine corbel arched room ceilings. Arches like this were common in Maya burial vaults, too. Moreover, this corbeled arch, typical of lowland Maya architecture, is found combined with a horizontal passage, a typical highland Maya trait, at Varajonal (Stone, *Pre-Columbian Man*, 1972, 130 and 136).

The Maya Palace of the Governors at Uxmal in the Yucatan is rated by some as "the most beautiful pre-Columbian building in America" and the top of its façade "is ten feet high and runs all around the Palace façade for a length of 2,275 feet" (Ivanoff, *Monuments*, 1973, 139). The two headed figure in front of the Palace is a monolithic throne which measures 39 inches across and stands 24 inches high.

Perhaps for many the Temple of the Magician is the symbol of Uxmal. It is also called the Wizard's Pyramid and the Divine Pyramid which "dominates the whole city with its impressive oval structure" (Wiesenthal, *Yucatan*, 1978, 66). Certainly it is one of the fabulous ruins in the archaeological zone. *Archeology in Mexico Today* (page 63) says, "The style of architecture and decoration at Uxmal is different from Chichen Itza [and is] no less beautiful and perhaps more forceful." The oval shape makes it unique. "The Pyramid of the Magician, supposedly built by a magic dwarf in a single day, is actually five buildings built one over another, standing more than 100 feet high" (*Mexico: Yucatan Peninsula*, Mexican National Tourist Council, 1975. Brochure).

Kabah

The Maya word for "arch," Kabah, is the name of one Maya archaeological zone. Here the arch, which is about 14 feet across, is unique. It is not a part of a building, it is the entrance to the town: "this monument marks Kabah's end of a paved causeway that connects the center with Uxmal" (Henderson, *Ancient Maya*, 1981, 190). An arch like this is unique, but the causeway is not, for "all of the Maya cities of the Puuc region were joined together by so-called *sacbeob* or sacred roadways. The first Spaniards to arrive in the country spoke of these roads and called them 'beautiful, broad and flat'" (Wiesenthal, *Yucatan*, 1978, 66).

Xlapac

At the entrance to the archaeological zone of Xlapac there is a fine example of a modern Maya house. If, on your next trip to Mexico, you do not have the opportunity to visit Xlapac, you can find a copy of a similar modern Maya house in Mexico City on the second floor of the National Museum of Anthropology. Those house models are complete, and you can see the cooking and sleeping facilities as well as the suspension of items from supporting roof poles (Cervantes, *Los tesoros*, 1978, 86).

If you want to explore ancient and modern Mexico, you can do so (in about a week!) in this Museum which has its fine collection of archaeological materials on the first floor. The second floor is dedicated to a superb assemblage of ethnographic materials. In a neat spatial distribution pattern, the modern Xlapac living people are portrayed on the second floor just about above the Xlapac who occupied the same places in prehistoric times. In those Xlapac ruins are some typical elephantine noses of the Puuc Maya style. They are particularly prominent on the corners of the Palace. The "Puuc structures are floridly decorated with rain god masks and earth monster façades. They are also characterized by alteration of the carved mosaic zones with severe or undecorated zones. Columns seem to set Puuc apart as well" (Adams, *Prehistoric Mesoamerica*, 1977, 151).

Sayil and Labna

The Puuc section of Mayaland is below Uxmal and is now served by the new "Puuc Route". This road leads to Xlapak, Sayil, and Labna—three archaeological zones that we visited in one day in both of our 1982 and 1984 Loyola Mayaland Tours.

"The Sayil Palace presents a completely new aspect of Maya architecture. The edifice (276 feet by 130 feet wide) has two stories; more precisely, it is built on two levels. The upper floor is set back from the lower one and rests on a nucleus of stones and cement, which act as a terrace. Chac masks, and other motifs characteristic of the Puuc . . . style alternate harmoniously with the façades of the palace . . . The Maya arch at Labna serves as a passage between two building complexes. It is thirteen feet long and ten feet deep and is flanked by two small halls . . . Sharply protruding cornices frame a mosaic frieze that is reminiscent of Uxmal . . . Greek style fluting, with a background of small columns, decorates the rear façade" (Ivanoff, *Monuments*, 1973, 155).

Palenque

The magnificent pyrimadal building at Palenque was called the Temple of the Inscriptions before it was discovered that it contained the incredible tomb of Lord Pacal. Actually, it is "the only monument in Maya architecture which is both a pyramid and a tomb" (Wiesenthal, *Yucatan*, 1978, 76). Here is one description: "The Temple of the Inscriptions contains the tomb of Pacal with a massive stone sarcophagus where archeologist Albert Ruz found a skeleton covered with almost one thousand pieces of jade under the 5-ton stone lid carved with hieroglyphs and a portrait of Pacal" (*Mexico: Archeology*, Consejo Nacional de Turismo. Brochure). Possibly the finest piece found in this tomb was the mask of Lord Pacal. "It was found broken in pieces, but has been perfectly reconstructed with all the mosaic pieces put together" (Fernandez, *Mexican Art*, 1967, 30). It is sad to mention that this human mask was stolen from the National Museum of Anthropology in Mexico City in December, 1985. It was made of about "200 pieces of jade, with eyes made of obsidian on a base of shell". This description and a picture of the Palenque mask can be seen individually among the 140 stolen pieces in the volume, (Museo Nacional de Antropologia, *Piezas arqueologicas robadas*, I.N.A.H., 1986, cover and 40).

Looking down from the Temple of the Inscriptions at Palenque, you see the Palace. The five-floor, 49-foot Tower in the Palace is unique in Maya sites. Our guide said that it was used as an astronomical observatory since the sun comes through the east-west windows only on the days of the equinox. Henderson describes the Palace as "a maze of interior courts and subterranean passages [which] is Palenque's most unusual building . . . A single glyph for the planet Venus painted on one of the landings of the Tower's interior stair may indicate that this was an astronomical observatory" (*Ancient Maya*, 1981, 177). In the Mexican National Tourist Bureau's film, *Sentinels of Silence*, narrated by the late Orson Wells, you descend in a helicopter into the courtyard of the Palace, which is "the largest single structure in this architectural complex" (Ivanoff, *Monuments*, 1973, 68).

Tulum

Eastern Yucatan has magnificent sandy beaches where one can just sigh and enjoy the white sand, sailboats, and picturesque clouds. Seventy miles south of Cancun is Tulum on the Caribbean. This first Mexican city discovered by the Spanish in 1517 is unique: it is the only walled coastal Maya city. (Wiesenthal, *Yucatan*, 1978, 74–75). The buildings have an odd architectural characteristic: the walls are slightly flared upward like some Greek columns (Ivanoff, *Monuments*, 1973, 167).

The main building of Tulum, El Castillo, the Castle, is also known as the Temple of Kukulkan, which is "the Maya name for Quetzalcoatl" (Adams, *Prehistoric Mesoamerica*, 1977, 237). Interestingly enough, the front of the castle does not face the Caribbean, but rather faces into the walled city. An inscription, which records a date translated 29 January, A.D. 654, places Tulum clearly in the classical Maya period, even though some of the monuments have a Toltec inspired nature as Ivanoff points out (*Monuments*, 1973, 170).

The Sacred Well at Tulum was a source of fresh water that was so necessary in this Maya city. One publication, of the Consejo Nacional de Turismo, says of Tulum "Most of the present structures are dated between A.D. 1200 and 1500 and several reflect a definite Toltec influence from that period. More than 50 buildings have been identified and many are well-preserved" (*Mexico: Archeology*, n.d., Brochure).

Afterword

This brief account passes over many aspects of a few archaeological zones. We have chosen to use some of the, perhaps, lesser seen or known places as we have been "Exploring Mexican Archaeology" to honor Father Schoder, S.J. We have formatted the slides and the complete paper used for the Schoderfest presentation onto a videotape, the first copy of which was happily presented to Father Schoder. There Dr. Susan Cavallo, the Director of the Latin American Studies Program, provides the introduction and the dedication to Father Raymond V. Schoder, S.J.

BIBLIOGRAPHY

Adams, Richard E.W. *Prehistoric Mesoamerica*. Boston: Little, Brown. 1977.

Archeology in Mexico Today. Mexico, D.F.: Petroleos Mexicanos. (n.d.).

Barbachano Ponce, Manuel. *Los Mayos. The Manuel Barbachano Ponce Mayan Art Collection. A Catalogue*. Rothmans. Canada: Pall Mall. (n.d.).

Bernal, Ignacio. *100 Masterpieces of the Mexican National Museum of Anthropology*. Mexico, D.F.: Jose Bolea 1969.

Bloomgarden, Richard. *The Easy Guide to Mexico City, Archeological Sites and Museums*. Mexico, D.F.: Lithografica Turmex. 1976.

Cantu, Garcia. *The Art in the Great Temple, Mexico: Tenochtitlan*. Text by Ruben Bonifaz Nuno. Photography by Fernando Robles. Mexico, D.F.: Instituto Nacional de Antropologia e Historia. 1981.

Caso, Alfonso. *The Aztecs, People of the Sun*. Illustrated by Miguel Covarrubias. Translated by Lowell Dunham. Norman: Oklahoma. 1958.

Cervantes, Maria Antonieta. *Los tesoros del antiguo Mexico*. 2nd ed. Museo Nacional de Antropologia. Barcelona: Geocolor 1978.

Covarrubias, Miguel. *Indian Art of Mexico and Central America*. New York: Knopf. 1957.

Fernandez, Justino. *Mexican Art*. Revised edition. Photographs by Constantino Reyes-Valerio. Feltham, Middlesex: Paul Hamlyn. 1967.

Henderson, John S. *The World of the Ancient Maya*. Ithaca: Cornell. 1981.

Ivanoff, Pierre. *Monuments of Civilization: Maya*. New York: Grosset & Dunlap. 1973.
Los codices de Mexico. Instituto Nacional de Antropologia e Historia. Mexico, D.F.: Imprenta Madero. 1979.
Mexico: Archeology. Secretaria de Turismo. Mexico, D.F.: Consejo Nacional de Turismo. (n.d.).
Mexico: Major Archeological Sites. Archeology: Mexico to Go. Mexico, D.F.: Ministry of Tourism. 1984.
Mexico: Major Archeological Sites. Mexico: Archeology. Mexico, D.F.: Ministry of Tourism. 1985.
Mexico: Yucatan Peninsula. Beverly Hills: Mexican National Tourist Council. 1987.
Mexico: Yucatan Peninsula. Mexico, D.F.: Secretaria de Turismo. (n.d.).
Meyer, Karl E. *Teotihuacan*. New York: Newsweek. 1973.
Museo Nacional de Antropologia. *Piezas arqueologicas robadas*. Mexico, D.F.: Instituto Nacional de Antropologia e Historia. 1986.
Pfeiffer, John. "The Life and Death of a Great City", *Horizon* 17, no. 1. (Winter) 1975.
Ragghianti, Carlo Ludovico and Licia Ragghianti Collobi (texts). *National Museum of Anthropology, Mexico City*. Great Museums of the World. New York: Newsweek. 1970.
Soustelle, Jacques. *The Olmecs: The Oldest Civilization in Mexico*. Translated from the French by Helen R. Lane. Garden City, N.Y.: Doubleday. 1984.
Stone, Doris. *Pre-Columbian Man Finds Central America*. Cambridge, Mass.: Peabody Museum. 1972.
Stuart, Gene S. *The Mighty Aztecs*. Washington, D.C.: National Geographic Society. 1981.
Wiesenthal, M. *Mexico City*. New York: Geocolor. (Crown). 1978.
Wiesenthal, M. *Yucatan and the Maya Civilization*. New York: Crown. 1978.

GREECE AND THE NEAR EAST: ART AND ARCHAEOLOGY

Eleanor Guralnick

The task of the archaeologist is to reconstruct history for times and places where written records do not exist or are insufficient. Too often the archaeological evidence from a single site is also insufficient to allow a clear picture of the development of complex phenomena such as international trade. To understand such issues it is essential to search out and order many kinds of information, including artifacts from many places. A full discussion of the relations between Greece and the Near East during the first half of the first millennium B.C. is beyond the scope of a brief article. What is possible to offer here is an overview of the kinds of evidence that archaeologists bring into consideration as they investigate the archaeological evidence for early contact and trade between Greece and the Near East and the art historical consequences of that contact for the development of Greek art.

A Near Eastern contribution to the art of archaic Greece has been accepted since 1912 when Frederik Poulsen's book, *Der Orient und die frühgriechische Kunst*, was published in Germany by Teubner. Using the limited evidence then available, Poulsen documented aspects of the Phoenician contribution and suggested relationships between Neo-hittite and Assyrian art and Greek art. Today we have a much broader knowledge of Near Eastern trade contacts with Greece (Fig. 1). Artifacts were imported into Greece from as far east as Luristan, as far north as the Caucasus and Urartu, from Assyria, Syria and Phoenicia, and from many Anatolian kingdoms, Neo-hittite, Phrygian, and Lydian. Greek art of the Orientalizing period, the seventh century B.C., is universally acknowledged to have incorporated motifs from the art of the Near East. It is not always recognized that the Geometric art of the eighth century B.C. already exhibits some motifs reflecting a Near Eastern connection. As we shall see, the earliest major eastern import after the Dark Age may have arrived in Athens ca. 950–900 B.C. Therefore, an eighth century reflection of the Near East in Greek art should not be surprising.

First let us look at the historical records. Herodotos wrote of the events leading to the Persian Wars. He focused mainly on Greek interaction with the peoples of Anatolia and on their late sixth century B.C. conquerors, the Persians. His accounts of the Anatolian kings tell of their dedications at Greek sanctuaries. Midas the Phrygian is said to have dedicated a throne at Delphi (Hdt. 1.14). The official inscriptions of the Assyrian king Sargon II mention a Mita of Muski who has generally been taken to be the same as Midas. If this is so, then Midas was a powerful ruler by 716 B.C., the fifth year of Sargon's reign.[1] He is mentioned repeatedly in Sargonid inscriptions and probably continued to rule

[1] D.D. Luckenbill, *Ancient Records of Assyria and Babylonia* II (Chicago: University Press 1926) 4, 7, 8, 11, 21, 22, 27, 36, 41, 51, 61, 111.

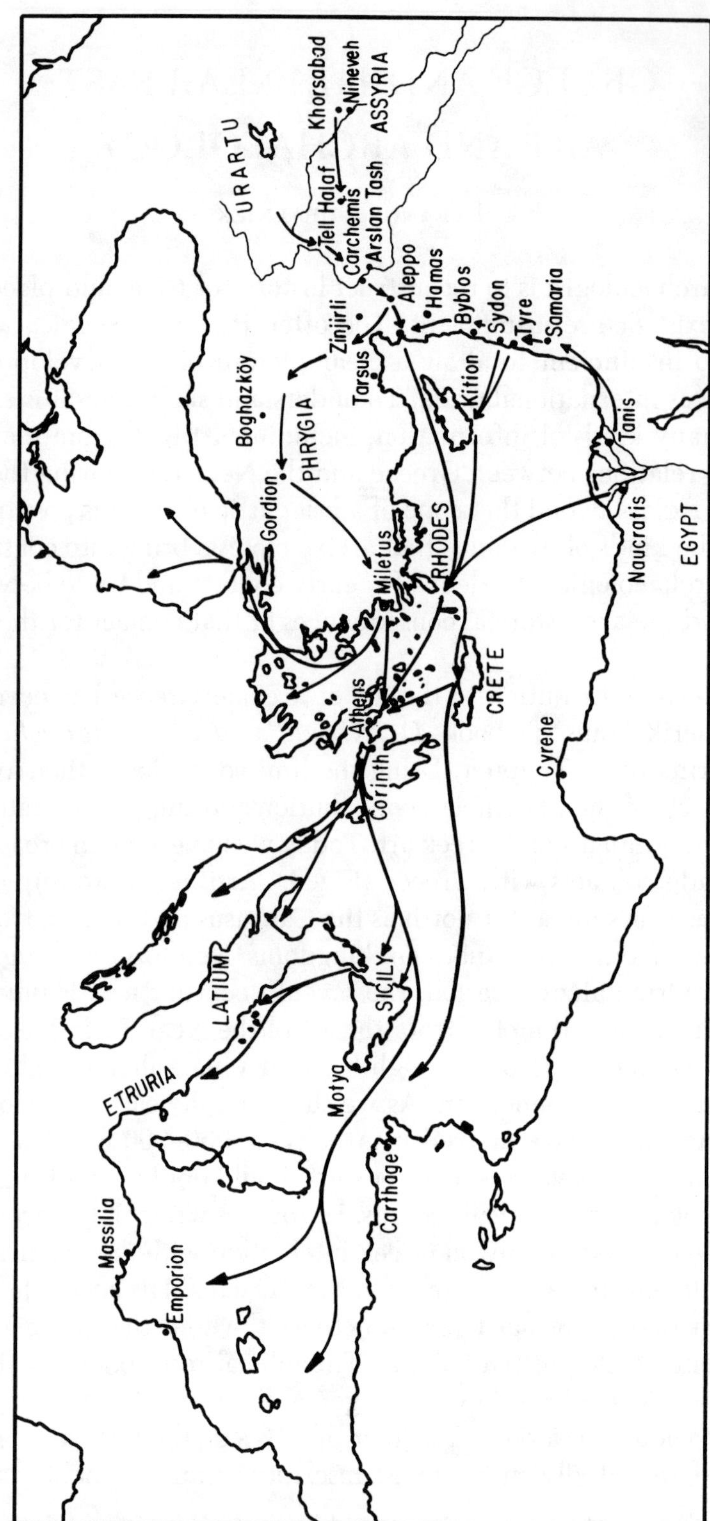

FIG. 1. Geometric Greece overseas trade routes.

through the end of the eighth century B.C., possibly into the early seventh. Gyges the Lydian, who died in 652 B.C., is said to have given much more than 30 talents of gold (Hdt. 1.14). Alyattes, who ruled Lydia perhaps ca. 600 B.C., was said to be the second Lydian Prince to give gifts to Delphi. His major gifts were a very large pure silver bowl and a remarkable iron stand, the work of the Ionian Glaukos of Chios (Hdt. 1.25). Croesus the Lydian is reported to have given gifts to Apollo at Delphi on more than one occasion. One such set of gifts is said to have included a sacrifice of 300 of every kind of beast, golden goblets, couches, and robes and vests of purple (Hdt. 1.50–52). Also he is said to have given 117 ingots of pale gold, a statue of a lion weighing 10 talents of refined gold, two enormous bowls, one of silver holding 600 amphorae and one of gold holding more than 5000 gallons and weighing 8 talents, 42 minae, 4 silver casks, 2 lustral vases, many round silver bowls, a female figure in gold some 4.5 feet in height, and the necklace and belt of his wife (Hdt. 1.51). Unfortunately not one of these early dedications has survived.

All of this suggests good friendly relationships between Greece and Anatolia during the centuries before Herodotos' own time. Except for a few brief anecdotes he tells us little which is clearly related to Greek Orientalizing or Geometric art, or the history of these times (Hdt. 4.152). Homer, writing perhaps about 700 B.C., makes brief mention of Phoenicians as traders (*Il.* 23. 740–45). Hesiod the Boeotian, son of an immigrant merchant from Kyme in Anatolia, himself ventured only across the narrow Euripus to participate in a poetry recitation contest and advises other Greeks to remain at home tilling the soil and foregoing overseas adventures (*W&D* 618–94). The earliest surviving literature offers very little real insight into the precise nature of trade and political interaction between early Greece and the Near East. Only the archaeological record can illuminate this question from a Greek perspective.

On the other hand, Near Eastern cuneiform inscriptional records speak repeatedly of contacts with "peoples from the islands of the west." It seems probable that at least some of these people are Greeks. The earliest references occur during the eighth century B.C. in Neo-Assyrian official letters from the reign of Tiglath-Pilesar III and records of Sargon II at Khorsabad. These refer to peoples called by Luckenbill "Iamana" and "Iawana" who lived in the "western sea" and are generally identified as the Ionians.[2] These and other inscriptions tell of battle, conquest, and paying of tribute. For instance, Luckenbill translates one passage as:

> And seven kings of Ia', a district of Iatnana (Cyprus),
> whose distant abodes are situated a seven days' journey
> in the sea of the setting sun, and the name of whose
> land, since the far-off days of the moon-god's time
> (era), not one of the kings, my fathers, who lived
> before my day, had heard, (these kings of Ia') heard

[2] See J.A. Brinkman, "The Akkadian Words for 'Ionia' and 'Ionian'," pp. 53–71 above. Recent scholarship has modified the reading of these names. Read "Yamnaya" (probably pronounced Yawnaya) for "Iamana" and "Iawana." Read "Yadnana" for "Iatnana" and "Atnana," and "Ya" for "Ia." These are separate names for three distinct and separate entities.

> from afar, in the midst of the sea, of the deeds which I was performing in Chaldea and the Hittite-land, their hearts were rent, fear fell upon them, gold, silver, (furniture) of maple (?) and boxwood, of the workmanship of their land, they brought before me in Babylon.[3]

True, there are no earlier direct references to the place "Ia'", however, the annals of Assurnasirpal II, 883–859 B.C., say that "The tribute of the kings of the seacoast, of the people of Tyre, Sidon, Gebail (Byblos), Mahalata, Maisa, Kaisa, Amurru, and Arvad, which lies in the midst of the sea. . .I received tribute from them. . .."[4] Arvad would seem to be a city on an island in the Mediterranean sea. Some modest contact or gift exchange between Assyria and a location in the Mediterranean sea is part of the ninth-century official Assyrian historical record. The most unequivocal and tangible evidence for an Assyrian presence in the west is the stele of Sargon II, 721–705 B.C., excavated on the island of Cyprus, and now housed in the Pergamon Museum in Berlin.[5]

In Greece, the eighth century was a time of renaissance. The archaeological record suggests that this century saw an end to the Dark Age which had followed the Mycenaean-Minoan civilization. Population was growing; technology was developing. Colonies of Greeks were settling on the eastern shores of the Aegean. The first trading emporia were established, at Pithecusae[6] in the Bay of Naples in the west, and at Al-Mina[7] on the Syro-phoenician coast in the east. Both were established about the same time as the conventional date for the first Olympic games, 776 B.C., or earlier. Near Eastern artifacts were brought into Greece still earlier than the establishment of these trading settlements. Although Greek trade to the Near East seems to have been mainly perishable goods which have not survived, Greek pots and sherds have been found at many sites (Fig. 2). Proto-geometric pottery of the tenth and ninth centuries B.C., has been excavated at Nineveh (Iraq), Hama (Syria), and Tell Abu Hawam (Israel). Geometric pottery of the ninth and eighth centuries B.C. has been found at the Greek emporion Al-Mina, Megiddo, and Askalon on the Syro-phoenician coast. Eighth and seventh century B.C. pottery has been found at a number of sites both on the coast and inland in country dominated by the Hittites. These sites include Sakcegeuzi, Carchemish, Tell Tainat, Çatal Hüyük, Aleppo, Neirab, Samaria, Tell Sukas, Deve Hüyük, and Ras Shamra.[8]

In contrast, the archaeological record in Greece suggests an extensive trade bringing luxury goods from many parts of the Near East to be dedicated as offerings at several

[3] Luckenbill (supra n. 1) 36, with other references to Ia, Iatnana, and Iamana on pp. 13, 22, 26, 31, 40, 41, 46, 50, 51, 52, 54, 61, 102–103, 105.

[4] Ibid. I, 166.

[5] Ibid. 100–103; E. Schrader, *Die Sargonstele des berliner Museums* (Berlin: Akademie der Wissenschaften 1882).

[6] J. Boardman, *Greeks Overseas* (London: Thames and Hudson 1980) 165–68 for extensive references to source publications.

[7] Ibid. 39–46.

[8] C. Clairmont, "Greek Pottery from the Near East," *Berytus* 11–12 (1954–1955) 85–141, pls. 20–25.

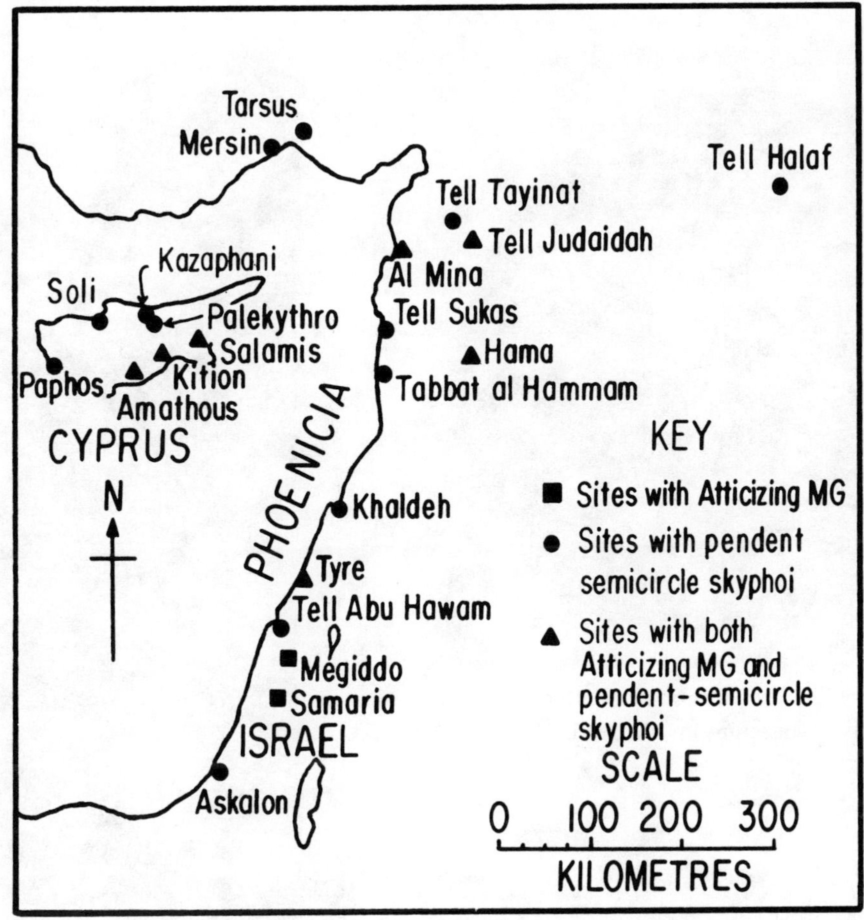

Fig. 2. Greek Middle Geometric exports to the Near East.

major sanctuaries. Relatively few artifacts were actually in everyday use. Some were buried with the dead as funeral offerings. Perhaps the earliest major example of Near Eastern bronze work excavated in Greece is the bronze bowl (Fig. 3, Pl. 12a)[9] with central rosette and surrounding frieze decorated with six male figures herding bulls, lions and goats. The frieze is framed with guilloche pattern. This repoussé hammered bowl of North Syrian workmanship is similar to others excavated on Cyprus. It was found in grave 42 of the Kerameikos cemetery at Athens. The Greek pottery found with the bowl was made very early in the Middle Geometric period and belongs to the late ninth or very early eighth century. The bowl itself was made earlier, some time between 950 and 900 B.C. The date of its import into Greece would seem to coincide approximately with

[9] A.M. Snodgrass, *The Dark Age of Greece* (Edinburgh: University Press 1971) fig. 56; J.N. Coldstream, *Geometric Greece* (New York: St. Martin's 1977) fig. 15; G. Markoe, *Phoenician Bronze and Silver Bowls from Cyprus and the Mediterranean* (Berkeley: California 1985) 203, 312–14, 149.

PLATE 12

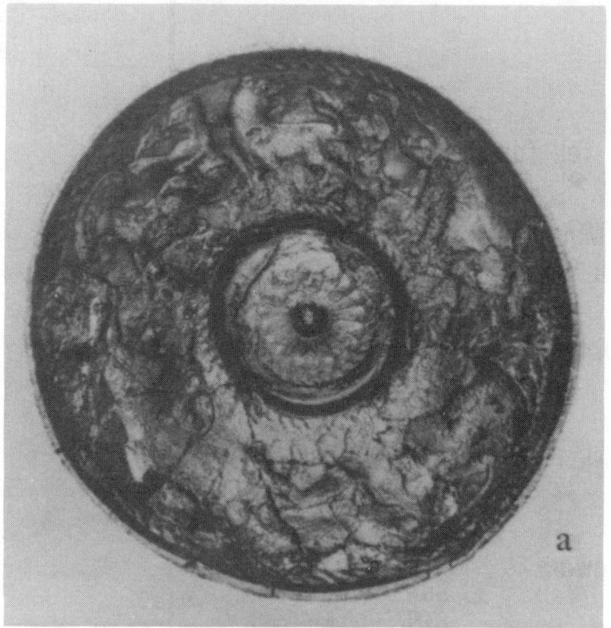

PLATE 12a. Phoenician bowl. Bronze. Ninth century B.C. Athens, Kerameikos Musseum, Inv. No. M5.

12b. Neo-hittite plaque. Bronze. Olympia. Eighth century B.C.

12c. Assyrian rider on camel. Bronze. Rhodes. London WA 135845. Bronzes Catalogue 222.

FIG. 3. Phoenician bowl. Bronze. From the Athenian Kerameikos. Ninth century B.C. Athens, Kerameikos Museum Inv. No. M5. Drawn after Kubler, *Kerameikos* V.1, fig. 5.

the founding of Al-Mina.[10] Its find place suggests that the earliest foreign acquisitions were by private individuals for private use.

Most fine foreign imports after the middle of the eighth century B.C. seem to have been dedicated as votive offerings at major Greek sanctuaries. Splendid bronzes and ivories of Near Eastern origin have been excavated from sacred ground at Olympia, Delphi, Delos, Crete, Rhodes, and Samos. The following are a few examples from among the many possible bronze imports. From Olympia there is a fine Late Hittite repoussé plaque (Pl. 12b) dated to ca. 700 B.C.[11] An Assyrian cast bronze male rider on a kneeling camel (Pl. 12c), dated to the seventh century was excavated in Rhodes.[12] A cast bronze Assyrian Ashur type cauldron attachment (Pl. 13a, b), dated 700–650 B.C., was excavated at Delphi.[13] These are simply examples selected from those which could have been catalogued, space permitting. The recent series of publications of imported artifacts from Samos[14] has suggested that this site be used as an exemplar illustrating the broad geographic distribution of the manufacturing workshops for imported artifacts excavated in Greece. The deposits in the Heraion of Samos provide an unusually precise chronology. The artifacts are from closed or sealed and undisturbed contexts dated by both Greek

[10] Boardman (supra n. 6) 43.

[11] P. Demargne, *The Birth of Greek Art* (New York: Golden Press 1964) fig. 422.

[12] Boardman (supra n. 6) fig. 56.

[13] E. Kunze, *Kretische Bronzereliefs* (Stuttgart: Kohlhammer 1931) Beilage 6.

[14] B. Freyer-Schauenburg, *Elfenbeine aus dem samischen Heraion* (Hamburg: Cramm, de Gruyter 1966); U. Jantzen, *Ägyptische und orientalische Bronzen aus dem Heraion von Samos*, Samos VIII (Bonn: Habelt 1972).

PLATE 13a, b. Assyrian cauldron attachment. Bronze. Delphi. Seventh century B.C.

13c. Assyrian god wearing horned crown. Bronze. Samos. Eighth century B.C.

13d. Assyrian man with seated dog. Bronze. Samos. Seventh century B.C.

PLATE 14

PLATE 14a. Luristan pitcher. Bronze. Samos. Eighth century B.C.

14b. Luristan horse trapping. Bronze. Samos. Eighth century B.C.

pottery sealed with the imports and by stylistic analysis with similar artifacts from the source location. The latter can occasionally be dated by association with inscriptional data. These circumstances together seem to provide artifacts from the Samian deposits with the least problematical absolute dating available for early Greek artifacts. The Near Eastern bronzes from Samos include a statuette of a bearded, helmeted, striding warrior wearing a kilt, imported from Syria.[15] A full-bodied pitcher with a long open pouring spout above a repoussé representation of a human head (Pl. 14a) comes from Luristan.[16] There are several fine examples of Assyrian male statuettes including one clean shaven courtier,[17] one bearded courtier,[18] and one clean shaven male wearing a horned crown (Pl. 13c).[19] There are two examples of the Assyrian statuette type of a standing man with his dog seated at heel (Pl. 13d).[20] In addition there are many examples of horse trappings of various types imported from Assyria, Luristan (Pl. 14b) and the Caucasus.[21] These artifacts date variously from ca. 750 to ca. 650 B.C.

Many of the Phoenician ivories excavated on Samos have parallels from other parts of the ancient world. They are testimonials to far reaching Phoenician trading contacts. For instance, a Phoenician ivory plaque with heraldically arranged seated women has a parallel excavated plaque from the North West Palace at Nimrud in Assyria.[22] Although there are some differences in detail, they are very similar in type and style, and are probably fairly close to one another in date. A small ivory perfume vase from Samos (Pl. 15a, b), has a parallel from the South East Palace at Nimrud (Pl. 15c), and yet another parallel from Carthage (Fig. 4).[23] These are each decorated with a single carved pendant acanthus flower on the shoulder. There is no reason to question the Phoenician origin of the five ivory objects mentioned so far, although the origins of ivories, their place of manufacture, is not always equally clear and unequivocal.

There is a fine small lion head (Pl. 15d) carved as a decoration on an ivory vase from Samos.[24] This head has generally been seen as Greek work in imitation of Phoenician prototypes, although one recent study considered it at Phoenician import. Two similar unattached lion heads have been excavated in Assyria. These have rather more emphatic Phoenician stylistic features. One was found in Fort Shalmaneser (Pl. 15e), the other in the North West Palace at Nimrud (Pl. 15f).[25] All three share certain features. The general shape is similar. All have double incised brow-lines and an incised circle on the forehead. Yet there are some differences. The incision is much deeper and much more emphatic on

[15] Jantzen (supra n. 14) pl. 64.

[16] Ibid. pl. 74, no. B274.

[17] Ibid. pl. 71, no. BB773.

[18] Ibid. pl. 70, no. B1594.

[19] Ibid. pl. 78, no. B1217.

[20] Ibid. 72, no. BB779; E.A. Braun-Holzinger, *Figurliche Bronzen aus Mesopotamien*, *Prähistorische Bronzefunde*, I, 4 (Munich: Beck 1984) 95, nos. 331–33, pl. 63.

[21] Jantzen (supra n. 14) pls. 61, 74, 75, 79, 80.

[22] Freyer-Schauenburg (supra n. 14) pl. 12.

[23] Ibid. pl. 27.

[24] Ibid. pl. 25.

[25] Ibid. pl. 25.

the Fort Shalmaneser lion head than on the Samian. The forehead circle is drilled completely though the head. In contrast, the lion head from the North West Palace has rather less emphatic incision. The Samian head is least emphatic in its carving. These stylistic differences need explanation. If an absolute chronology were certainly known, then the differences in the depth of the incision might be explained as earlier or later manifestations. Possibly it is simply a matter of individual workmen rendering a common type in slightly different ways. Does the rather charming innocence of the Samian head confirm it as a Greek work rather than a Phoenician? Whereas some of the imports clarify our understanding of early Greek art, chronology, trade and origin of some of the motifs in art, other artifacts provide tantalizing problems for study. These problems can be fundamental. Whether a particular object is Greek or foreign in origin is not always clear. The particular little lion head under discussion is a case in point. There is no consensus yet on whether he is of Greek manufacture in reflection of a Phoenician type or a Phoenician original. Why have we all not agreed to accept the artifact as one or the other? This small lion head perfectly illustrates the nature of the problems. While Greek works often reflect Near Eastern imported models, they never blindly copied. Usually Greek workmen added stylistic subtleties which appealed to Greek taste and which enable us to distinguish most Greek manufactures from their imported models, when both are known. Here is an instance where we do not have an unequivocal foreign model in Greece, and where the evidence for comparison provides puzzling features.

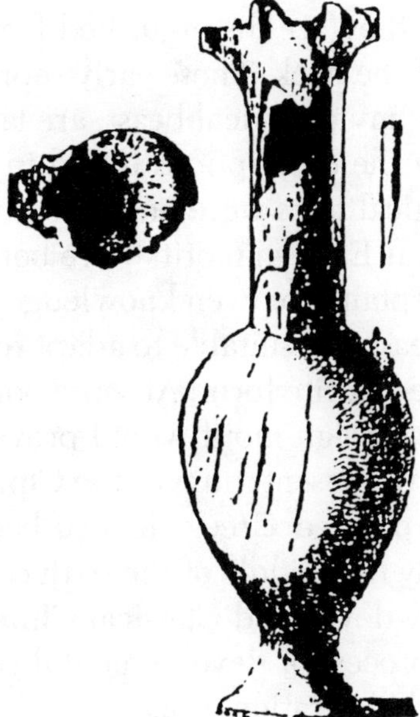

FIG. 4. Phoenician perfume vase. Ivory. Carthage. Mus. Lavigerie. Drawn after B. Freyer-Schauenburg, *Elfenbein aus dem samischen Heraion* (Hamburg: Cramm, de Gruyter 1966) pl. 27c.

FIG. 5. Corinthian vase with chimera. Seventh century B.C. Museum of Fine Arts, Boston. After J. Boardman, *Greeks Overseas* (London: Thames & Hudson 1980) fig. 79.

Many motifs used in early Greek art have a foreign original model, without a specific imported example recovered from Greece. This is the case for many of the mythological motifs which have their earliest graphic or plastic examples in the art of the Near East. For example, at Carchemish there is a splendid relief orthostate of Neo-hittite manufacture dating to ca. 750–700 illustrating a Chimera[26] depicted as a winged lion walking to left with tongue hanging out and upstanding tail ending in a duck head (Pl. 16a). A human male head wearing a hat grows out of its back at the shoulder. The earliest Greek representations of Chimeras are depicted on protocorinthian pottery[27] like this aryballos, ca. 650–600 B.C. (Fig. 5). Although these lions are generally not winged, their tails often terminate in a snake head, and they are distinguished from ordinary lions by the male human head which grows out of the back. These early representations, which are related to the Neo-hittite versions of the mythological beast, are later superseded by representations which follow more closely the descriptions found in later mythological literature. This suggests that the mythological tales were enhanced, with time, as imaginative details were added. Originally, Near Eastern motifs were borrowed as imaginative decorations without direct specific acceptance or even knowledge of the original meaning of the motif. Thus the Chimera-like beast was suitable to adapt for use as a vase decoration in a form very close to its original Neo-hittite form. At some point Greek artists noticed that a few small changes in this exotic foreign motif would provide an illustration for a developed Greek mythological beast. Representations of the Chimera evolved into a somewhat changed visual form that incorporated Greek details, becoming essentially Greek, no longer a bit of foreign exotica. By the middle of the sixth century B.C. this transformation was complete. The familiar fully developed Classical Chimera was the culminating step of a nearly two centuries long process of developmental evolution, perhaps of the story itself, but certainly for the visual illustration of it.

[26] Boardman (supra n. 6) fig. 80.
[27] Ibid. fig. 79.

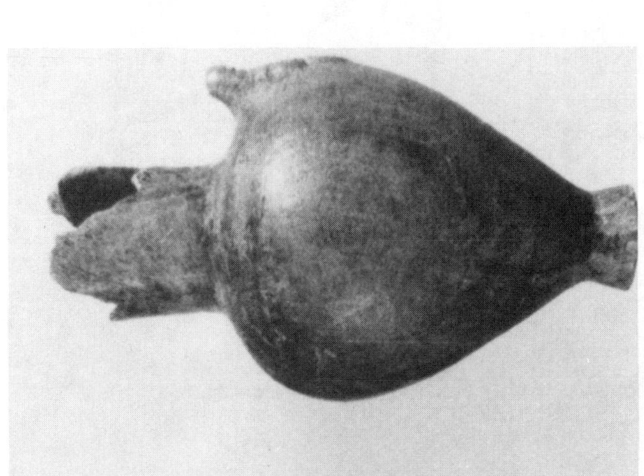

PLATE 15a, b. Phoenician perfume vase. Ivory. Samos.

15c. Phoenician perfume vase. Ivory. South-west Palace. Nimrud.

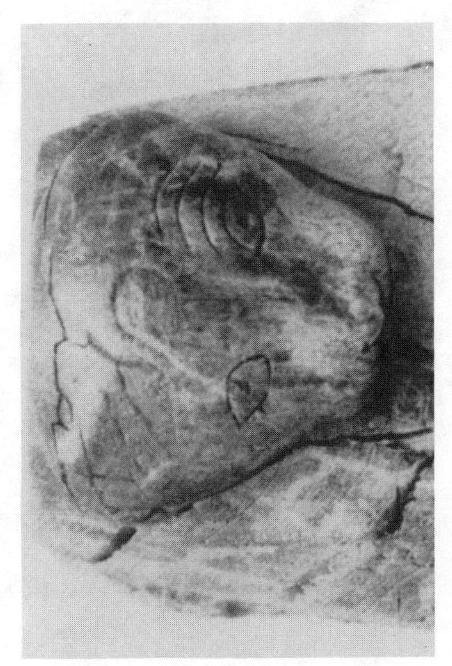

15d. Phoenician lion head. Ivory. Samos.

15e. Phoenician lion head. Ivory. Fort Shalmaneser.

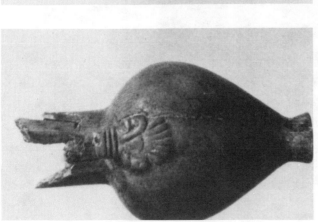

15f. Lion head. Ivory. North-west Palace. Nimrud.

PLATE 16

PLATE 16a. Neo-hittite orthostat relief.

16b. Middle Assyrian seal.

16c. Assyrian sealing with mythological themes.

A mythological motif which has a very long history in the Near East is the winged horse, familiar to Classicists as Pegasos. The Greek mythology connects this creature with Anatolia.[28] Yet, there are examples of this motif known from Middle Assyrian cylinder seals (Pl. 16b) from second millennium Mesopotamia.[29] In the illustrated Near Eastern example the winged horse is arranged heraldically with a lion, both standing upright on their hind legs with fore legs crossed. The word "heraldic" is used to describe a composition where the left and right sides are as mirror images arranged about an imaginary vertical center line. Such compositions, known for millennia in the Near East and the Bronze Age Aegean, reappear in Greek art during the seventh century B.C., the Orientalizing period. Many examples of such composition have been excavated at Olympia where they frequently decorate bronze shield straps.[30] Several of the shield straps have a particular heraldic composition, Pegasoi rearing up on hind legs, with front legs crossed (Fig. 6). The similarity of the Middle Assyrian seal motif to that of the Greek Orientalizing shield strap inspires speculation that the artist who made the bronze had seen and used as a model the motif from a similar seal or sealing. This is certainly a possibility. Several Syrian cylinder seals (Pl. 16c) approximately contemporary to the seal in question have been excavated from the Mycenaean palace at Thebes in recent years. Others have suggested that Mycenaean motifs incorporated into later Greek art had their source in artifacts accidentally or otherwise recovered from Mycenaean graves or tombs.[31] An early import might have been recovered in this way. To date, no actual prototype has been found at Olympia, or in Greece. Thus, nothing survives to illustrate the specific model followed by the seventh-century craftsmen in creating this rendering of an ancient Near Eastern motif.

The Syrian seal from Thebes (Pl. 16c) depicts a seated sphinx. The earliest representation of a sphinx in Geometric Greek art may be the one painted on the bowl from the Kerameikos (Pl. 19c) of the end of the eighth century. The complexity of dealing with questions of origins is highlighted by this example. Surely in this case it is not the rediscovery of an early seal which contributed to the purely Greek rendering of an ancient motif. Many examples of human headed, winged lions survive from Mycenaean contexts. This mythological beast has a long history in Egypt. Phoenicians used it decoratively. Many traditions in the Near East incorporated this motif into their mythological art repertoire. So, must we identify a single source? In this case at least, it might be better not to. The Geometric "sphinx" looks surprisingly like a winged centaur! Or a human headed Pegasos! Early Greek art has surprising originalities of purely Greek conception, even as it displays clear knowledge of the arts of its forebearers and neighbors.

How else may we bridge the gap of transmission when an essentially Near Eastern motif is used in a seventh-century B.C. context in Greece without a Near Eastern example from a Greek context to provide clear evidence for the model? Fabrics woven and embroidered in the Near East carried elaborate decorative programs. Assyrian kings are

[28] R. Graves, *The Greek Myths* (Baltimore: Penguin 1955) 75a–e.

[29] H. Frankfort, *Art and Architecture of the Ancient Orient* (Baltimore: Penguin 1956) pl. 75a.

[30] Emil Kunze, *Archaïsche Schildbänder, OlForsch* 2 (1950) Beilage 3.

[31] J. Boardman, *Island Gems* (London: Society for the Promotion of Hellenic Studies 1963).

FIG. 6. Plaque. Bronze. From Olympia. Seventh century B.C. Drawn after *OlForsch* 2 (1950) Beilage 3.4.

depicted as wearing elaborate garments on the wall reliefs of their palaces. Assurnasirpal II, 883–859 B.C., is shown several times wearing garments embroidered with mythological beasts (Fig. 7).[32] Later kings and courtiers have slightly simpler but still elaborately decorated garments. One splendid example in the Louvre shows Assurbanipal, 668–627 B.C., his charioteer and a page in a chariot under a magnificent umbrella (Pl. 17b).[33] All fabrics are shown as if woven or embroidered with concentric circles, concentric squares, rosettes, and checkerboard patterns. Other examples could be shown illustrating the use of floral themes. A late eighth-century Assyrian ivory panel (Fig. 8) illustrates a whole range of motifs.[34] Garment fabrics have checkerboard patterns with each square enclosing a smaller circle. Other motifs on this plaque are the heraldic arrangement of the central male figures, and the several framing elements including guilloche, rosette, and a type of pomegranate and acanthus frieze. This one small fragile ivory panel encompasses many of the motifs which are seen subsequently in fresh new uses and arrangements in Greek art of the seventh century.

Both fabric and ivory are fragile organic materials. The probability of cloth surviving from antiquity to the present under Greek weather conditions is extremely low, and no early examples are known to have survived. Some ivories have survived, but conditions not being favorable, many fewer survive than must have been brought into Greece during the period of interest. Decorated leather and wood products were probably also imported. These too have not survived. Perishable imports may well have provided a much richer repertoire of decorative motifs than those we know from surviving imported

[32] J. Canby, "Decorated Garments in Ashurnasirpals's Sculpture," *Iraq* 33 (1971) 31–53; Frankfort (supra n. 29) 104, fig. 41; S.M. Paley, *King of the World: Ashurnasirpal II, 883–859* (New York: Brooklyn Museum 1976) pls. 22a, 23c and 25a.

[33] Musée du Louvre, *Encyclopédie photographique de l'art II* (Paris: Editions "TEL" 1936) pl. 12.

[34] R.D. Barnett, *A Catalogue of the Nimrud Ivories* (London: British Museum 1957) pl. 114.

PLATE 17a. Daedalic Greek seated woman. Gortyn, Crete. Second quarter seventh century B.C.

17b. Assurbanipal with courtiers. Nineveh. 668–627 B.C.

17c. Auxerre kore. Auxerre, France. Third quarter seventh century B.C.

17d. King Warpalawas. Rock relief, Ivriz. ca. 720 B.C.

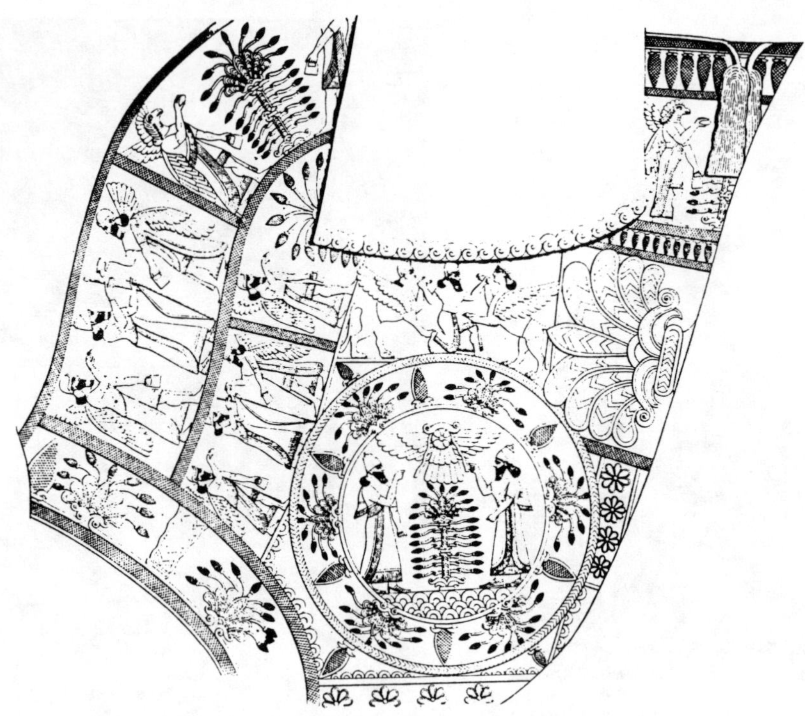

FIG. 7. Assyrian embroidered garment. From Nimrud. Ninth century B.C. British Museum no. 124565. *Monuments de Nineve* I, pl. 6 (cf. Layard's Drawing of b).

prototypes. Examples of carved and painted decoration on Greek garment representations in stone survive from the second quarter of the seventh century on. The most splendid early example is that of the seated woman from Gortyn (Pl. 17a), now in the Herakleion museum in Crete.[35] Her skirt is decorated with carved painted rosettes, acanthus and joined circles. Another example from later in the seventh century is the skirt of the Auxerre kore (Pl. 17c) in the Louvre which is decorated in concentric squares.[36]

Examples of some of the motifs under consideration can be seen in closer geographic proximity to Greece than Assyria. The rock-relief at Ivriz (Pl. 17d) shows the Neo-Hittite King Warpalawas, ca. 720 B.C., dressed in a garment which is partially decorated with concentric squares with central dot, partially with swastika patterns and bordered with diagonally placed squares enclosing a square spiral.[37] Weathering has long since removed any paint which might have originally enlivened the surface designs. It may seem rather tenuous to postulate from a rock relief to real Greek fabric. Yet, Greeks were known to have been in the area near Ivriz, which is reasonably accessible to Al-Mina and

[35] J. Boardman, *Greek Sculpture: The Archaic Period* (New York: Oxford 1978) fig. 30.
[36] Ibid. fig. 28.
[37] E. Akurgal, *The Art of Hittites* (New York: Abrams 1962) pl. 140.

Tarsus. The rock relief dominates the mountain pass which since ancient times has been the main route through the mountain range. One can hardly travel past without being aware of its dominating visual force. Whether from Neo-hittite rock reliefs, from knowledge of Late Assyrian palace decoration, from imported ivories, fabrics, leather or wooden manufactured goods, Greeks learned of the colorful elaborate fabric patterns used in the east and adapted these patterns for the decoration of their own garments, and to other decorative uses. Many examples of such decorated fabrics may be seen in the Greek art of the seventh century.[38]

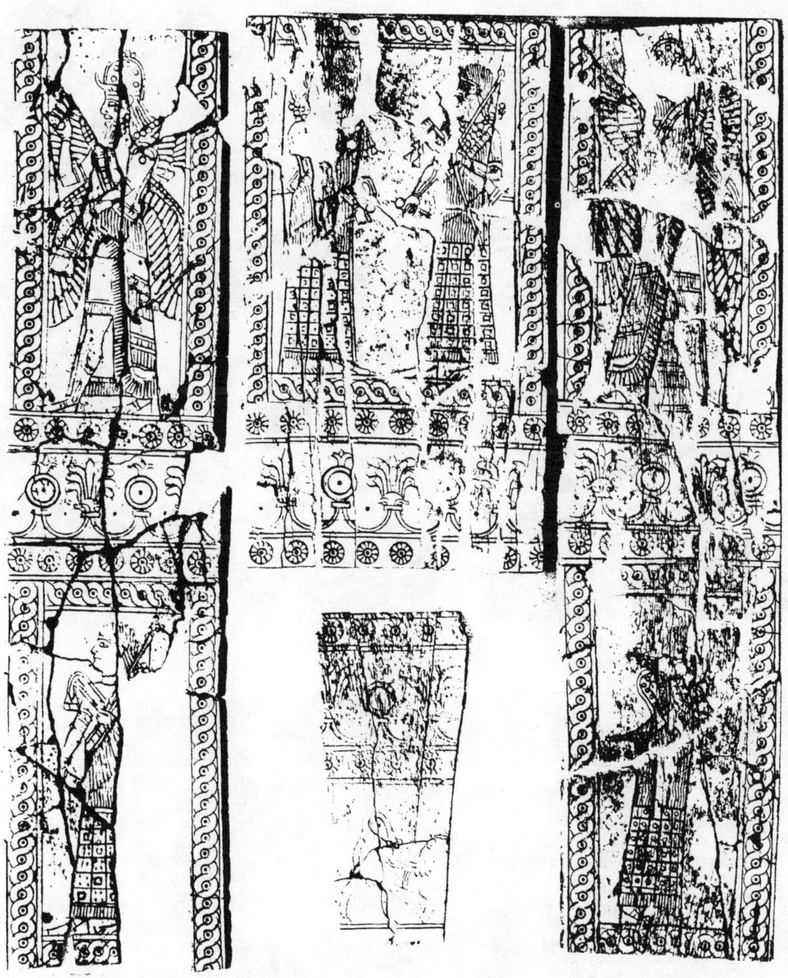

FIG. 8. Assyrian plaque. Ivory. Seventh century B.C. After R.D. Barnett, *Catalogue of the Nimrud Ivories* (London: British Museum 1957) pl. 114.

[38] G.M.A. Richter, *Korai* (London & New York: Phaidon 1968) pls. VId, VIIId, XXIIa, figs. 66–69, 76–79, 104–108, 113–16.

PLATE 18

PLATE 18. Shield. Bronze. Mt. Ida, Crete. Eighth century B.C. Complete view and details.

Among the earliest clear evidences for the adoption of a Near Eastern motif into the general repertoire of the Greek artist is a motif found on a number of early bronze shields, made during the eighth century B.C. and the early years of the seventh, and excavated during the nineteenth century from the cave on Mt. Ida on Crete. Among the earliest of these shields, perhaps from the middle of the eighth century, is shield no. 5 (Pl. 18).[39] About the central field is a circular field with a frieze of grazing animals. The animal file is so arranged that all stand upright, whether at the top of the shield or at the bottom. This seems to be the earliest example of grazing animals in a file from Greece. It is most likely the work of a Near Eastern workman. The earliest Near Eastern prototype for such an animal file as a shield decoration may be seen on the shield of the Urartian king, Argishti I, ca. 786–764 B.C., found at Karmir Blur (Fig. 9). Among the earliest appearances of this motif on an unequivocally Greek work of art is in Attic Geometric vase painting. The splendid Dipylon vase (Pl. 19a) has a geometric frieze about its neck representing grazing animals.[40] This vase belongs to the eighth century B.C., ca. 725–700. Another of the earliest examples of a painted frieze of grazing animals is on an Attic Geometric bowl from the Kerameikos (Pl. 19b) in Athens.[41] Here the frieze is circular, about the interior of the bowl. Viewed from above, the visual effect is not too dissimilar from that of the shield. One difference is that the animals are all walking on the same ground line about the central rosette. The design no longer has a clear top and bottom; the animals walk in the same single file about the center. Of course, the grazing animals are executed in Attic Geometric style, distinguishing them from the work of foreign craftsmen. Greek artisans never blindly copied foreign motifs. Always they translated that which they borrowed into their own local style, satisfying the taste of Greek patrons. Once a motif was incorporated into the Greek artistic repertoire its execution developed along the same lines in which Greek art generally was developing. Thus, by the seventh century, many Rhodian vases were decorated with friezes, often multiple friezes of grazing animals (Pl. 19d).[42] This particular style of decoration is called the "Wild Goat" style of Rhodian vase decoration. It dominated the decoration of Rhodian vases for more than fifty years. Variations of the same style were produced on Chios and at Clazomenae from ca. 650 down to ca. 600 B.C. This theme, of Near Eastern origin, is

[39] Kunze (supra n. 13) pl. 7. A number of bronze shields from Crete include the same motif. The earliest example was made during the eighth century B.C. A number of other examples, varying in decorative detail, were made in Crete during the last half of the eighth century and the first half of the seventh century. Shield no. 27, p. 34, from about 700 B.C., has an elaborate central rosette. This shield is reminiscent of the interior decor of Geometric bowls which often have an animal file arranged on a circular field about a central rosette. See ibid. pl. 53 and B. Schweitzer, *Greek Geometric Art* (London: Phaidon 1971) pls. 65–68. A bowl (pl. 67) from the Athenian Kerameikos actually has a file of grazing deer.

[40] H.A. Groenewegen-Frankfort and B. Ashmole, *Art of the Ancient World* (New York: Abrams 1977) 161, fig. 179. See also color plate 21 with another amphora from the Dipylon cemetery, Athens. In both cases the frieze on the vase neck is a file of grazing deer.

[41] N. Coldstream (supra n. 9) 116, fig. 37b and c; see also 111, fig. 33c and 112, fig. 34d; see 123, fig. 38 a, b, and c for gold diadems with the same motif and also of Late Geometric date from Athens.

[42] P. Mingazzini, *Greek Pottery Painting* (London: Paul Hamlyn 1969) 29, fig. 9; G. Becatti, *The Art of Ancient Greece and Rome* (New York: Abrams 1967) 35, fig. 23.

PLATE 19

PLATE 19a. Attic Late Geometric vase. Athens. Ca. 725–700 B.C.

19b. Attic Late Geometric bowl. Athens. Ca. 725–700 B.C.

19c. Attic Late Geometric bowl. Athens. Ca. 725–700 B.C.

19d. Rhodian oinochoe. Rhodes. Ca. 600 B.C.

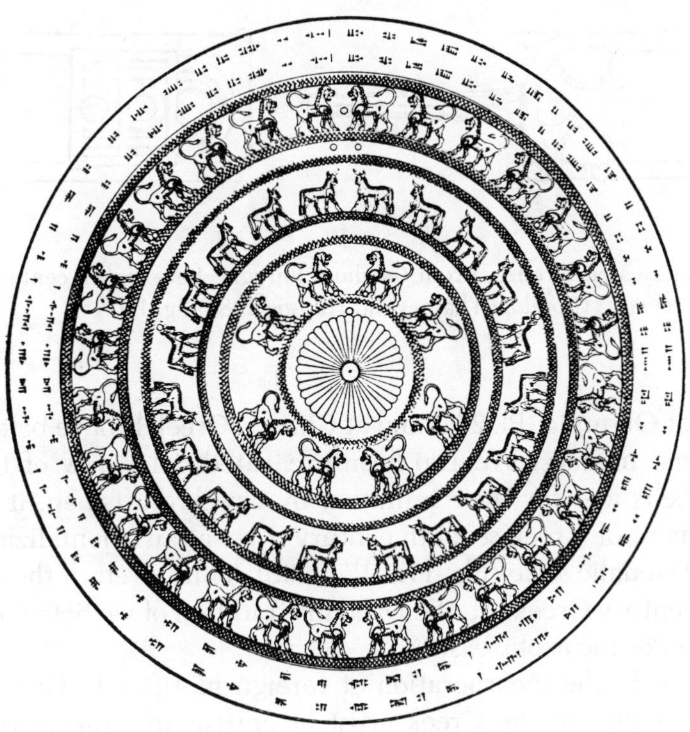

FIG. 9. Urartian shield of King Argishti I, Bronze. From Karmir Blur. Ca. 786–764 B.C. After Piotrovskii, *Iskusstvo Urartu* (Leningrad 1962) fig. 38.

one which was so thoroughly incorporated into early Greek art that there is a tendency to think of it as exclusively Greek forgetting its origins and the ways in which it was introduced to the Greek world.

One last example will illustrate that an element of seventh-century Daedalic sculpture also has its most probable roots in the Near East. During the seventh century, Greek art dropped its Geometric constraints and evolved in an increasingly pictorial fashion. Human representations became rather more lively and accurate. The dress of both men and women was shown in detail. One typical element of dress is the belt. Invariably it is wide, stiff, decorated, and with a buckle or catch fastening at the front (Fig. 10). The several details have suggested that it is a question of a metal or bronze belt, or possibly a belt with wooden or ivory appliques. Bronze belts have been excavated from sites in central and eastern Anatolia dating from the middle of the eighth century down into the seventh. The earliest such belts were found in Urartu, decorated with animal files. One such is on display at the Oriental Institute Museum in Chicago. Bronze belts with geometric decorations, dating to ca. 725, were found at Gordion in Phrygia (including that in Fig. 10). Recall Herodotos' report (1.51) that Croesus gave the belt of his wife to Apollo at Delphi. What is more to the point is that Phrygian belts have been excavated in

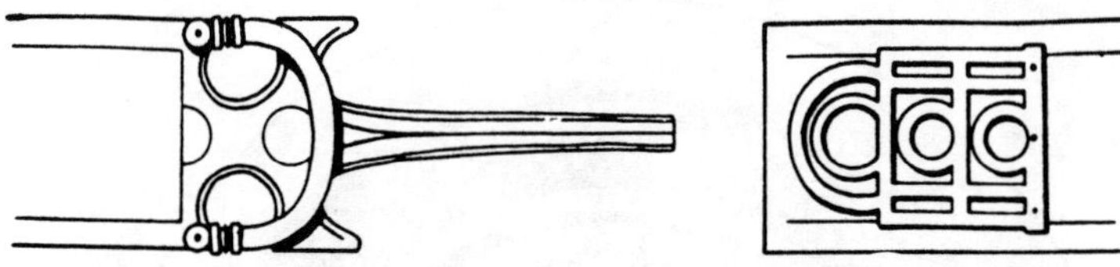

FIG. 10. Belt tongue and catch. Bronze. From Gordion, Phrygia. Late eighth century B.C. Drawn after J. Boardman, *Greeks Overseas* (London: Thames and Hudson 1980) fig. 100.

Greece, at Samos, at Olympia (Pl. 20a) and at Chios.[43] Greek bronze belts made in imitation of the imported models have also been excavated.[44] In view of the evidence for imported bronze belts and for their imitation by Greek craftsmen, it is reasonable to accept this component of Greek seventh century dress as an orientalizing element with an impact on the Daedalic style (Pls. 17a, 17c, 20b). Thus, even in the most indigenous aspect of seventh-century Greek art, the Daedalic tradition of ca. 660–600 B.C., it is possible to see the impact of the exotic east.[45]

A demonstration of the incorporation of foreign motifs into Greek art in no way denigrates the originality of the Greek artist or craftsman. During the Orientalizing period the Greek artists' imagination was constantly stimulated by new ideas and new visual experiences with imported artifacts and perhaps by tales told by travelers describing things not actually seen. The particular adaptations of the foreign motifs were the product of Greek creativity. The old motifs were used in new contexts, with new juxtapositions, with new color schemes, and with newly evolving stylistic details which are essentially Greek in nature. It is usually possible to distinguish the Greek from the foreign. The foreign models are reworked, transformed into something which suited Greek taste.

This article has mentioned only a few of the many seminal object types and motifs excavated in Greece, of Near Eastern origin. The discussion of the impact of such imported artifacts on Greek art and life is equally limited. Among imports which might have been discussed in terms of impact on Greek culture are the phialai mesomphaloi, which have a much longer history in Assyria and the Near East than in Greece, as do lion-headed rhyta, lotus-and-bud friezes, hugh cauldrons with conical stands. Lion and griffin head protomes, Ashur, bullhead and bird attachments for cauldrons, spool-handled bowls, ring-handled bowls, lion-head bowls, various architectural elements, Phrygian and Lydian fibulae and specific sculptural types all have substantial histories in the Near East prior to their advent in Greece. Many other motifs and artifact types can be traced

[43] Jantzen (supra n. 14) 49–51, pls. 47, 48; J. Boardman, "Chios," *AnatSt* 6 (1961) 179f.; Boardman (supra n. 6) 90–91.

[44] Boardman (supra n. 6) figs. 61, 73, 74.

[45] Boardman (supra n. 35). He illustrates a number of other seventh century B.C. Archaic figures wearing elaborate belts. These are figs. 28, 29, 32, 33, 45, 46, 49, 54, and 57–60. These include both korai and kouroi.

PLATE 20

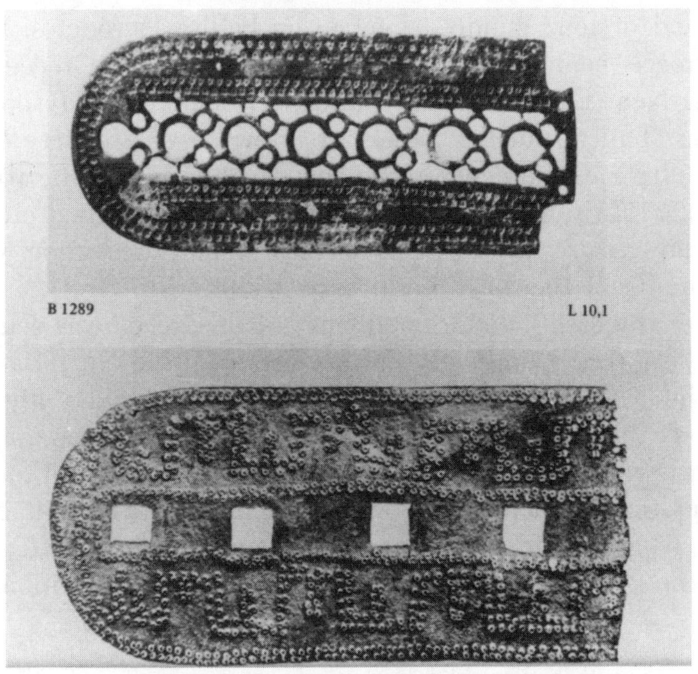

PLATE 20a. Belt tongues. Bronze. Olympia. Seventh century B.C.

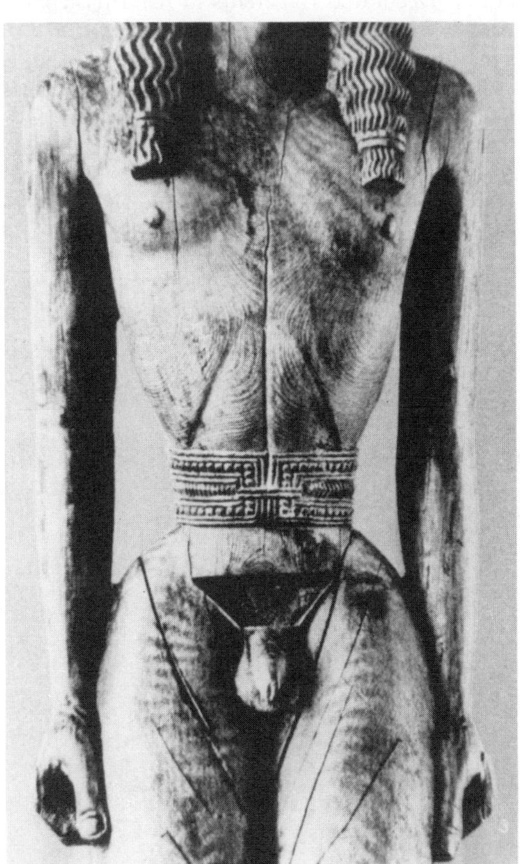

20b. Statuette. Ivory. Samos. ca. 630 B.C.

from their Greek renderings and use, to their unimported (or at least unexcavated) Near Eastern prototypes.

During a period of four hundred long years before Herodotos, Pericles and the Golden Age of Greece, contacts and trading patterns between Greece and the several civilizations of the Near East were many, and ever changing in response to changing political conditions. This stimulated Greek art to evolve in a variety of directions, responding to new influences and new motifs. There was nothing static about this contact, nor about its results. Early in our century scholarly work focused on the Phoenician contributions. Today, as a result of extensive research and excavation, we have a much broader understanding of the Near Eastern contribution to Greek art. Contributions came from all over the east. The Orientalizing art of Greece was eclectic, borrowing motifs from many sources, from every culture group in the Near East and also from Egypt. Some of these new ideas were incorporated into everyday life influencing the clothes Greeks wore, their personal decorations, the shape and decoration of their utensils, their grave goods and votive offerings at the major sanctuaries of the gods, and even the visual representations of their mythology. This contact had identifiable affects on the indigenous Greek art of the Geometric period, the eighth century B.C., and is traceable even in the art of the seventh century, the indigenous Daedalic tradition.[46]

[46] All illustrations are the author's original drawings and photographs except for those reproduced from earlier publications. The author wishes to acknowledge that some of the illustrations have been reproduced from the following publications: Akurgal, *Art of the Hittites*, 1960; Braun-Holzinger, *Figurliche Bronzen aus Mesopotamien*, 1984; Canby, "Decorated Garments in Ashurnasirpal's Sculpture," *Iraq* 33:1 (1971); Demargne, *Birth of Greek Art*, 1964; Frankfort, *Art and Architecture of the Ancient Orient*, 1956; Freyer-Schauenburg, *Elfenbeine aus dem samischen Heraion*, 1966; Jantzen, *Ägyptische und orientalische Bronzen aus dem Heraion von Samos*, 1972; Kunze, *Kretische Bronzereliefs*, 1931; Markoe, *Phoenician Bronze and Silver Bowls from Cyprus and the Mediterranean*, 1985; Musée du Louvre, *Encyclopédie photographique de l'art II*, 1936; Schweitzer, *Greek Geometric Art*, 1971. Full citations for each of these sources appear in the footnotes. Permission to reproduce these illustrations was generously granted by the following publishers and copyright holders: Editions Gallimard, the German Archaeological Institutes in Athens and Rome, Phaidon Press, and the University of California Press, Berkeley.

THE EXCHANGE OF LETTERS BETWEEN SAINT AUGUSTINE AND SAINT JEROME

Virginia K. Hellenga

An awkward, halting relationship between Saint Augustine and Saint Jerome developed slowly through an exchange of letters into a strong friendship. These letters, covering a period of twenty-five years, document the rocky path toward that friendship. Revealing very different personalities and contrasting temperaments, the letters show how quickly Augustine learned to use moderation and tact in dealing with Jerome, and how Jerome only gradually came to trust, respect, and value Augustine.

In desiring an exchange of ideas with Jerome, Augustine had little grasp of how difficult a character Jerome could be. Augustine was a man with an open mind, eager for real debate, for the clash of ideas by which both he and Jerome might arrive at the truth. Able to pursue a discussion with objectivity, Augustine was willing to be convinced by an argument stronger than his own. He assumed at the start that a man as learned and experienced in controversy as Jerome would be able to exchange ideas without involving personal feelings. Unfortunately, he did not know how sensitive Jerome was about his opinions, which to him were truth and not open to discussion. Nor did Augustine know how fiercely Jerome resented adverse criticism.

This lack of openmindedness in Jerome was closely related to his singlemindedness of purpose. After his uneventful conversion at the age of twenty, Jerome moved in the direction of the most extreme form of Christianity, asceticism. Renouncing the world completely, he became a monk in the desert of Chalcis, living a harsh life of fasting and mortification. With his emaciated body caked with dirt, his bones sticking into the earth floor of his cave, he began his life of intellectual labor for the Kingdom of God by writing the lives of the hermits. He became almost a recluse. Secluded in his monastery in Bethlehem, he devoted the rest of his life and strength to translating the Greek commentaries on the Bible, writing his own commentaries, attacking heresies, translating the New Testament from Greek, and the Old Testament from Hebrew. His translation of the Bible became the Vulgate.

Jerome's achievements were phenomenal, yet his brilliance had a darker side: jealousy, suspicion, brooding anger, and a fierce temper. When someone opposed him, he responded with biting satire and scathing attacks. "Polemics have nothing to do with truth," he explained. "Their only objective is to conquer, to crush one's adversary."[1] Even when his close friend and companion, Rufinus, disagreed with his views, Jerome attacked him viciously, and then rejoiced at his death, saying, "Now that the scorpion lies buried in Sicily . . . and the hydra with his numerous heads has ceased its hissing against us, and

[1] Quoted by Ferdinand Cavallera, S.J. in Francis X. Murphy, C.S.S.R, ed., *A Monument to Saint Jerome* (New York: Sheed & Ward 1952) 19.

time is given for other things than answering the inquiries of heretics, I will tackle the prophet Ezechiel."[2]

Jerome's feisty personality presented a real challenge to Augustine—one which he met with the strength of human understanding, patience, and steady Christian love. We are perhaps more familiar with Augustine's personality, especially through reading his *Confessions.* He was a profoundly original thinker, grappling with moral issues, searching, questioning, and seeking Christian truth. His compassionate understanding of human nature still speaks to the heart and soul. Consecrated Bishop of Hippo, North Africa, in A.D. 395, Augustine led an active life. Duties and responsibilities of his office made it impossible for him to pursue Scriptural studies full time. His sermons are brilliant and attest his competence in Scriptural exegesis, yet he was always eager to learn from those who dedicated their lives to Biblical scholarship. He was especially eager to learn from Jerome.

When Augustine's close friend Alypius, who was present in the garden at the time of his conversion, returned to Africa from visiting Jerome in Bethlehem, his glowing account of the visit inspired Augustine to write Jerome a letter. "You were made almost present to me by his description," he tells Jerome. Already familiar with Jerome's writings, he writes, "Never has anyone been so well known to another by face, as the quiet joy and scholarly pursuit of your studies in the Lord are known to me."[3]

Augustine knew Jerome's works, but he did not know Jerome's temperament. With an enthusiastic introduction, "My mind bubbles over with thoughts which I want to share with you about the studies we pursue," Augustine proceeds first to ask Jerome not to translate the Old Testament from the Hebrew (a task which Jerome had already begun), but rather to translate from the more familiar Greek Septuagint version (Parsons XII.94–95). Second, he presents strong arguments against Jerome's interpretation of Galatians 2:11–14. In his commentary on this passage, Jerome says Paul is telling a polite lie, or white lie, when he reprimands Peter for compelling the Gentiles to follow the Jewish law. Jerome assumes that Peter, being the first of the Apostles, could not do wrong, and therefore that Paul is not telling the truth. Augustine counters that Peter is human, and it is better to admire the gracious way in which he accepts correction than to claim that he could never do wrong. After all, he argues, Peter denied Christ. Augustine points up the danger of Jerome's opinion that Paul is telling a lie: it undermines the authority of absolute truth in the Scriptures (Parsons XII.95–97).

This first letter, written in A.D. 394 or 395, never reached Jerome. It did not even leave Africa. Profuturus, who planned to deliver the letter to Jerome, was made Bishop just before his proposed trip to the Holy Land, and died soon after. Jerome, on his own initiative, sent a short letter of greeting to Augustine in 397. Still eager for an exchange of ideas with Jerome, Augustine replied, inviting him to undertake a written debate.

[2] Quoted ibid. 9.

[3] Wilfrid Parsons, S.N.D., *Saint Augustine, Letters I. The Fathers of the Church* XII (Washington: Catholic University of America Press 1955) 93–94; cited infra as Parsons XII.

In this second letter, Augustine presents his arguments even more forcefully against Jerome's explanation of the passage in Galatians. "There is no need of many words to plead this case in your court;" he says, "a word to the wise is sufficient for one as far-seeing as you. Indeed, I should never presume to attempt to enrich with my pennies that genius of yours, divinely gifted with pure gold." Augustine argues his own position well, then asks Jerome to correct and revise his commentary. "Sing us a palinode," he says (Parsons XII.172–79). This request for a recantation was something Augustine would come to regret. Given in a spirit of goodwill, innocently, with no intent to offend, "sing us a palinode" would stir up such anger and resentment in Jerome that only with great difficulty would Augustine be able to placate him.

The fate of the second letter was worse than the first, and contributed to the misunderstanding. Paulus was to take it to Jerome, but became afraid of the dangers at sea and decided not to sail. He gave the letter to someone who gave it to someone else. Eventually, copies of the letter were circulating around Italy, especially in Rome. A rumor developed that Augustine had published a book against Jerome. Sisinnius found a copy of the letter, without a signature, along with other of Augustine's writings, on an island in the Adriatic, and took it to Jerome (Parsons XII.329).

Unaware of the fate of this letter, Augustine wrote for a third time (A.D. 402), nine years after first writing to Jerome—his hope of exchanging ideas still unrealized, his arguments on Galatians still unanswered. He begins,

> I have heard that my letter has reached you, but, as I have not deserved an answer, I do not blame this on your lack of love—no doubt there has been something to prevent it (Parsons XII.316).

He denies the rumor that he has written a book against Jerome and sent it to Rome (never suspecting that his second letter has ended up there), and adds, "If some chance statements are found in some of my writings, in which I am found to have views different from yours, that is nothing against you" (Parsons XII.316–17). Demonstrating an attitude toward criticism which is admirable, and just the opposite of Jerome's, he writes,

> Not only am I most ready to receive in a brotherly spirit any contrary opinion you may have to anything in my writings to which you take exception, but I ask and insist that you do so, and I will take pleasure in my own correction and your goodness (Parsons XII.317).

Receiving this letter, Jerome replied immediately. He has not heard that Augustine has sent a book against him to Rome, but says, "copies of a certain letter supposedly written to me came to me through our brother Sisinnius, the deacon, and in it you exhort me to sing my palinode" (Parsons XII.317–18). As for not writing, he explains,

> I did not want to put too much trust in copies of letters, lest you justly hurt and upbraid me for not proving that the letter was yours before I answered it (Parsons XII.318).

He asks for a more exact copy of the letter

> so we may engage in a debate over the Scriptures without any personal feeling and may either correct our mistake or learn that someone else made a heedless remonstrance (Parsons XII.318).

The implication is that Augustine's arguments on Galatians amount to "a heedless remonstrance," and that Jerome thinks of himself as a man who debates without involving personal feelings, although his reputation argued to the contrary. Rather self-righteously he continues,

> I could never go so far as to attack anything from the works of your Beatitude. It is enough for me to approve of my own and not to criticize those of others . . . It is a mark of childish boastfulness to act as boys are wont to do, and to seek credit for one's own name by depreciating famous men (Parsons XII.318–19).

Is he suggesting that Augustine is seeking credit for his own name by depreciating the famous Jerome? It would seem so.

With a reference to "the popular proverb about the tired ox setting his foot down more heavily" (which sounds like a veiled threat), Jerome stops himself. His attitude changes. "I have dictated this with sorrow," he writes. "How I wish I might deserve to embrace you, and that we might teach or learn something by mutual conversation!" This expression of friendship provided great encouragement to Augustine (Parsons XII.319).

Rancor, however, permeates Jerome's next letter, one which was obviously not intended to make Augustine happy. "Some of my close friends," he writes,

> have been suggesting that your conduct was not single-minded, but that your motive was a desire of praise and small renown and cheap popularity; that you wished to gain credit at my expense, so that many might know that you challenged, but I feared; that you, the learned one, were writing, but I, the unlettered one, had nothing to say; and that at last someone had appeared to put a stop to my chattering (Parsons XII.329).

That unfortunate second letter of Augustine, a copy of which was brought to Jerome, has angered Jerome. He continues,

> Cease to harass an old man who has retired to his cell. If you want to show off or practice your learning, seek out young, fluent, well-known men . . . who can or dare contest with you and can carry their weight with a bishop in a discussion on the Holy Scriptures (Parsons XII.329–30).

A few words near the end of the letter are in a friendlier tone, and Augustine's reply acknowledges, or rather capitalizes on them:

> I find many marks of your most kindly charity, and also some indications that I have offended you. So, then, I was charmed, as I read, and likewise constantly shocked. . . . When you answer so as to hurt me, what chance is left of us carrying on a discussion of the Scriptures without personal feeling? (Parsons XII.332–33)

This was a major problem to overcome. Augustine realized that the solution might simply be not to discuss interpretations of Scripture at all. Further along in the letter he says to Jerome,

> I ask you, if it can be done, that we inquire into and discuss some point, on which our souls may feed without any bitterness of dissension. But if I cannot mention what seems to me faulty in your writings, not you in mine, without suspicion of jealousy or injury to our friendship, then let us drop this for the sake of our lives and salvation (Parsons XII.339).

While this letter was on its way to Jerome, a very lengthy one was on its way to Augustine: Jerome's full answer to the interpretation of Galatians, which Augustine had first requested ten years before. Jerome approached the question from a much broader perspective, and Augustine was eventually able to show him how their views are basically in harmony.

Jerome was less hostile now, and gradually his letters assumed a friendlier tone. Augustine had shown him perfect Christian love, unconditional love, and an understanding which says, "Shall we take the good and not the evil?" Augustine loved the whole man, and with keen insight perceived that Jerome's faults were integrally connected with his virtues, as mere blemishes of a character which had such astounding strengths. Augustine's admiration for Jerome was steadfast throughout, from the beginning when he knew him only through the various works he had published, and remained undaunted by Jerome's antagonism and unkind remarks.

Augustine's supreme success with Jerome lay in his perception of the good heart behind the gruff exterior. He spoke to the inner man, reminding him of his kindness and affection. He writes Jerome (A.D. 405),

> I beg you to look in upon yourself, for a little while if you will, upon yourself, I say, in your attitude toward myself, and recall, or if you have a copy, reread your words in that short letter which you sent me . . . and note with how true, how brotherly, how affectionate a charity you reproached me for having offended you, and how you added gravely: 'By that conduct friendship is injured and the bonds of intimacy are broken . . . but let us not seem to be engaging in a childish contest, or to give grounds of contention to our mutual supporters or detractors.' I feel that these words were uttered by you from your heart and from a kind heart, for my best interest (Parsons XII.415).

Although, because of Jerome's reluctance, a lively exchange of ideas never came into being, a true friendship did develop between them, and this friendship was a great solace to Jerome at the end of his life. His last two letters show how his attitude toward Augustine has changed. In A.D. 418 he writes,

> I have always revered your Blessedness with the respect which befits you, and I have loved the Lord our Saviour dwelling in you, but now we add something to the heap, and

> if that is possible, we fill up what was full, so as not to allow one single hour to pass without mention of your name.[4]

In his final letter to Augustine, written shortly before his death, Jerome says,

> Every occasion is welcome to me which allows me to write to your Reverence, calling God to witness that if it were possible I would take the wings of a dove and fly to be enfolded in your embrace (Parsons XXX.405).

How marvelously changed is Jerome.

It is not easy to love someone who insults you or hurts you, but Augustine took Jerome's invective in stride, and passing beyond it, appealed to his inner nature, believing that Jerome was capable of loving even someone who had offended and antagonized him. Goethe observes,

> If we treat people as they are, we make them worse. If we treat them as if they were what they ought to be, we help them to become what they are capable of becoming.[5]

It is something of this sort which Augustine achieved with Jerome. He appealed to Jerome's virtues, and clung to the slightest indications of his affection, thus helping him to move from animosity toward a trusting friendship.

From the delicate way in which Augustine wrote to the volatile Jerome after the disastrous first two letters, we must think that Augustine somehow recognized that Jerome's faults were excesses of his strengths, mere defects and weaknesses accompanying such greatness. Perhaps Jerome, by exhausting his energy in his phenomenal intellectual labors, did not have enough emotional strength left to master his temperament. It is certainly a tribute to Augustine that he was able to win the affection which could say, "If it were possible I would take the wings of a dove and fly to be enfolded in your embrace."

[4] Wilfrid Parsons, S.N.D., *Saint Augustine, Letters IV. The Fathers of the Church* XXX (Washington: Catholic University of America Press 1951) 332; cited infra as Parsons XXX.

[5] Quoted in V. Frankl, *The Doctor and the Soul* (New York: Random House 1955) 8.

THIS CHILD 'IN MY NAME'

John J. Kilgallen, S.J.

Luke 9, 46–48 reads:

> 46 *εἰσῆλθεν δὲ διαλογισμὸς ἐν αὐτοῖς, τὸ τίς ἂν εἴη μείζων αὐτῶν,*
> 47 *ὁ δὲ ᾽Ιησοῦς εἰδὼς τὸν διαλογισμὸν τῆς καρδίας αὐτῶν ἐπιλαβόμενος παιδίον ἔστησεν αὐτὸ παρ᾽ ἑαυτῷ,*
> 48 *καὶ εἶπεν αὐτοῖς, ὃς ἂν δέξηται τοῦτο τὸ παιδίον ἐπὶ τῷ ὀνόματί μου ἐμὲ δέχεται, καὶ ὃς ἂν ἐμὲ δέξηται δέχεται τὸν ἀποστέιλαντά με. ὁ γὰρ μικρότερος ἐν πᾶσιν ὑμῖν ὑπάρχων οὗτός ἐστιν μέγας.*

My intent in this essay in honor of Father Schoder, S.J., is to identify what Jesus is teaching his disciples in these verses just cited. Before entering into the interpretative phase of this study, however, a few words should be said regarding introductory matters, the first of which touches upon the translation of these three Lucan verses.

First, the word *διαλογισμός* has been understood in a variety of ways by scholars. Zerwick, S.J., and Grosvenor suggest "speculation";[1] others recommend, for example, "discussion,"[2] "*Gedanken*,"[3] "*Überlegung*,"[4] "*Unterredung*,"[5] "*disputa*,"[6] " a thought,"[7] "*Erörterung*,"[8] "a reasoning,"[9] "argument."[10] From Luke's usage of this noun and its verb in his Gospel, the emphasis seems to be on the exchange of opinions with reasons given (cf. Luke 3, 15; 5, 21; 20, 14; 2, 35; 6, 8; 24, 38).[11]

[1] M. Zerwick, S.J., and M. Grosvenor, *A Grammatical Analysis of the Greek New Testament*, vol. 1 (Rome: Biblical Institute Press 1974) 215.

[2] *The New American Bible* (New York: Catholic Book Publishing 1970) 81.

[3] W. Schmithals, *Das Evangelium nach Lukas, Zurcher Bibelkommentare: Neues Testament* 3, 1 (Zurich: Theologischer Verlag 1980) 116.

[4] J. Ernst, *Das Evangelium nach Lukas, Regensburger Neues Testament* (Regensburg: Pustet 1976) 311.

[5] T. Zahn, *Das Evangelium nach Lukas, Kommentar zum Neuen Testament* III, 2nd ed. (Leipzig: Deichter 1913) 393.

[6] A. Valensin, S.J., and G. Huby, S.J., *Vangelo secondo San Luca, Verbum Salutis*, 3rd ed. (Rome: 1965) 200; cf. 'dispute': Wm. Manson, *The Gospel of Luke, The Moffat New Testament Commentary* (London: Hodder and Stoughton 1948) 117.

[7] A.B. Bruce, *The Synoptic Gospels, The Expositor's Greek Testament I* (London: Hodder and Toughton 1907) 534: "a thought of the heart, not a dispute as in Mark; one should make as little of it as possible."

[8] J. Chr. von Hofmann, *Das Evangelium des Lukas, Die Heilige Schrift neuen Testaments*, 8 Theil, Abteilung I (Nördlingen: Beck 1878). 254.

[9] R.C.H. Lenski, *The Interpretation of St. Luke's Gospel* (Columbus, Ohio: Wartburg Press 1951) 543; N. Geldenhuys, *Commentary on the Gospel of Luke* (Grand Rapids, Mich.: Eerdmans 1954) 287; cf. 'cogitatio': W.M.L. de Wette, *Kurze Erklärung der Evangelien des Lukas und Markus* (Leipzig: Weidmann 1848). De Wette notes that 'cogitatio' is Erasmus' choice and is to be preferred to 'disceptatio' suggested by Grotius, 74.

[10] J. Fitzmyer, S.J., *The Gospel According to Luke I–IX, The Anchor Bible*, vol. 26 (New York: Doubleday 1968) 815.

[11] It should be noted that Luke never uses the singular number of διαλογισμός except in Luke 9, 46.47; thus, to cite other Lucan uses of this word is a bit precarious.

DAIDALIKON: Studies in Memory of Raymond V. Schoder, S.J.

Secondly, though in the text αὐτῶν follows μείζων, scholars are few who understand that the two words belong together.[12]

Thirdly, there is not unanimity as to the translation of μείζων as "greater"; some scholars understand it to be under the influence of the semitic way of saying "the greatest."[13]

Fourthly, μικρότερος can be understood to mean "the smaller," but many prefer to see here, as with μείζων, the use of a comparative form to express the superlative sense.[14]

Finally, while some scholars translate the very last word of these three verses as "the greatest" (again under a semiticizing influence), many prefer to translate the word μέγας as "great."[15]

With this matter considered, it is permissible to ask about the rightness of taking these three verses as a unit unto themselves. There is general agreement that these three verses do belong to one another, but there is a range of opinion among scholars as to what other verses these three might belong. For J. Fitzmyer, S.J., these three verses merit a chapter of their own in his commentary, though within the commentary itself he notes, "The episode takes on a further nuance in the context in which it is found. Following on the preceeding passage, in which the disciples fail to comprehend Jesus' destiny, it suggests that part of that incomprehension comes from a rivalry among them that obscures real vision . . . . Again, in the following context, their incomprehension and rivalry are linked to an attitude about outsiders . . . ."[16] E. Schweizer, for his part, has divided his commentary into a unit which runs from 9, 37–50; K.H. Rengstorf, on the other hand,

[12] H. Schürmann, *Das Lukasevangelium, Herders Theologischer Kommentar zum Neuen Testament* III.1, 2nd ed. (Freiburg: Herder 1982) 575 n. 2: "Die Jünger suchen nicht jemand, der grösser ist als sie alle (gen. comparationis), wie B. Weiss, *Die Quelle*, p. 42, u.a. deuten; . . . αὐτῶν gehört zu τίς (gen. partitivus);" see also, e.g. E. Klostermann, *Das Lukasevangelium, Handbuch zum Neuen Testament* V (Tübingen: Mohr 1975) 109; A. Plummer, *Gospel According to Luke, The International Critical Commentary*, 4th ed. (Edinburgh: Clark 1901) 257; Bruce (supra n. 7) 534.

[13] E.g., suggested by Zerwick and Grosvenor (supra n. 1) 216; Fitzmyer (supra n. 10) 815; others prefer 'greater'; Schürmann (supra n. 12) 577, n. 2; Zahn (supra no. 5) 393; Lenski (supra n. 9) 544: "μείζων . . . should not be rendered by the superlative, cf. Luke 8, 51; 9, 19."

[14] E.g., Fitzmyer (supra n. 10) 815; Zerwick and Grosvenor (supra n. 1) 216; I. H. Marshall, *The Gospel of Luke, The New International Greek Testament Commentary* (Exeter: Paternoster Press 1978) 393.

[15] 'Greatest': Zerwick and Grosvenor (supra n. 1) 216; *The New American Bible* (supra n. 2) 81; Kostermann (supra n. 12) 472; 'great': Schmithals (supra n. 3) 116; E. Schweizer, *Das Evangelium nach Lukas, Das Neue Testament Deutsch* III (Göttingen: Vanderhoeck und Ruprecht 1982) 107; K. Rengstorf, *Das Evangelium nach Lukas, Das Neue Testament Deutsch* III (Göttingen: Vanderhoeck und Ruprecht 1958) 157; Ernst (supra n. 4) 311; Fitzmyer (supra n. 10) 815 (= 'really great'); Schürmann (supra n. 12) 577 n. 1: "Man darf also nicht—mit Wellhausen, *Einleitung*, 21; Black, *An Aramaic Approach*, 86 u.a.—superlativisch verstehen;" J. Boehmer, *Das Lukasevangelium, Das Neues Testament* III (Gutersloh: Bertelsmann 1909) 165; L. Marchal, *Les Saints Évangiles S. Luc - S. Jean, La Sainte Bible* X, 2nd ed. (Paris: Letouzey 1950) 130; A. Plummer (supra n. 12) 258: "Jesus does not say 'is the greatest'; and He thus gives no encouragement to the desire to be above others;" cf. Marshall (supra n. 14) 397: "Jesus says that the person who is least . . . among all the disciples . . . is either 'great' (La Grange 282; Schürmann, I, 577 n. 15) or 'the greatest' (Zerwick 146; cf. BD 245)."

[16] Fitzmyer (supra n. 10) 816.

suggests no linkage of Luke 9, 46–48 with any other verses.[17] H. Schürmann, under the title, "Abschliessende Weisungen für den Jüngerkreis," considers Luke 9, 46–50 as a unit;[18] T. Zahn prefers a unit title, "Mancherlei Belehrungen der Jünger und solcher, die es werden wollen," and includes therein Luke 9, 43b–62.[19]

Some scholars have given a more particular grounding to the disciples' speculation about greatness than, for instance, a wider incomprehension of the cross in a disciple's life. Basing himself on Luke 7, 28, wherein John the Baptist is distinguished from the least in the kingdom, A.R.C. Leaney is of the opinion that "Luke has taken the dispute of the Apostles as an occasion for arguing the pre-eminence of Jesus over John the Baptist."[20] A. Plummer long ago noted that "Bede explains, (the dispute among the disciples occurred) *quia viderunt Petrum Jacobum et Joannem seorsum ductos in montem, secretumque eis ibi aliquod esse creditum,*" thereby tracing Luke 9, 46 to Luke 9, 28–36.[21] Still longer ago W.M.L. de Wette noted the suggestions of Theophylactus and Chrysostom concerning the root of the disciples' disagreement, "die Jünger wegen der nicht gelungenen Heilung des Mondsüchtigen einer dem anderen die Schuld gaben."[22] T. Zahn prefers to see the disciples' discussion originating from an earlier preaching, "Dazu kam, dass die Ap. auf ihrer ersten Predigtwanderung (Luke 9, 1–6.10) . . . nicht all den gleichen Erfolg gehabt hatten."[23] A final example of scholars' concern to find a context for Luke 9, 46–48 shall be that of J. Boehmer, that the disciples were discussing their shares in the power of Jesus, since some of them had so recently seen the "Offenbarung des Reiches Gottes"[24] (= Transfiguration).

A number of scholars do not link Luke 9, 46–48 to events within the Gospel story, but prefer to offer as the immediate context of the verses the need for orderliness in Luke's contemporary church. Thus, whatever be the situation that gave rise to the original discussion about greatness, Luke chooses to tell the story because his contemporaries need to hear it to resolve their own community struggles concerning greatness. Thus, scholars speak of *Gemeindeordnung*, and explain certain features of the Lucan text in the light of this community problem, "Da Lukas 'unter euch allen' zufugt, denkt er dabei an Gemeindeglieder."[25]

I shall return to this discussion of contexts, but one can readily see from this brief presentation both the efforts of scholars to search in various directions for a context by which

[17] Schweizer (supra n. 15) 106; by entitling vv. 37–50 "Der Unverstand der Jünger," Schweizer links vv. 46–50 with the cure of the demonically possessed boy (vv. 37–43) and the inability of the disciples to grasp the need that Jesus must die (vv. 44–45); K. Rengstorf (supra n. 15) 128.

[18] Schürmann (supra n. 12) 574.

[19] Zahn (supra n. 5) 392.

[20] A.R.C. Leaney, A *Commentary on the Gospel According to St. Luke*, 2nd ed. (London: Black 1966) 59.

[21] Plummer (supra n. 12) 257.

[22] De Wette (supra n. 9) 74.

[23] Zahn (supra n. 5) 394.

[24] Boehmer (supra n. 15) 165.

[25] Schweizer (supra n. 15) 107; cf. Ernst (supra n. 4) 311; Schürmann (supra n. 12) 574.

to make Luke 9, 46–48 more intelligible and the lack of consensus about the context. Given that scholars are not in accord with one another regarding context, it may not be surprising to find that some even think that the three verses of Luke 9, 46–48 hang together badly. They insist that we have in these verses a lack of logic. To this insistence is added the view of some that Luke's problem of logic or coherence stems from a certain lack of logic in his Marcan source. Let us look briefly and more closely at these points of view.

In regard to the internal coherence of Luke 9, 46–48, de Wette wrote in 1846, "Diese ganze Rede bei Lukas ist ohne Haltung, denn *καὶ ὃς ἂν ἐμὲ δέξηται κτλ.* ist Reminiscenz aus Matth. 10, 40., und *ὁ γὰρ μικρότερος . . . οὗτος ἔσται . . .* sollte wie bei Matth. zu Anfang stehen. Nur bei diesem Ev. [= Matthew] ist Zuzammenhang und Klarheit . . . [Similarly] (dieses Kind) ist unpassend, da man nachder andern Evv. und der Natur der Sache einen allgemeinen Satz erwartet."[26] Sometime later, W. Dickson and W. Stuart took direct issue with de Wette, "the saying of Jesus in Luke 48b ought not to have been explained as 'wanting in point' (de Wette) or 'without explanation' (Strauss)."[27] It was many years later, in 1978, that I. Howard Marshall made coherence a central point of his study of these verses. He notes, "the connection of thought (between v. 48b and what precedes it) is obscure . . . the saying about receiving the child in Mark 9, 37 belongs to a different circle of ideas . . . . It seems probable that two originally separate traditions have been linked together by Mark in a section 9, 33–50 . . . . Luke has then tied them together more closely."[28] Since for Marshall, and perhaps for de Wette, the looseness of logic in Luke 9, 46–48 is traceable to the source of Luke's verses, we can proceed to the second point I proposed earlier to treat: the source (Mark) from which Luke draws his story.

It is Mark we have to deal with, particularly to note how he is perceived as struggling, not wholly successfully, to bring together two different traditions under title of the disciples' dispute. Rudolf Bultmann has indicated his belief that behind Mark 9, 33–37 (indeed, 33–50) lay a type of catechism of the Lord's collected sayings, that Mark took one of these sayings about care for children and created a story (for the benefit and need of his audience) about a dispute concerning greatness in the community and Jesus' response to it; Mark, Bultmann says, has not been altogether successful in converting a saying into a story.[29]

J. Fitzmyer suggests his agreement with Bultmann's analysis.[30] J. Ernst believes these verses to have had "eine komplizierte Vorgeschichte," i.e., the Marcan verses came from "zwei ursprünglich selbständige Stücke: I. Mark 9, 33–35 (sekundäre Dublette zu Mark 10, 35–45), II. Mark 9, 36f. (vgl. Mark 10, 13–15)."[31] I have already called attention to the remarks of I.H. Marshall concerning the different strands he notes in the Marcan source for Luke; he says further, "Mark in fact contains two separate lessons at this point, and

[26] De Wette (supra n. 9) 75 n.
[27] Wm. Dickson and Wm. Stewart, *The Gospels of Mark and Luke*, vol. 2 (Edinburgh: Clark 1880) 100.
[28] Marshall (supra n. 14) 395.
[29] R. Bultmann, *The History of the Synoptic Tradition* (Oxford: Blackwell 1963) 149.
[30] Fitzmyer (supra n. 10) 815-16.
[31] Ernst (supra n. 4) 311.

each has parallels elsewhere (Mark 9:35 = 10:43f. parallels Luke 22:26; and Mark 9:37 corresponds to Luke 10:16)."[32]

Obviously, the voices which speak of disharmonious union in Luke 9, 46–48 are few and tend to trace this disharmony to the Marcan source. One might tend to ignore these voices except for the fact that interpreters do reveal more than an ordinary difficulty and effort in bringing out the relationship they think should exist between the question of the disciples about greatness and Jesus's answer to it, and between Jesus' gesture of siding the child with him and his two statements, "to receive this child is to receive me," and "the lesser among you is great." Aware, then, of the possibility that the three verses of Luke might not hang together in perfect coherence, let us turn to consider the interpretation of Luke 9, 46–48. We should keep in mind, as well, earlier reflections on the meaning of certain vocabulary in this passage and the struggle to give these verses a proper context.

A survey of the prevalent commentaries reflects division of opinion among scholars. On the one hand, interpreters insist that Jesus answers the disciples' question about the greater among them by identifying the great disciple as one who makes himself small, like a child. "He who desires to be great must first learn to be truly small."[33] "He said that a person who was humble enough to receive a child would receive Himself and His Father; when men have that kind of attitude, questions of precedence will not arise."[34] "For (γάρ, introducing a confirmatory explanation) he who is less (than the others) among you all (to wit, subjectively, according to his own estimation of himself) is great (objectively, in accordance with his real worth)."[35] " . . . das Maass der Demuth das Maass der wahren Grosse ist."[36] In these quotations (and in others like them) interpreters are suggesting that the disciple becomes great by becoming the lesser, by becoming humble.

A particularly attractive and popular development of this interpretation suggests that the way to reflecting one's own "greatness" is to serve the least of society; to teach this, Jesus draws attention to the child (the least) with whom Jesus links Himself (the greatest). "Two ideas merge here: (1) The greatest is the one who confesses his greatest need before God, for God will proportionately satisfy his wants. (2) The greatest is the one who loves even the lowliest person."[37] " . . . humility must be revealed in this, that even to the least ones (the child is typical of what is 'smallest') service and aid shall be rendered in His name for His sake and for love of Him."[38] "True greatness consists in

[32] Marshall (supra n. 14) 395.

[33] Geldenhuys (supra n. 9) 287.

[34] I.H. Marshall, *The New Bible Commentary Revised*, 3rd ed. (London: Inter-Varsity 1970) 904.

[35] Dickson and Stuart (supra n. 27) 100; cf. Zahn (supra n. 5) 392 n. 16.: "Das zu diesen letzten Satz überleitende γάρ ist hier nicht in ein Kausales, 'denn,' auch nicht ein Explikatives 'nämlich,' sondern jense im Deutschen schwer wiederzugebende, von älteren Philologen mit *sane igitur, sane pro rebus, comparatis*, umschriebene 'Konfirmative Adverb': so ist ja wahrlich."

[36] B. Weiss, *Die Evangelien des Markus und Lukas*, 6th ed. (Göttingen: Vandenhoeck und Ruprecht 1901) 434.

[37] C. Stuhlmueller, C.P., *The Gospel of Luke, The Jerome Biblical Commentary* (London: Geoffrey Chapman 1968) 142.

[38] Geldenhuys (supra n. 9) 287.

willing service to all, even to those who appear least important in human eyes."[39] "Jesus points out that true greatness means humble service rather than precedence."[40] "To do a service that is considered as being least of all, which they therefore decline to do, is to do what is great in Jesus' eyes."[41] "Jesus is teaching that the person who is willing to take the lowest place is really great—such willingness being shown in caring for such despised members of society as children . . . . The person who is prepared to act as servant has abandoned all desire for greatness."[42] "Nach dem Masstab, der bei Gott gilt, zeigt jener wahre Grösse, der sich selbstlos in den Dienst des hilfsbedürftigen Mitmenschen stellt."[43] "Wer den Kleinen liebt, den Geringen herzlich zugetan ist, der ist gross."[44] "Wer unter euch der Grösste sein will, der muss vorher anscheinend zum Geringsten werden durch Liebesdienst auch an den Unbedeutendsten."[45] In all these interpretations, it is clear that Luke 9, 46–48 is teaching that true greatness is becoming the type of person who serves the least of this world, thus, encouragement to humility, to becoming the least, is encouragement to service of the humble, of the least in society.

On the other hand, however, there is a kind of interpretation which, though it may end up in agreement with those already cited, insists that Jesus is teaching that the littlest and most helpless person is the greatest. Thus, while the disciples, according to this interpretation, are concerned about degrees of greatness applied to themselves, Jesus downplays their concern to emphasize that the least of society, in His eyes, are the great ones. "Er ist weniger Mahnung an die Jünger, im Dienen 'klein' zu werden also Aussage über die Kleinen, die der Gemeinde die Wichtigsten sein müssen, weil sie vor Gott 'gross' sind."[46] "In einem derartig Kleinen ist Jesus selbst, ist Gott aufgenommen; von daher wird dann V48c verständlich: dass der Kleinste in der Gemeinde der eigentlich 'Grosse' ist."[47] "Wer von Herzen und beharrlich dem Urteil Jesu zustimmt, dass ein solcher Jünger auch wenn er der Geringste unter all seinen Mitjüngern ist, gross sei, überwindet alle Ehrsucht and Eifersucht."[48] " . . . le plus petit de tous ceux qui sont ses disciples est grand."[49] "Basti loro sapere che il più piccolo tra tutti quelli che sono i discepoli di Christo è grande."[50] " . . . the original point of the saying is concerned with the greatness of the child . . . .'The least' is the child in the midst of the disciples; the child is 'great' . . . ."[51]

[39] G.P.H. Thompson, *The Gospel According to Luke* (Oxford: Clarendon 1972) 156.

[40] E.E. Ellis, *The Gospel of Luke, The Century Bible* (London: Nelson 1966) 145.

[41] Lenski (supra n. 9) 548.

[42] Marshall (supra n. 14) 397.

[43] K. Staab, *Das Evangelium nach Lukas* (Würzburg: Echter Verlag 1956) 64.

[44] Boehmer (supra n. 15) 165.

[45] Klostermann (supra n. 12) 109.

[46] Schweizer (supra n. 15) 107; cf. A. Schlatter, *Die Evangelien und die Apostelgeschichte, Erläuterungen zum Neuen Testament*, vol. 1 (Stuttgart: 1908) 492: "Ihre Sucht nach der Grösse ist gestillt und auf die rechte Bahn gebracht, wenn sie die Kleinen so schätzen, wie Jesus sie schätzt, und bedenken, dass Jesus die ihnen erweisene Liebe als ihm getan annimmt."

[47] Schürmann (supra n. 12) 575.

[48] Zahn (supra n. 5) 395.

[49] Marchal (supra n. 15) 130.

[50] Valensin and Huby (supra n. 6) 200.

[51] Marshall (supra n. 14) 397.

From the above bevy of interpretations, one should conclude that, though the disciples concern themselves as to who of *themselves* is the greater, Jesus is concerned to teach them that the lowliest of the world (and the lowliest of their community) is to be recognized as great. This can be recognized by the placement of the child right beside Jesus.

We have, then, two understandings of this passage, Luke 9, 46–48. For some interpreters, these verses are meant to teach the disciples that their own greatness is to be found in their becoming the least (becoming a child), which 'becoming' is concretely expressed in service to others, particularly to the despised and least of this world. For other interpreters, these verses stress, not so much what makes the disciples great, but that, as far as Jesus is concerned, people whom the world considers to be least (and in particular disciples whom the community considers to be the least)—these are great; the disciples should adjust to this reality.

Without completely denying all the elements of the above-mentioned streams of exegesis, I would like to propose a slightly different understanding of these Lucan verses. There is some grounding in the history of interpretation for the opinion I express here, though it be quite tiny. Over a hundred years ago, J. Chr. von Hofmann suggested that Luke 9, 46–48 had to do with the disciples' dispute about their greatness *as apostles*. Jesus would have perceived the nature of their discussion; He answered in a way that would indicate that greatness stems from being ἐπὶ τῷ ὀνόματι 'Ιησοῦ. Thus, though greatness can be said to characterize the disciple who humbles himself, especially to serve the least person, or that the people considered to be the least by the world are to Jesus and to God truly great, what Luke 9, 46-48 underlines is that greatness flows from the fact that one is ἐπὶ τῷ ὀνόματι 'Ιησοῦ. As Hofmann notes, "So ist es also für den Beruf der Jünger, wenn sie ausgehen, ihn (Jesus) zu verkündigen, gleichgültig, ob Einer von ihnen irgendwie mehr ist, als der Andere; der Werth der Aufnahme, die sie finden, hängt lediglich davon ab, ob man deshalb aufnimmt, weil man den ehrt, in dessen Name sie kommen . . . .sein Grösse, die er mit ihnen allen theilt, darin besteht, dass es im Namen dessen kommt, den Gott gesandt hat."[52] Hofmann was curtly contradicted by the great scholar, B. Weiss;[53] Hofmann's opinion never flew again. Hofmann never offered arguments of a literary nature to defend his interpretation; it is to this task that I now set myself.

What I consider the key to interpreting Luke 9, 46–48 is the striking phrase: ἐπὶ τῷ ὀνόματι ἐμοῦ (v 48a = Mark 9, 37). Granted that the phrase is found in Luke's Marcan source, the phrase has its own meaning and impact in the Lucan works of Gospel and Acts of the Apostles.

In the Gospel of Luke we find the phrase ἐπὶ τῷ ὀνόματι(ί) (μου) twice, 21, 8 and 24, 47; in Acts we find it four times, 4, 17.18; 5, 28.40. In each case the sense of the phrase is best expressed by the translation: "to be a representative of Me." In the Gospel Jesus warns His followers concerning those many who "will come in My name" (21,8), clearly using the phrase to indicate that many deceivers will come "representing Jesus." At the end of his Gospel, Luke has Jesus appear to His disciples to show them that He is alive, to

[52] Hofmann (supra n. 8) 254.
[53] Weiss (supra n. 36) 434.

emphasize that the Scriptures had foretold both His death and His resurrection, and, finally, to point out that the same Scriptures now expect that there will be "preaching in My name" of repentance and forgiveness of sins "to all the peoples" (24, 47). Again, the phrase "in My name" is used here in such a way as to indicate that the task of preaching repentance which leads to forgiveness of sins is to continue the very work of Jesus, that the preachers will be representatives of the Jesus whose work continues, now that He is alive again.[54]

In the Acts of the Apostles, the four uses of *ἐπὶ τῷ ὀνόματι* are concentrated in the bitter story of strife between the apostles and the Sanhedrin, the same group which had, successfully, brought about an end to Jesus' preaching (Acts 4, 1–22; 5, 17–42). In the Lucan organization of the confrontation between apostles and Sanhedrin two points can be noted. First, the disciples are admonished "not to speak in that name" (4, 17), then "not to teach in the name of Jesus" (4, 18). It is certainly true that the Sanhedrin does not want the Christians to speak favorably or on behalf of the person it had terminated. But the disciples are not, for Luke, people who simply speak favorably of Jesus; in a real sense they are the means through which Jesus re-establishes the preaching and miracle-working which death had, momentarily, interrupted. The disciples are representatives of the Jesus who was raised from the dead to continue the offer of salvation. With this understanding of the role of the witnesses to Jesus, Luke again has the Sanhedrin censure the disciples; they are neither to teach *ἐπὶ τῷ ὀνόματι τούτῳ* (5, 28), nor are they to speak *ἐπὶ τῷ ὀνόματι 'Ιησοῦ* (5, 40). If the Sanhedrin can succeed in these commands, not only will Jesus not be spoken of favorably or defended, but His work will not continue; there will be no more representative through whom the offer of salvation can pass from Jesus to God's human beings.

Secondly, and from a slightly different perspective, one can note the difference of meaning in this disciple-Sanhedrin conflict story. When Luke wants to emphasize the means through which a miracle is worked, he is very careful to use consistently the preposition *ἐν*: *ἐν τῷ ὀνόματι 'Ιησοῦ Χριστοῦ τοῦ Ναζωραίου περιπατεῖ* (3, 6); *ἐν ποίᾳ δύναμει ἢ ἐν ποίῳ ὀνόματι ἐποιήσατε τοῦτο* (4, 7); *γνωστὸν ἔστω . . . ἐν τῷ ὀνόματι 'Ιησοῦ Χριστοῦ τοῦ Ναζωραίου . . . οὗτος παρέστηκεν* (4, 10). By describing the miraculous cure of the invalid as done *ἐν τῷ ὀνόματι*, Luke may well imply that the disciples are acting as representatives of Jesus, but he certainly and explicitly accentuates the means by which the lame man now walks; on the other hand, when Luke uses the preposition *ἐπί*, it is his intention to underline explicitly the role of the disciples as representatives of Jesus. In short, in the case of two prepositions which can often be used

[54] I cannot agree with I.H. Marshall's conclusions about the phrase *ἐπὶ τῷ ὀνόματί μου* (supra n. 14) 396–97: "The phrase has the meaning 'on the basis of' . . . and qualifies the action, not the recipient; elsewhere the phrase 'on/in my name' refers to the power to do mighty works that stem from Jesus, but here it suggests action based on discipleship; it is because the audience are disciples of Jesus who has just symbolically received the child that they are to do the same. They act under his authority and according to his will."

interchangeably by authors of this period, Luke is careful to maintain the individuality of the preposition ἐπί.[55]

The above analysis of a particular terminology makes one think that Jesus in Luke 9, 46–48 puts emphasis on the disciples' role as His representatives; it is as His representatives that they can be considered 'great.' This understanding of Luke 9, 46–48 fits well with the immediate Gospel context in which these verses are found. The story following upon Luke 9, 46–48—a story characterized by the *Stichwort* (ἐν) τῷ ὀνόματι (ί) (σου)—creates another opportunity for teaching about the disciple in his capacity as one who brings the power and teaching of Jesus into play in this world. The 'greatness' then of being a disciple who represents Jesus is a gift by the Jesus who chooses His representatives; it is to the advantage of the disciple to acknowledge the freedom of Jesus, the same freedom by which the disciple was chosen to represent Jesus, in Jesus' working a miracle when His name is invoked by one who is not His representative—it is also to the advantage of the disciple to recognize in this other an ally in the struggle to have Jesus (and His name) dominate all those powers which dominate human beings. In short, both stories relate best to the need to understand the role of disciple in the struggle between Jesus and Satan.

Luke 9, 46–48 also relates to the two stories which have to do with the Transfiguration of Jesus and the subsequent cure of the possessed boy. In the first story, it is clear that only three of the Twelve are witnesses of the astounding transfiguration of Jesus; it is also clear, from the second story, that none of the other nine was able to cure a demonically possessed boy (though presumably all of the Twelve had done just such a thing at an earlier juncture [Luke 9, 6.10]). One might conclude from these two stories (Luke 9, 28–36 and 9, 37–43) that greatness in discipleship is determined by being singled out, as in the first story, for special revelation, or by being more capable, as in the second story, in miracle-working. Luke 9, 46–48 makes clear that a disciple's greatness is determined by the fact that he represents Jesus. One can call himself great only because he represents Someone else than himself.

Indeed, Luke 9, 46–48 fits well with the entire chapter 9 (if we may be allowed to assume that the 9th chapter has its own inner logic). The beginning of the chapter speaks of the mission of the disciples; the accent is not on inner moral virtue, but on external activity in the name of Jesus. This mission story concerning the Twelve is followed by the story of the multiplication of loaves. This story finds its particular meaning in the fact that Jesus, before working a miracle, asks his Twelve to provide food for the crowds—and, in the feeding, it is the Twelve who mediate the bread and fish to the people (as they

[55] After Paul's conversion and preparation to be a representative of Jesus, he is found in Jerusalem where Luke twice describes him as ἐπαρρησιάσατο ἐν τῷ ὀνόματι 'Ιησοῦ (in Damascus), παρρησιαζόμενος ἐν τῷ ὀνόματι τοῦ Κυρίου (in Jerusalem itself) (Acts 9, 27.28). Though the use of in these verses might be understood to mean "as representative of," I would prefer to suggest that it mean "on behalf of." Also, Acts 16.18, where the phrase ἐν ὀνόματι 'Ιησοῦ Χριστοῦ is used, need not be understood as suggesting that Paul is giving an order to the demon, in the sense that Paul is acting to represent Jesus.

will eventually do in the Christian Eucharist), and it is to each of the Twelve that a full basket of the miraculous bread falls, as a foreshadowing of the Eucharistic future.

The subsequent confession of Jesus as the Messiah of God (Luke 9, 18–20), a confession which does justice to the wonders and wisdom of Jesus, must be integrated with the suffering implicit in Jesus' self-imposed title: Son of Man. The wonderful works of curing must make way for suffering and death, not only for Jesus, but for those who follow Him (Luke 9, 21–27). Peter deciphered part of the mystery of Jesus' being in calling Him Messiah of God; he still had to learn the fuller meaning of Jesus, and of discipleship of such a Jesus.

The positioning of the Transfiguration and the wonder-cure of the possessed boy (Luke 9, 28–43) after the dire forecast of Jesus' terrible fate is meant to comfort and give hope to the disciple who must suffer with Jesus. Yet, that hope is quickly sobered by a second reminder, amidst the praise at the cure of the possessed boy, that Jesus must die a death that seems to be the very contradiction of His wisdom and power (Luke 9, 44–45).

At this juncture, after all the stories of chapter 9 which relate to the role of the disciple as representative of Jesus, Luke places the teaching of Jesus that the greatness of the disciple is to be found in his being representative of the glorious and suffering Jesus.

If it is correct that the disciples are to look upon themselves as representatives of Jesus—in this is their greatness—one can even see the relationship drawn between this Gospel moment and the actual representation of Jesus in Acts. It is a representation of preaching forgiveness (e.g., 3, 16.19) and working wonders (e.g., 5, 12), combined with suffering as the representative urges audiences everywhere to call on the name of the Lord Jesus for salvation (2, 21; 4, 12; 8, 12; 9, 14.21; 15, 17; 22, 16). It is a general assumption today that Luke wrote the Acts as a completion to the Gospel and did it in such a way that Theophilus (Luke 1, 4; Acts 1, 1) might be able to realize the assuredness of what he had earlier been taught as a Christian. A part of this assuredness is the Lord's words that those who passed on His teaching to Theophilus are His representatives—and in this they find their greatness, for wherever they go, they are characterized as those who act ἐπί τῷ ὀνόματι Ἰησοῦ.

I received an M.A. in Classical Studies from Loyola University of Chicago under the direction of Father Schoder, S.J. Since then, he has been colleague, encouragement, consolation, guide, and inspiration. What has made him great is the Name to which he attached his own so many years ago and which he has borne so devotedly, lovingly and generously as a Companion of Jesus. May He whose Name you bear, Father Schoder, bring you the fullness of that Name!

THE ORIGIN OF VERGIL'S MYTH OF THE *BUGONIA*

KENNETH F. KITCHELL

For RVS: "Felix es, qui nos docuisti rerum cognoscere causas."

Few who have read the end of Vergil's fourth *Georgic* can readily forget it. Into what might easily have been a pedestrian account of bee breeding, the master poet has inserted an epyllion of vast scope and powerful poetry which tells of Aristaeus and his bees. After a discussion of diseases of the hive, Vergil moves on to the ultimate catastrophe for a bee-keeper—the total loss of his population. He then shares with his reader the formula for begetting bees from the carcass of a battered ox.

It is, he tells us, the invention of Aristaeus the Arcadian, but is Egyptian in origin (281–294). Vergil's instructions for the procedure are meticulous (295–314). In spring time (305–307) a narrow site is chosen and walled in. Into this a two-year old calf is led and its nostrils and mouth are blocked up. It is then beaten to a pulp, though care is taken not to break the skin. Aromatic herbs are spread around, the room is sealed, and the hopeful beekeeper waits for an unspecified length of time (though at line 552 we learn that Aristaeus waits for nine dawnings). Gradually the moisture within the softening bones heats and gives rise first to "animalia. . .trunca pedum," presumably larvae, which in turn give way to those which are "stridentia pennis" (308–09), and the lost bees are thus replaced. The rest of the book is devoted to a complicated epyllion which relates in some detail how Aristaeus came by this technique, followed by a brief description of how he first put it to use.

The motives and artistic aims of Vergil in this epyllion which, according to Servius,[1] was inserted at a later time by Vergil to replace now unacceptable verses on Gallus, have long been discussed.[2] But the aim of this paper is rather to study the origin of the belief that bees could come from a decaying bull. At the same time, the origin of another wonder found in the fourth *Georgic*, the attraction of swarming bees by clanging bronze, will be discussed. Both marvels were firmly believed by the ancients, yet both are based on biological impossibilities which preclude their having arisen from simple misobservation of nature. Their origin, then, is probably to be sought elsewhere.

Vergil's process for the creation of bees is generally called the *bugonia* or *bougonia* and has been so called by any number of scholars. The term appears nowhere in Greek and in Classical Latin but once in Varro. There, the aptly named Vaccius states that bees are called *bougenes* due to their birth from bulls and promises his friend that he, in his

[1] Serv. on *Ecl.* 10.1 and *G.* 4.1.

[2] Cf. L.P. Wilkinson, *The Georgics of Vergil. A Critical Survey* (Cambridge: University Press 1969) 108–11 and 325–26; more recently, J.S. Campbell, "Initiation and the Tale of Aristaeus in Georgics Four," *Ramus* 11 (1983) 105–108.

account, will be at least as entertaining "quam qui Bugoniam scripsit."[3] Eusebius gives us further information when he tells us that the author of the poem was one Eumelus, who also wrote a *Europia* and whose *floruit* was ca. 730 B.C.[4] Certain scholars choose not to believe that this *Bugonia* dealt with the birth of bees from oxen, and claim its topic was the origin of cattle.[5] In fact, neither claim can be demonstrated with certainty, but in light of Varro's context, it seems best to believe that it dealt with this miraculous generation and to accept it as the earliest mention we possess of belief in this practice. The next reference to it is in Columella (fl. 65 A.D.) who cites Democritus (b. ca. 460 B.C.?). It is only the overly conservative who do not wish to accept Columella's evidence, for Florentinus, in the *Geoponica*, also cites Democritus as a source for the practice.[6] Moreover, Democritus was an avid natural philosopher who is known to have written some twenty-four works on natural science, including one entitled Αἰτίαι περὶ ζῴων.[7] It seems clear, then, that we have here a fifth century reference to the practice as well.

Another fifth century reference may be found in Varro, who cites an Archelaos as a source for the belief.[8] Tilly and Storr-Best identify this author as the cultured king of Macedonia who ruled from 413–399 B.C. and who may well have written on natural matters.[9] But Varro's fragment is in verse, and it is probably best to identify Archelaos with the third century B.C. poet whose many works on marvels include a well-known, but lost, Ἰδιοφυῆ.[10] Modern investigators into the *bugonia* have been troubled by the fact that Aristotle does not mention it, some even hinting that the belief did not exist before his time. Given the evidence just cited, this is unlikely. Further, Aristotle himself was an avid bee watcher

[3] Varro *Rust.* 2.5.5. βουγενὴς is to be preferred to βουγόνας offered in *Thesaurus Graecae Linguae*, 3rd ed., ed. Henri Estienne, C.B. Hase, et al. (Graz: Akadämishe Druck 1954 repr. of 1831–65 ed.) s.v. βουγόνη.

[4] Euseb. *Chron.* 1254. C.R. Osten-Sacken, *On the Oxen-Born Bees of the Ancients (Bougonia) and their Relation to* Eristalis Tenax, *a Two-Winged Insect* (Heidelberg: J. Hoerning 1894) 20–22 n. 2 and 71 cites Georges *Latin-German Lexicon* as attributing Archelaos (infra n. 9) as the author of the *Bugonia*. It is to Osten-Sacken's credit that he noticed the true authorship since so many later scholars have missed the connection between Varro and Eusebius.

[5] W.D. Hooper, H.B. Ash, tr. and eds. *Marcus Porcius Cato on Agriculture. Marcus Terentius Varro on Agriculture* (Cambridge, Mass.: Harvard 1934) 369 n. 4, who do not cite Eusebius. Lloyd Storr-Best, tr. and ed., *Varro on Farming* (London: G. Bell & Sons 1912) 185 n. 2 holds for cattle as the subject, but cites Keil and Scaliger as opting for bees.

[6] Columella *Rust.* 9.14.6, Florentinus (infra n. 19) *Geoponica* 15.2. Will Richter, *Vergil, Georgica. Das Wort der Antike* V (Munich: Huber 1957) 370, doubts Democritus' identity. Osten-Sacken (supra n. 4) 40 n. 2 and 73 is also dubious. A.E. Shipley, "The Bugonia Myth," *JP* 34 (1918) 101 is undecided, while A.S.F. Gow, "BOUGONIA in *Geoponica* xv.2," *CR* 58 (1944) 15 calls the reference "highly suspect."

[7] See *RE* V 136–37 for a list of his works, including some twenty four works on natural history. *OCD*[2] 328 calls him "an avid biologist."

[8] Varro *Rust.* 3.16.4

[9] Archelaos is mentioned also by Varro at 2.3.5 on which see Bertha Tilly, ed., *Varro the Farmer* (London: University Tutorial Press 1973) 250 and Storr-Best (supra n. 5) 159, each with the incorrect citation of Pliny *HN* 18.3. The correct citation is given later by Tilly, 295 on 3.16.4 and is *HN* 18.5.22. On this Archelaos see *RE* II 446–48 no. 7.

[10] *RE* II 453–4 no. 34 and W. Smith, ed., *Dictionary of Greek and Roman Biography and Mythology* I (Boston: Little, Brown 1849) 264. The date of the poet is discussed in both places and by Osten-Sacken (supra n. 4) 71. Richter (supra n. 6) 370 claims without discussion that he is "Alexandriner."

who puzzled unsuccessfully over the problem of the generation of the bee. He ends his studies with a warning that a careful mind should rely on observation and not on rumor.[11] Apparently, the folk magic of the *bugonia* was beneath his mention. The fact remains that the practice is mentioned by every other writer on bees in antiquity.

After the time of Aristotle, the citations become very numerous indeed. Philetas of Cos, who lived just after Aristotle, is one of the first of a long line of poets who used the term *βουγενεῖς* as a synonym for *μέλισσαι*.[12] Other early writers whose language betrays a knowledge of the belief include Theocritus (ob. ca. 260 B.C.),[13] and Mago the Carthaginian. This last writer on agriculture is of unsure date, though should be placed prior to 146 B.C.[14] His twenty-eight books on agriculture were so prized that the Senate ordered them translated from Punic into Latin, and they were later rendered into Greek.[15] Nicander (fl. ca. 150 B.C.) mentions the practice twice in his extant works and is known to have written a *Melissurgica*.[16] Hyginus, Augustus's freedman, wrote on the subject, perhaps in a work entitled *De apibus* and was well thought of by Columella.[17] To these authors we can add Ovid, Bianor, Meleager, Plutarch, Galen, Pliny, Aelian, Porphyry, Servius, and a number of later Christian authors and Byzantine lexicographers who all know of the process.[18] A tenth century encyclopedia of agricultural matters, the *Geoponica*, has the longest description of the process and gives as its source one Florentinus who probably dates to the period A.D. 222–235.[19] This detailed account, which calls the process the *bougene*, follows closely that of Vergil but also elaborates upon it. Whether

[11] Arist. *Gen. An.* 3.10.760b 28ff. Aristotle's sections on bees are well covered by H.M. Fraser, *Beekeeping in Antiquity*, 2nd ed. (London: University Press 1951) 13–28.

[12] Cited by Antig. Car. 19.

[13] *Syrinx* 3. Cf. A.S.F. Gow, ed., *Theocritus* (Cambridge: University Press 1952) I 256 and II 555.

[14] On Mago see Tilly (supra n. 9) 135. Gow (supra n. 6) wishes, on too slender evidence, I feel, to emend the Greek *Βάρων* to *Μάγων* at *Geoponica* 15.2 (thereby providing another mention of Mago).

[15] Pliny *HN* 18.5.22–23, Columella *Rust.* 1.1.13 calls him the "father of agriculture."

[16] Nic. *Ther.* 741 f., *Alex.* 446–52, *Mellis.* = frgs. 92–94, p. 215, in A.S.F. Gow and A.F. Scholfield, eds., *Nicander, the Poems and Poetical Fragments* (Cambridge: University Press 1953).

[17] Columella constantly cites Hyginus in flattering terms, calling him his "paedagogus" in *Rust.* 1.1.13. He seems to mention the *De apibus* at 9.13.8, on which see *RE* X 630 and Smith (supra n. 10) II 535 no. 6. It was either a separate work or part of his *De agricultura*.

[18] Ov. *Fast.* 1.379f. (on Aristaeus), *Met.* 15.361–68, Bianor *Anth. Pal.* 9.548.2, Meleager *Anth. Pal.* 9.363.13, Plut. *Cleom.* 39, Galen "De compositione medicamentorum secundum locos" 9, vol. XIII 273, ed. Kühn, "An fit animal quod in utero geritur," vol. XIX 174–75, ed. Kühn, Pliny *HN* 11.22.68, Ael. *NA* 2.57, Porph. *De antr. Nymph.* 18, Servius on *Aen.* 1.435 (ed. Harv.). The citation in Fraser (supra n. 11) 98 to Lactant. *Div. Inst.* I.8 is incorrect; the passage refers to another belief that bees could find offspring among flowers and has nothing to do with the *bugonia*. Nor is the reference of Richter (supra n. 6) 370 to Empedocles frg. 61 useful; although the word *βουγονή* is used here it clearly refers to Empedocles' famed early monsters, in this case man-faced bulls. Further and later references can be found in *RE* III.434 where note that Hesychios cites, in addition to Callimachus, a source which specifies that the bees come from the ox's bones. A survey of sources is also given by Osten-Sacken (supra n. 4) 20–29.

[19] Johan N. Niclas and Peter Needham, *Geoponica, sive De re rustica libri xx* (Leipzig: C. Fritsch 1701) 1.58 date Florentinus to the early 200's under the emperor Macrinus, while *RE* VI 2756 no. 6 places him under Alexander Severus, A.D. 222–235. He is said to have written a *Georgica*.

Florentinus had the same source as Vergil or whether he is simply gilding the Mantuan's lily is unknown.[20]

The *bugonia*, then, enjoyed long-lived and unflagging popularity in antiquity. So strong was this belief that it was even claimed to have been accomplished as late as 1842.[21] And yet, this is odd, for the process is based upon a totally impossible premise. First of all, bees will have absolutely nothing to do with carrion. The ancients knew full well that foul odors can distress bees and specifically state elsewhere that they shun putrescent flesh.[22] Secondly, apart from Ovid's cryptic and undoubtedly tongue-in-cheek claim that the success of the process is a proven fact,[23] we have no hint that anyone ever tried the process. Each author who mentions it does not cite experience, but previous authors. The reason for this is simple—it does not work. The average beekeeper, ancient or modern, is, above all else, practical. It would have taken the loss of but a few bullocks for beekeepers to catch on to the fact that the *bugonia* did not work or, at the least, had only worked in the golden age of an Aristaeus. While ancients may have guessed this, they nonetheless had a strong respect for tradition and what was reported to have happened in bygone days.

Modern scholars have smiled at the ancients' supposed credulity and have attempted to find the origins of the *bugonia*. Some believe it arose from a custom of keeping hives in stables for warmth in winter.[24] This may be a point of contact between the two animals, but it is surely not enough to account for the complicated ritual the *bugonia* entails, and it is scarcely a fitting reward for the bees' host to be beaten to a jelly. Further, the practice of keeping bees in stables is not, to my knowledge, mentioned in antiquity.

Others have said that a dried carcass is meant and that while bees abhor rotting flesh they could, in a pinch, use a hollowed cadaver as a hive. This, incidentally, is the normal explanation given for Samson's miraculous lion.[25] Again, while this *may* happen occasionally, it neglects two facts. First, a rare occurrence would not give rise to such a pervasive story. Secondly, in the accounts of both Vergil and the *Geoponica*, the decaying flesh is stressed as an integral part of the process. This theory, then, is also unacceptable.

[20] This text, difficult to obtain, is also quoted in Greek in Shipley (supra n. 6) 100–101. English summaries appear in Osten-Sacken (supra n. 4) 40–41, A.B. Cook, "The Bee in Greek Mythology," *JHS* 15 (1895) 9 and also in his *Zeus. A Study in Ancient Religion* (New York: Biblo & Tannen 1964 rpt.) I 514. A complete translation appears in Fraser (supra n. 11) 8–10 who incorrectly calls Florentinus a Byzantine author. The fact that Florentinus cites Juba (ob. A.D. 23) as his source probably shows a tradition independent of Vergil's and thus yet another early source for the *bugonia*.

[21] Fraser (supra n. 11) 10. Hilda M. Ransome, *The Sacred Bee in Ancient Times and Folklore* (London: Allen & Unwin 1937) 204–206.

[22] To name a few, Arist. *HA* 9.40.625b, Ael. *NA* 1.59, Verg. *G*. 4.48–9, Varro *Rust*. 3.16.6 ("nemo has videt. . .in carne aut sanguine aut adipe"), Columella *Rust*. 9.14.3–4, Pliny *HN* 11.8.18. T.E. Page is simply wrong when he states "that bees will settle in a decaying carcass is well known," *P. Vergilii Maronis Bucolica et Georgica* (London: Macmillan 1965) 365 on *G*. 4.284. On the aversion to carrion, T.F. Royds, "Beekeeping in Classical Times," *Bee World* 5 (1923) 12.

[23] *Met*. 15.361–68

[24] DePauw, cited by Cook, "Bee" (supra n. 20) 18.

[25] T.F. Royds, *The Beasts, Birds, and Bees of Vergil* (Oxford: Blackwell 1914) 93–94, Ransome (supra n. 21) 114–16, Gow (supra n. 6) 15.

Many investigators have therefore resorted to a theory popularized by Osten-Sacken, who claimed that the origins of the *bugonia* lay in simple misobservation. The creatures which arose from the decaying flesh were not bees at all, but were drone-flies, the *Eristalis tenax*.[26] This fly is indeed one of nature's wonders of mimicry, for it so clearly resembles the honey bee that it fools not only many of its predators, but even trained entomologists at a distance.[27]

Osten-Sacken's theory is the one cited most commonly today,[28] even though it has been thoroughly disproven and despite the fact that it is entirely as implausible as the *bugonia* itself. For *Eristalis tenax* does not lay its eggs in carrion, but in stagnant water rich in organic matter. Its entire larval stage, in fact, is wondrously designed to enable it to prosper in just these conditions and not those a normal carrion larva encounters.[29] Osten-Sacken himself knew this, and often defended himself on the matter. His answer was that civilization has offered the insect dung heaps, sewers, and cesspools, whereas in antiquity it was forced to rely on carrion, laying its eggs in puddles of putrescent matter which collected as the carcass was almost totally gone. But this hypothesis is simply not borne out by observation.[30] Even if it happened rarely (which is doubtful), how could a theory such as the *bugonia* arise around such a hit and miss affair? And even if occasionally these drone flies were to arise, beekeepers would soon enough realize that they were minus one good ox and had instead a group of useless, non-honey producing flies. We must ask, with Wilkinson, "How did the elaborate, partly ritualistic, prescription achieve such wide currency when any experiment would have discredited it?"[31] No, *Eristalis tenax* as the source of the *bugonia* would be an even greater *dictu mirabile monstrum* than the thing it is supposed to have given rise to.

Other questions remain as well. If the *bugonia* is the result simply of a sort of misobservation of natural phenomena, why are not flies mentioned? Surely they are more plentiful than any other insect around corpses. Or why is the ox the only animal the bee (or for that matter *Eristalis tenax*) will deign to visit? Why must it be killed in this precise manner? The answer to these questions will not be found in misobservation of nature. Something else lay behind such an improbable tale which made it a part of the common folklore for centuries on end.

The same line of reasoning applies to another widely believed phenomenon concerning bees, which Vergil also reports. As is well known, hives deal with their excess population by sending out swarms in the spring. At this time it is most beneficial for a beekeeper

[26] Osten-Sacken (supra n. 4).

[27] An excellent drawing of *E. tenax* can be seen in Bernhard Grzimek, ed. *Grzimek's Animal Life Encyclopedia. Volume II, Insects* (New York: Van Nostrand Reinhold 1975) 395.

[28] Royds (supra nn. 22 and 25); *RE* III 435; Shipley (supra n. 6) passim; J.G. Frazer, ed. *Publii Ovidii Nasonis Fastorum Libri Sex* (London: Macmillan 1929) II 158; Wilkinson (supra n. 2) 269.

[29] Grzimek (supra n. 27) 508 and figs. 20–26.

[30] Osten-Sacken (supra n. 4) 32–33, 41, 57–60; letters to and from Osten-Sacken, published in W.M. Wheeler, *Social Life Among the Insects* (New York: Harcourt, Brace and Co. 1923) 311–19; A.D. Betts "Beekeeping in Classical Times" (letter in response to Royds, supra n. 22) *Bee World* 5 (1923) 12–13, and "Oxen-Born Bees," ibid. 111–12.

[31] Wilkinson (supra n. 2) 269. So too B.G. Whitfield, "Virgil and the Bees," *G&R* 25 (1956) 117, who opts, though, for the dried carcass theory.

if he can entice the swarm, led by its newborn queen, to settle on his land and enter his hives. It is certainly an easier way to obtain bees than the *bugonia*! We know that the swarming bees, which number from 5,000 to over 50,000, follow pheromones given off by both the new queen and certain "scout" bees.[32] One could thus lure them along by trapping the queen in a cage and using her as bait.[33] The ancients knew none of this, of course, and often suggested laying out tempting, odiferous herbs. But since wild herbs and flowers are plentiful enough in the Mediterranean springtime, this could hardly be a foolproof method. Thus, many ancient authorities recommend what is often called "tanging" or "ringing the bees". This process calls invariably for the clanging of bronze cymbals or vessels and was said to lure the bees down.[34] As with the *bugonia*, belief in tanging lasted well beyond antiquity and is reported until relatively modern times. Some authorities claimed the noise frightened the bees into staying put, but the general belief was that the noise was pleasing to them.

Unfortunately, just as the *bugonia* is based upon an impossibility, so too is tanging, for bees are quite deaf. They can feel vibrations transmitted over a solid surface, but they are incapable of hearing air-borne vibrations.[35] It is possible that in this case the natural habits of swarming bees helped the tradition stay alive, for the bees will at first travel a very short distance and then settle down, presumably to be sure the queen is with them. At such a time it is possible, but not easy, for them to be captured. But even if this is the case, why was noise felt necessary at all, when simple following would accomplish the deed? Secondly, why is the bronze necessary, and why is it so often specified that the bronze be cymbals? Will not iron do?[36] Why not the music of trumpets or harps? Again, something quite specific must lie at the basis of the belief, something which encouraged weary beekeepers

[32] R.A. Morse, "Swarm Orientation in Honeybees," *Science* 141 (1963) 357–58; R.A. Morse and R. Boch, "Pheromone Concert in Swarming Honey Bees (*Hymenoptera: Apidae*)," *Annals of the Entomological Society of America* 64 (1971) 1414–17; T.D. Seeley, R.A. Morse, et al., "The Natural History of the Flight of Honey Bee Swarms," *Psyche* 86 (1979) 103–13. I am indebted to Professor Morse for his sharing of his knowledge with me on this subject. See also the classic, Karl von Frisch, *The Dancing Bees*, 2nd ed. (London: Methuen 1966) 35–39.

[33] Illustrated in Morse (supra n. 32) 357, fig. 2.

[34] Cited by Varro *Rust.* 3.16.7, Verg. *G.* 4.64–6, Ael. *NA* 5.13, Columella *Rust.* 9.8.10, Arist. *HA* 9.617a 15–17, Pliny *HN* 11.22.68, Ov. *Fast.* 3.737ff., *Geopon.* 15.3, Luc. 9.284–92. See A.D. Betts, "Tanging a Swarm," *Bee World* 4 (1922) 126–27 and R. Nowogrodzki, "A Pied Piper of Bees?" *American Bee Journal* 117 (1977) 692–93 with a delightful sixteenth century representation of the act. The custom eventually was Christianized and charms invoking holy names were used. Cf. Ransome (supra n. 21) 163–68 and 225–26 with an excursus on the word "tanging". See also Frazer (supra n. 28) III 137 and A.D. Betts, "An Old Bee-Charm," *Bee World* 4 (1922) 140.

[35] Nowogrodzki (supra n. 34) 693, von Frisch (supra n. 32) 38–39, 129; Wilkinson (supra n. 2) 261–62; Sir J. Lubbock, *Ants, Bees, and Wasps* (New York: Appleton 1883) 290–91; C.R. Ribbands, *The Behaviour and Social Life of Honeybees* (London: Bee Research Association 1953) 51–54; R.E. Snodgrass, *Anatomy and Physiology of the Honeybee* (New York: McGraw-Hill 1925) 107; C.G. Butler, *The World of the Honeybee*, rev. ed. (London: Collins 1974) 117–18.

[36] It should be noted that Columella and Varro (supra n. 34) allow the substitution of handclapping and Aristotle (supra n. 34) refers to "rattling" with sherds and pebbles. He must mean they are in some container, presumably of bronze. All other authors specify bronze, often indicating cymbals are to be used.

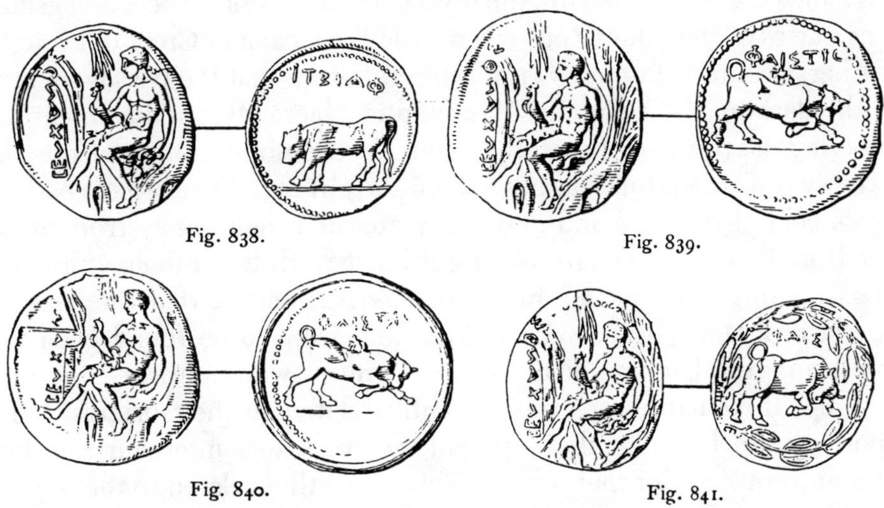

FIG. 1. Silver staters of Phaistos struck c. 360–300 B.C. After Cook, *Zeus* (supra n. 20) 946, figs. 838–841 (838, 839, 841 after Svoronos [infra n. 59] I 259f., pls. 23, 24–26).

to chase bees across the countryside with cymbals, or perhaps, if too tired, to accept with a nod a puzzling bit of folklore at face value based on its antiquity alone.

The long-lived, general respect for this tale and that of the *bugonia* is rooted, I feel, in the very old, long forgotten religious beliefs of Bronze Age Crete. This was already sensed by Betts and Wheeler[37] who, while overly zealous in their reconstructions, were nevertheless correct in searching for a religious origin for the *bugonia*. Many customs were and indeed are carried out, even in secular matters, because they once had a serious religious overtone. How many of us, for example, have participated in the ritual of carrying the bride across the threshold? As centuries pass, the reasons for a custom are usually forgotten, but the act remains surrounded with an aura of awe that is not dependent upon any understanding of its *aition*.

It is sometimes possible to deduce a cautious reconstruction of such a custom's origin. In this instance, I feel that we can find the origins of both the *bugonia* and of tanging in the myths which surround the birth of Zeus on the island of Crete. This Zeus, Zeus Kretagenes or Welchanos, shown here on coins of Phaistos (Fig. 1), has long been recognized as a survival of an ancient Minoan god of vegetation, one who died and was reborn each year.[38] It is an old myth, far older than its first telling in Hesiod,[39] and it has much to

[37] A.D. Betts, "The Earth Goddess and Her Bee Priestesses," *Bee World* 4 (1922) 52–53, and "Oxen-Born Bees" (supra n. 30). See also Wheeler (supra n. 30) 92–96.

[38] R.F. Willetts, *Cretan Cults and Festivals* (London: Routledge & Keagan Paul 1962) 79–81, 199–200; W. Burkert, *Greek Religion* (Cambridge, Mass.: Harvard 1985) 127; Cook, *Zeus* (supra n. 20) I 149f., 645f., II 925f.; M.P. Nilsson, *The Minoan Mycenaean Religion and its Survival in Greek Religion*, 2nd ed., rev. (New York: Biblo & Tannen 1974 reprint) 532ff.

[39] Hes. *Theog.* 477ff.

offer this investigation. To begin with, the myths commonly place bees alongside the goat Amaltheia as nurses of the infant Zeus when he lay in a cave in Crete to avoid the appetite of his father, Cronus.[40] In fact, Vergil himself tells us that the bees were attracted to the cave by the clashing of the Curetes' "crepitantia. . .aera,"[41] thus documenting the first tanging and tying the process intimately to Zeus Kretagenes. For their efforts the Cretan bees were amply rewarded, for Zeus gave them the gift of golden-bronze bodies to ward off the intense cold of the cave and personally guarded their honey from all intruders. Once a year from this cave, we are told, light burst forth to symbolize the birth of the god.[42] Aelian, quoting Antenor, an author of *Kretika*, tells us that the bees were well known into classical times (they were vicious) and were to be found even in his own day.[43] These bees were later rationalized into nymphs who nourished the infant Zeus using honey, but their names are transparently related to their origins.[44] In another curious report we are told that the apparent lack of sexual intercourse in bees was a reward to them from Zeus for their care.[45] This tale is thus related to the *bugonia*, for it was this lack of observed mating which so concerned the ancients about the bee.

This affiliation of bees with the oldest Cretan lore is also found in the myth of Glaukos, Minos, Polyeidos, and the bees, a clear story about rebirth and the bees' role in it whose portrayal on a gem was recognized by Furtwängler (Fig. 2), and in the roles the Curetes were said to have had in the invention of beekeeping.[46] We can also see it in the Cretan goddess Britomartis, whose name is probably to be derived from the pre- Greek verb *βλίττειν*, "to draw honey out of the hive."[47] There is more, but the pattern is clear. The honey bee held an important claim on the mythology, lore, and probably religion of classical Crete, with many elements undoubtedly extending well back into Minoan times.

We have, moreover, strong evidence that the bee and its honey were quite prominent from earliest times on Crete. Beekeeping as such is an ancient art,[48] and it is highly probable that the Minoans practiced apiculture.[49] The bee appears as hieroglyph number 86 in Evans' list (Figs. 3, 4), borrowed directly from Egyptian signs which are associated

[40] Many citations gathered by Nilsson (supra n. 38) 542 ff. and a remarkable dissertation (directed by Williamowitz and Diels), Ernest Neustadt, *De Jove Cretico* (Berlin: Mayer & Müller 1906) 18ff ("De Amalthea").

[41] Verg. *G.* 4.149–52.

[42] Ant. Lib. 19. Cf. Cook, *Zeus* (supra n. 20) II 928.

[43] Ael. *NA* 17.35. On Antenor see *FGrHist* IIIb no. 463.

[44] E.g. "Melissa". See the evidence in Fraser (supra n. 11) 7–8; Neustadt (supra n. 40) 44–58; W. Robert-Tornow, *De apium mellisque apud veteres signifcatione* (Berlin: Wiedmann 1893) 154 ff.

[45] Serv. on *G.* 4.150

[46] Diod. Sic. 5.65.2, Vergil (supra n. 41). Cook, "Bee" (supra n.20) 11.

[47] Cook, "Bee" (supra n. 20) 15; Willetts (supra n. 38) 179f.

[48] G. Clark, "Bees in Antiquity," *Antiquity* 16 (1942) 208–15, Ransome (supra n. 21) 19–42, 55–64; E. Crane, *The Archaeology of Beekeeping* (Ithaca: Cornell 1983) 19–27, 35–39.

[49] Ransome (supra n. 21) 61–64; S. Hood, "The Mallia Gold Pendant: Wasps or Bees?" in *Tribute to an Antiquary: Essays presented to Marc Fitch by Some of His Friends*, F. Emmison and R. Stephens eds. (London: Leopard's Head Press 1976), 92; C. Davaras, *Guide to Cretan Antiquities* (Park Ridge, N.J.: Noyes 1976) 144; cf. Crane (supra n. 48) 45, 48. I wish to thank Leverett Bogle who drew the sketches of the Minoan signs and sealings for this article.

FIG. 2. Scarab representing the Glaukos myth. After Ransome (supra n. 21) 108, fig. 19 (after Furtwängler, *Antike Gemmen* pl. XXII, 16).

FIG. 3. Minoan sealing with bee hieroglyph. After Evans (infra n. 50) 167 no. 86b.

FIG. 4. Minoan bee hieroglyphs. After Evans (infra n. 50) 212 no. 86.

with royalty (Fig. 5). Other signs depict honey jars (Fig. 6 a–e), and some sealings may depict tools used in beekeeping (Fig. 6 f).[50] Recent archaeological finds have even produced bee remains from a Minoan context.[51] Linear B tablets often mention honey (frequently as an offering), and the bee is quite evident in Bronze Age art (Pl. 21).[52] The bee, then, had a long history on Crete, one which culminates in the story of the birth of Zeus on Crete, nursed by the bees drawn by the first tanging.

What, then, of the bull? It too is met in the birth of this god on Crete. One does not wish to plunge too rashly into the often dangerous field of Bronze Age religion, and arguments can too easily be fought over exact interpretations of inexact scenes or over likely reconstructions of cults or beliefs which are shrouded in both time and silence. But even in these very cautious post-Evans times, it is well accepted to say that the bull played a very important part in Cretan religion. Nor is it excessive to identify this role as a representative of, manifestation of, or simply as an offering to, the yearly dying and reborn vegetation god of the Minoans.[53] Thus, while evidence for a bull-cult as such may be very weak, evidence for bull sacrifice (Fig. 7) and its probable connection with the famed Cretan double ax is quite strong.[54] Moreover, Çatal Hüyük has yielded highly suggestive and fairly well accepted evidence on the subject. Here, in clear cult centers, there is undeniable evidence that the Mother Goddess, the bull, and the bee were intricately bound up in the cycle of death and rebirth of the vegetation cult. Of special interest is the evidence from level six, where breasts, bulls, bees, and honey combs adorn the walls of the shrine.[55] Another parallel is to be found in Hittite myth, where the vegetation god Telpinu disappeared each year and was found again by a bee.[56]

All of these factors come together on Crete in the story of Zeus' birth. We may never determine the exact cave in which he was born and, in fact, its exact identification was probably argued over by the Cretans themselves.[57] But in various Cretan caves there is clear evidence of bull sacrifice to the young god who was, through his birth, closely associated with caves; other caves that have yielded offerings of arms call to mind the Curetes.[58]

[50] Sir Arthur Evans, *Scripta Minoa* (Oxford: Clarendon 1909) 212f., 165–67, 201; Hood (supra n. 49) 64–67; K. Kitchell, "The Mallia 'Wasp' Pendant Reconsidered," *Antiquity* 55 (1981) 10–13.

[51] My thanks to David S. Reese, who related in a private communication of 1981 that excavations in Kommos, Crete uncovered remains of at least two species of bees from a context dating them to perhaps 1600–1400 B.C.

[52] J. Chadwick and M. Ventris, *Documents in Mycenaean Greek*, 2nd ed. (Cambridge: University Press 1973) index s.v. "honey"; J. Zafiropoulo, *Mead and Wine* (New York: Schocken 1966) 39k; Hood (supra n. 49) passim.

[53] Nilsson (supra n. 38) 229f., 373f.

[54] "That the axe was used for the sacrifice of oxen is beyond doubt," Burkert (supra n. 38) 38; Nilsson (supra n. 38) 230–31.

[55] C. Dietrich, *The Origins of Greek Religion* (Berlin: De Gruyter 1974) 94ff., 104ff. (level six), and 107ff., (Dietrich's connection of the relationship to original cave worship in Crete). Cf. Burkert (supra n. 38) 37f., 40.

[56] Dietrich (supra n. 55) 120 n. 309.

[57] E.K. Platakes, Τό *σπήλειον τῆς γεννήσεως τοῦ* Κρηταγένους Διός, *Amaltheia* 7 (1976) 75–88.

[58] Dietrich (supra n. 55) 81 (ox skulls in the cave on Ida), 83 (bucrania and oxen-shaped rhyta at Psychro), 85 (weapons at Arkalokhori). Willetts (supra n. 38) 141–47 offers a survey.

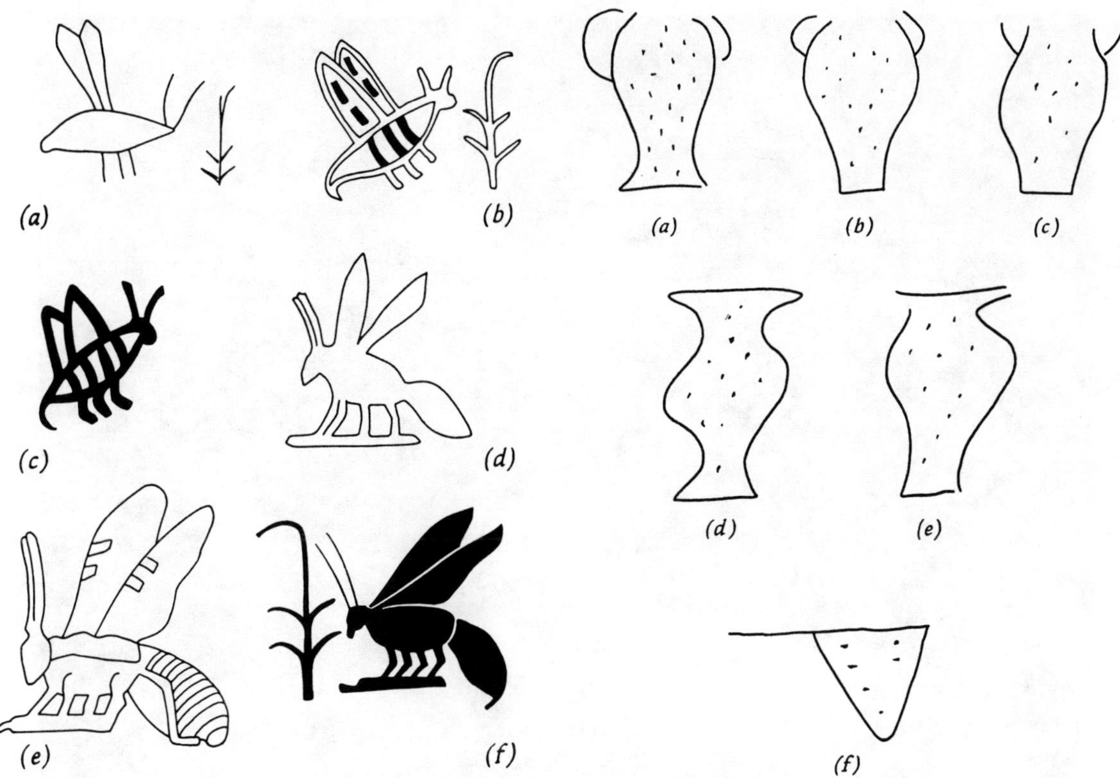

FIG. 5. Egyptian hieroglyphs of bees. After Ransome (supra n. 21) 25, fig. 3.

FIG. 6. Minoan jar hieroglyphs. After Evans (supra n. 50) 201 nos. 50, 51.

The Minoan god, then, whose name is known to us only as Welchanos or Zeus Kretagenes, had a strong association with the bull. Since bees are said to have nourished him, we begin to see a connection, one which was carried over into Classical myths. Cretan coins provide invaluable support for these myths. On the coins of Elyros and Hyrtacina, for example, a goat is on the obverse and a bee on the reverse.[59] On those of Phaestus the bull appears on the reverse of coins depicting Welchanos on the obverse (Fig. 1).[60] Other coins show Olympian Zeus with a bull, Dictaean Zeus with a goat or a bull, Demeter with a bull, Artemis with a bee, and even a bucranion such as those found in Minoan caves.[61]

It had long ago been suggested that the bee was a goddess herself on Crete or served as an emissary of the Great Goddess who was the consort of the young dying god.[62] There

[59] W. Wroth, *A Catalogue of the Greek Coins of Crete and the Aegean Islands* (Bologna: Forni 1963) 36, 50. These and the coins cited below can also be found in G. LeRidder, *Monnaies crètoises* (Paris: Guenthner 1966) and J.N. Svoronos, *Numismatique de la Crète ancienne* (Macon: Protat Frères 1890), using the indices of each.

[60] Wroth (supra n. 59) 63.

[61] Ibid. 10, 29, 37f., 66, 70f.

[62] Neustadt (supra n. 40); Betts (supra n. 37); Nilsson (supra n. 38) 360 n. 78.

PLATE 21

PLATE 21. The Mallia "wasp" pendant in the Herakleion Museum. Photo courtesy Museum.

FIG. 7 (above). Minoan sealstone in the Herakleion Museum showing a bull lying on a table for sacrifice. After Nilsson (supra n. 38) 230, fig. 113.

FIG. 8 (right). Statue of Artemis of Ephesos. After Ransome (supra n. 21) 57, fig. 8 (after C. Menetrius, *Symbolica Dianae* [Rome 1657]).

is not enough space here to analyze all the arguments, but copious linguistic and archaeological evidence has been collected to show that the bee, a constant symbol of rebirth, was closely associated with what is commonly called the "Great Mother." The evidence of the polymastic Artemis of Epheseus and her priests and priestesses called "essenes" and "melissai" is but one example. The coins of her city also show both the bee and the goat, and the famous statues of the deity show bees crawling next to bulls' heads (Fig. 8).[63] Further support is provided by the coins of Crete just cited where the young Zeus, the goat, the bees, bulls, and various female fertility goddesses[64] are present, often on coins of the same city.

[63] Fraser (supra n. 11) 98, fig. 13; Ransome (supra n. 21) 57ff. with pl. vi and fig. 8; Dietrich (supra n. 55) 120.

[64] One must remember that Cretan Artemis is not the later goddess of the Greeks; Willetts (supra n. 38) 179–98, 272–77.

It seems clear, then, that there is an undeniable relationship between Minoan culture and religion, the bull, the bee, and the later evidence of Zeus Kretagenes. How might they fit together? We must always remember that many centuries separate whatever the Minoan beliefs and rites were from their appearance in classical times. Much was forgotten in this span, much was added or deleted, and most was undoubtedly misunderstood. But one very interesting hypothesis seems to fit the known facts. Let us say, as is likely, that Minoan religion included a cult of an older form of Zeus Kretagenes seen as or merely associated with the bull. This animal was sacrificed each year to represent the god's demise. Later, most likely in the spring, the god was reborn to symbolize the rebirth of the crops. At the same time bees were seen as attending the rebirth. Their presence could have been merely mythical, or somehow enacted in ritual form (we recall the "melissai" and "essenes" as priests), or even an actual fact, for, as Antenor relates, they were said to exist into classical times in the very cave where the birth of Zeus was believed to have occurred. Whatever the mode, their "birth" was intimately connected with the slaughtered ox. As is common in such orgiastic cults, dancing and cymbals attended some part of the ritual and thus became associated with attracting newly swarming bees.

Tantalizing questions remain, of course. There are many details about which one could speculate to no good end. Why was the bull battered in later versions and not slaughtered as on Minoan artistic representations? Is Vergil correct in asserting that Egypt was the home of the *bugonia*, and if so, what has this to do with Herodotus' tale of the strange way the Egyptians buried their oxen and the fact that some ancient authorities say that the *bugonia* entailed burying the ox?[65] Is this why the Minoans copied their hieroglyph from the Egyptians? Is the fact that the bees in Zeus' cave so closely match Egyptian bees in color and temper an indication that apiculture came to Minoan Crete and thus Greece from Egypt?[66] Is our version of the *bugonia* a memory from Minoan days, or did classical authors pick it up externally from Egyptian sources, from Africa (Juba in the *Geoponica*), or Anatolia (Çatal Hüyük)? These questions are as intriguing as they are dangerous to answer. For now, if we may accept the barest outline as given above, the riddle of the *bugonia* and of tanging is solved at least in its basics. We now see why only a bull's body will produce the bees and why not just any noise, but specifically that of cymbals will attract them as they swarm. Moreover, the fact that both events are specific to spring is clear, for this is not only when bees naturally swarm, it is also when vegetation cults hold their ceremonies of rebirth. We may even know now why the bull in the *bugonia* is to be put away in an enclosure which so closely resembles a cave. Again, we even see something more than poetic elaboration when authors tell us the bronze cymbals used in tanging belonged to the Great Mother.[67] Much, of course, remains unanswered, but the ultimate origins of Vergil's *dictu mirabile monstrum*, the ox-born bees, may at last be clear.

[65] Hdt. 2.41, Antig. Car. 19 (23), Ov. *Fast.* 1.376–80, *Met.* 15.361–68.

[66] A.M. Sturgess, "The Golden Bee," *Bee World* 4 (1923) 182 on the temper of these bees. Fraser (supra n. 11) 6, 52, 90, 97.

[67] Vergil and Lucan (supra n. 34).

THUCYDIDES AND *IG* I³ 948: ἀμυδροῖς γράμμασι

B.M. Lavelle

Thucydides (6.54.7) describes the conditions of the Altars of the Twelve Gods and Apollo Pythios and their inscriptions in the following way:

> *καὶ τῷ μὲν ἐν τῇ ἀγορᾷ προσοικοδομήσας ὕστερον ὁ δῆμος Ἀθηναίων μεῖζον μῆκος τοῦ βωμοῦ ἠφάνισε τοὐπίγραμμα· τοῦ δ' ἐν Πυθίου ἔτι καὶ νῦν δῆλόν ἐστιν ἀμυδροῖς γράμμασι λέγον τάδε·*
>
> *μνῆμα τόδ' ἧς ἀρχῆς Πεισίστρατος Ἱππίου υἱός*
> *θῆκεν Ἀπόλλωνος Πυθίου ἐν τεμένει*

In May of 1877, the Greek archaeologist and epigrapher Koumanoudis recovered two well-preserved fragments of the latter Altar on the right bank of the Ilissos south of the Olympieion with the following inscription:

> Μνε̃μα τόδε hε̃ς ἀρχε̃ς Πεισιστ̣[ρατος hιππίο h]υιός
> θε̃κεν Ἀπόλλονος Πυθ[ί]ο ἐν τεμένει̣[1]

The only problem with the identification was that the letters of the recovered inscription, although not large or deeply cut, were well-formed, clear, and easily read.[2] Why had Thucydides described the letters as ἀμυδρά?

Suggested explanations followed closely upon publication of Koumanoudis' discovery. Among the first and now the most widely accepted (and so orthodox) explanation of the discrepancy is that the paint with which the Athenians colored inscribed letters to make them stand out from their white marble background had, through neglect and weathering, faded either partially or completely by Thucydides' day and so had caused him to term the letters "indistinct."[3] Other less well accepted explanations for Thucydides'

[1] This paper is dedicated to the memory of Father Schoder, whose superlative photographs of Greece and elsewhere have made much that once was *ἀμυδρὰ σαφέστατά τε καὶ φαεννότατα.*

On the inscription: *Eph. Ath.*, 7 May 1877; S. Koumanoudis, Ἀθήναιον 6 (1877) 149; K.D. Mylonas, "Νέα Προσκτήματα," *BCH* 1 (1877) 349–50; *CIA* IV, Suppl. 373e, 41; *IG* I² 761 (*SEG* 10, 318; 12, 56; 17, 11; 18, 9; 22, 56; 31, 9). Cf. E.L. Hicks and G.F. Hill, *Greek Historical Inscriptions* (Oxford: Clarendon 1901) 12, no. 10; M.N. Tod, *A Selection of Greek Historical Inscriptions* (Oxford: Clarendon 1933) 11, no. 8; R. Meiggs and D.M. Lewis, *A Selection of Greek Historical Inscriptions*² (Oxford: Clarendon 1975) 19–20, no. 11; P.A. Hansen, *Carmina Epigraphica Graeca Saeculorum VIII–V a. Chr. n.* (Berlin: de Gruyter 1983) 163–64, no. 305. Facsimiles: H. Roehl, *Imagines Inscriptionum Graecarum Antiquissimarum in Usum Scholarum*³ (Berlin: Reimer 1907) 73, no. 21; G. Welter, "Datierte Altäre in Athen," *AA* (1939) 23–35; J. Kirchner, *Imagines Inscriptionum Atticarum* (Berlin: Mann 1948) 11 and pl. 12; Travlos 102, 132–34. See also infra nn. 3–7.

[2] See Mylonas et al. (supra n. 1); the problem created by the relative elegance and sophistication of the inscription for its dating (cf. B.D. Meritt, "Greek Inscriptions," *Hesperia* 8 [1939] 62–64) has, I believe, been adequately resolved: cf. A.W. Gomme, "Athenian Notes," *AJP* 65 (1944) 327–28; H.T. Wade-Gery, "Themistocles' Archonship," *BSA* 36 (1936/37) 263, n. 2; Meiggs and Lewis (supra n. 1) 20.

[3] H. Heydemann, "Epigraphischen," *Hermes* 14 (1879) 317; E.S. Roberts, *An Introduction to Greek Epigraphy* (Cambridge: University Press 1887) 86; A. Wilhelm, *Neue Beiträge zur griechischen Inschrift-*

use of ἀμυδρά are that the letter-forms of the inscription were archaic and so old fashioned and obsolete at the end of the fifth century (Szanto),[4] that they were cut very narrowly and shallowly (Lauffer),[5] or that they were originally painted on the Altar, were faded by the time Thucydides read them, and were then cut into the stone sometime after (Löwy)![6] Arbanitopoulous' suggestion that the letters on the neglected Altar became filled with dirt (κόνις) has, as far as I can tell, been completely ignored.[7]

None of these explanations is convincing, least of all the "orthodox" one which seems to have evolved from mere wit as a tidying and a convenience. Its shortcomings are perhaps best demonstrated in the words of Jane Harrison who inspected Koumanoudis' finds in the basement of the Varvakeion: "[The fragments] stand at present [1888] at the end of a long dark passage full of inscribed slabs. They can only be examined in very indifferent light, but the letters are cut with such beautiful sharpness that there is no difficulty in reading them."[8] Indeed, another Athenian public inscription whose letters are described as ἀμυδρά (see below paragraph) should have been maintained and its letters recolored, if that were Athenian practice. For the inscription preserved a very ancient and important sacred law, not the name of an outlawed criminal, and should not have been unduly neglected. If, on the other hand, the Athenians did not in general maintain inscriptions (which is likely to have been the case), then Thucydides must have meant something other than "unpainted" when he used ἀμυδρά.[9] .

Explanation of Thucydides' meaning must devolve upon the meaning of ἀμυδρά as it can be applied to an inscription whose letters are now and must also have been clear and distinct in Thucydides' day. It so happens that ἀμυδρά is used in reference to other

enkunde (Vienna: Hölder 1909) 111–12; F. Hiller von Gaertringen, *Historische griechische Epigramme* (Bonn: Marcus & Weber 1926) no. 8; P. Friedlander and H. Hoffleit, *Epigrammata: Greek Inscriptions in Verse* (Berkeley: California 1948) 99, n. 2; M. Guarducci, *Epigrafia graeca I* (Rome: Istituto Poligrafico dello Stato 1967) 140. See also Hicks and Hill (supra n. 1); Welter (supra n. 1) 34–35; Kirchner (supra n. 1) 11; Meiggs and Lewis (supra n. 1) 20; Hansen (supra n. 1) 164. Cf. D. Page, *Further Greek Epigrams* (Cambridge: University Press 1981) 240: "The common explanation is that the paint with which the letters were filled had faded in his [sc. Thucydides'] day."

[4] E. Szanto, "'Αμυδρός," *WS* 3 (1881) 155–57; contra: Hicks and Hill (supra n. 1); Tod (supra n. 1); cf. W.B. Dinsmoor, "Greek Archaeology and History," in *Studies in the History of Culture* (Menasha, Wisc.: Banta 1942) 196. On the orthography of the inscription see G. Loeschke, "Altattische Grabstellen," *AM* 4 (1879) 43, and L. H. Jeffery, *The Local Scripts of Archaic Greece* (Oxford: Clarendon 1961) 75.

[5] S. Lauffer, "Zu den altattischer Weihinschriften," *AM* 62 (1937) 110; cf. K.J. Dover, *A Historical Commentary on Thucydides, IV* (Oxford: Clarendon 1971) 331: ". . . no doubt the letters of any inscription a hundred years old were faint to Thucydides by contrast with the great number of much more recent inscriptions to be seen in Athens." Cf. also Welter (supra n. 1) 34.

[6] E. Löwy, "Zu Datierung attische Inschriften," *SBMünch* 216, 4 (1937) 12–14; contra: Dover (supra n. 5) 332; Dinsmoor (supra n. 4) 198. It is quite impossible for me to conceive of a time after 510 B.C. when such a rescription would be possible. Cf. Roberts (supra n. 3).

[7] A.S. Arbanitopoulous, 'Επιγραφική (Athens: Typographeion "Estia" 1937) 111.

[8] Jane Harrison, *Mythology and Monuments of Ancient Athens* (London: MacMillan 1890) 204, who nevertheless adopts the explanation of faded paint (see supra n. 3). I am quite unsure why scholars infer that ancient Greek readers of inscriptions would not or could not vary the light and shadow on the surface of an inscription (cf. Welter [supra n. 1] 34–35).

[9] Cf. Hansen (supra n. 1) 304: " . . . ἀμυδροῖς (i.e., *'sine colore'*) γράμμασι . . . ."

inscriptions. Apollodoros in the speech against Neaira and Stephanos ([*Dem.*] 59.76) describes the state of a lithic stele set up near the Altar of Dionysos-in-the-Marshes, whose very ancient inscription made provisions for the wife of the king-archon: *καὶ αὕτη ἡ στήλη ἔτι καὶ νῦν ἕστηκεν ἀμυδροῖς γράμμασι Ἀττικοῖς δηλοῦσα τὰ γεγράμμενα.* The meaning of ἀμυδρά here is not altogether certain, but the stele was old and its surface is very likely to have weathered, perhaps altering some of the letters (see above paragraph).[10] Indeed, Remus' address to King Numitor (Plut. *Rom.* 7.8) supports the conclusion that the letter-forms themselves are altered either wholly or partially, for he says that the bronze trough that had carried the twin babies down the river Tiber was engraved with letters that had, by the time of Remus' majority, become ἀμυδρά.[11] Whether the bronze had oxidized or the letters were worn down, it is clear that the letters themselves, their shapes and legibility *unpainted*, were affected. A similar meaning is found in Plato's *Theaetetus* (194e) where Sokrates likens the soul to wax that can be imprinted: imprints made in soft wax, he says, become indistinct (obviously in respect of their shapes) because they melt together quickly (*ὑπὸ τοῦ συγχεῖσθαι ταχὺ γίγνεται ἀμυδρά*).[12] The general meaning of ἀμυδρός seems to be "indistinct or less distinct (and so less perceptible)."[13] Applied to letters in inscriptions, however, ἀμυδρά apparently means that their forms had been altered, that they were somehow not complete, and, consequently, that their message was less easily comprehended. How then can such a meaning be reconciled with letters that are quite distinct and very easily read even in "indifferent" light?

The answer must be found in the evidence we have of Athens' treatment of the Peisistratids in the wake of their expulsion from the city and of state criminals in general at Athens. Some short time after 510 B.C., the Athenians proscribed the tyrants and their children, and set up the proclamation of proscription upon the Akropolis for all and sundry to see.[14] The Peisistratids were condemned to death (obviously *in absentia*) and perpetually exiled (i.e., made *atimoi*);[15] rewards were appointed for their captors and their

[10] The inscription must have been more than two hundred years old, but how much older it is not possible to say. The sanctuary was "very ancient" (Thuc. 2.15.4; [*Dem.*] 59.76) and, although the earliest stone temple is to be dated to the sixth century, must have antedated the temple considerably (A.W. Gomme, *A Historical Commentary on Thucydides II* [Oxford: Clarendon 1956] 51): the *temenos* was important in the Anthesteria, a festival shared by the Athenians and Ionians (Thuc. 2.15.4), which may well have dated from Mycenaean times (cf. N. Coldstream, *The Formation of the Greek Polis: Aristotle and Archaeology* [Opladen: Westdt. Verl. 1984] 14, n. 19). On Dionysos-in-the-Marshes see Jane Harrison, *Primitive Athens as Described by Thucydides* (Cambridge: University Press 1906) 83–100; Travlos 332.

[11] *ἔστι δ' ἡ σκάφη καὶ σῴζεται, χαλκοῖς ὑποζώμασι γραμμάτων ἀμυδρῶν ἐγκεχαραγμένων, ἃ γένοιτ' ἂν ὕστερον ἴσως ἀνωφελῆ γνωρίσματα τοῖς τοκεῦσιν ἡμῶν ἀπολομένων.*

[12] Indistinct, unclear or imperfect in respect of shape: cf. Archilochus Fr. 231 West; Plato *Timaeus* 49a; Arist. *HA* 502b, 9; Paus. 10.28.1; Plut. *Alc.* 38.2.

[13] Indistinct affecting perceptibility, function, etc.: Plato *Rep.* 597a; *Phaedrus*, 250b; Arist. *Mete.* 343b, 13, 372a, 2, *HA* 537b, 12, 556b, 20; *Metaph.* 985a, 13, 988a, 23; Aretaeus (Hude) 16, 41; 127, 28; 47, 25; 53, 18; 50, 3. See also LSJ s.v. ἀμυδρός.

[14] Thuc. 6.55.1; cf. Dover (supra n. 5) 333; B.M. Lavelle, "Thucydides 6.55.1 and *Adikia*," *ZPE* 54 (1984) 17–19 and "*Adikia*, the Decree of Kannonos and the Trial of the Generals," *ClMed* (forthcoming).

[15] Condemned to death: Ar. *Birds* 1074–75; cf. Plut. *Sol.* 19.4 (on the law on tyranny before Solon; see also *atimia*, this note). Perpetual exile: Hdt. 5.65, 96.2; *Ath. Pol.* 19.6; Marcel. *Vit. Thuc.* 32; cf. also Andoc. 1.78 (cf. D. M. MacDowell, Andocides. *On The Mysteries* [Oxford: Clarendon 1962] 118). *Atimia*: *Ath.*

slayers.[16] Their property was confiscated, their homes were probably demolished and, it appears from the fact that Peisistratos and Hipparchos were also condemned, the bones of the dead were exhumed and cast beyond the borders of Attica.[17] These measures were standard for those convicted of tyranny or *prodosia* (treason) and constituted an *ignominia post mortem* or *post exilem*: they were obviously intended to obliterate all memory of criminals except that of their transgressions.[18] The Peisistratids, through the fifth century, were special objects of hatred for the Athenians and most especially execrated.[19]

The measures taken by the Athenians for state criminals very closely match the Roman practice of *damnatio memoriae* for criminals convicted of *perduellio* (treason) or *maiestas* (high treason) or for bad or tyrannical emperors.[20] This *ignominia post mortem* for such offenders included confiscation of property, denial of mourning for and burial of the criminal's body after execution, as well as destruction of the convicted's effigies and obliteration of his name from public and private inscriptions and monuments.[21] In regard to the latter, effacement seems to have ranged from excision to smearing with mud: when Heliogabalos had resolved to depose Alexander Severus (SHA, *Elag.* 13.6–7), he sent his minions to the Praetorian Camp with instructions to smear the inscriptions on Alexander's statues with mud "as usually happens to tyrants" (*ut fieri solet de tyrannis*).[22] This act was undoubtedly a prelude to a more formal and lasting obliteration, but its implications were at once perceived and resented by the Praetorians who rebelled and prevented Heliogabalos from carrying out his design.[23]

Pol. 16.10 (for tyrants; see also infra n. 18); cf. Dover (supra n. 5) 324; P.J. Rhodes, *A Commentary on the Aristotelian'* Athenaion Politeia (Oxford: Clarendon 1981) 222; and especially M.H. Hansen, Apagoge, Endeixis *and* Ephegesis *Against* Kakourgoi, Atimoi *and* Pheugontes (Odense: University Press 1976) 78–79.

[16] Ar. *Birds* 1074–75.

[17] Property confiscated: cf. Hdt. 6.121 and infra n. 18. Demolition of houses: see infra n. 18. Peisistratos and Hipparchos indicted: Thuc. 6. 55. 1.

[18] Condemnation for *prodosia*, confiscation of property, demolition of houses: Plut. *Mor.* 834a–b; *schol. ad Ar. Lysis.* 273. Proscription: Plut. *Mor.* 834a–b; *schol. ad Ar. Lysis.* 273; Lyc. *Leoc.* 117; *SIG* I³ 58 (= Meiggs and Lewis [supra n. 1] 105–107, no. 43). Progeny condemned: Plut. *Mor.* 834 a–b; *SIG* I³ 58. Denial of burial: Plut. *Mor.* 834 a–b; Thuc. 1.126.12. Flight: *SIG* I³ 58.

[19] See supra nn. 14, 15; cf. R. Parker, *Miasma* (Oxford: Clarendon 1983) 204. The institutional execration of the Peisistratids is likely to have been inversely propotional to the veneration accorded the tyrannicides: cf. *IG* I³ 131; Thuc. 6.53.3; Ar. *Lysis.* 631–34; *Ath. Pol.* 58.1 (and Rhodes' note ad loc. [see supra n. 15]). On the tyrannicides see M.W. Taylor, *The Tyrant-Slayers* (New York: Arno 1981).

[20] See S. Brasloff, *RE* IV.2, 2059–62 s.v. *damnatio memoriae*; F. Vittinghoff, *Der Staatsfeind in der römischer Kaiserzeit* (Berlin: Junker & Dünnhaupt 1936) 12–51.

[21] Cf. ibid. 18–41 on effacement.

[22] *misit et ad milites litteras, quibus iussit ut abrogaretur nomen Caesaris Alexandro. misit qui et in Castris statuarum eius titulos luto tegeret, ut fieri solet de tyrannis.*

[23] SHA, *Elag.* 14.2. Effacements: SHA, *Elag.* 17.4; Dio Cas. fr. 26.1; cf. Vittinghoff (supra no. 20) 21 ff. Removal of statues: Plut. *Cic.* 49.4 (Antony); Tac. *An.* 2.32.1 (Libo; cf. F.R.D. Goodyear, *The Annals of Tacitus, II* [Cambridge: University Press 1981] 281); 11.35.1 (Silius); 11.38.3 (Messalina); cf. Cic. *Rab. perd.* 24; Tac. *An.* 1.17.7; Suet. *Nero* 37 on the dangers of retaining outlawed statuary; cf. Vittinghoff (supra n. 20) 13 ff. Such damnation for treason or high crimes is undoubtedly very old at Rome (cf. Livy, 6.20; cf. also R.M. Ogilvie, *A Commentary on Livy, I–V* [Oxford: Clarendon 1965] 114–15 on *perduellio*).

Effacement and removal of memorials and inscriptions of evil kings, tyrants, and *prodotai* were also practiced at Athens. When the Romans and Attalos freed Athens from the control of Philip of Macedon in 199 B.C., the Athenians reacted by voting to remove all of the statues and inscriptions of Philip and his Macedonian predecessors from the city.[24] Even the places where memorials or inscriptions had been set up were accursed, and the Athenians went so far as to pass against Philip all of the decrees that had been passed against the Peisistratids (*postremo inclusum, ut omnia quae adversus Pisistratidas decreta quondam erant eadem in Philippo servarentur*).[25] In some cases, effacement appears to have been hastily accomplished or otherwise imperfectly carried out, for Macedonian inscriptions dated earlier than 199 B.C. have survived.[26] In the first flush of liberation, the Athenians may have done whatever they could to obliterate the inscriptions instead of bothering to excise each inscription. In many case, they may simply have rubbed mud into inscriptions, thus blotting out offensive letters and words. About one hundred years earlier, the people at Ilion in the Troad had passed a law on tyranny which provided for excision (*ἐκκόπτειν*) of the names of malefactors even if inscribed on holy objects, offerings, or tombs.[27] Athenian interests and influence in the area of the Troad were inveterate, and it may well be that the people of Ilion had borrowed the provision from Athens.[28] Not long before the promulgation of that law, the Athenians had removed and destroyed all of the statues of the tyrant Demetrios of Phaleron when the city was liberated in 307 B.C.[29] The bronze statues were either cast into the sea, sold, or melted down and made in to chamber-pots—the last a symbolic act of base contempt for the former tyrant.[30] But destruction of effigies as part of the *ignominia* must be dated much earlier. When Hipparchos, the son of Charmos, was convicted of *prodosia* shortly before 480 B.C., the Athenians voted to remove his statue from its place on the Akropolis, to melt it down, and to make it into a bronze stele on which were to be written his name and those of other traitors and sinners.[31] Hipparchos, who was a relative of Peisistratos and said to be the chief of the tyrants' friends in Athens before his trial, seems to have earned conviction for his defection to the tyrants-in-exile in Persia before Xerxes' invasion.[32] The removal of statues, inscriptions, or other reminders of state criminals from public view is a logical feature of a *damnatio* whose main purpose, after all, was to obliterate all but the

[24] Livy 31.44.4; cf. W.S. Ferguson, *Hellenistic Athens* (London: MacMillan 1911) 276–77.

[25] Livy 31.44.6–8.

[26] Cf. J. Briscoe, *A Commentary on Livy, XXXI–XXXIII* (Oxford: Clarendon 1973) 151: contra Ferguson (supra 24) who had suggested that the official imprecations voted against the Macedonians were rescinded by 188/87 B.C. Briscoe (151) assumes that the official imprecations were simply ignored and is more likely to be correct.

[27] *OGIS* I, 218, 12: *ὅτου ἄν τι ὄνομα ἦι τούτων ἐάν τε ἐν τοῖς ἱερ(τη)εύσασιν ἐάν τε ἐν ἀναθήματί τ' ἐπί τάφο<υ> ἐκκόπτειν πάντοθεγ.* Cf. Vittinghoff (supra n. 20) 19, n. 55.

[28] Cf. J.M. Cook, *The Troad* (Oxford: Clarendon 1973) 178 ff.

[29] Diog. Laer. 5.77 (Favorinus); cf. Ferguson (supra n. 24) 101. Demetrios may have been charged with tyranny, subversion, or treason, since the Athenians, from the end of the fifth century, seem to have made little distinction between such capital crimes (cf. the Demophantos-Decree: Andoc. 1.96–97).

[30] Supra n. 29; cf. Parker (supra n. 19) 162, n. 101.

[31] Lyc. *Leoc.* 117.

[32] *Ath. Pol.* 22.4; cf. Lavelle, "Thuc., " (supra n. 14) 18, n. 7.

worst memories of the convicted; effacement is most certainly in accord with the other aspects of Athenian *damnatio*, and its practice will have been older than its application in Hipparchos' case.[33]

Imperfect effacement of Peisistratos' inscription on the Altar of Apollo Pythios best explains Thucydides' use of ἀμυδρά. Peisistratos, along with his father, brothers, and relatives, was convicted of capital crime, proscribed, and so automatically held in execration by the Athenians. But that execration was greatly increased after the family's cooperation with the Persians in 490 and 480 B.C., and it is from that time that the Peisistratids were ranked in Athens' and democracy's worst enemies.[34] As with Hipparchos, the son of Charmos, Demetrios of Phaleron, and Philip of Macedon, the Athenians must have acted to extirpate the memory of these arch-criminals and, as with the Macedonians, very probably emotionally and hastily, effacing as they pleased, where and as they could.[35] Some special annoyance may have attached to the precinct of Apollo Pythios, itself the creation of the elder Peisistratos,[36] for, in one late tradition, the Athenians are said to have defecated in the *temenos*—an act of great contempt and profanation highly reminiscent of their treatment of Demetrios' statues and of the places where Macedonian memorials stood, as well as recollective of the law on tyranny from Ilion which did not spare even the sacred from execration.[37] If that is the case, and the Athenians did in fact openly profane the *temenos*, then they may have smeared the Altar with mud or anything else ready to hand *ut fieri solet de tyrannis*. But the late tradition, really the only proof we have for such conduct, may be unsound, for it is difficult to imagine why choregic monuments would have been set up in the precinct if it had been or continued to be defiled.[38] If the Athenians did not desecrate the *temenos* or Altar, but continued to respect them as holy, then they may have attempted to cover over the inscription with plaster, stucco, or some other inoffensive building material or substance.[39] Left neglected—did the *temenos* suffer damage in the Persian invasion?—the Altar will have weathered, exposing the epigram perhaps only partially, but enough for Thucydides or anybody else of his day to read.[40]

[33] Cf. supra n. 23. *Atimia* (i.e. outright outlawry) was earned for *tyrannis* or *prodosia* and was certainly older than Solon (supra no. 15).

[34] Supra n. 19.

[35] Building over the Altar of the Twelve Gods (Ferguson [supra n. 24] 277, n. 2; Dinsmoor [supra n. 4] 198, n. 19) was apparently not part of the *damnatio*, since the Altar was not modified until the third quarter (late?) of the fifth century (M. Crosby, "The Altar of the Twelve Gods," *Hesperia* Suppl. 8 [1949] 99 and 101). Dinsmoor's detection of a narrow, smoother band does not suggest effacement, but the original preparation of the stone (cf. Dinsmoor [supra n. 4], 198).

[36] On the Pythion see E. Curtius, "Das Pythion in Athen," *Hermes* 12 (1877) 491–99; Harrison (supra n. 10) 67–82; W. Judeich, *Topographie von Athen* (Munich: Beck 1931) 386, n. 5; Travlos 100.

[37] Hesychios s.v. ἐν Πυθίῳ χέσαι; Suda s.v. ἐν Πυθίῳ κρεῖττον ἦν ἀποπατῆσαι. For a fuller compilation of testimonia see J. P. Lynch, "Hipparchos' Wall in the Academy of Athens: A Closer Look at the Tradition," in *Studies Presented to Sterling Dow on his Eightieth Birthday*, *GRBM* 10 (1984) 177–79.

[38] Travlos (supra n. 1) 100–101.

[39] A. Orlandos, *Les materiaux de construction et la technique architecture des anciens grecs* (Paris: de Boccard 1966) 135–53. I thank the editor for pointing this work out to me.

[40] It is possible that only part of the inscription was effaced (e.g., Peisistratos' name), thus causing Thucydides' use of ἀμυδρά.

THE TIGRESS AND HER CUBS: TRACKING DOWN A ROMAN ANECDOTE

ALEXANDER P. MACGREGOR, JR.

Imagine, if you will, a tigress whose cubs have just been stolen, in hot pursuit of the horseman who has stolen them—this was a picture that moved, or amused, the Romans from the age of Nero to that of Justinian.[1] But, whenever it occurs, it has usually gone unrecognized for the commonplace it is. At first glance exclusively Roman—an interesting fact, were it true—on closer inspection it turns out to be a Roman reworking of a much older story, original to the lion, with the trail ultimately leading back to Homer. In any case, the *plot* of the story, if not its cast, remained much the same throughout the ancient world as a stock symbol of maternal fierceness and devotion, whatever variations might mark each retelling. And retold it was: at least sixty times in literature, at least ten times in the visual arts; what is more, there is a remarkable mutual influence between the two.

At the outset, the anecdote belongs to the lion, and is full of pathos. In the *Iliad*, when Achilles mourns Patroclus, he "uttered piteous groans, like a bearded lion when a huntsman has stolen his cubs from a thicket and he comes back too late, discovers his loss, and follows the man's trail through glade after glade, hoping in his misery to track him down" (18.318–22, tr. Rieu). Here, for the first and last time, the bereft parent is the father not the mother. But this is not to say that the later tradition is necessarily changing Homer; one could as easily say that Homer is accommodating the sex of the beast to that of Achilles. In any case, many of the later accoutrements of the story are here already, in the first telling: notably, the beast's failure to retrieve its cubs.

Despite the magnificence of Homer's treatment, later Greek authors were lukewarm to the tale:[2] Perdiccas, the companion of Alexander, is supposed to have stolen some lion cubs to demonstrate his daring, if we are to believe the much later account of Aelian (*V.H.* 12.39); Theocritus (*Id.* 9), followed by Ovid (*Met.* 13.789ff.), parodies the story by having the Cyclops Polyphemus, ever in the worst of taste, try to win the sea-nymph Galatea by offering her eleven bear cubs that he has presumably stolen. His gift plays off the love-gifts of fifth-century Athens (where the cheetah, tamest of the big cats, enjoyed a certain vogue);[3] and it is one of the few times that classical literature alludes to a bear-cub

[1] The author is grateful to Professors Arch Kristofferson and Anne Michelini of The University of Cincinnati and to Professors Susan Cole and Matthew Dickie of the University of Illinois at Chicago for their suggestions. Unless otherwise noted, translations are by this writer. The paper is presented here as delivered to the Chicago Classical Club, November 1984; originally delivered to the Cincinnati Classical Club, October 1982.

[2] Eur. *Med.* 187–89 may be an allusion: she "plays the wild bull, with the look of a nursing lioness"; see D.L. Page, ad loc. (Oxford, 1938).

[3] See A. Ashmead, "Greek Cats," *Expedition* 20.3 (1978) 38–47; and G. Koch-Harnack, *Knabenliebe und Tiergeschenke* (Berlin: Mann 1983) rev. R. Sutton, *AJA* 89 (1985) 183–84. I am grateful to the editor for these references.

theft: on the other hand, in the Old Testament it is the she-bear who regularly stands as the symbol of maternal fierceness and protectiveness: so *Proverbs* 17.12: "Better to encounter a bear robbed of her cubs than a fool enamored of his folly."

Eventually Homer's lion makes its way into Latin, where his mate enjoys a brief vogue in Horace and Ovid. Horace's treatment is sophisticated, even ironic (*Odes* 3.20): Pyrrhus, stealing his boy-love Nearchus away from an unnamed woman, is likened to a hunter pursued by a lioness, and warned to have a care. Ovid, a master at repeating himself without repetition, plays with the anecdote no fewer than seven times, notably at *Metamorphoses* 13.546–49, where he elevates Hecuba avenging Polydorus to the heroic level by likening her to a lioness defending her cubs—Achilles once again.[4] But he can make light of it as well: his Polyphemus, too, boasts of his gifts (*Met.* 13.834–37):

I found these twins, to play with you I hope—
So like each other you can't tell 'em apart;
Found you these shaggy cubs atop a cliff
And said right off, "I'll save 'em for my girl."

It is clearer here than in Theocritus that the cubs are an appropriate gift for Polyphemus to give precisely because they are the spit and image of the giver; Ovid is also playing off the old tradition that bear-cubs begin life as indistinguishable blobs "licked into shape" by the she-bear. In any case, Polyphemus does not *hunt* his cubs, as a proper hero should; he simply *finds* them, as Ovid's repetition of *inueni* emphasizes.

Elsewhere, too, Ovid has fun with the anecdote: in the *Fasti* (5.175–78) he creates an otherwise unknown hero, one Hyas. Still young, his *uirtus* had progressed to the point that he tried to steal lion cubs from their den; unfortunately, the mother ate him. Ovid tells the tale in four verses redolent of Saki, and with the same irreverent moral: heroic gestures only rarely work.

The anecdote occurs with the lion as principal character only one more time, in Statius (*Ach.* 1.168–72): the Centaur Chiron sets his pupil Achilles the task of stealing lion-cubs. The lion of Homer has come full circle, and disappears from Latin literature thereafter. The story originally his (or hers) had, a little earlier, been appropriated by a beast who perhaps better answered to the sanguinary temperament of the Romans—the tigress. When the story was transferred from the one beast to the other, the plot was expanded and romanticized; the resulting "Tiger Chase" was a peculiarly Roman product, unknown to Greek literature and uninfluenced by it.[5] The story first occurs in the days of Claudius, and proved an instant success; there is hardly a Latin poet who does not at least allude to it. It thus provides us with an excellent specimen of imitation, that is, of

[4] Echoed by Tiberianus *Anth. Lat.* 719b ed. Riese[2] (Leipzig, 1906) = 2.12–14 *Minor Latin Poets*, ed. Duff (London, 1934), where, pace Duff, the point is that gold can no more protect Polydorus than a lioness her cubs.

[5] The two apparent exceptions both wrote in the Roman court: Oppian (*Cyn.* 3.355–62), whose patron was Caracalla; and his contemporary Flavius Philostratus (*Vit. Ap.* 2.14), who wrote at the instance of Julia Domna.

the tension between tradition and originality, here, fortunately, working on material that did *not* rest on the authority of Vergil and Ovid. Moreover, the story makes its way into the visual arts, too, where it leads a life of its own even to the point where floor mosaics influence the later literary tradition.

Stripped of its individual embellishments, the story runs as follows: "A huntsman on horseback steals the cubs of a tigress; she pursues him at top speed, but he saves himself by one ruse or another; he finally manages to put water between himself and the beast, and thus makes his escape." The story enjoys many motifs found in folklore: the turn-about of the hunter hunted; the mother bereft; the ruses the huntsman employs; the water that stops the tigress just as the Doon stopped Meg the witch. There is much here to amuse children of all ages, and the anecdote afforded the poet the opportunity to display his ingenuity now by selective allusion, now by judicious innovation—judicious, in that the audience must be allowed the pleasure of recognizing the old story underneath the new twist that it has been given.

The tiger the Romans were to make so much of had been unknown to the ancient world before Alexander the Great; even Aristotle, sent specimens from India, only knew that "people in India say you get a fierce hunting dog if you cross a bitch and a tiger; that's what they say" (*H.A.* 8.28.13). Later Greek authorities add that the species is entirely female, and is impregnated by the West wind Zephyr: a relatively small stock of misinformation, even for ancient zoology.[6]

The first Latin writer to mention a tiger was the polymath Varro (*L.L.* 5.100); he calls it "a multicolored lion, so to speak, which has not yet been taken alive." Some sixteen years after Varro's death, Augustus exhibited the first live specimen—a tame one, no less—at the dedication of the theater of Marcellus in 13 B.C. (Pliny *N.H.* 8.25.65).

Poets were not slow to import the exotic into their own menageries. At the outset its epithets were undistinctive, pretty much the same as the lion's: *rabida*, *saeua*, *fera*, *irata*, and the like. With the tiger, though, brute savagery came to the fore: wrath (*ira*) is commoner of lions, sheer madness (*rabies*) of tigers; by the same token, lions can be *magnanimus*, *nobilis*, or *generosus*, but tigers never; on the other hand, only a tiger can be *atra*, *ferox*, *improba* or *stupida*.[7] Vergil makes good use of its reputation for utter savagery by having Orpheus capable of entrancing even a tigress (*G.* 4.510);[8] Ovid plays with the alleged fact that the beast loathes water when he has one flounder about in Deucalion's

[6] Cf. Arrian *Ind.* 15.1–3; Oppian *Cyn.* 1.323 and 1.432; Plutarch *Mor.* 144D and 167C; and Strabo 15.1.37.

[7] These comments are based on 160 passages that give the lion an attribute or epithet, and on 81 that give the tigress one; the latter collection is intended to be exhaustive. The lion enjoys 37 epithets, the tigress 28, with 21 in common. For the lion the most popular are *ira* (24 times), *saeuus* (21), *ferus* (18), *rabidus* (15); for the tigress this order is reversed (5, 7, 9, 12, respectively). That is to say, it is the mindless savagery of the tigress, not her righteous indignation, that is to the fore; pari passu, *cruentus* is frequent of the tigress (6), rare of the lion (3).

[8] The famous simile following likens Orpheus to the nightingale bewailing her own loss; it would heighten the pathos if the tigers here were likewise envisioned as bereft, but so enraged by their loss that only an Orpheus, suffering his own loss, could assuage them.

flood (*Met.* 1.305). Clearly, neither poet minds that the tiger did not exist in Europe, and never had; the beast was too useful poetically.[9]

In any case, Augustan poets limit themselves to allusions; the tigress will have no story of her own until the age of Nero. It would be pleasant to see in this turn of events the influence of Nero's pet tigress Phoebe, supposedly the only thing he ever loved;[10] but the real if prosaic reason is that a few years earlier Claudius, ever eager to follow in the footsteps of Augustus, had himself exhibited tigers, a set of four, thereby whetting public interest in the beast. It is surely no coincidence that in the same reign the geographer Pomponius Mela tells us, for the first time, the story of the tigress bereft of her cubs (3.5.7): "The forests of Hyrcania breed tigers, a savage sort of beast, and so speedy that it is easy and indeed normal for it to catch up with a horseman who enjoys a considerable headstart, and do this not just once but over and over again. The reason is because (*causa . . . est quod*) the horseman had snatched her cubs and is trying to carry them off, so he fools her by dropping one of them behind him; the tigress retrieves it and carries it back to her den; she then resumes the chase faster than ever, and goes through the same business over and over again until the fleeing thief reaches a more densely populated area than the tigress cares to approach." Now, Mela's account is notably repetitive, and even waits until halfway through before saying what had started the chase in the first place; moreover, his tigress renews the chase from Start over and over again: this serves to emphasize the supposed speed of the beast (based on Varro's derivation of *tigris* from the Persian word for "arrow"), but the repetition also suggests Zeno's paradox, if not an algebra problem. And Mela's account lacks a proper climax: the tigress simply gives up the chase when she reaches civilization, as indeed any wild beast would. Still, Mela's novelty became commonplace at once, and in the next reign both Seneca and Lucan allude to it. Seneca spins it into a simile for Medea (*Med.* 862 ff.): "This way she bears her step, and that, the way a tigress bereft of her cubs scours in her maddened course the forests of the Ganges . . . ." Lucan, as usual, says it in a word (5.405): Caesar races to Brundisium "faster than a tiger dam."

The polymath Pliny the Elder, the next to tell the story at length (*N.H.* 8.25.66), succeeds in smoothing out Mela's awkwardness: "Hyrcania and India both have tigers, an animal of awesome speed, which can be seen at its utmost whenever her entire litter is stolen . . . . The litter is snatched by stealth, and the thief makes his escape on a fast horse, on a relay of them in fact. Now, when the nursing tigress finds her lair empty . . . she is straight-way off, tracking by scent. When her caterwauling draws near, the thief throws one of the cubs behind him; she picks it up in her mouth, and, despite its weight, renews the chase even more swiftly, catching up to the thief a second time, and even a third,

[9] Roman poets locate the beast in Europe at least 16 times, usually in the company of Orpheus or Bacchus (but cf. Statius *Ach.* 2.124, where Chiron sets young Achilles a-hunting tigers); and in Africa perhaps 6 times (notably Verg. *Georg.* 3.248 and Petr. *B.C.* 15–18). Such passages regularly elicit an embarrassed silence from commentators—which is better than e.g. Conington on Verg. *Georg.* 4.510, "the existence of tigers in Thrace is of course a fanciful or mistaken notion" (London, 1865), or the editor whose note on 3.248 that Africa "abounds with the fiercest wild beasts" placidly assumes that the tiger is one of them.

[10] Cf. C.A.W. Guggisberg, *Wild Cats of the World* (London: David & Charles 1975) 180.

until he manages to board his ship, leaving the frustrated beast to rage upon the shore." Here, the tigress no longer has to return to her cave each time she recovers a cub (though Pliny's implication that the tigress reaches the seashore with three cubs in her mouth is bizarre enough in its own way); and the chase no longer merely peters out: it has been given a definite and appropriate *terminus*, the waters of the sea. Were these improvements original to Pliny? The barrier of water between pursuer and pursued is a stock folklore motif—compare *Uncle Tom's Cabin* or *Tam o'Shanter*—and the tiger supposedly could not swim (so Ovid). The tigress picking up her cubs as she goes is pretty clearly modeled on Ovid's Atalanta (*Met.* 10.649–80), who retrieves the golden apples cast behind him by Hippomenes. Pliny's three cubs seem to echo the apples three; moreover, in both stories the pursuer is burdened with the weight of what she picks up, presumably a symbol of maternity. Atalanta herself, like the tigress, was regularly a type of wild femininity (*Met.* 10.567, "unwedded through the shady woods"); the Greek tradition had had her nursed by a she-bear robbed of her cubs (Aelian *V.H.* 13.1; Apollodorus 3.12.5); Cybele, herself suckled by panthers, would eventually turn Atalanta and Hippomenes into lions for violating her sacred grove. The Atalanta myth, then, had much to offer Pliny, and pretty clearly it served him as a model. Mela's telling had been a simple and not wholly implausible piece of beast-lore, perhaps the creation of an animal trader out to inflate his reputation and his price; Pliny's reworking incorporates it into a sophisticated literary tradition, and the poets of the Flavian age would adopt it with enthusiasm and rework it in their turn.

So for example Martial, who alludes to the story twice: he transforms the Hyrcanian thief on a fast horse into a pale thief on a Hyrcanian horse: *raptor, in Hyrcano qui fugit albus equo* (8.26.2), and applies the image to people trying to avoid an incessant poetaster. Statius alters the tone by having his tigress succumb to grief (*Theb.* 10.820–26)—the very opposite of Vergil, where there had been no pleading with a tiger, unless the pleader was Orpheus: "thus, when her cubs are stolen, the harsh tigress, now bereft, lies down before her Scythian cave and licks their scent, still warm upon the rock; her wrath is gone, her ravening savagery stills, and herds and flocks may wander safely past." Valerius Flaccus reworks the anecdote twice, and at some length. Once, he has horsemen escaping with the cubs over a frozen river: "over the breakable waves," as he puts it (6.147 *fragilem . . . per undam*), while the grief-stricken mother shrinks back from the suspect surface. In a reworking yet more elaborate, he applies the story, in a simile almost Homeric, to the mothers of the Argonauts about to embark on their epic: "Jason cut the hawsers through with his sword. Not otherwise does the swift huntsman flee forests and desert tracts, urging on a horse that fears for its master, as he clutches to his breast tender tiger cubs which he has snatched away with trembling guile, the while their dam had left her cubs behind to go a-hunting. And so the ship pulls away, and on the shore stand the mothers . . . ." (1.488–94) Much of the effect of the passage depends on having an audience already familiar enough with the story to expect that the ship pulling away will be, as always, the ship bearing the huntsman and his trophies to safety. But Valerius has a surprise in store: the ship is so to speak a "double exposure," and turns out to be carrying not tiger cubs but tender Argonauts instead, once we hear that there is more than one mother grieving on the shore. The audience then admires the smooth transition between simile and actuality; admires, too, that un-Martial horse fearful for its rider, as well as the oxymoron "tender" (*teneras*) applied to the cubs, an epithet that adds to the pathos of the yet-untried young Argonauts, bewailed in advance.

Silius Italicus, too, turns the story into a Homeric simile, Homeric if only because of its palpable irrelevance to the subject at hand: his grief-stricken tigress has to represent Hannibal, the year after his victory at Cannae, casting about whether to attack Capua or march on Rome itself (12.458–62): "Scarce otherwise than when a tigress bristles at the loss of her litter, and the thunderstruck Caucasus is scoured in a few hours, and the Ganges leapt at a single bound, until in her lightning- fast course she finds the track of her offspring, and sates her rage upon the enemy." This reworking is novel in several ways, not all of which add to its appeal: Silius' is the only huntsman luckless enough to be caught; his is the only tigress, too, able to cross the barrier of water, and at a bound. Silius is trying to achieve an effect, too, when he tells us, with bogus precision, that tigers are fast enough to cross Armenia "in a few hours"; perhaps, though, the words "Ganges" and "Caucasus" were merely exotic music to Silius' ear, to be juxtaposed like musical notes with no thought of *vraisemblance*.

With Silius the story ends its career in Silver Latin, apart from a terse allusion in Juvenal; one of his viragos is "worse than a bereft tigress" (6.270), and he can let it go at that, so much had the story become part of the esthetic baggage of his age. For the next three centuries, nearly, the story lives on in the visual arts, not literature. It somehow became part of the repertoire of stock scenes that the journeyman artist could repeat over and over.

In the mid-second century it occurs in a mural painting, now lost, from the tomb of the Nasonii at Rome; it had been accompanied by a mural of the Rape of Proserpina—a curious juxtaposition that led one student to suggest that the Tiger-chase in some way symbolized immortality.[11] Not immortality, as we shall see; rather mortality and loss, as both pagan and Christian were to take it centuries later.

The Tiger-chase is also depicted on a sarcophagus relief from the Villa Medici in Rome around A.D. 270 (Pl. 22a).[12] A new element enters the story: one of the cats pauses to paw a round object that can be construed as a convex mirror: if so, the first occurrence of mirrors in the tale; where they would have come from, we do not know.[13] A late

[11] The "curious juxtaposition" of Proserpina with the tigress may well have influenced Claudian; v. infra. In any case, cf. A.M. Toynbee, *Animals in Roman Life and Art* (London: Thames & Hudson 1973) 72, based on P.S. Bartoli and G.P. Bellori, *Picturae Antiquae Cryptarum Romanarum et Sepulchri Nasonum* (Rome 1791) 55, pl. 15, fig. 1; and R.P. Hinks, *Catalogue of the Greek, Etruscan, and Roman Paintings in the British Museum* (London: British Museum 1933) 48, no. 72a.

[12] Cf. Toynbee (supra n. 11) 81; M. Cagiano de Azevedo, *Le antichità di Villa Medici* (Rome: Tip. del Stato 1951) 61, pl. 31, fig. 50 (sic; read "49"): "un leone e due pantere . . . . Questa rarissima scena illustra chiaramente quel sistema di caccia . . . ," which is wrong in all particulars; cf. n. 18.

[13] An anecdote of Pliny's (*N.H.* 29.12.52–53) may shed some light on this iconographical problem: "There is a kind of egg in Gaul, quite unknown to the Greeks . . . a sort of wind-egg (*urinum*) produced by snakes. The Druids say that it should be caught in a military cloak (*sagum*) lest it touch the ground, and the

PLATE 22a. Sarcophagus in the Villa Medici, Rome. After Cagiano de Azevedo (supra n. 12) pl. 31, fig. 50 (read "49").

22b. Piazza Armerina, the Great Hunt mosaic, detail. After Toynbee (supra n. 11) pl. 24.

PLATE 23a. Worcester, Mass., Hunt Mosaic from Antioch, detail. After Toynbee (supra n. 11) pl. 23.

23b. Meleager; detail from the mosaic of the Hall of Megalopsychia, Antioch. After Toynbee (supra n. 11) pl. 22.

variant of the Atalanta myth, perhaps, in which Hippomenes distracts her by dropping something more appropriate to feminine vanity than apples: in the *Gesta Romanorum* (c. 60, "*De Avaritia*") Abibas outraces Rosamunda by dropping gold coins behind him. In any case, the Villa Medici sculptor balances the Tiger-chase scene with another depicting the ship itself, laden with cages for its prey. This scene, likewise an innovation as far as we know, will become quite popular in its own right.

The next century would enjoy no fewer than four reworkings of the story in the visual arts. Two, unfortunately, remain unpublished; apparently the scene was used on the floors of *triclinia*, one in Antioch, the other in Cyrene.[14] A published Antiochene mosaic (Pl. 23a),[15] the Worcester hunt, has its horseman follow the older tradition: he simply holds onto his cub, like the horseman in Valerius Flaccus (though he seems to be enjoying his work a good deal more). There is another small novelty here: unlike Mela and Pliny, the artist puts the released cubs to work chasing the horseman. This was a clever touch, and the motif proved popular enough to be introduced into stock hunting scenes, where the cubs originally had no business. It is not surprising that the three hunt scenes with intrusive tiger cubs are all from the same place, Antioch; we are, after all, in the world of the journeyman mosaic-layer, filling up empty space with cartoons from his catalogue. One can easily imagine the man's employer giving him his instructions, too—"I want one just like Julius Alexander's out near Daphne, only less Maenads and more tigers."

In any case, the three Antiochene mosaics are very similar. The best executed (Pl. 23b)[16] is from the "Hall of Megalopsychia," named after the emblem of Heroism at its center; one of its embodiments is Meleager, here given a tigress to spear, not the traditional boar. The tiger cubs are in the van, defending their mother (a pleasant turnabout); the rearmost looks back, as if to take a cue from its dam. Exactly the same pose occurs with one of the cubs in the Dumbarton Oaks hunt, only there it is pointless because the tigress is now placed too far forward of the cub for it to be looking at her, and there is nothing to the rear of her for the cub to be looking at.[17] The result is nonsense, iconographically speaking; pretty clearly the figure of the cub had been uncritically copied out from a book of cartoons.

---

catcher rides off on horseback (*raptorem equo*: cf. Martial 8.26.2); the snakes pursue until they are deterred by the barrier of running water (*amnis alicuius interuentu*)." He adds that such wind-eggs supposedly confer victory in law-suits; indeed, a Vocontius was executed under Claudius (!) for smuggling one into the courts under his toga. Clearly this is the Tiger-chase with a different animal; snakes in pursuit of humans are known from folk-lore; cf. K.P. Schmidt, "The Hoop-Snake Story," *Natural History* 25 (1929) 76–80. Pliny's account of the theft of the snake-egg seems to explain one detail in the visual tradition of the Tiger-chase: the huntsman there is always in uniform, with his *sagum* whipping in the wind behind him. Moreover, any visual representation of Pliny's snake-chase might well have been the source for the discoidal mirrors (or globes) in the Tiger-chase later; but it would have been enough for a diligent reader of Pliny to have noticed the similarity between the two anecdotes and simply "combined his information."

[14] Toynbee (supra n. 11) 346 n. 51 and 359 n. 84.

[15] Ca. 500. Cf. ibid. p. 72; D. Levi, *Antioch Mosaic Pavements* (Princeton: University Press 1947) pl. 172b.

[16] Ca. 450. Cf. Toynbee (supra n. 11) 71; Levi (supra n. 15) pl. 77a.

[17] Ca. 500. Cf. Toynbee (supra n. 11) 71; Levi (supra n. 15) pl. 86a.

Far the most spectacular representation of the Tiger-chase occurs in the Great Hunt mosaic at Piazza Armerina, in the heart of Sicily, discovered only in 1946 (Pl. 22b).[18] Someone of means, perhaps the retired tetrarch Maximianus, erected a vast villa here at the beginning of the fourth century; it was expanded over the next hundred years. Its Great Hunt mosaic, the most elaborate of its kind, depicts the trapping of all manner of exotic animals and their subsequent embarkation for Rome, there to make a Roman holiday—a business that the government seems to have devoted more and more attention to while the real world crumbled around them. The Piazza Armerina mosaic depicts the activity in all of its aspects. Lion, tiger, rhinoceros, gazelle, aurochs, elephant are all on display—indeed, scarcely an animal known to antiquity is omitted, or the means for catching them; and it is thanks to the scenes showing the loading of the animals on board ship for their voyage to Rome that we enjoy our best contemporary depictions of the Roman merchant marine, *obiter picta* though they were.

Presiding over all is the deity that has given Rome such bounty, Africa herself (Pl. 24a), flanked by the greatest beasts of her realm, an elephant and . . . a tigress. It would be cavalier to complain that there are in fact no tigers in Africa; after all, in the tidy world of the Roman geographers, Africa included Western Ethiopia, while India comprised the Eastern; and one can always argue that the mosaic simply reflects the artificial world of the Colosseum, where tigers did in fact consort with giraffes. The literature of the age was equally free and easy with its geography: so Claudian ends his panegyric of Stilicho with a set-piece describing the animals shipped from Africa to Rome, and then likens them to the troupe that sailed with Bacchus, led by a "tiger unaccustomed to the sea, amazed at all the sails" (24.369).

The tigress beside Africa may well be a piece of whimsy, like the scene of the tigress chasing the huntsman at the same end of the hall. And in between the two lies a scene that can only be artistic fancy at play: another cage, only with the huntsman inside, this time, and his intended prey perched triumphant on top of the cage—a griffin (Pl. 24b). Likely enough, then, that this end of the mosaic was intended to be fantasy pure and simple: as the proverb had it, *semper aliquid noui Africam adferre* (Pliny *N.H.* 8.17.42).

In any case, the Tiger-chase scene here (Pl. 22b) is splendidly executed. The tigress has reached the shore; no cubs accompany her—that motif occurs only at Antioch. Here, as at Rome (but never at Antioch), she is depicted pawing a round object, surprised by what she sees in it—herself in miniature. We should not automatically call the object a

[18] For the most recent survey see R.J.A. Wilson, *Piazza Armerina* (Austin: Texas 1983); cf. also Toynbee (supra n. 11) 72–81, who notes that "the mosaic illustrates very clearly a passage of Claudian," which is not strictly true—Claudian is later—and is indeed quite misleading in its implication that Claudian and the mosaic correspond detail by detail. Toynbee adds that "a favorite method . . . for obtaining tigers and tigresses for pets or for show . . . was to steal the cubs on the hunting field." Not on a hunting field, as we have seen; and her pet tigers rest on the insubstantial basis of Sen. *Ep.* 85.41, where a tiger lets herself be kissed by her keeper. But not because Seneca has ever seen it happen; rather, because the tiger-tamer stands as a simile for the Stoic Sage, who is himself a "master at taming evils" (*artifex . . . domandi mala*). In the Stoic system, however, the Sage does not yet exist; if so, the keeper who can kiss his tiger must be equally unreal. In any case, Seneca presupposes not the tractability of the beast but rather its utter intractability. For a similar play with ἀδύνατα, cf. Sen. *Med.* 376–79.

PLATE 24

PLATE 24a. Africa; detail from the Great Hunt mosaic at Piazza Armerina. Courtesy of The National Geographic Society.

24b. Piazza Armerina, the Great Hunt Mosaic, detail. Courtesy of The National Geographic Society.

mirror; there was another explanation possible, as we shall see. Enough for the moment that the object, whatever it is, has succeeded in stopping the tigress by making her think that she has recovered a cub dropped by the fleeing horseman. While she stops to paw the object, though, the horseman to her left makes his escape up the gangplank of the waiting ship once again, just as in Pliny and the Villa Medici relief (Pl. 22a).[19]

We must return to the world of literature to end our discussion of the Tiger-chase. The literature of the fourth century was a renaissance in its way; and two of its greatest names, one pagan, one Christian, each saw in the story of the tigress bereft only an emblem of undeserved loss.

St. Ambrose, who died in 397, Father of the Church and of the hymn, saw the bereft tigress as a symbol of a soul that suffers from an excess of piety and will in consequence be undone by deceit (*Hex.* 6.4.21): "But the thief sees that he is being overtaken by the speed of the beast; he has no hope of getting away, so he devises the following ruse: when he sees that the tigress is almost upon him, he tosses her a globe made of glass. She is deceived by her own reflection, and thinks that it is one of her cubs; she stops short to pick up her offspring . . . ." Ambrose adds that the beast sees through the trick, and renews the chase; the horseman tosses her a second globe (as opposed to the second cub of Pliny); no wiser than before she stops for this one too, and even attempts to nurse it. Ambrose then draws the moral of the piece: "Thus was she deceived by the zeal of her piety, and in consequence failed either to save or to punish."

What is noteworthy here is that his is the very first time a literary account of the Tiger-chase has the tigress deceived by mirrors. They will become a stock motif in later retellings of the tale; and, very curiously, Ambrose's innovation was to influence earlier authors as well—or rather their editors: many a commentary on Martial and Juvenal assumes that the mirror-trick was a part of the story in *their* day.[20] In any case, Ambrose must have been influenced by a visual representation of the Piazza Armerina type, if not that particular mosaic. As noted above, at Piazza Armerina it is not immediately obvious that the tigress is looking into a mirror; a visitor could be sure of it only if he compared the scene with the one in the Sala dell'Imperatrice (Pl. 25a) where Amphitrite regards her own charms in a bronze mirror while a sea-green tigress looks on in amazement. Perhaps that is what Ambrose did; whatever his exact source, his version owes its mirror to the visual tradition, and to some extent he is putting a mosaic into words. In so doing he would not be unique: two centuries later the rhetorician Timothy of Gaza, apparently unaware of the literary tradition, would retell the tale based solely on a mosaic of the Piazza Armerina

[19] A badly damaged fourth-century mosaic from Dermech, near Carthage, duplicates this much of the Piazza Armerina scene; no tigress is in evidence. The young animal may be a baby elephant; cf. K. Dunbabin, *The Mosaics of Roman North Africa* (Oxford: Clarendon 1978) 53–54 and pl. XIII no. 26.

[20] So Freidländer ad loc. (Martial 8.26.2; Juvenal 6.270); so also most of the variorum editions of the authors discussed here. Toynbee (supra n. 11) 72 refers to the "famous 'mirror-trap'"; but she bases this solely on Claudian 36.263–68. Two authorities do not so much as mention the Tiger-chase, with mirrors or without; so O. Keller, *Die antike Tierwelt* (Leipzig: Teubner 1909 and 1913) and S. Thompson, *Motif-Index of Folk Literature* (Bloomington: Indiana 1958), but such omissions only illustrate that the Tiger-chase has indeed gone unrecognized.

Plate 25a. Amphitrite; detail from the mosaic of the Sala dell'Imperatrice, Piazza Armerina.

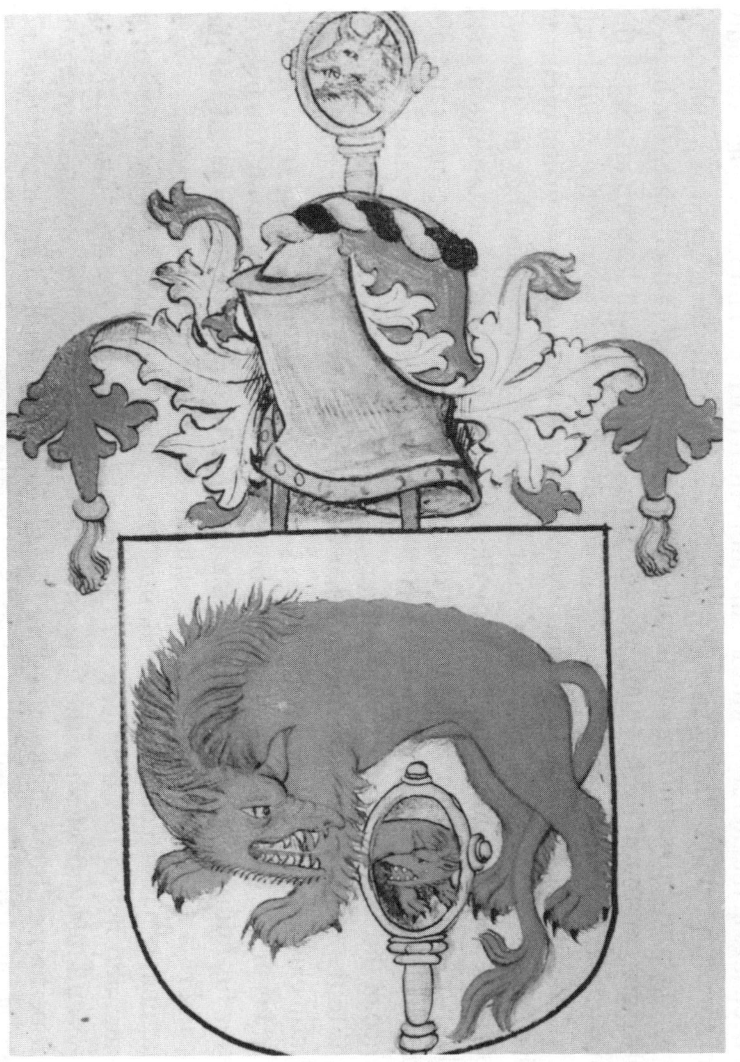

25b. Arms of Thomas Sybell. After Dennis (infra n. 22) 145

type: "after the hunters steal the cubs of the tigress they stuff them into glass jugs and then toss one jug behind them . . . " (Tim. Gaz. 9 = M. Haupt *Opuscula* 3.282). There had never been jugs in the literary tradition, any more than mirrors; Timothy's "jugs" can only be a misinterpretation of the mirror in a mosaic—a circle misinterpreted as a sphere, in other words. And the mosaic may well have been Piazza Armerina itself, since the hapless Timothy goes on to tell us that "into the bargain, the tigress will leap up and seize the griffin when the griffin tries to steal her cubs, and she does not let go until the griffin hurls itself, along with the tigress, into the sea." Never before have tigress and griffin occurred together, except in the Great Hunt mosaic at Piazza Armerina, where they are the two beasts who remain uncaught. But Timothy did not let their fortuitous juxtaposition go at that; he works up a tale that serves to link the two. That of itself is interesting; far more significant is the fact that in Timothy, as in St. Ambrose, we enjoy striking examples of the influence of the visual tradition on the literary.

It is to the Sicily of Piazza Armerina that we must return to end our discussion. The "last Latin classic," as he has been called, was Claudius Claudianus, a Greek from Alexandria; he began his meteoric career shortly before the death of St. Ambrose. Lukewarm whatever his faith, he became nonetheless a client of the great Christian family of the Anicii, and rose to become the laureate of Stilicho, the power behind the throne.

Claudian's masterpiece is the *de Raptu Proserpinae*, composed bit by piece over ten years, and not so much an epic in three books as three books worth of glittering speeches and *tableaux vivants*: the epic equivalent, that is, of a play by Seneca or a mosaic whose figures, individually arresting though they are, still float in empty space, no common ground at all beneath their feet. So Claudian's simile for Ceres distraught on discovering that her daughter has been snatched away in the shadow of Mount Aetna (*R.P.* 3.263–68 = 36.263–68):

> Thus steep Niphàtes by th' Hyrcanian dam
> Is shak'n, whose nurselings all the timid horse
> Snatched to amuse an Achaemenian king;
> She presses on, more fleet than erst her mate
> Zephyr: yea, all her stripes do splash green rage
> And would engulf the man within the depths
> Of her capacious maw, but that she stops,
> Entrancèd by her glass reflexiòn.

There is no calling a thing by its right name in Claudian: the "Hyrcanian dam" is simply our old friend the tigress, stopped this time, as in Ambrose, by the novelty of seeing her face in a mirror. Perhaps Claudian, too, took his inspiration from Piazza Armerina; we know that the imperial favorite traveled to Africa for his honeymoon, and it is easy to imagine him stopping over at the imperial palace on the way. And Claudian does describe the tourist attractions of Sicily: Aetna, of course, and a statue of two pious (!) brothers from Catina who saved their father from one of Aetna's eruptions (*Carm. Min.* 17). It is hard to imagine as observant an eye as Claudian's missing the other great sight in the vicinity: Piazza Armerina, too, lies in the shadow of Mount Aetna.

In any case, Claudian's tigress stops short when she sees her reflection: that much is clear in the Latin. But it is unlikely that she is actually looking into a mirror of *glass*, though that might be our own impression at first glance. Given the Latinity, and technology, of Claudian's age, his phrase "glass reflection" (*uitrea forma*) can in fact only mean a reflection the *color* of glass—our "bottle-green."[21] If the thing that mirrors the tiger were an artifact of any kind, it would have had to be made of metal, like Amphitrite's and the others of the ancient world.

All that Claudian needed to make his tigress glass-green was to have her stop where she had been stopping for over three hundred years—at the edge of water, water glassy-green, as the poets so often have it, for it is the water that had always stopped her short. In sum, Claudian found the perfect solution to the poetic "problem" inherent in the anecdote that he had been bequeathed, this by giving *his* tigress every possible reason to stop. The literary tradition had interposed a body of water on the (false) belief that tigers could not swim; the visual tradition, followed by Ambrose, had substituted the business of the mirrors. Claudian's poetic achievement was to combine these two images into one, without the least discord between them. As a result, the end of the Tiger-chase no longer seems forced and arbitrary; when Claudian's tigress looks into the sea and finds not her cubs but only herself, the story has regained the pathos and grandeur with which Homer had invested it more than a millennium before.

Understandably, the Middle Ages, well though it knew its Claudian, preferred the straightforward and suitably moralized account of St. Ambrose, mirror and all. *His* tigress, indeed, eventually degenerates into a wretched symbol of feminine vanity—the Tyger of heraldry, as red as a blush, who holds a mirror to her own admiring face (Pl. 25b).[22] What St. Ambrose would have thought of this development—or Claudian, Homer, and Atalanta—can only be imagined.

[21] In Latin *uitreus* most often means "glass-green": so 75 times of the 118 occurrences examined by this writer. It connotes shininess or translucency (but not transparency), and is regularly applied to things wet and slick: off-shore shallows and rocks, rivers, nymphs, etc. It regularly appears in color-medleys with *caeruleus* (for deeper waters) or *uiridis* (rarely of other waters); more often of sea-weed or on-shore vegetation). A precise color-value is fixed by SHA *Elagab.* 19.2, which gives the sequence *prasinum* (the Circus-color, = *uiride*), *uitreum*, *uenetum* (the Circus-color = *caeruleum*). There is no good example of *uitreus* or its nominal being applied either to hand-mirrors of any kind, or to transparency as such. Greg. Tur. *Vit. S. Juliani* (*MGH* 569.35 and 576.2) seems the first to refer to glass window panes, but they may well have been "bottle green"; so also the glass globes at e.g. Sen. *N.Q.* 1.3.9 and 1.6.5; also Claudian 68.2; such globes will have been small enough to be transparent in fact, but the material itself was the point.

[22] Cf. R. Dennis, *The Heraldic Imagination* (London: Potter 1975) 144, who gives the arms of Sybell (s. XVI): "Argent a Tyger statant tail cowed gules, gazing at its reflection in a hand-mirror erect." The Renaissance emblem-tradition provides a huntsman tossing hand-mirrors to distract the tigress: so Joachim Camerarius (1500–74) ap. *Emblemata* 2.36, A. Henkel and A. Schöne edd. (Stuttgart: Metzler & Pösch 1967) 403.

SOME COLLOQUIALISMS IN THE GOSPEL ACCORDING TO MARK

Richard M. Mackowski, S.J.

The Gospel according to Saint Mark contains 1345 words. Of these, forty-two occur only in Mark and do not appear in any other Biblical book.[1] Eighteen words are ordinary expressions, and there are seven *ἅπαξ λεγόμενα*.[2] Of the eight proper names, six are names of persons and two are place-names.[3] Mark uses ten foreign words which are peculiar to his Gospel: seven of these are Semitic words of either Hebrew or Aramaic origin; and there are three Latinisms.[4]

The intent of this paper is to analyze only the ordinary expressions and the seven *ἅπαξ λεγόμενα*. This article, therefore, is naturally divided into two parts: Part One is an analysis of the eighteen common words in Mark: ἀλεκτοροφωνία (13.35), ἀλλαχοῦ (1.38), ἀνακυλίειν (16.4), ἀπόδημος (13.34), ἀφρίζειν (9.18), εἶτεν (4.28 *bis*), ἐσχάτως (5.23), θανάσιμον (16.18), θυγάτριον (5.23; 7.25), κωμόπολις (1.38), μυρίζειν (14.8), νουνεχῶς (12.34), παρόμοιος (7.13b), προαύλιον (14.68), προσορμίζεσθαι (6.53), σμυρνίζειν (15.23), στασιαστής (15.7), and τηλαυγῶς (8.25), Part Two deals with the seven ἅπαξ λεγόμενα. These are ἔννυχα (1.35), ἐπιράπετιν (2.2), ὑπερπερισσῶς (7.37) and ἐκπερισσῶς (14.31), ἐπισυντρέχειν (9.25), κεφαλ(α)ιόω (12.4), and προμεριμνᾶν (13.11).

The vocabulary of Mark's Gospel has a special place in the study of first-century colloquial Greek. The present analysis shows that the words which appear only in Mark and in no other book of the entire Greek Bible are colloquialisms for the most part, naturally taken from the spoken language of everyday Greek, as opposed to the more literary idiom of the Hellenistic authors. Colloquialisms are words and/or expressions[5] employed by the ordinary, common people in the street, which would never be used in

[1] See R. Morgenthaler, *Statistik des Neutestamentlichen Wortschatzes* (Zürich & Frankfurt am Main: Gotthelf-Verlag 1958) *passim*; but for total figure of "1345" see p. 164.

Supplemental Abbreviation: *P.G.* = *Patrologiae Graecae* (Paris: Migne 1857). For modern Greek translations, see infra n. 29.

[2] Vincent Taylor, *The Gospel According to St. Mark* (London: Macmillan 1959) 44, citing H.B. Swete, *The Gospel According to St. Mark* ed. 3 (London: Macmillan 1909) xlvii.

[3] The personal names are Ἀβιαθάρ (2.26), (ὁ υἱὸς) Τιμαίου Βαρτιμαῖος (10.46), Ἰωσῆς (6.3; 15.40, 47), Σαλώμη (15.40; 16.1), Συροφοινίκισσα (7.26). The geographical names are Ἰδουμαία (3.8) and Δαλμανουθά (8.10). Of these proper names only Ἀβιαθάρ and Ἰδουμαία appear in the Septuagint.

[4] The words considered Semitic (Hebrew and/or Aramic) are Βοανηργές (3.17); ἐλωῒ ἐλωῒ λαμὰ σαβαχθάνι (15.34), ἐφφαθά (7.34), κορβάν (7.11), οὐά (15.29), and ταλιθὰ κοῦμ (5.41). The Latinisms are κεντυρίων (15.39, 44–45), ξεστῶν (7.4) and σπεκουλάτορα (6.27).

[5] Such as: ἀμφιβάλλοντας (1.16), δύο δύο (6.7), εἷς κατὰ εἷς (14.19), ἐπιβαλών (14.72), ἔσονται γὰρ αἱ ἡμέραι ἐκεῖναι θλῖψις (13.19), ἤφιεν (1.34; 11.16), λέγων . . . ἵνα . . . ἐπιθῇς (5.23), οἱ κατέσθοντες (12.40), ὅταν δὲ ἐγένετο (11.19), ὅτι = *why?* (2.16; 9.11, 28), πρασιαὶ πρασιαί (6.40), συμπόσια συμπόσια (6.39), σύσσημον (14.44), and σχιζομένους οὐρανούς (1.10).

higher circles of the courts, for instance, or in finer literature, the literature of the period that imitated the classical authors.

Part One: The "Common" Words in Mark

Internal evidence shows that Mark wrote his Gospel for non-Palestinian Christians, and most authorities agree that he wrote his Gospel in Rome. Below is a brief study of the eighteen "common" words in Mark. In parentheses I offer the Modern Greek translation which, in some cases, preserves the ancient Κοινή of the New Testament.

Ἀλεκτοροφονία (ὅταν λαλοῦν οἱ πετεινοί) (13.35). The word means "cock-crowing" and is derived from ἀλέκτωρ (rooster) and φωνέω (to produce a sound or tone). The Old Testament records a three-fold division of the night,[6] while the New Testament knows of a four-fold division.[7] Ἀλεκτοροφονία is a common, popular expression for the more technical τριτὴ φυλακή.[8] The term perseveres into the Patristic period to indicate either one of the six hours of prayer or the end of the Paschal fast.[9]

Ἀλλαχοῦ (ἄς πᾶμε). This adverb is censured by the Atticists,[10] but it is found in Sophocles' *Oedipus at Colonus*,[11] where it was most likely borrowed from common Greek for literary effect. It appears in the Patristic period and survives in Modern Demotic Greek.

Ἀνακεκύλισται (εἶχε κυλισθῆ) (16.4). Κυλίειν is a later form of the common, classical κυλίνδειν.[12] Compound verbs are characteristic of the Κοινή; hence, ἀνακυλίειν is just such an example. It is interesting to note that both Matthew and Luke change the verb to ἀποκυλίεν, thereby showing that ἀνακυλίειν must have been too colloquial for their renditions of this Gospel passage. There are numerous examples of uncompounded κυλίειν in the writings of the Church Fathers. The verb is also used in Modern Greek.

Ἀπόδημος (ὁ ὁποῖος ἔφυγε εἰς τὴν ξενιτιὰ καὶ ἄφησε τὸ σπίτι[13] του) (13.34). Although ἀπόδημος occurs in the classical authors, it is still less literary than the more classical ἔκδημος which is Attic Greek. Matthew uses the cognate ἀποδημεῖν (25.14) and Luke

[6] For example in Judges 7.19. The four-fold division of the night was known to Euripides (*Rhesus*, 5). In Mark the fact that μεσονύκτιον (13.35; cf. Luke 11. 5; Acts 16.25 and 20.7) is in the accusative, indicating duration, and ἀλεκτοροφονίας in the genitive, indicating the moment, is "un peu subtil pour Marc," is a good observation, writes M.-J. Lagrange, *Évangile selon Saint Marc* (Paris: Gabalda 1929) 352, n. 35. See also H.J. Rose, "Time-Reckoning," *OCD*² 1075f.

[7] Matthew 14.25 and Mark 6.48. Re the "first watch" see Josephus *B.J.* 5.45.6; and for references to the first, second and third watch, see 5.506.2.

[8] Luke 12.38.

[9] See *Didascalia et Constitutiones Apostolorum* I (ed. Funk, 1905; 1962 reprint) *ad Const. Apost.* 5.18.2; Didymus Alexandrinus *De Trinitate* 3.22 (*P.G.* 39.920 A); Origen in *P.G.* 11.825 B. For other references to the *Const. Apost.*, see 8.34.1 and 7; and for Dionysius of Alexandria see *Epistola Canonica* (*P.G.* 10.1273 A) and *The Letters and Other Remains of Dionysius of Alexandria* (ed. Feltoe, 1904) 94.

[10] For example, *The New Phrynicus* (ed. Rutherford, 1881) and *Moeridis Atticistae Lexicon Atticum* (ed. J. Pierson, 1759). Both Atticists, Moeris and Phrynicus, belong to the second century after Christ.

[11] Cf. *Oed. Col.* 42–43 and cf. Xen. *Hell.* 6.1.11 and 2.3.20.

[12] In Homer cf. *Od.* 9.147; 11.11, 598, etc.; κυλινδέω is the Attic form, as in Plato *Rep.* 479d.

[13] It is interesting to note that the Modern Greek word for "house" = σπίτι is derived from the Latin HOS*PITIUM* (ὁσπίτιον; cf. Palladus *Laus* 1019 B).

employs ἐκπορεύεσθαι (19.12). Evidence of the use of ἀπόδημος in Patristic literature is lacking; however, both ἀποδημία and ἀποδημεῖν do occur.[14] The ancient ἀπόδημος survives in Modern Demotic Greek, but it defines a person who is "living abroad."

'Αφρίζει (ἀφρίζει) (9.18, 20). This verb describes a condition of epilepsy or hysteria. Matthew explains it by σεληνιάζεσθαι (4.24; 17.15), meaning "to be moon-struck." 'Αφρίζειν appears to be used for the first time in Sophocles.[15] It is not found in the non-literary papyri nor in the writings of the Fathers of the Church. But it must have been in constant, colloquial usage, because it is a common Modern Demotic Greek verb.

Εἶτεν . . . εἶτεν (ἔπειτα . . . ἔπειτα) (4.28). Phyrnicus condemns this Ionic form as ἐσχάτως βάβαρα.[16] But it is not an uncommon form in the non-literary papyri; it fell into disuse with the reappearance of ἔπειτα, which is also used today.

'Εσχάτως (εἰς τὰ τελευταῖα του). (5.23). Classical Greek generally employs an adverb of manner with ἔχειν to express a condition of being. The Κοινή, however, is much more liberal in this respect. 'Εσχάτως is basically an adverb of time, defining a state of being in a given period. But this late usage is censured by the Atticists because it was too commonplace. It should be noted that both Matthew and Luke change the expression: Matthew 9.18 reads "ἄρτι ἐτελεύτησεν" and Luke 8.42 has "ἀπέθνησκεν." In Mark 1.32 the evangelist uses a similar idiom in his "οἱ κακῶς ἔχοντες" to describe "those that are sick," which is good Greek idiom. 'Εσχάτως appears in both Hellenistic and Patristic Greek, and, although it is not used in the above version, it survives in Demotic Greek today. Further, the expletival use of ἔχει (= there is, *c'è*, *il-y-a*, *gibt es*) seems to be a vestige of its ancient use as εἶναι (e.g., ἔστι).

Θανάσιμον (θανατηφόρον) (16.18) is a classical term which must have become colloquial Greek in the later periods.[17] It also perseveres in Modern Greek. Θανατηφόρος was used simultaneously with θανάσιμος and the two adjectives are interchangeable, the latter being used especially to describe poisonous drugs (φάρμακα), beasts (θήρια, ἕρπατα), and the like. Sources show that it was a very common word in the first century.[18] The Church Fathers offer substantial evidence of the frequency of θανάσιμος in the early post-Biblical period.[19]

Θυγάτριον (τὸ μικρό μου κοριτσάκι) (5.23; 7.25). This common diminutive is also a term of affection. It is interchangeable with θυγάτηρ, as is common with diminutives in

[14] Hermas *Similitudines* 5.2.2.; 5.58.3, in F.X. Funk, ed., *Patres Apostolici I* (Tübingen: Laupp 1901) 531, 539; Clement of Rome *Stromatum* 7.11 (51), in *P.G.* 9.489 A; Athanasius of Alexandria *Oratio contra Gentes* 31.98 in *P.G.* 25.64 B.

[15] Soph. *El.* 719; cf. Hippocrates 2.123 and Theophrastus *De Causis plantarum* 6.1.5.

[16] *Phrynicus* 101. The second century grammarian Aelius Dionysius considers it an Ionic form; see *Aelii Dionysii et Pausanii Atticistarum fragmenta* (ed. Schwabe, 1890) *Ael. Dion. ap. Eust.* 1158.38.

[17] Swete (supra n. 2) 406 and Taylor (supra n. 2) 613.

[18] Dioscorides *De Materia Medica* (ed. Wellmann, 1906–14) 4.106 (cf. Eur. *Ion* 616); Polyb. 1.56. 4; Philo the mechanic *Excerpta aus Philons Mechanik* (ed. Diels and Schramm, Berlin: Abhandlungen der Preussischen Akademie der Wissenschaften 1919) II.162.23 and V.177.5, 18 (sing.) and V.229.1 (pl.); Philo the philosopher *De legibus specialibus* 3.95; Josephus *Ant.* 17.74.

[19] Ignatius of Antioch *Epistola and Trallianos*, in *P.G.* 6.2. See also Dioscorides (supra n. 18). Hermas (supra n. 14) 78. 9; cf. Polyb. (ed. Paton, 1966–68) p. 26 and 9.1.

Mark.[20] Θυγάτριον occurs in the classical authors and is a common word in the papyri. It is not attested in the Fathers; however, it was certainly known in that period, since it was employed by the Emperor Julian in the IV century.[21] The word exists in colloquial Greek today.

Κωμοπόλεις (χωριά) (1.38). This is one of the four expressions which Mark uses to define a "city," a "town," a "hamlet (or farm)," and a "market-town." Κωμόπολις, strictly speaking, translates the last of these definitions. It belongs to late Greek, first found in Strabo,[22] then employed rather frequently in the later periods. It survives in Modern Demotic Greek.

Μυρίσαι (νὰ ἀλείψῃ μὲ μῦρον) (14.8). Μυρίζειν has radically changed its meaning since antiquity. Its fundamental meaning in ancient Greek was "to anoint"; in Modern Greek it signifies "to smell." Greeks today prefer to use χρίειν or ἀλείφειν, when they wish to speak of an anointing. In Biblical Greek μυρίζειν is a genuine ἅπαξ λεγόμενον, but the verb is as old as Herodotus. Its modern connotation is traceable to at least the III century after Christ: in Heliodorus, for instance, we find the phrase "μυρίζεσθαί τινί," meaning "to be fragrant with." It is a common word in the literature of the Fathers: it means "to anoint" or "to spread sweetness upon."

Νουνεχῶς (συνετά) (12.34). This common adverb, derived from νοῦν + ἔχειν, is correctly rendered "prudently" in English. It does not appear in literature earlier than Aristotle. Luke interprets the adverb as ὀρθῶς (10.28), which is more literary. It is interesting to note that the Modern Greek version has συνετά, following MS 28, συναιτῶς, an otherwise non-existent form.

Παρόμοια (παρόμοια) (7.13b). This is strictly a colloquial word, signifying, according to Pollux, that something is "somewhat similar (but not exactly so)."[23] The Latin *similia* is etymologically parallel to the Greek word, from which the basic notion of similarity is derived. The only form accounted for in the Patristic age is the doubled *iota* in παρομοίιος. As is clear from the translation above, the word exists in Modern Demotic Greek.

Προαύλιον (προαύλιον) (14.68). This word appears rather late in the development of Greek, when the style of houses changed, particularly when it was fashionable to build a fore-court which preceded the courtyard (αὐλή, *atrium*). The word is rendered best as a "hall" or the German "*Vorhof.*" In the literature of the Church Fathers, it designates either the room before the court of a house, which connotation survives in Modern Greek, or the *antechamber* of a church, where the candidates were prepared for baptism.[24] In Mark's time προαύλιον specifically denoted the "vestibule" (*vestibulum*) which led from the street into the inner court (αὐλή).

Προσωρμίσθησαν (ἀγκυροβόλησαν) (6.53). In general, the early writers use the middle voice of this verb (προσορμέω → προσορμεῖσθαι); the later authors employ the passive.

[20] The use of diminutives in Mark are not necessarily diminutive in sense: cf. Taylor (supra n. 2) 45.

[21] See his *Orationes*, ed. F. C. Herlein (Leipzig: Teubner 1875–76) 7. 226b; cf. Plut. *Ant*. 33.

[22] Strabo (ed. Jones 1960–67) 12.2.5.

[23] Pollux *Onomasticon* (ed. W. Dindorf, 1824) 24.

[24] Cyril of Jerusalem *Catecheses mystogogicae*, in *P.G.* 87.3713 A.

A rather close parallel to our text is in Aelianus' "τῇ Νάξῳ προσωρμίσθη."[25] In Matthew 14.34 we read "ἦλθον ἐπὶ τὴν γὴν εἰς Γεννησαρέτ." Προσορμεῖν is common in the non-literary papyri. The ("causative") προσορμίζειν is used in conversational Greek today.

Ἐσμυρνισμένον (ἀρωματισμένο μὲ σμύρναν) (15.23). A similar word has already been discussed above (see μυρίζειν = *to anoint*). Σμυρνίζειν means "to mix with myrrh." Matthew uses the less colorful μεμιγμένον (27.34) meaning that the wine was "drugged" (lit. "mixed") with gall or bile: "οἶνον μετά χολῆς μεμιγμένον." John, in informing us that the sponge was soaked in vinegar (σπόγγον οὖν μεστὸν τοῦ ὄξους; 19.29), seems to be following Luke who states that the soldiers offered Jesus vinegar to drink (23.36). Scholars agree that σμυρνίζειν is a late verb, but it should be noted that it is not attested in the papyri or inscriptions. The Fathers of the Church employ it to signify either "to mingle with" or "to preserve (in myrrh)"; hence it comes to mean "to embalm." Apparently, the verb is rare in Modern Greek, and found only in the *Katharevousa*.

Στασιαστῶν (στασιαστᾶς) (15.7). This word is generally used in a causative sense and defines "one who instigates a revolt." It belongs to late Greek, succeeding the classical στασιωτής. Matthew uses λησταί (27.38); Luke reads κακοῦργοι (23.32); but John has only "two others" (ἄλλους δύο in 19.18). Neither the later form στασιαστής nor the classical στασιωτής is verifiable in the Patristic period; but στασιαστός, meaning "rebellious" or "factious," is found in the *Acta Apostolorum Apocrypha*, published by C. Tischendorf in the second half of the last century.[26] In current Modern Greek στασιαστής defines a "rebel" or a "revolutionary".

Τηλαυγῶς (καθαρά) (8.25). This is a rare adverb, expressing the idea that something is visible "clearly though from a distance." The adjective, however, is common. A parallel use of the adverb appears in a non-literary papyrus of the third century after Christ from Oxyrhynchus.[27] Otherwise, it is not found in the history of the Greek language, although it is sometimes used in Modern Greek.

Part Two: Markan ΑΠΑΧ ΛΕΓΟΜΕΝΑ

One of the great Markan scholars of our century, Vincent Taylor, states that Mark's Gospel contains seven ἅπαξ λεγόμενα.[28] I list them below with their Modern Greek, Latin Vulgate, and English translations,[29] in the order in which they appear in the Gospel.

1.35 ἔννυχα = νύχτα = DILVCVLO = *that evening, after sunset*
2.21a ἐπιράπτει = ῥάβει = ASSVIT = *(no one) sews*

[25] Aelianus *Var. Hist.* (ed. Herscher 1864–87) 8.5.

[26] *Acta Pilati* (ed.C. Tischendorf 1876) p. 210, cf. 9.2, p. 242.

[27] The form χρημαθισθήσῃ in *P.Oxy.* VI.886[24] (III A.D.) should, no doubt, read χρηματισθήσῃ as in *P.Giss.* I.20[18] (II A.D.), the regular aorist passive of χρηματίζω.

[28] Taylor (supra n. 2) 44.

[29] The translations and/or versions which I have used are as follows: Ἡ Καινὴ Δισθήκη: Τὸ πρωτότυπον κείμενον μὲ νεολληνικὴν μετάφρασιν (Athens: Βιβλικὴ Ἑταιρεία 1967); *Novum Testamentum Graece et Latine*, ed. E. Nestle, E. Nestle, et al. (Stuttgart: Deutsche Bibelstiftung 1981); *The New Jerusalem Bible*, gen. ed. Henry Wansbrough (London: Darton, Longman & Todd 1985).

7.37 ὑπερπερισσῶς = μεγάλην = AMPLIVS = *unbounded*
9.25 ἐπισυντρέχει = μαζεύεται = CONCVRRENTEM = *was gathering*
12.4 ἐκεφαλίωσαν = τὸν ἐτραυμάτισαν εἰς τὸ κεφάλι = IN CAPITE VVLNERAVERVNT = *thrashed (him on the head)*
13.11 προμεριμνᾶτε = φροντίζετε = PRAECOGITARE = *(do not) worry beforehand*
14.31a ἐκπερισσῶς = περισσότερον = AMPLIVS = *still more earnestly*

The intent of this section, therefore, is twofold: a) to explain these ἅπαξ λεγόμενα in terms of first century colloquialisms and b) to show that perhaps their number can now be reduced to three, for there seem to be parallels for ἐπιράπτει, ἐπισυντρέχει, ἐκεφαλίωσαν, and προμεριμνᾶτε. It should be noted from the start, however, that in the treatment of these ἅπαξ λεγόμενα it was necessary to concentrate for the most part on the composite forms of these words. In this respect we follow the theory of M.-J. Lagrange that these words are ἅπαξ simply because a prepositional prefix was joined to an already existing form, as each of the above except ἐκεφαλίωσαν, an augmented aorist, clearly demonstrates.[30] But, whether compounded or not, we must accept the word as it is in the text, and, therefore, consider it as a form used in the ordinary, everyday Κοινή of the first century after Christ. Furthermore, it is true that a study of any ἅπαξ λεγόμενον and/or λεγόμενα may be more a matter of statistics rather than philology; nevertheless, the question "precisely why are these words ἅπαξ λεγόμενα?" must be addressed. And this I attempt to do in the twofold purpose of the following analysis.

ἔννυχα (νύχτα) (1.35). The adjective ἔννυχος, from which the adverb ἔννυχα is formed, occurs as early as Homer. It is formed according to the regular rules for forming adverbs from adjectives. But the adverb ἔννυχον, or more commonly ἐννύχιον, belongs to the later classical period. In general, it means "nightly" or "by night." *The Jerusalem Bible* is correct in rendering this adverb as "in the morning, long before dawn," as the context would require, rather than as the translations of the *Revised Standard Version* ("that evening, at sundown") or of the *New American Bible* ("after sunset, as evening drew on"). The reason is that ἔννυχα describes or defines the early "nightly" hours of the *morning* in this passage rather than the early "nightly" hours of the *evening*. The basic meaning of πρωΐ points to the morning hours in contrast with ἑσπέρα = the evening. In an inscription of the fifth century after Christ, the adjective ἔννυχος defines the "day of death."[31] The Modern Greek νυχτά, a "contracted" colloquial form, perpetuates the ancient expression.

Ἐκπερισσῶς (περισσότερον) (14.31) and ὑπερπερισσῶς (μεγάλη) (7.37). The common element in these two adverbs is the preposition περί with the -σσῶς ending, formed

[30] He expresses his own view as follows: "Ces *hapax legomena* ne peuvent naturellement manifister l'unité de style. On remarquera seulement qu'ils n'ont rien de recherché. Le plus grand nombre n'est *hapax* que par l'addition d'une préposition. Ce sont donc probablement des expressions populaires; c'est le cas surement de κεφαλιοῦν *et probablement de* ἔννυχα. Il n'a rien là de technique ni de raffiné" (supra n. 6) lxvii; see also 307.

[31] *IG* VII (1892) 584.5.

on the analogy of ἔπισσαι, μέτασσαι, and περισσεύειν. The adjective περισσός, ή, όν, and the adverb περισσῶς formed from it, are directly derived from the preposition περί as to form and meaning. These are old forms; though they do not appear in Homer, they occur in Hesiod[32] and Herodotus.[33] In late Greek they appear rather frequently on inscriptions,[34] in papyri,[35] in the Septuagint,[36] as well as in the philosopher Philo (c. 20 B.C.–c. A.D. 54)[37] and the historian Flavius Josephus (A.D. 37–c. 100).[38] The adverb περισσῶς is used by John Chrysostom.[39]

Originally prepositions were free-standing adverbs, related directly or indirectly to a verb. By themselves, ἐκ could mean "therefrom"; περί could indicate something "around" or "about" and in a superlative sense "above others" or "exceedingly"; and ὑπέρ would describe something done "over-much" or "above-measure". In the course of time, the ending -σσός, ή, όν, was added to some prepositions in order to make adjectives and adverbs out of them.

The function of these prepositional prefixes is exclusively adverbial, used to strengthen the original meaning of περί which fundamentally denoted the idea of something (done) "above others" in the sense of "exceedingly," when it is employed absolutely as an adverb. In Mark's Gospel both adverbs signify the same idea, and the fact that they appear only once (ἅπαξ λεγόμενα) in literature must in this way define them as strict colloquialisms which never entered into any type of writing. Neither ἐκπερισσῶς nor ὑπερπερισσῶς, in either adverbial or adjectival form, has entered into Modern Greek speech. But it is interesting to note that George C. Divry's Modern Greek dictionary lists the various forms of περισσός.[40]

As I have stated above with reference to V. Taylor's listing of seven ἅπαξ λεγόμενα in Mark, I rather suspect that their number may now be reduced to only three, the three briefly analyzed above. The following four (ἐπιράπτει, ἐπισυντρέχει, ἐκεφαλίωσαν, and προμεριμνᾶτε) seem to have at least one other occurrence in literature.

'Επιράπτει (ῥάβει) (2.21). The verb ῥάπτω, meaning "to sew" or "to stitch," is seen as early as Homer; its compound ἐπιράπτω or perhaps more accurately ἐπιρράπτω, however, does not. The form in Mark 2:21 is a genuine ἅπαξ λεγόμενον if the reading of the older manuscripts (ℵ A B* C E, etc.) preserves the correct spelling of the verb. But if the reading of the later manuscripts (B^2 K M U Γ, etc.), which have ἐπιρράπτει, corrects the

32 Hesiod *Th.* 399, where the expression means "beyond the regular number (size)."

33 Herodotos 2.32; see also 2.129.

34 *Ägyptische Urkunden aus den königlichen Museen zu Berlin: Griechische Urkunden* I–VIII (Berlin 1895–1926) 380.10 (where the comparative -εροv is employed as an adverb).

35 See *P.Amh.* II.132.2 (early II A.D.) and *P.Teb.* II.488 (A.D. 121–2) where the meaning is as that in Acts 26.11.

36 The following examples occur in the Septuagint: Exodus 10.5; Numbers 4.26; 1 Kings 30.9; Proverbs 14.23; Ecclesiastes 2.15; in the Greek Old Testament see 1 Maccabees 9.22, *al.*

37 Philo *Quod deterius potiori insidiari soleat* 15, *al.*, while the comparative is used 1.14.

38 Josephus *Ant.* 1.258.

39 John Chrysostom *P.G.* 7.813 B, on Matthew 27.23 (περισσῶς).

40 George C. Divry, *English-Greek and Greek-English Dictionary* (New York: Divry 1969): περίσσεια, περίσσευμα, περίσσευσις, περισσεύω, περισσότερος, and περισσῶς, see p. 640, *ad loc.*

original spelling of the verb, it ought not be considered any longer a real ἅπαξ λεγόμενον. I suspect that the latter is the case, for the composite form (with a doubled *rho*) is actually the more frequent, even in many other compounds of ῥάπτω. Examples are certainly not lacking from the classical to the non-classical authors. G.C. Divry even lists ῥάπτω and some of its compounds, such as περιρράπτω ("to hem, sew around") and ὑπορράπτω ("to line, sew under") in his dictionary of Modern Greek.[41]

Ἐπιρράπτω is not found in the literature of the Patristic period. But it is indeed noteworthy that the second aorist form of the verb appears in Nonnus the epic poet of the fifth century after Christ. In his *Dionysiaca*,[42] the following two examples occur, thereby proving the existence of this verb in a later period and illustrating, after all, that ἐπιρράπτω is no longer an ἅπαξ λεγόμενον in Greek literature. The first example is: Ζεὺς δὲ πατὴρ . . . δεξάμενος Διόνυσον ἐπέρραφεν ἄρσενι μηρῷ (9.2–3). The second example, which illustrates the use of (ὑπορ)ράπτω in the sense of making up a story (λόγον), reads: ἀλλὰ δόλῳ δόλον ἄλλον ἐπέρραφεν Εἰραφιώτης (42.315).[43] Ἐφέρραφεν (ἐπέρραφεν) is not listed by the fifth century lexicographer Hesychius, probably because he was more or less a contemporary of Nonnus. (One would expect him to cite only the ancient authors known up to his time.)

In the parallel passages of Matthew 9.16 and Luke 5.36, ἐπιράπτει is replaced by ἐπιβάλλει. From this we can perhaps conclude that ἐπιράπτω was too vernacular or colloquial for the more elegant ἐπιβάλλει at the time.

Ἐπισυντρέχει (μαζεύεται) (9.25a). Both ἐπιτρέχειν and συντρέχειν are classical. Ἐπισυντρέχειν, however, a composite verb that is characteristic of Hellenistic Greek, belongs to the Κοινή. Its occurrence in the *Acta Thaddaei* proves that it is no longer a Greek ἅπαξ λεγόμενον. The sentence which contains the consequential verb is: ἐπὶ πολλὰς δὲ ἡμέρας ἐπισυντρεχόντων τῶν λαῶν ἐκ διαφόρων χωρίων καὶ θεωρούντων τὰ γινόμενα ὑπὸ Θαδδαίου, καὶ ἀκούοντες τῆς διδασκαλίας αὐτοῦ πολλοὶ ἐπίστευσαν καὶ ἐβαπτίζοντο ἐξομολογούμενοι τὰς ἁμαρτίας αὐτῶν.[44] This is a very colorful verb: ἐπί, when employed as an adverb (or prepositional adverb used as a prefix to a verb) means "as well" or "besides", also containing the idea of a place, e.g., to a place; σύν as an adverb, like ἐπί, denotes accompaniment, "together", "at once" or "along with." Moreover, the composite prepositional adverb ἐπισυν–, which is quite common in the papyri, prefixed to τρέχω, offers us a descriptive picture of how the crowds "came running together to" Jesus.

Ἐκεφαλ(α)ίωσαν (ἐτραυμάτισαν εἰς τὸ κεφάλι) (12.4). If the reading ἐκεφαλίωσαν of ℵ B L Ψ 579 and 892 is accepted, then we have another genuine Markan ἅπαξ

[41] Ibid. 666, *ad loc.*

[42] Nonnus *Dionysiaca* (ed. Ludwich 1909–11) 9.2–3.

[43] Ibid. 42.315, and cf. Eur. *Alc.* 537 "ὡς δή τί δράσων τόνδ' ὑπορράπτεις λόγον;". Relative to the principal parts of ἐπιράπτω, as far as I can judge, one can find the following forms: ἐπιρ(ρ)άπτω, ἐπιρράψω, (ἔρραψα), a 2 aorist in ἐπέρραφον, . . . , (ἔρραμαι), and an aorist passive in ἐρράφην.

[44] In the *Acta Apostolorum Apocrypha* (ed. Lipsius and Bonnet, 1891–1903), see *Acta Thaddaei* in vol. I. No. 7, pp. 227 to 228.

λεγόμενον. But if ἐκεφαλαίωσαν of A C D N X Δ Π Σ Φ ϧ 22 and even of Θ (ἐκεφαλέωσαν) and W (κεφαλεώσαντες) be correct, then again the verb is not a real ἅπαξ. (It is interesting to note that the *epsilon* in Θ and W preserve the first century sound of αι as ε, as in Modern Greek.) I favor the former reading particularly because of the manuscript evidence and the fact that κεφαλιόω (κεφλιοῦν) is legitimate, based on the analogy of γνάθοῦν = to strike on the cheek (from γνάθος); κεφαλιοῦν comes from κεφάλιον, which we strongly suggest, must have been a localism, because both Matthew and Luke had to explain it for their readers: Matthew 21.35 has ἐλιθοβόλησαν, and Luke 20.12 reads τραυματίσαντες ἐξέβαλον. If a decision is to be made in favor of manuscript evidence, κεφαλιοῦν has the stronger authority; from a philological point of view, however, κεφαλαιοῦν might also be reconsidered.

Προμεριμνᾶτε (φροντίζετε) (13.11). In the parallel pericopes Matthew (10.19) and Luke (12.11) both read, according to the best manuscripts, μεριμνήσητε, which would be the more correct grammatical form here, μή with the subjunctive expressing better Greek in such imperatival situations. With respect to Mark's use of προμεριμνᾶτε, however, it should no longer be considered an ἅπαξ λεγόμενον, because it can now be illustrated in Hippolytus of Rome, who employs the verb twice in his *Philosophoumena*. The first example is ἐν τοῖς προμεριμνήσθεισιν ὑμῖν ἐκκειμένων τούτων δογμάτων (*PG*. XVI. 3282 B); and the second is Ταῦτα μὲν οὖν ἐκείνοις, οἷς οὐκ ἀνάγκην ἔχομεν τὰ παρ' Ἕλλησι προμεμεριμνήμενα παρατιθέναι οὖσι προδήλοις τοῖς ὑπ' αὐτῶν λεγομένοις τὴν σύστασιν ἔχειν ἐκ γεωμετρικῆς τέχνης καὶ ἀριθμητικῆς (ibid., 3363 A). In view of the fact that προμεριμνᾶν does not appear in literature prior to the first century after Christ, it ought to be defined as a colloquialism during this time; but it found acceptance in a subsequent period, like many words and expressions in various languages. The Modern Greek φροντίζετε bears the same meaning as (προ)μεριμνᾶν. The uncompounded form is found in Modern Greek dictionaries.[45]

Conclusion

I have proposed conclusions after each entry. The catalogue of Markan colloquialisms, words which are generally classified as rare, strange or unusual, and the ἅπαξ λεγόμενα, even though I have now reduced their number, when taken as a whole, must clearly show that the special vocabulary of Mark was taken from the colloquial Greek of his time. Mark, therefore, is an early witness of first century "conversational" Greek, the common language of just ordinary people. In this brief study one gleans a special insight into this ordinary language, an insight which cannot be so easily and so specifically derived from either Matthew or Luke in the study of the language of the New Testament.

Prior to the redaction of his Gospel, Mark must have spoken and perhaps even written in this everyday idiom. He used the vocabulary which was most familiar not only to himself, but especially to his audience. These were the choice words which his hearers

[45] Divry (supra n. 40); and Θ. Τζαννέτατος, Νεὸν ὀρθογραφικὸν καὶ ἑρμηνευτικὸν λεξικόν (Athens: Γιοβάννης 1970).

and readers would not only understand immediately as their very own, but which would transmit to them the reality of the true Evangelical message. This is the impact of Mark's vocabulary and descriptive style.

The words which occur only in his Gospel and not in any other book of the Greek Bible must illustrate the fact that these were extremely common, non-literary, everyday words and expressions which were changed or corrected by Matthew and Luke and their redactors. All must have realized the extraordinary banality of the words studied above. For "literary" purposes, all of Mark's "followers", including his own redactors, felt obliged to "improve" on this very rich source of first-century colloquialisms.

LOVE'S LABOR'S LOST: WOMEN IN THE *ODYSSEY*

PATRICIA A. MARQUARDT

This paper is dedicated to Fr. Schoder's lifelong love of Homer and to his own epic success in teaching Homeric Greek to countless students over a period of forty years. Fr.Schoder's newly revised text on Homeric Greek will inspire generations of students to come not only with Homer's immortal words but also with a sense of his great humanity. The scholarly work of Fr. Schoder on behalf of Homer is truly "love's labor's won"!

Odysseus' adventures are played against a backdrop richly hued with strong feminine characters. Four, in particular, command our attention here—Circe and Calypso, a pair of seductive goddesses, who detain Odysseus for over eight years, and Helen and Penelope, two legendary wives. Faithless Helen has returned at last to hearth and husband, while Penelope faithfully awaits her husband's return. Despite the preponderance of romantic interest in the *Odyssey*, Homer presents in the end a bittersweet picture of love. Circe and Calypso perform leading roles and establish the scenario which is replayed poignantly on the human stage by Penelope and Helen. These thematic echoes are the subject of this paper. The similarity of Calypso and Helen has already been established and illuminates part of the picture.[1] We must also establish the parallel between Circe and Penelope before we can see the larger stage on which Homer has commented touchingly and perceptively on the human condition.

I. MAGIC IN ITHACA

Although the general likeness of Penelope and Circe has been noted in passing by several critics, the similarity, as reflected in details of the narrative, has not been fully explored.[2] Let us consider briefly the extraordinary situation on Ithaca. A mortal woman with only private messages of encouragement (e.g. 13.380–81) and infrequent public appearances (15.516–17) has kept dangling for three to four years (2.89–90), possibly

[1] Cf. William Anderson, "Calypso and Elysium," in *Essays on the Odyssey*, ed. Charles H. Taylor (Bloomington: Indiana University 1963) 73–86.

[2] Charles Beye, notably, has observed: "Circe is dominant and malign in a way which can be related to Penelope . . . [who] descends the stairs, seduces the suitors with her beauty, writes them notes, strings them along while weaving the shroud. They in their impatience, their desire and boisterousness have become animal-like in their behaviour" ("Male and Female in the Homeric Poems," *Ramus* 3.2 [1974] 97–98). The Circe-Penelope likeness has also been commented on by E.A.S. Butterworth in *Some Traces of the Pre-Olympian World in Greek Literature and Myth* (Berlin: de Gruyter 1966) 97–98; and by Charles Segal in "Circean Temptations: Homer, Vergil, Ovid," *TAPA* 99 (1968) 422.

The text of the *Odyssey* used throughout this paper is that established by William Stanford (*The Odyssey of Homer*, 2 vols.; [London: Macmillan 1959]). Some of the ideas expressed in this section were presented in an earlier form at the 1983 Meeting of the Classical Association of the Midwest and South in Columbus, Ohio. I would like to thank Professor H. James Shey of the University of Wisconsin-Milwaukee for his helpful suggestions and encouragement in developing these ideas.

longer, more than 100 wealthy and important men from Ithaca and the surrounding islands (1.245–47; cf. 24.108: *κατὰ πτόλιν ἄνδρας ἀρίστους*). Ostensibly paying court to Penelope, they have, in effect, laid siege to Odysseus' home and have been living it up in his absence, feasting nightly in the palace and carousing with the serving girls. Penelope has been putting them off with her ruse (*δόλος*) of weaving and unravelling the shroud for her father-in-law Laertes. It puts heavy demands on the reader's willing suspension of disbelief that one of the unnamed suitor, at least, would not have grown weary of the daily ritual of waiting around and feasting in the palace and have returned to his own kingdom until Penelope finally resolved upon removing the impasse by selecting one of them as her husband.

The fact is that the suitors, for all their boisterous arrogance, have little individuality and act, in a folkloric manner, as though spellbound, not unlike the men enthralled by Circe, who reduced her captives literally to the level of animals (10.237–43; 432–34). The motif of the enchantress and spellbound captives would help to account for the cartoon quality of Penelope's suitors, whose very numbers and slavish doggedness have not been satisfactorily accounted for by speculation about Penelope's politcal position in Ithaca or her ability to confer kingship.[3] Clearly it was not only Odysseus' property which attracted the suitors. When Penelope, enhanced in beauty by Athena, appears before the suitors in Book 18, the stunned suitors react at once as though Aphrodite herself has appeared before them. Their limbs are loosened (*λύτο γούνατα*; 18.212), Homer tells us, and bewitched by love (*ἔρῳ. . . ἔθελχθεν*), each prays to share the lady's bed (18.212–213).[4]

Like Circe's victims, the suitors of Penelope, for all their outward show, seem to have lost the ability to leave Ithaca of their own free will. They talk boldly, plot against Telemachus' life and angrily threaten to stay around consuming Odysseus' property until Penelope chooses one of them without delay and breaks the spell, so to speak (2.85–128).[5] In a general way, the suitors do have freedom of action, but from the time they enter

[3] E.g. Martin Nilsson, *Homer and Mycenae* (New York: Cooper Square 1968 [1933]) 225–26. The text of Homer does not present a clear picture of the political situation on Ithaca. For a discussion of some of the problems, see M.I. Finley, *The World of Odysseus* (London: Chatto and Windus 1978, 2nd rev.) esp. 88–91 and 129–30; and J.V. Luce, *Homer and The Heroic Age* (London: Thames and Hudson 1975) 73–74. The position of women in general in Homeric society is discussed by James Redfield, *Nature and Culture in the Iliad* (Chicago/London: University of Chicago 1975) 119–23.

[4] The sense denoted by *θέλγω* is regularly an attribute of divinity in the *Odyssey* (e.g. Calypso 1.57; Hermes 5.47; the Sirens 12.40, 44; and Athena 16.298) and suggests bewitchment or enchantment through the power of a greater than human agency. Cf. 16.194–95: *ἀλλά με δαίμων θέλγει*. The strongly magical sense of *θέλγω* is discussed by Jacqueline de Romilly in *Magic and Rhetoric in Ancient Greece* (Cambridge, Mass.: Harvard University 1975) 3–4, 83, 91. A provocative study by Marie-Madeleine Mactoux (*Pénélope, Légende et Mythe* [Paris: Université de Besançon 1975] 203–14, 245–46) concludes that Penelope possesses some of Helen's characteristics as a goddess of fertility.

[5] For the folkloric tradition underlying the suitors' waste and profligacy (the unjust-guest tale), see H.L. Levy, "The Odyssean Suitors and the Host-Guest Relationship," *TAPA* 94 (1963) 147–53. Comic aspects of the suitors are noted by Douglas Stewart in *The Disguised Guest: Rank, Role, and Identity in the* Odyssey (Lewisburg, Pa.: Bucknell University 1976) 100–101. The suitors'foolishness is highlighted by Daniel Levine in "*Odyssey* 18: Iros as Paradigm for the Suitors," *CJ* 77 (1982) 200–204; and their baseness in "Homeric Laughter and the Unsmiling Suitors," *CJ* 78 (1982–83) 97–104.

Penelope's palace to eat and drink (2.55–57), like the victims of Circe who enter her enchanted palace to feast on "abundant meat and mellow wine" (10.468), the suitors are trapped, in effect, not without the help of their own natures, in a situation which leads inexorably to their destruction. Penelope weaves a web of destruction and eventual death for the suitors, stringing them along as she spins her thread (ἐγὼ δὲ δόλους πολυπεύω 19.137), weaving and unravelling an actual garment of death, the shroud of Laertes, such a garment of death as the suitors themselves will eventually need. Penelope, as we shall see, by virtue of the coveted status (γέρας) she holds as Odysseus' wife and her own compelling presence, has become their Circe.

Homer suggests the suitors' likeness to animals at first in muted tones. They are ever present in large numbers (cf. 22.299: βόες ὥς ἀγελαῖαι), for the most part nameless and speechless (a veritable "flock" of suitors), and like sheep and geese, they look to the palace for their daily feeding. In Book 17, the sheep, as night falls, return in flocks from the countryside, obedient to their herders (170–71). At the same time, the herald Medon goes to summon the suitors who are sporting themselves on the lawn (174–75). Homer states that the suitors, summoned by Medon, left their games at once, obedient to the voice of the herald, and made their way to the palace: οἱ δ' ἀνστάντες ἔβαν πείθοντό τε μύθῳ (17.177). The artful juxtaposition of the homecomings of sheep and suitors is striking. Later, in conversation with the beggar, Penelope establishes the equation of suitors with animals as a full-blown motif. Penelope has had a disturbing dream in which her pet geese (who come in daily from the pond to eat their grain; 19.536–37) were slain by an eagle who was really Odysseus exacting vengeance on the suitors (19.538–50).[6] In the dream, the eagle expressly states that the geese are functioning as analogues to the suitors: χῆνες μὲν μνηστῆρες, ἐγὼ δέ τοι αἰετὸς ὄρνις (19.548).

The description of the suitors' destruction in Book 22 fulfills Penelope's vision in the dream. Assembled in their customary dining quarters with the expectation of eating, the suitors are trapped in an enclosed area and slaughtered by Odysseus very like the geese which Penelope likened them to earlier in the poem. Homer says that the suitors "rushed panic- stricken (ὀρινθέντες) about the room, searching the solid walls on every side" (22.23–25), trying desperately to escape their inevitable fate. The first suitor killed is Antinous, their leader, pierced through the neck by an arrow (22.15–16). Although many of the suitors put up a fight, their efforts avail them nothing (e.g. 22.255–56). Not a one marked for slaughter is allowed to escape (22.383–89). The suitors, unlike geese, share a moral culpability for their destruction, as Homer makes clear (e.g. 22.50–53; cf. 16.364–92), but their similarity to geese in outward circumstances, and in the innate fierceness which makes geese excellent guard animals, is nonetheless striking.

[6] However Penelope's dream is to be understood, it cannot be disputed that on some level of her mind, the suitors are identified with geese. For a summary of the major interpretations of the dream, see A. H. M. Kessels, *Studies on the Dream in Greek Literature* (Utrecht: HES 1978) 91–110. The author concludes that Penelope's dream is an example of wish-fulfillment. Dreams as similes in Homer are proposed by Norman Austin in *Archery at the Dark of the Moon* (Berkeley: University of California 1975) 122–24.

TABLE

	CIRCE (BK. 10)	PENELOPE (BK. 23)
Testing:	Circe's magical potion (φάρμακον; 317) and wand (ῥάβδος; 319)	(Testing and sign are the same.)
Signs:	The magical herb (μῶλυ; 305) carried by Odysseus	The secret of the marriage bed (πυκινὸν λέχος; 177) known to Odysseus (202)
Identity:	Circe recognizes Odysseus (330)	Penelope recognizes Odysseus (230)
Bed:	Circe and Odysseus go to bed (εὐνή; 347)	Penelope and Odysseus go to bed (εὐνή; 289)
Leave-taking:	Odysseus journeys to consult Teiresias (492)	Teiresias prompts Odysseus' journey (251)
Nekyia:	Odysseus visits land of the dead (Bk. 11)	Suitors go permanently to underworld (Bk. 24)

Penelope's likeness to Circe is strengthened by thematic echoes in the poem. The sequence of events which occurs in Odysseus' meeting with Circe reappears in connection with his reunion with Penelope and nowhere else in the *Odyssey*. Although the plot requirements of each sequence differ, the order of ideas and motifs is similar (see Table).

In the case of both Circe and Penelope, Odysseus' reception occurs in an atmosphere of death (the apparent "death" of Odysseus' men; the recent slaughter of the suitors) and is followed, one book later, by a journey to the land of the dead (in the first instance by Odysseus himself; in the second, by the suitors, at the hands of Odysseus). Odysseus possesses the herb moly as an antidote for Circe's spells; the knowledge he possesses about the construction of the marriage bed acts as an "antidote" for Penelope's disbelief and reserve. After Odysseus successfully meets their challenge, both women happily acknowledge his identity and procede with him to bed—Circe, so that they "may come to trust" (φιλότητι πεποίθομεν ἀλλήλοισιν; 10.335), Penelope because she no longer mistrusts (23.215–18; cf. 230: πείθεις δή μεν θυμόν). In each instance, the progress to bed is temporarily halted—by the oath which Odysseus demands Circe take (10.342–47) and by the account of his trials yet to come, which Penelope insists that Odysseus relate (23.256–62).

Both Circe and Penelope see Odysseus off on a divinely commissioned journey, essentially different in purpose from his other journeys. Odysseus leaves Circe to journey (at her instructions) to the land of the dead to consult the seer Teiresias (10.490–93). Odysseus leaves Penelope on a journey of atonement and reconciliation with Poseidon

(23.266–81), as directed by Teiresias (23.249–253). Circe, possessed of a powerful occult knowledge, prompts the first *nekyia*. The "very prudent" (περίφρων) Penelope is closely involved in the second *nekyia*—that of the suitors in Book 24 (98–204), inasmuch as their ardent but arrogant wooing of her resulted in their own journey to the underworld. Amphimedon, in fact, complains bitterly in the underworld (24.125–90) that Penelope's encouragement led to the melancholy circumstances in which they find themselves.[7]

Although the depiction of Penelope is colored by the traditions surrounding the Circe-figure, Odysseus was after all correct in his assessment of his wife to Calypso: "She is mortal while you are immortal and ageless" (5.218). A woman of great complexity, Penelope suffers much in Odysseus' absence and, despite her ambiguous relationship with the suitors, for the most part conducts herself in an all too human way (e.g. 17.102–103; cf. 18.174).[8] Penelope, though Circe-like in her effect upon the suitors, was, after all, a woman and not a goddess, although we shall see that in matters of the heart, these two are not widely separated in the *Odyssey*.

II. Calypso and Circe: The Divine Prototypes

Circe and Calypso, the divine women encountered by Odysseus, have much in common. Each makes her appearance in the poem singing sweetly and working at the loom (5.61–62; 10.221–23). Each is beautiful, unattached, passionate, and an aggressive paramour who offers Odysseus a seductive respite from his troubles. Each dwells apart from the world of men in an idyllic island setting. Calypso lives in a picturesque grotto on the lush and verdant Isle of Ogygia (5.63–74). Circe inhabits an inviting house in a dense thicket on the heavily wooded Isle of Aeaea (10.150). There is a magical sense of wildness and unreality about the physical surroundings of both goddesses in keeping with their divine natures. Each, accordingly, is potentially dangerous—a δεινὴ θεὸς αὐδήεσσα ("terrible goddess with human voice"), as Homer tells us (12.150; 12.449). Circe would have reduced Odysseus' humanity or his manhood (e.g. 10.339–41). Calypso would have smothered him emotionally with her cloying attentiveness, as she kept him a virtual prisoner of love. Hermes, moreover, appears in both accounts as Odysseus' immediate protector. He supplies Odysseus with the herb moly as an antidote to Circe's malevolent spells (10.281–306) and delivers the ultimatum to Calypso (5.97–115) which results in Odysseus' release.

Despite superficial similarities, however, Circe and Calypso represent fundamentally different types of women, I think. Calypso is the protective mother-figure, who retrieved Odysseus from the sea and determined to care for him forever, as she explains to Hermes: "I loved (φίλεον) and cared for (ἔτρεφον) him; I was even planning to make him immortal and unaging all his days" (5.135–36). She would hide Odysseus from the world as

[7] The thematic unity of Book 24 to the rest of the poem is demonstrated by Agathe Thornton in *People and Themes in Homer's Odyssey* (London: Methuen 1970) 93–114; and Dorothea Wender in *The Last Scenes of the Odyssey* (Leiden: Brill 1978) 72–75.

[8] For a comprehensive study of Penelope, emphasizing her intelligence and emotional dilemma, see my "Penelope Πολύτροπος" in *AJP* 106 (1985) 32–48.

she lavished on him affection and the promise of immortality (cf. 8.453). In her desperation to hold on to Odysseus, she even conceals from him the real reason for her sudden willingness to let him go. She never mentions directly Hermes' visit and command but suggests rather that she herself has (at last) been touched by Odysseus' obvious discontent and will help him to leave her island, if that is what he really wants. True to her word, she patiently assists Odysseus in the construction of his boat, willingly supplying the necessary materials and advice (5.233-61).

Hoping still to hold onto Odysseus, Calypso demonstrates her superiority to ordinary women, but her insecurity is evident. Convinced that Odysseus' unhappiness over his situation with her is rooted in his desire for another woman, his wife Penelope (whom, in her mind, he "longed for always every day"; 5.210), she cannot resist reminding him that only a mortal woman (and one twenty years older at that) awaits him in his beloved Ithaca. How human of Calypso at this time of impending loss to need to hear her own superior beauty acknowledged by Odysseus—which he is prudent to do (15.215–20)—but the tribute is a hollow one. Calypso's efforts to rekindle Odysseus' desire for her are useless; the nymph quite simply no longer pleased Odysseus: οὐκέτι ἥνδανε νύμφη (5.153). Self-centered in her own desires, Calypso can only imagine that the gods demand Odysseus' release because they are jealous of the happiness she has found with the hero. She angrily mentions the gods' role in the ultimately unhappy affairs of Eos and Orion and Demeter and Iasion (5.118–29). Identifying with the two other amorous/fertility figures, Eos (the Dawn) and Demeter (the Cultivated Earth), Calypso is herself the archetypal mother, sensual and instinctive, but also clinging and touchingly vulnerable. Perhaps another Odysseus will never wash ashore to fill her empty life. There is no hint that Calypso would ever leave her remote island domain. She seems fated passively to receive and cling fast to whoever comes her way.[9]

In contrast with Calypso, the mother/lover figure, is Circe, the enchantress and guide. Sexually generous also, her chief appeal is her occult knowledge, powerful to transform the bodies of men and to illuminate the way to the netherworld. Unthreatening and alluring to the eye, she is, in reality, a formidable goddess, who keeps her victims captive in the cruelest form of imprisonment: human minds in animal bodies (e.g. 10.239–40). Her home is a veritable menagerie. Some of her "pets" are confined to pens; others roam around freely (10.212–19). But all are unable to leave the home of Circe. Ever the attentive hostess, Circe personally sees to the feeding of all of her "guests". After the goddess' drugged wine and magical wand transform Odysseus' men into bristly swine (10.233–40), Circe promptly feeds them a meal designed to please their new, less refined palates—acorns, chestnuts, and cornel-berries (10.241–43)!

[9] For Calypso's connections with death, see Barry B. Powell's *Composition by Theme in the Odyssey* (Meisenheim am Glan: Hain 1977) 4–7 and accompanying notes. Calypso as the "Concealer" is described by Thornton (supra n. 7) 125–26. The threat posed by Calypso and Circe is discussed in the context of Odysseus' other temptations by James H. Hogan in "The Temptation of Odysseus," *TAPA* 106 (1976) 187–210. The author's conclusions hint at something of the paradoxical vulnerability of these goddesses in the face of the hero's own inner strength and resolve: e.g. "Odysseus manages to enjoy the sexuality of Calypso and Circe without inclining toward permanent seduction" (p. 209).

Once Circe realizes, however, that resourceful (πολυμήχανος; 10.401) Odysseus has met her challenge and that her spells are useless against him (e.g. 10.326: "You drink this potion and are not enchanted!"), she places aside her cruel tricks and amiably restores Odysseus' men to their former shapes (only taller, younger, and more handsome than before; 10.391–96). For a full year, there are lavish feasts in Circe's palace (10.467–68). With or without magical potions, Circe is a witty and enchanting hostess, and in the end, Odysseus' comrades must remind their "possessed" (δαιμόνιος) captain of the need to sail on (10.472–74).

More overtly complex and exciting than Calypso, Circe accepts with equanimity Odysseus' decision to leave her but insists that he must first make a trip to the realm of Hades to consult the soul of Teiresias (10.490–95). Compelling Odysseus to seek his own immortality, she sends him on a greater, spiritual journey before releasing him to the perils of his physical journey. "Unflinching (σχέτλιος), you descended alive to the house of Hades. You will have two deaths when other men have but one" (12.21–22). Circe, then, is the intellectually stimulating female, thriving on challenge, who enchants and inspires, although her call to growth and transformation is not without its own dangers. This is seen on the lowest level by her animal transformations and on the highest level by Odysseus' harrowing journey to the netherworld, which she directs. It is Odysseus' fate to meet death in some way at Circe's hands, and the actual death of Elpenor (12.10) symbolizes this fact.[10]

Neither Circe's occult knowledge nor Calypso's soft possessiveness can hold Odysseus forever. As a virtual prisoner of love on Calypso's island ("cold lover with an ardent dame" in Rieu's translation) and as a fascinated lover in Circe's palace, Odysseus retains hold of his individuality and rejects the limited existence awaiting him in an extended relationship with each. Are we to feel sympathy for these goddesses who loved Odysseus (in their fashion) and would gladly have removed from him the burden of mortality? Homer intends us to feel some sympathy for Calypso, I think, in her lonely Elysium, who in the end apparently has nothing to offer Odysseus but emotional stagnation. Still, remembering the days when her love did in fact please Odysseus, she is content to hold onto her unwilling lover forever.

There is less sympathy for Circe, who seems stronger than Calypso and more overtly malign, although Homer does say that Circe, on at least one occasion, was capable of feeling pity (ἐλέαιρε καὶ αὐτή; 10.399). Circe, however, will always be surrounded by men, in one form or another. After Odysseus, other travellers, no doubt, who were defenseless against her spells, made their way to her palace and stayed on indefinitely (to say nothing of her earlier victims who may not have fared as well as Odysseus' men). It is unlikely, though, that Circe ever found her match among mortal men. There can be no

[10] For Circe as ψυχοπόμπος ("soul-guide"), see Charles Mugler, "Circe et la nécessité," *Annales de la Faculté des Lettres et Sciences Humaines de Nice* 35 (1979) 59–65. Circe as a folkloric type is examined at length by Denys Page in *Folktales in Homer's Odyssey* (Cambridge, Mass.: Harvard University 1973) 51–69. Andrew R. Dyck focuses on Circe's sexual challenge in "The Witch's Bed But Not Her Breakfast: An Odyssean Paradox," *RhM* 124 (1981) 196–98. For a discussion of the ambivalent erotic power of Circe and Calypso, see Michael Nagler, "Dread Goddess Endowed with Speech," *ArchNews* 6 (1977) 77–85.

doubt that, for a period of time, Odysseus benefitted from his contact with each goddess. Calypso rescued him from the sea and restored him to vigor. Circe gave him unparalleled vision and adventure. In the end, however, Odysseus chooses to leave the warm embraces of each for an uncertain future. It is safe to conclude that, in so doing, Odysseus touched the lives of these immortal women, in varying degrees, with something of his own mortality—feelings of unfulfillment and loss.[11]

III. Helen and Penelope

While it is not unexpected for goddesses to lose their mortal lovers, as Calypso complains, the script of love's loss in the *Odyssey* is replayed with subtlety on the human level. The two fundamental types (mother/lover and enchantress/guide), as embodied in Calypso and Circe, reappear in the depictions of Helen and Penelope. Helen, sensuous and amorous, at least in former days, has returned to her husband Menelaus after the war and lives with him at Sparta in a kind of grim and unhappy Elysium, lightened by the use of drugs (4.219–26). Calypso's idyllic cave is replaced by an opulent palace worthy of the gods (4.71–75), but a similar sense of boredom and dissatisfaction are present. The languid domestic scene, which Menelaus must endure as the price for the immortality which will eventually come to him through marriage with Zeus' daughter, has been discussed at length by William Anderson.[12]

There are personal parallels between Calypso and Helen as well. Self-centered like Calypso, Helen seems unconcerned about wearying or tormenting Menelaus with casual,

[11] The intrusion of the mortal world upon the immortal world in Homer has been described eloquently by Paolo Vivante in *The Homeric Imagination: A Study of Homer's Poetic Perception of Reality* (Bloomington: Indiana University 1970), who, speaking of Calypso, Circe, and Polyphemus, says: "[T]hese mythical beings are eternally bound up with the places which are their abodes, untouched by any searching experience, until on a certain day Odysseus arrives and they feel all the friction of human life. Love, hatred, stir them from their divine state. A spell appears to be broken, the human moment is vindicated so Circe's magic can no longer work . . . she has become a woman, ready to fall in love and to feel the suspense of time rather than its revolving flux" (p. 139). Circe's emotional transformation has also been described by Cedric H. Whitman in *Homer and The Heroic Tradition* (New York: Norton 1965 [1958]) 300: "Circe . . . distillate of woman that she is . . . becomes, from a witch, a woman of gentle compassion . . . with a sympathy unusual in goddesses." For a study of Odysseus as the man who chooses trouble as a means of establishing his own identity, see George E. Dimock, Jr., "The Name of Odysseus" in *Essays on the Odyssey* (supra n. 1) 54–74.

[12] Anderson (supra n. 1) compares the relationship of Calypso and Odysseus with that of Helen and Menelaus. Both Calypso and Helen hold out, with their beauty and sensuality, the promise of Elysium. Odysseus ultimately rejects the kind of Elysium which Calypso offers him and chooses instead the uncertain perils of a sea-voyage and homecoming. Menelaus, in contrast, by reuniting with Helen at war's end, has insured his own place in Elysium after death. In outward circumstances, life with the semi-divine Helen is indeed a paradise on earth; Menelaus' palace overflows with unimaginable riches. Anderson has perceptively grasped the hollowness of this idyllic scene and the paradoxical unhappiness Menelaus feels as he contemplates an eternity of Elysium with the beauteous Helen forever at his side. A sensitive study of Helen in the *Odyssey* is also presented by Johannes Kakridis in *Homer Revisited* (Lund: Publ. of the New Society of Letters 1971) 40–53. For some minor character doublets in the *Odyssey* (e.g. Eumaeus and Philoitios, Eurykleia and Eurynome), see Bernard Fenik's discussion in *Studies in the Odyssey* (Wiesbaden: F. Steiner 1974) 172–207. The author states: "Repetition on almost every level . . . is one of the fundamental stylistic features of Homeric poetry" (p. 231).

almost boastful talk about her former days of infamy when she was the darling of Aphrodite (e.g. 4.260–64). Helen's need to relive past glories parallels Calypso's need for reassurance from Odysseus of her superiority to Penelope (5.211–13). Helen clings to the past the way that Calypso clings to the present. Helen, unlike Calypso, presumably retains a sexual hold over her mate, but Menelaus' pronounced discontent and ready tears (e.g. 4.77–108), although attributed to thoughts of his lost comrades, recall Odysseus' feelings of discontent with Calypso. Helen's life with Menelaus echoes sadly the relationship of Calypso and Odysseus. It is clear that Helen, though essentially possessing what Calypso lost, has won little either.

Penelope also regains her husband, but Odysseus' long absence has exacted a heavy toll. For years, Penelope has lived with loneliness and anxiety and suffered the estrangement of her son (e.g. 17.102–106; 23.97–103) and the irretrievable loss of her youth (18.180–81). Circe-like in her effect upon the hoards of persistent suitors, who daily flocked to the palace, Penelope, and the beloved home she represented, also inspired Odysseus with an unwavering resolve to return to Ithaca, no matter what the immediate distraction or obstacle in his path. It may be too much to conclude (as jealous Calypso did) that Odysseus "longed for [Penelope] always every day" (5.210), but it is clear that the memory of Penelope survived the formidable likes of Circe and Calypso. Circe was more of a threat, perhaps because Odysseus' stay was too short to admit of boredom or perhaps because Circe's appeal, once she put aside her mischievous spells, was reminiscent of Penelope's.

The echoes in the depictions of Circe and Penelope, as discussed earlier, continue in muted tones with Odysseus' return to Ithaca. Circe sends Odysseus to the land of the dead before directing him homeward to Ithaca. The presence of Penelope's suitors destroys the possibility of a joyous homecoming and demands that Odysseus himself send scores of men to death (22.383–89). Like Circe, Penelope accepts as a given Odysseus' need to continue his journey. Although she has Odysseus only briefly before he embarks on another journey of indeterminate length (ἀμέτρητος πόνος; 23.248–53), Penelope understands, like Circe, the nature of the man she loves, and she prudently puts no obstacles in his way.

Calypso and Circe, two dominant female types in the *Odyssey* establish the scenario of love and loss which Helen and Penelope replay with tragic nuance and broad implication.[13] The parallels between Helen and Penelope and their divine counterparts, subtly drawn by Homer, lend a dynamic symmetry to the poem. Circe and Calypso are Odysseus' two most formidable opponents because the threat they pose is psychological—Circe challenging his spiritual/intellectual self and Calypso his sensual/physical self. Penelope and Helen carry the essence of these remote and powerful goddesses into the world of men and play important, similar roles there. The parallels between Calypso and Helen, on the one hand, and Circe and Penelope, on the other, exemplify, I think, a

[13] Homer sounds the overture to this same theme with Nausicaa, who also experiences a romantic stirring for the hero (e.g. 6.243–45; 8.458–62) but is spared the realization of her desires.

fundamental unity in Homer's cosmos. The worlds of gods and men, goddesses and women, are not far apart in Homer but intersect on many levels. Just as the gods are not immune to human emotions, so too men may lay claim to a certain share of divinity. Such is the humanity of Homer that Calypso, for example, can feel human emotions of loneliness and loss, and Penelope can partake in some measure of the divine power of enchantment. Homer's portrayal of human and divine love is marked by keen insight and tinged with sadness. "Love's labor" in the case of Calypso and Circe may belong to the fantastic and unreal world of Odysseus' adventures. But their human counterparts, Helen and Penelope, experience a similar sense of loss from their love's labors.

VERGIL'S AEOLUS EPISODE

ALEXANDER G. McKAY

Recent discussions of the Aeolus episode in Vergil's *Aeneid* I, 50–156, have concentrated on political aspects and breaches of authority on the part of both Juno and Aeolus.[1] The political simile attaching to Neptune's role as pacifier of the dissident winds and their unruly steward certainly underlines the political implications of the episode. I propose, however, to shift attention to the inner dynamics and poetics of the tableau, to explore Vergil's use of imagery, mythological allusion, and Lucretian illustration in designing the memorable piece, and to illustrate how deeply affected Horace was in his drafting of the *propemptikon* to Vergil's ship (*Odes* I, 3).

Let me begin with another storm in waters far removed from Vergil's cyclone at the outset of the epic:

> If by your art, my dearest father, you have
> Put the wild waters in this roar, allay them.
> The sky, it seems, would pour down stinking pitch
> But that the sea, mounting to the welkin's cheek
> Dashes the fire out. O, I have suffered
> With those that I saw suffer: a brave vessel,
> Who had, no doubt, some noble creature in her,
> Dash'd all to pieces.

The verses are drawn, of course, from the second scene of Act I of Shakespeare's *The Tempest*. Miranda addresses her magician father, Prospero, imploring him to use his arts to calm the waves that seem to overwhelm the ship of Alonso, King of Naples, while thunder and lightning provide their special effects to highlight the prelude to the main action.

Vergilians are quick to sense sympathetic bonds between Vergil's and Shakespeare's opening storms. Vergilian echoes,[2] which are frequent in Shakespeare's drama, seem distinctly more than fortuitous, and the verdict of modern Shakespearean scholarship is strongly in favor of the closest conceivable ties between the Elizabethan playwright and the Augustan epic poet.[3] My concern, however, is not so much with the influence of Vergil's storm on later literature and art as with the cumulative power of reminiscences

[1] For political and governmental aspects see Oliver Phillips, "*Aeole, namque tibi*," *Vergilius* 26 (1980) 18–26, and John Sarkissian, "The Idea of Imperium in *Aeneid* I. 50–296", *Augustan Age* 4 (1985) 51–56.

[2] See A.D. Nuttall, "Virgil and Shakespeare," in *Virgil and his Influence: Bimillennial Studies*, ed. Charles Martindale (Bristol: Bristol Classical Press 1984) 71–93.

[3] On Vergil's storm episode and Shakespeare's Tempest consult D.D. Carnicelli, "The Widow and the Phoenix: Dido, Carthage and Tunis in The Tempest," *Harvard Library Bulletin* 27 (1979) 389–433; R.S. Conway, "The Classical Elements in Shakespeare's Tempest," *New Studies of a Great Inheritance* (London: John Murray 1921) 165–89; Jan Kott, "The Aeneid and The Tempest," *Essays in Criticism* 34 (1984) 193–215.

DAIDALIKON: Studies in Memory of Raymond V. Schoder, S.J.

and of models in Vergil's creation of what stands out as the most memorable of many storms in Latin poetry.[4]

Homer's *Odyssey* is undeniably a primary source:[5] Odysseus' encounter with Poseidon's storm after the Ogygian interlude unquestionably inspired the Vergilian counterpart;[6] and Juno's seduction of Aeolus certainly reflects Hera's seduction of Hypnos in her continuing campaign against Zeus' will and Trojan resistance.[7] In many respects, the divergences from the Homeric prototypes are characteristically more arresting than the detectable reverberations. For one, the Homeric palace on the floating island, proper locale for a deity whose name, Aiolos, suggests "variable, shifty" yields to a new locale, a cave "pregnant with suppressed frenzy of southern winds," as ominous and potentially as destructive as the Greeks lodged in the belly of the Trojan horse.[8] The winds are contentious and straining at the bit, and Vergil signals their impending outburst with sonority and clatter (*magno cum murmure montis/circum claustra fremunt*, 55–56). Only Aeolus, master of the winds, perched above them in splendid isolation, is able to regulate and control the rampant blasts.

Caves are a favorite resort of Vergil throughout his poetic career, from his bucolics to the epic, sometimes in association with diabolic, frenzied creatures, like Cacus in *Aeneid* VIII, sometimes more serenely for comforting and prophetic agents like Cyrene and Proteus in the Fourth *Georgic*, or Deiphobe, the Apolline Sibyl, in *Aeneid* VI.[9] Vergil's description of the place of confinement for the fractious winds stresses the massive scale and weight of the mountain laid over them by divine intervention, and the reader is reminded of a comparable sentence passed on the rebellious Titans. Hesiod's prison, designed by Zeus and Poseidon to contain the Titans, shimmers through the cave of the winds and certainly provided incentive for Vergil's account of Tartarus in *Aeneid* VI:[10]

> A wall of bronze is driven around it, and night is drifted
> about its throat in a triple circlet, while upward from it
> there grow and branch the roots of the earth, and of the barren sea.
> There the Titan gods live buried under the darkness
> and the mists, and this is by the decree of Zeus the cloud-gatherer,
> in a moldy place, at the uttermost edges of monstrous
> earth. There is no way out for them; Poseidon has fitted
> brazen doors, and the walls run around enclosing everything.[11]

[4] On the epic background of the storm, see M.P.O. Morford, *The Poet Lucan: Studies in Rhetorical Style* (Oxford: Blackwell, 1967) 20–58; for renderings in art see Reuben A. Brower, "Visual and Verbal Translation of Myth: Neptune in Virgil, Rubens, Dryden," *Daedalus* 101:1 (1972) 155–82.

[5] Homer, *Odyssey* 10, 1–76 (Aiolos episode).

[6] Homer, *Odyssey* 5, 282–332 (sequel to Calypso's island paradise).

[7] Homer, *Iliad* 14, 225–79 (the seduction of Hypnos).

[8] Vergil, *Aeneid* 2, 238.

[9] Caves are locales of elemental powers, reckless in the case of Aeolus, responsible from the standpoint of technology in the Cyclopean case (*Aeneid* 8, 419, 424). Tenants include Proteus (*Georgics* 4, 429), Cerberus (*Aeneid* 6, 400), and Cacus (*Aeneid* 8, 210).

[10] *Aeneid* 6, 548–627 (Tartarus).

[11] Hesiod, *Theogony* 726–33, translated by Richmond Lattimore, *Hesiod: The Works and Days, Theogony, The Shield of Herakles* (Ann Arbor: Michigan 1959) 166–67.

The Titanic offensive against the Olympians, in the *Theogony* account, brings the universe to the brink of catastrophe and disorder, just as Aeolus' reckless winds confound the elements and threaten the downfall of heaven.

Homer supplies the patronymic Hippotades, "son of Horseman," for Aiolos in the *Odyssey*, a name well suited to the subordinate of Poseidon whose own association with horses was mark of his identity.[12] Vergil seems to align himself completely with the equine tradition of the winds in his version of the tale; Aeolus performs as master or overseer of fractious horses, of race horses anxious for the event which had become a staple of popular entertainment in Rome. Tacitus observes that "there are special vices, peculiar to this city, which children seem to absorb, almost in the mother's womb: a partiality for the theater and a passion for horse-racing and gladiatorial shows."[13] Lucretius provides a scene taken directly from the circus to illustrate the finite time taken by the atoms of will to travel from the brain to the limbs: "In the moment of time when the starting gates are opened, surely you observe that the horses, however strong and ambitious, are unable to break out as suddenly as their spirit longs to do?"[14] Horse-racing was as deep-seated with Lucretius as with Vergil who refers to chariots and the *aurigae* with particular relish. Vergil's portrayal of the winds as racehorses appears, however, to be a deliberate reaction to the Lucretian image. Whereas Lucretius, in his account of winds and storms, compares them to the snarling, aggressive creatures of the *venationes*, awaiting their release from cages on the eve of a production,[15] Vergil imagines them as stallions, rampant creatures of circus *quadrigae* whose reckless speed and vigor captivated the Roman *ignobile vulgus*. Certainly Vergil's language has clear implications of circus games: the winds, confined like chargers, like those of the Lucretian circus image, impatient for their freedom, straining and snorting (*sonoras*, 53) against the starting gates (*carceres*) while Aeolus, the starter, or president of the spectacle, watches from overhead, as though from the *pulvinar* on the Palatine side of the Circus Maximus in Rome. And Aeolus, in Vergil's description, handles his scepter as though it were a charioteer's whip, designed on the one hand to mollify the spirits and passions of the steeds, and, on the other hand, following Juno's command, as an instrument likely to instigate and excite their energy for the course. Juno's order rings with the frenzy of the race track: *incute vim ventis* (69), *age diversos* (70) "drive them on in all directions". In short, Vergil seems to juxtapose and combine several fictional and realistic elements in his description of the winds and of their master: the winds are like suppressed Titanic demons but, in the image of restless circus creatures whose energies presage excitement and widespread disruption and ruin—apocalyptic counterparts to the restrained magisterial steeds of Neptune's chariot which eventually restores order to the storm-tossed sea.[16]

[12] Homer, *Odyssey* 10, 2.

[13] Tacitus, *Dialogus* 29.

[14] Lucretius, *De Rerum Natura* 2, 263–65.

[15] Lucretius, *De Rerum Natura* 6, 189–203, especially 198–200.

[16] James Henry, *Aeneidea* (1873–92), conjectured that the *Ludi Circenses* influenced Vergil's choice of metaphor: *imperio premit* (53); *vinclis et carcere* (54), *frenat* (54), *claustra fremunt* (56), *premere* (63), *laxas . . . habenas* (63), *clauso ventorum carcere* (141). R.G. Austin, *P. Vergili Maronis Aeneidos Liber Primus* (Oxford: Clarendon 1971) loc. cit., admits that Vergil's adopted imagery derives mainly from the

The locale of the Aeolus encounter is noteworthy. Where does the cyclone center? Scholars generally agree that the storm breaks at the opposite extreme of the Aeolian Islands, namely off the west coast of Sicily as the Trojans sail towards the toe of the boot and the promised shores of Hesperia.[17] Anchises' lamented death occurred at Drepanum (modern Trapani) under Mount Eryx, and after the obsequies the fleet turned towards the Tyrrhenian Sea and the promised land. To accentuate the hostile nature of the storm Vergil departs from his predominant horse imagery to suggest a military formation at verse 82: *venti velut agmine facto qua data porta*. But the deviation is only momentary, for immediately after their release, all semblance of order is dissipated and destruction is let loose on the waters.

Vergil announces the forthcoming winds in the manner of a racetrack reporter: they come forth from their starting gates like named stallions: Eurus, Notus, Africus, and Aquilo, the shrieking nor-wester, followed by Zephyrus. Because Eurus is the most repeatedly cited and gains the spotlight in Neptune's forceful reprimand (140), we may suppose that the fleet had been diverted from its westward course by the Easterly which directed it towards the Tunisian shores. Vergil, with a pilot's zeal and precautionary concern, actually provides a detailed account of the menace, the so-called *Arae*, where the fleet, entire or in part, may be sacrificed. They are pictured as a huge ridge, just beneath the water level, with sandbanks, shallows and hidden rocks. Their location seems certain: they must surface in the fairway channel between the Tunisian and Sicilian shorelines. Although Roland Austin preferred to discard any positive identification for the "Altars," mariners and recent scholarship tend to identify them with the Skerki Bank, south-west of Lilybaeum and Motya on the western side of Sicily, and en route to Tunisian waters.[18]

Aeolus' rocky domain is generally identified with the Aeolian Isles off the north-east of Sicily.[19] Ancient testimony certainly suggests the existence of a cult figure for the archipelago,[20] and Bernabò Brea, the excavator, has connected a fragmentary pottery find, with the graffito AIO, with the name of the wind deity.[21] Although some scholars

race-horse (and prison) but "without intending any one connected, or uniform, series of metaphors." P.R. Hardie, "Some Themes from the Gigantomachy in the *Aeneid*," *Hermes* 111 (1983) 311–26, supposes that the winds are anthropomorphic, because Neptune uses rational speech to them!

[17] R.G. Austin (supra n. 16) 60, locates the storm center southwest of Lilybaeum on the west coast of Sicily.

[18] Pliny, *N.H.* 5, 42 and Varro, *De ora maritima* (quoted by Servius) identify the *Arae* in the waters west of Sicily towards Africa; Kenneth Wellesley, "Virgilian Places" in *Vindex Humanitatis: Essays in Honour of John Huntly Bishop* (Armidale: University of New England 1980) 146–69 (especially 161–3), provides precise topographical details of the Skerki Bank.

[19] Vergil identifies the realm of Aeolus without hesitation: *nimborum . . . patriam . . . Aeoliam* (*Aeneid* 1, 51–52), *Aeoliam . . . Liparen* (*Aeneid* 8, 416–17), an island *Sicanium iuxta latus* (*Aeneid* 8, 416). See also L.G. Pocock, *Reality and Allegory in the Odyssey* (Amsterdam: Hakkert 1959) s.v. Aeolus, Aeolian Islands; and Jenny Strauss Clay, "Aeolia, or Under the Sign of the Circle," *CJ* 80 (1985) 289–91.

[20] For Aeolus cult, see Diodorus Siculus 20, 101.

[21] For the graffito consult Bernabò Brea and M. Cavalier, *Il castello di Lipari e il museo archeologico eoliano* 2 (Palermo 1976) 90.

have preferred to associate Aiolos with the western reaches of Sicily, Vergil's age was less suspicious. Strabo, in particular, associates weather forecasts specifically with the Aeolian group and with Polybius as his authority:

> Some of the people of the Aeolian isles, when ships were unable to sail, used to predict what wind would blow (from cloud effects in the Aeolian volcanic archipelago) and were not misled. Polybius deduced from this that what seems to be (Homer's) most mythical account was not unfounded, and that Homer spoke the truth through riddles when he called Aeolus the steward of the winds . . . They say that Aeolus lived on Strongyle (Stromboli), an island with a circular shape that sends forth flames.[22]

Storm warnings and weather probabilities are not part of Vergil's dramatic event of *Aeneid* I, and Aeolus does not emerge as a volcanic figure. Strabo's subscription to the popular view, and his assignment of Aeolus to the volcanic island rather than to Lipara where the cult has been positively identified, suggest, however, that there was a growing confusion of winds and volcanic fire in the Augustan mind. Elsewhere, Vergil associates himself with the same belief: Cacus, the fire-breathing demon and opponent of Hercules at Pallanteum, is a graphic embodiment of the chthonic forces of fire and wind that inhabit volcanoes.[23]

From the standpoint of descriptive powers, Vergil's narrative of the storm and its impact on the Trojan fleet is particularly memorable and an impressive embodiment of the generalization of the *prooemium*: *multum ille et terris iactatus et alto* (3), *iactatos aequore toto* (29), and *acti fatis maria omnia circum* (32). The technique, repeated in *Aeneid* II, where it has been sensitively noticed by Fred Mench,[24] is surprisingly cinematic. T.M. Andersson has noticed the camera technique most suggestively:

> "The reader . . . observes the scene from every angle and level, from a distance in which the fleet can be conceived of as a group of dots and, in reverse, from the foreground perspective of Aeneas' own view, from the shore on which the waves tumble, from the sky on which the clouds gather and the lightning flashes, and even from the sandy depths of the uprooted sea."[25]

Contemporary response to the artistry and the drama of the opening episode was not lost on Vergil's contemporaries, most notably, on his *animae dimidium meae*, Quintus Horatius Flaccus.

Scholars are generally agreed that Horace's *propemptikon* ode, I, 3, was designed to compliment Vergil as he embarked on an Adriatic crossing from Italy to Greece. There is also general agreement, by reason of the details that Horace attaches to the vessel, the passage overseas, and the passenger, that the trip was historic and actual. But there is no documented notice of the crossing, only assumptions that Vergil knew the Adriatic from

[22] Strabo 6, 2, 10.

[23] For Cacus as flame-thrower see Vergil, *Aeneid* 8, 198–99; 251–55; 259–67. Evander directs Aeneas to the ruined cave on the Aventine where Hercules wrestled with the fire-demon (*Aeneid* 8, 190–305).

[24] Fred Mench, "Film Sense in the Aeneid," *Arion* 8 (1969) 381–97.

[25] Theodore M. Andersson, *Early Epic Scenery* (Ithaca: Cornell 1976) 57.

experience, from repeated visits to Greece. His final crossing, from Greece to Brundisium, was prelude to his death in 19 B.C.; it seems in some way the rejection of Horace's earlier entreaty that his poet friend be spared and that his person should be delivered safe and sound to Greece and the environs of Athens. A literal, however imprecise, reading of *Odes* I.3 shatters, or at least partially dissipates, when the ode is associated with the Vergilian storm scene of *Aeneid* I. The ode seems to be as much a compliment to Vergil's stormy tableau and storm-tossed hero as a farewell expression directed at Vergil's transport vessel embarking on the boisterous Adriatic. Nisbet and Hubbard have curiously denied any association with the Aeolus episode: "Horace's Ode is an accomplished piece of versification, but little more. The poet may protest his affection for Virgil but he shows none of his usual tact and charm; there is not a hint of Virgil's poetry."[26] On the contrary, Horace's *propemptikon* repeatedly exhibits factors and vocabulary familiar from the Aeolus episode. The agents of Vergil's storm reappear, only slightly diminished in number and emphasis, in Horace's counterpart; Aeolus, regulator of the winds, and the windy trio of Africus, Notus, and Aquilo all feature in Horace's ode, to be sure in a fresh context, the stormy Adriatic, which for Horace, and many of his traveling contemporaries, was repeatedly a stage for discomfort or disaster.[27] Aeolus, in Horace's version, has a function entirely comparable with that assigned to him by Vergil; Horace's *tollere seu ponere volt freta* (16) is a manifest derivative from Vergil's: *mulcere dedit fluctus et tollere vento* (66). Reverberations sound again in Horace's use of *incubo*. Vergil's usages are malign, sinister, even nightmarish in their several appearances: *incubuere mari* (84), *ponto nox incubat atra* (89) and in *Aeneid* II, describing the advance of the twin serpents from Tenedos: *angues/incumbunt pelago* (205f). Horace's echo (and the priority of Vergil's first books to the Horatian *propemptikon* seems most likely),[28] transforms the race-horse imagery of Vergil's winds into a company (*nova febrium cohors*) of novel diseases which have settled like some awesome incubus over the earth. Vergil's imagery seems to derive from the *ludi circenses*; Lucretius' winds and storms are pictured as amphitheater animals; Horace transcends both when he identifies his host of diseases with a military formation (Vergil let the *agmen* flicker into his own description) and so invests his particular terror with a greater sense of order and discipline than Vergil's rampant, uncontrolled winds and waves. Imitation was Horace's best compliment to his poet friend, and the parade ode consigned to Vergil's ship was a tribute less to a circumstance than to the impressive artistry of a master poet. The Roman *Odes* offer additional insights into

[26] R.G.M. Nisbet and Margaret Hubbard, *A Commentary on Horace Odes Book 1* (Oxford: Clarendon 1970) 44.

[27] Cf. M. Owen Lee, S.J., *Words, Sound, and Image in the Odes of Horace* (Ann Arbor: Michigan 1969) 19–20; D.A. Kidd, "Virgil's Voyage," *Prudentia* 9 (1977) 97–103; Ronald Basto, "Horace's *Propemptikon* to Vergil: A Re-examination", *Vergilius* 28 (1982) 30–43; and C.F. Saylor, "Horace's C.1.2 and Vergil's Storm (*Aen.* 1.81ff)," *Vergilius* 25 (1979) 20–25.

[28] Scholars tend to place Horace *Odes* I, 3 among the later poems published in 23 B.C.C. The *propemptikon* no doubt followed upon Vergil's reading of the first books of the epic.

Horace's indebtedness to Vergil generally, and to the Aeolus and Allecto episodes as well; Juno's character in *Odes* III.4 exhibits striking reminiscences of her temperament and dauntless will as counter-destiny as portrayed in *Aeneid* I and VII.[29]

The ensuing action to the tempest is summary, and the tone peremptory. Neptune's double province, of waves and winds, has been trespassed upon by Juno, the airy celestial Hera; her invasion of his territory, with Aeolus as instrument, confuses and perverts the natural order. Venus does the same when she trespasses on Juno's Punic territory, but she conceals her trespass by assuming the guise of a huntress, Diana-like, to safeguard her future and to escape Juno's notice. As god of the sea, where wind and water come visibly into contact, Neptune is supreme, and means to maintain his suzerainty. During his epiphany Vergil has him pay more attention to the winds than to the waters of the sea.

Vergil marshals extraordinary forces in the conflict over Aeneas' future—Jupiter, Juno (with Aeolus), and Neptune with his marine associates—and the poet's pictorial imagination is as vivid as the stupendous conflict between Athena and Poseidon for the mastery of Attica, the theme of the west pediment of the Parthenon. Neptune, with his splendid chariot, is an impressive response to Juno, and the marine deities that escort the sea divinity are both counterparts and antagonists to the bestial embodiments of the cyclone in Vergil's dramatic design.

Neptune's response to Juno's intervention begins with rage and ends in speechlessness, or more properly, *aposiopesis*: *quos ego* . . . . His bluster extends only to threatening gestures and warnings (135–36), and Vergil has clearly elected to introduce a god whose *vis temperata* (*Odes* III, 4, 66) brings peace. Vergil conceives of Neptune as a redeemer, active for Aeneas' sake and cause, a role which suggests political redemption more than epic encounter or even gigantomachy. W.S. Anderson has caught the intention:

> "Neptune's activity . . . indicates the goal of peace and political stability to which Aeneas is groping; then beyond that, points to the achievement of Augustus, who, like Neptune and the statesman of the simile, quieted the storm at sea and the mob at Rome."[30]

The political and magisterial symbolism of the opening episode has never been in question. Highet noted, too, that Vergil distrusted oratory in every instance, save one where its salutary effect is signalled: in the striking simile where Neptune's subduing of the riotous waves is compared with the sudden change when a riot is suppressed by the appearance of a single man, known for his rectitude and service to his country, one who asserts the power that had been assigned in part to Aeolus: *ille regit animos et pectora mulcet* (153).[31] Cato Uticensis and Octavian vie for identification with Vergil's ideal statesman; the latter seems altogether more opposite given the circumstances of storm

[29] For reminiscences of Vergil in the *Odes*, see G.E. Duckworth, "*Animae dimidium meae:* Two Poets of Rome," *TAPA* 87 (1956) 281–316; and Ronald Basto, "Horace *Odes* 3.2 and *Aeneid* 12," *CJ* 78 (1982–3) 127–30.

[30] William S. Anderson *The Art of the Aeneid* (Englewood Cliffs: Prentice-Hall 1969) 25.

[31] Gilbert Highet, *The Speeches in Vergil's Aeneid* (Princeton: University Press 1972) 283–84.

and near disaster involving the forefather of the Julians.[32] Octavian's naval encounters and mishaps before the victory at Actium were repeatedly associated with the Tyrrhenian and Sicilian waters, and Lipari, the ostensible site of Aeolus' windy realm, actually served as a naval base for Sextus Pompey during the hostilities with the second triumvirate.[33] The loyalty of the Liparaeans to Sextus Pompey's cause led to their deportation to Campania in 37 B.C. The islands were a thorn in the side of the Julian cause until their recapture by Octavian and Agrippa after the naval victory at Naulochus.

The way of allegory is beset with problems and need not be pursued here. More important is the recognition of the Aeolus episode as a dramatic, memorable tableau of the adversities of the hero beset, a vivid token of the personal enmity of Juno, and a graphic illustration of the cosmic implications of the hero's quest. The storm helps to visualize and summarize the hero's *labores*, to convey an impression of the persistent misfortune that assails him. The focus on the elements, on winds and waves, personalized in Aeolus, and in celestial Juno, and brutalized in the frenzy of the winds as reckless racehorses, heightens the sense of Aeneas' isolation. The spiritual collapse which he endures and eventually triumphs over, his cry of anguish and of thwarted heroism in the midst of the storm, the sound and light effects that enhance the episode, are as deeply etched on our minds as on Horace's impressionable genius. The sequel, the continuation of Juno's role as counter-fate in Carthage, comes not unexpectedly; the *furor impius* which she embodies and encourages in her patronage of Dido has already caught the spotlight in Vergil's Aeolus episode.

The foregoing paper is a tribute to Father Schoder's devoted, constructive services to Vergilian studies, and to the enlightened understanding which his lectures, field guidance, and incomparable photographs have brought to bear on them. Our association has lasted for more than a quarter century, and it is a privilege to salute his labors and our unanimity during many years of service to the Vergilian Society Incorporated, to the Classical Summer School at Cumae, and to The Vergilian Society's Classical Tours.

[32] R.S. Conway, ed., *Virgil, Aeneidos Liber Primus* (Cambridge: University Press 1935) ad 1, 148–53 prefers Cato Uticensis; Douglas Laurel Drew, *The Allegory of the Aeneid* (Oxford: Blackwell 1927) 66–72, favors Octavian. His statement, page 67, accents the allegorical properties of the storm passage with some precision: "I would urge that Virgil is alluding to the series of disasters, some of them due to bad weather, suffered by Augustus in the protracted naval war waged against Sextus Pompeius, 38–36 B.C., in general, and to the great storm of the first year's operations, in particular."

[33] For the naval action in the Aeolian and Tyrrhenian waters see Appian, *B.C.* 5, 84–90, and Dio Cassius 48, 47–48.

GERARD MANLEY HOPKINS AND THE CLASSICS

PETER MILWARD, S.J.

At this distinguished Schoderfest it falls to my lot to be the one representative of Father Schoder's outstanding extra-classical interest in the poetry of Gerard Manley Hopkins. It is perhaps natural that I should be so, seeing that we have collaborated on no fewer than two books concerning this Jesuit poet: namely, *Landscape and Inscape*, published by Paul Elek of London and William Eerdmans of Grand Rapids in 1975, and *Readings of the Wreck*, published by the Loyola University Press of Chicago the following year. Even before then, the name of Raymond Schoder was well-known among Hopkins scholars as the assistant editor of yet another book on the poet, the immortal *Immortal Diamond*, published by Sheed and Ward in 1949, to which he also contributed two chapters: "An Interpretive Glossary of Difficult Words in the Poems", and "What Does *The Windhover* Mean?"

My own acquaintance with Ray goes back to this very time, when he came to post-war England, partly for his tertianship at St. Beuno's College, partly to take those color slides of the places in Hopkins' poems which we used for the illustrations of *Landscape and Inscape*. Thus he may be said to have contributed the "landscape" part of the book, while it was my endeavour to fill in the "inscape". I was then a young Jesuit student of philosophy at Heythrop College in the wilds of Oxfordshire; and I particularly recall the reputation which this eccentric American Father left behind him in our province. It was said that he would hang from trees at impossible angles to take just the right photo of the front of St. Beuno's College; and that he would go all the way to Harwich to take another photo of the sea—though it must be the same all over the world—just because this happened to be the spot where the *Deutschland* foundered one fateful day in December 1875. Both these pictures, incidentally, may be admired in our volume, besides another of a stuffed bird formerly at Stonyhurst College that purports to be a "Windhover"—and may even have inspired Hopkins' famous poem of that name.[1]

Anyhow, not to stray too far from the main theme of this conference, which is naturally classical, and to comply with Ray's own wishes, I have chosen for my topic this

[1] Such is the theory I have ventured to propose in an article for *Hopkins Research* (Tokyo, 1982) No. 11, under the title, "Poet of Landscape and Inscape".

The following abbreviations will be used in this article:

Dixon — *The Correspondence of Gerard Manley Hopkins and Robert W. Dixon*, ed. C.C. Abbott (London: Oxford 1955).

Bridges — *The Letters of Gerard Manley Hopkins to Robert Bridges*, ed. C. C. Abbott (London: Oxford 1955).

Journals — *The Journals and Papers of Gerard Manley Hopkins*, ed. H. House and G. Storey (London: Oxford 1959).

Sermons — *The Sermons and Devotional Writings of Gerard Manley Hopkins*, ed. C. Devlin, S.J. (London: Oxford 1959).

afternoon the obvious subject of "Gerard Manley Hopkins and the Classics". I say "obvious", not only because this put together two of Ray's main academic interests, but also because Hopkins was himself a classicist—and because I, too, may lay some claim to this title, at least in my Jesuit and Oxford formation. After all, Hopkins was educated in the old humanist tradition both at Highgate Grammar School and especially at Balliol College, Oxford, where he achieved the high academic distinction of a Double First in Classical Mods and Greats. Subsequently, he taught Rhetoric to young Jesuit students at Manresa College in 1873–74; and he was Classics master at Stonyhurst College for a brief period in the spring of 1878 and again for 1882 to 1884. Finally, in what should have been the climax of his academic career, he was sent to lecture on the Classics at University College, Dublin, in the newly reconstructed Royal University of Ireland.

In view of this lifelong preoccupation of Hopkins with the Classics, it is surprising that so few Hopkins scholars have explored this aspect of his genius, which might well deserve full-length treatment in a book.[2] Yet Hopkins himself is largely to blame, the way he seems to downgrade his own indebtedness to the Classics. Almost from the beginning of his poetic career he seems intent on keeping his professional studies apart from his private poetic interests, as it were in separate compartments of his mind. In contrast to the early poems of Shakespeare or Milton or Keats, the three English poets who had most influence on his poetry, one can peruse the undergraduate poems of Hopkins without a suspicion that here is a brilliant student of the Greek and Roman Classics. The references and allusions in these early poems of his are for the most part religious and Biblical, not classical. The same impression may well persist through most of his mature poems, apart from "Andromeda", which is obviously based on the Greek myth of Perseus and the Gorgon's head.

At a deeper level, however, the influence of his classical education may be perceived in that new rhythm which, as he told his friend Canon Dixon, had long been haunting his ear and which he finally realized on paper in his revolutionary poem *The Wreck of the Deutschland*.[3] This poem he later described, in a letter to his other friend Robert Bridges, as a "Pindaric Ode";[4] and in his "Author's Preface" (written some years later) he speaks of "Greek and Latin lyric verse" as earlier examples of what he now for the first time calls "sprung rhythm".[5] How long he had been meditating on this new rhythm is a matter of conjecture; but it may well have gone back to the time when he was teaching Rhetoric to

[2] There is, of course, Todd K. Bender's study *Gerard Manley Hopkins*, sub-titled *The Classical Background and Critical Reception of His Work* (Baltimore: Johns Hopkins 1966); but this is rather a collection of special studies, such as Hopkins' adaptation of the Pindaric Ode and his use of Greek Hyperbaton, than a full-length treatment of the classical influence.

[3] In a letter dated October 5, 1878; *Dixon*, 14.

[4] As Hopkins tells Bridges in a letter dated April 2, 1878: "The Deutschland would be more generally interesting, if there were more wreck and less discourse, I know, but still it is an ode and not primarily a narrative. There is some narrative in Pindar, but the principal business is lyrical" (*Bridges*, 49).

[5] In editions of Hopkins' Poems, "Author's Preface" is regularly placed before *The Wreck of the Deutschland* at the beginning of "Poems (1876–89)". It is dated around 1883.

Jesuit students at Manresa, for whose benefit he prepared detailed lecture notes on "Rhythm and Other Structural Parts of Rhetoric—Verse".[6] In these notes he has much to say on pitch and stress and accent, with special mention of the "richer rhythm" of "Greek and Latin lyrical verse", though he refrains from using the term "sprung rhythm".

Subsequently at Stonyhurst, from 1882 onwards, he took up the idea of writing a whole book on Greek lyrical meters; and this remained a major interest of his till the end of his short-lived academic career. In Dublin he returned to this project with such eagerness that he could write as follows to Canon Dixon, in a letter of January 1887:[7]

> I have done some part of a book on Pindar's metres and Greek metres in general and metre in general and almost on art in general and wider still . . . . What becomes of my verses I care little, but about things like this, what I write or could write on philosophical matters I do; and the reason of the difference is that the verses stand or fall by their simple selves and, though by being read they might do good, by being unread they do no harm; but if the other things are unsaid right, they will be said by somebody else wrong, and that is what will not let me rest.

This passage seems to me deeply significant, not just as evidence of Hopkins' continuing interest in the Classics, but also as a symptom of that deep psychological frustration that plagued his years both in England and even more acutely in Ireland. He was indeed a great poet with a fine ear for poetic rhythm, finer perhaps than that of any other Englishman after Shakespeare and Milton; but one has to admit that he was essentially too much of an amateur, if not a dabbler, to become a great scholar. It is my firm opinion that with all this attention to the minutiae of Greek meter Hopkins was sadly frittering away his unique poetic and philosophical talent; and this opinion of mine I find corroborated in scholarly detail by John Louis Bonn in another chapter of *Immortal Diamond*, entitled "Greco-Roman Verse Theory and Gerard Manley Hopkins"[8]—which is regarded by Todd K. Bender as "the best study of the accuracy of Hopkins' classical metrics".[9]

So now let me divert my own attention from this wearisome topic of metrical and rhetorical analysis, which seems to me an academic cul-de-sac, to the true nature of Hopkins' indebtedness to the Classics, which is more precisely philosophical. For this I have to go back to his classical studies at Oxford, where he was engaged not only on literature (in Classical Mods) but also and much more on philosophy (in Greats). From this period we have little evidence of his interest in the lyrical meters whether of Pindar or of the Greek tragedians, but much of his interest in Greek philosophy, in the form of essays written for his various tutors. Notable among them is the fragment on "Parmenides", which contains the first recorded use of his characteristic coinages, "inscape"

[6] *Journals*, 267–90.

[7] *Dixon*, 150.

[8] *Immortal Diamond* (supra p. 257) 73–92. Bonn's conclusion is "that Hopkins was following a most misleading trail in the Dorian theory and that no solution could have been forthcoming"; and so, "as a theorist in metric, particularly in Greek and Latin metric, Hopkins holds no great place" (91–92).

[9] Supra n. 2, 73.

and "instress". In explaining the meaning of Parmenides, the young undergraduate remarks that "all things are upheld by instress and are meaningless without it"; and he expresses admiration for this old philosopher's "feeling for instress, for the flush and foredrawn, and for inscape", which is why he was revered by Plato "as the great father of Realism".[10]

This fragment is significant not just for its first use of these celebrated terms, but also and chiefly for the way it reveals the basic intuition of the poet, which may be described as "an intuition of being". For in the same passage Hopkins goes on to speak for himself in words that seem to echo through his later poems and prose writings: "But indeed I have often felt when I have been in this mood and felt the depth of an instress or how fast an inscape holds a thing, that nothing is so pregnant and straightforward to the truth as simple *yes* and *is*." On this point I find a particularly penetrating comment by James Finn Cotter in his study of *Inscape*:[11]

> *Instress* is man's *yes* in response to Being felt and known; *inscape*, the *is* that marks not individuality but Being itself; it 'holds' each object whole within the plenitude of IS.

I also find a notable illustration of this idea in the later poem, *The Wreck of the Eurydice*, where the poet says of one of the drowning men:

> It is even seen, time's something server,
> In mankind's medley a duty-swerver,
>   At downright 'No or Yes?'
> Doffs all, drives full for righteousness.

And before then, at the heart of the *Wreck of the Deutschland*, he has said the same of himself:

>   I did say yes
> O at lightning and lashed rod . . .
>   I whirled out wings that spell
> And fled with a fling of the heart to the heart of the Host.

In other words, Hopkins' response to the Being or "inscape" of Christ is the simple utterance of what he calls "the best word", which is "yes".[12]

Of course, this philosophy of Being, which is so central to the poetry of Hopkins, is not entirely derived from the Greek thought of Parmenides, in which he recognizes "an

[10] *Journals*, 127.

[11] *Inscape: the Christology and Poetry of Gerard Manley Hopkins* (Pittsburgh: University of Pittsburgh Press 1972) 13.

[12] This point is further developed by Hopkins in his Commentary on the *Spiritual Exercises*: "There must be something which shall be truly the creature's in the word of corresponding with grace; this is the *arbitrium*, the verdict on God's side, the saying Yes, the doing-agree (to speak barbarously), and looked at in itself, such a nothing is the creature before its creator, it is found to be no more than the mere wish, discernible by God's eyes, that it might do as he wishes, might correspond, might say Yes to him." (*Sermons*, 154).

undetermined Pantheist idealism". It is rather his Christian interpretation of Parmenides, as shown by Cotter in terms of the enlightened teaching of Clement of Alexandria, for whom philosophy "was a schoolmaster to bring the Hellenic mind, as the law the Hebrews, to Christ".[13] And this interpretation is also derived from the revelation of the Divine Name made to Moses, as "I AM WHO AM", which may well (according to an opinion widespread among the Church Fathers) have been echoed in the Greek philosophy of Parmenides and Plato.

It would, however, take me too long, and too much out of my way, to explain how far this simple philosophy of Being influences the poetic output of Hopkins. To my mind, once it is pointed out, it becomes surprisingly obvious, enabling all the various pieces of his poems to fall into harmonious and appropriate place. I would even maintain that, without a realization of this philosophical key-concept, the meaning of Hopkins' poems cannot but remain obscure; and the interpreter who overlooks it or despises it condemns himself to linger in the shallows and miseries of mere imagery or phonetics or what is nowadays called semiotics. After all, I dare to add, there is no great poet, whether Virgil or Dante or Shakespeare, who is not also a great philosopher, at least in desire; just as, conversely, there is no great philosopher, whether Aristotle or Aquinas or even Kant, who is not also a great poet, at least in desire. So for the appreciation of their poetry it is necessary to have some understanding of their philosophy.

But now let me come at once to the end of my paper and turn to the final poems of Hopkins, which he composed in his Dublin years. I speak particularly of his series of so-called "dark sonnets", which fall in between two exceptionally long sonnets entitled respectively "Spelt from Sibyl's Leaves" and "That Nature is a Heraclitean Fire and of the Comfort of the Resurrection". Or rather, it is of these two sonnets I now wish to speak, because of the obvious mention of the Classics they contain in their very titles. In the first place, the "Sibyl" is, of course, the Cumaean Sibyl who figures in Virgil's *Aeneid* VI, where she is described as writing her oracles on different leaves of paper and scattering them in the wind that blows through her cave. She is also associated in mediaeval legend, and in the mediaeval hymn *Dies Irae*, with David in foretelling the coming of Christ; and as such she figures in the other poem of Virgil, the "messianic" *Eclogue* IV. For the poet in his present mood, however, her oracle points not so much to the comfort of Christ as to "a rack/Where, self-wrung, self-strung, sheathe- and shelterless, thoughts against thoughts in groans grind".[14]

On the other hand, this pessimistic poem—in which Todd Bender also notes the influence of Greek lyric verse for its use of a heightened diction[15]—is counterbalanced at the end of the series by that other, more optimistic poem, in which Hopkins recurs to the

[13] *Stromata* 1.5, quoted by Cotter (supra n. 11) 13.

[14] There is a particularly fine commentary on "Spelt from Sibyl's Leaves" by Ray Schoder himself in *Thought* 19 (December 1944) 633–48.

[15] Bender (supra n. 2) 51, 157; cf. also W.H. Gardner, *Gerard Manley Hopkins*, Vol. II (London: Oxford 1949) 130.

thought of that other pre-Socratic philosopher, Heraclitus. In many ways Heraclitus of Ephesus stands in contrast to Parmenides of Elea, particularly in his emphasis on the flux of things under the element of fire. It is to this flux in the world of nature that Hopkins pays special attention in this poem, first with delight but then with "pity and indignation" as he reflects on its implication for individual men, for whom "all is in an enormous dark" "Drowned". Here precisely, however, is the *peripeteia* or turning-point of his poem, as he goes on to exclaim: "Enough! the Resurrection"—and so he ends on the Schoderian theme of the "immortal diamond" in man.

To this I must add, in terms of my classical theme, that this *peripeteia* need not imply a rejection of Heraclitus or a reaffirmation of Parmenides (in his Mosaic or Clementine interpretation). Heraclitus, too, in so far as one can make anything out of his "dark" sayings, seems to have looked from the perpetual flux to the eternal fire in things, and so to the divine Word above things. Thus he may be seen as a pagan precursor of St. John the Evangelist, who introduces his Gospel of Christ with the inspired declaration: "In the beginning was the Word, and the Word was with God, and the Word was God . . . .And the Word was made flesh, and dwelt among us." If the pagan philosophers of St. Augustine's time had come to recognize the truth of the former sentence, it was in no small measure thanks to Heraclitus and his followers among the Stoics, as well as the later Platonists.[16] But it was the philosophy of Christ that revealed the truth of the latter sentence, as confirmed by what Hopkins calls "the comfort of the Resurrection."

There I may bring my remarks on Hopkins and the Classics to a timely conclusion, in keeping with this season of Easter. What they all lead up to is, I think, the point at which the influence of the Classics merges into that of Christianity. In this way, as T.S. Eliot says at the end of *Four Quartets*, "The fire and the rose are one"—namely, the fire of Heraclitus and the mystic rose of Christ.[17] In this way, too, I may add, light may be thrown not only on G.M. Hopkins but also on Ray Schoder, as a priest-scholar whose classical interests and studies are ultimately directed—as Hopkins dedicated his immortal poem on "The Windhover"—"to Christ our Lord".

[16] This is how St. Augustine speaks of "the books of the Platonists" in his *Confessions* VII.9.

[17] In "Little Gidding", 1.259, though, in Eliot's meaning "the fire" may mean the fire of divine love and "the rose" may refer to human love; for these symbols are convertible.

HEROIC TEMPER IN CONTEXT: ACHILLES, OEDIPUS, SOCRATES

Helen E. Moritz

Like many others, I was first influenced by Father Schoder in learning ancient Greek through his *Reading Course in Homeric Greek*, and, more fortunate than many, got to meet the man himself when he gave guest lectures at Rosary College, my undergraduate institution. We got to be personal friends while I was a graduate student at the University of Chicago, a friendship we maintained through my successive moves about the country. Father Schoder was always a great support and mentor to me in my career in Classics. I offer this paper, which incorporates an admiration of Homer for which Father's Greek text planted the seed, as a small token of my sincere gratitude and affection.

The characters of my title—the Achilles of Homer's *Iliad*, Oedipus of Sophocles' *Tyrannos*, and Socrates of Plato's early dialogues—are certainly among the best known figures of the ancient world. They achieve the distinction of familiarity as protagonists in the masterpieces of three paramount authors, but, on deeper consideration, they may also be seen as ideally suited to be emblematic of Greek culture more generally. Separated by era and genre, the figures display a persistent Greek ethos while simultaneously mirroring the effects of political and intellectual evolution. In this paper I hope to show how an analysis of both fundamental and incidental similarities in their histories may serve to elucidate the characters themselves and significant changes in Greek values over time.

It might be objected that the characters named are not commensurate, since one is an actual historical figure while the other two are literary constructs. My response is that, on the one hand, each captures the spirit of an age, real or regarded as real, and that, on the other, the Socrates we encounter in the *Apology*, *Crito*, and *Phaedo* of Plato is as effective and affecting a literary creation as Homer's Achilles or Sophocles' Oedipus.[1] What we shall deal with in each case, in good Aristotelian fashion, is not the sequential narrative of a character's life, but the artistic unity consisting in his choices and the tragic consequences of those choices.[2]

The fundamental similarity that obtains among all three of my subjects is that each is in his own way a hero. The observation is not original: it is noted, in passing, by Bernard Knox in the book whose title I borrowed for this paper.[3] But the fact is worth

[1] The Socrates of Plato's *Apology* is himself aware of having become a literary fiction in Aristophanes' *Clouds*, cf. 18b–d. (All citations on Socrates in this paper, unless otherwise specified, are to the *Apology*.)

[2] Cf. Aristotle, *Poetics* 1451 a 15–35.

[3] Bernard M. W. Knox, *The Heroic Temper. Studies in Sophoclean Tragedy*. Sather Classical Lectures, Volume 35 (Berkeley and Los Angeles: California 1964) 50–52, 58. (All page references to Knox in this paper are to *The Heroic Temper*.) Some of the connections are also suggested in the titles of Cedric H. Whitman's successive volumes, *Sophocles. A Study of Heroic Humanism* (Cambridge, Mass.: Harvard 1951) and *Homer and the Heroic Tradition* (Cambridge, Mass.: Harvard 1958). On the nature of Sopho-

demonstrating in detail, as it will underpin my later analysis of that which constitutes the heroic commitment of each of the three.

In that afore-mentioned book, *The Heroic Temper*, Knox has given us the canonical and abiding description of the typical Sophoclean hero. While his analysis is generally familiar, a brief precis of the principal characteristics of such a hero will facilitate my discussion. Knox defines the Sophoclean hero, represented by the principal characters of six of his extant plays, as one who,

> unsupported by the gods and in the face of human opposition, makes a decision which springs from the deepest layer of his individual nature,. . .is faced with a choice between possible (or certain) disaster and a compromise which if accepted would betray the hero's own conception of himself, his rights, his duties. The hero decides against compromise, and that decision is then assailed, by friendly advice, by threats, by actual force. But he refuses to yield;. . .[he holds] firm against the massive pressure of society, of friends as well as enemies (pp. 5, 8–9).

In his struggles, the hero himself bears full responsibility, the gods none; though one feels the presence of the gods at every turn, their relationship with the hero is enigmatic (pp. 5–7). The opinions of others are irrelevant to this hero (p. 28). He is alone (p. 5), isolated not only from men but by the gods (pp. 32–33), considered strange or δεινός by others (p. 23) and himself fully aware of his own sharply differentiated individuality (p. 38). He is often angry (p. 21), invariably considered rash or insolent by others (pp. 21–23), thought by himself to be treated intolerably, without respect, often as a laughing stock (pp. 29–30). He chooses death, or at any rate is indifferent to it in the face of his chosen course of action (pp. 34–36). Most often his actions bring him to a fall which is "both defeat and victory at once" (p. 6).

The archetype of such a hero is, of course, Oedipus, "Oedipus at Thebes" as Knox would say,[4] the king who, determined to save his people by ridding Thebes of plague, is consequently also determined to fulfill Apollo's command to find and expel Laius' killer (p. 10). The role of the gods is ambivalent here; they readily respond to Oedipus' questions, but the responses only produce more questions, and Oedipus faces in the god's own representative Teiresias an iron will not to cooperate. Having posed a riddle and given a command, Apollo takes no responsibility for solution or fulfillment; these lie with Oedipus alone (pp. 4–7, cf. 33). There are other attempts to dissuade him from his mission: Creon counsels a private discussion of the matter and appears to plot against him; Jocasta and the shepherd who had rescued him as a boy plead with him to let the matter lie, all to no avail (pp. 12–14). In his rage against such impediments Oedipus isolates himself successively from those nearest to him, Creon and Jocasta (pp. 18–20, 32). Oedipus knows himself different from other men, by his unique ability to answer the riddle of the

---

clean heroes Knox acknowledges a debt to Whitman, inter alios, in n. 18, pp. 166–67; on the heroism of Achilles, Knox cites chapter 9, "Achilles: Evolution of a Hero," in Whitman's book on Homer (n. 75, p. 173).

[4] Notably in the title of his book, *Oedipus at Thebes. Sophocles' Tragic Hero and His Time* (New Haven: Yale 1957), but also throughout *Heroic Temper* (supra n. 3) e.g., pp. 8, 10, 15, etc.

Sphinx, and by his terrible portended destiny to kill his father and marry his mother (cf. pp. 23–24). At the moment of learning the dread truth of his identity, Oedipus is fully cognizant of the potential for disaster, but insists on knowing, nonetheless (p. 8). The consequence is, indeed, "both defeat and victory at once," the utter loss of family, status, and community that accompanies his being identified as Laius' killer, the victory of solving the second riddle, greater than that of the Sphinx, that of his own identity (p. 35).

Achilles in the *Iliad* displays much the same pattern. Knox remarks this, observing that in this way Sophocles' plays, too, as otherwise those of Aeschylus, were "slices from the banquets of Homer" (p. 52). Knox catalogues Achilles' conviction that he has been treated dishonorably in being deprived of Briseis, the iron will he displays in withdrawing from battle, his angry rejection of the attempts, by Odysseus, Phoenix, and Ajax, to persuade him to alter his resolve, his "strangeness" (δεινότης), his indifference to death in the decision to kill Hector and so avenge the death of his friend Patroclus (pp. 50–52).

Other features of the characteristic heroic profile may be added. Achilles' relationship with the gods is peculiar: his mother is a goddess and he has, through her, the ear of Zeus himself;[5] he effectively compels the high god to alter the course of the Trojan war to do him honor (1.495–530). But the gods are silent on the possible consequences of this privilege, and fail to restrain him from letting Patroclus take the field in his armor;[6] even Thetis, who can reveal her son's choice of destinies to him, is unable to prevent his dying "soon after Hector" (18.54–62, 95–96).[7] For his actions he alone is responsible. Achilles is isolated, in his tent on the shore alone with the elements, like Sophocles' Philoctetes (e.g., 1.348–50, 488–92, etc.).[8] The isolation effectively continues even when Achilles returns to the war effort: sharply differentiated from the run of humanity he would reject the rituals of reconciliation and material compensation were he not compelled to abide by accepted forms; impervious to the common human need for food, he is nurtured by the gods on nectar and ambrosia (19.137–275, 352–56). Finally, though it is not for this reason that Achilles confronts Hector, in doing so he elects the hero's ambiguous destiny of "defeat and victory at once," which in his case means a short life with unending glory (18.98–125, cf. 9.412–13).

[5] *Iliad* 1.348–427. All citations on Achilles in this paper are to book and line numbers in Homer's *Iliad*.

[6] When Achilles, prior to sending Patroclus out to the battlefield, prays to Zeus that his friend might both drive Hector back from the ships and return unwounded, Zeus grants one prayer and not the other (16.233–52), but gives *Achilles* no indication of his response to the prayers. It is interesting in this connection that, in making the appeal on behalf of Patroclus, Achilles reminds Zeus that he had granted the hero's earlier prayer for honor, in conventional prayer form seeking to bind Zeus to the new request, though without success. Patroclus himself, when earlier appealing to Achilles for assistance against the Trojan onslaught, had raised the possibility that Achilles was holding back because of some prophecy told him by Zeus' will (16.36–37), and Achilles had answered, with ironic truth, "I have not any prophecy in mind that I know of; there is no word from Zeus my honoured mother has told me" (16.50–51, trans. by Richmond Lattimore in *The Iliad of Homer* [Chicago: University Press 1951] 331).

[7] On the ambiguity of Achilles' relationship with the gods, see also Seth L. Schein, *The Mortal Hero. An Introduction to Homer's Iliad* (Berkeley: California 1984) 91–96 and 120.

[8] Cf. Knox (supra n. 3) 32–33, 141–42.

Even Socrates, as Knox himself notes, compares himself in court with Achilles and other Trojan heroes in that, like them, he would not abandon the "post" to which Apollo had "assigned" him; he also undertakes a heroically stubborn commitment to a course of action from which he will not be dissuaded even in the face of death.[9] Again we may flesh out the profile. Once more the gods are enigmatic: Apollo seemingly shows special favor to Socrates in asserting that no one was wiser, but the god does not elucidate his own meaning; he remains aloof as Socrates increasingly creates enmity against himself in the very act of trying to fulfill the oracle's implicit command (20e–22e). It is Socrates alone who elects to publicize the oracle's meaning by demonstrating to his fellow citizens their lack of awareness of their own ignorance (22e–23c).

Community and individual friends alike send strong signals that Socrates must desist or pay the penalty. This was evident even before his trial in Socrates' cognizance of his growing unpopularity with the citizens he examined, among them influential politicians and poets. It is evident in the offer Socrates hypothetically imputes to the jury to acquit him on condition he abandon his constant interrogation of his fellow citizens (29c, 37e). It becomes outright threat in the prosecution's proposal of the death penalty (36b). At each assault on his resolution Socrates remains steadfast, and since he sees his god-given mission as one of enlightening his fellow Athenians, he even rejects offers to help him escape from prison and execution.[10] For Socrates, however, consistent with the heroic profile, the opinions of others are irrelevant. In the *Crito*, the dialogue in which Socrates declines the opportunity to escape prison, the validity of popular opinion is explicitly examined, and found wanting (esp. 46c–48d, 44c–d).

Socrates is also δεινός.[11] Not only "satyr-like" in appearance, given to trances, and capable of drinking all night with no visible effect the following day,[12] Socrates is atypical among Athenians in ignoring his economic well-being and eschewing political activity (23b–c, 31b–c). He is himself aware also of being eccentric in both the mission imposed by Apollo (28a–30c) and in receiving admonitions from a personal internal voice, the famous δαιμόνιον σημεῖον (31c–d, 40a–b). Because of this strangeness, Socrates, like other heroes, becomes the butt of disrespectful treatment; while other heroes resent "being laughed at" in general terms, Socrates has actually been made the subject of comic drama in the *Clouds* of Aristophanes, and is aware that his comic characterization is among the most damaging factors in the case against him (18a–19c).[13]

[9] Ibid., 58. Cf. *Ap.* 28c–d.

[10] 30b–c, 37e–38a; most definitively in *Crito* 54d.

[11] A point made repeatedly by Alcibiades in the *Symposium*, although the term used there is θαυμαστός, cf. 216c, 217a, 220a, 221c, and especially 215b-c and 219c.

[12] *Symp.* 215b on Socrates' "Silenus-like" appearance, 174d–175d and 220c–d on his trances, and 223b–d, cf. 220a on his capacity for drink.

[13] Interestingly, in light of his own analysis of the intolerance of the Sophoclean type of hero for being mocked, Knox notes that Socrates misquotes Achilles, making his rationale for being willing to die after exacting vengeance a desire not to remain καταγέλαστος ["ridiculous"] beside the ships (supra n. 3, 175, n. 89). Alvin W. Gouldner, on the other hand, says that although "Greeks commonly manifest a profound tendency to concern themselves with what others think of them,. . .It is Socrates' mission to redirect and

For his failure to conform, Socrates finds himself isolated from his community. The indictment by Anytus and the others marks him as socially aberrant, especially in not believing in the gods the state believes in (24b); the jury's verdict confirms the indictment; and the imprisonment and execution ultimately reify the citizens' judgment by removing Socrates finally from their midst. The hero dies, but feels his choice vindicated in the silence of the voice which has always restrained him from any false step (40a–c).

Thus, in different times and disparate circumstances, the manner of the hero remains surprisingly constant. The consistency in depiction suggests that, by the Athenians, at least—for it is they who incorporated the *Iliad* into the Panathenaea, produced Sophocles' *Oedipus*, and convicted Socrates—the figure of the hero was regarded with a deep-seated ambivalence. He was invariably a creature of both wonder and dread: his courage and steadfastness in the face of opposition were admirable and set a standard to which to aspire; but the level of his commitment to moral purpose, exceeding what ordinary mortals could achieve, roused in them too uncomfortable an awareness of their own shortcomings to be tolerated long.[14] Thus the hero became separated from his society, but the cause and effect relationship remains ambiguous, necessarily. To the community, the hero, by his non-conforming behavior, appeared to reject the communal standards; the hero saw himself as rejected.[15] To a society fearful of *hybris* and of excess in general, the hero's very standing with the gods was suspect. In literature the special divine recognition accorded the hero was both privilege and curse, the hero simultaneously blessing and pariah;[16] similarly, Socrates' self-proclaimed mission from Apollo was countered by the allegation of atheism (24b, 26b–d).

The ambivalence in literature about the exceptional character found its practical corollary not only in the treatment accorded the historical Socrates but also in the institution

oppose this inclination, telling the Greeks, in effect, 'let them mock'" (*The Hellenic World. A Sociological Analysis*, Part I of *Enter Plato: Classical Greece and the Origins of Social Theory* [New York: Harper and Row 1969] 85).

[14] Cf. Knox (supra n. 3) 42–44, on the congruence of the Sophoclean hero with Aristotle's description of the man incapable of working in common as "either beast or god" (*Pol.* 1253a), and 57–58, on the Sophoclean hero assuring the potential for greatness while generally failing to provide a model for human conduct.

[15] Achilles, for example, while himself rejecting Agamemnon's offer of compensation and resisting public reconciliation and the army's need to eat before joining battle, interprets Phoenix' attempt to persuade him to return to the field as disloyalty (9.611–15) and seems to take it as an affront that the Greeks have managed to build a fortification without his assistance (9.348–50). Though Oedipus rejects counsel from Creon, Teiresias, and Jocasta, he suspects the men of a plot against *himself* (*Oedipus Tyrannos* 383–403, 532–42; all citations on Oedipus in this paper are to the *OT*) and his wife of inability to accept a husband of potentially less than noble birth (1062–63, 1069–70, 1076–79). Besides those aspects of Socrates' character already mentioned as perceived by the Athenians as aberrant, such as his abstention from politics and disregard of material prosperity, note his refusal to follow the accepted practice of pleading for the jurors' mercy (34c–35d, cf. 38d–39a). But Socrates feels keenly the Athenians' fundamental desire to be rid of him, the fact that they look upon him as no more than a pesky gadfly when he has neglected his own interests for their sake (30d–31c).

[16] Cf. Knox (supra n. 3) 54–57 on the similarly ambiguous character of those worshiped by the Greeks in hero cults.

of ostracism. The outstanding, prominent man was admired, but, because he threatened the social equilibrium, was expelled, sometimes to be recalled again prematurely.[17] In the case of Socrates himself, of course, the community would have preferred the reversible penalty of exile, had Socrates only given them the opportunity to impose it.[18]

If the manner of the hero and the community's reaction to him remained constant over time, however, the content of heroism did not. It is now time to trace the differences among the similarities already adumbrated and, in so doing, to observe the identifying features of three quite different moments in man's intellectual and moral history.

While all three heroes commit themselves to a cause, the focus of commitment varies considerably from case to case. Achilles' goals are two-fold: first, adequate recognition of his personal honor, without regard to the cost for the Greek army (1.352–54, 407–12); then, vengeance for the death of a personal friend, without regard to the cost for himself (18.90–100, 114–16). Both reflect a primary focus on the self, on individual pride and private friendship.[19] To a point, that orientation is approved in the *Iliad*. Despite the disastrous losses to the Greek army occasioned by Achilles' withdrawal from the fighting, public opinion turns against Agamemnon rather than Achilles until the latter rejects what the group considers in fact *to be* adequate material recognition (9.103–13, 626–42, 697–703). Achilles is also aware, when he goes to kill Hector, that in avenging his friend he is simultaneously winning unfailing glory, individually garnering the immortality of song (18.114-25). That avenging Patroclus also benefits the Greek army is irrelevant to Achilles' decision. Apparently composed in and for the aristocratic society of the Archaic Age, and purportedly recreating the milieu of the princes of palace-dominated Mycenaean culture, the *Iliad* conveys the values of privilege and status for the few who can assert and maintain their position.[20]

With Oedipus, on the other hand, the heroic commitment is to saving the community, from plague, and from the pollution of Laius' murderer (58–77, 93–94, 132–46). As king, as guarantor of the city's safety, a role first assumed in his contest with the Sphinx, and since maintained (35–53), Oedipus sees his duty to the community as paramount over personal interest.[21] As Achilles' purpose is characteristic of epic values, so is Oedipus' goal, albeit somewhat anachronistically, reflective of the demands of the democratic society in which the tragic drama developed and flourished.[22] In a mirror-reversal of

[17] Cf. Gouldner (supra n. 13) 57–58, 95–96, and Chapter 2, "The Greek Contest System. Patterns of Culture," 41–77, in general.

[18] Cf. 37c–e and *Crito* 44b–c, 45b–c, and esp. 52c–54a.

[19] Cf. Gouldner (supra n. 13) 54.

[20] Cf., e.g., Whitman, *Homer* (supra n. 3) 17–86. Knox (supra n. 3) 121–25, discusses the aristocratic nature of the Achillean standard; Knox notes on 52 that the *polis* "hardly exists in the *Iliad*," and on 53 that in Sophocles' "heroes who assert the force of their individual natures against their fellow men, their *polis*, and even their gods, he recreates. . .the loneliness, terror, and beauty of the archaic world."

[21] Oedipus extends the curse on Laius' killer even to his own household (249–54), and gives way to the chorus on his intention to execute Creon despite the belief that this will lead to his own death (646–72).

[22] Cf. Pericles' Funeral Oration, as reported in Thucydides 2.34–46, esp. 42.3–43.6, a speech almost certainly delivered only a year or two prior to the production of the *OT* (cf., e.g., Whitman, *Sophocles* [supra n. 3] 49–50).

Achilles' case, the fact that in identifying the cause of the community's pollution Oedipus incidentally resolves some long-unanswered questions about himself is irrelevant to his initial decision.

For Socrates, the commitment is, in an odd way, oriented to both self and community; the philosopher devotes himself primarily to virtue, ἀρετή, improving the excellence of his own soul; but, to do that, as he sees it, it also becomes necessary for him to turn "gadfly" and try to direct his community on the same path (28b, 29d–30c, 30e, 38a). Personal and social outcomes once again become inextricably intertwined, but in this case the community never recognizes or acknowledges its benefit.[23] If in Achilles we see aristocratic values and in Oedipus those of the *polis*, in Socrates we see an early phase of a development which arose from the incipient decline of the *polis* and the disillusionment that accompanied Athens' defeat in the Peloponnesian Wars.[24] To the Athenians at the beginning of the fourth century it seemed as if the gods had abandoned them and, while their initial collective response, evident in the accusations of impiety brought against Socrates, was to blame a weakening in the state religion,[25] people subsequently turned increasingly to forms which offered more personal satisfaction, to mystery religions or ethical philosophy.[26] Socrates, though clearly punctilious about the forms of worship in both the traditional Greek pantheon and in local cults,[27] was, with his persistent investigation into the nature of virtue and his private voice, on the leading edge of that change.

A development in views about the gods is as apparent in the tales of these heroes as is the changing face of heroism. Substantive differences become evident as one examines certain incidental similarities in religious apparatus that link these stories one to the other. The *Iliad* and *Oedipus Tyrannos* both open with a plague (*Il.* 1.9–52, *OT* 22–30), and, in both cases, the hero consults the spokesman of Apollo for an explanation and solution (*Il.* 54–73, *OT* 68–77). How different the responses! Although vestiges of the social values reflected in the *Iliad* may still have been current when that poem received its monumental composition, the world of the *Iliad* is primarily one of wishful memory, a golden time in which gods and mortals still occasionally associated face to face. And while not many had a divine mother at their beck and call as did Achilles, the prophets could see clearly the will of the gods. Thus Calchas pronounces unambiguously both the cause and the cure of the plague afflicting the Greek army (1.92–100), and, despite the human problems to which this pronouncement gives rise, the problem of the plague itself

[23] His proposed "penalty" of public maintenance equivalent to that accorded Olympic victors, argued on the basis that he had benefited the city more than such athletes did, was, of course, summarily rejected (cf. 36b–37a).

[24] For a brief account of this process, cf. J. J. Pollitt, "The World Beyond Control," in *Art and Experience in Classical Greece* (Cambridge: University Press 1972), esp. 111–14.

[25] Cf. Thuc. 8.1, on Athenian response to news of the Sicilian disaster.

[26] Cf. Pollitt (supra n. 24) Chapter 5, "The World of the Individual," esp. 136–43, and Gilbert Murray, *Five Stages of Greek Religion* (New York: Doubleday 1955) "The Great Schools of the Fourth Century, B.C.," 76–115.

[27] Just before dying for his heroic commitment to vindicating the truth of Apollo's panhellenic oracle, Socrates took pains to insure that a modest cock "owed to Asclepius" would be offered as required (*Phaedo* 118a5–8).

is quickly disposed of (1.308–17, 430–74). The cosmos of the *Oedipus* is that with which fifth-century Athenians were all too familiar, one in which the will of the gods was hard to interpret and, often enough, did not bode well for mortals.[28] While the cause and cure of the Theban plague, too, is stated readily enough—avenge the murder of Laius! (96–107)—the key to the solution, the identity of the murderer, is unknown, and the god not only gives no direction but in fact seems, in the person of his prophet Teiresias, willfully to impede compliance with his own command.[29] Still, the oracle is public in nature, as was that of Calchas in the *Iliad*, and directed to the lawful authority in the community, the king himself. The public mission imposed on Oedipus leads, of course, to a very personal quest, but the occasion and focus of the oracle are public. On Socrates, as on Oedipus, Apollo imposes an enigmatic mission (21b). But the oracle in question here, reflecting the incipient decline of the *polis* in which Socrates lived, is a response to a private query, and concerns a private citizen.[30] The oracle has no apparent concern with the *demos* and in fact brings the private citizen into conflict with the state.

Looking at the modulations in the relationships between gods and mortals over time in another way, we find that in a sense we have come full circle. Achilles had personal and privileged communication with a goddess, his mother Thetis; in that heroic age, god met mortal in the flesh in open exchange. Oedipus looked out on an opaque universe, in which the gods were neither apparent nor direct. With the δαιμόνιον σημεῖον of Socrates, the communication is once again personal and privileged, but now internal and incomplete: Socrates' voice only restrains him at need from the wrong course of action; it does not make positive encouragement or engage in dialogue or consolation (31c–d, 40a–b).

Tracing one final constant among the heroes will also enable us to observe perhaps the greatest single change in the conception of heroic excellence, ἀρετή, and its demands which was witnessed by the ancient world. Despite differences of focus, Achilles, Oedipus, and Socrates all committed themselves, each in his own way, to intellectual and moral integrity. Achilles, with sufficient leisure from the war to contemplate the matter, begins to question the reason for the war and the basis of the heroic code itself: for a single woman, for Menelaus' single marriage, is all the effort and disruption of countless other marriages warranted (9.337–43)? and, if its price is death when one might live, does the term "honor" hold any meaning (9.318–22)? Achilles comes to no simple answers to these questions, but the point is that, unlike his fellows who refuse to engage such issues, he insists on raising them.[31] On the moral side, when Achilles does return to the

[28] Both points are well illustrated in the Cassandra scene of Aeschylus' *Agamemnon*, esp. 1242–55, which ends with Cassandra's frustrated expostulation to the chorus which is incapable of understanding her and highly uneasy at her words, "I know well the Greek language," and the chorus' response, "So also are Pythian oracles Greek, but hard to understand, nonetheless."

[29] The god's only hint is the cryptic "what is sought is graspable, what is unheeded gets away" (110f.). On Teiresias' obstinate refusal to help see 316–44, esp. 332–33 and 341, and 376–77. Teiresias only speaks the clear truth to Oedipus when the king has been provoked to such rage as to be incapable of receiving it (362), and the prophet's parting words to the king are no more than another riddle (449–62).

[30] Chaerephon had on his own initiative asked the god whether anyone was wiser than Socrates (20e–21a).

[31] Cf. Schein (supra n. 7) 105–110.

fighting, it is from the duty to avenge a friend (18.90–93, 114–16), not for goods or honor, regardless how these follow in train.

Neither can Oedipus let go the riddle Apollo sets him, or the retribution for the murder of a king. Others urge a cognitive dissonance, a disregard of oracles, though this can lead only to further suffering for the people in the continuation of the plague and to untenable uncertainty for Oedipus.[32]

Finally, Socrates insists on explicating the oracle of Apollo in a way which is both true to his knowledge of his own limitations and consistent with the god's words, and makes a career of looking to the soul and investigating the nature of ἀρετή (21b–d, 29d–30b). And therein lies the difference. For Socrates' predecessors the moral imperative was vengeance, for him an explicit questioning, as we see in the *Crito*, of the morality of doing evil even in return for evil (49a–e). While they set out to redress wrong, Socrates sought a positive course of right action. We notice that, atypically, Socrates was not an angry hero, and, at the end of the *Apology*, explicitly denies any anger even against those who had accused or condemned him (41d). His end, too, seems to achieve the greatest "strange success"[33] of the hero: he dies, but, unrestrained by that inner voice, is confident that he goes to something better, either to eternal rest or to an endless dialogue with the wise (40c–41c).

[32] Teiresias advises Oedipus to drop the matter, esp. 320–21 and 332–33; Oedipus is incredulous at the prophet's apparent lack of concern for the city, 322–23, 330–31. Jocasta urges skepticism about oracles, 707–25, esp. 723–25, but Oedipus becomes all the more distressed at her story which was supposed to demonstrate their inefficacy, 726–27; she begs Oedipus not to follow up the news brought by the Corinthian messenger, 1056–57 and 1060–61, but Oedipus *must* track down the clues which have appeared, 1058–59, 1065. The Theban herdsman pleads with him not to pursue his questions, 1146, 1165, but he *must* hear the truth, no matter how dreadful, 1170.

[33] Cf. Knox (supra n. 3) 6.

THE PAN-HELLENIZATION OF THE "DAYS" IN THE *WORKS AND DAYS*

Gregory Nagy

The Alexandrian concept of *krisis*, in the sense of *separating, discriminating, judging* (verb *krīnō*) those works and those authors that are to be preserved and those that are not,[1] is crucial to the broader concept of "canon" in the Classical world.[2] The Alexandrian scholars who were in charge of this process of separation, discrimination, judgment, were the *kritikoi* "critics,"[3] while the Classical authors who were meant to survive the *krisis* were called the *enkrithentes*,[4] a term that corresponds to the Roman concept of the Classics, the *classici*, who are authors of the "first class," *primae classis*.[5]

The *krisis* of the *enkrithentes*, however, starts not with the Alexandrian scholars, nor even with the likes of Aristotle.[6] The "crisis" of *krisis* is already under way in the Archaic period of Greece. But criteria of the crisis are different. In the Archaic period, what is at stake is the survival or non-survival not merely of specific works or specific authors but of tradition itself. What must be preserved and what may be lost is decided by an ideology that can be reduced to a basic question: what is pan-Hellenic and what is not. I have explored this ideology at length elsewhere,[7] with a focus on the following lines in the *Theogony* of Hesiod:

> We know how to say many false things that are just like real things.
> But we know also, whenever we are willing, how to announce things that are true [*alēthea*].[8]
>
> Hesiod *Theogony* 27–28

In this passage, the Muses promise to teach Hesiod to speak in a mode that they describe as the absolute truth, the noun for which is *alētheia*. The ideology of pan-Hellenism

[1] For a discussion of this usage, see R. Pfeiffer, *History of Classical Scholarship: From the Beginnings to the End of the Hellenistic Age* (Oxford: University Press 1968) 117.

[2] For a history of the usage of "canon" to designate a selective listing of authors and works, ibid. 207.

[3] Ibid. 89, 242.

[4] Ibid. 206. Cf. Horace *Odes* 1.1.35: see Pfeiffer (supra n. 1) 206.

[5] Ibid. 207.

[6] Ibid. 117, 205.

[7] G. Nagy, "Hesiod," in T.J. Luce, ed., *Ancient Writers* (New York: Scribners 1982) 43–73.

[8] "'Truth', which itinerant, would-be oral poets are 'unwilling' to tell because of their need for survival (*Odyssey* xiv 124–125), is 'willingly' conferred by the Muses ['whenever we are willing' at *Theogony* 28]. We see here what can be taken as a manifesto of pan-Hellenic poetry, in that the poet Hesiod is to be freed from being a mere 'belly'—one who owes his survival to his local audience with its local traditions: all such local traditions are 'lies' in face of the 'true things' that the Muses impart specially to Hesiod. The conceit inherent in the pan-Hellenic poetry of Hesiod is that this overarching tradition is capable of achieving something that is beyond the reach of individual local traditions" (Nagy [supra n. 7] 48). The pan-Hellenic nature of Hesiodic poetry is conveyed by the absolutist concept of *alēthēs/alētheiē* 'true/truth' (= 'what is not subject to forgetting or mental disconnection,' as expressed by *lēth-* 'forget, be mentally disconnected').

in archaic Greece is a relative one, though it presents itself as absolute: to be pan-Hellenic, a given composition must highlight those aspects of Greek tradition that are shared by *most* Greek locales, while all along shading over those aspects that vary from locale to locale.[9] In the process of aiming at a consensus, such an ideology is clearly relative; still, in claiming that it represents *all* Greek locales, it is presenting itself as absolute.[10]

In this presentation, I hope to shift the focus to the *Works and Days*, specifically the *Days*. What follows is a working translation, with notes that supplement the commentary of M.L. West.[11] It is hoped that this evidence will help elucidate the process of pan-Hellenization.

The "Days" part of the *Works and Days* begins thus:

> Take care to mark the days[12] [of the month], which come from Zeus, giving each day its due.
>
> Hesiod *Works and Days* 765

The very first day of the month to be mentioned is a crisis-point for the pan-Hellenic perspective, since it is the day when each polis is most idiosyncratic, with local traditions prevailing:

> Do this for your servants. The thirtieth day of the month is best
> for inspecting different kinds of work that have to be done and for apportioning food-supplies.
> This is the day that people spend by sorting out [= verb *krīnō*] what is truth [*alētheia*] and what is not.
>
> Hesiod *Works and Days* 766–768

West in his commentary on the *Works and Days* remarks: "Civil calendars often fell out of step with the moon [. . .], and it was on the 30th that errors arose. Each month had to be allowed either 29 or 30 days, but the last day was called *triakás* (or in Athens *henē kai neā* [meaning 'the old and the new']) in either case, the preceding day (?) being omitted in a 'hollow' month. So it was always a question of when to have the 30th."[13] In other words, each *polis* had its own traditions about the calendar (West here calls these traditions "civil calendars"). At the time of the 30th, then, there is a crisis about arriving at a pan-Hellenic norm from the standpoint of each polis. This norm is conveyed here by the notion of *alētheia* "truth," which, I have argued, is the criterion of pan-Hellenism. Then the poet embarks on a catalogue of those days of the month that share the highest degree of consensus in local traditions, with the catalogue proceeding in a descending order of consensus. The 30th may be a crisis point, varying from *polis* to *polis*, but the crisis leads to a shared pan-Hellenic perspective. The poet has blotted over the differences, simply noting that *alētheia* "truth" is being sorted out [= is in a crisis: to repeat, the verb is *krīnō*] on the

[9] Nagy (supra n. 7) 48–49.
[10] Ibid.
[11] M.L. West, ed., *Hesiod: Works and Days* (Oxford: Clarendon 1978).
[12] First we had the "works"; now we have the "days."
[13] Ibid. 351.

30th. After the 30th, it is possible to arrive at a fixed sequence of given days traditionally spent in given ways by all Hellenes.[14] The poet will now highlight this fixed sequence, which is the pan-Hellenic perspective. Zeus, as the god who is the planner of the universe, is an appropriate symbol for the organizing principle that underlies the pan-Hellenic perspective, and it is with Zeus that the poet begins the catalogue:

For what I now tell you are the days of Zeus the Planner.
To begin with, the first,[15] fourth,[16] and the seventh[17] are each a holy day
(it was on the seventh that Leto gave birth to Apollo of the golden sword).
So too the eighth[18] and the ninth.[19] And yet these two days of the waxing part of the month
are particularly good for various kinds of work by mortals.[20]
The eleventh and the twelfth are both good
for shearing sheep and for gathering the benign grain.
But the twelfth is much better than the eleventh.
It is on that day that the spider, levitating in the air, spins its web
in full day,[21] while the Knowledgeable One[22] amasses her pile.
On that day a woman should set up her loom and get on with her work.
Avoid the thirteenth day of the waxing part of the month
for beginning to sow. But it is the best day for getting your plants bedded in.
The sixth day of the middle of the month is very unfavorable for plants,
but it is good for giving birth to male descendants. As for females, it is not at all favorable
either to be born at all on that day or to get married.
Nor is the first sixth day an appropriate one for a girl to be born.
But, for gelding kid goats and sheep
it is a kindly day. Also for making an enclosure for the sheep.
It is good for the birth of a boy, but such a child will grow up liking to utter words of mocking reproach,
which are lies, crafty words, and stealthy relations.[23]
On the eighth day of the month geld the boar and the loud-roaring bull.
Do the same with the work-enduring asses on the twelfth.

[14] For the apparent exception on the Cycladic island of Keos, see the passages quoted ibid.

[15] In the *Odyssey*, the new moon is the context for a festival of Apollo (xiv 162 = xix 307; xx 156, 276–278, xxi 258).

[16] For example, Aphrodite was specially worshiped on this day.

[17] The most important holy day of Apollo.

[18] For example, the eighth at Athens was the day for honoring Poseidon and Theseus.

[19] For example, the ninth at Athens inaugurated the City Dionysia.

[20] That is, they may be holy days, but they are not necessarily holidays. This hedge suggests that the eighth and the ninth are less "pan-Hellenic" than the first, fourth, and seventh.

[21] The waxing and waning of the day are in symmetry with the waxing and waning of the moon.

[22] That is, the ant. Cf. the cicada at line 582. Note the Aesop fable "The Grasshopper and the Ant," which is really "The Cicada and the Ant" (no. 373 in the edition of B.E. Perry, *Aesopica* [Urbana: Illinois 1952])

[23] The stealthy relations may include sexually suggestive "sweet-talk." The features enumerated here are characteristic of a traditional persona such as Perses, or such as portrayed in the poetry of Archilochus.

On the Great Twentieth, a full day,[24] a knowledgeable man
should be born.[25] Such a man is very sound in his mind [*noos*].
The tenth is favorable for a boy to be born; for a girl, it is the fourth
of the mid-month. On that day, sheep and shambling horned oxen,
as well as the sharp-toothed dog and work-enduring asses,
are to be tamed to the touch of the hand. But take care in your *thūmos*
to avoid the fourth of the beginning and ending of the month.
Do not have your heart eaten away with troubles on this day, which is very much a day when the gods bring things to fulfillment.
On the fourth of the month bring home your wedded wife,
having sorted out the bird-omens, which are best for doing this.
Avoid fifth days. They are harsh and ominous.
For they say that it was on the fifth that the Erinyes assisted
at the birth of Horkos (Oath), to whom Eris (Strife) gave birth, to be a pain to those who break an oath.
On the seventh of the mid-month cast the sacred grain of Demeter
upon the smoothed-over threshing floor, looking carefully about you.
Have the woodman cut beams for the rooms in your house
and plenty of ship-timbers which are suitable for ships.
On the fourth, begin to build sleek ships.
The ninth of the mid-month is better when evening approaches.
But the first ninth is the most painless for humans.
It is good for conception and for being born
for man and woman alike. It is never a completely bad day.
Or again, few people know that the thrice-nine of the month is best
for opening a wine-jar and for putting yokes on the necks
of oxen, mules, and swift-footed horses,
or for hauling a swift ship with many oars down to the wine-colored sea.
Few give it its true [*alēthēs*][26] name.
Open your jar on the fourth. The fourth of the mid-month is the most holy of them all.
Again, few do it [= give it its true name].[27] I mean the after-twenty
[= the twenty-first],[28] which is best
when dawn comes. As evening approaches, it is less good.
These, then, are the days, a great blessing for earth-bound men.
The others fall in between. There is no doom attached to them, and they bring nothing.
Different people praise different days,[29] but few really know.[30]

[24] See supra n. 21 on line 778.

[25] The characterization seems to suit the persona of Hesiod himself.

[26] The Hesiodic name "thrice-nine" would be the pan-Hellenic designation, as implied by the word *alēthēs*. Note the observations about *alētheia* at line 768. Local designations of this day may have been subject to tabu. The number thrice-nine is particularly sacred: see the references collected by West (supra n. 11) 361.

[27] This interpretation differs from what is found in the standard editions.

[28] Note again the periphrasis, as in the case of thrice-nine at line 814.

[29] Here we see the localized perspective.

[30] Here we see the pan-Hellenic perspective. "Know" in the sense that we have seen at line 792.

Sometimes the day is a step-mother, and sometimes it is a mother.[31]
With respect to all of these days, fortunate and blissful is he who knows all these things as he works the land, without being responsible to the immortals for any evil deed,
as he sorts out [= verb *krīnō*] the bird-omens, and as he avoids any acts of transgression.

Hesiod *Works and Days* 769–828

[31] This riddle can be better understood by reading Georges Dumézil, *Camillus: A Study of Indo-European Religion as Roman History* (Berkeley and Los Angeles: California 1980).

ANOTHER LOOK AT CHARACTER IN SOPHOCLES

Anthony J. Podlecki

I make this small offering of affection and gratitude to one who, through his life, his teaching and his ministry, exemplified Terence's *dictum* "homo sum: humani nihil a me alienum puto."

Aristotle attributes to Sophocles the autobiographical statement that he "fashioned characters as they ought to be, whereas Euripides made them as they were" (*Poet.* 1460 b 34). This cryptic remark has attracted rather less attention from critics than it perhaps deserves.[1] There are two other pieces of ancient evidence that connect Sophocles with the portrayal of character. In the capsule-summary that Plutarch has Sophocles give of his own development as a dramatist, he describes the third and final, and his own most distinctive phase, as "that most concerned with character and best" (*ἠθικώτατον καὶ βέλτιστον*)[2] and according to the anonymous *Life of Sophocles* transmitted in the manuscripts along with the text of the plays (this may in fact go back to a Peripatetic source),[3] we read that he "knew how to take into account the right moment and the events, so that from a short half-line or single expression he could fashion a whole character."[4]

In what way, exactly, is the fashioning of character an important part of Sophoclean dramaturgy? In the simplest and most obvious sense, it seems to me that Sophocles' characters are memorable, they make an impression, if for nothing else then at least by their gigantic stature, the self-possessed and even arrogant way they tower above the other *dramatis personae*. What mainly contributes to this impression of majestic uniqueness is their single-minded adherence to a very individual moral code, which sets them off from, and invariably drives them into opposition to, the ordinary world of "mere mortals," those of us who are ready when necessary to trim and compromise and bend if not

[1] D.W. Lucas in his Commentary on the *Poetics* (Oxford: University Press 1968) thinks the reference is to the idealization commended by Aristotle at *Poet.* 1454 b 10–15: "though not concealing their faults, he makes his characters finer than those of real life; they are worthy of the heroic world in which they move" (Lucas, 238). S.H. Butcher explains: "the meaning is that the characters of Sophocles answer to the higher dramatic requirements; they are typical of universal human nature in its deeper and abiding aspects; they are ideal, but ideally human; whereas Euripides reproduced personal idiosyncracies and the trivial features of everyday reality" (*Aristotle's Theory of Poetry and Fine Art* [New York: Dover 1951] 370–71). "Es besagt nicht mehr und nicht weniger, als daß Sophokles sein Personen idealisierte, was mit einer Typisierung nicht identisch ist, und auch keineswegs zutrefft, während Euripides veristische Ziele verfolgte. . . . " (A. Gudeman, *Aristoteles Peri Poietikes* [Berlin: de Gruyter 1934] 427).

[2] Plutarch, *de profectibus in virtute* 7 (*Mor.* 79 B). (This and the passage from the *Poetics* cited in the preceding note are discussed by P.E. Easterling, "Character in Sophocles," *G&R*, 2nd. ser., 24 [1972] 121–29 at 123.) See C.M. Bowra, "Sophocles on his own Development," *AJP* 61 (1940) 385–401 (repr. in C.M. Bowra, *Problems in Greek Poetry* [Oxford: University Press 1953] 108–25); M. Pinnoy, "Plutarch's Comment on Sophocles' Style," *QU* n.s. 16 (1984) 159–64.

[3] See my article, "The Peripatetics as Literary Critics," *Phoenix* 23 (1969) 114–137 at 134–35.

[4] *Vita Sophoclis* 21 (the significance of the first part of the sentence, *οἶδε δὲ καιρὸν συμμετρῆσαι καὶ πράγματα*, is obscure); Easterling (supra n. 2) 123.

actually break moral "laws." Sophocles' heroes, by contrast, "march to a different drummer." When put to the test, they magnificently decide to remain true to themselves. They are prepared to leave behind the world of ordinary humans rather than yield. We know that we would not have the courage to follow them along their solitary and ultimately fatal path, but we admire them greatly for their fierce and unswerving determination.[5]

But if the Sophoclean hero cuts himself or herself off from the world of ordinary human behavior, does not this very fact create a gap between them and us? How can we reach across the divide between the commonplace and the heroic to understand and "feel with" them? More important, how do *they* reach across to make *us* believe that they are real people whose unwillingness to compromise, lonely and self-destructive though it be, nevertheless has something to say to us? How is that evocation of fear and pity which Aristotle saw as the kernel of the experience of tragedy actually achieved? (We should not forget that it was also Aristotle who saw that the tragic hero must be enough like us—he uses the term ὅμοιος—to elicit our sympathy and understanding.)[6] I wish to explore here a significant but often overlooked technique used by Sophocles to overcome the remoteness of his heroes, to make them more believable, more "like us."

In an interesting discussion of various aspects of characterization in Sophocles, Mrs. P. E. Easterling points to the "impression of depth, of a solid individual consciousness behind the words" used by Sophocles' characters.[7] She notes that characters like Odysseus in *Philoctetes*, or Ajax, often make ambiguous statements, just the way people do in real life, and she points to the language employed by the characters as "one of the most important means of creating an impression of depth."[8] In a paper that ranges more widely than character in Sophocles John Gould remarks that "the language of the dramatic persons does not give clues to or 'express' their personality, their inward and spiritual being: it *is* their personality and their being. . . . It is a major function of dramatic language and form to determine (and above all to limit) the range and nature of the questions we are encouraged to ask of dramatic persons."[9] Gould's purpose is to mark the distance between the techniques of character protrayal in Sophocles and Euripides on the one hand and on the other (say) Shakespeare, Racine and Eugene O'Neill (in fact, I think he overdoes the differences),[10] but I find his and Mrs. Easterling's comments about the impor-

[5] B.M.W. Knox remarks, "In his plays [Sophocles] explores time and again the destinies of human beings who refuse to recognize the limits imposed on the individual will by men and gods, and go to death or triumph, magnificently defiant to the last" (Introduction to R. Fagles, *Sophocles, the Three Theban Plays* [New York: Viking 1982] 35; cf. also Knox, *The Heroic Temper* [Berkeley: California 1964]). Karl Reinhardt said of the Sophoclean hero that "it is his discovery that he is abandoned and alone that makes him realize his human condition" (*Sophocles*, English trans. [Oxford: Blackwell 1979] 2). R.P. Winnington-Ingram sums up the thesis as follows: "A man or woman of excess, an extremist, obstinate, inaccesible to argument, [the Sophoclean hero] refuses to compromise with the conditions of human life" (*Sophocles, an Interpretation* [Cambridge: University Press 1980] 9).

[6] *Poet.* 1454 a 24, cf. 1453 a 5.

[7] Easterling (supra n. 2) 125.

[8] Ibid. 127.

[9] J. Gould, "Dramatic Character in Greek Tragedy," *PCPS* 204 (1978) 43–67 at 44.

[10] For example, Gould's comment on O'Neill's dialogue, "in its staccato angularity, stopping, starting and constantly shifting into new and unexpected emotional keys" (ibid. 45) seems to me a not inapt way of

tance of the language used by the characters helpful and suggestive. Only they have missed an important corollary: language is used not only by Sophocles' heroes to describe their own motivations, resolution to act, etc., it is also used *by others about them*. Particulary significant, it seems to me, for our understanding of these men and women as real people is the language used by those closest and dearest to them. To point out the difference between Greek tragedy and real life, Gould observes epigrammatically: "We do not expect to get up from our seats in the theatre and follow a character off-stage. . . . We may follow an everyday person home, but not a dramatic person."[11] In fact, it is my contention that we do, in a certain sense, "follow Sophocles' characters home," for the poet gives us ample opportunity to hear them described in terms of the most intimate family-oriented, "homelike" surroundings. Through the medium of the language used about them by others and, to a less extent, through the language they themselves use to those with whom under other circumstances they might have been expected to feel the closest and most intimate ties of affection, we get a glimpse of what these gigantic, towering, unapproachable individuals might have been, if they had not been pushed into the extreme situations which they are now in. We hear them talked about, and at times also talking, as "people like us."

Antigone

Critics have generally taken Sophocles' main purpose in the opening scene of *Antigone* to oppose sharply Antigone's attitude with that of her sister; by contrast then Antigone appears "the intransigent . . . heroine whose refusal to compromise is set off by the sympathetic ordinariness of an associate."[12] Antigone remains unmoved by her sister's plea, "we must remember that nature meant us to be women (*γυναῖχ' . . . ἔφυμεν*), not fighters-against-men" (61–62). But another, perhaps even more important purpose of the dramatist is to remind us that Antigone's present rigidity is assumed, not a permanent and rather unpleasant quality but a role that she is now forcing herself to play in order to meet the unexpected and unasked-for challenge which her uncle's edict presents. She, like Ismene, is "only a woman," and she would at other times and under ordinary circumstances yield most gladly to the urging not to try to go against her nature in "acting in despite of

---

characterizing Creon's exchanges with his son. Gould insists (p.46) that "there is nothing in Greek tragedy . . . like that self-analytical, self-exploring mode of language which is the distinguishing mark of Shakespeare's soliloquies," but many would feel that Ajax's great speeches, or Medea's, not to mention the disputed passage *Ant.* 891 ff., soon to be considered, come very close. And I pesonally feel that the distinction between "inner" and "public" spaces, the Greeks allegedly being unable or unwilling to recognize the difference, is overdone. Sophocles offers an "inner" exchange of intimacies at the beginning of *Ant.* and has one of his characters cover up (more or less successfully) the convention of "public" utterance ("so that we can speak privately," *Ant.* 19). It is likewise easy to overemphasize the gap allegedly created between characters and audience because of the masks: "In masking, we lose the *flickering* procession of *ambiguous* clues to *inaccessible* privacy; in its place, personality is presented in the *changeless*, public continuity of mask" (ibid. 49; my italics). Each of the italicized words is loaded and could, space permitting, be challenged.

[11] Ibid. 44.

[12] Easterling (supra n. 2) 124.

the citizens" (79). Besides drawing a contrast between the two girls, the scene has the additional effect of showing Ismene's genuine sisterly affection for Antigone. "Oh, poor girl, how I fear for you," Ismene tells her (82) and, after she has heard of her sister's plan to bury their brother—a rash act of defiance which she does not approve and cannot yet bring herself to share responsibility for—she assures her that she is embarking on her venture "foolish, but truly dear to your dear ones" (99; compare Antigone's remark to her sister later, "I do not love a 'dear one' whose love is returned in words only." [543]). When Ismene has brought herself round to the point where she even asks to share the fatal consequences of Antigone's deed, an eleventh-hour conversion which the latter stiffly and even angrily rejects, Ismene asks pathetically, "What life could be dear bereft of you?" (548), and to Creon, "Is my life liveable deprived of her?" (566). Here too, I suggest, we are being shown something to compensate for the unnatural and ultimately vulnerable rigidity which at first sight seems to be Antigone's main characteristic: there must be something gentler about her (real) nature, we now begin to see, to call forth such deep and apparently genuine affection from Ismene. Significantly, it is precisely in this scene and in response to these affectionate remonstrances that Antigone for a brief moment lets down her guard and utters a normal, even a loving, reassurance to her sister: "Save yourself, I do not grudge your getting away safe" (553), and again, "Take heart [*θάρσει*, a "gentle" encouragement], you live, but my life-force died long ago . . . " (559–60).[13]

We the audience, then, see Antigone reflected in her relationship to her sister. We are also given fleeting glimpses of the love between her and Haemon. This is first alluded to in the scene we have just been considering. Ismene to Creon: "You really mean to kill your son's intended bride?" Creon (in a remark so crude and unfeeling that it can hardly be matched elsewhere in Greek literature): "There are other furrows for him to sow." Ismene: "Yes, but no bond so close as that linking the two of them" (568–70). The issue of the engagement has at least been broached (*νυμφεῖα*, 568). Unfortunately, a serious doubt about line-attribution blurs somewhat the impression made by the lines which follow:

Cr. I loathe the thought of evil women as daughters-in-law.
572 [ ] Haemon, dearest, how your father dishonors you.
Cr. You and that marriage of yours give me a pain!
574 [ ] You really intend to rob your own son of this girl?
Cr. Hades is the one naturally suited to stopping this marriage.

A residual uncertainty about who spoke lines 572 and 574 is annoying,[14] but the fact remains that the poet chose again to draw attention to the love between Haemon and Antigone.

[13] Mrs. Easterling discusses the passage *Ant.* 536 ff. but leaves things up in the air: " . . . at least Sophocles has given us something real in this ambiguous little scene" (supra n. 2, 126), nor do I understand the thrust of her remark that "the picture is complicated by Ismene's reiterated claim that life without Antigone is not worth living" (ibid.).

[14] The MSS assign 572 and 574 to Ismene, but most edd. (Campbell, Jebb, Pearson, Kamerbeek) give them to Antigone and the Chorus respectively (Dawe gives 574 also to Antigone). (In view of the tenor of my own argument Kamerbeek's rationale is of interest: "It is a gain in connection with the latter part of the play if Antigone may once be allowed to give utterance to her love for Haemon" (*The Plays of Sophocles*

How strong this love is we are allowed to see in the scene between Haemon and his father. A model of almost superhuman composure, the boy's civility and filial respect finally break down when Creon threatens to have Antigone brought out and executed before her fiancé's eyes: "You will never look upon this face again!" (764). The strength of the love between them is precisely the theme of the choral ode that follows. "Love unconquered in battle," the Chorus sing, ". . . you sleep on a maiden's soft cheeks" (781–84), and again, "Desire, shining clear from the eyes of a bride ripe for marriage, conquers all" (795–96). This romantic emphasis seems a little surprising, but we hear it again almost immediately as Antigone is brought out by the guards on her way to her rocky prison. She laments that she is going to her death "with no dowry of wedding songs, nor does any bridal song attend me, but I shall marry Acheron" (814–16; at 654 Creon had said, coarsely, "Let the girl marry someone in Hades"); and again, "I go (to my grave) cursed, unwed . . . no tears, no friends, no wedding song (attends me)" (867, 876).[15] In the scene that follows, Antigone begins the long speech—to which we shall return in a moment—with an address to "my tomb, my bridal chamber" (891), and at the end of the play, long after our dramatic interest has shifted to Creon, Sophocles takes the opportunity of reviving the theme. The Messenger thus describes Haemon's reaction to Antigone's suicide: "lamenting the ruin of his bridal that was to be found only in death [Campbell's translation of 1224], his father's actions, his ill-fated marriage . . . "; and the details of their last moments reinforce the image of "what might have been": Haemon "enfolded the maiden in his languishing embrace, his death-blood spurting out upon her white cheek . . . poor man, his only share of marriage-rites there in Hades" (1236–41).

We ought to look again, then, in light of this late-developing humanity of Antigone, at a passage around which a great deal of scholarly controversy has swirled, verses 904–20. In these lines which many editors have condemned, but which Aristotle had in his text,[16] Antigone attempts to come up with reasons to explain—to herself, first of all, and only secondarily to the Chorus—why she took so bold, so unexpected, and so unprecedented a step as to act in defiance of duly constituted authority. "I would not have done it," she says in effect, "if the loss that I suffered in my brother's death could have been

III. The Antigone [Leiden: Brill 1978] 115). M.L. West ("Tragica III," *BICS* 26 [1979] 108) argues convincingly against reattributing 574, and I believe a strong case can be made for leaving Ismene with 572 also, as I hope to argue elsewhere.

[15] On this important theme see H.J. Rose, "The Bride of Hades," *CP* 20 (1925) 238–42; S. Wiersma, "Women in Sophocles," *Mnemosyne*, 4th ser., 37 (1984) 25–55 at 45–6, citing R.F. Goheen, *The Imagery of Sophocles' Antigone* (Princeton: University Press 1951) 37 ff., "The Marriage Motif." I believe R.W.B. Burton is mistaken, in his otherwise enlightening discussion of this kommos, to write off these utterances by Antigone as being made "in purely general terms of regret that she cannot fulfill her womanhood in marriage, and they express no personal feeling for [Haemon]" (*The Chorus in Sophocles' Tragedies* [Oxford: University Press 1980] 124). See, most recently, L.J. Jost, "Antigone's Engagement: A Theme Delayed," *LCM* 8 (1983) 134–36, although he perhaps overstresses Antigone's "repression."

[16] *Rhet.* 3. 16, 1417 a 32. Jebb, who condemns the passage, notes that although Aristotle cites only vv. 911 and 912 (with a variant, βεβηκότων for κεκευθότοιν, in 911), he "certainly had the whole passage in his text of Soph." It is excised and relegated to an endnote in the influential trans. by D. Fitts and R. Fitzgerald (*Sophocles: the Oedipus Cycle* [New York: Harcourt Brace 1958] "dismal stuff . . . a series of limping verses whose sense is as discordant as their sound," p. 240).

made up in any other way; children, husbands can (in principle) be replaced, brothers, not, at least when parents are dead." The logic is faultless, but juvenile; but have we not had repeated references throughtout the play to Antigone's youthfulness? She now finds herself facing a terrible prospect—death, and a particularly horrible, because lingering, one at that. She is trying to make herself understand why she acted, to try to comprehend her own motives, and this is the pathetic best that she can do. The reasoning is feeble, the expression at times faulty (passing, as many commentators feel, especially in verses 909–10, beyond the bounds of acceptability even for the sometimes erratic syntax of Sophocles),[17] but the heart, especially Antigone's heart, has its own reasons, and they are unamenable to rational exposition. Knox has commented with justice that a decision on the authenticity of this passage "is of vital significance for the interpretation of the play as a whole."[18] I agree, and in light of the case I have been trying to make for an Antigone whose humanity and vulnerabilty are revealed gradually as the play proceeds, and especially in view of the additonal reference they contain to Antigone's dying "without bridal bed, with no wedding song and no share in marriage or the nursing of children" (917–18), I join the side of those critics who adjudge the lines authentic, if awkward.[19]

Her sister and her fiancé talk about an Antigone of whom we, the audience, have only the merest inkling. It is, I believe, one of the primary functions of Haemon and Ismene in this play to "compensate" for the otherwise rather one-sided and austere characterization of the heroine, who is so unlike Anouilh's Antigone with her sand pail and her pet dog. Her sister and her lover have found something intrinsically loveable in Antigone's nature—indeed, in a clear echo of Ismene's words earlier about their "nature as women" (61–62), Antigone proclaims to Creon, "It is my nature to join in mutual loving (συμφιλεῖν ἔφυν, 523) not in mutual hating"—and so we, too, should be prepared to make allowances for the rigidity, even the stridency, she has had to assume to meet the present challenge.

[17] Thus, G. Müller in his *Antigone* (Heidelberg: Carl Winter 1967) castigates the lines' "stillistische Besonderheiten" (p. 208) and Winnington-Ingram speaks of their "contorted argument and awkward locutions" (supra n. 5, 145). Jebb pronounced 909–12 "unworthy of Sophocles", but of the three points which he mentions—and the offending words are in fact confined to 909–10—only the first, the "defective" and somewhat confusing genitive absolute κατθανόντος in 909, seems to me to be of any moment (but compare *O.T.* 629, cited by L. Campbell in his *Introductory Essay on the Language of Sophocles* [Oxford: Clarendon 1871] 13 as an example of genitive absolute with subject omitted). (The argument from the alleged dependence on Herodotus 3. 119 is worthless; see my article "Herodotus in Athens?" *Greece and the Eastern Mediterranean in Ancient History and Prehistory, Studies presented to F. Schachermeyr* [Berlin: de Gruyter 1977] 246–65 at 248–49.)

[18] Knox, Introduction to Fagles' translation (supra n. 5) 31.

[19] The passage as a whole is accepted by G.M. Kirkwood who, however, thinks that 909–10 "are not exactly what Sophocles wrote, for the obscurity of expression that characterizes them is most un-Sophoclean" (*A Study of Sophoclean Drama* [Ithaca: Cornell 1958] 163); likewise Reinhardt (supra n. 5, 83–84) and Kamerbeek (supra n. 14, 159, "not without some lingering misgivings"). There is an extended analysis and defense of the passage by H. Rohdich, *Antigone, Beitrag zu einer Theorie des sophokleischen Helden* (Heidelberg: Carl Winter 1980) 170 ff. See also D.A. Hester, "Sophocles the Unphilosophical, a Study in the *Antigone*," *Mnemosyne*, 4th ser., 24 (1971) 11–59, at 36–38 and 55–58, and T.A. Szlezák, "Bemerkungen zur Diskussion um Sophokles, Antigone 904–920," *RhM*, n.f., 124 (1981) 108–42.

Ajax

A Sophoclean hero very close to Antigone in some of the characteristics we have been considering is Ajax (the similarity of effect that the two plays make, which has led many critics to date them together as relatively "early" works, in fact results mainly from the kinship of the leading characters). It is fair, I think, to say that Ajax is one of the coldest and least approachable of heroes in Sophoclean, if not in all Greek drama. There is only one moment when he acknowledges the immense loss which his concubine, Tecmessa, and their son will feel at his death: "I feel pity that she will be left a widow among enemies, and the boy an orphan" he says at the beginning of the second of his three great soliloquies (652–53), but even here it is prefaced with the harsh comment, "This woman here turned my language into a woman's"—he is referring, presumably, to the "gentleness," or as he would consider it, weakness, which he showed in the preceding scene with Tecmessa and the child Eurysakes[20]—the gentleness appearing to the average reader as nothing more than a grudging willingness to answer her questions in half-civil tones, peppered with such rebukes as "it is a good thing to be modestly quiet" (586) and "you're too bothersome to me" (589). His language has moderated, but in a hardly noticeable degree, from such earlier comments to her as "get out of here at once" (369) and "woman, what becomes women best is silence" (293).

What is Tecmessa's reaction to all this? She might have been portrayed as a cowering inferior, a mere chattel, mother of Ajax's child but little more. In fact, what we are given is a dignified and self-assured woman, the second most important character in the play, spear-won and ostensibly nothing more than a bed-mate, but in what she says and how she bears herself a wife in everything but name. Here we have a most striking and successful use of "compensation": the Ajax whom we see on stage is hardly more than a shell of his former self, and yet even at his best we wonder what he may have done to deserve the fierce loyalty and genuine devotion he receives from Tecmessa. When he prays to Zeus for death she retorts, "Pray for my death at the same time, for why should I live when you are dead?" (393–394). In her long speech trying to get him to accept the bonds of necessity, in which she uses her own case as an example of how *Ananke* works in human lives, she remarks: "The gods decreed I should come under your power, and so from the time I first came into your bed, my thoughts have been for your welfare . . . " (490–91),[21] and towards the end of this speech she says, "I have nowhere to look except to you; you made war on and annihilated my country; another fate overtook my mother and father, who are now dead and dwell in Hades. What country, then, do I have except

[20] Winnington-Ingram remarks that the extent to which Ajax feels "pity and a conflict between tough and tender emotions in himself—must be a matter of individual judgement" (supra n. 5, 31). The phrase *ἐθηλύνθην στόμα* in 651 is given a subtly nuanced interpretation by P.E. Easterling, "The Tragic Homer," *BICS* 31 (1984) 1–8 at 6, a paper which came to my notice after my own views reached final form. I am happy to find that our interpretations concur in several important respects and I note these agreements where possible.

[21] Mrs. Easterling remarks that "she appeals by Zeus *'Εφέστιος* v. 492 to the bed they shared, laying great emphasis on the reality of this union and her devotion to Ajax, giving it therefore the same kind of weight as a marriage relationship" (ibid. 3).

you? What wealth? My whole salvation is in you." And then she issues a most tender and piteous appeal to him (one we know is bound to fail): "Have remembrance of me; surely a man should have remembrance, if he has ever experienced some pleasure. For, so goes the saying, favor, *charis*, always begets favor; a man who lets remembrance slip away when he has been done some good is not entitled to be considered 'nobly born'" (514–24). It is precisely this that hurts her most deeply when, after the arrival of the Messenger from the Greek camp, she understands the real meaning of Ajax's words and how cruelly he has deceived her: "I know . . . that I have been expelled from our old *charis*" (808). Here and there we hear the faintest hint of this strong and passionate and (we almost wish to say) redeeming relationship from Ajax's side. Early in the play the chorus of sailors remark to Tecmessa: "Impulsive Ajax continues in his love for you, though you were won by his spear" (211–12), and it appears to me to be significant that when he begins to return to his senses after his mad attack it is to her that he turns to demand an explanation (312). Later she does what she can to protect his dignity even in death,[22] interposing herself between his badly disfigured corpse with its jets of blood issuing from the nostrils, and the morbidly curious chorus (918 ff.). Her last words onstage echo simply and touchingly the depths of her feelings for him: "(As far as the gods and the Greeks are concerned) Ajax is no more, but is gone, leaving me a legacy of pain and tears" (972–73).

The other relationship we see portrayed very vividly and movingly is that between Ajax and his son Eurysakes. Even before he is shown in the degrading position of a slayer of cattle we hear Ajax cry out in anguish, and his first cry is for his son: "O, boy—my boy!" (339). At Ajax's insistence and in spite of Tecmessa's misgivings that he is not in a fit condition to deal with his son, the boy is brought forth. "He'll not be afraid," Ajax remarks, "to cast his gaze at this new-shed blood, if he is right and properly my son; like a colt he must be broken in to his father's savage ways, his nature made like mine" (545–49). No one in the audience who remembered his Homer could have missed the cruel perversion of the identical scene at the end of the sixth book of the *Iliad* involving Hector and his young son Astyanax. The language Sophocles uses shows clearly, as critics have noted,[23] that he had the earlier, Homeric scene in mind. For our present purposes it is important to note that both fathers allude to the joy which the two sons bring to their respective mothers (*Il.* VI. 481 = *Aj.* 559; Mrs. Easterling, perhaps exaggerating somewhat, calls this "the only glimpse Ajax gives us of tender feelings for Tecmessa"[24]). There is, however, one striking difference in the prayers of the two fathers for their sons. Hector envisages a hypothetical bystander's remark[25] to the effect that Astyanax is "far better

[22] "She, we feel, is the right person to find Ajax's body: she knows what to do and say . . . " (ibid. 6).

[23] Winnington-Ingram (supra n. 5) 16. Note especially *Iliad* VI. 469 ταρβήσας *Aj.* 545 ταρβήσει . . . οὐ. (The influence of this scene on Sophocles' conception of Ajax and Tecmessa, and the consequent deepening in the characterization of the latter, are the principal themes of the study by Mrs. Easterling mentioned in n. 20 above. She rightly advises [p. 6] that "the analogy appears to be more complex than critics have normally allowed").

[24] Ibid. 5.

[25] Cf. J.R. Wilson, "Καί κε τις ὧδ' ἐρέει: An Homeric Device in Greek Literature," *ICS* 4 (1979) 1–15 at 14.

than his father" (VI. 479), whereas Ajax's comment reveals a more limited but also a more touching vision: "Child, may you be more fortunate than your father, but in all other respects the same" (550–51).

This hope that the boy Eurysakes may somehow be a prolongation of his father's life and heroic deeds is symbolized by the boy's actions in the last part of the play, the obstructed funeral of Ajax's corpse. Teucer bids the boy "stand near and put your hand on your father" (1171–72). He cuts a lock of the child's hair as an offering, and urges him to resist any efforts to dislodge him from his father's bier (1180 ff.) and at the very end of the play tells the lad, "Boy, touch your father's body lovingly and use what strength you have to help me lift it" (1409–11). It may be noted that one of the effects of this parallelism (although it is not directly connected with the main point of my argument) is that we are invited to compare Ajax himself with Hector, and it seems clear that it is for the purpose of reinforcing the comparison that Sophocles introduces the recurring detail of the exchange of armor between the two heroes (verses 661, 817, 1027).[26]

If the poet asks us to moderate our view of the harshness of Ajax's temperament by letting us see him through the eyes of his wife and child (thus showing him in the position of a husband and father who "might have been") he stands also in two other relationships, and both of these are given secondary emphasis in the play. As Telamon's son he feels keenly his failure to live up to his father's *aristeia* on the occasion of the previous expediton to Troy (the note is struck several times[27] and serves to emphasize one of the play's important themes, genuine vs. spurious nobility of birth, with which I am not here concerned).[28] Ajax's feelings of shame at having failed to live up to what he imagines to be his father's expectations have displaced almost every other emotion towards his parents, but at a significant point in his first soliloquy he shows that his sense of responsiblity towards them has not been totally obliterated. He tells the Chorus to have Teucer make sure to "take the boy home and show him to my mother and father, that he might be their sustenance in old age" (568–70). But for his own part he is deaf to Tecmessa's appeal that he should "have the decency not to surrender" his father and mother to an old age of continuous grief at his death (505 ff.). As a woman and mother Tecmessa is able to add a moving reminder to him of how his mother Eriboea "often prayed to the gods that her son come home again alive" (508–9). Although Ajax, now locked in his tent, is not there to hear them, the Chorus in the First Stasimon reiterate the point: his mother's laments will be shriller than the nightingale's (625 ff.); in Telamon's eyes his son's ruin will appear greater than any that has struck the line of the Aiakidai (641 ff.). In his last speech Ajax drops a hint that, although Tecmessa's attempt to dissuade him from his suicidal purpose by reminding him of his filial obligations have proven unsuccessful, they have at least

[26] So, too, Easterling (supra n. 20) 6–7.

[27] Vv. 462 ff., 1299 ff. The importance of this failure to live up to his father's expectation is perhaps underscored by early references to him as "son of Telamon" by the Chorus (134, 183) and Tecmessa (204), and in part explains the emphasis Ajax himself puts on having his own son taken back to the boy's grandfather (568 ff.).

[28] On this, see now Easterling (supra n. 20) 7–8; Wiersma (supra n. 15) 34.

made some impression on him. He calls upon the Sun to stop its progress through the heavens at Salamis to "announce my ruin and my death to aged father and ill-starred mother. Poor woman, when she hears this news she will shriek her lamentation through the whole city" (845–51).

The third most important character in the play after the hero himself and Tecmessa is Teucer, Ajax's bastard half-brother. He plays a significant role in the action in standing up to the Atreidae to secure Ajax's burial, to be sure, but he also lets us see the hero, apparently so cold and aloof, in yet another human relationship. An aspect which has to be taken into account (as with Tecmessa) is an element of selfishness in their attempts to dissuade Ajax from killing himself. At 1008 Teucer remarks wryly, "I suppose Telamon will receive me with a smile and open arm, when I go home without you." "My enemies are many," he says later, "my safeguards few; that's what I have got for myself now that you are dead" (1022–23). But this apparent selfishness is, I suggest, only superficial; the things said about Ajax by Tecmessa and Teucer strengthen our impression that he has been an absolutely indispensable support to them both. They almost literally cannot survive without him. Moreover, their grief is heightened by the thought that they have been able to do nothing for him in return; they have not been able to reach across the abyss his colossal pride has created and bring him back from his utter despair. "Where can I go," Teucer asks pitifully, "among what men can I show myself, since I did nothing to aid you in your sufferings?" (1006–7), and the Chorus of Ajax's seamen lament, in a similar vein, "How you have bloodied yourself, unprotected by your friends!" (910). All this is canceled by the tone of genuine affection with which Teucer addresses Ajax (*φίλτατ'*, 977, 996, 1015), an affection the more unexpected in that Teucer is a bastard, and would certainly have been overshadowed by his full-born brother who was clearly their father's favorite (contrast Edmund and Edgar in *King Lear*). The sincerity of the eulogy which he pronounces at the play's close is palpable: "This man . . . , in all things best, and none among mortals better than he" (1415–16).

The sterling qualities of Ajax as a leader can be clearly seen in the mixture of admiration, affection and utter dependence felt for him by the Salaminian seamen who comprise the Chorus. "When things go well for you," they tell him in their opening song, "I rejoice; when some blow from Zeus or vicious rumor by the Greeks assails you, I am overcome by fear and trembling, like the eye of a dove" (126–40). To Ajax in turn they are his "beloved" seamen (349), "helpers in his seamanship" (356); they alone, he says, can help him in his suffering (360). When Tecmessa informs them that he has stabbed himself, they wail, "O for my return, O sire, you have slain us too, your shipmates" (900–2; we may note again the mingling of "selfish" motives). They sum up their loss, simply and sadly, in their last stasimon: "Before, impulsive Ajax was my protection from terrors by night and enemy weapons. Now, he lies sacrificed to an evil daemon. What pleasure, what pleasure will I ever have again?" (1211–16). Ajax's own men represent a small nucleus within the larger organism of the Greek army before Troy and here, too, we are meant to "fill in" our estimation of him on the basis of the positive contribution he has made to the war-effort before his denial of Achilles' arms and its humiliating aftermath.

In fact, it is precisely this that is at issue in the last part of the play; Ajax is entitled to burial, his brother Teucer argues, for the benefits he had done to his comrades-in-arms (1269 ff.; cf. *Iliad* XV. 415 ff., XVI. 101 ff.). The Atreidae, of course, must ignore or deny his contribution. Menelaus insists that he is just a common man, a δημότης.[29] Agamemnon is more brazen: "Where did he go, where did he stand, that I did not?" (1236). To ask the question is to answer it—and not in Agamemnon's favor. A decision about Ajax, then, must not be based on the harm that in his mad rage he tried to inflict on his former comrade (and would have succeeded, had not Athena deflected his homicidal mania into so ludicrous and humiliating an outcome). His characterizing epithet is θούριος, "full of the impetus of battle," and it is a label which his men use both of him (212, 1213) and of the War god, Ares, whom he used to serve (613),[30] performing "works of the greatest manliness with his hands" (616–17). "I will make a large boast," he tells his men—modesty not being among the repertory of Greek virtues—"Troy never saw my equal coming from the land of Greece" (423–27). The remembrance of what he had been adds to the poignancy of his present state, and Ajax himself is keenly aware of how far he has fallen. "Do you see," he ask the Chorus bitterly, "the man once bold, and stout of heart, who never flinched in battle with the enemy, who have now turned my hand to inspire terror in—harmless beasts!" (364–66). Tecmessa uses a word of him which regrettably no longer applies: χρήσιμον, "of use to his fellows" (410); thus, one of the alternative courses he deliberates upon is to make one last suicidal dash among the Trojan enemy to "perform some useful service" (468). And Tecmessa reverts to this theme when she pleasurably envisions how his enemies among the Greek chiefs will, "now that he is dead, groan for him in the need [χρεία] of battle" (963).

Finally, Sophocles uses another, hightly effective technique of rehabilitation: the objectively favorable testimony of personally hostile, or at lease unfriendly, witnesses. Even his arch-enemy, the goddess Athena, admits it when she asks her favorite, Odysseus, "Did anyone have better plans, or was anyone better at executing them when the opportunity arose?", and Odysseus must agree: "I know of no one" (119–21). Ajax insists that "if Achilles were alive and making a judgement of excellence concerning his armor, no one would have got them instead of me" (442–44). We might be tempted to discount this claim as just another of Ajax's "loud boasts," until Odysseus confirms it at the play's close: "I could not dishonor him by refusing to admit that he was the one best man of those of us who came to Troy, after Achilles" (1339–41). I feel fairly confident that we are meant to assume that there are grounds to the charge made by Ajax (448–49) and by Teucer (1137), that the ballotting was rigged by the Atreidae. For Plato, at any rate, Ajax was a prototype of one who had "died because of an unjust decision" (*Apol.* 41 B).

When all is said, however, Ajax remains one of Sophocles' most impenetrable creations: curt, aloof, cold—save for the passionate fire of his mortally wounded pride and venomous hatred which is nothing more than comradeship-gone-sour. Although the poet

[29] V. 1071. Stanford *ad loc.* notes that his "false assumption" is presently answered by Teucer (1097 ff.).

[30] Jebb *ad loc.* notes the parallel with Aesch. *Pers.* 137, but the epithet is also used of Xerxes at *Pers.* 73, 718 and 754.

has employed the various relationships we have been considering—with his all-but-wife, his son, his half-brother, his men, even his adversary, Odysseus—to modify his austere portrait, it requires a real effort on any audience's part to remember that this gigantic, now humiliated, warrior had been in many important respects, and would presumably have continued to be, were it not for the intervention of a malign Fate, a "man like us."

Philoctetes

We look—almost, but not quite, in vain—for any ameliorating touches in the portrayal of Philoctetes. Here is a man who for over nine years has been totally alone (the uninhabited nature of Lemnos seems to have been an innovation of Sophocles', for in the versions of Aeschylus and Euripides the Chorus was composed of citizens of Lemnos).[31] In fact, the poet goes out of his way to stress Philoctetes' "remoteness" (*μόνος* or *μοῦνος*, 172, 183, 227, 286, 470, 688, 954; *ἔρημος*, 265, 269, 471, 487, etc.).[32] It is not quite correct to say that Philoctetes has been entirely alone; he has had one companion, of the sort, however, that no rational person would have chosen—his disease.[33] Through a striking pattern of metaphors, Sophocles presents the festering sore in Philoctetes' foot as possessing almost an external and independent presence, a grim substitute for the human company whose lack he feels so sorely. "I looked all around" (Philoctetes is recounting to Neoptolemus his early days on Lemnos) "and found nothing at hand but suffering" (283). "My sickness," he tells Neoptolemus later, "longs to take you as a follow attendant" (647–75, *ξυμπαραστάτην*), and shortly afterward Neoptolemus asks him whether he is suffering the pain of his "attendant disease" (734). Philoctetes hands over the bow "until there is remission of this now attendant suffering of my disease" (765), and he sees the young boy as somehow a substitute or replacement for his illness: "I never expected that you would have had the courage to take pity on me, and abide my sufferings, standing by and assisting me" (869–71; cf. 885, where Neoptolemus refers to Philoctetes' "attendant misfortune"). Once, this notion of attendance or companionship extends beyond the disease to Philoctetes' natural surroundings. In the depths of despair at his betrayal by Neoptolemus he calls on the "harbors, headlands, company [*ξυνουσίαι*] of mountain beasts . . . rocky cliffs . . . I cry aloud to you, my customary attendants" (936–39). The theme is rounded off effectively by the Chorus later when they remark to Philoctetes, "Your Destiny [Κῆρ] has not learnt how to endure the endless suffering with which it cohabits" (1167–68, *ξυνοικεῖ*).

[31] Dio Chrysostom remarks that "both [Aeschylus and Euripides] made their choruses consist of Lemnians" (*Orat.* 52.7; on the importance of this treatise in the history of literary criticism, see M.T. Luzzatto, *Tragedia greca e cultura ellenistica: L'or. LII di Dione di Prusa* [Bologna: Patron 1983]). For a symbolic interpretation of this isolation see P. Vidal-Naquet, "Sophocles' *Philoctetes* and the Ephebeia," in J.P. Vernant and P. Vidal-Naquet, edd., *Tragedy and Myth in Ancient Greece*, trans. J. Lloyd (Sussex: Harvester 1981) 175–299 ("Philoctetes thus finds himself situated on the borderline between humanity and animal wildness", p. 180).

[32] Mrs. Easterling remarks that Philoctetes' loneliness "is both literal and symbolic" (supra n. 2, 128; cf. also her article, "Philoctetes and Modern Criticism," *ICS* 3 [1978] 27–39). See also C. Segal, *Tragedy and Civilization, an Interpretation of Sophocles* (Cambridge, Mass.: Harvard University Press 1981) 296.

[33] Winnington-Ingram (supra n. 5) 291.

Philoctetes' long isolation, and the deep sense of aggrievement he has nursed throughout it, have made him much less than a man, almost a beast.[34] The one chance Neoptolemus has of reaching across the chasm, to try to rescue what shred of humanity and sympathy may remain in him for the suffering Greek army at Troy, is through *logos*, rational human speech, but this is frustrated. Philoctetes' first reaction of joy at hearing human voices, and Greek voices at that (232 ff.), after so many years of nothing but inanimate nature to which to pour out his cries (687–88, 694–95, 936 ff., 1458–60), turns to even more bitter distrust of human relationships, when he realizes that he has been deceived by the perverted use of speech.[35] How to make contact with a man like this? Every vestige of humanity must surely have been destroyed in one who would rather suffer a lifetime of unendurable pain than return to Troy, to the firm assurance of healing but only at the risk of (as he imagines it) being laughed at by his enemies. Very little remains to remind us that he was once human. He is addressed or referred to several times in the play as "son of Poias" (5, 263, 318, 453, 461, 1230), true, and in his long speech of entreaty to Neoptolemus, he begs to be taken home to his "dear father," to whom, he says, he sent many requests for a ship to fetch him home, but to no avail (488 ff.). In the divine *fiat* with which the plays ends (it is this, and not any change of heart on Philoctetes' part, that finally reverses his intransigence and makes him rejoin the expedition at Troy), Herakles promises that he shall send the spoils of victory and the prize of valor home to his father (1428 ff.). We thus see a technique similar to that in *Ajax* being used to hint at another, more human, side of Philoctetes' character, but it does little to temper our view of him as a "loner," one who has self-destructively and even pathologically cut himself off from human converse, who is prepared to go even to the point of sacrilege in his refusal to fit in with Zeus' plan for the taking of Troy. "Never, never will I yield, not even if the fire-bearing Hurler of Lightning comes to set me aflame with his blazing bolts! Let Troy be damned . . . " (1197–1200; cf. 1400–1401). It is an outburst more worthy of an impious desecrator like Capaneus than of the leading figure of a Sophoclean play.

Electra

Some of these same techniques of amelioration or modification are used in *Electra*, but with (to may taste, at least) only dubious success. "You are wasting away with your insatiable lamenting," the Chorus of young women from the neighborhood caution her (123); "instead of moderation, you have brought yourself to unmanageable grief—your lamenting will destroy you" (140–41). And this is precisely the impression we get: there is something morbid, unbalanced, about the way she has given herself over to suffering. "I weep, I waste away, I shrilly denounce the ill-fated festal day [decreed by Clytemnestra] for my father, but only privately and for myself, for I could never weep openly to the extent that would bring my *thumos* pleasure" (283–86). But the trouble is precisely here,

[34] Segal (supra n. 32) 297, 301, 315.

[35] I have developed this point in "The Power of the Word in Sophocles' Philoctetes," *GRBS* 7 (1966) 233–50; cf. Winnington-Ingram (supra n. 5) 294 with n. 96.

with her *thumos*, which her excessive devotion to misery has warped beyond repair. "You are falling into self-caused disaster . . . ," the Chorus warn her, "You have acquired a great excess of misfortune by always breeding wars in your warped soul" (215–19, δυσθύμῳ ψυχᾷ). "I am being destroyed in misery," she tells them, "as I wait for Orestes to put a stop to these abuses [she means her maltreatment at the hands of Clytemnestra and Aegisthus] . . . In such circumstances, it is not possible to be either moderate or pious; amongst evils it is very necessary also to practice evil" (303–309). And of course "practice evil" is exactly what Electra and Orestes do, when the two are reunited and finally find their opportunity for revenge.

Electra's single-minded devotion to suffering, and the insatiable desire for vengeance that it gives rise to, are only momentarily relieved by a few glimpses of what she might have been if circumstances had allowed her to live a different, more ordinary, life. "I am childless," she tells the Chorus, "without a husband, I live in perpetual misery, bathed in tears . . . " (164–66). "Most of my life has gone past without hope, and I can hold out no longer. I waste away without children, no beloved husband stands near to protect me, I am like an alien settler (ἔποικος), without worth, a mere housekeeper in my ancestral home, in these ugly clothes that you see, hanging about at empty tables" (185–92).[36] Electra's words are meant to suggest that she might have been a normal girl, with normal feminine interests and pastimes, but this seems to me difficult to believe. The endless moaning and lamenting which are merely the surface manifestations of the deeper smouldering hatred that has warped her personality have obliterated practically every trace of any other human emotion.[37] The scene between Electra and her sister Chrysothemis has several obvious similarities with that between Antigone and Ismene, but the effect made on the audience is (in my opinion) very different. Chrysothemis pleads that she "has not the strength" to show Clytemnestra and Aegisthus her true feelings, and Electra throws the plea back at her: "You've said that, if you could have got the strength, you would manifest your hatred of them; but while I'm taking vengeance for father for all he suffered, you do nothing at all to help, and you are trying to deter me from acting" (347–50). It does not seem possible that Sophocles is asking us to equate Electra's undertaking to hate her mother and Aegisthus with Antigone's to bury her brother.[38]

Electra's confrontation with her mother, for all its closeness to the encounter between Antigone and Creon, simply makes us cringe. Electra's vile abuse has clearly taken its toll, for Clytemnestra alludes to it several times (641, 798). Clytemnestra for her part longs to live out her days "in the company of those I love, in happiness, with children who will not assail me with their ill-will or bitter pain" (652–54). When the false report of

[36] As Gould observes, "Electra's sense of her own situation as a unique outrage against nature focusses sharply upon the physical feel and texture of her daily experience," (supra n. 9, 52–53).

[37] The point is made by George Gellie: " . . . living long with hatred has made it something even more potent than her love; it has turned her into something that we can hate" (*Sophocles: a Reading* [Melbourne: University Press 1972] 127).

[38] Reinhardt calls attention to other differences between Antigone and Electra, whom he well describes as "alienated from herself, disfigured, and consumed by her own fires" (supra n. 5, 138 and 143 ff.); see also Winnington-Ingram (supra n. 5) 241 ff.

Orestes' death comes, Clytemnestra grasps at the specious hope that she will now at last be rid of the one "whose presence was a greater harm to me, always drinking blood from my soul undiluted; now we shall spend our days at ease and free from this girl's abuse" (785–87). Electra tries to slough the blame off on her mother: "Have me proclaimed to all as evil, reviler, full of shamelessness; if I am naturally skilled in such acts, at least I do not at all disgrace *your* nature" (605–609). But the charge rings hollow; she has scored merely a point in the debate, not a victory based on fact.

Sophocles' version, as much as those of the other two dramatists, cannot escape the basic weakness inherent in the plot: Orestes is *not* dead and the audience knows it; therefore, the moment which was no doubt intended to be the crowning point of her tale of woe, and most evocative of sympathy from the audience, Electra's reaction to her brother's death, can only be a rather hollow exercise in drumming up pseudo-tragic emotions:

> Dearest Orestes, how in dying you have killed me too!
> You have gone away and torn from my heart
> the last remaining hopes that were my companions,[39]
> that you would some day come to avenge your father
> and my wretchedness. Now where ought I to go?
> I am alone . . .
> I must return again a slave
> to these most hated of humans, my father's
> murderers. No! . . .
> I shall let my life dry up[40]
> here by the gate, without friends.
> Let those inside kill me if they like.
> If they do, it will be a favor; if I live,
> more pain. There is no more desire for life.
> (*Elec.* 808–22, slightly abridged)

Since we know that Orestes is really alive, all this is empty, vapid. Electra is not to have even this moment of genuine, and so ennobling, grief.[41]

Oedipus Coloneus

In the encounter between Oedipus and his son Polyneices in *Oedipus at Colonos* we have a reversal of the motif I have here been exploring. Earlier in the play a picture has emerged of affectionate concern, not to say dependence, by Oedipus on his daughters, especially Antigone, and a correspondingly deep, abiding and truly filial solicitude for him on their part.[42] Now, all this is thrown to the winds. So far from revealing a more human side to Oedipus' daemonic character through the language used by and to "dear

[39] Compare Philoctetes' references to his sufferings as his "attendants", p. 290 above.

[40] Jebb *ad loc.* notes that Philoctetes uses a similar image at *Phil.* 819.

[41] C. Segal, "Visual Symbolism and Visual Effects in Sophocles," *CW* 74 (1980/81) 125–42 at 134 observes that "Orestes' ashes are supposedly in the urn while the living Orestes stands before her."

[42] Vv. 353 ff., 361, 445 ff., 508–9, 1108 ff. (cf. also 1607–9, 1614 ff.).

ones," the interview between father and son brings out not a trace of any human affection in Oedipus. If anything, it shows him hardening into a more monstrously unfeeling force, without any trace whatever of fatherly instincts towards the boy. Polyneices makes a fairly long speech by way of introduction (in which, admittedly, his sincerity is put open to question, for his language is extravagant and his images ring somehow false[43]). But surely his appeals to his father by "Zeus' partner and coadjutor, *Aidôs*" (1268) will have some effect? Not at all. Oedipus remains stonily silent (1271 ff.). Antigone intervenes on his behalf, not only as a delicate allusion to her later staunch defense of the right of burial for his corpse, but also to enlist the audience's sympathy for his case. Oedipus finally condescends to speak, but only, he says, because Theseus has sent the boy to him to be given a hearing (1349 ff., another point in Polyneices' favor). Furthermore, the "justice" (relatively speaking) of Polyneices' case is emphasized: he is the elder brother (374–76, 1293–95). He has some justification, then, for his claim that he has been wrongfully deprived of the Theban throne.

None of this makes any impression whatever on Oedipus. He denounces his son with a vehemence that shocks us (as no doubt the poet intended that it should). "Go to perdition: I spit you out and unfather you, you vile creature" (1383–84). He then imprecates mutual self-slaughter on the brothers with a triple curse: "I call upon the horrid paternal gloom of Tartarus . . . , I call upon these goddesses [the Eumenides], I call upon Ares . . . " (1389–91). What could be more offensive to an audience's sensibilities than to hear a father cursing his sons in such violent terms? True, they have done wrong and Oedipus has been wronged. But the effect this scene has is to show us what a gulf now separates Oedipus from ordinary humankind. All ties of human affection between him and his sons are severed. But we cannot judge Oedipus by human standards, for he is now something superhuman, elemental, akin to those nameless divinities who, at play's end, call him to themselves (1626 ff., 1661–62), to the final resting place that his long years of suffering have earned him. So far from being an exceptional individual whom the poet has attempted, almost as an afterthought, to humanize, Oedipus is the measure of divinity against which we must judge the more "normal" heroes we have here been examining.

[43] His very first words are for "my own sorrows" (1254). Oedipus' squalor he describes as "an aged coresident of the old man" (1259; but his reference to Oedipus' meagre nourishment as "ἀδελφά to his unkempt appearance" is less unusual than it might at first appear; cf. *Ant.* 192 with Jebb's note *ad loc.*).

NEW LIGHT ON THE CULTS OF ARTEMIS AND APOLLO IN MARSEILLES

PAUL PROPERZIO

An article in the *AJA* by M. Euzennat provides the most complete and up-to-date report on the excavations conducted at Marseilles.[1] Euzennat remarks that prior to the March 1967 excavations of the Bourse area, north of the *Vieux-Port* (ancient harbor of Marseilles), little was known about the ancient city. The meager epigraphical evidence produced by the earlier and more recent excavations has furnished virtually nothing of historical value, while several layers of pottery have contributed only tangentially to our knowledge of the history of Marseilles. The new information gained by the excavations has enhanced what we know about the economic and political development of the city in ancient times, but it has advanced little our understanding of Marseilles' religious history.

My study of the cultic and mythic history of Marseilles attempts to present all the presently known evidence for the religious tradition of the ancient city.[2] What surfaces is a notably different picture of Marseilles, which traditionally has been described as "*la cité antique sans antiquité.*"[3] It is now clear that Marseilles supported numerous cults, many of which were a mixture of Graeco-Roman, native, and Eastern elements; and the presence of so many diverse cults in the city created a cosmopolitan atmosphere hardly equalled anywhere in the ancient world except perhaps in Athens, Corinth, Alexandria, and Rome.[4]

Extant evidence indicates that Artemis and Apollo were among the oldest and most prominent deities venerated in Marseilles. The principal cult of Artemis there was the ancient and widespread Ionian cult of Artemis Ephesia; that of Apollo the old and important cult of Apollo Delphinios of the Ionian Greeks.[5] Artemis Ephesia, whose Archaic

[1] "Ancient Marseille in the Light of Recent Excavations," *AJA* 84 (1980) 133–40.

[2] P. Properzio, *Evidence for the Cults and Mythology of Marseilles from Its Foundation to the Fall of the Roman Empire in the West from Ancient Literary, Epigraphical, Numismatic, and Archaeological Testimonia* (Diss. Loyola University of Chicago 1982). M. Clerc, *Massalia: Histoire de Marseilles dans l'antiquité des origines à la fin de l'empire romain d'occident*, 2 vols. (Marseilles: A. Tacussel 1927–1929) devotes only two chapters of his monumental work on Marseilles to the cults of the city, for which additional relevant information has been gained since the publication of his second volume in 1929.

This paper derives from my doctoral dissertation; I am grateful to Professor Al. N. Oikonomides for suggesting the topic and for guiding me through the two inscriptions discussed here.

Special thanks are due to Professor Raymond V. Schoder, S.J., for his valuable advice, criticism and encouragement both as one of my major professors and as a member of my dissertation committee. Father made it possible for me to go to Antibes (ancient Antipolis) in Southern France as a Condon Fellow (summer 1974) in order to research my dissertation. Subsequently Father Schoder often visited my wife Debbie and me in New Jersey and lectured frequently at Drew University. We traveled to France and Greece with Father and valued his friendship highly. He will be greatly missed.

[3] A.G. Woodhead, *The Greeks in the West* (London: Thames and Hudson 1962) 68.

[4] Properzio (supra n. 2) 270.

[5] Ibid. 48–66, 28–44.

temple at Ephesos (the Artemision) was one of the most famous monuments in antiquity, was worshiped in Marseilles as a goddess of natural fertility in the Oriental manner; Apollo Delphinios was venerated there chiefly as a god of sailors and maritime cities, and in this context the epithet reveals his worship as the dolphin god. New epigraphical evidence, in the form of restorations proposed below to two inscriptions, augment what is now known by suggesting that, in addition to the well-established cults of Artemis Ephesia and Apollo Delphinios, other cults were dedicated to these two deities in Marseilles.

I.

An important Greek inscription, dating before the middle of the first century B.C., was found at Marseilles before the 1850s, then sent to Paris and never recovered by the Museum Borély in Marseilles:[6]

ΘЄΑ·ΔΙΚΤΥΑ
ΔΗΜΟϹ·ΜΑΣΣ

θεᾷ Δικτύᾳ | δῆμος Μασσ(αλιωτῶν)[7]

The dedication is to the goddess Diktya (Diktynna), a Cretan divinity also called Britomartis, who is identified with the Greek Artemis.[8]

Previously this inscription has been thought to have no significance for Marseilles because it was interpreted as a dedication by the δῆμος Μασσ(αλιωτῶν).[9] The δῆμος would not have figured in such an offering, since we know from Strabo (4.1.5) that a democracy did not exist in Marseilles: *Διοικοῦνται δ' ἀριστοκρατικῶς οἱ Μασσαλιῶται πάντων εὐνομώτατα*. In 49 B.C., after collaborating with Pompey, Marseilles was besieged and forced to submit to Julius Caesar and his lieutenant Trebonius. The Romans, however, allowed the Massaliotes to remain relatively independent, governed by a council of 600 senators and scrupulously observing laws in keeping with their Ionian heritage, until the first century after Christ.[10]

[6] *CIG* III, 6764 = *IG* XIV, 357° (*Inscriptiones falsae vel suspectae Galliae Hispaniae Germaniae*). Cf. also Clerc (supra n. 2) I 451 n. 1. The inscription is thought to be from a terracotta vase fragment now lost.

[7] *CIG* (supra n. 6). The same reading is found in E. Cougny and M. Lebègue, *Gallikōn Syngrapheīs Hellenikoí: Extraits des auteurs grecques concernant la géographie et l'histoire des Gaules* (Paris: Renouard 1890) VI 164–65. Μασσ[ιλιωτῶν] is the reading of the fourth word in L.R. Farnell, *The Cults of the Greek States* (Oxford: Clarendon 1896) II 589 n. 131h.

[8] For Diktynna identified with the Greek Artemis cf. Cougny and Lebègue (supra n. 7) 165 n. 3. For the Greek Artemis identified with Diktynna, Britomartis, and the Ephesian goddess see Farnell (supra n. 7) II 473–82; Properzio (supra n. 2) 56–60.

[9] Cf. *IG* (supra n. 6), also noted by Cougny and Lebègue (supra n. 7) 164 n. 1 and by Clerc (supra n. 2) I 451 n. 1.

[10] For the government of the Massaliotes and their hostilities with Caesar cf. Clerc (supra n. 2) I 424–34, II 65–156; W.H. Hall, *The Romans on the Riviera and the Rhône: A Sketch of the Conquest of Liguria and the Roman Province* (London: Macmillan 1898) 132–48; Properzio (supra n. 2) 14–15.

The restoration proposed here eliminates such objections:[11]

ΘϵΑ·ΔΙΚΤΥΑ [- - - name of dedicant - - -]-
ΔΗΜΟϹ·ΜΑΣΣ[ΑΛΙΗΤΗΣ ΑΝΕΘΗΚΕΝ]

θεᾳ̃ Δικτύᾳ [- - - name of dedicant - - -]-
δῆμος Μασσ[αλιήτης ἀνέθηκεν]

This restoration supposes that a Massaliote whose name ends in -δῆμος made the dedication. It conforms both in the customary dedicatory phraseology and in the shapes of the letters, notably the rounded *epsilon* (line 1) and the lunar and tetraskeles *sigmas* (line 2), to the form and style of Greek inscriptions of the first century B.C.[12]

Although the principal cult of Artemis in Marseilles is considered to have been that of Artemis Ephesia as already noted, this inscription, supported by other archaeological and numismatic evidence,[13] suggests that a cult of Artemis Diktynna was also observed in the city.

II.

A second Greek inscription of the Roman period, now lost, was found on a marble pedestal at Marseilles before 1830:[14]

ΚΗΜΙ
ΑΠΟΙ
ΠΑΙΩ
ΟΠΑΙ

'Αποτροπαίῳ as a reading of the eight letters of lines 2–3, was rejected in *IG*.[15] A new restoration of the inscription is proposed:[16]

[- - - - -]ΚΗΜΙ [- - genitive - -]-
[- - - - -]ΑΠΟΛ̣ [ΛΩΝΙ Α]-
[ΠΟΤΡ Ο]ΠΑΙΩ [Ι- - - - - -]
[- - - - -]ΟΠΑΙ [- - - - - -]

[- - - - -]κη Μι [- - genitive - -]-
[- - - - -]'Απόλ̣ [λωνι 'Α]-
[π ο τ ρ ο]παίῳ [ι- - - - - -]
[- - - - -]οπαι [- - - - - -]

[11] Ibid. 56. Μασσαλιήτης (line 2) = Μασσαλιώτης.

[12] Cf. A.G. Woodhead, *The Study of Greek Inscriptions* (Cambridge: University Press 1967) 41, 63–65, 72, 91–92; Properzio (supra n. 2) 56–57.

[13] Ibid. 60–66.

[14] *CIG* I, 464 = *IG* XIV, 2464.

[15] Ibid.

[16] Properzio (supra n. 2) 37. The restoration proposes that the original eight letters of lines 2–3 belong to

This tentative restoration assumes that both sides of the marble pedestal have been broken off. Although the fourth letter of line 2 is printed as an *iota* in *IG*,[17] the new reading supposes that it might have been a *lambda*. No specific date of the Roman period has been assigned to the inscription. The shapes of the letters, however, particularly the *mu*, *pi* and rounded *omega*, seem to point to the first centuries after Christ but no earlier than the first century B.C.[18]

The dedication would have been by a lady whose father's or husband's name appeared in the genitive (lines 1–2).[19] This reading also interprets the dedication to be to Apollo Apotropaios, "Averter of Evil" (lines 2–3).[20] Ἀποτρόπαιος is a frequent cult epithet of Apollo, and Apollo Apotropaios continued to be worshiped according to Greek ritual in Roman times.[21] It follows that the dedication, if made to Apollo Apotropaios, may indicate that this cult as practiced in Marseilles involved certain rites of purification and human sacrifice related to an early Ionian festival of Apollo known as the *Thargelia* and connected with his Apotropaic cult.[22] Lactantius Placidus on Statius (*Theb.* 10.793) recounts that it was a Gallic custom to purify the city by sacrificing a human victim who, having been sustained for a year at the public expense, was stoned to death by the citizens. Servius on Vergil (*Aen.* 3.57) connects such an expiatory rite directly with Marseilles. The author relates that in a time of pestilence in Marseilles one of the poorest citizens offered himself to be fed for a year at the public expense. Then, dressed for sacrifice, he was led around the entire city and cursed so that he might absorb all evils. Finally, he was driven out of the city or sometimes even thrown down a cliff to his death.[23]

---

two separate words, [- - - -]Ἀπόλ̣[λωνι Ἀ]|[ποτρο]παίω[ι- - - - - - -], not just one; cf. *IG* (supra n. 14). Thus, the reading Ἀποτροπαίωι = (Ἀποτροπαίῳ) of lines 2–3 rejected by *IG* is considered possible by the new restoration.

[17] Supra n. 14.

[18] Cf. Woodhead (supra n. 12) 9, 64; Properzio (supra n. 2) 38.

[19] Properzio (supra n. 2) 37. [- - - -]ΚΗΜΑ̣[ΣΣΑΛΙ]|[ΗΤΗΣ] is perhaps another possible reading of lines 1–2 which would identify the dedicant only as a Massaliote lady: [- - - -]κηΜα̣[σσαλι]|[ήτης]. Μασσαλιήτης (lines 1–2) = Μασσαλιώτης (cf. supra n. 11).

[20] Properzio (supra n. 2) 37. It is tempting to restore after Apollo's epithet (lines 2–3) καί (line 3) and the name of another 'Apotropaic' deity (lines 3–4), since there remain the four letters οπαι (line 4) which conceivably could form the same epithet of another god or goddess who performed the same function. However, since the number of 'Apotropaic' deities from antiquity is still indeterminable, such a restoration is not here attempted. Still another possible reading of lines 3–4 after Apollo's epithet (line 3) could be [καί So and So] ὁ παῖ[ς ἀνέθηκαν]. This would allow the inscription tentatively to read: "So and So (a lady), daughter or wife of So and So (or a Massaliote lady whose father's or husband's name is not given), and So and So, (her) son, made the dedication to Apollo Apotropaios."

[21] Aristophanes (*Eq.* 1307, *Av.* 61, *Pl.* 359); *CIG* 464; Apollo is so invoked in a fourth-century B.C. Attic inscription. Cf. Farnell (supra n. 7) IV 255, 430 n. 274d; Properzio (supra n. 2) 37–38.

[22] Ibid. 38–40.

[23] The passage of Servius also informs us that Petronius was aware of this ritual in Marseilles: *hoc autem in Petronio lectum est.* J.P. Sullivan, *The Satyricon of Petronius: A Literary Study* (Bloomington: Indiana 1968) 39–42, 78–80 says there is reason to believe that Marseilles may have been the setting of the beginning and some other episodes of the *Satyricon* which are now lost. According to Sullivan, it has been conjectured that Petronius himself was from Marseilles.

These literary sources suggest that the Massaliotes performed a rite closely resembling the Attic (originally Ionian) *Thargelia* in honor of Apollo during which a citizen who was chosen as a scapegoat (*φαρμακός*) absorbed all evils and was then removed.[24] From the evidence at hand it is possible, though not conclusive, that the *Thargelia* in honor of Apollo was celebrated in Marseilles.[25] If so, the proposed restoration of the Massaliote inscription as a dedication to Apollo Apotropaios who was honored during the celebration of the Ionian *Thargelia* provides further testimony of diversity in Apollo's cult in Marseilles.[26]

[24] Encolpius, the narrator of the *Satyricon*, several times in the story alludes to having offended the god Priapus who stalks him until he has made atonement for the violation (cf. esp. *Sat.* 133.3). Sullivan (supra n. 23), citing the passage of Servius on Marseilles as evidence, argues that the *Satyricon* may have begun with some sort of plague sent by Priapus which was afflicting Marseilles, and Encolpius, the apparent offender, had to serve for a time as a 'scapegoat' to rid the city of the plague. Encolpius' ultimate escape or removal from the city takes him, hounded by the god, on a series of adventures until he has made final reparation to Priapus and returns home again, perhaps to Marseilles. In further support of his contention that Encolpius may have been a scapegoat in Marseilles, Sullivan makes mention of the practice of using a scapegoat during the Ionian *Thargelia* in Graeco-Roman times.

[25] On the *Thargelia*, other rituals related to it, its connection with Marseilles, and Petronius' knowledge of the festival in Massaliote tradition cf. Farnell (supra n. 7) IV 267–84, esp. 279–80 and 419 n. 245; Clerc (supra n. 2) I 454–57, II 259–61; H. Ternaux, *Historia Reipublicae Massiliensium* (Göttingen: Huth 1826) 65, n. 161, and 66, n. 162; J.G. Frazer, *The Golden Bough* (New York: Macmillan 1942) 578–83.

[26] It is not possible to determine whether the cults of Apollo Apotropaios, Apollo Delphinios and Apollo Thargelios were all observed during the celebration of the *Thargelia* in Marseilles. It is, however, likely that Apollo's prominent Delphinian cult there may have included aspects of other ceremonies, such as the *Thargelia*, performed in his honor. There is no direct evidence that a cult of Apollo Thargelios actually existed in the city. The Massaliote dedication to Apollo Apotropaios, then, is the only testimony we now have which would enable us to suggest that his cult was also associated with a *Thargelia* in Marseilles.

TWO GEORGIC POETS: V. SACKVILLE-WEST AND VERGIL

Harry C. Rutledge

Homer and Hesiod and Virgil knew
The ploughshare in its reasonable shape,
Classical from the moment it was new.
The Land (89)

Here the old Bacchic piety endures,
Here the sweet legends of the world remain.
Homeric waggons lumbering the road;
Virgilian litanies among the bine.
The Land (106)

In 1926 the British literary world bestowed upon V. Sackville-West the Hawthornden Prize for her poem, *The Land.*[1] This poem, one hundred seven pages long, is a celebration of agricultural life in the part of England which Sackville-West knew intimately, County Kent. Sackville-West had been born at Knole, the ancestral seat of the Sackville family. At the time *The Land* was written, Sackville-West and her family (her husband the diplomat, Harold Nicolson), were living in Long Barn, an old manor house not far from Knole. It was at Long Barn that Sackville-West began her great hobby of gardening, an avocation which would have its now famous culmination in the gardens of nearby Sissinghurst Castle, which the author acquired in 1930.

As suggested by my epigraphs from Sackville-West's poem, *The Land* is imbued with classical allusion and takes not a little of its distinction from the classical presence. The poem itself begins with an epigraph from the *Georgics*

Nec sum animi dubius, verbis ea vincere magnum
quam sit et angustis hunc addere rebus honorem.
(3.289–290)

[1] For this paper the Latin text of Vergil is that of R. A. B. Mynors (Oxford: University Press 1969); the English translations are my own. *The Land*, V. Sackville-West (London: Wm. Heinemann 1926). References to Vergil are to lines, those to Sackville-West to pages. I owe special gratitude for fresh views to Michael C. J. Putnam, *Virgil's Poem of the Earth: Studies in the Georgics* (Princeton: University Press 1979). For the life of V. Sackville-West I am indebted to Victoria Glendinning, *Vita: The Life of V. Sackville-West* (New York: Knopf 1983), but also to Vita Sackville-West's novel which reflects the country seat, Knole, *The Edwardians* (New York: Doubleday, Doran 1930) and to Philippa Nicolson, *V. Sackville-West's Garden Book* (New York: Atheneum 1983). The greatest thanks is to the Vergilian Society of America, which Father Raymond Schoder helped found. At the VSA's invitation I served on its Naples faculty in 1963, 1967, 1977, returning to Italy as president of the VSA in 1978. This paper is a tribute to all concerned.

> I have no doubt how great a task it is to conquer such subjects with words and to add glory to a restricted subject.

Sackville-West might well have added the next two lines from Vergil to her epigraph so as to include the phrase, *raptat amor* (3.292), inasmuch as her own love for Knole and the Kentish countryside was almost a passion. The author declared that when she began *The Land* she did not have Vergil in mind. She picked up Vergil's poem as she was writing *The Land*,[2] but her design and purpose remained unique.

Whereas Vergil's poem is arranged topically, *The Land* conforms to the seasonal year, beginning with winter. The four primary sections of *The Land* go from winter through autumn. Both poems are marked by a mass of agricultural detail, though neither would serve as a manual from a federal department of agriculture. Both poems are full of humanity in general and the farmer in particular. *The Land*, however, does not have the concentration on large animals which we find in the Third Georgic, nor does it have such a climax as Vergil provides in the Fourth Georgic with the tale of Aristaeus and Orpheus. On the other hand, Sackville-West's poem is more even in its description of humanity in a country life. The yeoman himself, in all of his occupations, is ever present in *The Land*. The farmer has no less esteem in *The Land* that he does in the *Georgics*, despite the lack of such a panegyric, an apotheosis, as Vergil provides in *Georgics* Four with Orpheus, Proteus, and Aristaeus.

The Land opens to a soliloquy, the speaker singing "the cycle of my country's year" (3), a "Classic monotony" (3), whether "oats in Greece/Or oats in Kent" (3). The shepherd, "Like his Boeotian forebear" (3) could be in either Thebes or Lombardy (3). It is winter. The poet intends to celebrate nothing more than the "pious yeoman" (4) whose grave will support the epitaph, "'He tilled the soil well'" (4).

The pensive speaker continues this meditation, twice noting "The country habit has me by the heart" (5). An Homeric solemnity takes over the poem as the speaker remarks on "shepherds and stars" as "quiet with the hills" (6), there being "a bond between the men who go/From youth about the business of the earth" (6). The narrator knows only "the battle between man and earth" (7), and thus the note is struck of the presence in the rustic life of *labor* and *vis*, terms which Michael Putnam regards as two of Vergil's "signature words."[3]

Finally the narrator enters the world of country life in winter, the "rainy dark" (8) of December, whereupon the narrative pauses for the sake of a "Winter Song" (9–11), the first of several apostrophes set off by italics within the fabric of the longer poem. When the narration resumes, we are on the Weald of Kent and the poem becomes a Kentish winter. In due course Sackville-West gives us the yeoman housebound, making plans and calculations for the spring and summer ahead.

[2] Glendinning (supra n. 1) 166.
[3] Putnam (supra n. 1) 39.

The passage concerned with the provident yeoman matches in tone the lines from *Georgics* One regarding the farmer and his wife (291–296):

et quidam seros hiberni ad luminis ignis
peruigilat, ferroque faces inspicat acuto.
interea longum cantu solata laborem
arguto coniunx percurrit pectine telas,
aut dulcis musti Volcano decoquit umorem
et foliis undam trepidi despumat aëni.

One man watches at the late winter firelight, sharpening torches with a keen blade. In the meantime, his wife, lightening her unending work with song, runs through her loom with a humming reed, or boils away on a fire the sweet liquid of new wine and skims with leaves the foam of the shivering kettle.

Sackville-West:

Then pencil in hand beneath the hanging lamp
The farmer ponders in the kitchen's hush
. . . .
The year revolves its immemorial prose
(21)

Since time immemorial farmers have thus reckoned, certainly, in English terms, since "Drake played bowls at Plymouth" (23). And for this farmer, "Experience [is] his text-book" (25).[4] Long ago Jupiter set us to worry

. . . primusque per artem
mouit agros, curis acuens mortalia corda,
nec torpere graui passus sua regna ueterno.
(*Georgics* 1.122–124)

He first made us work the fields as an art, sharpening mortal perception with worry, not permitting his world to become listless from lethargy.

In the final analysis, the farmer—whether yeoman or shepherd—must be able to survive, and manage, alone. The words of Sackville-West sum up the picture presented by Vergil in *Georgics* One and Two, and by Homer in the *Iliad* (8.533–565), shepherds and soldiers by firelight:

The power of being alone;
The power of being alone with earth and skies,
Of going about a task with quietude,

[4] Putnam (supra n. 1) 17 points out that the word *experientia* is used only twice in the *Georgics*, in the prologue (1.4) and at the beginning of the Aristaeus epyllion (4.316). Yet, ultimately, in my opinion, the term is the fundamental subject of both the *Georgics* and *The Land*.

Aware at once of earth's surrounding mood
And of an insect crawling on a stone.

(25)

Hereupon spring enters *The Land.* We are in a world of "recurrent patterns on a scroll" (30). The yeoman struggles with his soil—

He knows the clay,
Malevolent, unkind, a spiteful slave;
Has he not felt its rancour in his bones?
Gashed it with share and mattock? torn its flesh?

(32)

As Vergil says,

labor omnia vicit
improbus et duris urgens in rebus egestas.

(1.145–146)

Hard work conquers everything, as does pressing need in hard times.

The experienced farmer knows to rotate his crops, the art "known to the Roman" (33), "to keep his land in kindly heart" (33). Vergil makes the same point early in *Georgics* One (79–83). Spring is the season for blossoming orchards, an important concern for the Kentish farmer. Sackville-West focuses on apple trees, which can make

A ghostly orchard standing all in white,
Aisles of white trees, white branches, in the green

(36)

Vergil provides the same colorful touch in his reference to the almond tree

. . . cum se nux plurima silvis
induet in florem et ramos curvabit olentis

(1.187–188)

. . . when the luxuriant
almond tree arrays itself in the forest at
blossom-time and bends its scented branches . . .

The flower of the almond has the same pinkish-white color familiar in peach blossoms. Both Vergil and Sackville-West suddenly imbue their narratives with a stroke of gleaming color.

Following a soliloquy on the birth of young animals in the springtime and the dangers existing for the young (37–39), Sackville-West concentrates on the "Bee-Master" (39–44), a major part of the Spring section of *The Land.* Here Sackville-West dramatizes beekeeping with references to the Orient

The Syrian queens mate in the high hot day,
Rapt visionaries of creative fray
. . . .
I have known bees within the ruined arch
Of Akbar's crimson city hang their comb

(40)

But then she turns from that exotic scene saying

But this is the bee-master's reckoning
In England.

(40)

We are reminded of Vergil's "Praise of Italy" in *Georgics* Two (136–176).

Sed neque Medorum siluae, ditissima terra,
nec pulcher Ganges atque auro turbidus Hermus
laudibus Italiae certent . . .

But neither the forests of Media, richest
of lands, nor the beautiful Ganges nor
the Hermus swollen with gold can vye in
praise with Italy . . .

Sackville-West thereupon dilates on the art of apiculture including the making of honey. Here she offers a distillation of the many details presented by Vergil in *Georgics* Four (314 lines, covering a little more than ten Oxford pages, as opposed to Sackville-West's 114 lines, over less than five full pages). Her purpose is different. In *The Land*, Sackville-West wanted to present a tapestry of Kentish farming life, season by season. Her poetry is close in spirit and purpose to such a work in another medium as the calendar pages from the *Très Riches Heures* made by Paul de Limbourg and his brothers for the Duc de Berry in the early fifteenth century.[5] Those lustrous pages also combine country and courtly life over the twelve months of the calendar year. Vergil's purpose is to show aspects of rural life, with man ever present in the landscape. The wonderful feature of Vergil's bee book is that it leads up to and culminates—a culmination for the whole of the *Georgics*—in the epyllion on Aristaeus and Orpheus, a celebration of art and man.[6] Vergil knew perfectly well that apiculture is at its height in the springtime—

[5] *The Très Riches Heures of Jean, Duke of Berry* (New York: George Braziller 1969).

[6] Putnam (supra n. 1) 276 observes that the Aristaeus epyllion from its beginning at 4.315 with its apostrophe to the Muses is in "epic high style." He goes on to suggest that Aristaeus is a latter-day Achilles—"Virgil presses the kinship of troubled hero-sons seeking the support of divine mothers who happen to be water nymphs" (ibid., 282). If Vergil's "Aristaeus-Orpheus" was not a brilliant earlier poem set into the Fourth *Georgic*, then we can only assume that Vergil wanted the Fourth *Georgic* to give a sublime conclusion to the whole poem, and chose the legend of Orpheus with all of its macabre and poignant drama for his purpose. This opinion is shared and elaborated on by Brooks Otis, *Virgil: A Study in Civilized Poetry*

qualis apes aestate noua . . .
(*Aeneid* 1.430)

as bees in fresh summer—but in the *Georgics* the country tapestry is a background for a study of life and main features of the human condition, with death and life intermingled, as in the plague narrative of *Georgics* Three (478–566) and the deaths of Orpheus and Eurydice in *Georgics* Four (485–526). Sackville-West is simpler. Near the end of her spring book she observes:

My life was rich; I took a swarm of bees and
found a crumpled snake-skin on the road,
All in one day, and was increased by these.

I have not understood humanity.
But those plain things, that gospel of each year,
Made me the scholar of simplicity.
(55)

Her "simplicity," of course, is that of earth and life.

And so to "Summer" in Kent. Summer is the time of sheep shearing in the "genial meadows of the Weald" (63). Sheep require shepherds. Shepherds remind Sackville-West of the world of the Old Testament. Abel, Jacob, Leah and Rachel are evoked, and then David, shepherd and harp-player[7]

Come from the wilds to sooth dark Saul to sleep.
(64)

Instead of evoking Iron Age Greece, or Italy, Sackville-West chooses, instead, the Palestinian counterpart to that agrarian world of pre-classical times. As far as world culture is concerned, the name of David is no less impressive than that of Romulus. Thus Sackville-West makes Kent and her world of Knole one with the ancient world by analogy to that most famous of shepherds, David, his world not so very far removed from that of Homer's Troy.[8]

Whereupon the Kentish summer proceeds. In due course, Sackville-West takes up the thatcher and other craftsmen (80-82). These people knew scythes, hammers, and knives (81). These occupations and tools direct us to the craft of the poet. Here Sackville-West is more in the Eclogue-world of carved wooden cups and willow baskets (*Eclogues* 3 and 10), than in the Georgics-world where the poet triumphs before a marble temple

(Oxford: University Press 1963) 211–214. The "fairy story" (ibid., 211) to which Aristaeus belongs would not have suited in any way the purpose of Sackville-West. Vergil himself ennobles the conclusion of *The Land*, as Orpheus ennobles the *Georgics*.

[7] Abel, Genesis 4; Jacob, Genesis 25; Leah and Rachel, Genesis 29; Saul and David, Samuel 1.16.

[8] Another striking example of a point of view which combines the Aegean world and that of the Near East is found in the short stories of Marguerite Yourcenar, *Feux* (Paris: Librarie Plon 1957), a collection of tales begun in the 1930's, with vignettes ranging from Phaedra to Mary Magdalene.

(*Georgics* 3.13–39). Both Vergil and Sackville-West cannot resist comparing the arts of country life with the work of the self-conscious artist. The Vergilian georgic expression which most closely links the ancient poet to the modern is

> felix qui potuit rerum cognoscere causas.
>
> (3.490)

With this judgment the great gardener, V. Sackville-West, could only agree. And just before that verse, Vergil had said

> Me uero primum dulces ante omnia Musae,
> quarum sacra fero ingenti percussus amore,
> accipiant, caelique uias et sidera monstrent
>
> (3.475–477)

> For me in truth the sweet Muses are above
> everything, whose sacraments I observe,
> struck with deep passion—may they
> accept me, showing me the ways of the
> heavens and the stars.

Sackville-West's love of writing and of the farms and gardens of Kent is wholly attuned to Vergil's love of poetry and Italy.

Sackville-West concludes *The Land* with the season of autumn. In this part of the poem there is a heaping up of classical allusion, a crescendo occurring in the final salute to Vergil.

The first subject of "Autumn" is plowing. Our poet begins

> Homer and Hesiod and Virgil knew
> The ploughshare in its reasonable shape,
> Classical from the moment it was new
>
> (89)

—then she refers to "the slow Egyptian" turning "the dark/Loam in his narrow valley" (89) and then to "the Mede across his Asian plain [who] scores the poor furrow for his meagre wheat" (89). Once again Sackville-West sees the world of the Fertile Crescent and that of the Aegean basin as one.

Thereafter the Kentish farmer is busy with threshing, hedging, ditching, cutting fence poles. The poet's tone becomes somber as she approaches December. There is a pause in the narrative as Sackville-West relates the folk of her Kent to an older time:

> Dark was the ilex in the Grecian vales
> . . . .
> No woodsman but had heard the Dryad cry,
> No girl but knew the goat-foot faun was nigh
>
> (95)

and on to a recollection of Daphne

Fleeing before a god, and, all but spent,
Slipped from his arms, herself become a tree.

(96)

The poem's coda follows. The poet reviews her subjects and their year. She goes on to comment on the superiority of life in the country to life in London (103–104).[9] She moves into her final rustic image, the taking of the vintage—

Here the old Bacchic piety endures
Here the sweet legends of the world remain.
Homeric waggons lumbering the road;
Virgilian litanies among the bine

(106)

Who could so watch, and not forget the rack
Of wills worn thin and thought become too frail,
Nor roll the centuries back
And feel the sinews of his soul grow hale,
And know himself for Rome's inheritor?

(106)

And quickly, almost with a leap, we are brought to Vergil

O Mantuan! that sang the bees and vines,
The tillage and the flocks
. . . .
Then all my deep acquaintance with that land,
Crying for words, welled up . . .

(107)

Finally,

Then thought I, Virgil! how from Mantua reft,
Shy as a peasant in the courts of Rome,
Thou took'st the waxen tablets in thy hand,
And out of anger cut calm tales of home.

(107)

Suddenly Sackville-West offers us an extraordinary illumination of both her world and that of Vergil. It was in 30 B.C. that Vergil published the *Georgics*. The world of the

[9] Viewed in terms of literary history *The Land* (1926) is between T. S. Eliot's *The Waste Land* (1922) and D. H. Lawrence's *Lady Chatterly's Lover* (1928), both of which works condemn the modern industrial world and celebrate the old—and more natural—life of the country. For the opinion that *The Land* is a reaction against *The Waste Land* see Michael Stevens, *V. Sackville-West: A Critical Biography* (New York: Scribners 1974). *The Land* had a flurry of popularity during the hard years of World War II (Glendinning [supra n. 1] 325). The great interest in recent years in the literary circle known as "Bloomsbury," in which V. Sackville-West and Virginia Woolf were devoted friends, has prompted a renewed interest in the works of Sackville-West.

Georgics, that rural world, had not changed since Hesiod and would not change before V. Sackville-West wrote *The Land*. Vergil's world had, however, been seriously threatened and fractured as in an earthquake by the civil wars of the first century B.C. and the struggle between Antony and Octavian. The magisterial chronicler of this era is Ronald Syme in his *The Roman Revolution*. Sackville-West's world was the years between the wars, World War I and World War II. She preserves the world that she knew in *The Land* and in her novel of 1930, *The Edwardians*, a tale of Knole. Sackville-West did not see the end of an era so acutely or so astringently as did T. S. Eliot in *The Waste Land* (1922). In fact, however, *The Land* is a memorial to a way of life. Vergil is more realistic. The *Georgics* end with the deaths of Orpheus and Eurydice. Aristaeus will recover his bees. What then? Octavian Caesar (not yet Augustus in 30 B.C.)

> ad altum
> fulminat Euphraten bello victorque volentis
> per populos dat iura viamque adfectat Olympo
> (4.559-561)

> fulminates in war beside the deep Euphrates and
> as victor gives laws to a willing people and
> prepares his way to Olympus.

The world was changing. Vergil recognized the coming of a new day in the *Georgics*, emphatically describing it in the *Aeneid*. The daughter of Knole felt herself to be in the same transitional position as she finished *The Land*. Both georgic poems celebrate a paradise about to be lost. That paradise is captured and made everlasting in these two great works.

THE SHROUD OF TURIN IN CONSTANTINOPLE: THE DOCUMENTARY EVIDENCE

Daniel Scavone

Foreword

In October, 1988 three radiocarbon facilities (University of Arizona, Zurich, Oxford) arrived at a date 1260–1390 for the Turin Shroud. The Vatican's inexplicable acquiescence should not close the books on the issue of the antiquity of the Shroud and its possible authenticity as Jesus' burial cloth.

In fact, the C^{14} testing of the Shroud had many flaws. Against the best advice of the C^{14} scientific community, samples came only from the most contaminated part of the Shroud. Threads from other areas should have been included. All three labs dated bits from the same area of the Shroud, reputedly using the same decontaminating solvent: of course their dates agreed. Also, only the accelerator (AMS) method was used, when the more experienced decay (SPC) technique was available as "second opinion" and is often used to verify AMS findings. Most C^{14} testing uses an average date retrieved from several objects in the same stratum of a "dig." The single Shroud could not provide this kind of certainty. Objects from a "dig" are scrupulously kept out of cigarette smoke to maintain their true carbon-counts; the Shroud has been handled for at least 630 years and absorbed smoke from a church burning down around it. All this renders it unique in C^{14} dating history. Whence comes the certainty of its C^{14} "date"? Indeed, C^{14} experts universally warn against too great a reliance on C^{14}.

A strong case is made against the 14th-century date by the following paper. Moreover, a 6th-century icon of Christ from St. Catherine's Monastery on Mt. Sinai (Pl. 27b), certainly copied from the Shroud, is evidence that the Shroud (itself not a painting) originated much earlier. The 170 points of precise congruence between icon and Shroud face include congruence of the wrinkle lines seen on the Shroud cloth, which the icon artist faithfully copied. This is not proof that it is Jesus' Shroud, but it does refute a 14th-century date.*

The absence of a firm historical record for the Shroud of Turin (Pls. 26, 27a) prior to ca. 1355 has been a major obstacle in any efforts to know whether this 14 by 3.5 foot linen cloth bearing the bloodied frontal and dorsal image of a crucified man is indeed the burial wrapping of Jesus Christ. Still, the positive indications of authenticity found in the copious reports of the October, 1978 scientific examination of the Shroud, as well as the acknowledged inability of the examining scientists to refute its genuineness and the physical details of the Shroud itself, all militate to virtually compel continued historical research.

* See Alan and Mary Whanger, "Polarized image overlay technique: a new image comparison method and its applications," *Applied Optics* 24 (March 15, 1985) 766–72.

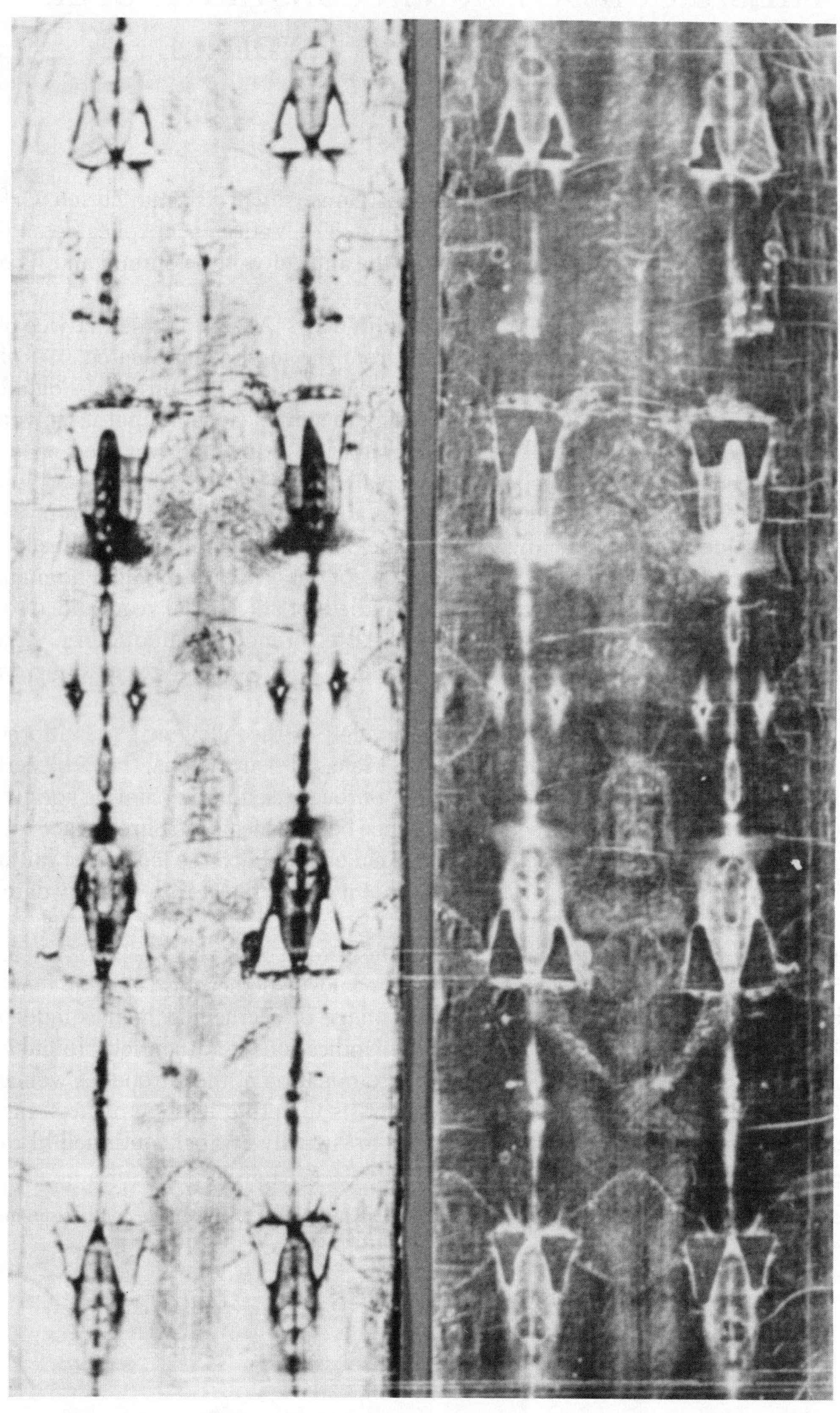

PLATE 26. Photograph of entire Shroud, both positve and negative.

Since the Shroud's history is a matter of solid record after ca. 1355, the major thrust of the historian must go to the preceding centuries. Although the documents adduced in the present paper from the period prior to ca. 1355 are quite speculative and only make indefinite reference to the Shroud present today in Torino, Italy, they represent something in the nature of a few bright lights in a dark void of information. Without them there would be a total absence of documentation. If the Shroud was not in Constantinople from the 10th century to about 1204, though it may indeed have been elsewhere, we would have no proof that it even existed. In Constantinople we at least have (to alter the metaphor) a smoking gun.

At least ten documents of a secular nature refer to the presence in Constantinople of a cloth which in 944 had come from the city of Edessa, modern Urfa in southern Turkey, a cloth miraculously imprinted with a likeness of the face of Jesus. These documents span the period 944 to 1247. Six of them, dating from 1150, 1190, 1200, 1201, 1203, and 1207, also assert the presence in Constantinople of Christ's burial wrappings. Two documents, dated 1190 and 1247, identify *part* only of the burial wrappings along with the imaged face cloth. Finally, six different documents from 958, ca. 1095, 1157, 1171, 1205, and 1207, attest the burial wrappings but *not* the face cloth. There are sixteen documents in all.

In addition, numerous other documents beginning from the period of the Fourth Crusade, 1204, record the *transfer* of fragments of Christ's burial linens to various cathedrals in western Europe.[1] These include the 1247 document which is also the only record of the departure of the Edessa towel from Constantinople.[2]

One difficulty which presents itself to the historian is the great variety of terms used by these medieval sources to designate these two objects, the imaged face cloth and the linen(s) of burial. For the first we get *sancta toella, imago Christi Edessena, linteum faciem Christi repraesentans, mantile, soudarion, mandylion, manutergium, sudarium super caput*, and *cheiromaktron*. For the latter we have *sindon, sudarium, linteamina, fasciae, panni, spargana, othonai kai ta soudaria, entaphioi sindones.*[3] Most of these latter are plurals, evidencing the likelihood that besides a large shroud other auxiliary linens associated with the burial were present.

Historians of the Turin Shroud are hard put to reconcile these references, though they are nearly unanimously agreed that the Shroud present today in Turin did sojourn in Constantinople prior to its arrival in Lirey, France ca. 1355, where the earliest document, of the year 1389, describes it "about thirty-four years ago."[4] The present paper is an attempt to make such a reconciliation.

[1] Paul Edouard Didier, comte, Riant, *Exuviae sacrae constantinopolitanae*, 2 vols. (Geneva: Societé de l'Orient Latin 1878). See also Riant, *Dépouilles religieuses enlevées à Constantinople au XIIIe siècle par les latins et documents historiques nés de leur transport en occident* (Paris: Societé Nationale des Antiquaires de France 1875). Jean Ebersolt, *Sanctuaires de Byzance: recherches sur les anciens trésors des églises de Constantinople* (Paris: Editions Ernst Leroux 1921).

In this paper the following abbreviation will be used: *SSI* = *Shroud Spectrum International*.

[2] Riant, *Exuviae* (supra n. 1) II 133–35.

[3] These terms will be found in their appropriate contexts in the notes to this paper. The list is probably not exhaustive.

[4] The *Memorandum* of Pierre d'Arcis, Bishop of Troyes. Original text in Luigi Fossati, *La santa sin-*

Document I

On August 15, 944, amidst great celebrations, the *mandylion*, i.e. the towel bearing Christ's portrait not made by hands (*acheiropoieta*), arrived in Constantinople from Edessa. It was still stretched out and sealed inside its oblong frame, the face visible in the circular central opening. Its presence in Edessa is attested with some certainty back to 544 when, according to the historian Evagrius, its miraculous powers saved that city from the siege imposed by King Chosroes of Persia.[5] A legend describes its coming to Edessa during Christ's lifetime, accounting thereby for about 500 more years, but this must be taken with great care and strictly as a legend.

Briefly, the legend states that Jesus cured the illness of his contemporary, King Abgar of Edessa, by sending him a towel with which He had wiped his face. This cloth now bore the miraculously formed portrait of Jesus. Abgar was immediately converted, and Edessa became largely a Christian city. Abgar's descendant, however, returned to paganism, and the cloth was kept safe by being sealed in a niche in the city wall above the Sacred Gate. In time it was forgotten. About 525,[6] during the reparation of the walls after a great flood, the cloth was rediscovered; its accompanying candle was still lit, and a tile placed protectively over the cloth now contained an identical miraculous image.

The entire cycle of legend and history can be found in our first document from Constantinople, the lengthy *Narratio de imagine Edessena*, written shortly after 944 under the auspices of Byzantine Emperor Constantine VII Porphyrogenitus. What interests us now is the description of the image as being extremely faint, more like a "moist secretion without pigment or the painter's art."[7]

Equally curious—and increasingly significant in light of Documents III and IV—is a second version of the origin of the Edessa cloth which comes later in this same *Narration*.

> There is another story. . . . When Christ was about to go voluntarily to death . . . sweat dripped from him like drops of blood. Then they say he took this piece of cloth which we see now from one of the disciples and wiped off the drops of sweat on it.

This version would be inexplicable unless we suppose that traces of blood were noticed on the face. Since the oldest Abgar story excludes any idea of blood, the *Narratio* offers this variation along with the original version. When combined, the elements of the two versions describe quite accurately the image on the Turin Shroud (Pl. 27a): apparent absence of artist's colors, faintness of image, traces of blood.

---

done, nuova luce su antichi documenti (Torino: Borla 1961) 213–19. English translation in Ian Wilson, *The Turin Shroud* (London: Victor Gollancz 1978) 230–35.

[5] Evagrius, *HE* 4.27 in Ernst von Dobschuetz, *Christusbilder, Untersuchungen zur christlichen Legende* (Leipzig: Hinrichs'sche 1899) 68** and 70**, introduces the image during the siege in 544, omitting its miraculous rediscovery. See too Robert Drews, *In Search of the Shroud of Turin* (Totowa, N.J.: Rowman and Allanheld 1984) ch. 5. Averil Cameron doubts the presence of any sort of image in Edessa in the 6th century since Procopius does not mention one: "The Sceptic and the Shroud," Inaugural Lecture at King's College London, 29 April 1980.

[6] Wilson (supra n.4) 117.

[7] Constantine Porphyrogenitus, *Narratio de imagine Edessena* 1 in von Dobschuetz (supra n. 5) 41**: *ἐξ ἰκμάδος ὑγρᾶς δίχα χρομάτων καὶ τέχνης τῆς γραφικῆς ἐναπεμορφώθη*. English translation in Wilson (supra n.4) 235–51.

PLATE 27

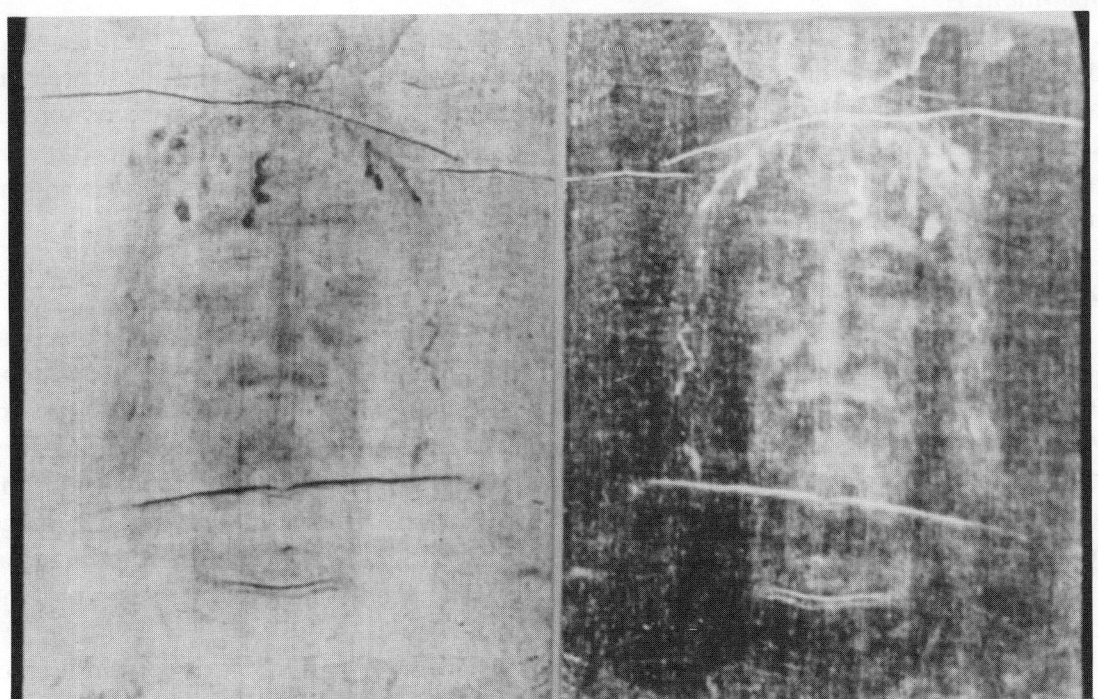

PLATE 27a. Photograph of the face on the Shroud, positive and negative.

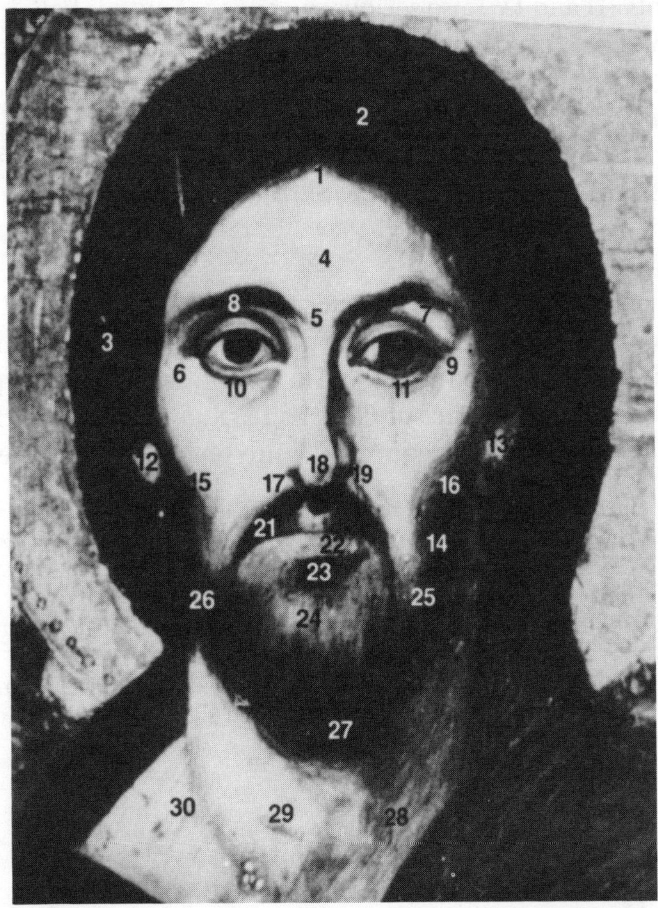

27b. A 6th-century icon of Christ from St. Catherine's Monastery, Mt. Sinai.

Document II

The above account is embellished by Symeon Magister, writing his *Chronographia* sometime in the late tenth century. He asserts that while Constantine VII could see the faint image in its details, his two brothers-in-law and rivals for the throne as sons of Romanus I Lecapenus, the reigning Emperor, could barely make out an outline. Symeon thus confirms the similarity in appearance between the Edessa image and the face of the man of the Turin Shroud.[8]

Document III

The possible identity of Shroud and Mandylion has recently received strong corroboration. In 1986 the Italian sindonologist, Zanninotto, discovered a Greek MS of a sermon delivered by one Gregory, Archdeacon of Hagia Sophia in Constantinople, on August 16, 944, the day after the arrival of the Mandylion. As an eyewitness of the events, Gregory gives the names and ranks of those who participated in the celebration. He mentions the crowning of the image with the emperor's crown and the honorary placing of the image on the imperial throne. After reciting the Abgar legend, Gregory describes the image as formed by "the perspiration of death on his face." Then comes the most arresting part: he speaks of Jesus' side wound and the blood and water found there.[9]

It was Ian Wilson's now famous view that the face seen on the Mandylion was in fact the facial portion of the Shroud, whose folded remainder was hidden by being enclosed in an elaborate frame (infra, Doc. IV; cf. Pl. 28a). The present paper subscribes to this view. But Documents III and IV raise serious questions about his belief in a late (ca. 1100) discovery of the folded Shroud behind the enframed Mandylion. He argued that that date coincides with the appearance in Byzantine iconography of a new style in the depiction of the events of Easter: the *threnos* or "Lamentation." Jesus is now shown lying upon a full-length shroud after being removed from the cross; in many versions his hands are folded just as the hands appear on the Turin Shroud (Pl. 28b).[10]

Document IV

In this connection one should note another text of Constantine VII Porphyrogenitus. It is his letter of encouragement to his troops then under arms and campaigning around Tarsus in 958. The letter announced that the Emperor was sending a supply of holy water consecrated by contact with the relics of Christ's Passion which were then in the capital. No mention is made of the recently acquired Mandylion: it would have been out of place

[8] Symeon Magister *Chron.* 52 in I. Bekker, ed., *Corpus scriptorum historiae Byzantinae* (*CSHB*) (Bonn: Weber 1838) 750: *καὶ γὰρ πρὸ ὀλίγων ἡμερῶν τουτῶν πάντων καθιστορούντων τὸν ἄχραντον χαρακτῆρα ἐν τῷ ἁγίῳ ἐκμαγείῳ τοῦ υἱοῦ τοῦ θεοῦ, ἔλεγον οἱ υἱοὶ τοῦ βασιλέως μὴ βλέπειν τι ἢ πρόσωπον μόνον, ὁ δε γαμβρὸς Κωνσταντίνος ἔλεγεν βλέπειν ὀφθλαμοὺς καὶ ὦτα.*

[9] Werner Bulst and Heinrich Pfeiffer, *Das Turiner Grabtuch und das Christusbild* (Frankfurt am Main: Knecht 1987) 134.

[10] The manner in which the Mandylion was enframed is verified by pictorial examples from the 10th to the 13th centuries. Ian Wilson, *The Mysterious Shroud* (Garden City, NY: Doubleday 1986) color plate 28; also Bulst and Pfeiffer (supra n. 9) ills. 118, 119, 121, and 122.

PLATE 28

PLATE 28a. Three copies of the Edessa Mandylion from the 11th and 12th centuries.

28b. *Epitaphios* (embroidered cloth) in Belgrade, Yugoslavia, dating from the 13th century.

among the relics of the Passion. Reference is made, however, to "the precious wood, the unstained lance, the precious inscription (*titulus*?), the reed which caused miracles, the life-giving blood from his side, the venerable tunic, the sacred linens (*spargana* here must mean burial linens), the *sindon* which God wore, and other symbols of the immaculate Passion." The precise identity of this *sindon* has been enigmatic, but acquires some clarity with Zanninotto's find.

Documents III and IV strongly suggest that the Edessa icon was unfolded in Constantinople almost immediately and not, as Wilson urges, about 1100. In fact, Kurt Weitzmann had already demonstrated that the *threnos* appeared much earlier and gradually evolved into the fully developed shroudlike representation. Wilson's thesis, however, remains cogent even if it may have to accept this small compromise. It now seems correct to suppose that while an unfolding may have occurred already in 944 which disclosed the larger folded cloth, its *recognition* as Jesus' burial wrapping was not immediate or generally broadcast. One last alternative is available: if the Shroud was folded, as Wilson illustrates, could not the chest-with-side wound section be visible on the opposite side without requiring an early unfolding/recognition? In any case the Byzantines would have been too much under the spell of the Abgar cycle to have considered the immense implications, as is evidenced by the absence of any hint of a shroud in Gregory's sermon (Doc. III).

Whatever the chronology, and indeed the truth, of an unfolding and recognition, the Mandylion/Shroud does not appear again in the sources for more than a century.[11]

Document V

A letter which bears the date 1095 falls next under our purview. It purports to be an invitation sent by the Byzantine Emperor Alexius I Comnenus (1081–1118) to his friend Robert the Frisian, Count of the Flemings (1071–1093) and to all the princes of the realm (Flanders? the Holy Roman Empire?). He announces that the Greek Empire was under constant siege throughout by Patzinaks and Turks, and he bemoans the atrocities perpetrated by these pagans. They are lately invading the area of Constantinople itself and will soon take the capital. Alexius then asserts his preference that the capital should be captured (sic) by western Christian knights rather than by the abominable Turks, more so because the city houses great treasures as well as the precious relics of the Lord. These are

[11] See A.M. Dubarle, *Histoire ancienne du linceul de Turin jusqu'au XIII siècle* (Paris: O.E.I.L. 1985) 55f. Kurt Weitzmann, "The Origins of the *Threnos*," *De artibus opuscula XL, Essays in Honor of Irwin Panofsky* (New York: New York University Press 1961) 476–90 and Wilson (supra n. 4) 133–47. Perhaps Weitzmann's research allows us to accept the possibility raised by the letter of 958 that Constantine VII Porphyrogenitus had already seen the Shroud unfolded, despite the elaborate discussion of the Edessa Mandylion in Document I above. See too Carlo Maria Mazzucchi, "La testimonianza piú antica dell'esistenza di una Sindone a Costantinopoli," *Aevum* 57 (1983) 227–31, which provides the original Greek of the salient portions of the letter of 958: *τῶν ἱερῶν σπαργάνων, καὶ τῆς θεοφόρου σινδόνος*. A date around the start of the 12th century for the recognition of the burial linens is strengthened by an oath of the year 1108, reported by Anna Comnena *Alexiad* 13.12. This oath was sworn "by the Passion of Christ . . . by his invisible cross (which) I associate with . . . the Cross of Christ, the Crown of Thorns, the Nails, the Spear . . . ." No mention, and very likely no recognition yet, of a shroud in 1108.

then named, and include "the linen cloths found in the sepulcher after his resurrection." To dismiss this letter as spurious is to miss its significance as a Byzantine document referring to the presence of Jesus' burial wrappings in Constantinople. Indeed, were it not for the enigmatic Document IV, this letter would be the first such reference. Most historians have agreed that Alexius would not have written such words, but they also concur that the *epistula* probably "depends on an authentic letter of the basileus" written with another end in mind and that it dates, variously, from 1091 to 1105.[12] It is the contemporaneity of this *epistula* and the developed *threnos* or Lamentation in art which is striking, for it signals with a twin corroboration the presence of the large burial *sindon* of Christ in the capital.

Three western sources, all variously borrowing from a discourse of Pope Stephen III in 769, but with one significant modification, provide an important clue in this connection. In the eighth century discourse in which the Pope was opposing himself to the iconoclast movement then current in the Greek church, Christ responded to Abgar's request for a cure: "Since you wish to look upon my physical face, I am sending you a likeness of my face on a cloth . . . "[13] The first of the three later variants is a sermon of the twelfth century, Wilson thinks from before 1130.[14] The second text derives from the *Ecclesiastical History* of the English monk Ordericus Vitalis, ca. 1141.[15] The third is a passage from the *otia imperialia* of Gervasius of Tilbury, dating from ca. 1211.[16] In all three texts, that which Abgar received was not just a facial image, but one which enabled the viewer to discern the form and stature of Jesus' entire body. Again, a chronological relationship seems to exist between the alteration in these western texts of image from face-only to entire body and the emergent *threnos* scenes in the East which suggests a knowledge of the Shroud of Christ. In none of these accounts, note, is the cloth recognized as a burial sindon.

[12] See the overview of interpretations in Einar Joranson, "The Problem of the Spurious Letter of Emperor Alexius to the Count of Flanders," *AHR* 55.4 (1950) 811–32 and in A.A. Vasiliev, *A History of the Byzantine Empire 324–1453* (Madison: Wisconsin 1964) II 386ff. Anna Comnena assures us in *Alexiad* 8.3–5 that her father did write to seek mercenaries from every quarter including Europe, and she singles out the Count of Flanders.

[13] See von Dobschuetz (supra n. 5) 191*: *quod si faciem meam corporaliter cenere cupis, en tibi vultus mei speciem transformatam in linteo dirigo* . . . .

[14] Wilson (supra n. 4) 135; von Dobschuetz (supra n. 5) 133**f: *si vero corporaliter faciem meam cernere desideras, heu tibi dirigo linteum, in quo non solum faciei mee figuram, sed tocius corporis mei cernere poteris statum divinitus transformatum* . . . .*Nam isdem mediator dei et hominum, ut ipsi regi in omnibus et per omnia satisfaceret, supra quoddam linteum ad instar nivis candidatum toto se corpore stravit, in quo, quod est dictu et auditu mirabile, ita divinitus transformata est illius dominice faciei figura gloriosa et tocius corporis nobilissimus status, ut qui corporaliter in carne dominum venientem minime viderunt, satis eis ad videndum sufficiat transfiguratio facta in linteo.*

[15] von Dobschuetz (supra n. 5) 224*: *Abgarus Toparcha Edessae regnavit, cui dominus Jesus sacram epistolam destinavit et pretiosum linteum, quo faciei suae sudorum extersit et in quo eiusdem salvatoris imago mirabiliter depicta refulget; quae dominici corporis speciem et quantitatem intuentibus exhibet.*

[16] *Otia imperialia* 3.23 in von Dobschuetz (supra n. 5) 131**ff: *sed quia me corpor aliter videre desideras, en tibi dirigo linteum, in quo faciei meae figura et totius corporis mei status continentur.* . . . *Traditur autem ex archivis auctoritatis antiquae, quod dominus per linteum candidissimum toto corpore se prostravit, et ita virtute divina non tantum faciei, sed etiam totius corporis dominici speciosissima effigies linteo impressa sit* . . . .

Document VI

The Edessa cloth is not mentioned again until 1150 by an English pilgrim to Constantinople. He saw what he describes as a gold container, *capsula* (*aurea*), in which "is the *mantile* which, applied to the Lord's face, retained the image of his face."[17] He also itemizes "*sudarium* which was over his head": yet another reference to Jesus' burial cloth in Constantinople, though not clearly a body shroud.[18]

Document VII

Seven years later (1157) this confusion of terms continues when Nicholas Soemundarson (Thingeyrensis), an Icelandic pilgrim, lists in his very detailed inventory of the palace relics the "*fasciae* with *sudarium* and blood of Christ." He makes no mention of the container holding the cloth of Edessa, and indeed, the reference to blood demands that we interpret these as burial cloths. Meanwhile, concerning *fasciae* as distinguished from *sudarium*, one of the terms must denote a body cloth.[19]

Documents VIII, IX, X

In 1171 Archbishop William of Tyre, who was admitted, he says, into the imperial treasury, saw the *syndon* of Christ. This is the ordinary word for a body shroud and is never used in these contexts to denote the Edessa cloth.[20]

The anonymous inventory of 1190 hardly solves the historian's perplexity by listing: a) "part of the linens in which the crucified body of Christ was wrapped"; b) *Syndon*; and c) "the towel sent to King Abgar at Edessa by the Lord, on which the Lord himself transferred his image."[21] But from this time on, both objects, Edessa cloth and burial linens, regularly appear in the same inventories.

In 1200 the inventory of Antonius of Novgorod similarly identifies both *linteum* and "*linteum* representing the face of Christ."[22]

Document XI

The plot thickens when Nicholas Mesarites, *skeuophylax* (overseer) of the treasuries in the churches of the Great Palace in Constantinople, lists the

[17] Riant, *Exuviae* (supra n. 1) II.211f: *Mantile, quod visui Domini applicatum, imaginem vultus eius retinuit . . . sudarium quod fuit super caput eius.*

[18] Now Bruno Bonnet-Eymard, "Le Soudarion Johannique negatif de la gloire divine," in Lamberto Coppini and Francesco Cavazzuti, eds., *La Sindone, scienza e fede* (Bologna: Editrice CLUEB 1983) 75–89, argues that the word *soudarion* (used by John 20:5–7) and its late Latin variant used here (supra n. 17) may derive from *soudara*, a middle eastern word of the O.T. period (Ruth 3:14), which indicated not a sweat cloth or chin-band but a large poncho of linen which was placed over the head, which covered the entire body, and came down to the feet. This striking interpretation is countered by Jean Pirot, "Soudarion mentioniére," *Sindon* 32 (Dec., 1983) 74f., who also produces texts urging the meaning, "chin-band."

[19] Riant, *Exuviae* (supra n. 1) 214: *fasciae cum sudario et sanguine Christi.*

[20] Ibid. 216.

[21] Ibid. 217: *pars linteaminum quibus crucifixum Christi corpus meruit involvere . . . syndon . . . Manutergium regi Abgaro a Domino . . . Edesse missum, in quo ab ipso Domino sua . . . transfigurata est ymago.*

[22] Ibid. 223: *linteum faciem Christi repraesentans.*

> Burial sindones of Christ: these are of linen. They are of cheap and easy to find material, still smelling of myrrh, and defying destruction since they wrapped the uncircumscribed, fragrant-with-myrrh, naked body after the Passion.[23]

Has he seen a naked man's image on one of these cloths? Can his word "uncircumscribed," "indescribable," or "mysterious," signify that this image was strangely lacking an outline? If so, this would be the first clear evidence that the burial wrappings so often cited in Constantinople, but never before with image, may indeed be the Turin Shroud. But Nicholas also specifically mentions the towel (*cheiromaktron*) with a "prototypal" image of Jesus on it made "as if by some art of drawing not wrought by hand."[24]

Document XII

A burial *sydoines* certainly bearing the figure of the Lord is described in the Church of Our Lady of Blachernae by Robert of Clari, knight of the Fourth Crusade on tour in Constantinople in 1203–04.[25] This passage has long been regarded as the *locus classicus* attesting the presence in the Eastern capital of the Shroud of Turin. Robert also saw elsewhere, in the Pharos Church, the two urns which supposedly contained the famous Edessa towel (*touaile*) and the imaged tile (*tiule*).[26] He concludes by saying that after the sack of Constantinople by the knights of the Fourth Crusade in April, 1204 this *sydoines* was no longer seen.[27]

Père A.M. Dubarle has noticed on a *threnos* scene in an illuminated psalter of Pray, Hungary dating from 1192, and thus roughly contemporary with the texts of Mesarites and Clari, a configuration of four holes on an object which may be the lid of Christ's sarcophagus, but which is strangely decorated in a pattern similar in appearance to a woven cloth. Remarkably, the same configuration of burn holes of unknown origin and date appears on the Turin Shroud. If the holes in the Pray MS and those on the Shroud are related it would be stunning visual evidence supporting a date for the Turin Shroud earlier than the fourteenth century.[28]

[23] August Heisenberg, ed., *Nikolaos Mesarites, die Palastrevolution des Johannes Komnenos* (Würzburg: Königl. Universitaetsdruckerei von H. Stuertz 1907) 30. *'Εντάφιοι σινδόνες Χριστοῦ· αὗται δ'εἰσὶν ἀπο λίνου ὕλης εὐώνου κατὰ τὸ πρόχειρον, ἔτι πνέουσαι μύρα, ὑπερτεροῦσαι φθορᾶς, ὅτι τὸν ἀπερίληπτον νεκρὸν γυμνὸν ἐσμυρνημένον μετὰ τὸ πάθος συνέστειλαν* (13.25–28). Shortly after this Mesarites again refers to *τὸ σουδάριον σὺν ταῖς ἐνταφίοις σίνδοσιν* . . . .(14.13–14).

[24] Ibid. 31: *τόν νομοδότην αὐτὸν ὡς ἐν πρωτοτύπῳ τετυπωμένον τῷ χειρομάκτρῳ καὶ τῇ εὐθρύπτῳ ἐγκεκολαμμένον κεράμῳ ὡς ἐκ ἀχειροποιήτῳ τέχνῃ τινὶ γραφικῇ* (14.33–35).

[25] Robert de Clary, *La conquête de Constantinople*, ch. 92, in Charles Hopf, *Chroniques greco-romaines inedites ou peu connues* (Paris: 1873. Repr. Brussels: Impression Anastaltique Culture et Civilisation 1966) 71: *Et entre ches autres en eut un autre des mousters que on apeloit medame Sainte Marie de Blakerne, ou li sydoines la ou nostres sires fu envelopes, i estoit, qui cascuns desvenres se drechoit tous drois, si que on i pooit bien veir le figure nostre seigneur, ne seut on onques ne Griu ne Franchois que chis sydoines devint, quant le vile fu prise*. Engl. tr. in E.H. McNeal, tr., *Robert de Clari, The Conquest of Constantinople* (New York: Columbia 1936) 112.

[26] Robert of Clari ch. 83, in Hopf (supra n. 25) 65 and McNeal (supra n. 25) 104.

[27] On the interpretation of these texts see Peter F. Dembrowski, "Sindon in the Old French Chronicle of Robert of Clari," *SSI* 2 (March 1982) 13–18: *le figure* means "entire body," not "face-only."

[28] Dubarle (supra n. 11) 55f. That the object perforated by the four-hole configuration might be the sarcophagus lid is suggested by G. Millet, *Richerches sur l'iconographie de l'Evangile aux XIV*^e^*, XV*^e^ *et*

Before going on to the next document, it may be well to recite here the hypothesis of Ian Wilson by which the imaged face cloth from Edessa is made to be identical with the imaged burial cloth, which emerges almost surreptitiously—well, at least quietly and without fanfare or ceremony—from 958 with no mention of an image, and with image in the texts of Mesarites and Clari. He argues that: a) the first descriptions of the Edessa towel, as a moist secretion very difficult to see, closely describe the appearance of the Turin Shroud; b) the manner of displaying the Edessa cloth (Pl. 28a), in a frame wider than it is tall, with a circular central opening in which the apparently disembodied or neckless face is visible, flanked by decorative panels on either side, may have been the result of folding the actual burial wrapping in half three times and sealing it in a frame to remove from view the blood and nakedness of the Lord's body; c) in this form it came to Constantinople, not to be restored in a new frame until 1150 or thereabouts (Doc. VI). As the old frame was removed, Wilson goes on, and the entire fourteen-foot burial cloth was unfolded, the Byzantines became aware that a far greater relic was present, one which derived from the actual (Biblical) burial of Jesus, and not from the Abgar story, a mere apocryphal and anachronistic aetiological legend. Indeed, the fact that the arrival in the capital of the burial wrappings, so prominent in the relic collection, was not heralded by the usual great processions and viewings, seems to support its rather unorthodox discovery as suggested by Wilson's hypothesis.[29] Finally, the continued presence of a portrait of Christ's face on a towel may (by the hypothesis) point to an artist's copy from the original shroud face simply to keep up appearances or to have something to display on the feast day. Wilson surmises that it was this copy which was kept in one of the golden urns of the Pharos Church.[30] But leaving aside all question of hypothesis, the documents firmly place a shroud of Jesus in Constantinople from ca. 958 to 1204, the year when the city was looted in the Fourth Crusade.

XVIe siècles (Paris: Fontemoing 1916) 527, where we are informed that marble plaques were placed over the Holy Sepulchre containing three (sic) little round windows through which one could see the holy stone.

[29] Wilson (supra n. 4) 92–103 and 133–47. Documents III and IV, adduced here, would require us to reassess the supposed time of Wilson's reframing along the lines of n. 11 supra.

[30] The assumption made here, that the cloth which Clari described in 1203 in the Blacherne Chapel is identical to the one Mesarites guarded in the Pharos Church in 1201, with his hints of an image, and thus also with the burial linens named in early inventories back to 1150 (and possibly to 958), is accepted by most sindonologists. But as is usual in the study of the Turin Shroud, nothing is sacred. Even the *locus classicus* has been called into question. Werner Bulst, "Christusikone-Edessabild/Turiner Grabtuch," *Hermeneia* I.2/3 (August 1985) 56f, warns that there are three candidates for the Turin Shroud in Constantinople at this time: Clari's *sydoines* in the Blacherne Chapel, the *touaille* in the urn cited by Clari and Mesarites in the Pharos Church, and the burial shroud mentioned by Mesarites, also in the Pharos Church (supra nn. 24, 25, 26, and 23). He opts for the cloth in the urn, which Mesarites had called a *cheiromaktron* with a "prototypal" image. This is an unlikely choice since Mesarites does refer to the "mysterious (or non-outlined) naked body" on the burial wrapping. Also, Bulst would leave us with a Clari credulous enough to believe that an ordinary painted *epitaphios* cloth was the actual shroud of Jesus. This must be rejected and was, by Clari himself, so to speak, for he is very clear in calling the *sydoines* Jesus' burial linen, and equally clear when referring to something painted, as in ch. 83 just after the *touaille* passage, when he describes an "image of St. Demetrius painted on a panel." See Hopf (supra n. 25) 66 and McNeal (supra n. 25) 105.

The remaining four documents bear upon the vexed question of the Shroud's departure from Constantinople. Three of them have been used by sindonologists as proof that the Shroud was still in that city as late as 1207 and possibly (Doc. XVI) still there until 1241. The present paper urges that upon examination these documents do not prove this at all, and in fact one of them (Doc. XIV) strongly suggests the Shroud's presence in Athens already by 1206. Document XV asserts that it was indeed in Athens in 1205.

Document XIII

In 1207 Mesarites, former overseer of relics, was pronouncing his eulogy (*Epitaphios*) for his deceased brother, John. We must suppose that for the last three years he had been totally excluded from any official function in the capital, and certainly from the relic treasury. Indeed, Latin clerics had replaced Greeks in every important capacity including that of Patriarch.[31] In the midst of this speech, he conjured up for the Greeks then present in Hagia Sophia a reminiscence of the greatness of their city which his brother had served so loyally, and of the atrocities of the looting by the crusaders, which he, himself had witnessed. In this speech Mesarites again refers to Constantinople as possessing the burial wrappings of Jesus, and this reference has been used as evidence that the Shroud was still present in the city in 1207.[32] The latter position breaks down when it is noticed that in fact, Mesarites' words in the *Epitaphios* are largely a direct quote from his 1201 report (Doc. XI) and are used here only for rhetorical effect.[33] A comparison of the two documents reveals:

[31] On this very important point, essential in the present argument, there is ample certainty. The eunuch Constantine Philoxenites was "minister of imperial treasuries" for the unfortunate Isaac II on his brief restoration to power in 1203 (Nic. Chon. 550). Mesarites was thus out of that post. Once the crusaders had taken the city the Greek clergy was utterly displaced in important posts. See Ernst Gerland, *Geschichte des lateinischen Kaiserreiches von Konstantinopel* (Darmstad: Wissenschaftliche Buchsgesellschaft 1966. Repr. of 1905) 10–17 and 118–54. Also Walter Norden, *Das Papstum und Byzanz* (New York: Burt Franklin 1958. Repr. of 1903). The discussion of the new Latin power structure in Constantinople in Robert Lee Wolff and Harry W. Hazard, *A History of the Crusades* (Madison: Wisconsin 1969) II 194–99 precludes any possibility of doubt. Finally, there is the evidence of Villehardouin that when the city was captured, the Bucoleon was occupied and secured by the troops of the Marquis de Montferrat while those of Henri de Flandre did the same at the palace of Blachernae. No place for Greeks in this context. M.R.B. Shaw, tr., *Joinville and Villehardouin: Chronicles of the Crusades* (New York: Penguin 1963) 92.

[32] Pietro Savio, *Ricerche storiche sulla Santa Sindone* (Torino: Società Editrice Internazionale 1957) 121. This collection of texts is a work of immense scholarship and of inestimable value to sindonology. Dorothy Crispino, "1204: Deadlock or Springboard?" *SSI* 4 (March 1982) 24–30, follows Savio.

[33] Thus, the Greek text of Mesarites' *Palastrevolution* (supra n. 23) 31–32 (Column A) should be compared to that of the *Epitaphios* in August Heisenberg, *Neue Quellen zur Geschichte des lateinischen Kaisartum und der Kirchenunion. I. Der Epitaphios des Nikolaos Mesarites auf seinem Bruder Johannes* (Munich: Bayerischen Akademie der Wissenschaften 1923) 27f. (Column B). (Italics below are by the present writer.)

Column A	*Column B*
[He lists ten relics of the Passion corresponding to the Ten Commandments and including the 'Eντάφοι	[He lists ten relics of the Passion present in Constantinople.] "Christ is known in Judea but

a) In both places Mesarites lists the relics of the Passion of Jesus, including the burial wrappings.

b) Both texts employ the symmetrical contrast of Constantinople and Judaea: the Passion occurred *there*, but the relics are *here*.

c) Both texts add, identically, "Why should I go on and on? . . . (The Lord himself) is here, as if in the original, his impression stamped in the towel and into the easily broken clay (tile) as if in some graphic art not wrought by hand."

d) He completes both texts by stating in each, but in a different order, that this place (Constantinople) is another Bethlehem, Jerusalem, Tiberias, Nazareth, Bethany, Mount Tabor, Golgotha.

Since every existing document dealing with the Latins' disposition of the relics and with the diminished role of the Greek clergy after the sack is evidence that Mesarites no longer had any knowledge of the whereabouts of the relics of which he had been the solicitous guardian in 1201, the *Epitaphios* of 1207 clearly is not a proof that the Shroud was still in Constantinople at that time, but only that Mesarites and his audience of Greek prelates thought it was.

Document XIV

In the years immediately after the Latin takeover of Constantinople in 1204, a series of discussions took place between Greek clergy and papal envoys, often presided over by the Latin Patriarch, dealing with their disagreements over dogma and how to reconcile them and bring the Greek Orthodox Church back into the Roman fold. These included the *filioque* issue, the use of leavened vs. unleavened bread in the Eucharist, and the general but ultimate question of papal primacy.[34]

σινδόνες and later *τὸ σουδάριον* and *ἐντάφιοις σινδόσιν*.] " . . . *καὶ τί δεῖ με τῷ λόγῳ μακρηνορεῖν τὰ πολλά*; The Lawgiver himself is *here* . . . *ὥς ἐν πρωτοτύπῳ τετυπομένος τῷ χειρομάκτρῳ καὶ τῇ εὐθρύπτῳ ἐγκεκολαμμένον κεράμῳ ὥς ἐν ἀχειροποιήτῳ τέχνῃ τινὶ γραφικῇ*. . . . *ναὸς οὗτος, τόπος οὗτος Σίναιον ἄλλο, Βηθλεέμ*, ᾿Ιορδάνης, ῾Ιεροσόλυμα, Ναζαρέτ, Βηθανία, Γαλιλαία, Τιβεριάς, *νιπτήρ, δεῖνος*, Θαβώριον *ὄρος*, Πιλάτου *πραιτώριον, καὶ τόπος κρανίου μεθερμηνευόμενος* ῾Εβραϊστὶ Γολγοθᾶ."

the Lord is not absent from us. His tomb is *there*, but the *ὀθόναι καὶ τὰ σουδάρια* have been brought *to us*; *κρανίου τόπος ἐκεῖ* but the cross is *here*. *καὶ τί δεῖ με τῷ λόγῳ συνείρειν πολλά*; He who is *ἀπερίγραπτος*, who appeared to us in the form of a man, *περιγραπτὸς, ὥς ἐν πρωτοτύπῳ τετυπωμένος τῷ χειρομάκτρῳ καὶ τῇ εὐθρύπτῳ ἐγκεκολαμμένος κεράμῳ ὥς ἐν ἀχειροκμήτῳ τέχνῃ τινὶ γραφικῇ. τόπος οὗτος, ὦ τέκνον*, ῾Ιεροσόλυμα, Τιβεριάς, Ναζαρέτ, Θαβώριον *ὤρος*, Βηθανία *και* Βηθλεέμ . . . "

[34] Gerland (supra n. 31) 133-37; Norden (supra n. 31) 183–87; Heisenberg (supra n. 33) 8–12.

One of the interpreters at these meetings, a man fluent in both Latin and Greek, was Nicholas of Otranto, abbot of Casole monastery in southern Italy. In 1205 he greeted the new papal legate, Benedict of St. Susanna,[35] then on his way to Constantinople via Brindisi, and accompanied him through Greece to the capital. There he served as Benedict's personal interpreter and translator. The literary legacy of this little-known scholar includes some poetry and at least three reports of the disputations in which he served as interpreter. These were written in Greek and in his own Latin translation.[36]

His reference to the Shroud of Jesus comes in the midst of his discussion in 1207 of the use of yeast in the Eucharistic meal of the Last Supper. A portion of that very bread had been present, he said, in the imperial relic collection. Among the relics of the Passion, which he now enumerated, were the *spargana*, "linens." This word normally renders infant's swaddling clothes, and the *fascia* of his Latin translation does not help in this context; however, since Nicholas is listing relics of the Passion, he must mean burial linens. Here is the crucial passage:

> When the city was captured by the French knights, entering as thieves, even in the treasury of the Great Palace where the holy objects were placed, they found among other things the precious wood, the crown of thorns, the sandals of the Savior, the nail (sic), and the burial linens (which we later saw with our own eyes) . . .[37]

This passage too has been assumed by sindonologists to prove that the Turin Shroud was still in the capital in 1207.[38] Certainly Nicholas Hydruntinus, as he is called, was more likely than Mesarites to know the contents of the relic treasury in 1207. It is possible that he may have been admitted among the relics, not because he clearly claims so, but only as

[35] This Cardinal Benedict was then Bishop of Porto and Selva Candida (also called S. Rufina), the two hamlets having been united by Pope Callixtus II (1119–1124). Porto is located on the bank of the Tiber opposite Ostia. Nicholas of Otranto (ca.1155–1235), Abbot of Casole, should be distinguished from a younger contemporary poet of the same name. The latter is customarily referred to in the MS tradition as the son of an imperial notary named Giovanni Grasso, a friend and disciple of our Nicholas. The Abbot of Casole is also known as Nectarius. See Augusta Acconcia Longo and Andre Jacob, "Poesie di Nicola d'Otranto nel Laur. Gr. 58.2," *Byzantion* 54 (1984) 371–379 and Johannes W. Hoeck and Raimond J. Loenertz, *Nikolaos-Nektarios von Otranto, Abt. von Casole. Beiträge zur Geschichte der ost-westlichen Beziehungen unter Innocenz III und Friedrich II* (Ettal: Buch-Kunstverlag 1965).

[36] Johannes Albertus Fabricius, *Bibliotheca Graeca* (Hildesheim: Olms 1967; Repr. of 1808) vol. XI. 288f. Heisenberg (supra n. 33) especially 10, n. 1, from the first treatise of Nicholas of Otranto on the procession of the Holy Spirit: *καὶ ἅ μάλιστα ἐνωτίσθημεν παρὰ τῶν ἐν Θεσσαλονίκῃ καὶ τῇ βασιλίδι τῶν πόλεων οὐ μὴν ἀλλὰ καὶ ἐν ᾿Αθήας σοφωτάτων καὶ ἱερῶν ἀνδρῶν τῶν μετὰ τοῦ κὺρ Βενεδίκτου καρδιναρίου . . . διαλεχθέντων συναγραψάμεθα . . . ἅτινα τῇ παραγγελίᾳ ἐκείνου ἐν λατινικῇ ἐξ ἑλληνίδος μετεστρέψαμεν γλώττης.*

[37] Riant, *Exuviae* (supra n. 1) II. 233f gives both the Greek and Latin versions, presumably equally by Nicholas of Otranto: *quum capta esset a Francigenis regalis civitas . . . et in scevophylachium Magni Palacii tamquam latrones intrantes, ubi sancta posita erant, scilicet: preciosa ligna, spinea corona, Salvatoris sandalia, clavus et fascia (que et nos postea oculis nostris vidimus), aliaque multa invenerunt* . . . . (Riant's parentheses). The Moscow MS published by Bishop Arsenij, Greek only, with Russian translation (Novgorod 1896), does not have the word *postea*, Greek *ὕστερον*, "later."

[38] Savio (supra n. 32) 118–20. Crispino (supra n. 32) so believes the Shroud was still in Constantinople in 1207 that she has converted Nicholas' reference into an "official" list.

an inference from Benedict's high rank among Latin prelates, as papal legate, who himself shipped a large consignment of relics to Pope Innocent III in the spring of 1205.[39] More promising, however, is the fact that Nicholas says something in another context which may be decisive in our efforts to discover the whereabouts of the Shroud after 1204: Benedict and he had in 1206 traveled in Thessalonika and Athens debating the same questions of Church unification with the Greek theologians in those places.[40] It is the reference to Athens which is significant, for it may be there that Nicholas saw the burial linens with his own eyes, which is such a peculiar part of the passage cited at length above.[41] The next document fortifies this possibility.

Document XV

In the wake of the Fourth Crusade large portions of Greece fell into the hands of or were awarded to western knights as fiefs from the Latin Byzantine Emperor Baldwin, and later Henry of Flanders. Thus Boniface of Montferrat occupied the Kingdom of Thessalonika; William of Champlitte and later Geoffrey of Villehardouin, nephew of the historian, controlled the Morea (Peloponnese) as Prince of Achaea; and Othon de La Roche became Lord of Athens, to which Thebes was later added. The territory of Epirus, however, remained a center of Greek power under Michael Angelus as Despot. Michael and his brother, Theodore, were nephews of Isaac II Angelus, one of three Byzantine Emperors who were deposed during the Fourth Crusade. The document in this instance is a letter dated 1 August 1205 from Theodore in the name of Michael to Pope Innocent III. The letter was published in 1902 but was not noticed by sindonologists; here are the pertinent passages:

> Theodore Angelus wishes long life for Innocent, Lord and Pope at old Rome, in the name of Michael, Lord of Epirus, and in his own name. In April of last year a crusading army, having falsely set out to liberate the Holy Land, instead laid waste the city of Constantine. During the sack, troops of Venice and France looted even the holy sanctuaries. The Venetians partitioned the treasures of gold, silver, and ivory while the French did the same with the relics of the saints and the most sacred of all, the linen in which our Lord Jesus Christ was wrapped after his death and before the resurrection. We know that the sacred objects are preserved by their predators in Venice, in France, and in other places, the sacred linen in Athens . . . Rome, Kalends of August, 1205.[42]

[39] The fact of this shipment alone encouraged Riant *Dépouilles* (supra n. 1) 43 and 39f, to think that Benedict might even have been a successor to Garnier de Trainel, Bishop of Troyes, and Nivelon de Cherisy, Bishop of Soissons, as officially designated overseer of the relics of the imperial treasury. The documents, however, which he cites for Garnier (37, n. 5) and for Nivelon (38, n. 2) are definitive by comparison. Many other individuals shipped consignments of relics to Europe, but it was the function of these official overseers to receive requests, mete out fragments of relics, and authenticate them.

[40] Supra, n. 36.

[41] See supra n. 37. The present interpretation takes his relative pronoun *que*/*ἅτινα* to refer only to *fascia*/*σπάργανα*.

[42] Pasquale Rinaldi, "Un documento probante sulla localizzazione in Atene della Santa Sindone dopo il sacheggio de Costantinopoli," in Coppini (supra n. 18) 109–113. (Engl. transl. by the present writer.)

If this letter is authentic, and its publication is accompanied by a very convincing authentication, then it is extremely probable that it was in Athens that Nicholas of Otranto saw this cloth. If so, instead of the previously frustrating total absence of documentation concerning the Shroud's departure from Constantinople, we now possess two documents which place it in Athens after the sack and already by 1205.[43]

To these must be related a third, though not from Constantinople. It is a long-disputed MS referring to the year 1208, which contains an account of a donation on the part of Ponce de La Roche to the Archbishop of Besançon, Amedee de Tramelai, of the Holy Shroud, which his son, Othon de La Roche, Latin Duke of Athens and one of the most prominent knights of the Fourth Crusade, had sent him. For literally centuries sindonologists have been periodically reviving what is known as the Besançon theory on the basis of this last MS (No. 826 of the Library of Besançon). They could never prove that Othon de La Roche ever possessed the Shroud. Now it would seem, this attractive thesis, that the Shroud sojourned in Besanon from ca. 1208 to 1349, must again be urged but with the new evidence of Documents XIV and XV.[44]

Document XVI

The final document in this series has been used by Shroud historians to place the Shroud in Constantinople as late as 1247.[45] Here is its background. The Latin Empire of Constantinople was destined to end in 1261 when the Greek Lascarids expelled the crusaders. But by 1238 Bulgars and Greeks were closing in on the capital, and the last Latin Byzantine Emperor, Baldwin II, was sorely in need of funds to maintain his armies. In order to raise these funds he was driven to the extremity of pawning his treasures, most notably among which was the crown of thorns, mortgaged to the bankers of Venice in 1238. In the following year this precious object was redeemed by King St. Louis IX of France and duly transferred to Paris (St. Denis).

In 1241 two other shipments of relics were sent by Baldwin to Louis as surety for another loan. A cutting from the shroud of Jesus figured among these latter relics. Finally

[43] The authenticity of this letter has been doubted primarily because it lends credence to the theory that the Shroud may have gone from Othon de La Roche in Athens to Besançon, France and resided there until 1349. In fact it does, and the present paper tends in that direction. But to condemn the letter on those grounds seems unjust; after all, the letter of Theodore says nothing at all about Besançon. Its authenticity should be judged on sounder principles. See Don Piero Coero Borga in his review of Rinaldi (supra n. 42) in *Sindon* 32 (Dec. 1983) 106.

[44] It will be useful to note that the plaint of Rev. Paul de Gail, S.J., *Histoire religieuse du linceul du Christ de Jérusalem à Turin* (Paris: Editions France-Empire 1973) 122, that since Othon never acknowledged possession of the Shroud so that it has been posthumously foisted upon him against his will, so to speak, may similarly be made regarding Geoffroy de Charny I, first reputed owner of the Lirey Shroud. It is ironically the d'Arcis *Memorandum* which first imputes the Shroud to him. But if his possession may be accepted from the evidence of secondary documents, then Othon's silence may not be held as decisive when secondary documents similarly point to his earlier possession. De Gail is enthusiastic but inaccurate when he says Geoffroy de Charny *"a expressément affirmé l'avoir reçu en cadeau."* This was a claim of his son, Geoffroy II. His grand-daughter Marguerite asserted that the Shroud came to Geoffroy I as a reward for valor in war, as de Gail well knew, 123.

[45] Ibid. 100–11. Crispino (supra n. 32) 27 follows de Gail.

our document, a Golden Bull of Baldwin II, cedes all these relics, which are enumerated, to the French King in perpetuity, in consideration for still another loan. In view of the letter of Theodore of Epirus which complained that the Shroud had been removed to Athens by 1205, it is important to examine this Bull carefully. And in fact when this is done, we learn that the Bull does *not* assert the Shroud's presence in Constantinople in 1241. Rather, it merely lists among the relics ceded to Louis "part of the *sudarium* in which Christ's body was wrapped in the tomb."[46] Far from stating that Baldwin cut a section from the Shroud still in his possession, it suggests a corroboration of what we know from numerous other sources: that portions of relics were often removed in order to be shared with other churches, and that what Baldwin had to send to Louis in 1241 was more likely a portion cut off before the Shroud was hustled away to Athens.[47] Indeed, if Baldwin was willing to part with the entire crown of thorns, from which individual thorns might be and were more easily removed, each thorn of infinite monetary value, why should we suppose he would hesitate to part with the entire Shroud, if he had had it?

The Bull of 1247 also cedes the "holy towel inserted in a frame" (*sanctam toellam tabule insertam*), and so it does seem to document the departure from Constantinople of that object to which Nicholas Mesarites and Robert of Clari referred in 1201 and 1203 as the cloth from Edessa bearing the face of Jesus, and which Wilson argues might have been a copy after 1150, once the Edessa cloth was unframed and discovered to be an impression of the entire body of Jesus.[48]

Conclusion

To sum up the points made in this paper: a linen cloth or cloths described as the burial wrappings of Jesus are attested in many documents, twice with his image if one counts Mesarites (Doc. XI), in Constantinople from 944 to 1203. Other documents in Constantinople suggest that the Edessa towel always with the image of Jesus' face may be identical with Jesus' shroud in folded form, enclosed in a frame. Before that, from 544 to 944, this towel was certainly in Edessa. The Shroud of Turin thus may have a pedigree back at least to 544, and if the Abgar legend has any historical worth, to the very time of Christ. If the pieces of this elaborate puzzle truly fit as they seem to, the Turin cloth may in fact be the tomb wrapping of Jesus.

The three documents which have been customarily adduced by Shroud savants to prove that the Shroud was in Constantinople after the crusaders' sack in 1204 are seen on examination of their contents and context not to do so. And in fact, one of them, the treatise of Nicholas of Otranto, may support the Shroud's presence in Athens with Othon de La Roche, where the letter of Theodore of Epirus places it in 1205. Pointing ahead in time, it may now be worthwhile to explore again the possibility that the Shroud was located in Besançon from ca. 1208 to 1349. The cloth of Besançon disappeared when the Church of St. Etienne which housed it was struck by lightning and burned. Six years later the securely documented career of the Turin Shroud began at Lirey.

[46] Riant, *Exuviae* (supra n. 1) II 133–35: *partem sudarii quo involutum fuit corpus eius in sepulchro.*
[47] Ibid. I 20 and II 67–227 *passim.*
[48] Wilson (supra n. 4) 133–35.

Other hypotheses of the Shroud's whereabouts 1204–1355 include Wilson's[49] that the Shroud resided with the Knights Templar from 1204 to 1314 and then with the family of its first certain owner, Geoffroy de Charny, from 1314 to 1355 when it was placed in his church at Lirey. Wilson's argument is very convincing, drawing upon depositions from the Templar heresy trial 1307–1314.

Another is that of Père de Gail, writing before Wilson's book appeared.[50] He argues that since Geoffroy is known to have campaigned in the Smyrna Crusade of 1346, he must have acquired it as a military reward somewhere in the Middle East on that occasion. Unaware of the Templar documents or of the new implications presented here, however, de Gail was unable to produce a single document supporting his otherwise plausible supposition. Nor do the records of Smyrna or Cyprus, his choices, claim the Shroud was ever in those places.

Finally, a word about the highly subjective but cleverly and elaborately contrived reconstruction of Currer-Briggs.[51] He supposes that the Shroud was removed from Constantinople by Margaret of Hungary, daughter of King Bela III and widow of Isaac II Angelus and soon after of Boniface of Montferrat, crusader who became King of Thessalonika. In July of 1204 the newlyweds, Margaret and Boniface, departed from Constantinople for their new kingdom, presumably with the Shroud. The chief evidence, which attracts even Wilson,[52] is her rededication of a church in Thessalonika in honor of the image not made by hands (*Acheiropoietos*) and her third marriage to Nicholas de St-Omer, who was related to Geoffroy de St-Omer, one of the founders of the order of the Knights Templar. Other than this, no document ascribes the Shroud to her keeping, nor did she ever claim to have had it. But it is true also that neither did Geoffroy I de Charny nor Othon De La Roche ever claim to have possessed the Shroud (supra n. 44).

[49] Wilson, ibid., 152–65, is energetically, if not conclusively, rebutted by Malcolm Barber, "The Templars and the Turin Shroud," *SSI* 6 (Mar. 1983) 16–34.

[50] De Gail (supra n. 44) 131–41.

[51] Noel Currer-Briggs, *The Holy Grail and the Shroud of Christ* (Maulden, G.B.: ARA Publications 1984) 71–82.

[52] Forward to ibid., vi f. However, the present writer has discovered that the epithet *acheiropoietos* was applied only to churches devoted to Mary Theotokos (Mother of God), particularly to this church in Thessalonika and to her church in the monastery of the Abramites in Constantinople. There are no churches to Christ under this epithet. Jean Ebersolt, *Monuments d'architecture byzantine* (Paris: Les Editions d'Art et d'Histoire 1934) 15f. and R. Janin, *Les églises et les monastères* (Paris: Centre National de la Recherche Scientifique 1953) 9f.

ON THE CLASSICAL ATHENIAN WEDDING: TWO RED-FIGURE LOUTROPHOROI IN BOSTON

ROBERT F. SUTTON, JR.

Athenian wedding practices of the Classical period are still imperfectly understood, despite rich evidence and scholarly attention.[1] Although a great many nuptial customs are attested in contemporary literature, with fuller detail provided in later scholia and lexical works, no adequate comprehensive account of the wedding survives from antiquity.[2] While this evidence is generally reliable, its value is limited by its piecemeal and lexical nature and especially by the absence of a context through which the full significance of individual details can become clear. Illustrations of weddings in contemporary art therefore represent a welcome additional source long recognized but rarely studied systematically.[3] During the Archaic and Classical periods such artistic representations are found

[1] Comprehensive modern discussions: R. Hague, "Marriage Athenian Style," *Archaeology* 41.3 (May/June 1988) 32–36, 64; R. Seaford, "The Tragic Wedding," *JHS* 107 (1987) 106–30; H.P. Foley, *Ritual Irony. Poetry and Sacrifice in Euripides* (Ithaca: Cornell 1985) 65–105; I. Jenkins, "Is There Life after Marriage: A Study of the Abduction Motif in Vase Paintings of the Athenian Wedding Ceremony," *BICS* 30 (1983) 137–45; J. Redfield, "Notes on the Greek Wedding," *Arethusa* 15 (1982) 181–201; J.-P. Vernant, "Le mariage en Grèce archaïque," *PP* 28 (1973) 51–74, reprinted in *Mythe et société en Grèce ancienne* (Paris: Maspero 1974) 57–81, trans. J. Lloyd as *Myth and Society in Ancient Greece* (Sussex, N.J.: Harvester 1980); V. Magnien, "Le mariage chez les grecs anciens. L'initiation nuptiale" *AntCl* 5 (1936), 115-138; W. Erdmann, *Die Ehe im alten Griechenland. Beiträge zur Papyrusforschung und Antikenrechtsgeschichte* 20 (Munich: Beck 1934); E. Pernice, "Griechisches und römisches Privatleben," in A. Gercke and E. Norden, *Einleitung in die Altertumswissenschaft*, 4th ed. (Leipzig: Teubner 1932) 1–87; Heckenbach, "Hochzeit," *RE* XVI (1913) 2129–33; E. Samter, *Geburt, Hochzeit, und Tod* (Leipzig: Teubner 1911); idem, *Familienfeste der Griechen und Römer* (Berlin: Reimer 1901); M. Collignon, "Cérémonies du mariage," DarSag III.2 (1904) 1647–54; P. Stichotti, "Zur griechischen Hochzeitsgebräuchen" in *Festschrift für Otto Bendorff*, ed. K. Masner (Vienna: Hölder 1898) 181–88; W.A. Becker, *Charicles*, revised by H. Göll (Berlin: Calvary 1878) vol. 3; idem, *Charicles*, ed. 4, trans. F. Metcalf (London: Longmans Green 1874).

For vases attributed by Beazley in *ABV* and *ARV*², consult also *Paralipomena* and *Beazley Addenda*. This paper derives from my dissertation (North Carolina) *The Interaction between Men and Women Portrayed on Attic Red-figure Pottery* (Ann Arbor: University Microfilms 1981) currently under revision. Subsequent research was made possible by a Fellowship from the American Council of Learned Societies in 1984 with additional support from Loyola University of Chicago. I am indebted to John H. Oakley for generously sharing his knowledge and opinions with characteristic good humor; I am grateful to him, H.A. Shapiro, J.G. Keenan and S.B. Sutton for criticizing earlier drafts, to J. Bremmer, J. Vaio, and H. Schibli for discussing particular details, and K. DeVries for comments on the article in galley proof. C. Patterson's manuscript, "Athenian Marriage," with good discussion, arrived too late to be considered.

[2] The most extensive treatment is that of Pollux (*Onomastikon* 34–48), known only in later epitomes; like most of the secondary ancient sources, this is concerned mostly with terminology. As this paper demonstrates, the Atticist tradition represented by scholia and lexica has greater authority for Classical Athenian practice than do non-Attic, Hellenistic, and Roman literature. The unfortunate tendency to fuse traditions of different periods and places is most obvious in the work of Magnien (supra n. 1).

[3] For comprehensive discussion of Attic nuptial scenes see the dissertations: Sutton (supra n. 1) 145–275 (only scenes with bride and groom together); E. Götte, *Frauengemachbilder in der Vasenmalerei des 5.*

primarily on Attic vases whose discovery, licit and illicit, continues steadily. The abundant evidence of these vase paintings, although as piecemeal and problematic as the literary evidence, confirms the accuracy of literary notices, occasionally portrays practices not mentioned in surviving texts, and provides welcome chronological and geographical control for the practice of various customs and attitudes. Furthermore, these vase representations, which were meant to be viewed in the Attic nuptial context they portray (to judge from their overwhelmingly Attic provenience and appearance on special nuptial vase shapes), can be accepted without reservation as valid expressions of accepted popular attitudes towards marriage uncolored by the demands of a particular dramatic, judicial, or philosophical context.[4] Better understanding of the wedding can be anticipated with the forthcoming publication of thousands of vase fragments found in the late 1950's at the shrine of Nymphe, site of a great nuptial cult in Athens.[5] Even as we await the appearance of this new material, however, much can be gained through the detailed study of imperfectly published vases and the synthesis of accessible material in a modern interpretive framework. This paper presents in detail two red-figure vases in the Boston Museum of Fine Arts that illustrate the value of such representations for understanding the Classical Athenian wedding and its social significance.

Weddings belong to a class of rituals which attend major transitions in life described by A. van Gennep eight decades ago in his classic *Rites of Passage*.[6] Such rites have a

---

Jahrhunderts (diss. Munich, publ. Aachen 1957) 33–71; E. Zevi, "Scene di gineceo e di idillio nei vasi greci della seconda metà del secolo quinto" *MemLinc* 6 (1937) 291–369 at 351–69. C. Bérard, "L'ordre des femmes," in *La cité des images: religion et société en grèce antique* (Lausanne & Paris: Fernand Nathan 1984) 85–103 at 94–99 is schematic. For related later material from Sicily see P. Deussen, "The Nuptial Theme of Centuripe Ware," *OpRom* 9 = *Skrifter Svenska Institutet i Rom* (4°) 33 (*Studies Sjöquist*; 1973) 125–33 and U. Wintermeyer, "Die Polychrome Reliefkeramik aus Centuripe," *JdI* 90 (1975) 136–241, espec. 170ff. Two articles by C. Sourvinou-Inwood discuss wedding iconography in relation to abduction and pursuit: "The Young Abductor of the Locrian Pinakes," *BICS* 20 (1973) 12–21 and "A Series of Erotic Pursuits: Images and Meanings," *JHS* 107 (1987) 131–53, the latter with references to forthcoming studies not available to me.

[4] Customs not otherwise attested: the tossing of shoes at the wedding procession on the name vase of the Painter of the Athens Wedding, Athens NM 1388, *ARV*² 1317.1, P. Perdrizet, «Ἀττικὸν ἀγγεῖον μετὰ παραστάσεως πόμπης γάμου», *ArchEph* 1905, 209–14; and the groom lifting the bride into the wedding carriage on the red-figure loutrophoros Berlin F2372 (now in the East, according to Oakley), A. Furtwängler, *Collection Sabouroff*, pl. 58–59; DarSag I.2, p. 1528, fig. 1992 and III.2, p. 1652, fig. 4866; G. von Lucken, *Griechische Vasenbilder* (Berlin: Staatliche Bildstelle 1921) pl. 20; for the interpretation, Stichotti (supra n. 1) 183, and somewhat differently Sutton (supra n. 1) 175–77, W.14, pl. 10; Sourvinou-Inwood (supra n. 3, 1973); Jenkins (supra n. 1) passim, fig. 1. Classical red-figure scenes showing bride and groom are overwhelmingly Attic in provenience and occur largely on loutrophoroi (Sutton [supra n. 1] 214–15, 235–36); in the Archaic period black-figure scenes follow a different pattern (T.B.L. Webster, *Potter and Painter in Classical Athens* [London: Methuen 1972] 105–108), though the discoveries from the shrine of Nymphe (see infra) will surely alter the picture.

[5] R.E. Wycherley, *The Stones of Athens* (Princeton: University Press 1978), 197–200; Travlos 361–63. Beazley's 150+ attributions "do not even skim the material," *ARV*² viii, 1747f. The black-figure material is being studied by Charikleia Kanellopoulou-Papadopoulou, the red-figure by Maria Tsoni-Kyrkou.

[6] A. van Gennep, *The Rites of Passage*, trans. M. Vizedom and G. Caffee (Chicago: University Press 1960, after French ed. of 1908), esp. 10–12, 106, 116f.; more recently, V. Turner, *The Ritual Process: Structure and Antistructure* (Ithaca: Cornell 1977) 94ff., 166–72, and passim. See Jenkins (supra n. 1).

tripartite structure which effects first the participants' separation from their original ("preliminal") status, then the actual transition to a new status (the "liminal" process), and finally their incorporation into a new ("postliminal") state of existence. This basic ritual structure is embellished with a variety of practices appropriate to the specific occasion; for weddings these regularly include rites for fertility, expiation, and purification, as well as those invoking divine blessing. Most illustrations of weddings on Attic vases either portray events connected with the bridal bath and toilet, a thematic bias probably reflecting ritual use of the vases they decorate,[7] or show the act of transition itself through a procession. As van Gennep noted, weddings tend to emphasize the act of transition since the change of status from single to married involves an actual physical relocation of at least one member of the couple to a new house. In Archaic Attic wedding scenes the couple generally journey from the bride's natal home to their new house in a chariot, a heroic vehicle that elevates the scene, transcending normal experience. During the Classical period, however, they more often travel on foot, and the setting may move within the new house as the bridegroom leads his new wife to the bedroom (*thalamos*) for the consummation of the wedding (the *gamos* proper). These changes are typically Classical, for they result in a more profound representation that expresses the inner mental, emotional, and spiritual processes that underlie and sustain the action.[8]

Although both vases under consideration entered the Museum of Fine Arts during the first decade of this century, neither was illustrated until recently, and neither has yet received satisfactory discussion. Both are loutrophoroi, impractically elongated versions of the hydria and amphora, the two shapes regularly used to transport and hold water.[9] These were special vessels produced for use in two Athenian family rituals where purification by bathing played an important role, namely weddings and funerals. Examples known to date are illustrated with scenes pertinent only to one or the other of these rituals, although vessels with nuptial scenes were frequently deposited in and at graves. The first of our loutrophoroi is decorated with one of the finest examples of the bridal couple's procession to the *thalamos*, and with another scene that is possibly a unique

[7] Götte and Zevi (supra n. 3); on loutrophoroi, infra n. 9; for lebetes gamikoi F. Harl-Schaller, "Zur Entstehung und Bedeutung des attischen Lebes gamikos," *ÖJhBeibl* 50 (1972–1975), 151–70 and M.B. Moore and M.Z.P. Philippides, *Attic Black-figured Pottery*, *Agora* XXIII (Princeton: American School of Classical Studies 1986) 27–29; Richter and Milne (infra n. 9) 11, xxi. On present evidence the two shapes are remarkably divergent in their illustration of nuptial themes: lebetes generally show the bride among other women, loutrophoroi the bride and groom together.

[8] Sutton (supra n. 1) 160–97; on chariots, I. Krauskopf, "Eine attische schwarzfigurige Hydria in Heidelberg," *AA* 1977, 13–37, P.J. Connor, "A Marriage Procession," *AA* 1979, 158–61, and R. Hague, "The Chariot and Procession Scenes in Greek Art and Literature," abstract *AJA* 90 (1986) 180f. On the symbolism see Jenkins (supra n. 1) and Sourvinou-Inwood (supra n. 3). The motif of the bride awaiting the groom in the thalamos (Magnien, supra n. 1, 119f.) seems to be post-Classical or non-Attic.

[9] Pollux 3.43; Hesychios and Harpokration svv. *λουτροφόρα ἄγγη* and *λουτροφόροι*. First identified by A. Milchholfer, "Gemälte Grabstelen," *AM* 5 (1880) 164–94 at 174–79; G.M.A. Richter and M. Milne, *Shapes and Names of Athenian Vases* (New York: Metropolitan Museum 1935) 5–6, xxii; R. Ginouvès, *Balaneutikè: recherche sur le bain dans l'antiquité grecque*, *BEFAR* 200 (1962) 268–76; Moore and Philippides (supra n. 7) 18–20.

representation of the *engye* (ἐγγύη), the agreement between the groom and the bride's *kyrios* that made the marriage legal. The other vase has a unique illustration of the *katachysmata*, a ritual of incorporation performed when the couple first entered their new home. Both vessels date approximately to the 420's B.C., the decade that followed the outbreak of the Peloponnesian War. Their illustrations are important both for confirming the accuracy of the lexica and scholia, and even more for their eloquent and undeniable expression of new, romantic attitudes towards marriage that emerged under the Radical Democracy, attitudes whose appearance in contemporary literature has been debated.

I

We start with an amphora version of the loutrophoros, illustrated with the aid of an unpublished slide by Father Schoder and an unpublished drawing known from a photograph in the Beazley Archive in Oxford (Pls. 29–33, Fig. 1).[10] Though reconstructed from many fragments, the vase is virtually complete. Under the A-B handle (Pl. 29b) it has sustained damage, and only ghosts of the black glaze remain in a crucial section of the scene. These details and others executed in added colors which are barely visible today are fortunately recorded in the old drawing (Pls. 31–32).[11] The slender shape (Fig. 1), with elongated neck, body and handles capped at the ends by spreading foot and flaring mouth, is typical of large loutrophoroi of the second half of the fifth century.[12] Although Beazley knew the piece, he did not identify any other vase painted by the same hand, and I can do no better. Its drapery is typical of the early Rich Style which emerged shortly before ca. 425 B.C., to judge by the appearance of its initial phase on a few vases from graves relocated during the purification of Delos (Thuc. 3.104),[13] though it is not as

[10] Boston Museum of Fine Arts 03.802, Francis Bartlett Donation; height as restored, 0.753 m. Illustrated in Sutton (supra n. 1) pls. 13, 14; E. Keuls, *The Reign of the Phallus: Sexual Politics in Ancient Athens* (New York: Harper & Row 1985) 118, fig. 102; Hague (supra n. 1) 32 (color); profile L.D. Caskey, *Geometry of Greek Vases* (Boston: Museum of Fine Arts 1922) 81, whence Fig. 1. Mentioned in Boston, Museum of Fine Arts, *Annual Report*, 1903, 71 no. 62; U. Wintermeyer, (supra n. 3) 171, n. 141; A Hermary, H. Cassimatis, and R. Vollkommer, "Eros," *LIMC* III (1986) 850–942 at 905 no. 639e. I examined the vase through glass in 1978. For further information I am indebted to Florence Wolsky, Assistant in the Museum's Department of Classical Art, who kindly compared vase and drawing, and to John Oakley who examined the vase out of the case without benefit of the drawing. I am grateful to the Beazley Archive and Donna Kurtz for hospitality in 1984 and for a copy of their photograph.

[11] The drawing, signed with a monogram composed of the letters FHG and the date 1/02, was evidently made before the vase entered the museum. To adapt the composition to a flat surface there has been some rearrangement of feet (in particular those of the *nympheutria* which on the vase overlap the bride's) and other minor changes; the drawing indicates the extent of restoration. Other omissions and errors in the drawing are noted infra.

[12] After Caskey (supra n. 10). Comparison with photographs indicates that the artist slimmed the lower body slightly. Cf. a contemporary loutrophoros in the British Museum 1923.1-18.1, by the Painter of London 1923; *ARV*², 1103.1, described Sutton (supra n. 1) 247, W.37. The slightly earlier loutrophoros in E. Berlin (supra n. 4) is related, as noted in *Annual Report* (supra n. 10).

[13] C. Dugas, *Les vases attiques à figures rouges. Délos* XXI (1952); for recent discussion, A. Lezzi-Hafter, *Der Schuwalow-Maler* (Mainz: von Zabern 1976) 4.

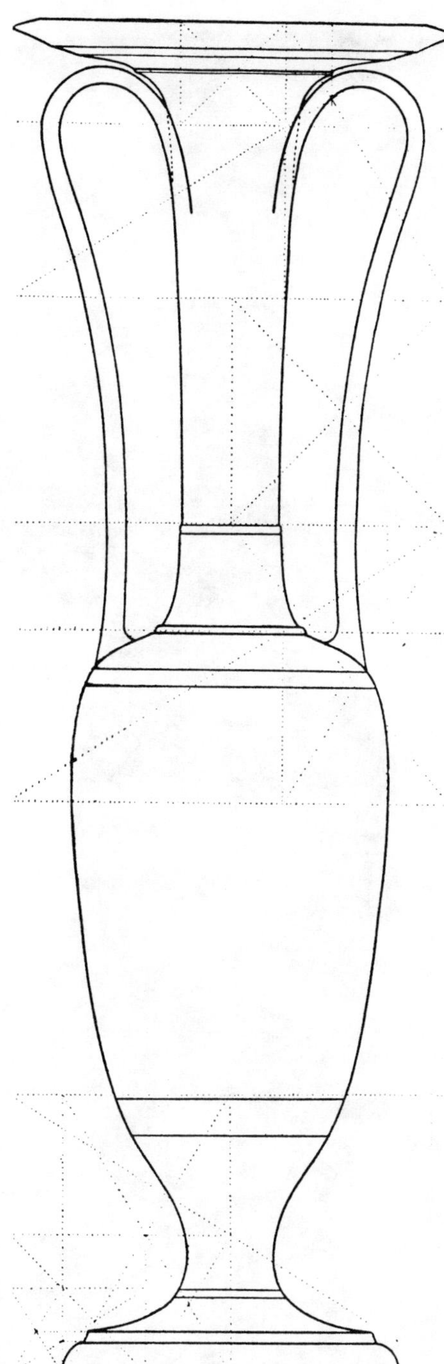

Fig. 1. Profile drawing of Boston 03.802. After Caskey (supra n. 10) 81.

florid as the developed style of the Meidias and Dinos Painters. Particularly noteworthy is the absence of modeling lines similar to those in sculpture which impart volume by curving across rather than running along rounded anatomical forms, a stylistic device encountered in the works of the Meidias Painter but not of the Eretria Painter, an older master whose later works are contemporary with the early Meidias Painter.[14] For our loutrophoros, therefore, a date ca. 425–420 B.C. is indicated.

The major decorative field is a continuous zone that runs around the body of the vase below the attachment of the handles. While the handles on a loutrophoros amphora often define the division of two separate fields below, here the major scene of the front has been expanded far beyond these natural borders, leaving room for only two figures in the separate composition on the back (Pl. 30a). We start with the major scene which represents the climax of the wedding as bride and groom, attended by various women and personifications of Love, are about to enter the bridal chamber for the consummation of the wedding. On the far left (Pls. 30b, 31), at the tail of the procession, a woman stands right holding a fan in her left hand and in her right a plemochoe, a toilet vessel used to hold perfumed liquids.[15] At her feet stands a goose, a common

[14] Rhys Carpenter, *Greek Sculpture* (Chicago: University Press 1960) 124ff. Cf. e.g. the name piece of the Eretria Painter (*ARV*² 1247–1257), P. Arias and M. Hirmer, trans. and revised by B. Shefton, *A History of 1000 Years of Greek Vase Painting* (New York: Abrams 1961) pl. 203 and the name piece of the Meidias Painter (*ARV*² 1312–1332) Arias and Hirmer pls. 214f., and his Phaon hydria, ibid. pls. 216, XLVI.

[15] Also called kothon and exaleiptron by archaeologists, the latter perhaps the ancient name; the use is clear in any case. Moore and Philippides, (supra n. 7) 49; Sutton (supra n. 1) 334; B. Sparkes and L. Talcott,

a. Side A; courtesy Museum, negative no. BC 9714.

b. Side A-B; courtesy Museum, negative BC 9711

PLATE 29. Red-figure loutrophoros, Boston, Museum of Fine Arts 03.802, Francis Bartlett Donation.

domestic animal often shown on red-figure vases with women, children, and also Aphrodite.[16] The next woman to the right, standing under the handle, corresponds to the door under the other handle and seems to serve a similar, almost architectural purpose as she turns back to her companion. In her lowered hand she carries a small rectangular wooden chest shown almost successfully foreshortened in three-quarters view; she apparently holds it by the cords that sealed the lid. Such chests held a variety of household objects, including fillets and cosmetics, and often appear in scenes showing the dressing of the bride.[17] The round-bottomed object she holds up by her left shoulder, despite resembling a wicker basket, is probably a metal phiale, a shallow bowl used for drinking and pouring libations, an item with considerable use in a wedding.[18] Wreaths with pointed leaves (myrtle, olive, bay, or the like) hang on the wall framing her head on either side. The drawing records the word ΚΑΛΗ in Ionic letters running down from the right of her head, though this inscription is not easily seen on the vase today.[19]

On the front of the vase (Pls. 29a, 31–33) a closed group of four full-sized figures is accompanied by two miniature Erotes. These six figures constitute the fully elaborated core group of the most popular type of wedding scene found on red-figure vases, a group that is set in a variety of locales, indoors and out. Each of the main figures represents a generally recognized role in the wedding. Bride and groom stand in the center, framed between two women who turn towards them. The woman on the left, dressed in an ungirt peplos and wearing on her head a diadem of vertical leaves and a pendant earring, raises her hands to adjust the bride's veil and himation.[20] We recognize her as the *nympheutria*, a generic term defined by Hesychios simply as a bridal attendant chosen by the bride's parents, perhaps even the *nymphokomos*, a *nympheutria* charged specifically with adorning the bride.[21] She is balanced on the right by a woman bearing torches who stands

---

Black and Plain Pottery of the Sixth, Fifth, and Fourth Centuries B.C., *Agora* XII (Princeton: American School of Classical Studies 1970) 180f; Richter and Milne (supra n. 9) 21–23, xxiif.

[16] Cf. the boys with goose (not swan) on the chous Athens NM 1224, H. Rüfel, *Kinderleben in Klassischen Athens* (Mainz: von Zabern 1984) 133. Aphrodite, identified by inscription, rides a goose on the Pistoxenos Painter's white ground cup in the British Museum D 2, *ARV*² 862.22, M. Robertson, *Greek Painting* (New York: Rizzoli 1979) 113.

[17] G.M.A. Richter, *Furniture of the Greeks, Etruscans, and Romans*, 2nd ed. (New York: Phaidon 1966) 72–76; Sutton (supra n. 1) 335f.

[18] Moore and Philippides (supra n. 7) 56f; Sparkes and Talcott (supra n. 15) 105f; H. Gericke, *Gefässdarstellungen auf griechische Vasen* (Berlin: Hessling 1970) 27–31; Richter and Milne (supra n. 9) 29, xxii; Sutton (supra n. 1) 339–41. Cf. the wedding scene on the monumental pyxis by the Penthesilea Painter from the Acropolis, Athens, National Museum Acr. 569, *ARV*² 890.172, E. Langlotz et al., *Die antiken Vasen von der Akropolis zu Athen* II (Berlin: de Gruyter 1933) pl. 43, and Sutton (supra n.) W.64 (pl.15), 201–203.

[19] Ms. Wolsky (personal communication, supra n. 10) thought she might see the K and A, but was not certain. Possibly the letters have faded since the drawing was made.

[20] Oakley reports that what appears in the drawing as a fillet is actually the eighth-inch strip of glaze with which the painter outlined the figure before painting in the background.

[21] Pollux , *On.* (ed. E. Bethe, 1900) 3.41: *ἡ δὲ διοικουμένη τὰ περὶ τῶν γάμων γύνη, νυμφεύτρια. ἡ αὐτὴ δὲ καὶ θαλαμεύτρια.* Hesychios (ed. K. Latte, 1966) s.vv.: *νυμφεύτρια· ἡ συμπεμπομένη ἀπὸ τῶν γονέων τῇ νύμφῃ παράνυμφος* (repeated verbatim s.v. by Photios [ed. S. A. Naber, 1864]). *νυμφοκόμος· ἡ νυμφεύτρια*

PLATE 30. Boston 03.802 (pl. 29). **a.** Side B; courtesy Museum of Fine Arts, Boston, negative BC 9713. **b.** Side B-A; courtesy Museum, negative BC 9712.

by the partly open door of the *thalamos*. This woman is elaborately dressed in himation over chiton and fancy diadem; a crack through her ear makes it uncertain if she originally lacked an earring. Such female torchbearers are the most common attendants at weddings on red-figure vases.[22] The figure here is probably to be identified as the groom's mother. In literature it is a recognized privilege of the two mothers of the wedding couple to carry torches in the wedding: the bride's mother to light the couple's procession to their new home, and the groom's mother to conduct them to the *thalamos*.[23]

Between these female representatives of the two families, the groom leads his bride towards the *thalamos* in an old compositional type dating back to the Geometric period. During the Classical period this type becomes a regular feature of nuptial scenes and is adapted with minor variation to portray different events of the wedding set in several locales.[24] The groom strides right, looking back towards his bride as he leads her forward, grasping her left hand in his right. He wears a fancy himation sprinkled with dots, and a nuptial wreath of pointed leaves, probably of myrtle, though olive and other species cannot be excluded. Above his head the drawing shows the letters ?]ΑΛΣΟ in Ionic script. This was presumably originally the meaningless K]ΑΛΣΟ which occurs on other vases of the period and probably represents a scrambling of the common ΚΑΛΟΣ ("handsome"); if so, it is not a proper kalos inscription, irrelevant praise of a named individual, but rather an appropriate comment that enhances the scene.[25] The bride seems to have been similarly praised by inscription, for in Father Schoder's photograph (Pl. 33) one can see above her head a painted A or Ionic Λ (for ΚΑΛΟΣ or ΚΑΛΗ) between irregular white patches that represent crackling of the glaze. The bride, wearing chiton and himation, reaches out to her husband and meets his gaze with slightly downturned head. In her hair she wears a wreath or crown of delicate vertical leaves, perhaps a metal diadem. The back of her head and shoulders is covered by a short veil decorated with stars, the

ἡ κοσμοῦσα τὴν νύμφην. Cf. also *νυμφοπόνος· ἡ περὶ τὴν νύμφην πονουμένη*. See further Magnien (supra n. 1) 120–23. This figure was described as the *nympheutria* already in *Annual Report* (supra n. 10); see Sutton (supra n.1) 158, 193-194 and Oakley (infra n. 62) 116.

[22] Sutton (supra n. 1) 191–93.

[23] E. Samter, *Geburt* (supra n. 1) 72, citing Eur. *Medea* 1028 and a scholion to Apollon. *Argon*. 4.808. For the bride's mother: Eur. *Iph. Aul*. 732–35 and scholion to id., *Troad*. 315. For the groom's mother: Erdmann (supra n. 1) 258 citing a scholion to Eur. *Phoen*. 344.

[24] Sutton (supra n. 1) 177–96; infra n. 36.

[25] Cf. *καλος* written over the heads of both bride and groom and a third spinning woman (possibly the bride repeated at a different moment) on the roughly contemporary hydria by the Orpheus Painter, New York M.M.A. 17.230.15, *ARV*² 1104.16, G.M.A. Richter and L. Hall, *Red-figured Athenian Vases in the Metropolitan Museum of Art*, New York (New Haven: Yale 1936) no. 138, pls. 140–41. *καλος* and *καλε* are applied to a woman and man who are possibly, though not at all certainly, a nuptial couple on earlier Nolan amphora by the Providence Painter in Harvard's Fogg Museum 1972.45, *ARV*² 638.43, *The Frederick M. Walters Collection* (Cambridge, Mass.: Garland 1973) 64f. For *καλος* used of a woman see Munich 2345, *ARV*² 496.2, Arias and Hirmer (supra n. 14) pl. 158. It is perhaps easier to believe that when applied to a woman the simple exclamatory *καλος* stands for the neut. noun *κάλλος* ("a beauty,", LSJ s.v. 2) than *καλός* treated as an adj. of two endings, though the formulaic nature of kalos inscriptions may be to blame, as DeVries reminds me. On kalos inscriptions see D.M. Robinson and E.J. Fluck, *A Study of the Greek Love-Names* (Baltimore: Johns Hopkins 1937), *ABV* and *ARV*², K.J. Dover, *Greek Homosexuality* (Cambridge, Mass.: Harvard) 111–24, and H.A. Shapiro, "Kalos Inscriptions with Patronymic," *ZPE* 68 (1987) 107–18.

PLATE 31

PLATE 31. Drawing of Boston 03.802 (pl. 29), side A (left); courtesy The Beazley Archive, Ashmolean Museum, Oxford.

PLATE 32. Drawing of Boston 03.802 (pl. 29), side A (right); courtesy The Beazley Archive, Ashmolean Museum, Oxford.

PLATE 33. Boston 03.802 (pl. 29), side A, detail; after color slide by Father Schoder, courtesy Loyola University of Chicago.

kredemnon or *kalyptra*.[26] This receives final adjustment from the *nympheutria* as two miniature Erotes, personifications of Love, bestow further adornment upon her head. These gifts, painted in added color that has escaped artist and camera lens, are, as Oakley indicates, a necklace held by the Eros on left, and a wreath by his fellow. These are usual gifts from Erotes in such scenes and reflect the general attention accorded the bride's coiffure in the literary sources.[27]

The *thalamos* door to which the couple move is shown in detail, though the handling of perspective is not entirely successful. The doorway is set back and raised above the ground on which the figures walk by two steps or, more likely, a deep step and a high threshold; the low lintel is crowned by a cornice in three degrees. The slight taper of the doorjambs cannot be ascribed entirely to the demands of the pictoral field, since the vase swells in the middle, and it is likely that the artist intended to represent a trapezoidal doorway.[28] The leaves of the door are constructed of three panels framed by studded rails and thin stiles. The artist slanted the rails on the open leaf to show its recession into space but mistakenly slanted several rails of the closed leaf as well. The round object on the closed leaf is probably a keyhole; the hook-like form on the open leaf is perhaps a latch or handle, or even a hook.[29] Neither item is the pestle that Pollux (3.37) says was fastened to the *thalamos* door during a wedding. Through the doorway we see a round, lathe-turned leg of the bed, part of its horizontal frame, the chevron pattern of the bedclothes, and part of a scabbard hanging on the wall above. The representation of the marriage bed is relatively rare on vases, and none shows the elaborate decoration or canopy mentioned in the literary evidence.[30] The most arresting detail of the scene is the figure of Eros who has

[26] Magnien (supra n. 1) 122; Redfield (supra n. 1) 195f; A. Krug, *Binden in der griechischen Kunst* (diss. Gutenberg, Mainz: Hösel 1967) 134, Type 7; Sutton (supra n. 1) 319; C.M. Edwards, "Aphrodite on a Ladder," *Hesperia* 53 (1984) 59–72 at 61f.; D. Armstrong and E.A. Ratchford, "Iphigeneia's Veil: Aeschylus; *Agamemnon* 228–48," *BICS* 32 (1985) 1–12; Seaford (supra n. 1) 124f.

[27] Sutton (supra n. 1) 187. The wreath is most common, reflecting its acknowledged role in the wedding: see M. Blech, *Studien zum Kranz bei den Griechen* (Berlin: de Gruyter 1982) 75–81. The necklace, common in toilette scenes, is offered on the loutrophoros Berlin F 2373 (*ARV*² 1322.20, Manner of the Meidias Painter; Sutton [supra n. 1] W.51, pl. 12) and may represent some sort of diadem in this context. On the literary theme see Magnien (supra n. 1) 121–23.

[28] Though vases more often represent rectangular doors in homes, trapezoidal doors are regular for temples, tombs, and other impressive structures; cf. Vitruvius 4.6, 6.6. On doors generally, C.B. Gulick, *The Life of the Ancient Greeks* (New York: Appleton 1903) 22, 26 and recent discoveries in Macedonian tombs, M. Andronicos, *Vergina. The Royal Tombs* (Athens: Ekdotike Athenon 1984) 3f., 36, 76, 101, 198f.

[29] The photographs suggest that the drawing is not reliable here: both leaves appear to be washed with dilute glaze to indicate wood, and the upper curve of the keyhole seems to survive above the crack.

[30] Magnien (supra n. 1) 115f.; Wintermeyer (supra n. 3) 170 n. 134; Keuls (supra n. 10) 118–21; Collignon (supra n. 1) fig. 4869; add: the black-figure tripod pyxis Warsaw 142319 MN, *CVA* Goluchow, Czartoryski (Poland 1) pl. 16.1; black-figure hydria Leningrad 2067 (B235), *ABV* 364.59 (Leagros Group), K.S. Gorbunova, *Chernofigurn'ye atticheskie vazy v Ermitazhe. Katalog* (Leningrad: I Skusstvo 1983) no. 84, pl. 117; red-figure hydria recently on the London Market (Spink) dating ca. 430–420 B.C., kindly brought to my attention by D. von Bothmer: a groom standing frontal reaches and turns back to lead the bride to a bed partially emerging on right as a *nympheutria* adjusts her veil; above his head a two-line inscription: ΚΑΛΗ/ .Α . . . . ., possibly stoichedon.

just burst through the door, apparently leaping down from the bed. To emphasize the extraordinary nature of his apparition a woman to the right, dressed simply in peplos with pendant earring, throws up her hands in surprise at this vision of Love himself bursting from the wedding chamber.

The refined erotic imagery of this picture is typical of contemporary nuptial and domestic representations. Although some may object to calling the image of marriage presented here romantic, it is difficult to know how else to describe such an idealized picture of the physical and emotional bond between husband and wife. This treatment is something new in the Classical period, and it is worth showing how and in what terms this romantic vision is constructed.

First, both bride and groom are idealized as beautiful young adults, the bride physically mature, and the groom still beardless. W.K. Lacy has pointed out that while philosophers might recommend that men marry at age thirty and women in their teens, the vase painter Polygnotos shows the two figures equal in age on his loutrophoros in Toronto.[31] Polygnotos is not idiosyncratic, for in weddings on Classical vases the groom is far more often represented as a beardless youth, like ours, than as a bearded man.[32] While Beazley has noted a general tendency in the Classical period to youthen figures, in the context of weddings, such preference for a young, more *kalos* groom (a quality here enhanced by inscription, as noted above) is part of the generally romantic air of these scenes. For women and brides, who may have constituted the major audience for these scenes, the groom was shown to be as attractive as possible. Grooms who viewed the scenes would naturally be pleased to identify with the *kalos* ideal represented here. While other grooms of the same period have shoulder length hair, the short hair of ours possibly reflects a more democratic or athletic ideal.[33]

We turn next to the positions of bride and groom, a compositional type whose Geometric pedigree has already been mentioned. He grasps her hand or wrist, and turns back as he leads her forward. This type is commonly used in Archaic abduction scenes, and during the Classical period becomes common for weddings and for the figure of Hermes Psychopompos leading souls to the nether world. In all it serves, in the words of G. Neumann, as "the sign of the grasp of possession which, through the leading position of the

[31] W.K. Lacy, *The Family in Classical Greece* (Ithaca: Cornell 1968) 106, 162, caption to fig. 24, Toronto 635, *ARV*[2] 1031.51; Sutton (supra n. 1) pl. 11, W.34.

[32] Ibid. 213: 82% of the grooms in the red-figure weddings studied are beardless where this detail can be made out, and some of the beards belong to gods for whom they are part of the figure's iconographic identity.

[33] Male hair length colors a representation rather than serving as a strict iconographical marker; its employment, moreover, seems to vary with individual painters. Furthermore, it is impossible to define any sharp division in the continuum between long and short hair, although one can note the extremes. On beardless grooms, one may note at the short end those on Pl. 34 infra, NY 17.230.15 (supra n. 25), Toronto 635 (supra n. 31), and London 1923.1-18.1 (supra n. 12); true longhairs include Pl. 35 infra, Berlin F 2373 (supra n. 27), and Athens 1388 (supra n. 4). To Aristophanes long hair seems to be an aristocratic symbol (V. Ehrenberg, *People of Aristophanes* [New York: Schocken 1962] 97). Though longish hair serves also as an heroic or mythological marker, the rule is not firm; see Sourvinou-Inwood (supra n. 3, 1987) 133 with n. 17.

one figure, contains an element of mastery and domination."[34] The earliest known wedding in which this scheme occurs is a fragmentary cup by Euphronios from the Athenian Acropolis showing the mythological wedding of Peleus and Thetis; the cup should date ca. 510 B.C., though possibly earlier lost monumental scenes behind it.[35] It does not, on available evidence, occur in non-mythological weddings on vases until after ca. 480 B.C. In the context of a wedding this compositional type effectively expresses male legal domination and leadership in marriage (*kyreia*), while at the same time expressing the groom's sexual possession of the bride and the emotions he feels for her. The groom's grasp on his bride's hand (or, on other vases, her wrist), the Homeric χεῖρ' ἐπὶ καρπῷ which served, among much else, to solemnize legally a transaction or agreement (cf. *Il.* 24.671; *Od.* 18.258), was a recognized part of the Attic wedding.[36] There it expressed perhaps not agreement as much as the groom's sexual possession of the bride. The compulsion implicit in his grasp is effectively moderated by his backward glance to catch her eye. The bride extends her arms towards him and slightly lowers her head while meeting his glance; she expresses the ideal of willing female submission to masculine authority, a modest woman, yet one who does not obliterate her own proper subjectivity. This traditional element of the abduction scheme in weddings is translated into a mutual gaze of desire tempered by reassurance and consent that shows the emotions required of both husband and wife for the foundation of a new *oikos* (household).

There can be no doubt that love is in this glance between bride and groom, for the artist has included two Erotes buzzing around the bride's head, and a third tumbling out of the bedroom, in a complex of imagery that can be parallelled in the contemporary poetry of Euripides and even of the more austere Sophocles.[37] Such miniature winged boys had been known in Greek art for over a century.[38] All were not called Eros, for when they are labeled, one finds as well the names of Pothos and Himeros (Longing and Desire). In literature and art, however, these names are virtually synonymous, and it is not misleading to apply the conventional label Eros to all. Although in fourth-century vase painting such Erotes become epidemic and vapid, turning up in almost any context, here they still retain considerable power as images. In many High Classical wedding scenes such Erotes are closely associated with the bride, like the two shown buzzing around her here. Yet vase painters also show considerable ingenuity in using a single,

[34] G. Neumann, *Gesten und Gebärden in der griechischen Kunst* (Berlin: de Gruyter 1965) 59: "das Zeichen des Besitzergreifens, welches durch den Vorrang der eine Figure etwas Herrisches und Gewaltsames hat"; on the gesture generally, 59–66.

[35] Athens Acr. 176, *ARV*² 17.18; E. Svatik, "A Euphronios Kylix," *ArtB* 21 (1939) 251–71; new fragment and reconstruction by B. Philippaki, «*Καί πάλι ἡ κύλικα τοῦ Εὐφρονίου στήν 'Αθήνα*», *ArchEph* 1980, 'Αρχ. *χρον*. 62–65.

[36] Neumann (supra n. 34); S. Flory, "Medea's Right Hand," *TAPA* 108 (1978) 69-74; Jenkins (supra n. 1) 138ff.; Davies (infra n. 52); Sourvinou-Inwood (supra n. 3, 1987), esp. 139–41; cf. Eur. *Alc.* 916 and *Medea* 21f.

[37] Cf. *Hipp.* 525–564 and passim; *Ant.* 781–800.

[38] Hermary et al. (supra n. 10); A. Greifenhagen, *Griechische Eroten* (Berlin: de Gruyter 1957) esp. 34–49 on their naming; H.A. Shapiro, "The Origins of Allegory in Greek Art," *Boreas* 9 (1986) 4–23, at 19 and 11 on distinctions between Eros and Himeros; in weddings, Sutton (supra n. 1) 186–89.

larger Eros otherwise. The third Eros on our vase who bounds from the wedding bed transfers attention from the person of the bride to the bed and *thalamos*, two very concrete symbols of the sexual act in marriage. This vigorous figure, much more massively built than his two fellows and resembling a long jumper in pose,[39] bursts from the bedroom. He suggests the vigorous male offspring that should hopefully result from the union of bride and groom in an original and effective image.

Thus through a variety of means this vase painting builds a consistently romantic view of marriage, one that explicitly emphasizes the importance of the emotion Eros as a positive force that binds husband and wife together. In this respect our scene is not unique but rather representative of general trends in nuptial and domestic iconography of the second half of the fifth century B.C. Erika Götte has sensitively traced how ordinary scenes of respectable women at home become progressively and politely eroticized, in part through the inclusion of Eros and Aphrodite, a process that culminates in the extravagant creation of the Meidian style that are akin in their general spirit to the poetry of Sappho.[40] Moreover, the iconography of Helen becomes a major theme during the fifth century, one that converges with the iconography of weddings and general domestic scenes.[41] What is remarkable is not that Helen should adopt the appearance of a bride, but that brides and wives should regularly be treated in the same manner as Helen. Finally, Eros, in the Archaic period a figure of mythical scenes also found in connection with pederasty and occasionally with *hetairai*, during the second half of the fifth century B.C. is domesticated and brought into the service of the *oikos*, the basic social unit of the Athenian state.[42] J.-P. Vernant has suggested on other grounds that there was a reassessment of the institution of marriage in Athens following the establishment of the Democracy in 508 B.C.[43] The evidence of available vase representations suggests that it was not an immediate result of the Cleisthenic reforms, but rather a long-term effect that did not appear until after the Persian Wars, and one that evolved gradually. The new pedestrian wedding type is in common use from the 460's B.C. on; with it comes an increasingly romantic tone, but Eros himself does not appear with bride and groom until the 430's.[44] Like the reforms of 461 B.C. that established the Radical Democracy and like Pericles' Citizenship Law passed a decade later,[45] this new domestic imagery on Classical

[39] N. Yalouris, ed., *The Eternal Olympics* (New Rochelle: Caratzas 1979) 176–87; E.N. Gardiner, *Athletics of the Ancient World* (Oxford 1930, repr. Chicago: Ares 1980) 144–53.

[40] E. Götte (supra n. 3) 39–61.

[41] L. Ghali-Kahil, *Les enlèvments et la retour d'Hélène*, École Francaise d'Athènes, Travaux et mémoires 10 (Paris: Boccard 1955) 53–70, 157–77, esp. no. 11, pp. 53, 55f., Makron's skyphos Boston MFA 13.186, *ARV*[2] 458.1, where Helen's abduction is shown as a wedding with Aphrodite and Peitho (Persuasion) serving as *nympheutriai*.

[42] Sutton (supra n. 1) generally 232f., 463–465 and esp. 224f., F.7, pl. 19 on the unattributed epinetron Athens NM 2179 (C. Robert, «Ὄνοι πήλινοι», *ArchEph* 1892, 247–56) which I take as an anticipation of the Xenophontic economic view of marriage; Hermary et al. (supra n. 10) 935f.

[43] Supra n. 1.

[44] Sutton (supra n. 1) 177ff., esp. 183, 186, appearing in weddings by the Peleus and Washing Painters, but not (to date) by Polygnotos, their common master.

[45] C. Hignett, *A History of the Athenian Constitution* (Oxford: Clarendon 1952) chapter 8, appendixes 8, 10; C. Patterson, *Pericles' Citizenship Law of 451–50 B.C.* (New York: Arno 1981).

vases is a symptom of the deep and gradual revolution in Athenian life set in motion by the political restructuring of the state at the end of the sixth century B.C. In short, vase paintings present a visual expression of the new ideology that derived from and sustained the Radical Democracy in Classical Athens.

Turning from the major scene on the vessel, we consider next the separate two-figure composition on the back of the main frieze (Pl. 30a), a representation whose significance is not readily apparent. The two figures overlap the end figures of the main scene, and although they have no obvious formal or iconographical connection to the wedding, it is likely that they are to be related in some fashion. On the left a bearded man, holding a scepter and wearing long chiton and himation, shakes the hand of a youth dressed as a traveler or ephebe.[46] The youth carries two spears and wears a traveler's shoes (*endromides*), cloak (*chlamys*), and hat (*petasos*; here hung over his back) with a patterned *chitoniskos* over a second plain one whose edge is visible hanging down over his left knee (no bottom hem line is indicated for this undergarment).

On available information it is impossible to say with certainty who these two figures are meant to represent, or even that the painter had any very precise notion himself (an idea that is less shocking today than it was a generation or two ago).[47] The scepter held by the older man, whether he is a mortal king or divine, indicates that the action belongs to the mythological world. The staff's height, smooth sides, horizontal banding, and finial indicate a royal scepter rather than an ordinary staff. Gods, goddesses, and kings carry such staffs in scenes that are safely mythological or religious; while the walking sticks of contemporary men and youths in genre scenes on red-figure vases assume a variety of forms, none shares these features.[48] This king is further distinguished by the long chiton he wears under his himation. Normal male dress in the Classical period is the plain himation without undergarment worn by the groom on the obverse of this vase. The long chiton for males was considered a luxury of a vanished aristocratic past (Thuc. 1.6) that occasionally appears in the representation of older gods and heroes.[49] His young companion, though dressed as a normal ephebe or traveler, is also distinguished from the ordinary by his decorated chitoniskos, which, though not recognized as a mythological

[46] Sourvinou-Inwood (supra n. 3, 1987) 135.

[47] Cf. the comments of H. Metzger, "Beazley et l'image," *AntK* 30 (1987) 109–18; Sourvinou-Inwood (supra n. 3, 1987).

[48] Sorlin Dorigny, "Sceptrum-Grèce," DarSag IV [n.d.] 1115–17; Hug, "Sceptrum," *RE* II.2 (1921) 368–72; Brueckner (infra n. 68) 82; Sourvinou-Inwood (supra n. 3, 1987) 143f. For the mythological scepter see e.g., Arias and Hirmer (supra n. 14) pls. 131 (Croesus on the pyre, Louvre G 197, *ARV*² 238.1, Myson), 139–40 (Priam and Phoenix, Louvre G152, *ARV*² 369.1, Brygos Painter), 156 (Zeus, Louvre G175, *ARV*² 206.124, Berlin Painter), 158 (Kekrops, Munich 2345, *ARV*² 496.2, Oreithyia Painter), and those held by various gods in *Cité des images* (supra n. 3) figs. 157 (surely not a priestess), 159 (Demeter), 160b, 161–63. For staffs in genre scenes see e.g., ibid. figs. 10, 37, 61, 73, 105, 113–15, 118, 125, 170, and the cloaked satyrs in figs. 192–93; Arias and Hirmer (supra n. 14) pls. 138 and XXXIII (Würzburg 479, *ARV*² 372.32, Brygos Painter), 148 (Paris, Cab. Méd. 542, *ARV*² 438.133, Douris), 161 (Palermo V 778, *ARV*² 550.2, Pan Painter).

[49] M. Bieber, *Entwicklungsgeschichte der griechischen Tracht*, ed. 2, ed. F. Eckstein (Berlin: Mann 1967) 26f., 28f., 32f., pls. 13, 14, 15.2, 16.

marker, fits well in the heroic world of the gentleman with the scepter.[50] This figure corresponds to the ephebic type employed generally in fifth century B.C. vase painting for young heroes and (despite the absence of sword or club) especially for Theseus, the acknowledged hero of the Athenian Democracy.[51] Whether he is meant to be recognized specifically as Theseus or any other hero is not crucial for understanding the scene, for the action is of a generic type that could fit almost any mythical (or non-mythical) biography.

The gesture of shaking hands has a long history of use in a variety of contexts in Classical art and signified meanings which might all be subsumed under the Greek terms *homophrosyne* and *philia* ("common accord" and "friendship").[52] Thus it is employed in scenes of arrival and departure to express greeting and farewell, in weddings between bride and groom (as we have seen), and on votive reliefs and elsewhere to symbolize the formalization of treaties and other formal agreements. In the Classical period the most common use of the motif is in genre scenes of farewell and greeting, scenes which often have an implicit mortuary meaning through their appearance on vases that were put to funerary use and on grave reliefs (though most of the latter belong to the following century). The gesture is ambiguous, however, and much of its appeal to Classical vase painters wishing to market their products was probably that it would be an appropriate sign for any number of occasions for which a customer might buy a vase. Several explanations suggest themselves for the gesture's meaning here.

At first glance ours is a conventional scene of a departing warrior, a popular stock theme on contemporary and earlier vases.[53] The popularity of this subject is at least partially explained by its suitability to a funerary context, where the viewer is invited to understand that the warrior is setting off on his final journey from which he will not return alive, a meaning that is not required, however, if the scene is viewed in other contexts. The use of the subject here might therefore have been suggested by the mortuary use of loutrophoroi, with no intention of direct thematic connection between the two sides of the vase. I cannot, however, point to any other loutrophoros whose decoration

[50] Cf. Apollo in erotic pursuit on the hydria London E 140, ibid. pls. 13.3 and 4, 14.1 (*ARV*[2] 1042.2 [top], Coghill Painter), the groom on the Oxford loutrophoros 1927.4067, *ARV*[2] 1179, below (related to the Painter of Athens 1454), *CVA* (Ox. 2, GB 9) pl. 59.3 and 4; Pelops on the amphora in the Manner of the Dinos Painter, Arezzo Mus. Civ. 1460 (*ARV*[2] 1157.25), Arias and Hirmer (supra n. 14) pls. 212, 213; Castor on the name vase of the Meidias Painter (supra n. 14).

[51] C. Sourvinou-Inwood, *Theseus as Son and Stepson. A tentative illustration of the Greek mythological mentality*, *BICS* Suppl. 40 (1979) 3; ead. (supra n. 3, 1967) 132ff.; J.P. Barron, "Bakchylides, Theseus, and a Woolly Cloak," *BICS* 27 (1980) 1–8 at 1 n. 3.

[52] On the gesture G. Davies, "The Significance of the Handshake Motif in Classical Funerary Art," *AJA* 89 (1985) 627–40; Neumann (supra n. 34) "Verbundenheit", 49–58; neither identifies it with an ancient term. For ὁμοφροσύνη see Redfield (supra n. 1) 186, 197f.; for φιλία, abstracts of papers delivered at a special session on this concept by D. Halperin, E. Stehle, S. Schein, and G. Richert, American Philological Association, *Abstracts of Papers. Annual Meeting 1987*, 141–44.

[53] The general type Sutton (supra n. 1) 228–32; E. Pemberton, "The Name Vase of the Peleus Painter," *JWalt* 26 (1977) (Studies to D.K. Hill) 62–72; with handshake, Davies (supra n. 52) 628 and n. 8; briefly discussed with illustrations by F. Lissarrague, "Autour du guerrier," in *Cité des images* (supra n. 3) 34–47 at 41f., fig. 61.

explicitly combines the themes of marriage and death. Vase painters evidently recognized loutrophoroi as either nuptial or mortuary, and left it to their customers (if they wished) to follow tragedians and authors of epitaphs in combining the imagery of the two rituals for pathetic effect. Until parallels can be found, other explanations should probably be sought for our scene, for it is unlikely that such a combination occurs here merely because the artist forgot which type of loutrophoros he was painting.

If this representation is taken in close connection with the wedding on the obverse, it might be thought to represent the departure of the bridegroom after the wedding[54] (on the model of Troilos and Cressida, evidently not an ancient tale, or perhaps Amphitryon), though one might expect the bride to be shown to heighten the pathos, and one would expect inscriptions (which admittedly could have faded or been overlooked) to clarify identities. Conversely, it could represent the *arrival* of the bridegroom, or better yet the sealing of the *engye*,[55] the agreement between the bride's *kyrios* ("guardian", her father if he was alive) and the groom which made the marriage legal. The *engye*, which necessarily preceded the *gamos* (sometimes by years), normally involved the transfer of the dowry to the groom and was sealed by a handshake before witnesses. The king in our scene would be the *kyrios* and the youth his prospective son-in-law, a hero just arrived from afar, as his clothing suggests. Interestingly, the figures cited with decorated chitoniskos (supra n. 50) include four bridegrooms and a sole divine rapist (their structural equivalent on the divine level), and the garment may have had nuptial associations. Nevertheless, the bridegroom on the other side of our vase is not so dressed, and although one *might* identify the two figures on either side of the vase as the same individual (both share short hair), such identification is not *required* by the iconography; in fact, their different clothing discourages it as might the lack of witnesses. Nevertheless, an *engye* set in the mythological world seems to be the most attractive identification for the scene on this vase.

If this represents an *engye*, can the principals be more precisely identified? We have noted that the youth appears in a form regularly used for Theseus, a hero whose sexual liaisons and marriages were recognized as problematic already in antiquity (cf. Plutarch *Theseus* 28–29). The marriage to Minos' daughter Phaedra was clearly recognized as legitimate (cf. Euripides *Hippolytos*), and Minos might be the king in our scene. Barron, however, has recently argued that under Kimon, a politician of the 470's and 460's B.C. who consciously fostered Theseus as the Democratic hero, another legitimate marriage was concocted for Theseus to a Megarian known variously as Epiboia, Eriboia, Phereboia, Periboia, and Meliboia in order to provide a mythological connection through her son Ajax between Theseus and the aristocratic Philaid family to which Kimon belonged.[56] If Barron's complicated chain of reasoning is correct our king could be her

[54] A suggestion of J.G. Keenan.

[55] A.R.W. Harrison, *The Law of Athens, Vol. 1: Family and Property* (Oxford: Clarendon 1968) 3–9; H.J. Wolff, "Marriage Law and Family Organization in Ancient Athens," *Traditio* 2 (1944) 43–95 at 51–53; Vernant (supra n. 1) 57–64; but see now the important discussion by C. Patterson (supra n. 1).

[56] Supra n. 51, pp. 2f.

father Alkathoos. Whoever the king is, our scene can be connected to other contemporary scenes showing the family life of Theseus; these scenes where identities are established by inscriptions have, nevertheless, only tenuous connection to mythological reality. On an unpublished pelike Aison shows the grown hero between his parents Aigeus and Aithra although they were never married and lived on opposite shores of the Saronic gulf after the illicit encounter that engendered the hero; the Codrus Painter decorated a cup with the even more unlikely gathering of Aigeus, Theseus, Medea, Phorbas, and Aithra (Medea was Aigeus' wife who sought to poison Theseus on his arrival in Athens).[57] Such scenes are to be understood not strictly as illustrations of myth, but rather as attempts to provide mythological paradigms for contemporary Athenian social institutions by employing the hero of the Democracy in groupings analogous to the contemporary family ideal, however incompatible these may be with the facts of mythic biography.[58] On our loutrophoros, however, without inscriptions (unless they have escaped detection) it would be unwise to insist that the youth must be Theseus, as likely as that may be, or any other specific figure of myth. Given the ambiguous, polysemic nature of Classical representation, which fuses mythic and "every-day" events into an single interpenetrable continuum,[59] the scene can be seen as a generalized, paradigmatic encounter in which a hero/ephebe contracts marriage with a king/aristocratic, authoritative older man.

Further support for recognizing the *engye* can probably be found in the single figures found on either side of the vessel's narrow neck. Though isolated on either side of the vase, two women face each other across the intervening handle and relate compositionally to one another in a manner which indicates that they belong together. The woman above the wedding faces left; she wears chiton, himation, and a decorated head-covering. Cradled in the crook of her left arm is a loutrophoros hydria, and in her lowered right a wreath. While both items might belong to a funeral as well as a wedding,[60] that possibility is probably excluded here by her dress and coiffure. The second woman, dressed similarly to the extent preserved, faces right holding a torch diagonally in her right hand and slightly raising her left beneath the mantle. On her head she carries a flat wicker basket which probably represents the *pherne*, the bride's trousseau, an item

[57] Aison: Athens 1185 (*ARV*[2] 1176.26); on the inscriptions, J.D. Beazley, "Some Inscriptions on Vases. III," *AJA* 39 (1935) 475–88 at 488. Codrus Painter: Bologna PU 273 (*ARV*[2] 1268.1); see C. Robert, *Archaeologische Hermeneutik* (Berlin: Weidmann 1919) 145–47. On Theseus and Medea see Sourvinou-Inwood (supra n. 51). U. Kron, "Aithra I," *LIMC* I 420–31, nos. 48, 49, pls. 330–31, discussion pp. 429 ff. Cf. an amphora by the Mannerist Oinanthe Painter showing Theseus with Aigeus, Poseidon and a woman persuasively identified by Sourvinou-Inwood (supra n. 51, n. 122 [p. 69]) as Aithra rather than Medea: London E 264, *ARV*[2] 579.1; *CVA* pl 7.1; Neumann (supra n. 34) 24; Kron (supra) no. 46 = Aigeus 29, pl. 279.

[58] For the term "mythological paradigm" as employed here, Webster (supra n. 4) passim (see the index s.v.); see further Sutton (supra n. 1) 229–32.

[59] Cf. V. Zinserling, "Zum Problem von Alltagsdarstellungen auf attischen Vasen," *Beiträge zum antiken Realismus*, ed. M. Kunze (Berlin: Akademie-Verlag 1977) 39–56; Sourvinou-Inwood (supra n. 3, 1987) 135f.; Götte (supra n. 3) 39–61; Krauskopf (supra n. 8).

[60] Cf. the neck of the funerary loutrophoros by the Kleophrades Painter, Louvre CA 453, *ARV*[2] 184.22, Arias and Hirmer (supra n. 14) pl. 126 and *Cité des images* (supra n. 3) fig. 143.

that recurs sporadically in wedding scenes from the sixth century on.[61] Together these figures relate to the wedding below and probably indicate that the scene with handshaking figures should be connected as well, and probably shows the *engye*. Yet given the polysemic nature of vase representation noted above, it should be admitted that while the nuptial context of the vessel urges one to recognize here the *engye* as the scene's primary denotation, the mortuary and other connotations of the handshake cannot be entirely excluded, especially if the vase was placed in a grave, as seems likely.

In summary, the major scene on this vase is a fine representation of the Attic wedding that shows the romantic ideal of marriage that emerges in the Periclean age. Though evidently set in the contemporary world, it employs the language of allegory. The two figures on the neck clearly echo its nuptial theme and suggest that the small scene on the reverse is probably nuptial as well. There we find what is apparently a unique representation of the *engye* set in the mythological world, one that may serve as the founding act of the wedding on the other side. The free juxtaposition of images drawn from myth, allegory, and daily experience found on this vase makes it a good example of the Classical style in art.

II

The second vase considered here is a fragmentary loutrophoros hydria by the Phiale Painter recently published by John Oakley (Pl. 34).[62] While Oakley argues that its unusual representation illustrates the *anakalypteria*, an important, but problematic ritual in which the bride unveiled before her husband and received gifts, its details accord better with the *katachysmata*, a less important, but more precisely described event. There are three non-joining fragments from the upper part of the main scene which once continued all around the vase. Our plate illustrates only the largest, from the front. The setting is inside a home, indicated by the objects hanging in the background, which include lekythos, a feminine head covering conventionally called a sakkos, and fillets. Under the hydria's vertical handle on the back (not illustrated) begins a line of three women moving right with items for the bridal toilet. The last in line holds a mirror, the next a wooden chest like that in Pl. 30b but with open lid, and the foremost figure the remains of what is surely a wicker basket and a fillet. This last figure stands behind the woman at the left of our illustration who is a *nympheutria* holding a short veil over the bride's head. Of the bride, seated right on a stool, only the upper head remains, showing the diadem in her hair. A small Eros flies down towards her bearing a fillet. Facing the bride on the right of the illustration is the head and upper torso of the beardless groom who wears a himation

[61] Connor (supra n. 8) 160, figs. 1 and 2, with references to earlier literature. In red figure see the pyxis by the Marlay Painter, London 1920.12-21.1, *ARV*[2] 1277.23; *JHS* 41, pl. 6.1, 2, 4, 5; Sutton (supra n. 1) pl. 10, W.15; I. Jenkins, *Greek and Roman Life* (Cambridge, Mass.: Harvard 1986) 38.

[62] Boston, Museum of Fine Arts 10.223, James Fund and Special Contribution; *ARV*[2] 1017.44; J.H. Oakley, "The Anakalypteria," *AA* 1982, 113–18; Sutton (supra n. 1) 197–201, pl. 15, W.63; Hermary et al. (supra n. 10) pl. 645, no. 639a. I have benefitted from discussing this vase with Oakley since 1980.

PLATE 34

PLATE 34. Red-figure loutrophoros by the Phiale Painter, Boston, Museum of Fine Arts 10.223, James Fund and special contribution; detail. Photograph courtesy Museum of Fine Arts, Boston, negative B 12052.

and wreath of myrtle or olive; he also sits, as his position makes clear. Between the couple is a boy wearing himation and wreath who stands frontally but turns to hold out something now lost to the bride. Above the heads of the two male figures a woman, of whom only the arms and some drapery survive, holds up a shallow basket containing small rounded forms. Behind on the wall hangs a scarf with straight fringed ends and dotted decoration painted in thin glaze. On the far right of the scene there is room for another figure of whom nothing remains, by all rights probably a woman with torches.

These details and other elements of the scene agree with the description of the *katachysmata*, a rite of incorporation performed when bride and groom first entered their new home. The most detailed and relevant description is found in a scholion to Aristophanes *Ploutos* 768:

> When newly purchased slaves—or those on whom they wished to call down some blessing, especially a bridegroom—first entered the house, they would shower them with tasty treats beside the hearth as a sign of prosperity. As Theopompos [a comic poet of the fourth century B.C.] says in *Hedychares*:
>
> > Come on, you [sing.], quickly pour the *katachysmata* over the groom and bride . . . .
>
> . . . .The *katachysmata* consist of dates, small coins [or cakes], fruits, dried figs, and nuts which the fellow slaves would snatch up. They [the *katachysmata*] were mentioned mainly when they bought a slave. For they would bring him to the side of the hearth and, sitting him down, they would pour coins [or cakes], dried figs, dates, fruits, and other tasty treats down over his head, and the other slaves would snatch them up. These were therefore called *katachysmata* [καταχύσματα, "things poured down," from καταχέω, "pour down"].[63]

Photios, Harpokration, and Suidas add that this rite was also performed, presumably on behalf of the polis, to inaugurate *presbytai* and *theoroi*, the city's secular and sacred

[63] τῶν γὰρ νεωνήτων δούλων τῶν πρώτως εἰσιόντων εἰς τὴν οἰκίαν, ἢ ἁπλῶς τῶν ἐφ' ὧν οἰωνίσασθαί τι ἀγαθὸν ἐβούλοντο καὶ τοῦ νυμφίου, παρὰ τὴν ἑστίαν τραγήματα κατέχεον εἰς σημεῖον εὐετηρίας, ὡς καὶ Θεόπομπός φησιν ἐν Ἡδυχάρει

φέρε σὺ τὰ καταχύσματα
ταχέως κατάχει τοῦ νυμφίου καὶ τῆς κόρης . . . .

. . . σύγκειται δὲ τὰ καταχύσματα ἀπὸ φοινίκων, κολλύβων, τρωγαλίων, ἰσχάδων καὶ καρύων, ἅπερ ἥρπαζον οἱ σύνδουλοι. κύριως δὲ ἐλέγοντο, ὅτε δοῦλον ἠγόραζον· ἔφερον γὰρ αὐτὸν παρὰ τὴν ἑστίαν καὶ καθίζοντες κατὰ τῆς κεφαλῆς κατέχεον κόλλυβα καὶ ἰσχάδας, καὶ φοίνικας, καὶ τρωγάλια καὶ ἄλλα τραγήματα, καὶ οἱ σύνδολοι ταῦτα ἥρπαζον. ἐλέγοντο οὖν ταῦτα καταχύσματα. *Scholia Graeca in Aristophanem*, ed. Fr. Dübner (1877, repr. Hildesheim: Olms 1969) 366. For the text of the Ravenna codex, see W.G. Rutherford, *Scholia Aristophanica* (1896) 79–80 with translation. Suidas (ed. Adler, 1967, vol. 3) s.v., vs. 878 repeats most of the scholion verbatim, but vs. 877 derives from a different tradition and omits reference to the wedding. Tzetzes repeats the scholion with minor variations, *Scholia in Aristophanem. Pars IV, Fasc. 1 Jo. Tzetzae, Commentarii in Aristophanem. Prolegomena et Commentaria in Plutum*, ed. L. M. Positano (1960) 173; more briefly, Pollux (3.77), Hesychios (s. v.), I. Bekker, *Anecdota Graeca* I (Berlin: Nauck 1814) 269, and L. Bachmann, *Anecdota Graeca* II (Leipzig 1823, repr. Hildesheim: Olms 1965) 378 vs. 16. For the translation of κόλλυβα as "coins" (contra LSJ "cakes") see L. Deubner, "Καταχύσματα und Münzzauber," *RhM* 121 (1978) 240–54 at 240 n. 2, repr. in id., *Kleine Schriften zur klassischen Altertumskunde* (Königstein/Ts.: Hain 1982) 772–786.

ambassadors, Photios explicitly describing the contents of the shower as *panspermia*, a mixture of all seeds.[64] The word *katachysma*, in both singular and plural, was used also for seasoning or sauce applied to food.[65]

We have identified the *katachysmata* as a rite of incorporation since it attended the entry of bride, slave, and the city's ambassadors into a new status. Its specific function is clear from the scholion: a prosperous outcome for *oikos* and polis. Although Samter (followed by Burkert) has seen the rite as an expiation of household gods and chthonic spirits, Deubner, in a posthumous article, rehabilitates Mannhardt's earlier connecting it to fertility and regards this as a *Segenritus*, a general invocation of blessing.[66] The specific choice of fruits, nuts, and coins does suggest that fertility was the primary motive which was later generalized to prosperity. The emphasis on the groom in the sources cannot be an objection, for he is the leading figure of the new *oikos*; the fertility and fruitfulness invoked are not specifically that of the bride but of the new *oikos* and the patrilineage to which it belongs. Eros, included in the loutrophoros scene, personifies the physical and emotional force that will achieve this fertility and prosperity in the marriage. In other contexts, the new slave, like the bride, is merely an outsider brought into the *oikos* to serve its ends through his toil, while in the case of ambassadors the extension from household to polis is natural. One would like to know where the civic rite took place; presumably it was at the Prytaneion, site of the civic Hestia.[67]

Returning to our vase, one is struck by the close correspondence between its details and the scholion's description of the *katachysmata*. The most crucial item is the basket held over the groom's head, an item which deserves fuller description. It is a shallow, flat bottomed basket shown in partial perspective which displays its interior and contents; diagonal stripes of dilute glaze used in and out probably indicate the pattern of the wicker rather than shading. Attached to the outside is a sprig of myrtle or the like whose leaves are painted with somewhat darker dilute glaze. The shapes of the basket's contents are drawn in outline, and the interiors of some are painted with dilute glaze, though in some cases this is probably the wicker design showing through. Their shapes vary in size and contour: some are round; others, which are dark and almond shaped, but larger with bent over ends, must be figs, possibly dried; at least one has the bilobed shape of an apple or quince. This variety corresponds closely with the mixture described by the scholiast. The basket is held at an angle over the heads of the central figures, and its contents seem in motion, as if about to spill out over those below. That the woman with the basket acts alone corresponds to the singular *σύ* in the fragment quoted from Theopompos. Her

[64] S.vv. *καταχύσμα* and *καταχύσματα*; Harpokration s.v. *καταχύσματα*; Suidas (supra n. 63).

[65] Pollux 6.56; cf. also *καταχυσμάτιον* also 6.59, 6.68; cf. also Suidas (supra n. 63) vs. 876.

[66] Samter, *Familienfeste* (supra n. 1) 7–14; Deubner (supra n. 63); both citing Mannhardt, *Mythologische Forschungen* (1884) 351ff. These earlier discussions are hampered by non-structural approaches to comparative material. W. Burkert, *Greek Religion*, trans. J. Raffan (Cambridge, Mass.: Harvard 1985) 76 and n. 8 discusses it as a purification rite; our representation shows that the basket was not a *liknon* as he assumes.

[67] Wycherley (supra n. 5) 45f.; S.G. Miller, *The Prytaneion. Its Function and Architectural Form* (Berkeley & Los Angeles: California 1978) 13–16.

position by the groom reflects the greater prominence given to the bridegroom in the ancient notices, where the bride is mentioned as an afterthought if at all. That bride and groom are seated also is in agreement, and we would be justified in restoring a hearth between the couple in the missing lower section of the vessel, though it would have to overlap or be hidden behind the legs of the three figures that must converge here. In short, the scene represents the *katachysmata* as described in the scholion with a precision that proves the reliability of both sources.

Brueckner had seen an allusion to the *katachysmata* on a somewhat earlier white ground pyxis in London by the Splanchnopt Painter, one of the finer colleagues of the Penthesilea Painter (Pl. 35).[68] There a pedestrian wedding party approaches a burning altar. Beside it stands a woman with scepter who holds out a small round object in added clay and gilt that was identified by C. Smith as a fig.[69] Brueckner identified the sceptered woman by the altar as the Hestia of the new home and took her offered fruit to be an allusion to the *katachysmata*. While he is surely right about Hestia,[70] direct connection to the *katachysmata* is vitiated by the Phiale Painter's more explicit representation. On the pyxis the couple are not seated, nor are seats provided for them. More serious, the single fruit (whatever its species) is merely held out by the goddess and not poured over the couple. As the scholion indicates, the act of pouring, from which the ritual takes its name, is the essential feature of the rite, without which it cannot be recognized. The object offered on the London pyxis is better identified with the quince or other fruit that the bride ate before retiring to the *thalamos* with the groom.[71] Brides are sometimes shown holding a fruit in red-figure procession scenes,[72] and it is even possible that the bride on our vase was offered one by the boy who stands before her.

This last suggestion deserves consideration. It is tempting (with Oakley) to connect the boy with the *pais amphtales* (a boy with both parents living) who at the wedding, according to Zenobios (3.98), carried bread around in a *liknon* (winnowing basket) repeating the phrase ἔφυγον κακόν· εὗρον ἄμεινον ("I fled evil, I found a better thing"); both phrase and *liknon* recurred in the Eleusinian Mysteries, though it is difficult to know

[68] London B. M. D 11, *ARV*² 899.146; A. Brueckner, "Athenische Hochzeitsgeschencke," *AM* 32 (1907) 79–122 at 80–84; Jenkins (supra n. 61) 2, 3 (color). Keuls (supra n. 10) 124, fig. 112, has suggested that the *katachysmata* (discussed ibid. p. 6) might appear on the hydria London E 192 (*ARV*² 548.54; Painter of London E 489) though the details do not correspond with the rite as described: this is a simple toilet scene.

[69] Quoted by Brueckner (supra n. 68) 83, with illustration. The form is much less precisely defined in fact, as D. Williams confirms (personal communication).

[70] Accepted with reservations by W. Fuchs, "Hestia," *EAA* IV (1961) 18–22 at 19f.

[71] Plutarch, *Solon* 33.4 (89C), *Mor.* 138D (*Gam. Parang.*) and 279F (*Rom. Quaest.*); Erdmann (supra n. 1) 258.

[72] Bride holding fruit: Louvre G 226, *ARV*² 250.15 (Syleus Painter), *CVA* (Louvre 6, Fr. 9) pl. 44.4–7 and 9; Toronto 635 (supra n. 31); Athens 14504, *ARV*² 539.44, described Sutton (supra n. 1) 252, W.61. On a late Archaic amphora once Basseggio, a woman (*nympheutria*?) holds a fruit beside a woman resembling a bride whose veil is adjusted from behind by a third woman (*nympheutria*?), as a youth (groom?) with staff looks on from the right; *MonInst* 8.35, whence *Wiener Vorlegeblätter* 1888, 8.4 and Sutton (supra n. 1) pl. 12, W.60.

PLATE 35

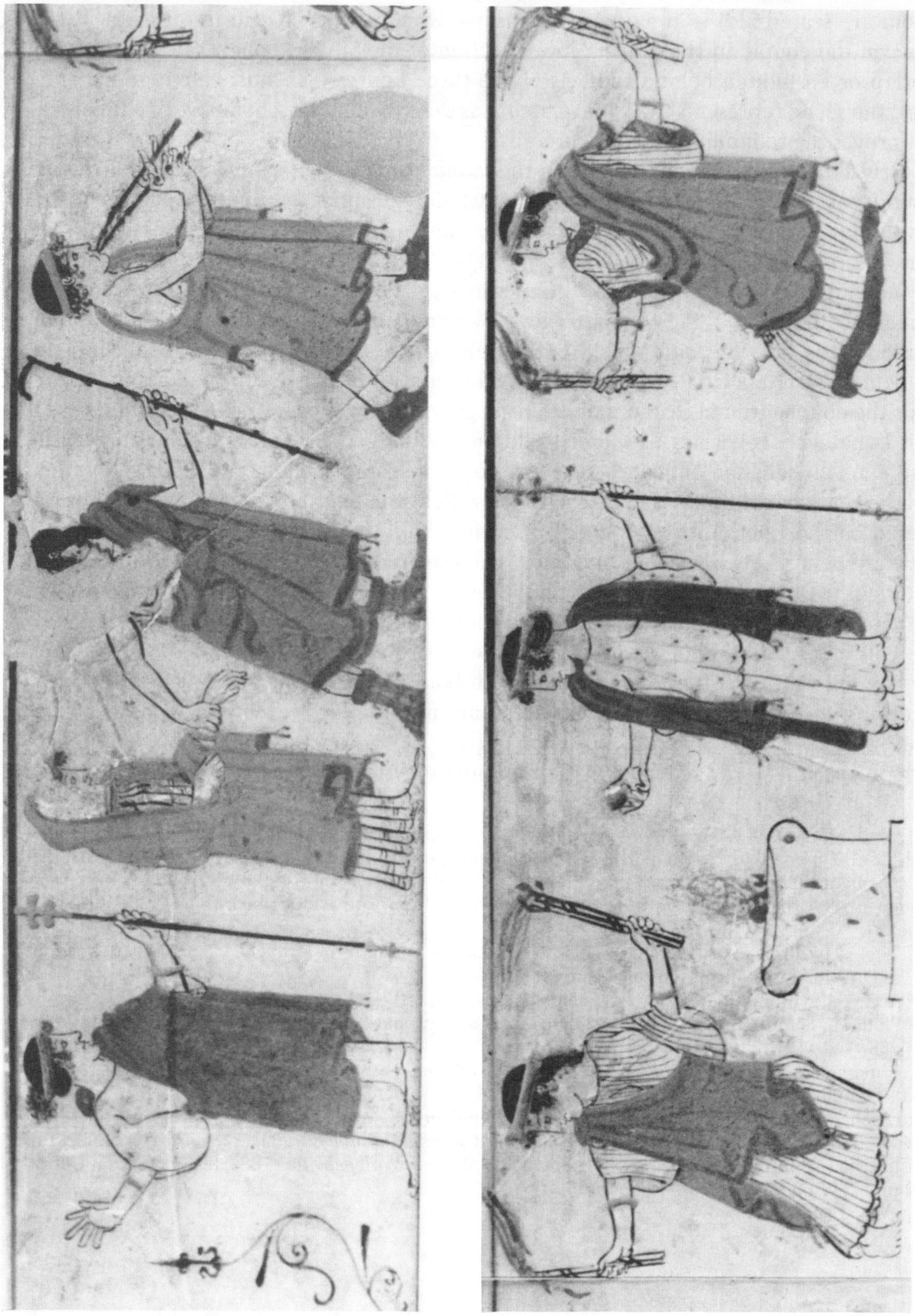

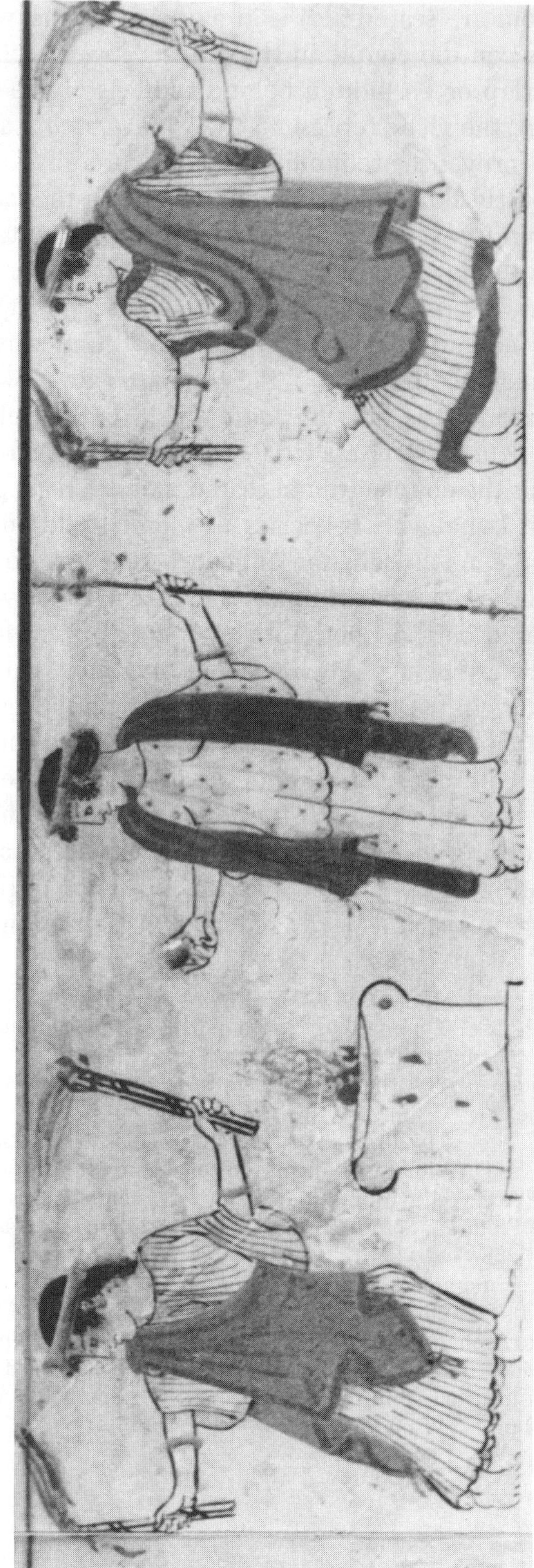

Plate 35a, b. White ground pyxis by the Splanchnopt Painter, London, British Museum D11; after Jenkins (supra n. 61) 2–3, courtesy the Trustees of the British Museum.

whether they or weddings were the origin of the practice.[73] Although Pernice and others place this activity at the wedding banquet, it fits equally well at the new house as a ritual of incorporation in conjunction with the *katachysmata*, suggesting as it does a journey and implying that the thing found is arrival at a new state. Since, however, the boy here is not crowned with a wreath of acanthus and acorn as Zenobios describes, this vase cannot illustrate his account literally. The offer of foodstuff would accord well with the custom that the bride eat something not long after entering her new home.[74] We have already mentioned the quince that Plutarch says Solon decreed she eat before retiring to the *thalamos*, and there is some mention as well of sesame cakes (*plakous*, *pemmata*). The primary symbolism is probably the bride's acceptance of sustenance, *trophe*, in the house of her husband, an act that signifies her transfer to his *kyreia*, and serves, like the sexual act, to incorporate the new household. That this was a token meal can be extrapolated from *The Homeric Hymn to Demeter* (371–74, 412–13) where Persephone was bound as wife to Hades by eating in his home the most minimal of meals, a single pomegranate seed. The Hymn is quite clear that it was the act of eating that bound Persephone to Hades, and not the pomegranate seed per se. The preference for fruit at weddings reflects its association with both fertility and sexuality. Returning to our scene, it is likely that the boy in our scene is *amphithales*[75] and a strong possibility that he offers the bride some food, most fittingly a fruit. This gift has the support of the London pyxis mentioned above (Pl. 35), where the donor is the personification of the household hearth, an item that was probably represented here as well as noted above. Such juxtaposition of two rituals of incorporation, the *katachysmata* and the ritual meal, in a single scene would be appropriate.

Another good possibility remains, however, namely that the boy held instead a wreath, fillet, perfume vessel, or similar item for use in the final preparations of the bride, the activity that occupies Eros and the four women behind the bride. Oakley argues that this attention to the bride indicates the *anakalypteria*, the ritual unveiling of the bride before the groom. Understanding of the *anakalypteria* is clouded by apparently contradictory notices in the ancient literature.[76] As its name indicates, the event focused on the public unveiling of the bride before her new husband and guests, an occasion that was attended by the *anakalypteria dora*, gifts from the groom to his bride. While most authorities place the rite at the banquet at the bride's natal home which immediately proceeded her transfer to her new home, others, notably Pherekydes of Syros (sixth

[73] Samter, *Familienfeste* (supra n. 1) 19; M. Nilsson, "Wedding Rites in Ancient Greece," *Opuscula Selecta* vol. 3, *Skrifter, Svenska Institutet i Athen* (8°), no. 2 (1951) 243–50 at 248f. argues that it dates from the Roman era; Redfield (supra n. 1) 193 with n. 12 defends an earlier date.

[74] Magnien (supra n. 1) 133f.; Erdmann (supra n. 1) 260, n. 61; for more on the erotic associations of fruit see Sutton (supra n. 1) 320–26.

[75] A. Oepke, "Ἀμφιθαλεῖς in griechischen und hellenistischen Kult," *ArchRW* 31 (1934) 42–56 at 46f., 56; L. Robert, "ΑΜΦΙΘΑΛΗΣ," *HSCP* Supp. 1 (*Studies ... Ferguson*; 1940) 509–19.

[76] J. Toutain, "L'anakalypterion," *REA* (1940) 345–53; L. Deubner, "ΕΠΑΥΛΙΑ," *JdI* 15 (1900) 144–54 = *Kleine Schriften* (supra n. 63) 1–11; further literature cited by Oakley (supra n. 62) n. 3; add Redfield (supra n. 1) 192; Pernice (supra n. 1) 58; and C. Patterson (supra n. 1).

century B.C.),[77] seem to indicate that it occurred on the third day, following the wedding night. Vase paintings do little to resolve the matter, for while most show the bride unveiled in procession, apparently indicating that the *anakalypteria* has already occurred, a small number show her head completely covered, including a fully realistic representation complete with mulecart rather than the chariot which usually replaces it on the vases.[78] We cannot resolve such conflicting evidence here, evidence which may reflect variant local or familial practice and nomenclature. It is sufficient only to note that there is no evidence that connects the *anakalypteria* with the couple's arrival at their new home, a moment fixed for our scene by the *katachysmata*.

Moreover, our scene does not show the act of *unveiling*, but rather, as Beazley thought, of *veiling*; this is a crucial point, and the only one on which Oakley and I still differ.[79] The *nympheutria* lowers a short veil onto the bride's head as Eros flies down from above with a fillet. This action could not be more different from the traditional gesture found in black figure and later wedding scenes, sometimes called *anakalypsis* or *apokalypsis*, in which the bride stiffly pulls her mantle away from her face.[80] The *nympheutria's* action is, indeed, strikingly like the motif of decking the bride found on the other Boston loutrophoros (Pls. 29–33) and related scenes. There is nothing in the attitude of any of the figures to suggest a revelation of the bride (cf. the gesture of the woman at the door who catches sight of Eros on Pls. 29b and 32). Furthermore, the motion of Eros *towards* the bride with a fillet is consonant with the decoration of the bride but rather at cross-purpose to any unveiling or disclosure. Both veil and fillet have evidently just been taken from the chest with open lid and the wicker basket held by the women on the left, while the last woman in line stands by with a mirror to assist in their arrangement.

We may then reconstruct the scene as follows. The couple, freshly arrived in their new home, are seated by the hearth and showered with the *katachysmata*. Meanwhile, the bride, still wearing the relatively simple clothing required for the journey, receives final embellishment at the hands of *nympheutriai* and Love himself before being led to the *thalamos* for the *gamos* proper, the consummation of the marriage. There we might anticipate that she will unveil herself to the groom or that he will unveil her himself, a

[77] *Die Fragmente der Vorsokrater*, ed. Diels and Kranz, 6 ed. ([n. p.]: Weidmann 1951) sect. 7.2. Without the full context, it is difficult to know if this divine wedding might have been longer than a normal human wedding, and the third day does not have here its usual significance of "on the day after the *gamos*."

[78] The red-figure saltcellar Bonn 994, L. Deubner, "Eine Hochzeitsvase in Bonn," *JdI* 51 (1936) 175–79 = *Kleine Schriften* (supra n. 63) 556–60; *CVA* (Ger. 1) pl. 28.1–4. Fragments of loutrophoroi from the Shrine of Nymphe described in Sutton (supra n. 1) 242 (W.21 = *ARV*² 526.61 [Orchard Painter]?), 251 (W.55, W.56), mentioned by Oakley (supra n. 62) n. 7.

[79] *ARV*² 1017.44. Oakley now accepts the identification of the *katachysmata* on the right of the scene, but maintains that the *anakalypteria* is shown simultaneously on the left.

[80] References cited by Oakley (supra n. 62) n. 16; add the abstract M. Mayo, "The Gesture of Anakalypsis," *AJA* 77 (1973) 220; J.-M. Dentzer, *Le motif du banquet couché dans le proche-orient et le monde grec du VIIe au IVe siècle avant J.-C.*, *BEFAR* 246 (1982) 484–489, while rejecting a specific connection to the *anakalypteria* and taking a broad interpretation of the motif, admits the possibility that the motif had a special significance in certain scenes, including, one assumes, those that are explicitly nuptial.

private moment found in Hellenistic terracottas[81] that should not be connected with the public *anakalypteria*. The items with which she is adorned may have been brought along in procession as part of her trousseau. Whether the boy offered her a fruit or some other item, it was the focus of the scene. It should have provided a needed compositional link between the figures of bride and groom while uniting the theme of incorporation represented by the *katachysmata* with the polite sexual imagery seen in Eros and implicit in dressing the bride.

The Phiale Painter created a serious and contemplative scene out of what must have been a noisy and merry event as members of the household scrambled to grab up the treats falling over the couple. This unrealistic quiet mood is shared with the first loutrophoros discussed and most contemporary wedding scenes. Such vases are strikingly different in spirit from the raucous *epithalamia* and noisy goings on that attended weddings as actually celebrated. Earlier we argued that this tone expressed a new perception of marriage and the *oikos* under the Athenian Radical Democracy. This view could have no better support than the observation that such romantic illustrations, though remarkably accurate in the portrayal of the *Realien* with which they are constructed, nevertheless alter the mood of the event to create a more profound image that reflects a new ideology rather than social reality.

The value of vase paintings, therefore, for enhancing our understanding of the ancient Athenian wedding is not as simple documentary illustrations of Classical life, or merely in providing confirmation of the accuracy of the scholiasts, but rather as evidence for how ancient Athenians interpreted their own experience through art, and how this led them to play the roles their society dictated. In particular, their depiction of Eros at the liminal stage of the wedding may have encouraged many an uneasy bride and groom as they approached an arranged marriage, serving as both something to expect and a model to emulate. The conception of Eros as a positive social force binding together husband and wife to form the *oikos*, undeniable here in visual form, lends support to those scholars who find such romantic attitudes expressed in contemporary Athenian drama and shows the popular wisdom on which Xenophon, Plato, and other Socratic philosophers were able to draw when they turned their attention to love and marriage a generation later.

[81] Toutain (supra n. 76) 348ff., fig. 2.

BOETHIUS ON THE "INDIVIDUAL": PLATONIST OR ARISTOTELIAN?

Leo Sweeeney, S.J.

The fact that the word "individual" looms large on many levels of the contemporary scene needs no documentation, and Ralph Harper's description in 1955 of what "individual" means remains true today. In his book *Modern Philosophers and Education* he states: "To see another man as an individual is to treat him as if he personally mattered, as if he was irreplaceable, as if he was different from all others. This requires a sensitivity to differences, a humor, and even a certain tenderness that one does not extend to a person insofar as one is thinking of him as one of a type."[1] From those statements we realize that an

[1] *Modern Philosophers and Education* (Chicago: National Society for Study of Education 1955) 250. For "individual" in contemporary educational, social and political theory, which gives "priority in value or worth to the individual over all else," see R.W. Hall, *Plato and the Individual* (The Hague: Martinus Nijhoff 1963) 11–17, where he gives helpful references to writings of R.B. Perry, F.A. Hayek, F. Knight, J.M. Clark, W.E. Hocking, C.L. Becker, E. Baker, H. Kelsen, R.H. Tawney, H.A. Myers, and others.

For more directly and technically philosophical reflection on "individual," see these two articles of J.J.E. Gracia: "Boethius and the Problem of the Individual in the Commentaries on the 'Isagoge'," *Atti del Congresso Internazionale di Studi Boeziani* (Roma: Herder 1981) 169–70, where he lists the six basic issues involved in the problem of individuation as the intension of individuality, the extension of individuality, the ontological status of individuality in the individual and its relation to the nature, the cause or principle of individuation, the discernability of individuals, and the function of proper names and indexical terms; "Individuals as Instances," *Review of Metaphysics* 37 (1983) 37–59, where he dismisses five features traditionally assigned as constituents of individuality (distinction, division, identity, impredicability, indivisibility) as failing to serve as its necessary and sufficient conditions, which (he concludes) are best satisfied by conceiving individuality as incommunicability (to use the language of Boethius, Aquinas, and other medievals) or non-instantiability (a contemporary word): "What is meant by saying that individuals are incommunicable [is the same as saying that it is impossible] that they be instantiated. Socrates, for example, cannot become instantiated in the way 'man' can. It is, then, non-instantiability that provides us with a precise understanding of individuality, since it is both a necessary and sufficient condition of it. Individuals cannot be instantiated as universals can. They are instances of instantiables and, therefore non-instantiable themselves" (57). See infra n. 25.

Also see K.R. Popper, "Symposium: The Principle of Individuation," *Proceedings of Aristotelian Society for the Systematic Study of Philosophy*, Supplementary Vol. 27 (1953) 97–120; P.F. Strawson, *Individuals: An Essay in Descriptive Metaphysics* (London: Methuen 1965) 23 sqq., 121 sqq., 227 sqq. One also may profitably consult the chapters in Michael J. Loux (ed.) *Universals and Particulars: Readings in Ontology* (Garden City, N.Y.: Doubleday 1970), especially Loux's own two chapters, "The Problem of Universals" (3–15) and "Particulars and Their Individuation" (189–203) as well as David Higgins, "The Individuation of Things and Places" (307–335); also the chapters in M.K. Munitz (ed.) *Identity and Individuation* (New York: New York University Press 1971) especially Munitz's "Introduction" (iii–viii) and H. Hiz, "On the Abstractness of Individuals" (251–61). On Aristotle's position on "individual" see L. Sweeney, S.J., *Authentic Metaphysics in an Age of Unreality* (New York/Bern: Peter Lang 1988) 181–86; G.E.L. Owen, "Inherence," *Phronesis* 10 (1965) 97–105; R. E. Allen, "Individual Properties in Aristotle's *Categories*," *Phronesis* 14 (1969) 31–39 (see 32, n. 4, for references to W.D. Ross; G.E.M. Anscombe, J.L. Ackrill, and K. von Fritz); B. Jones, "Individuals in Aristotle's *Categories*," *Phronesis* 17 (1972) 107–123; J. Annas, "Individuals in Aristotle's *Categories*: Two Queries," *Phronesis* 19 (1974) 146–52.

individual is someone who personally matters, who is different from all others, who is irreplaceable. That last word should be taken seriously: an individual is he who is so important, whose contribution to others is so unique, whose influence is so widespread that no one else can take his place: he is, literally, "irreplaceable." Names of several prominent people easily come to mind: Einstein in physics, Hegel in philosophy, George Balanchine in ballet, Johann Sebastian Bach in classical music, Abraham Lincoln in government, Martin Luther King, Jr., in civil rights, Mother Teresa of Calcutta in charitable works, Pope John Paul II in religion, Michael Jackson on the current music scene, and so on.[2]

But individuality is not to be restricted to prominent people. It may and should, if taken seriously, be applied to every human existent because each one of us differs from all others (parents, spouses, children, students, neighbors, friends), each one of us is unique and, therefore, each is irreplaceable: absolutely no one is identical with me, no one else is me, no one is numerically the same. The twofold result is that no one can fill my shoes or replace me and, secondly, that, because I am unique and because I am, I have a right to be. This last result can perhaps be best gathered from a description which a young lady gave of her experience when confronted with the fact that she had been an illegitimate child.

> I remember walking that day under the elevated tracks in a slum area, feeling the thought, "I am an illegitimate child." I recall the sweat pouring forth in my anguish in trying to accept that fact. Then I understood what it must feel like to accept, "I am a Negro in the midst of privileged whites," or "I am blind in the midst of people who see." Later on that night I woke up and it came to me this way, "I accept the fact that I am an illegitimate child." *But* "I am not a child anymore." So it is, "I am illegitimate." That is not so either: "I was born illegitimate." Then what is left? What is left is this, "*I Am.*" This *act* of contact and acceptance with "I am," once gotten hold of, gave me (what I think was for me the first time) the experience "Since I Am, I have the right to be."[3]

From such a description one realizes that viewing an individual as he/she who is literally "irreplaceable" issues into our contemporary awareness of the legitimate claim everyone has to civil and personal rights in all fields, of freedom as our precious and inalienable property.[4]

Several questions can now arise. For instance, whence came this appealing notion of individuality? What is its source within the history of ideas?[5] Another inquiry is how early in the history of thought that conception of individual can be found.

[2] Such people are outstanding (and thus unique) in some sort of excellence, but one may easily list others outstanding in evil—e.g., Hitler, Stalin, Mao Tse-Tung, Fidel Castro, Idi Amin, Ayatollah Khomeini, Muammar Qaddafi, Jim Jones of Guyana.

[3] See Rollo May, *Existence: A New Dimension in Psychiatry and Psychology* (New York: Basic Books 1958) 43. The girl continues her account by turning the tables on Descartes: "[My experience of be-ing] is my saying to Descartes, 'I *am*; *therefore* I think, I feel, I do.'"

[4] Such awareness of rights and freedom must, of course, be balanced by awareness of the responsibilities they also entail. Lack of such concern for the rights of others would produce a "*Me*-Generation" with tendencies to manipulate, bully or, even, enslave others.

[5] Certainly one major origin is the Judeo-Christian Scriptures, which emphaszie God's knowledge and love of each human person. As instances see Psalm 139, 1 sqq.; Psalm 147, 1, 3 and 4; Isaiah, 43, 1 sqq.; Paul,

PLOTINUS

Anyone reading the *Enneads* of Plotinus (205–270) is struck not only by the absence of the notion but by its explicit denial. See *Enneads*, VI, 5 (23), 12, 16 sqq., where he addresses a human soul and explains how it acquires and also frees itself from individuality: "[In ascending back to Intellect] you have come to the All and not stayed in a part of it, and have not said even about yourself, 'I am so much.' By rejecting the 'so much' you have become all—yet you were all before. But because something else other than the All added itself to you, you became less by the addition, for the addition did not come from real being (you cannot add anything to that) but from that which is not. When you have become an individual by the addition of non-being, you are not all till you reject the non-being. You will increase yourself then by rejecting the rest, and by that rejection the All is with you."

Ἢ ὅτι παντὶ προσῆλθες καὶ οὐκ ἔμεινας ἐν μέρι αὐτοῦ οὐδ' εἶπας οὐδὲ σύ «τοσοῦτός εἰμι», ἀφεὶς δὲ τὸ «τοσοῦτος» γέγονας πᾶς, καίτοι καὶ πρότερον ἦσθα πᾶς· ἀλλ' ὅτι καὶ ἄλλο τι προσῆν σοι μετὰ τὸ «πᾶς», ἐλάττων ἐγίνου τῇ προσθήκῃ· οὐ γὰρ ἐκ τοῦ παντὸς ἦν ἡ προσθήκη—οὐδὲν γὰρ ἐκείνῳ προσθήσεις—ἀλλὰ τοῦ μὴ ὄντος. Γενόμενος δέ τις καὶ ἐκ τοῦ μὴ ὄντος ἐστὶν οὐ πᾶς, ἀλλ' ὅταν τὸ μὴ ὂν ἀφῇ. Αὔξεις τοίνυν σεαυτὸν ἀφεὶς τὰ ἄλλα καὶ πάρεστί σοι τὸ πᾶν ἀφέντι·)

By liberating itself from the body, then, a soul discards the individuality which physical existence had put upon it and which prompted it to say: "I am so much," "I am this definite human being distinct from all else," "I am this individual." Thereby the soul regains its place within the Soul and, eventually, within the Intellect, where nonetheless it retains its other sort of individuality—its distinguishability or divisibility from Intellect, Soul, and other souls.

But even this individuality is set aside when a soul ascends beyond Soul and Intellect to become one with the One and thereby achieves happiness above being. In that beatifying union, Plotinus states in VI, 9 (9), 11, 4 sqq., "there were not two, but the seer himself was one with the Seen (for It was not really seen but united to him) . . . He was one himself then, with no distinction in him either in relation to himself or anything else; for there was no movement in him, and he had no emotion, no desire for anything else when he had made the ascent, no reason or thought; his own self [= what he was on a lower level: soul] was not there for him, if we should say even this" (lines 4–12: *'Επεὶ τοίνυν δύο οὐκ ἦν, ἀλλ' ἓν ἦν αὐτὸς ὁ ἰδὼν πρὸς τὸ ἑωραμένον, ὡς ἂν μὴ ἑωραμένον, ἀλλ' ἡνωμένον,*

Galatians, 2, 20; Gospel of Matthew, 25, 40 and 45. Another ultimate source of contemporary individualism is the stress put on "person" and "supposit" *vs.* "essence" and "nature" in early Ecumenical Councils and Creeds of the Church. For documentation see Sweeney (supra n. 1) 173–78. Also see M.F.X. Millar, S.J., "The History and Development of the Democratic Theory of Government in Christian Tradition," *The State and the Church* (New York: Macmillan 1924) 99–144.

ὃς ἐγένετο ὅτε ἐκείνῳ ἐμίγνυτο εἰ μεμνῷτο, ἔχοι ἂν παρ' ἑαυτῷ ἐκείνου εἰκόνα· Ἦν δὲ ἓν καὶ αὐτὸς διαφορὰν ἐν αὐτῷ οὐδεμίαν πρὸς ἑαυτὸν ἔχων οὔτε κατὰ ἄλλα—οὐ γάρ τι ἐκινεῖτο παρ' αὐτῷ, οὐ θυμός, οὐκ ἐπιθυμία ἄλλου παρῆν αὐτῷ ἀναβεβηκότι—ἀλλ' οὐδὲ λόγος οὐδέ τις νόησις οὐδ' ὅλως αὐτός, εἰ δεῖ καὶ τοῦτο λέγειν). In fact, his contemplation of God was perhaps "not a contemplation but another kind of seeing, a being out of oneself [= what one is as a distinct and lower existent], a simplifying, a self-surrender [a surrender of what one is as a distinct, less real being], a pressing towards contact, a rest, a sustained thought directed to perfect conformity" (lines 22–25: *Τὸ δὲ ἴσως ἦν οὐ θέαμα, ἀλλὰ ἄλλος τρόπος τοῦ ἰδεῖν, ἔκστασις καὶ ἅπλωσις καὶ ἐπίδοσις αὑτοῦ καὶ ἔφεσις πρὸς ἁφὴν καὶ στάσις καὶ περινόησις πρὸς ἐφαρμογήν*). Those lines apparently explicate the identity between man when fully real and primal Reality: man then is one with the One.

Plotinus then recapitulates the entire process of descent and ascent (lines 36–51). "When a soul goes down it comes to evil and so to non-being . . . When it travels the opposite way it comes, not to something else but to itself; and so when it is not in anything else it is in nothing but itself. But when it is in itself alone and not in being, it is in That; for one becomes oneself not as being but beyond being by that intercourse . . . When a man falls from that vision [and union with the One], he wakes again the virtue in himself and considers himself in all his order and beauty, and is lightened and rises through virtue to Intellect and through wisdom to Divine. This is the life of gods and divine and blessed men, deliverance from the things of this world, a life which takes no delight in the things of this world, escape in solitude to the Solitary."

Inspiring and consoling as that text is, it leaves little doubt but that an individual human soul is most truly real when it is no longer individual at all. This occurs when it has shed all particularity, uniqueness, distinction, otherness by rising above not only the physical universe but also the psychic and intelligible realms, by transcending thereby being and knowledge, by losing itself in the One, by somehow literally becoming the One. Consequently, individuality is for Plotinus unreality, nonbeing, negation, evil almost, since it is equated with otherness, distinction, separateness, all of which are inimical to unity, wherein alone reality resides.[6]

BOETHIUS

On the other hand and a full two and a half centuries later, the Latin author Anicius Manlius Severinus Boethius (ca. 480–525) apparently does not hold individuality in such low repute—at least he uses the term in his very definition of "person" as "naturae rationabilis *individua* substantia" (*Contra Eutychen et Nestorium*, Sect. 3, 4–5). This

[6] See Danièle Letocha, "Le statut de l'individualité chez Plotin ou le miroir de Dionysos," *Dionysius* 2 (1978) 76: "Chez Plotin individualité n'est rien du point de vue ontologique: elle manifeste la distance à l'Un, le non-être, l'evil;" and 78: "Les grandes hypostases du *Nous* et de la *Psychē*, le multiplicité progressive qui semble submerger la perception première, c'est l'Un lui-même fragmenté par cette illusion du regard." The entire article deserves attention. Also see P.J. About, *Plotin* (Paris: Editions Seghers 1973), esp. 63–88.

definition he applies not only to men but to angels and even to God,[7] and hence "individua" therein would seem to imply perfection.

Let us set that definition within the context provided by the theological tractate itself. As its title indicates, that tractate aims at answering criticisms against the position put forth in the Council of Chalcedon in 451 that Christ consists of two natures (divine and human) and one person.[8] In contrast, Nestorius saw in Christ two natures and two persons, Eutyches one nature and one person.[9] In his reply Boethius elaborates what "natura," "substantia," and other key Latin terms in the definition mean. "Natura" means "the specific difference which informs anything": "natura est unamquamque rem informans specifica differentia" (ibid., Sect. 1, 57–58).[10] Both Catholics and Nestorius agree (Boethius adds) with "nature" so defined: in Christ there are two such natures because the specific difference which makes Him be God cannot be the same as that which makes Him be man (ibid., 59 sqq.: "tam Catholici quam Nestorius secundum ultimam definitionem duas in Christo naturas esse constituent; neque enim easdem in deum atque hominem differentias convenire").

[But in the face of this agreement why do Catholics not also agree with Nestorius that He is two persons? Because of the meaning they give to "persona,"] which is (Boethius concedes) a "matter of very great perplexity" (ibid., Sect. 2, 1–2: "Sed de persona maxime dubitari potest quaenam ei definitio possit aptari"). Nonetheless, these points are clear. "Natura" is a substrate of "persona" and thus is always involved whenever "persona" is predicated (ibid., 9–12: "Nam illud quidem manifestum est personaeG subjectam esse naturam nec praeter naturam personam posse praedicari"). But unlike "natura," which is

[7] See ibid., Sect. 2, 25–28 and 36–37, quoted infra p. 366. In our references to Boethius' tractate the final numbers indicate the relevant lines of the Section as found in the Loeb edition first put out by E.K. Rand and H.F. Stewart and revised by S.J. Tester in 1973. In my translations or paraphrases brackets will indicate the interpolations needed to explicate the movement of Boethius' thought so as to clarify his meaning.

[8] See Henry Chadwick, *The Consolations of Music, Logic, Theology and Philosophy* (Oxford: Clarendon 1981) 190: Boethius' "prime objective is to reconcile the critics of Chalcedon by assuring the hesitant that Chalcedon's 'two natures' is both necessary to avert Eutychianism and altogether distinct from Nestorianism." Chadwick's discussion of *Contra Eutychen et Nestorium* (180–202) is most helpful and informative, as is his bibliography, pp. 261–84.

[9] This simplified statement is drawn from Boethius' own tractate, corroborated however by Chadwick (supra n. 8, 182), who sees it as filling the then current need of a "middle way between Nestorius and Eutyches."

[10] Boethius illustrates "nature" here with gold and silver: it is that form which specifically and properly differentiates the two metals (ibid., 54–56). This definition of "natura," based on Aristotle's *Physics* 193a28–31 (see Chadwick [supra n. 8] 191) is contrasted with several other meanings, the first of which is applicable to anything that exists and which appears in Syrianus, Ammonius, and other Neoplatonists: "nature is a term for those things which, insofar as they exist, can in some way be apprehended by the intellect" (ibid., 8–10: "natura est earum rerum quae, cum sint, quoquo modo intellectu capi possunt"). In another sense, based on Plato's *Phaedrus* 270d and *Sophist* 247e, nature is "that which can act or can be acted upon" (ibid., 25–26: "natura est vel quod facere vel quod pati possit"). In still a third sense, based on Aristotle's *Physics* 192b20, nature is "the principle of movement per se and not as accident" (ibid., 41–42: "natura est motus principium per se et non per accidens").

applicable to substances and to accidents (e.g., whiteness, blackness, largeness), "persona" is said only of substances (ibid., 17–18: "relinquitur ergo ut personam in substantiis dici conveniat").

But one can take substances in a twofold manner—either as they are found in actual existents [this let us call "Schema One"] or according to our way of predicating them ["Schema Two"]. According to Schema One actually existing substances are twofold insofar as they are either corporeal or incorporeal.[11] Corporeal substances are either living or nonliving (e.g., a stone); living substances are either rational [a man as a composite of soul and body] or irrational (e.g., a horse or an ox).[12] Let us now return to the second member of the initial division of Schema One and subdivide it. Some incorporeal substances are rational, others not so (e.g., the life-giving principles in subhuman animals; ibid., 23–24: "[substantiae incorporeae irrationales] ut pecudum vitae"). Rational substances are either by nature immutable and impassible (e.g., God) or because of their status as creatures mutable and passible except through grace, e.g. angels and human souls; ibid., 18–28:

> Sed substantiarum aliae sunt corporeae, aliae incorporeae. Corporearum vero aliae sunt viventes, aliae minime; viventium aliae sunt sensibiles, aliae minime; sensibilium aliae rationales, aliae inrationales. Item incorporearum aliae sunt rationales, aliae minime, ut pecudum vitae; rationalium vero alia est inmutabilis atque impassibilis per naturam ut deus, alia per creationem mutabilis atque passibilis, nisi inpassibilis gratia permutetur ut angelorum atque animae.

These last alone (God, angels and human souls) are "personae" (ibid., 36–37: "at hominis dicimus esse personam, dicimus dei, dicimus angeli").

But what if we understand "substance" precisely as a predicable (Schema Two)? Then substances are either universal or particular. Universal substances are such as can be predicated of many individuals and thus are genera and species. For instance, the genus "animal" can be said of several individual [sorts of] animals (e.g., horses, oxen, snakes), "stone" of individual [sorts of] stones (e.g., pieces of granite, diamonds, limestones), "wood" of individual [sorts of] sticks of wood (e.g., oak, maple, walnut), the species "man" of individual men (ibid., 37–44):

> Rursus substantiarum aliae sunt universales, aliae particulares. Universales sunt quae de singulis praedicantur ut

[11] The methodology which initiates and constitutes Schema One, as it will Schema Two also, Chadwick relates to "the so-called Porphyrian tree" (ibid. 192). It also could easily be reduced back to the dialetctics of division/collection Plato introduced in *Phaedrus* 265e sqq. and utilized not only in that dialogue but also in *Sophist*, *Statesman*, and *Philebus*.

[12] Boethius gives no example of a rational corporeal substance, but one may infer it to be a composite of human soul and body from his instancing a human soul itself as a rational incorporeal substance.

> homo, animal, lapis, lignum ceteraque huiusmodi quae vel genera vel species sunt; nam et homo de singulis hominibus et animal de singulis animalibus lapisque ac lignum de singulis lapidibus ac lignis dicuntur.

On the other hand, particular substances are such as not to be predicable of things other [than what each is but only of itself]—e.g., "Cicero" is said only of this Roman citizen, "this rock" only of this marble statue of Achilles, "this wood" solely of this oaken table.

Accordingly (Boethius now draws his first conclusion), "persona" can never be said of "substance" taken universally (e.g., genus, species) but solely of particulars and individuals, e.g., Cicero, Plato, and any other single rational existent; ibid., 44–52:

> Particularia vero sunt quae de aliis minime praedicantur ut Cicero, Plato, lapis hic unde haec Achillis statua facta est, lignum hoc unde haec mensa composita est. Sed in his omnibus nusquam in universalibus persona dici potest, sed in singularibus tantum atque in individuis; animalis enim vel generalis hominis nulla persona est, sed vel Ciceronis vel Platonis vel singulorum individuorum personae singulae nuncupantur.

Secondly, "persona" is definable as "naturae rationabilis individua substantia" because "persona" belongs to rational substances solely and because "substantia" here entails a nature which is individual;[13] ibid., Sect. 3, 1–5:

> Quocirca si persona in solis substantiis est atque in his rationabilibus substantiaque omnis natura est nec in universalibus sed in individuis constat, reperta personae est definitio: "naturae rationabilis individua substantia."

But what does "individua" in the definition indicate? That the nature or substance so described is such as to be in a single and unique existent (see ibid., Sect. 2, 44 sqq.), which moreover is either divine or angelic or human (ibid., 24–28). This last fact—namely, that "individua" applies not only to men but to angels and God as well—guarantees that individuality is a perfective and positive factor of such existents and that Boethius thereby

[13] In the rest of Sect. 3 Boethius discusses the Greek terms *πρόσοπον*, *οὐσία*, *ὑπόστασις*, and *οὐσίωσις* and their Latin equivalents. In Sect. 4, 6–9, he re-affirms his definitions in Section 3, 4–5, of "natura" and "persona." According to Chadwick a comparison of *Contra Eutychen et Nestorium* "with Boethius' other writings shows that his treatment of 'person' varies according to the degree to which Aristotelian language about primary or individual substance is enfolded within a Platonic metaphysic of universals" (supra n. 8, 194). On Maxentius of Constantinople, theological leader of a group of monks known as "Scythian" and influential at Rome also in the early sixth century see ibid. 186–88: his definition of "persona" is "una res individuae naturae," the last word signifying the substrate of person. For reactions to Boethius' definition of "persona" beginning with his own century and extending up to Aquinas see ibid. 195.

differs from Plotinus (see above). Hence, in this area he is not Platonic but, as we shall see, Aristotelian. In order to establish this let us turn to Plato and then to Aristotle.

PLATO

The core of Plato's metaphysics is that subsistent Forms or Essences (e.g., Beauty, Justice) are primary realities, and that individual existents (human souls included) are real only to the extent that they transiently participate in those Forms. Let us look at that metaphysics a bit more closely.

In our interpretation metaphysics is the knowledge of the real as real;[14] but to be real for Plato is to be immutable; therefore, Platonic metaphysics concerns that which is immutable. But two sorts of existents are immutable:

1) primarily and in and of themselves subsistent Forms of Essences are immutable,

2) derivatively individual sensible existents share in immutability insofar as efficient causes make-them-be-images of Forms, which also cause them as models and goals.[15]

Several aspects of that participational situation deserve comment. The participated perfection never becomes an intrinsic and stable constituent of the participant.[16]

[14] "Real" means "that which has value, worth, perfection." Most philosophers would agree with that answer, but disagreement begins in deciding what factor ultimately causes objective value, worth, and perfection. For Plato that cause is immutability. See Sweeney (supra n. 1) 26 sqq. and 80, n. 33.

[15] For the contrast between Forms and sensible things in terms of the former's immutability and the latter's mutability see *Phaedo* 74A–B and 78D; *Symposium* 210E–211B; *Timaeus* 27D–28A and 51E–52A; *Philebus* 58A. In the first two dialogues mentioned, immutability resides in the fact that a Form is simple (μονοειδές—see *Phaedo* 78D5; *Symposium* 211B1); in the last two dialogues Forms are composite because they participate in other Forms (see *Timaeus* 30C–D; *Philebus* 23C–D as answering the second of three questions Plato asks earlier in 15B: how can Forms be one-many? His reply: they are *ousiai* which are combinations each of *peras* and *to apeiron*; see also *Sophist* 251E–252D) and yet they are immutable.

In *Phaedo* 100B–E participation of things in a Form is designated simply as its presence in and association with them. In *Parmenides* 131A–D participation is further explained as the process by which things are made-to-be-images of Forms—a process which is later disclosed to consist in the exemplary and telic causality of the Forms themselves and in the efficient causality of the Craftsman (*Timaeus* 28A–29A and 29D–C; *Philebus* 26E–27C and 28C–30D). See L. Sweeney, S.J., *Infinity in Plato's Philebus: A Bibliographical and Philosophical Study* (forthcoming) chs. IV–VI.

[16] The participated perfection is the second of three factors in the participational situation of which Plato speaks in *Phaedo* 102B and *Parmenides* 130B:

the form of (say) Beauty itself, which is a single Essence subsisting apart from the physical world but which is the radical cause (as model and goal) of why these petunias are beautiful;

the beauties present in the flowering plants, which are the multiple participated perfections immanent in the petunias and through which the Form itself is present to them;

the plants themselves,which are the participants.

To them Plato adds a fourth factor—the craftsman as efficient cause—when he realized that he must explain further how those multiple participated perfections come about (for references to *Timaeus* see supra n. 15). Reflection upon the nature of participants induced him to add a fifth factor, which in the *Timaeus* (47E–49A, 50A–51B and 52D–53C) he called receptacle or space and in the *Philebus* (23C, 24A–25A) the indefinite or unlimited (τὸ ἄπειρον).

On the three-factor theory of participation see L. Sweeney, S.J., "'Safe' and 'Cleverer' Answers in Plato's Discussion of Participation and Immortality," *Southern Journal of Philosophy* 15 (1977) 242–51; idem, "Participation in Plato's Dialogues: *Phaedo, Parmenides*, and *Timaeus*" (forthcoming); Richard Patterson, *Image and Reality in Plato's Metaphysics* (Indianapolis: Hackett 1985).

Secondly, the participated perfection (e.g., beauty) is that which each participant has in common with the Form and, what is especially relevant, *with other participants*—in fact, such common perfections and the common names we use to designate them lead to our awareness (through recollection) that the Form itself exists and of what it is.[17] Thirdly, that which distinguishes one participant from other participants (and, of course, from the Form itself), that which is uniquely its own, that which makes it other than them is its "individuality." And what does that consist in? It is aligned with unreality because the reality of this individual participant is whatever participated perfection it has in common with other participants transiently and (so to speak) on loan. It is linked with negation: beauty (e. g.) in participant A is not the beauty in participants B and C. It is other than their beauties. But that otherness is not something positive but simply the observable fact that somehow and for some inexplicable reason beauty in A *is not* beauty in B or in C.

Already one can begin to see how individuality in moral agents is unreal and negative. Why so? Philosophers (let us restrict ourselves to this sort of human soul, since what is true of them is also true *a fortiori* of soldiers and tradesmen in the *Republic*) are just, temperate, courageous, and morally good only by participating in the Form of the Good and, thereby, in the Forms of Justice, Temperance, and Courage. What such philosophically gifted participants have in common (however impermanently and on loan) is the participated perfections of goodness, justice, temperance, and courage, which make them be authentically moral agents. What distinguishes one such participant from others, what makes him be other than them, what is unique to him would constitute his individuality as a moral agent. And what does that consist in? It could not be anything real since the justice, temperance, courage, and goodness which he has in common with other moral agents are the participated perfections, which alone are real. Again it must not be anything positive but simply the negative fact that somehow the morality precisely of Socrates *is not* precisely that of Plato. And what "is not" expresses is actually and really nothing.[18]

[17] On recollection as a human soul's recalling (on the occasion of sense-experience) the awareness which it achieved by contemplating (and thereby participating in) the Forms before entering the physical world, see *Meno* 81A sqq.; *Phaedo* 74A sqq.; *Phaedrus* 246D–252C. Also see Jacob Klein, *A Commentary on Plato's Meno* (Chapel Hill: North Carolina 1965) 108–172; J.C.B. Gosling, *Plato* (London: Routledge and Kegan Paul 1973) 125–27 and 160–66; N.P. White, *Plato on Knowledge and Reality* (Indianapolis: Hackett 1976) 47–61.

[18] Apparently what corresponds in the realm of Forms to this negation is the Form of Otherness and Nonbeing in *Sophist* 255C–E and 256D–258C, a Form which accounts for the fact that the Form of Rest is *other than*, and thus, *is not* the Form of Motion by their participating in Otherness and Nonbeing. More relevantly: the Form of Otherness and Nonbeing accounts for the fact that the Form of Justice is other than and is not the Form of Courage by their participating in Otherness and Nonbeing. So too Plato's Justice is other than Socrates' by their participating in the Form of Otherness or Nonbeing. But their being other than one another constitutes their individuality. Hence, the Form of Otherness and Nonbeing in the *Sophist* can be called the Form of Individuality, by participating in which individual existents are individual, even though their individuality as such is negation, unreality, absence.

Consistently, Plato will no longer equate individuality with negation, unreality, and absence in *Philebus* 23C sqq., where an individual physical existent is no longer form or image or reflection solely (see

Accordingly, the outcome of Plato's metaphysics is that individuality *as such* is not a perfection: in and of itself it is merely negation, unreality, nonbeing. An individual existent *qua* individual is unreal, worthless, insignificant. Consistently, then, Plato's position cannot have been an ancestor of our current dedication to the "infinite reality" (Kierkegaard) of each individual. Even if he had never written the *Republic* with its subordination of all ranks of citizens to philosopher-kings, themselves subordinate to the Form of the Good, his metaphysics would locate whatever reality individual human souls have in the perfections which they share in common and not in their individuality.

This is the metaphysics which helps produce the downgrading of individuality we have already met in Plotinus' *Enneads*, VI, 5 (23), 12, 16. For here, as with Plato, metaphysics is the knowledge of the real as real; but to be real for Plotinus is to be one, and, hence, Plotinian metaphysics deals with oneness.[19] But unity is found in two sorts of existents:

1) primally and fully in Plotinus' highest hypostasis—the One/Good, who is God and Who is sheer and subsistent unity;

2) derivatively in all other existents—the Intellect (and the intellects it contains) and the Soul (and its contents: the World Soul, astral souls, human souls, subhuman souls). The Intellect and intellects come about by the One overflowing and by that overflow (which is intelligible matter and power) turning back to contemplate its source; the Soul and souls come about when the Intellect in turn overflows and the resultant overflow looks back at the Intellect and the One and fashions itself. In all those existents other than the One, reality is unity and nothing else: each is real to the extent that it *is the One on a lower level*.[20]

But each existent is individual to the degree that it is *other* than the One and, thus, each is thereby unreal. Take as an example an individual human soul: when embodied it is distinct and separate from other human souls and intellects, from the Soul and the Intellect and, of course, from the One. Even when it puts off matter and ascends to the higher realms of reality, it is not separate from the Soul, Intellect, and One, but is at least distinguishable from (and thus other than) them and, hence, remains individual. It puts

---

Timaeus 50B6, where τὸ σῶμα is only the εἴκων itself), but is a composite of πέρας and τὸ ἄπειρον, the latter serving as participant, the former as the formal determinant which directly affects the *apeiron*, which in turn receives, limits, and thereby individuates the *peras*. Obviously in the Philebus Plato is closely approaching Aristotle's doctrine of individuation—see the paragraphs infra corresponding to notes 21–22.

[19] In Plotinus metaphysics is the knowledge of the real as real and not (as Aristotle expresses it) of being as being, since reality is not being but unity. Were Aristotle's formula taken literally, metaphysics would be restricted to reflection on Intellect, Soul, and the physical world since the One transcends being. Actually, though, such a restriction is unnecessary when the object of metaphysics is taken to be the real as real and the real is oneness and not being.

[20] On reality as identified with unity, which is primarily found in God as the One/Good who is the source of all other existents, see VI. 9 (9). 9. 1–8; III. 8 (30). 10. 14–31; V. 2 (11). 1. 10–21. For translation and commentary on those texts see L. Sweeney, S.J., "Are Plotinus and Albertus Magnus Neoplatonists" in L. P. Gerson (ed.) *Graceful Reason: Essays in Ancient and Medieval Philosophy Presented to Joseph Owens* (Toronto: Pontifical Institute of Mediaeval Studies Press 1983) 182–88; on monism as the essence of Plotinus' metaphysics see ibid. 188–91.

off even this individuality by becoming one with the One and thus is truly real, but only when no longer what it was as a distinct existent.

ARISTOTLE

But what of Aristotle (384–321 B.C.)? On the "individual" has Plato influenced him as he did Plotinus?

However alike Plato and Aristotle may be in other areas,[21] their positions on the individual diverge rather radically. Consider the interpretation each would give to (say) two beautiful blooming cherry trees. Both philosophers agree that tree A is other than tree B, that A is not B: they are two individual trees. But, as we have suggested earlier, that otherness and, hence, individuality is, for Plato, simply a negation and unreal because the reality of each tree resides in what they have in common (the immanent perfections of beauty, treeness, color, etc.) through participating in the subsistent Forms of Beauty, Treeness, Color, and the rest. Those immanent participated perfections are not received, literally and permanently, by and in their participants and are not entitatively affected by them: in brief, those perfections are not individuated (in any positive sense) by the participants.

The situation is quite different in an Aristotelian approach. The otherness, distinction, uniqueness—in a word, individuality—of the two trees is a positive factor in them. Why so? Because it arises when the forms (accidental and substantial) which help constitute them are educed by efficient causes from the potency of the substance and of prime matter, which also are real constituents of the trees and which entitatively affect the forms (perfections, acts) thus brought forth and continuing on within them for at least some duration. Those forms do not subsist apart from actual cherry trees, but they actually are and are what they are only as present and concretized in those trees. In a word, those forms (both accidental and substantial) are *real* only when and *as individuated* by the substance or matter within which they are present.

But are not those forms the perfections which the two trees have in common? Yes, but they have that commonness only *as known*: only as the content of our awareness of them and, hence, only as specifically alike; only, therefore, as universals (both direct and reflexive). In the actual trees such forms are not common but individual: their being is itself permeated by the distinctiveness, uniqueness, individuality issuing from the components from which they have been educed, which are limiting and thereby determining them and which are formally perfected and thereby determined in turn.

For Aristotle, then, individuality of forms and of the existents they help constitute is the positive entitative state of uniqueness and differentiation in which all material things find themselves.

[21] One position which they have in common is that knowledge in one of its apsects is a πάθημα inasmuch as the object known is its content-determining-cause. See L. Sweeney, S.J., "Plato, Plotinus and Aristotle on the Individual" in John Furlong, Wm. J. Carroll, and Stephen Mann (eds). *Roots of Western Civilization: The Emergence of the Individual* (Baltimore: Coppin State College Press 1988) Appendix C: "Plato and Aristotle on Knowledge."

Individuality is, then, not negation or nonbeing (as it is for Plato and Plotinus). No, it is a positive state of reality within material existents which arises when substance receives accidents and prime matter receives substantial form. When that substantial form is a human soul, conceived as spiritual and immortal, then a structure within which the infinite value and dignity of each individual human person resides can be built upon the speculative foundation Aristotle has at least in part laid.[22]

CONCLUSIONS

In our exegesis above of Boethius' definition of "persona" as "naturae rationabilis idividua substantia," we inferred that individuality there is a perfection and expresses a positive state of reality within the divine, angelic, and human existents of which it is predicated. Secondly, the Latin author's position is thereby akin to Aristotle's rather than to Plato's.

This kinship become even clearer if one turns to Section 6 of *Contra Eutychen et Nestorium*, where Boethius deals with Eutyches' contention that even if Christ's body was taken from Mary, the human and divine nature did not last (and, thus, Christ consists of one nature and is one person; ibid., Sect. 6, 3–8) because His humanity was transformed into divinity.[23] But (Boethius replies) such a transformation is impossible because Christ's human substance consists of a human soul and body and thus is corporeal; but no corporeal substance can be changed into an incorporeal one or *vice versa* because change or transformation can occur only if the two substances share a common subject which is matter (ibid., 24–26: "sola enim mutari transformarique in se possunt quae habent unius materiae commune subjectum").[24] Obviously what is human and what is divine have nothing entitative directly in common and thus cannot be transformed into one another (ibid., 66–77).

What interests us is not the validity of Boethius' reply to Eutyches but his positing matter as a necessary principle of change and, by implication, as also involved in individuating the human soul. Giving matter that function is what Aristotle explicitly does. As we have stated above, individuality arises when forms (substantial or, for that matter, accidental) that constitute physical existents are educed by efficient causes from the potency of prime matter and of substance, which as real components of such existents entitatively affect the forms thus brought forth. These latter are what they are solely as present and concretized in those existents. In brief, those forms are real only when and as

[22] On the primal role the Judeo-Christian Scriptures and the Ecumenical Councils and Creeds of the Church played in building that structure, see supra n. 5.

[23] This reason is the second of three, the first of which is that the divinity is changed into humanity, the third that divinity and humanity are both so modified that neither retains its proper reality. But only the second reason is directly relevant for our purposes.

[24] Boethius adds a second requirement for such transformation: the two substances must also have the ability to act upon and be acted upon by each other. Examples of substances which do not have this reciprocal ability are bronze and grass, whereas wine and water do. Hence, even if two things have a common matter, they still need this additional characteristic in order to be transformed (ibid., 26–65). The second requirement is not immediately relevant and hence I give it no special attention.

individuated by the matter of substance within which they are present. Thus, the individuality of forms and of the existents they help constitute is a positive entitative state of uniqueness, differentiation, and perfection, in which all physical things find themselves by reason of matter and substance.

Such is Aristotle's position on individuality. Such also is perhaps implied in Boethius' description of "persona" as "naturae rationabilis individua substantia" when joined with his characterization of matter as the subject which renders possible the change of one physical thing into another.[25] I make this suggestion even though James Shiel has rather convincingly shown that Boethius had no other Aristotelian Greek text than the *Organon* and this in a single codex, which however did contain marginal quotations from Aristotle's other treatises.[26] If my reading of Boethius on individuality as a positive perfection in an existent is accurate, Aristotle's *Physics* 226a10 and *De generatione et corruptione* 329a24 must have been among the passages quoted.[27]

[25] According to Gracia (supra n. 1, "Boethius . . . ") the Latin author speaks of "individual" "in his two editions of the *Commentary on Porphyry's 'Isagoge'*, the two editions of the *Commentary on Aristotle's 'De Interpretatione'* and the theological tractate commonly known as *De Trinitate* . . . None of these five works contains a systematic treatment of individuality . . . The comments pertinent to our discussion are scattered throughout the texts and contain little to suggest that Boethius had a clear and comprehensive view of individuality." But see Gracia's summary, 180–82. Unfortunately he does not attend to *Contra Eutychen et Nestorius.* Likewise Gracia appears to pay little attention to that tractate in his *Introduction to the Problem of Individuation in the Early Middle Ages* (Washington: Catholic University of America Press 1984)—references seem to occur only on 55, n. 7; 155 (this as well as the next two references are to Gilbert of Poitiers' commentary on the tractate) 184, n. 80; 189, n. 114; and 257. Although Gracia's book became available only after I had written my paper and deserves more study, it seems clear that his initiating it by discussing twentieth-century approaches to the problem of individuation so as to secure a framework for early medieval authors (see ch. I., pp. 17–63) is questionable methodology, which he follows also in the two articles cited supra n. 1. Nonetheless, his chapter on Boethius (65–121) is significant—see especially pp. 109–110 on the contrast between metaphysical and logical approaches to individuality; also see p. 259: Plato "downgraded individuality to the realm of the unreal and, concerned as he was with the realm of the real, paid little attention to it. And even Aristotle, whom one would have expected to have paid more attention to it, was so concerned to attack his former teacher's views that he seems often to have forgotten about this fundamental feature of the world. There are only a handful of passages in his works in which individuality is discussed, and then only incidentally and briefly."

[26] "Boethius' Commentaries on Aristotle," *Medieval and Renaissance Studies* 4 (1958) 217–44. Also see J. Shiel, "A Recent Discovery: Boethius' Notes on the Prior Analytics," *Vivarium* 20 (1982) 128–41. For a list of his other articles, see Chadwick (supra n. 8) 280.

[27] See ibid. 199: "Change is possible only to entities that share a common substrate of the same matter, a proposition Boethius has learnt from Aristotle's treatise 'On coming to be and passing away' (226a10) . . . Boethius' argument . . . presupposes that in matter lies the root of all mutation, an opinion which Augustine once records as maintained by 'some' (*City of God* 8.5). Among late Neoplatonists it is the general view, as, for example, in Simplicius' commentary on Epictetus."

WHO STANDS BEHIND AENEAS ON THE ARA PACIS?

THEODORE TRACY, S.J.

Since imitation is the most convincing form of homage, I shall try to offer homage to Father Raymond Schoder, a long-time friend and colleague, by venturing into his own field of archaeology and art history, perilous though that may be for one whose special interest has been Greek philosophy. My attempt to answer the question posed in the title is offered simply for consideration and comment by those who are specialists in Roman art and archaeology.

Paul MacKendrick has remarked that "the Altar of Peace is universally acknowledged to be the greatest artistic masterpiece of the Augustan Age."[1] Even now, however, there is no general agreement on all of its elements. The remains of the *Ara Pacis* (Pl. 36a) are badly mutilated, and the identity of many, perhaps most, of the personages carved on the enclosure walls has long been a matter of controversy. Yet full appreciation of the artistic integrity of the *Ara* depends upon these identifications. In this paper I shall focus principally upon the identification of one personage whose representation survives only partially on the sculptured remains, but whose identity is, I believe, of capital importance to the artistic integrity of the *Ara*. I refer to the figure now represented only by an arm and hand holding a staff, and with shoulder draped in a long outer garment, standing behind the figure generally identified as Aeneas on the panel to the right of the main entrance of the altar enclosure (Pl. 37). The personage originally represented there in its unmutilated form was, I submit, the goddess Venus.

In building a case for this hypothesis I shall assume, first, that the entire complex, as reconstructed, represents a harmonious whole, planned so that the architectural and sculptural elements fit appropriately to emphasize the principal functions of the entire structure, i.e., to serve as a monumental altar for annual ritual sacrifice, celebrating the peace achieved by Augustus in 13 B.C., as decreed by the Senate and recorded in the *Res Gestae*.[2] It was designed to honor Augustus, depict the origins and contemporary representatives of the Julian gens and the Roman people, and propagate the values espoused by Augustan ideology, past, present, and future.

Secondly, I shall assume that the artistic conventions of the designer and artist are consistent for the entire structure, so that those evident in the extant sculptural remains may be presumed to have been observed in the sculptural elements now lost.

[1] P. MacKendrick, *The Mute Stones Speak* (New York: New American Library 1966) 162.

I wish to thank especially Professors Elizabeth Gebhard and Alexander MacGregor of the University of Illinois at Chicago for their generous help with details of this paper, and Professor Edwin Menes of Loyola University, Chicago, for rendering the manuscript legible.

[2] Chapter 12. S. Weinstock, "Pax and the Ara Pacis," *JRS* 50 (1960) 44–58, contests this identification with the modern reconstruction. But see J. Toynbee, "The 'Ara Pacis Augustae'," *JRS* 57 (1961) 153–56; M. Torelli, *Typology and Structure of Roman Historical Reliefs* (Ann Arbor: Michigan 1982) 29–30.

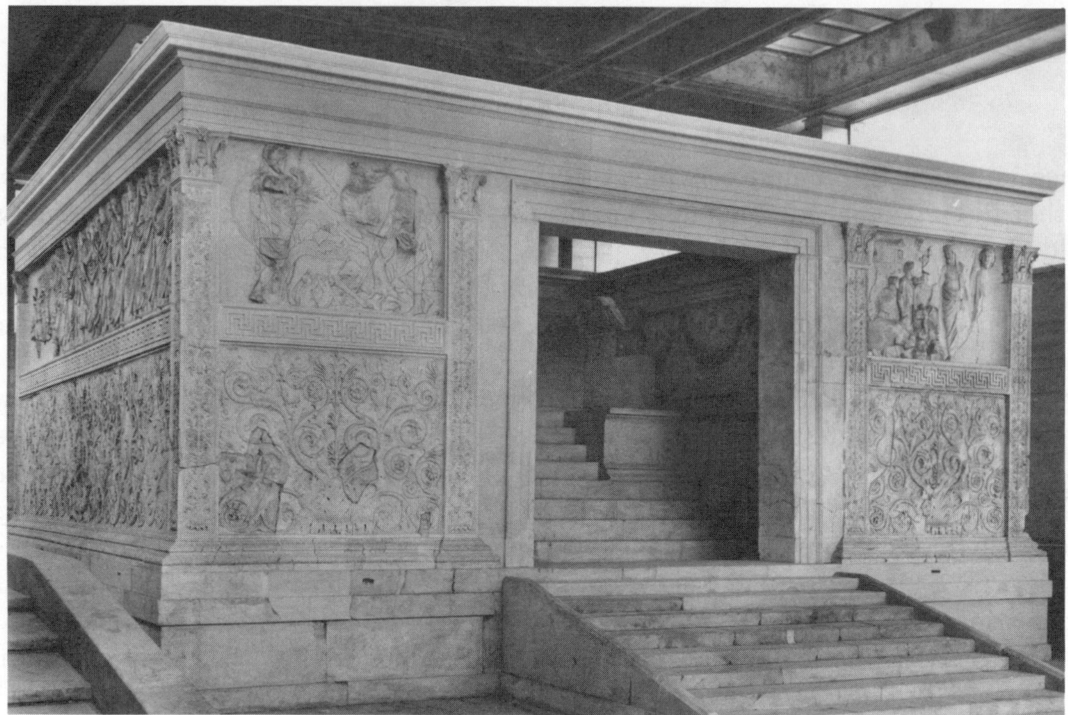

PLATE 36a. Ara Pacis Augustae seen from the northwest. Photo E. Richter 1115.

36b. Ara Pacis Augustae, the south procession. Photo E. Richter 1120.

Thirdly, I assume that consideration of the content and function of any missing part of a sculptural element must take into account its relation to the purpose and function of the carefully designed whole.

Finally, while the overall structure was designed as an altar surrounded by an enclosure wall with two entrances, I shall assume that the *front* of the complex, the principal approach and entrance, originally faced the Campus Martius on the west, while the *back*, a secondary or rear entrance, was approached from the old Via Flaminia on the east. I believe this is consistent with the asymmetrical structure of the altar and approaches on the east-west axis, with the long series of steps on what was originally the west side of the structure leading up to the altar platform itself, but only a short series of steps on the east side, and these falling short of the altar platform. Moreover, the figures of the sculptured friezes on both north and south sides of the enclosure, representing a ritual procession going to sacrifice, faced in the direction of the original *west* entrance, not the east. MacKendrick observes that the procession is "imagined as turning the corner of the enclosure and entering the west doorway to sacrifice at the altar."[3] The location of the principal entrance on the west is of some importance, as we shall see.

Approaching the reconstructed *Ara Pacis* as it exists today,[4] by way of what I presume to be this principal entrance, we find a very fragmented panel on the upper left of the main doorway (Pl. 36a). At the upper left of this panel is the helmeted head of a male figure, now identified with the god Mars, ruler of the Campus Martius, "paternal god of the city", and "progenitor of the Romans."[5] The remaining fragments and other parallels indicate that he was standing next to a gnarled tree, the *ficus ruminalis*, at the center, under which the infant Romulus and Remus are suckled by the she-wolf, while the shepherd Faustulus observes them on the right. The scene seems to suggest that Mars, the divine progenitor of the Roman people, here entrusts his twin sons to the care of the human Faustulus.

Turning to the upper right of the main entrance, we find the panel which is the focus of our interest (Pl. 37). It is described by Moretti, who directed the reconstruction of the *Ara*, as follows: "On the right panel, perhaps the masterpiece of the monument, an austere bearded figure, his head covered by his mantle, is in the act of offering a sacrifice upon the rustic altar, with one *camillus* holding the offerings and another leading a sow. Above, on the left, there is a shrine containing the Penates. To the right of the sacrificer,

[3] MacKendrick (supra n. 1) 163–164, following Moretti (infra nn. 4, 6, 11). E. Simon, *Ara Pacis Augustae* (Greenwich, Conn. 1967: New York Graphic Society) 8: "In antiquity, one climbed the stairs from the direction of the Campus Martius, that is, from the west . . . [W]e shall speak of the front and back (originally west and east) . . . ." See also E. La Rocca, *Ara Pacis Augustae* (Rome: Bretschneider 1983) 14; Torelli (supra n. 2) 31. On the other hand, G.K. Galinsky, *Aeneas, Sicily, and Rome* (Princeton: University Press 1969) 194, speaks of a slab on the *east* side of the enclosure as significant because "it is part of the front of the Ara Pacis."

[4] Reconstructed under the direction of Giuseppe Moretti in 1937–38. For a brief account of the recovery of the extant remains and their reassembly, see MacKendrick (supra n. 1) 156–62 and Simon (supra n. 3) 7–8.

[5] Simon (supra n. 3) 25.

who is recognized as Aeneas, there is preserved part of another figure . . . .[I]t has been suggested that here we have a youthful divinity (Honos or Bonus Eventus) or Achates, the faithful companion of Aeneas."[6]

This description suggests the problems, and the long case- history, of this mysterious figure with staff and sleeved arm appearing to the right of "Aeneas". We may recall that the reconstructed panel consists of three fragments: one large block containing the *camilli* and the sow; a second huge block with "Aeneas" and the remains of his companion; and the fragment of a youthful head with long hair, now set in place as the head of that companion. This has presented scholars with two long-standing problems:

1) Who is the mysterious figure behind "Aeneas"?

2) Does the head set above it really belong to that figure?

To these much debated problems I would like to add a third: What of the "*camilli*"?

Only a sampling of the long and complex debate over the first two questions can be presented here. In 1907 Sieveking first suggested that the person offering sacrifice was Aeneas. That is now generally accepted. He identified the figure behind simply as "a subordinate companion of Aeneas" and assigned the head to a hypothetical figure of "Pax Romana" on a rear panel.[7] Two years later Studniczka saw the sleeved arm and long garment of the missing figure as belonging to Aeneas' Trojan companion Achates. He assigned the head to a hypothetical Honos, seated on a back panel.[8] In 1917 Sieveking declared that the sleeved arm was "neither Phrygian nor Trojan," identified the figure behind Aeneas as Genius Populi Romani, and restored the head to it, finding it "in size and workmanship like that of Aeneas."[9] In 1938 Mustilli suggested that both figure *and* head belonged to Achates.[10] This was enthusiastically affirmed and supported by Moretti in 1948, in his full report of the restoration.[11] The identification was generally accepted until Weinstock pointed out that the figure occupied far too important a space and position to be Achates (largely a creation of Vergil) and identified it as Iulus-Ascanius, now *fully-grown* and in Trojan garb. Weinstock rejected the head as belonging to the figure.[12] This is the identification now followed by commentators like Simon, who also regards the "youthful head with curly locks" as "stylistically in keeping with the *Ara Pacis* but out of place in this context."[13]

Before discussing my own identification of the figure and the head, I would like to complete the circuit and mention other relevant features of the altar enclosure as a whole. Turning from the front to the right (south) side of the complex, we find the long

[6] G. Moretti, *The Ara Pacis Augustae*, trans. Veronica Priestly (Rome: Libreria dello Stato 1939) 10. Moretti (idem 9) located this panel as one of the two framed "between the entrance jambs of the principal entrance (the west end, toward the Campus Martius)." See supra n. 3.

[7] J. Sieveking, "Zur Ara Pacis Augustae," *ÖJh* 10 (1907) 186–88.

[8] F. Studniczka, *Zur Ara Pacis*, *AbhLeip* 26 (1909) 921–23, 936–40.

[9] J. Sieveking, "Die Kaiserliche Familie auf der Ara Pacis," *RM* 32 (1917) 93, n. 10.

[10] D. Mustilli, *L'Arte Augustea* (Rome: Istituto di studi romani 1938) 320.

[11] G. Moretti, *Ara Pacis Augustae*, 2 vols. (Rome: Libreria dello Stato 1948) I 153.

[12] Weinstock (supra n. 2) 57.

[13] Simon (supra n. 3) 23. LaRocca (supra n. 3) 40 follows Weinstock and Simon literally in this identification. So also Torelli (supra n. 2) 37f.

frieze (Pl. 36b) depicting figures now identified as Augustus, Agrippa, Livia, Tiberius and others representing the Julian *gens*. Coming to offer sacrifice, they are garbed in formal ritual attire, some of the notables (Augustus, Agrippa, Livia) with heads already veiled for sacrifice.

Turning from this we come upon the panel (Pl. 4a, p. 36 above) to the left of the rear (east) entrance with the beautiful central figure of a seated female dandling two infants and surrounded by symbols of fertility and abundance. This has been, and is, generally identified as Tellus/Saturnia Tellus or Italia.[14] Galinsky and Booth, however, in 1966 made a vigorous case for the identification of the central figure with Venus instead;[15] and in 1983 Thornton supported this by documenting the necessity of the presence of Venus on any major construction honoring Augustus, who prided himself on his descent from Venus through Anchises and Aeneas.[16]

Most fragmentary of all is the panel to the upper right of the rear entrance. The surviving fragment shows the upper leg of a figure seated above the remains of weapons, enough to identify it as the goddess Roma seated in parallel position facing the goddess on the left panel. To the ample empty space of this panel is generally assigned the youthful head by those who deny it belongs to the Aeneas panel.

Turning from here to the original north side of the complex, we find another processional frieze headed toward the west entrance, consisting of citizens, magistrates, priests, and perhaps other members of the imperial family, both male and female. Again, they are formally attired for a solemn religious ceremony, some with heads veiled. We now return to the principal questions.

Who Stands Behind Aeneas?

If we examine the original sculptural remains as they exist in the friezes of the north and south walls, three general artistic conventions can be observed:

1) All else being equal, the *importance* of the personage is indicated by the location, amount of space occupied, and the depth of relief in which the figure is sculptured. Describing the dynastic procession, Moretti points out that the personages that follow Augustus "are ranged upon two or even three planes. Those in the foreground are always the most important . . . "[17] High relief signals high importance.

2) Details of dress are important and carefully observed. Again Moretti observes of the south wall frieze (Pl. 36b), "All the figures in this frieze are of an almost hieratic austerity, due not only to the character of the ceremony in which they are taking part but also to the etiquette regarding dress and comportment on ceremonial occasions, especially formal when the Emperor was present."[18]

[14] E.g., Simon (supra n. 3) 26–29.

[15] G.K. Galinsky, "Venus in a Relief on the Ara Pacis Augustae," *AJA* 70 (1966) 223–44; expanded by the same author in his *Aeneas, Sicily, and Rome* (supra n. 3) 191–241. The case is made largely on iconographic parallels with Greek representations of Aphrodite. A. Booth, "Venus on the Ara Pacis," *Latomus* 25 (1966) 873–79, proposed the idea independently.

[16] M.K. Thornton, "Augustan Genealogy and the Ara Pacis," *Latomus* 42 (1983) 619–28.

[17] Moretti (supra n. 6) 11. Simon makes the same point (supra n. 3) 15–16.

[18] Moretti (supra n. 6) 12.

We have observed already that some of the most prominent figures have heads veiled for sacrifice. But there is another detail of dress that is observed consistently: all the *male* adults in both friezes wear a short-sleeved undergarment that leaves their forearms bare; all the *female* adults wear an undergarment that covers the arm to the wrist in a *sleeve*. This is clear in the case of Livia and the female figures that follow her, especially those that reach down toward a child. Close examination of the left arm of the Livia figure reveals that it is sleeved under her draped mantle. Likewise, the two female figures that follow with young children reach down to them with arms that are sleeved under their mantles. Similarly, the fragmentary female figures on the north frieze present forearms well covered. This suggests the traditional modesty of the Roman matron, a virtue which Augustus was hoping to revive.

3) Male and female figures are distinguished by relative height; i.e., the males are consistently taller than the females, as might be expected. The frieze showing Agrippa, Livia, and followers (Pl. 36b) illustrates this, where males and females on the same level of relief show this difference consistently at the shoulder level and top of the head. Moreover, major figures in high relief of *both* sexes are taller than those behind them, male and female. Hence *height* as well as high relief indicates importance.

With these three artistic conventions in mind we now turn to the Aeneas panel and the mysterious figure behind Aeneas (Pl. 37):

1) The space occupied by the missing figure—1/4 or 1/5 of the entire panel—must indicate a personage of high importance. Moretti was uneasy with assigning all this space to Achates, and suggested that a figure of Ascanius-Iulus might have appeared at his side or behind him, to balance the *camilli* in composition.[19] Again, as mentioned earlier, Weinstock later considered Achates far too unimportant a character, and a purely literary one at that, to occupy so important a space, and so substituted Iulus-Ascanius, grown up but still in Asiatic costume with long sleeves. "What we need is an important personality, and this can only be Ascanius . . . ."[20] Not necessarily Ascanius, but certainly important.

Looking at the *level of relief* in which the arm, hand, and staff are carved, we can say that the personage must have been at least as important as Aeneas, since those features, as well as the remnant of the shoulder and garment, are carved in relief at least as high as the corresponding features in Aeneas. As we have seen, high relief signals high importance.

Finally, the *position* of the figure at the extreme right of the panel parallels the position of Mars at the extreme left of the opposite panel; which should lead us to expect it be occupied by a personage of corresponding dignity if the whole front of the enclosure is to present a balanced composition, both aesthetically and conceptually.

2) The arm of the missing figure is *sleeved to the wrist*. This had led several commentators to assume it must belong to Asiatic dress (Phrygian or Trojan), since no Roman male would appear thus clothed. But according to the conventions we have seen, an arm

[19] Moretti (supra n. 11) I 127; Studniczka (supra n. 8) 923 had made the same suggestion in 1909.

[20] Weinstock (supra n. 2) 57; Simon accepts this identification (supra n. 3) 23.

PLATE 37

Plate 37. Ara Pacis Augustae, the Sacrifice of Aeneas. Photo E. Richter 1116.

so sleeved should belong to a *female* figure, especially on the occasion of solemn ritual.[21] Aeneas is represented as observing the dress required by ritual, sacrificing with head veiled. He becomes the prototype in this detail for Augustus and the other males behind him on the adjoining frieze. Could not the missing figure be a corresponding model or prototype for the long-sleeved *females* in the same frieze?

3) But the *height* of the missing figure at the shoulder seems roughly *equal* to that of Aeneas (compare right shoulders for each), and so it has always been presumed to be *male* (Bonus Eventus, Achates, Iulus Ascanius). How is this to be reconciled with the sleeved arm indicating a *female*? According to the convention of the artists, human females are presented consistently as shorter than males. Then a corollary of the same convention would be that a female presented as equal to or taller than a male would be more than human—a divinity. The same notion is carried by Vergil in *Aeneid* II, 591–92, where Venus appears to Aeneas . . . *confessa deam, qualisque videri / caelicolis et quanta solet* (" . . . manifesting the goddess, in beauty and stature such as she is wont to appear to the lords of heaven"—Fairclough). The implication of *quanta* is that Venus appears "god-size", i.e., greater than human. On the basis of the artistic conventions of the *Ara* itself we must conclude, then, that the long-sleeved figure roughly as tall as a human male could only be female and divine both—a goddess.

That the missing figure behind Aeneas did indeed represent a *goddess* seems confirmed by the presence of the staff of knotted wood in her hand. This is the *sceptrum*, commonplace in the iconography of divinity, originally a long, lance-like staff of wood, with twigs and bark removed, just as represented here. In the Greek tradition it was carried especially by Zeus, Hades, Hera, Aphrodite, Nereus.[22] In the Roman tradition, as evidenced by the coinage of Julius Caesar and Augustus, it is the constant mark of the goddess Venus.[23]

The designer of the panel recognized that the *sceptrum* was also carried by rulers and priests participating in the authority of the gods, as is clear from the staff held by Aeneas. But note the difference in thickness and careful modeling of the staff held by the figure behind Aeneas. It is relatively as large and prominent in the composition as the scepters held by the gods seated in the temple above the *camilli*. A staff of such thickness, prominence, and careful modeling can hardly be explained as the spear of an Achates or the shepherd's staff of an Ascanius; particularly if the broken markings in the extreme upper right of the panel be interpreted as the remains of attached fillets, appropriate to a scepter (cf. *Iliad* I, 14–15) but hardly to a spear or shepherd's staff.

[21] M. Southard, a professional artist friend, quite unaware of the identity problem, has suggested spontaneously that the hand and arm holding the staff on our panel should belong to a female personage, since upper- and forearm are not heavily muscled (as is the arm of Aeneas) but slender and tapering, the wrist loose, and the hand holds the staff lightly with fingers open and relaxed, in what is much more a feminine gesture than the firm grip characteristic of the male.

[22] A. Hug, *RE* IIA, 1 (1921) col. 369.

[23] E. Babelon, *Monnaies de la république romaine* (Bologna: Forni 1963) II 21, no. 34; 22, nos. 35, 36; etc.

The great variety in the length, thickness, modeling, and ornamentation of scepters found on the coins, paintings, and sculpture of this period leads one to believe that there is no standard iconography, but that the style in each case was left to the choice of the artist. The rustic wooden scepter represented here suggests that the artist was consciously archaizing, as he clearly does in details of the dress, a topic we shall discuss below.

Who, then, is the personage that stands behind Aeneas? I suggest it can only be *Venus*, for a variety of reasons:

1) As Thornton has abundantly documented, Venus *must* have been represented prominently on a civic altar dedicated to honor Augustus. "If Augustus is as consistent a man as his propaganda shows him to be, and if he has established a programmed genealogy of divinity in the historical, literary, and numismatical recordings as the evidence shows he has, then he cannot leave Venus off the *Ara Pacis* . . . "[24]

2) We have noted that the artistic and conceptual balance of the two panels flanking the main entrance to the *Ara* demands that the position of Mars at the extreme left of the one panel be balanced by a personage of equal dignity facing Mars at the extreme right of the opposite panel. Again, in the light of Augustan ideology this could only be Venus. Robert Schilling, in his detailed study *La réligion romaine de Vénus*,[25] has established that the young Octavian, in the ideological struggle against Antony and Cleopatra, went even beyond Julius Caesar in separating the cult of Venus from the eastern elements associated with the Greek Aphrodite by joining Venus in strong bond to the cult of an ancient national Roman divinity—Mars. At Augustus' behest, for example, the Pantheon was consecrated (25 B.C.) in particular to Mars and to Venus. Again, the two are joined on the front of the temple of Mars Ultor constructed in the Forum of Augustus (2 B.C.), with cult statues inside where, in Ovid's phrase (*Trist.* II, 296) *Stat Venus Ultori iuncta* . . . If this is the case, it would seem certain that only Venus, and no other goddess, could have been joined to Mars on the front of the *Ara Pacis* honoring Augustus. In fact, the presence of Mars on the one front panel would seem to *demand* the presence of Venus on the other.

3) Only Venus is related to Aeneas as Mars is related to Romulus and Remus on the opposite panel. And it is both artistically and ideologically appropriate that she should occupy the panel on the side of the dynastic procession in which her "descendant," Augustus, and the most prominent members of the Julian *gens* appear.

4) The sow being brought to sacrifice provides another link to Venus. The victim is generally recognized as a pregnant sow. As Weinstock has remarked, however, it is not the white sow mentioned in *Aeneid* VIII as guiding Aeneas to the site of Lavinium, since

[24] Thornton (supra n. 16) 628.

[25] R. Schilling, *La réligion romaine de Vénus* (Paris: de Boccard 1954) 324–42. The details are documented in Schilling, who concludes (337): "En quoi consiste en définitive l'innovation d'Auguste? L'empereur ne s'est pas contenté de juxtaposer les deux divinités. Il les a soumises . . . à une sorte de contamination reciproque: Mars a pris un charactère 'julien' par sa mission d'*Ultor parentis patriae* ; Vénus, sans cesser d'être *Genetrix*, a pris un charactère plus militaire pour se rapprocher de Mars. Ainsi, le couple Mars-Vénus à reçue une signification nouvelle: en réaction contre le syncrétisme, le culte officiel accentue la romanité des deux divinités; bien plus, il leur attribue la protection de la dynastie impériale."

she is always represented with her 30 piglets.[26] Rather, this sow is about to be sacrificed before a shrine of the "Penates," implying a setting of established homeland and ritual. Lily Ross Taylor has pointed out that "Venus, particularly as the Julian *gens* honored her as the mother of the race, was closely allied to the all-embracing Mother Earth. Indeed, all the great female divinities of Italy . . . were local goddesses of fertility." To them, a common sacrifice was a porca; and Taylor properly criticizes Sieveking for associating the sacrifice pictured on the Aeneas panel with the *Penates*. "He too recognized in the victim a pregnant sow, but he failed, as have other scholars, to realize that by the fixed laws of Roman sacrifice such a victim could not be offered to any divinity except the mother goddess earth under one of her many forms."[27] Venus, as a fertility goddess and mother of the Julian *gens*, was an appropriate recipient of such a sacrifice. The panel, then, would depict Venus present as her son proposes to sacrifice in her honor—a strong reminder of the divine origins of the Julian *gens*.

5) Finally, the arm with sleeve to the wrist, far from creating an iconographical problem, accords perfectly with the fully clothed and matronly Roman Venus promoted by Julius Caesar and Augustus. Schilling has pointed out that Caesar commissioned the artist Arcesilaus to create a new and dignified Venus type for the temple of Venus Genetrix in his forum. Though there is much debate on details, scholars agree that this new Venus Genetrix was dressed with the dignity of a matron in a tunic held by a cincture and in a long outer garment. "Ainsi, César avait opté pour une déesse entièrment vètue. Peut-être Sylla l'avait-il précédé dans ce choix iconographique . . . . En tout cas, César a créé le premier type de la statuaire romain officielle, qui rompt nettement avec la nudité grecque . . . . Mais la statue cultuelle de Venus Genetrix était destinée à inspirer un sentiment de respect; elle portera toujours la *longa vestis* des matrones."[28] That Vergil conceived of Venus as dressed in the *longa vestis* is clear from the scene in *Aeneid* I, 404, where she puts aside her disguise and reveals her divinity: . . . *pedes vestis defluxit ad imos / et vera incessu patuit dea* . . . . And that the undergarment could indeed be sleeved to the wrist is evident from a number of surviving wall paintings of the matronly Venus, which present her dressed in a long and ample outer garment over a tunic with sleeves that come to the wrist. The best known of these, the "Pompeiian Venus", shows these features clearly (Pl. 38a). She is also crowned with a diadem and carrying a staff or scepter, as elsewhere.[29] Thus, the sleeved arm and staff of the figure behind Aeneas fit well the iconography of the modest Venus type created under Caesar for official portrayals of Venus as *genetrix* of the Julian *gens* and taken over by Augustus in his promotion of a Roman Venus, freed of all Greek and oriental features. She is the matronly

[26] Weinstock (supra n. 2) 57.

[27] L.R. Taylor, "The Mother of the Lares," *AJA* 29 (1925) 304, 310. La Rocca (supra n. 3) 40 follows Sieveking and is open to the same criticism. The common identification of the seated divinities as the Penates has been questioned, on iconographical grounds, by Professor Elizabeth Gebhard.

[28] Schilling (supra n. 25) 310–13.

[29] For illustrations, see ibid. pls. IX, XV, XVII, XXIII.

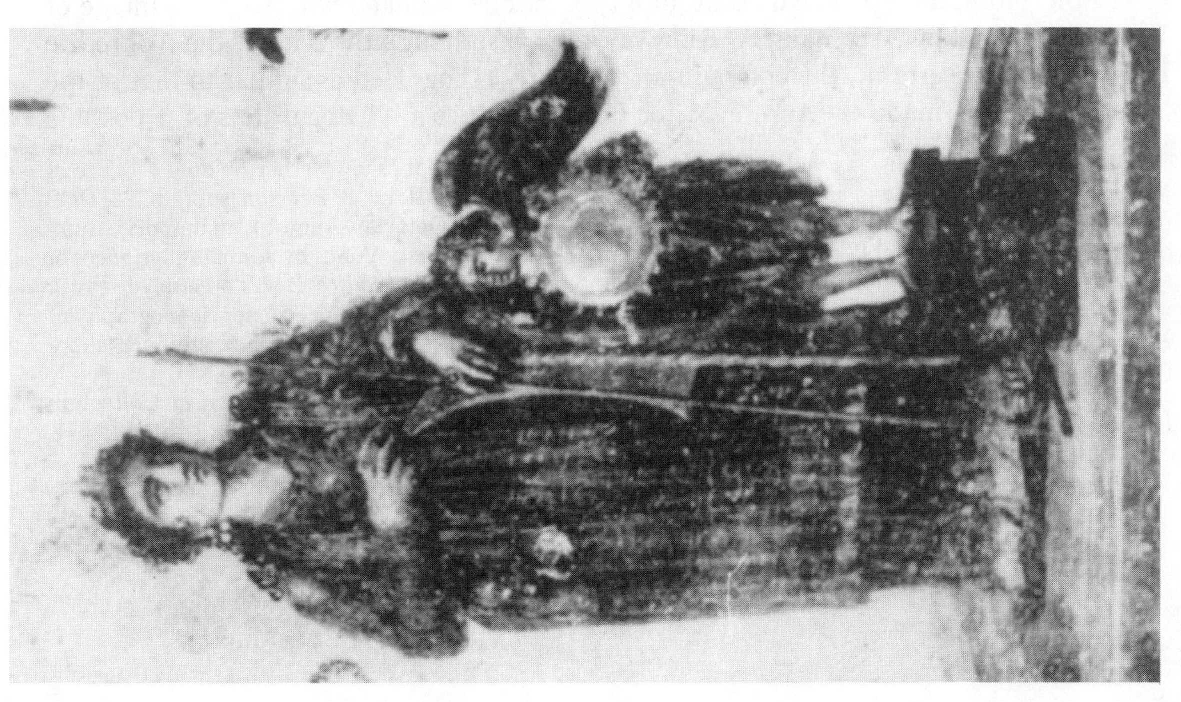

PLATE 38a. The Pompeian Venus. After Schilling (supra n. 25) pl. 15.

38b. The Aphrodite of Fréjus Type. Providence, Museum of Art, Rhode Island School of Design no. 23.351, Museum Appropriation and Special Gift. Photo courtesy Museum.

Venus, the Venus of peacetime and fecundity.[30] Her modest attire set the norm, presumably, for the long-sleeved matrons pictured on the friezes.

It must be noted, however, that the outer garment of the *Ara* figure, unlike that of the female figures on the frieze and the wall paintings of Venus, is secured by a clasp on top of the right shoulder. What are we to make of that? Actually, it provides a final confirmation that the *Ara* figure does indeed represent Venus.

A sculptured standing female figure (Pl. 38b) preserved in the Museum of the Rhode Island School of Design in Providence wears an outer garment strikingly similar on the right side to the fragmentary remains of the garment worn by the *Ara* figure.[31] It is secured by a clasp on the right shoulder and falls in full folds along the right side, while lesser folds move diagonally across the front of the torso. This peculiar gathering of the garment under the right arm is due, in the Providence figure, to the fact that the garment is stretched diagonally across the right breast, under the left, and caught up in a knot at the left hip, forming a short mantle over a full inner garment or chiton.

Brunilde Ridgway has identified the Providence figure as a Roman adaptation of the "Aphrodite of Fréjus type," named after a Greek original in the Louvre[32] In the original, however, the chiton has slipped from the left shoulder, leaving the left breast bare, a feature which the Roman adapters changed in various ways through fuller clothing. Ridgway remarks: "The Romans were particularly attracted by this type and often used it as a stock body for portrait statues; but the mannerism of the slipped strap . . . seems to have offended their sense of modesty."[33] Subsequently, a more "modest" type was developed, featuring a short diagonal mantle or himation, used especially where the sculptor sought to archaize. Ridgway points out that "short diagonal himatia appear in archaistic statues, and the period of the first century B.C. and the first century A.D. saw the peak of this archaistic production."[34] This would fit precisely the time when the archaistic panel was produced showing Aeneas in primitive garb sacrificing at a rustic altar.

Futhermore, this particular Aphrodite type has been linked with the new image of Venus developed by Arcesilaus. As Ridgway remarks, though the date of the Aphrodite Fréjus type is uncertain, "the composition was early recognized as similar to that of the 'Venus Genetrix' made by Arkesilaos for Caesar in 46 B.C."[35] Regardless of a possible

[30] The long-robed Venus of peacetime appears on a coin of Octavian, showing her holding a figure of Victory in her right hand and a cornucopia in her left (ibid. pl. XXXIII, no. 3; Babelon [supra n. 23] II 43 no. 86). This distinctive iconography of Venus under Caesar and Octavian-Augustus undercuts, in my opinion, the attempt to establish the identification of the "Tellus" figure as Venus by adducing instances of similarity between the "Tellus" figure and Hellenic representations of *Aphrodite*. It was precisely to break with the iconography and frivolity of the Hellenic Aphrodite that Caesar introduced a new iconography of Venus more suitable to the *gravitas Romana* and the dignity of the Julian *genetrix*. See Schilling (supra n. 25) 87.

[31] Inv. no. 23.351; Brunilde S. Ridgway, *Classical Sculpture. Catalogue of the Classical Collection* (Providence: Museum of Art, Rhode Island School of Design 1972) no. 14, pp. 159–61.

[32] Ibid. no. 14, p. 40.

[33] Ibid.

[34] Ibid. 41.

[35] Ibid.

connection with Arcesilaus, Ridgway favors the position of Margarete Bieber, that the Fréjus type represents a classicizing-eclectic creation of early imperial times.[36]

Thus, the fragmentary outer garment of the *Ara* figure, secured by a clasp on the right shoulder and falling in full folds along the right side, with smaller folds moving in a diagonal direction toward the left hip, suggests that it belongs to an archaicizing-classicizing Venus Genetrix type popular at precisely the time the *Ara* was constructed. She is the fully modest Roman Venus, her modesty underscored by the long sleeved undergarment or chiton, and imitated by the female figures on the friezes. Though the chiton of the Providence figure is sleeveless, Ridgway notes that a female figure with sleeved chiton and diagonal mantle, exhibiting a comparable mixture of classical and archaic elements, can be found in the Vatican Magazine.[37]

Finally, it may be relevant to note that in 16 B.C., three years before the *constitutio* of the *Ara Pacis*, a silver coin issued under Augustus celebrated the symbols of his priestly offices on the reverse, and on the obverse, the claim of the Julian *gens* to descent from Venus Genetrix. The obverse shows a bust of Venus. Her head is diademed, her hair falls in rich folds down the back of her neck, and her garment is secured by a clasp on the right shoulder.[38]

Does the Head Belong to the Figure?

If the figure behind Aeneas be identified as Venus, then what of the *head*? This I consider a subordinate question; and I believe the answer to the first question in no way depends upon its resolution. Still, though we may be on less secure ground here, I think a good case can be made for the identification of the head as that of *Venus*, belonging to the figure over which it is presently in place.

The head was discovered in 1859 with the left half of the Aeneas panel.[39] It is universally recognized as "stylistically in keeping with the Ara Pacis" and belonging to it.[40] As we have seen, some commentators assign it to the position it now occupies on the front of the *Ara*. Others assign it for various reasons to the empty spaces of the Roma panel. While Mustilli, Moretti, and Riemann join head to figure on the Aeneas panel and identify them as belonging to the (human) Achates,[41] scholars who assign the head to the rear panel generally recognize it as belonging to a *divinity*—Pax, Bonus Eventus, Genius Populi Romani, Honos, etc.[42]

[36] Ibid. 41–42.

[37] Ibid. 42, n. 6.

[38] Grueber (infra n. 54) II 55, no. 4490 and note.

[39] Sieveking (supra n. 9) 93, n. 10.

[40] Simon (supra n. 3) 23; see Studniczka (supra n. 8) 936.

[41] Mustilli (supra n. 10) 320; Moretti (supra n. 11) I 153; H. Riemann, *RE* 18, 1 (1942) col. 2090.

[42] Pax: Sieveking (supra n. 7) 188; Bonus Eventus: E. Peterson, *Ara Pacis Augusti*, Sonderschriften des Österreichischen Archaologischen Instituts II (1902) 121; Genius Populi Romani: Simon (supra n. 3) 29; Honos: Studniczka (supra n. 8) 940; any of the above: J.M.C. Toynbee, "The Ara Pacis Reconsidered and Historical Art in Roman Italy," *ProcBritAc* 39 (1953) 80. La Rocca (supra n. 3) 40 thinks it belongs to Honos who, with Virtus, flanked the goddess Roma on the rear panel.

Generally the head is seen to be "the curly head of a young man" or male divinity, who "carried a horn of plenty (cornucopia) on his left shoulder."[43] This suggested to Simon and others that it belonged to the Genius Populi Romani, often represented with a horn of plenty. Not all commentators, however, saw the head as belonging to a male personage. Sieveking, who first identified Aeneas on the monument, initially believed the head belonged to a *female* personification of the Pax Augusta, remarking that "the long locks on the neck appeared to correspond more to a female figure (*ein weibliche Figur*) resembling the Augustan coinage on which the head of Peace (Pax) appeared."[44] Though the presence of the cornucopia led him later to revise his opinion and assign the head and figure to the Genius Populi Romani "with staff and cornucopia,"[45] I believe Sieveking's initial insight was correct.

For the sake of comparison we might look at the two heads that presently face each other on the panels flanking the principal entrance to the *Ara*, namely, the head of Mars and the head attached to the Venus figure. Simon presents accurate views of both in convenient form and viewed from the proper angle, that is, from below.[46]

Careful examination of the fairly well preserved head of Mars reveals some characteristic male features:[47]

1) the beard, obviously;
2) *angularity* of brow and cheek contours;
3) the clear line or crease joining nostril lobes to lip level;
4) relatively small and deep set eyes, shielded by brows;
5) brow-line fairly straight joining nose;
6) ears completely exposed (as in all other male heads on the friezes, when not veiled or covered by wreath);
7) hair relatively short on neck (as on all other male heads).

These male characteristics, except for beard and exposed ears, can be found verified, for example, in the well defined and carefully modeled head of Agrippa on the south frieze, though this, of course, is a portrait.

In contrast to these, the head opposite Mars, though badly battered, shows:

1) no beard;
2) rounded, rather than angular, features, with soft lines;
3) no hard line from nostril to level of lips;
4) relatively small mouth with full, curved lips;
5) comparatively large, open, and prominent eyes, with gracefully curving lids;
6) brow-line gracefully curving to join nose;

[43] Simon (supra n. 3) 29.
[44] Sieveking (supra n. 7) 188.
[45] Sieveking (supra n. 9) 93, n. 10.
[46] Simon (supra n. 3) pls. 28 and 29.
[47] The professional artist mentioned supra n. 21 also spontaneously identified the head opposite Mars as female and, when asked the reason, pointed out most of the features cited here as distinguishing male from female characteristics.

7) long hair, covering the ears and flowing down the neck (all female heads on the enclosure walls, where not veiled, show hair flowing at least over the upper ear and in some instances, notably the "Tellus" panel, flowing down the back of the neck);

8) clear traces of a *headband* or *diadem* in the folds of the hair above the forehead. This detail is hardly appropriate for a *male* head in the Roman tradition, and so is explained by commentators as an eastern or oriental costume attributed to an assumed male personage. It would be most appropriate for Venus, however, who is generally portrayed on coins and paintings as crowned in some fashion. These female characteristics may be verified by comparing the features of the female heads on the "Tellus" (Pl. 4a) relief. Despite the badly battered lips, nose, forehead, and hair, the head now placed opposite Mars could have belonged, I believe, to a beautiful female personage.

But a *divinity*? Here Studniczka provides some helpful details.[48] Examining the comparative vertical (chin to top) measurement and height of relief of this head with that of the others sculptured on the enclosure walls, he reported:

1) A line from brow to mouth-opening on the Mars head measured about .06 m. while that on this head, now opposite Mars measured .07 m.

2) Since the beard on Mars made vertical (chin to top) head measurement difficult, Studniczka moved to the beardless figures on the friezes having the same brow-mouth-line measurements as Mars and found that their vertical measurement averaged .18 m. That of the head now opposite Mars measured .20 m.

3) The only head of comparable measurement (.20 m) is that of the central figure on the "Tellus" panel.

4) Only the head of the central figure on the "Tellus" panel is sculptured *in relief* as *high* as that of the head now opposite Mars. Studniczka concluded that the head therefore belonged to a god, and assigned it to a hypothetical figure of Honos seated on the rear panel with Roma.

J.M.C. Toynbee also, assuming the figure behind Aeneas to be Achates, assigned the head to a back panel on the ground that it "not only differs in style and execution from the other heads on the panel, but is also on slightly too large a scale to match them."[49] Her objection about the "style of execution" probably refers to the *high relief* of the head as compared to that of Aeneas and the *camilli*. Her objection about the size comes from her assumption that the person behind Aeneas is simply another human being (Achates) and so should have a head of comparable size. But in examining the artistic conventions of the *Ara* we have found that both extraordinary size and high relief were used to indicate a personage of great importance and, when larger than human, a divinity. This principle would certainly be verified in the head of the central figure of the "Tellus" panel, which alone matches the size and height of relief of the head now opposite Mars. If the one is universally acknowledged to belong to a divinity, we should be justified in making the same assumptions about the other.

[48] For the measurements given here cf. Studniczka (supra n. 8) 936.

[49] Toynbee (supra n. 42) 78.

Furthermore, if the head we are discussing is of proportions matched only by the head of the central figure on the "Tellus" panel, it must belong to a *major* female divinity. It is obviously not the head of Roma, who would be helmeted. It would be too large to belong to a *subordinate* figure on the Roma panel, somehow balancing or parallel to the Aurae on the "Tellus" panel.[50] Hence, it would seem to belong in the only other space available, namely, where it is presently, set in the Aeneas panel.[51] And, from all we have seen, the only possible major female divinity to whom it might belong is Venus.

One curious question arises from a study of the dimensions and location of the head now opposite that of Mars: if this is the head of Venus, intended to balance that of Mars on the opposite panel, why is it of larger dimension, and set in higher relief, than the head of Mars? The explanation may possibly go back to the fact that the altar was erected principally to honor Augustus who, like Julius Caesar before him, took his greatest pride in his family's Trojan ancestry and descent from Venus. This is attested, as Taylor has remarked,[52] by the constant appearance of Venus on the coins of the Julian house. Some coins showed Mars, from whom the family also traced descent through the Alban Kings although this was a claim less well attested. Hence the connection with Venus was always emphasized more than the less well authenticated descent from Mars. This may help to account for the greater eminence accorded Venus by the artist who designed the *Ara Pacis Augusti*.

As has been mentioned, commentators generally recognize the fragment of a *cornucopia* at the left side of the head, which led some to identify the head on iconographical grounds as belonging to the Genius Populi Romani. If, however, we can judge by the numismatic evidence, the cornucopia had much broader associations and was by no means the exclusive attribute of the Genius Populi Romani. For example, in the fateful year 82 B.C., when he defeated the Marians and became dictator of Rome, L. Cornelius Sulla had gold and silver coins struck with the diademed head of Venus on the obverse and a double cornucopia filled with fruits on the reverse; another with the head of Hercules on the obverse, a ship with double cornucopia on the reverse; another with the head of Mercury obverse, a double cornucopia reverse: another, the goddess Roma obverse, a double cornucopia reverse.[53] Grueber conjectures that "the double cornucopiae may be

[50] The dimensions of this head, comparable only to those of the central figure on the "Tellus" panel, would seem to rule out the possibility of Simon's suggestion that it belonged to a Genius Populi Romani "who stood behind Roma. Similar to the Aurae of the 'Tellus relief', he was shown smaller than the main figure." See Simon (supra n. 3) 29. The same objection can be brought against the assumption that the head belongs to a subordinate figure (Honos) flanking Roma and balancing, with another figure (Virtus), the Aurae of the opposite panel, as proposed by Torelli (supra n. 2) 37–38, and La Rocca (supra n. 3) 40, 49.

[51] Though the head, in my opinion, has been located in the proper *place* above the figure behind Aeneas on the reconstructed altar, it may not have been set in position by Mustilli at exactly the correct height or angle, since he assumed that it belonged to the human Achates and must parallel somehow the head of Aeneas.

[52] L.R. Taylor, *The Divinity of the Roman Emperor* (Middletown, Conn.: A.P.A. Philological Monographs 1 1931) 58–59.

[53] Babelon (supra n. 23) I 408–10, nos. 32, 33, 35, 36, 37. As early as 99 B.C. the double cornucopia appeared associated with the goddess Roma. See ibid. I 540–41, no. 4.

intended to refer to the cessation of hostilities after the second Mithridatic War."[54] A coin issued in the same year (82 B.C.) by Q. Fufius Calenus, however, celebrates the final pacification of Italy and the real end of the Social War (91–82 B.C.) with images of Honor and Virtue on the obverse, and identified figures of Italy and Rome clasping hands on the reverse. Italy bears a cornucopia.[55] Two years later, when Sulla celebrated his triumph in Rome, another coin was struck *ex senatus consulto* bearing the diademed head of Venus obverse, and a cornucopia filled with fruit, adorned with bandalettes, and crowned with laurel on the reverse.[56] The cornucopia in these contexts seems to symbolize cessation of hostilities, peace, and the abundance that comes with peace; and, in these two important issues of Sullan coins, all of this is associated with Venus.

Of the Sullan coins Grueber remarks "that it may be noticed that the treatment and form of the head of Venus . . . is very similar to that on the coins of Julius Caesar."[57] The Sullan type of diademed Venus head with outward gazing eyes does indeed appear abundantly through the coinage of Julius Caesar and into that of Octavian-Augustus, though with considerable minor variations on hair-style, diadem, and other adornments.[58] There seems to be little evidence of the cornucopia, however, on the coins of Julius Caesar.

The cornucopia reappears very early on the coinage of Octavian-Augustus, and seems to be regarded as symbol of some special aspect of his destiny. An aureus issued in Rome in 39 B.C. shows head of Octavian obverse and a cornucopia tied with a fillet reverse.[59] A memorial coin to Julius Caesar, issued the same year, shows Caesar laureate obverse, and cornucopia, celestial globe, rudder, etc. reverse.[60] These became special personal attributes of Augustus, as we shall see. The significance of the cornucopia, again, comes clear the next year (38 B.C.) when an aureus appears showing the head of Lepidus obverse and,

[54] H.A. Grueber, *Coins of the Roman Republic in the British Museum* (London: British Museum 1910) II 464.

[55] Babelon (supra n. 23) I 512, no. 1.

[56] Ibid. I 412, no. 44.

[57] Grueber (supra n. 54) II 464.

[58] For comparison, see H.A. Seaby, *Roman Silver Coins* (London: Seaby 1952) I 96–97 (Julius Caesar): no. 1—hair long, simple diadem; no. 12—hair very long, simple diadem and necklace; no. 13—hair tightly up (elaborate diadem, ear pendant, and necklace), cupid on shoulder; no. 14—hair tightly up, with flower, simple diadem, ear pendant, and necklace, cupid and *lituus* before, scepter behind; no. 15—hair long, headband, no jewelry.

For similar variations in Venus heads on Augustan coins, see ibid. I 120, 121, 129, nos. 70–72, 348. In all these the hair is long behind the neck and the diadem simple, as on the *Ara* Venus head. One (no. 348) shows her garment held by an ornamental shoulder clasp, as on the Venus figure behind Aeneas. Another (no. 72) has a laurel branch before, and behind, a cornucopia! Hence, Seaby identifies the head as "Venus or Peace" (p. 120). She may be *both*—Venus Genetrix, Patroness of Augustan Peace—just as Venus Victrix was invoked by August as patroness in the time of battle. See ibid. I 120, nos. 62, 63.

The same minor variations in hairstyle, adornment, and attributes are evident in the Venus Genetrix types on the wall paintings. Note, for example, the long hair flowing over the shoulders in the "Pompeiian Venus" (Pl. 38a), in contrast to the neatly coiffed Venus of other paintings. See Schilling (supra n. 25) pl. XV, XVII, IX, XXIII, pp. 190, 222, 126, 286.

[59] Grueber (supra n. 54) no. 4231. See H. Mattingly and E.A. Sydenham, *Roman Imperial Coinage* (London: Spink; reprint 1962) I 41.

[60] Grueber (supra n. 54) nos. 4237–41.

reverse, a *female figure, draped, diademed*, bearing a *scepter in her right hand* and a *cornucopia in her left*. She might be the archetype of the figure behind Aeneas on the *Ara*. Grueber identifies her tentatively as "Concordia" and suggests the coin celebrates the recent reconciliation between Lepidus and his colleagues, Octavian and Antony.[61] An aureus issued the following year (37 B.C.) shows the head of Octavian obverse and, reverse, "Fortuna" standing with rudder in right hand and cornucopia in left.[62]

Following the victory at Actium, Octavian was honored by coins issued in the East. One of these, a denarius (31–29 B.C.), shows his head obverse and, reverse, a draped female with olive branch in right hand and cornucopia in left; Mattingly identifies her as Pax.[63] Another denarius of similar date shows a diademed Venus-type head with olive branch before and cornucopia behind; commentators seem undecided whether this is Venus or Pax.[64] The association of Octavian, Venus, the cornucopia, and peace is important for what follows.

The cornucopia as a symbol clearly attached to the personal destiny of Octavian begins to appear in a series of coins issued first in 27 B.C., the year he received the title *Augustus*. That year a new style coin was issued from mints controlled by him in Ephesus and Pergamum. These show his head, bare or laureate, obverse and, reverse, a Capricorn with cornucopia on its back, or holding a globe and rudder with cornucopia above, and the title *Augustus* below.[65] Capricorn was the month of Octavian's conception, now introduced as a coin type which "varies slightly in its meaning according to its attributes. Its reference is primarily to Augustus himself . . . "[66] Thus, Octavian deliberately links his destiny with the attributes symbolized by the cornucopia, globe, and rudder. And in two of these early issues, the cornucopia *alone* rides on the back of the Capricorn.[67]

What do the three types symbolize? Grueber explains that "the globe and rudder (land and sea) are emblematic of the extended influence of Augustus, and the cornucopiae of the abundance and prosperity which resulted from the restoration of peace to the Empire."[68] Mattingly simply remarks: "The rudder and globe signify world-rule, the cornucopiae plenty."[69] He tends, however, to identify any female type associated with a cornucopia as Pax, even when identical to or clearly resembling the traditional Venus-type head with diadem.[70] "The two diademed heads of female deities probably represent

[61] Ibid. I 582–83, n. 29, 584.

[62] Ibid. no. 4313. Fortuna, with rudder and cornucopia, seems to have occupied, with Venus and Mars, the pediment of the temple of Mars Ultor, erected by Augustus in 2 B.C. See Peterson (supra n. 42) 62.

[63] H. Mattingly, *Coins of the Roman Empire in the British Museum* (London: British Museum 1976) I 99, no. 605. These coins honored Octavian as beginning a new era of peace. See Taylor (supra n. 52) 145.

[64] Mattingly (supra n. 63) I 100, nos. 611–14.

[65] Ibid. I 107, no. 664; 113, nos. 696, 698.

[66] Mattingly and Sydenham (supra n. 59) I 48. Professor Gebhard has called my attention to the cornucopia that appears on the Gemma Augustea, where it is held by the goddess Earth. See G. Hanfmann, *Roman Art* (Greenwich, Conn.: New York Graphic Society [n.d.]) XVII. Hanfmann notes that Capricorn, which also appears on the cameo, signifies the month of Augustus' conception, not birth.

[67] Mattingly (supra n. 63) I 113, no. 696, 698.

[68] Grueber (supra n. 54) II 19, note 1.

[69] Mattingly (supra n. 63) I cx.

[70] Ibid. I 99, no. 605; 100, no. 611, and cf. no. 609.

Venus and Peace; Peace is differentiated by the branch and cornucopia."[71] Thus, both Grueber and Mattingly regard the cornucopiae as symbolizing primarily *peace* with its attendant abundance and prosperity. And in linking the three types to Capricorn, Octavian seems to proclaim it his personal destiny to establish world rule and peace, and thus to merit the title *Augustus*.

The Capricorn type, with globe, rudder, and cornucopia, continued to appear at later dates from Augustus' mints in Spain. Mattingly lists two issues, one from Emerita, dated 22–19 B.C., another from Colonia Patricia (?), dated 19–16 or 15 B.C.[72] But perhaps most significant for the generally recognized connection of the cornucopia symbol with Augustus are two coins issued by the official senatorial mint, over which Augustus could claim no direct control.

Perhaps it is coincidence, but in 9 B.C., the year of the *dedicatio* or consecration of the completed *Ara Pacis* a quadrans was issued bearing a large cornucopia flanked by the letters S and C (*senatus consulto*) on the obverse; on the reverse, an altar hung with a wreath. The same was issued the following year under different moneyers.[73] Then in 7 B.C. an unusual coin was issued under three separate moneyers. The reverse is normal, bearing SC and the moneyer's name. But the obverse shows Augustus' head laureate; behind it a small winged Victory fastens the wreath with her right hand while holding a cornucopia in her left; below, Augustus' titles as Pontifex Maximus and holder of the tribunician power. Mattingly considers the style "on a far higher level than the average of the time."[74]

Clearly, then, the cornucopia seems important to include on a coin honoring Augustus. Would it not be important to include it on an altar complex honoring Augustus? And especially on an altar honoring Augustus specifically as *dux pacificans*[75] it would seem essential that his personal symbol of peace appear. But where more prominently and appropriately than on the right side of the right-hand panel flanking the principal entrance to the altar complex, and carried by Venus, *genetrix* of the Julian *gens* and patroness of the Augustan peace? Which is where the cornucopia would appear on the monument if the head bearing its fragment be recognized as the head of Venus and its present position be acknowledged as correct.[76]

[71] Ibid. I cxxiii.

[72] Ibid. I 56, no. 305; 62, no. 344.

[73] Ibid. I 40, no. 202; 41, no. 207.

[74] Ibid. I c; for the coins, see I 41, no. °; 42, no. 217; 43, no. 224.

[75] See Simon (supra n. 3) 8.

[76] That Venus can be portrayed with one or other of Augustus' personal symbols without losing her identity as Venus seems clear from the painting of the diademed "Pompeiian Venus", where she carries the staff of divinity but leans on a *rudder*, generally an attribute of "Fortuna". See Pl. 38a. Another wall painting from Pompeii shows Venus, draped and with scepter, carried on the wings of Cupid, who bears her *cornucopia* in his arms. See Galinsky (supra n. 3) 234 and fig. 140. It seems risky, then, to identify Venus-types on coins simply as "Pax" or "Fortuna" because they are portrayed with one or other symbol. Perhaps a conflation of the two (Venus-Pax, Venus-Fortuna) is intended.

As to the cornucopia as symbol of peace, it may be that Augustus and/or the designer of the *Ara* had in mind the famous statue of Eirene, goddess of peace, ascribed to the elder Kephisodotos and dated c. 350–320 B.C., which stood in the Areopagos and was often copied. The goddess was portrayed as draped,

What of the Camilli?

One last suggestion, and this most tentative. What of the figures of the two young boys on the Aeneas panel? They are always identified simply as *camilli* assisting at the sacrifice—and, of course, they are that. But why are they there at all? And why *two*? They occupy at least a third of the panel, are carved in the same height of relief as Aeneas, with carefully modeled features and almost free-standing heads. And they are *individualized* as Simon remarks: "The two attendants are finely differentiated: the one with the fruit gives an impression of nobility, and the other, leading the animal, of robustness."[77] As we have seen, these are indications, according to the artistic conventions of the *Ara*, of important personages.

Furthermore, the "noble" figure is obviously taller, more grave, more mature; the "robust" figure, though a little bent, seems clearly shorter, more boyish. It seems reasonable to assume, then, that the artist intended to present them as being of different ages, possibly five or six years apart, the older being perhaps twelve or thirteen, the younger seven or eight. Why the difference in age?

Again, they are portrayed as actively involved in the central action of sacrifice, which is the focus of attention in the panel. They are not just background figures, functioning attendants, filling space between altar and shrine. They wear tunics and are crowned with laurel wreaths, models in dress and type for the *pubes Romana* of historic times.[78] They actively assist Aeneas with the fringed cloth, the fruits and libation jar, and the sow ready for sacrifice.

If the artist presents these two boys as individualized personages of equal importance with Aeneas, of different personalities and ages, and engaged with Aeneas in the central action of sacrifice, who are they meant to portray? I venture to suggest that the older and taller may be *Iulus Ascanius* and the younger the son of Aeneas and Lavinia. These would parallel Romulus and Remus on the opposite panel, just as Venus parallels Mars and, in some sense, the human Aeneas parallels the human Faustulus (though Aeneas is the "real" father of the first offspring of the Julian *gens* while Faustulus is only foster-father of Mars' Roman offspring).

Portraying the two sons of Aeneas might also be intended to underscore the parallel between Aeneas and Augustus who, as Moretti points out,[79] at the time of the *constitutio* of the Altar (July 4, 13 B.C.) had two (adopted) sons, Gaius and Lucius (though these were popularly assimilated to Iulus-Ascanius and Romulus, as Augustus was to Aeneas). The prominent cheekbones, broad foreheads, firmly rounded chins, and prominent ears on

---

holding the infant Ploutos (wealth, abundance) in her arms, a knobbed scepter, and a cornucopia. See L. Lacroix, *Les reproductions des statues sur les monnaies grecques* (Liège: Faculté de Philosophie et Lettres 1949) 295–97 and pl. XXVI, 8–11. For a broad discussion of the deified virtues that served as moral underpinning of Augustus' regime, see J.R. Fears, "The Cult of the Virtues," *ANRW* II Principat, 17.2 Religion (1981) 884–89.

[77] Simon (supra n. 3) 24.

[78] Ibid. 23.

[79] Moretti (supra n. 11) I 313.

each of the boys' sculptured heads may perhaps be intended to recall the physical characteristics of Augustus, whose remote ancestors they would be.[80] In any case it seems to me more satisfactory, artistically, conceptually, and ideologically, to identify the two boys as the sons of Aeneas rather than simply as two anonymous *camilli* introduced by the artist to fill out the panel.

Conclusion

If what has been suggested is valid, the important panel to the right of the principal entrance to the *Ara* complex would portray Aeneas in the act of offering sacrifice, assisted by his two sons. And the main sacrifice, a pregnant sow, is to be offered to his mother, the goddess Venus, who stands behind him, unnoticed, her scepter in her right hand, and in her left a cornucopia, symbol of peace and the prosperity that follows peace. Aeneas is not the heroic warrior of the *Aeneid*, but *Pater Aeneas*, mature, bearded, veiled for sacrifice, established in his new homeland, Lavinium, as indicated by the temple of the "Penates" in the distance, upper left. His battles are over, he is at home, at peace. He has two sons, the older of ancient noble Trojan stock, the younger of more recent, robust Latin stock. And just as Venus had been Aeneas' companion and savior in time of war, she stands behind him as patroness of his peace and prosperity.

The parallels with Augustus, who appears on the processional frieze behind Venus, must be obvious. He has emerged victorious from the civil war and subsequent wars of pacification. He now returns to a homeland firmly established in peace. He rejoices in his two adopted sons. He approaches to sacrifice with head veiled like Aeneas. He has been declared Augustus and, most recently (12 B.C.), *Pontifex Maximus*. Venus, from whom he proudly claims descent, has been his patroness in time of war (Venus Victrix); he how approaches her, who bears his symbol of the cornucopia, as *genetrix* and patroness of the *Pax Augusta*. Thus Venus, goddess of peace, positioned near the right corner of the enclosure wall, provides a visual and conceptual link between Aeneas and Augustus, and a presence most appropriate for the *Ara Pacis Augustae*.

Finally, the suggested identifications make possible, I believe, a more complete interpretation of the entire sculptured series that adorn the enclosure walls. On each side of the principal entrance the front panels balance in the ways we have mentioned: Mars with Faustulus and the twins, Romulus and Remus, on the left: Venus with Aeneas and his two sons on the right. The helmeted Mars, god of armed might and power, on the left; Venus with cornucopia, goddess of peace and plenty, on the right. On the left (north) side frieze, behind Mars, father of the Roman people, stands the civic procession, largely magistrates and priests; on the right (south) side frieze, behind Venus, *genetrix* of the Julian *gens*, stands the dynastic procession, largely Augustus, his family and household. On the left rear panel, behind Mars, god of war, sits the warrior-goddess Roma, symbol of Rome's victorious armed might; on the right rear panel, behind Venus, patroness of peace, sits the goddess Tellus-Saturnia, symbol of Italy's fertility and abundance in peace.

[80] For these features in Augustus, see Simon (supra n. 3) 16 and plate 31: veiled head of Augustus from the Terme Museum.

The sculptured series forms a consistent whole, and the total composition with its balanced two-fold theme reflects Augustus' personal vision of his destiny, symbolized on his coinage by the globe and rudder (power over land and sea) between the forelegs of the Capricorn, and by the cornucopia (peace and plenty) carried on its back. It is the same ideal and destiny proposed by Vergil for the entire Roman people (*Aeneid* VI, 851–52):

tu regere imperio populos, Romane, memento
(hae tibi erunt artes), pacisque imponere morem.

MNESIKLES' PROPYLAIA ON THE ATHENIAN AKROPOLIS

Jos de Waele

These pages are dedicated to Father Raymond V. Schoder, S.J., who, as a Fulbright professor, was my teacher of Classical Archaeology at the Catholic University of Nijmegen (The Netherlands) during the academic year 1956–1957. This article,[1] which virtually constitutes my inaugural address at Nijmegen University of October 10, 1986, was also presented on occasion of the Schoderfest at Loyola University of Chicago, when I was invited there as a Condon Symposiast from April 10–13, 1986. The results are meant as a token of gratitude for a 30-year friendship with the distinguished scholar.

In the spring of 431 B.C., when hostilities between Athens and Sparta culminated in the Peloponnesian War, which would bring both sides more than once to the brink of economic disaster, the consequences for the Athenian building program were severe. The embellishment of the Akropolis that had been begun by Perikles in 449 B.C. was suddenly interrupted, and financial contributions, paid primarily by the Allies of the Athenians, were once again reserved for their original goal, the upkeep of army and fleet. With the outbreak of war a 17-year period of great achievement that had witnessed the construction of the most splendid buildings of Hellenic antiquity came to an abrupt end. During this time first the Parthenon was built according to the design of Iktinos and Kallikrates, while Pheidias, heading a host of craftsmen, finished the building—in particular its sculptural decoration: the metopes, the frieze with the Panathenaic Procession, and both pediments, sculptures which now mainly, as the Elgin Marbles, adorn the galleries of the British Museum in London. Within the temple itself, moreover, the colossal cult statue of Athena Parthenos was wrought in gold and ivory, an extravagance which has inspired the ironic description of the shrine as a "weather-proof statue-box".[2] This statue is generally held to have been completed in 438 B.C.[3]

In the following year, 437 B.C., construction was started on the monumental entrance to the Akropolis, the Propylaia, a gateway that adorned the Akropolis like a crown. For five years building operations took place until the Peloponnesian War brought construction to a halt. As we shall see later, several indications point to the conclusion that the building was never finished as originally planned.

Within the brief scope of this article several aspects of the Propylaia will be discussed. First we consider the nature of the literary sources which have established the reputation of the Propylaia until modern times, next the function of the inscriptions referring to the construction of the building. Finally the Propylaia itself will be analyzed

[1] Translated by Bastienne Otten (Nijmegen) with revision by the editor.
[2] C.J. Herington, *Athena Parthenos and Athena Polias* (Manchester: University Press 1955) 38.
[3] B. Wesenberg, "Parthenosgold für den Parthenonbau?" *AA* 1985, 53.

according to a system developed at the Department of Classical Archaeology of the Catholic University of Nijmegen. This metrological analysis will enable us to reconstruct the line of thought followed by the architect Mnesikles as he first drew up his plan of the Propylaia and later during the course of the building's construction, so that his true architectural intent may be revealed. It will serve as well to illustrate how this method of analysis can contribute to a better understanding of ancient buildings.

I. The Propylaia in Ancient Literature[4]

In ancient Greek literature the Parthenon and the Propylaia are both classified as monuments which were erected more or less as votive offerings after the victory over the Persians following their invasion in 480 B.C. To the orators of the fourth century B.C., the generation of Demosthenes (384–322 B.C.), these monuments are a symbol of the Athenian golden age and thus serve as vehicles of propaganda. In 355 B.C. Demosthenes refers in his speech against Androtion[5] to "the men who built the Propylaea and the Parthenon, and decked our other temples with the spoils of Asia, trophies in which we take a natural pride," and states further on (c. 76), "Hence the People inherits possessions that will never die; on the one hand the memory of their achievements, on the other the beauty of the memorials set up in their honour,—yonder Propylaea, the Parthenon, the stoas, the docks— . . . ."[6] One cannot escape the notion that Demosthenes, in referring to these monuments during his speeches pointed to the Propylaia from the Pnyx which faced them: *Προπύλαια ταῦτα*, i.e. "the Propylaia over there, the Parthenon, stoas, and ship docks."

The orator Aischines[7] (390–315 B.C.), Demosthenes' principal opponent, even reports that Epameinondas, showing blatant disrespect for the reputation of Athens, bluntly proposed before the Theban Assembly to transfer the Propylaia from the Akropolis in Athens to the Kadmeia, the stronghold of his native Thebes which at that moment possessed hegemony over Greece.[8] To Athenian ears this must have sounded like transferring the Statue of Liberty from New York to Moscow as spoils of war.

Specific information can further be found in the lexika and scholia which sought to explain references in the texts of the orators such as the aforementioned passages. Harpokration, a lexicographer living in Alexandria in the second century after Christ, writes that

[4] The literary sources have been collected in: O. Jahn and A. Michaelis, *Arx Athenarum a Pausania descripta* 3 (Bonn: M. Weber 1901) 42–46.

[5] *Contra Androtionem* 22, 13.

[6] Elsewhere Demosthenes uses almost the same buildings as examples: *Contra Aristocratem* (23, 207): "On the other hand, both the structure and the equipment of their public buildings were on such a scale and of such quality that no opportunity of surpassing them was left to coming generations. Witness those Propylaia, docks, stoas, the great harbor, and all the edifices with which you see the city adorned." (translation Vince with alterations).

[7] Aischines, *On the Embassy* 105: "Epameinondas was a Theban, and he did not cower before the fame of the Athenians, but spoke right out in the Theban assembly, saying that they must remove the Propylaia of the Akropolis of Athens and set it up at the entrance to the Kadmeia." (trans. C.D. Adams).

[8] Harpokration, s.v. *Προπύλαια ταῦτα*. Cf. *FGrHist* 328, fr. 36; ibid. 373, fr. 1, and Jacoby's commentary ad loc.

the construction of the Propylaia was begun in Athens under the architect Mnesikles during the archonship of Euthymenes (437/6 B.C.). He refers this information to two earlier authors whom he actually names: Philochoros (340–267 B.C.), the last Atthidographer, i.e. an author of Attic local history, and Heliodoros (ca. 125 B.C.), the author of a *periegesis* or guidebook in which the Akropolis of Athens was described in detail. In the first book of his work—apparently dealing with the entrance of the Akropolis—Heliodoros writes: "The building was built in five years, and 2012 talents were spent."[9] In modern times doubts have been expressed as to whether this amount is correct.[10] In any case, if we can define the nature of their sources more precisely, we can presume that the information given by Philochoros and Heliodoros is reliable, since they had access to epigraphical documents which were originally to be seen near the Propylaia.

II. The Inscriptions[11]

The text of these inscriptions has come down to us badly damaged on 20 fragments. The nature of these inscriptions is quite clear. They are not specifications for a building to be built like those for the arsenal of Philon at Piraeus,[12] but, like those surviving for the Parthenon and Parthenos, accounts of money received and spent for its construction.[13] From these financial accounts it becomes apparent that the cost of the building was met from several sources including:[14]

1. Money from the sale of surplus building materials such as roof tiles and timber. This entry probably occurs mainly in the first year when the former gateway was torn down to produce second-hand building materials, but perhaps also occasionally later as scaffolds came down.
2. The sum remaining from the previous year carried over to the current year. This entry naturally does not occur in the first year.
3. Contributions from various boards including the treasurers of Athena and the Hellenotamiai, treasurers of the Athenian Alliance.
4. Revenues from house rent and from the silver mines at Laurion.
5. Private donations.

In the heading of the inscription, only partially preserved, the name of the magistrate Euthymenes occurs at the outset. He is the Eponymous Archon who held office in the Attic civil year 437/6 B.C. It is clear that the inscription also included a summary of

[9] *ἐν ἔτεσι μὲν ε′ παντελῶς ἐξεποιήθη, τάλαντα δὲ ἀνηλώθη δισχίλια ιβ′.*

[10] A.W. Gomme, *A Historical Commentary on Thucydides II* (Oxford: Clarendon 1956) 20–23; J.J. Keaney, "Heliodorus F. 1 and Philochorus F. 41," *Historia* 17 (1968) 507–508.

[11] *IG* I², 363–67; *IG* I³, 462–466; R. Meiggs and D. Lewis, *A Selection of Greek Historical Inscriptions to the End of the Fifth Century B.C.* (Oxford: Clarendon 1971) no. 60.

[12] J.A. de Waele, "Het scheepsarsenaal van Philo in Piraeus (*IG* II², 1668)," in: G.J. Bartelink and J.H. Brouwers (eds.), *Noctes Noviomagenses J. Nuchelmans oblatae* (Bussum: Unieboek 1985) 150–70.

[13] Cf. J.S. Boersma, *Athenian Building Policy from 561/0 to 404/3 B.C.* (Groningen: Wolters-Noordhoff 1970) 105.

[14] W.B. Dinsmoor, "Attic Building Accounts," *AJA* 17 (1913) 371–98 at 382–83.

receipts and expenditures. Although roughly the first 22 letters are lost, the lacuna can most probably be filled in with: Μνεσικλε̃ς ἀρχιτέκτον καὶ, following Dinsmoor who here draws an analogy with the somewhat later Erechtheion inscription, although in the latter the architect's name is not mentioned at the outset.[15]

Mnesikles is named in ancient sources only as architect of the Propylaia. While he has been credited tentatively with other buildings, including the Erechtheion and the Stoa of Zeus Eleutherios in the Agora,[16] it is the Propylaia which must serve to define Mnesikles' genius.

III. The Propylaia and Previous Analysis

Before turning to its analysis, we must briefly describe the plan of this complex building which unites within a single structure several disparate elements (Pl. 39a).[17] Only the Central Building has the form of what the Greeks call a *propylon*, a monumental gateway. Its nucleus is formed by an H-shaped construction in which two side walls are united by a central screen wall that is pierced by five doorways leading to the Akropolis (Fig. 1). These doorways could originally be shut with wooden doors, as we know from Comedy.[18] The central doorway, also the largest, is framed on either side by two symmetrically disposed openings which are reduced both in width and height as one moves from the center. Corresponding to the deep antechamber, the West Hall, is the shallower East Hall on the Akropolis side of the building. Both are faced with Doric porches similar to hexastyle temple façades, although their central intercolumniation is markedly wider than the others in order to span the ramped central passageway. The roof and ceiling of the deep West Hall are supported by a double row of slender Ionic columns.

We turn now to the other rooms attached to the Central Building. On the left as one enters the Akropolis lies the Pinakotheke, whose plan superficially resembles that of a temple *in antis*. A porch is supported by three Doric columns between antae, while the door behind is located asymmetrically within its wall, flanked by a window on either side. Pausanias (1.22.6) calls this wing the Pinakotheke, and, unless we are prepared to accept that it was given another function in the course of its existence, this name must refer to its original function: a room in which, like a treasury, votive tablets, *pinakes*, were hung. According to our spokesman Pausanias the paintings to be seen here included ones by the renowned Polygnotos of Thasos and therefore dated back as far as the fifth century B.C. Use of the room as a banquet hall, recently proposed by Travlos,[19] is unlikely.

[15] *IG* I², 372–74.

[16] The Erechtheion by Dörpfeld, *BPW* 48 (1928) 1073; the Stoa of Zeus Eleutherios by H.A. Thompson, *Hesperia* 6 (1937) 53: "The design of the building . . . if it was not directly due to Mnesicles, was at any rate influenced by the free and ingenious spirit (evidenced in the works) of the master on the hill above." H.A. Thompson and R.E. Wycherley, *Agora* XIV, *The Agora of Athens* (Princeton: American School of Classical Studies 1972) 100 n. 95; Travlos, 527.

[17] See for extensive bibliography: Travlos 482–93; R. Bohn, *Die Propyläen der Akropolis zu Athen* (Berlin-Stuttgart: Spemann 1882); J.A. de Waele, *Mnesikles' Design of the Propylaia in Athens* (forthcoming).

[18] Aristophanes, *Lysistrata* 259 ff. " . . . with block and bolt and barrier vast,/ Making the Propylaea fast" (trans. Rogers, Loeb ed., vol. 3 [London: Putnam 1924]).

[19] W.B. Dinsmoor, Jr., "The Asymmetry of the Propylaia for the Last Time?" in *Studies in Athenian*

PLATE 39. Reconstruction of the Propylaia by Luckenbach. **a.** As finally executed.

b. The "intentional" plan of Dörpfeld. After H. Luckenbach, *Kunst und Geschichte* I. *Altertum*. 13th ed. (Munich & Berlin: Oldenbourg 1922) 47.

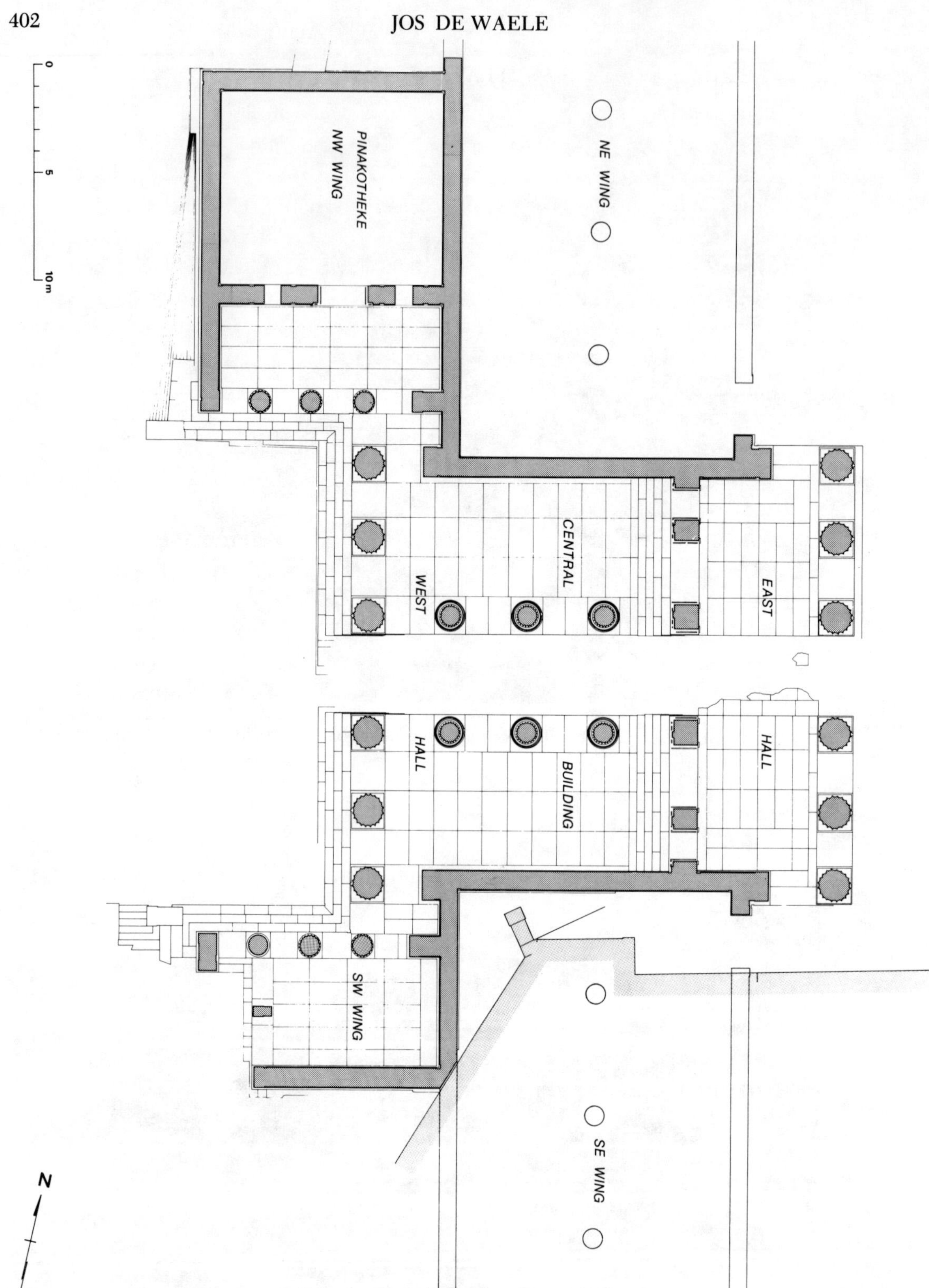

FIG. 1. The Propylaia. Plan showing the different elements and reconstructing the intentional plan. Drawing Peterse.

The smaller Southwest Wing, located on the right as one enters the Akropolis, presents a colonnaded façade corresponding to that of the Pinakotheke opposite. Behind the colonnade lies an open rectangular hall providing access to the sanctuary of Athena Nike.

These three structures comprise the Propylaia as it stands today, but there is evidence that this is not how the building was originally conceived by its architect. Wilhelm Dörpfeld (1853–1940), founder and grandmaster of the study of architecture, described in German as *Bauforschung*, through his precise observations, initiated modern research on the Propylaia. He rightly concluded that the entire building was never completed.[20] His evidence is as follows. First, lifting bosses visible on wall blocks in some inconspicuous parts of the exterior were never removed, as was normally the case during a building's final finishing. Similarly, the protective mantle of stone that had served to protect the surface of the stylobate against minor damage during construction was likewise never removed, as was usual. Furthermore, Dörpfeld concluded from antae located on the northern and southern flanks of the East Hall and from the stump of a wall north of the Pinakotheke that two halls were originally planned on the eastern, Akropolis side of the Propylaia, but, unlike their counterparts on the west, were never built according to plan (Pl. 39b, Fig. 2). Finally, as evidence for some construction on the east Dörpfeld pointed to the presence of cuttings for the ridge beams in the outside of the walls of the Central Building. Concerning these unrealized wings Dörpfeld presented an explanation which has been of crucial importance for later studies. Noting the complex building history of St. Peter's Basilica in Rome, Dörpfeld[21] concluded that in the study of ancient architecture as well one must take into account changes made during the course of construction, "Abänderungen, welche der ursprüngliche Entwurf eines Bauwerkes während der Bauzeit oder später erfahren hat."[22] According to Dörpfeld, then, the Central Building and the Pinakotheke alone were constructed according to Mnesikles' design, while his Southwest Wing and two eastern wings were curtailed.[23]

Since, in Dörpfeld's view, the Propylaia was intended as a strictly symmetrical structure in Mnesikles' original design, and since two sanctuaries already existed in the south, for him the explanation for the present plan was self-evidently the opposition of religious authorities: "Die Priester haben sich gewiss, so bald Mnesikles sein Project öffentlich bekannt gab, dieser Verkleinerung der Bezirke widersetzt und auf eine Abänderung des Entwurfes gedrungen."[24] This view is clearly repeated and elaborated in later studies by other scholars, and through this large unison chorus, solo voices in opposition are barely audible. The current consensus is well expressed by Gruben[25] who writes, "Wegen des

---

Architecture, Sculpture, and Topography, *Hesperia* Supplement 20 (Princeton: American School of Classical Studies 1982) 18–33.

[20] W. Dörpfeld, *AM* 10 (1885) 38–56; ibid. 131–44.

[21] Ibid. 38.

[22] Ibid. 38.

[23] Ibid. 41.

[24] Ibid. 45.

[25] G. Gruben, *Die Tempel der Griechen* (Munich: Hirmer 1980) 180; H. Bankel, *Haller von Hallerstein in Griechenland* (Berlin: Reimer 1986) 96–99.

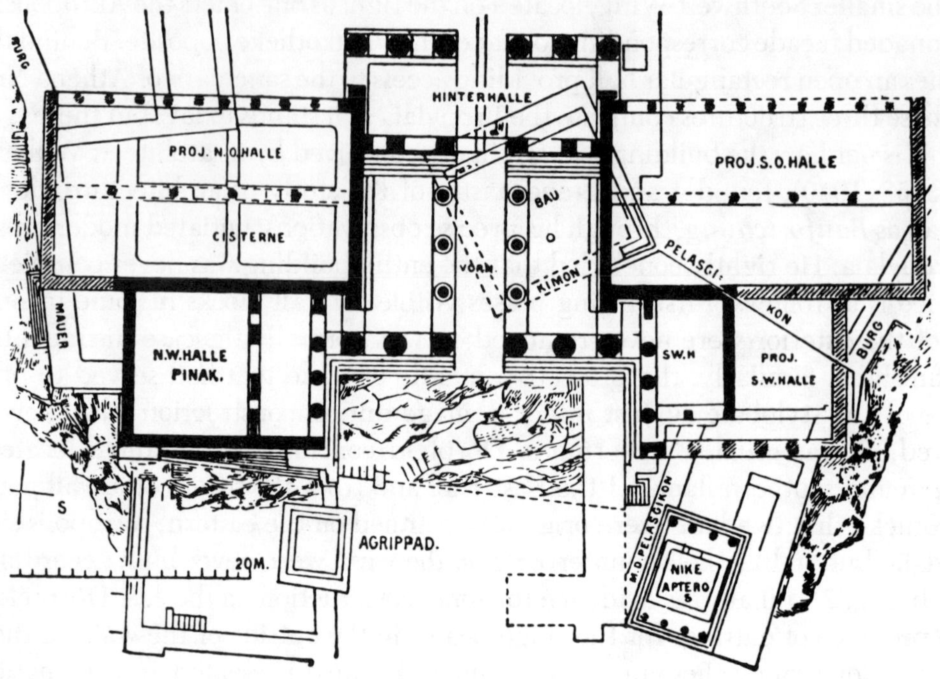

FIG. 2. Plan of the Propylaia after Dörpfeld. The hatched parts would be the intentionally symmetrical plan. After F. Winter, *Kunstgeschichte in Bildern* (Leipzig: Kröner) p. 136, 2.

Widerstandes der konservativen Priesterschaft des angrenzenden Nike- und Artemis-Bezirkes wurde sein Entwurf beschnitten." When Dörpfeld postulated perfect symmetry he was clearly led by ideas which originated under the strong spell of Classicism, doubtless first felt during his training at the Berliner Bauakademie. Comparing the plans of the Propylaia in Athens with the Propyläen on the Königsplatz in Munich designed by von Klenze,[26] one notes in the latter the same symmetry that can also be detected in the Brandenburger Tor in Berlin.[27] The influence of the Athenian Propylaia on both German structures can be traced to the persistent influence of *The Antiquities of Athens* by James Stuart (1730–1788) and Nicholas Revett (1720–1804) where, indeed, both wings are reconstructed symmetrically.[28] Their reconstruction can be excused, however, by the fact that the so-called Frankish Tower (Pl. 40), probably erected by the Venetian Acciaioli shortly after 1401, was then situated on the Southwest Wing where it remained until Schliemann provided the funds for its demolition in 1875.[29] Only then did it become possible to examine the foundations closely.

[26] O. Hederer, *Leo von Klenze. Persönlichkeit und Werk* (Munich: Callwey 1981) 342–47.

[27] R. Bothe, in W. Ahrenhövel (ed.), *Berlin und die Antike-Katalog*, (Berlin: Deutsches Archäologisches Institut 1979) 294–98.

[28] J. Stuart and N. Revett, *The Antiquities of Athens* (new edition, London: Macmillan 1893) pl. XLIII, facing p. 88.

[29] M.C. Hellmann and P. Fraisse, *Paris—Rome—Athènes: Le voyage en Grèce des architectes français aux XIX et XX siècles* (Paris: École Normale Supérieur 1983) 188–93; 204–11.

PLATE 40

PLATE 40. The Propylaia from the southwest, ca. 1750; in the foreground, the Frankish Tower. After Hellmann-Fraisse (supra n. 29) 34, fig. 12.

This Classicistic image has determined opinion about the Propylaia for a long time, even as research has continued on other lines. The most promising of these new lines is the attempt to discover the basic units used in the structure's construction. It was W.B. Dinsmoor who, proceeding along the path laid out by Dörpfeld, converted the latter's metric measurements into a Doric foot of 32.72 cm. which he derived from the block height of 49 cm.[30] Other scholars have found different measurements as the basis of construction. Most notably the Danish scholar Bundgaard[31] in a monograph on Mnesikles based his analysis on the frieze of triglyphs and metopes, postulating that its elements would have consisted respectively of 2 and 3 units.

Other studies in a similar vein likewise enable the conversion of only a few distances and provide no insight into the architect's general design.[32] This seems the appropriate point to introduce a special excursus on a phenomenon which a German colleague once described to me as a "Zeitvertreib für pensionierte Bauräte," a phenomenon which could also be defined, in analogy with theosophy, as "metrosophy." By this term I mean the way in which all kinds of "sacred" geometric figures such as the pentagon, hexagon, golden section and the like can be drawn onto a ground-plan; under this label one could refer to every solution that has been tried out in relation to the Parthenon.[33] Individual authors like to prove how a carefully presented mysticism was applied at the construction site.[34] The German Bauforscher Armin von Gerkan (1884–1969) tried with his sharp wit to banish this many-headed hydra, but his effort has, unfortunately, proven to be in vain.[35] Time and again one must note how studies based on these methods stubbornly persist. An anecdote related by Dinsmoor[36] illustrates this best:

> As an example of the universal applicability of "dynamic symmetry" I might note a curious instance of a clash between this and the "module system." To illustrate the latter was published a plan of the Heraeum at Olympia (*Architecture* XLII, 1920, 209), apparently drawn by an office boy without knowledge of the fact that the flank columns are actually more closely spaced than those on the façades by 0.31 m (more than 12 inches); for he represented them as uniformly spaced on all sides. In an attempt to convert this system an ardent student of "dynamic symmetry" worked over the erroneous plan and found that it perfectly fitted his own theories. But when his attention was drawn to the fact that the net result of his success was merely the proof that it was not the ancient Greek architect, but the irresponsible office boy, who had unwittingly designed the Heraeum on the "dynamic" system, he refrained from publication.

[30] 1½ DF × 32.72 cm. = 49.08 cm.

[31] J.A. Bundgaard, *Mnesicles. A Greek Architect at Work* (Copenhagen: Scandinavian University Books 1957) 75.

[32] H. Riemann, *Gnomon* 31 (1959) 309–19.

[33] A.K. Orlandos, *The Parthenon* (Athens: Greek Archaeological Society 1978) 669.

[34] T. Brunés, *The Secrets of Ancient Geometry* (Copenhagen: Rhodos 1967) 260: "The temple brotherhood . . . has . . . a secret ritual which must on no account be passed to anyone whom the master has not initiated in the appropriate degree."

[35] A. von Gerkan, *Gnomon* 14 (1939) 529–34; id., *Gymnasium* 64 (1957) 359–64.

[36] W.B. Dinsmoor, "How the Parthenon Was Planned," *Architecture* 47 (1923) no. 6, 179, n. 4.

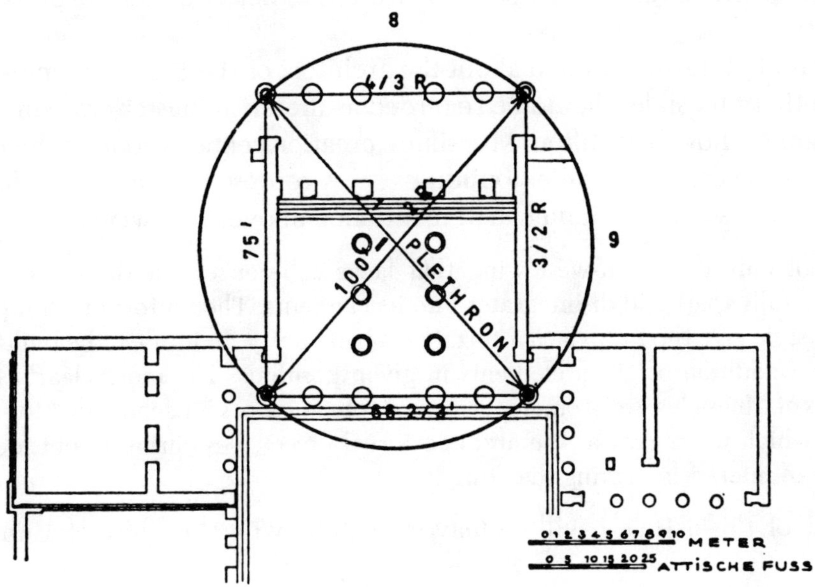

FIG. 3. Plan of the Central Hall after Wedepohl (supra n. 37), based on a circle of 100 Attic feet.

The Propylaia has not escaped the "metrosophists'" quest either. Wedepohl[37] assumed the architect's ground-measurement and starting point to be the hypotenuse of 100 Attic feet (29.5 cm), which would be measured from the center of the corner column to the center of the diagonally opposed other corner column (Fig. 3). From this, the depth and width of the main building could be construed; then the architect would have computed the position of the screen wall, columns, and the other walls.

Tiberi[38] proceeds from Wedepohl's theory, but instead of 100 Attic feet, he uses 100 Doric feet (32.72 cm.). However, if Wedepohl's theory is wrong, then Tiberi's cannot be right either. In 1984 we checked Tiberi's measurements and ascertained that his measuring points have no constructural significance at all.[39] Here too von Gerkan's criticism stands firm.

[37] E. Wedepohl, "Maßgrund und Grundmaß der Propyläen," *BonnJbb* 161 (1961) 252–62.

[38] C. Tiberi, *Mnesicle architetto* (Rome: Officina Edizioni 1964); id., "Osservazioni sulla cosiddetta Pinacoteca dell'Acropoli di Atene," *Τιμητικός τόμος εἰς μνήμην* Γ.Θ. *Ζώρα*, *Parnassos* 25 (1983) 821–46.

[39] Thanks to a contribution from the Netherlands Organization for the Advancement of Pure Scientific Research (Z.W.O.) Ing. (= engineer) C.L.J. Peterse and the author were able to remeasure the building. Our thanks go to the Ephor of the Acropolis, Dr. Evi Touloupa, and her staff for their generous help.

In the same way one should reject the hypothesis that ancient architects were higher mathematicians and that their ground-plans bear witness to an apparently advanced knowledge of Greek mathematics.[40] Nor were the measurements expressed in irrational numbers.[41]

In current literature opinion about the architect of the Propylaia moves between two poles: whether Mnesikles should be regarded as merely a master craftsman or rather as a master planner. For J.J. Coulton, Mnesikles' creation remains "one of the most ingenious, unusual, and successful of Greek buildings."[42] A representative of the opposing, master-craftsman view would be Bundgaard, mentioned above, who writes:[43]

> It is not only the south-west wing that lacks coherence, but the design as a whole that . . . falls apart and disintegrates into its elements. The uniform technique and consistent style give the Propylaea a certain external unity. In its idea, the building is a mechanical addition of given elements in given positions. The more clearly the circumstances of Mnesicles' work emerge, the more obvious does it become that the artistic synthesis which we regard as the architect's real object, lies curiously outside Mnesicles' sphere of interest in making the design.

In the rest of this article I will endeavor to show why this view of Bundgaard cannot stand.

IV. Metrological Analysis of the Propylaia

Using the method employed over the last ten years in our department, one can demonstrate the simple way in which the groundplan of the Propylaia arose.[44]

It is fair to state that until now we have gained little insight into the planning methods of the ancient Greek architect because we have proceeded on a fundamentally wrong basis. If, for example, we were to analyze every building of the Renaissance using the same unit of measurement, e.g. the English-American foot of 30.45 cm., we would never be able to realize our goal because each building is based on slightly different units. That may be taken for granted, for from the middle ages until fairly recent times the foot used as a standard of measurement varied from town to town.[45] While it is commonly thought that the Greeks used only two or three different standard feet,[46] one may wonder if the

[40] J. Bousquet, *Le trésor de Cyrène*, *FdD* II (Paris: E. de Boccard 1952) and Dinsmoor's review, *AJA* 61 (1957) 402–11.

[41] P. Gros, "Nombres irrationels et nombres parfaits chez Vitruve," *MEFRA* 88 (1976) 669–704, esp. 682, where Gros deals with irrational numbers in Vitruvius. In Book VI.3.3 Vitruvius gives the ratios of three atrium types, the latter of which has a ratio of $1{:}\sqrt{2}$. This value of $\sqrt{2}$, however, is derived from the diagonal of the square with sides of 1. This method is clearly derived from the use of cords, which can also be found in the Egyptian right triangles (3,4,5, and 5,12,13).

[42] J.J. Coulton, *Greek Architects at Work* (London: Elek 1977) 119.

[43] Bundgaard (supra n. 31) 75.

[44] This is worked out in a more extensive publication: De Waele (supra n. 17).

[45] R. Klimpert, *Lexikon der Münzen, Maße und Gewichte*² (Berlin 1896, repr. Graz: Akademische Druck 1972) 111–12.

[46] E.g., W.B. Dinsmoor, "The Basis of Greek Temple Design: Greece, Asia Minor, Italy," *Atti del VII Congresso di Archeologia Classica I* (Rome: Erma di Bretschneider 1961) 355–68. H.H. Büsing, "Metrologische Beiträge," *JdI* 97 (1982) 9.

ideal of the Greeks formed by Winckelmann and Goethe has wrongly fostered the view that, *in this respect*, ancient Greek civilization was closer to eighteenth century Europe than to the middle ages (and observe in passing that the metric system was not introduced until after the French Revolution). Furthermore, since attention to accuracy in measurement was strongly inconsistent in antiquity, even within a particular city, one must allow for possible variation in the value of foot measurements.[47] Commerce would call for standardized measure long before architecture. Therefore, in the study of ancient architecture it is absolutely essential to assume, at any rate for the fifth century B.C., that *each building has its own unit of measurement*; whether the term used to describe this unit is "foot," "module," or "unit" is immaterial in this context, and hereafter "unit" (abbreviated as "u.") will be used strictly for the sake of convenience.

Following this fundamental assumption the next problem is how to compute this unit for each building. In some cases this computation is a relatively easy matter. When blocks for a particular building are ordered with a standard length of four feet, as occurs often in inscriptions, and the length of the building consists of 25 blocks, it is clear that building is exactly 100 feet long.[48] One observes a tendency in this direction in the fourth century B.C. In the preceding century, however, while the Doric foot of 32.72 cm. may have been applied regularly to the size of blocks, it can be deduced from the wall structure that block length and overall length of a wall are not based on the same unit of measure. If a wall consists of uniform blocks except for the last one—obviously an odd spacer block—we may conclude that two different units were employed in the building. While it would take too long to work this out in detail here, it may suffice to present the results of our analysis of the Propylaia as an illustration of this approach.

The basic unit of measurement used in the construction of the Propylaia is a unit of 0.302 m. In the East Hall of the Central Building the sides of the square stylobate slabs on which the columns rest measure 1.81 m. in length, equal to 6 units of 30.2 cm. (Fig. 4):
6 × 0.302 m. = 1.81 m.
Two such blocks form the penultimate "normal" interaxial spacing, the *Normaljoch*:
12 × 0.302 m. = 3.624 m.
The central interaxial spacing is:
18 × 0.302 m. = 5.436 m.
Thus these interaxial spacings, which are carefully marked by scratches indicating the center of each column preserved on the surface of the stylobate which was carefully cut away on this very spot, when expressed as simple multiples of the basic unit of 0.302 m., can be used to illustrate the placement of the six columns in the east porch, represented by their respective interaxial spacings:
14 u. + 12 u. + 18 u. + 12 u. + 14 u. =
14 u. + 42 u. + 14 u. = 70 u.

[47] E.g., in Pompeii: J.A. de Waele, "Der römische Fuß in Pompeji: Der Tempel des Juppiter Capitolinus," *BABesch* 59 (1984) 1–2; C.L.J. Peterse, "Der oskische Fuß in pompejanischen Atrien," ibid. 9–10.

[48] E.g., in the temple of Demeter in Agrigento: J.A. de Waele, "Der Entwurf der dorischen Tempel von Akragas," *AA* 1980, 210–11.

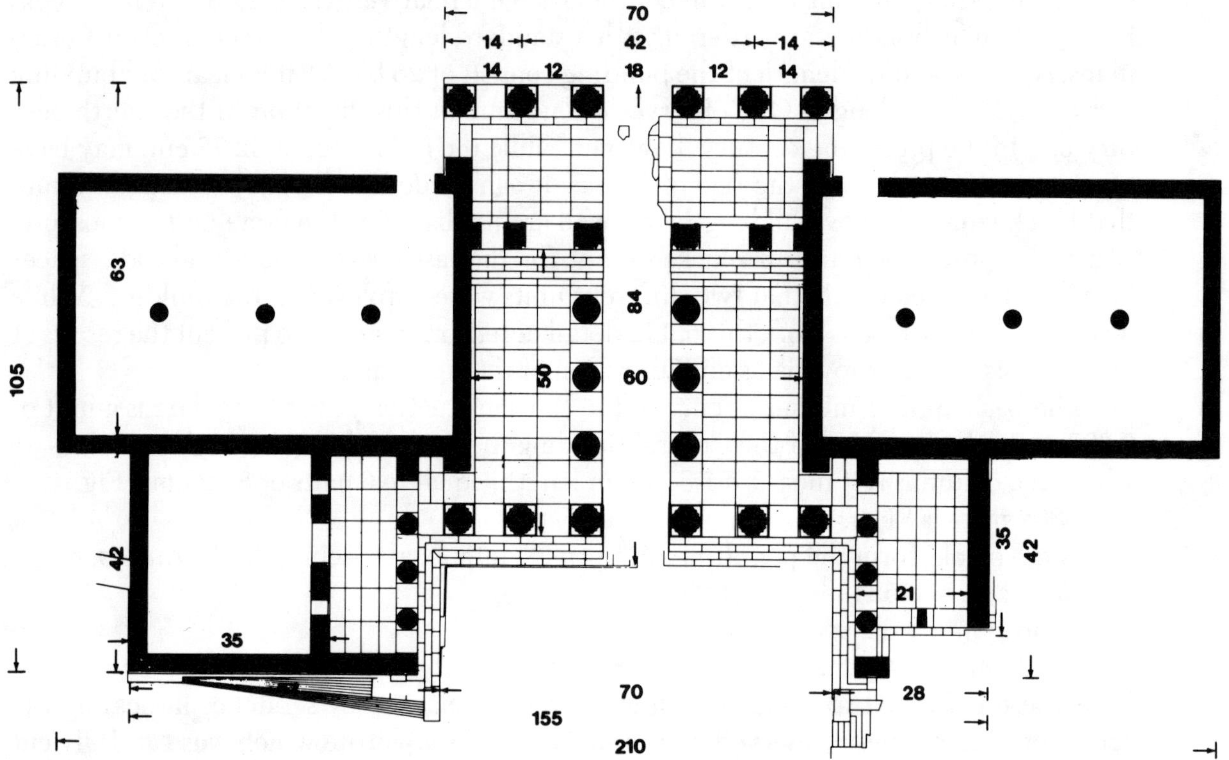

Fig. 4. Stages in the design of the Propylaia. Drawing Peterse.

The depth of the entire Central Building is 84 u. (25.41 m.). Thus the ratio of 5:6, already recognized before[49] for the relationship between the building's width and depth, can be expressed in the building's own units as 70 u.: 84 u.

[49] Riemann (supra n. 32) 315 s.

This ratio of 5 : 6 is also found in the West Hall which measures 50 u. × 60 u. (Fig. 4). The dimensions of the Pinakotheke too have been laid out in this same proportion, this time as multiples of seven: 35 u. × 42 u. (Fig. 4). Finally, the width of the Southwest Wing also consists of multiples of 7: façade 42 u.; rear 35 u. Since its depth, including the rear wall (3 u.) and the steps (4 u.), is 28 u., the interior depth is 21 u. from the edge of the stylobate to the wall plane. Thus the interior depth (21 u.) is half the width of the north façade (42 u.).

The different elements of the Propylaia are likewise related to each other in simple numerical proportions of the basic unit (Fig. 4):

Central Building : Pinakotheke depth
63 u. : 42 u.
3 : 2

Almost the same relation can be noted with regard to the structure's overall measurements. The depth is 105 u. (= 63 u. + 42 u.). The total width of the Central Building plus those of the two western wings can be calculated as follows (Fig. 4):

28 u. (= 4 u. × 7)
70 u. (= 10 u. × 7)
57 u. (= [8 u. × 7] + 1 u.)

155 u.

It will be observed that these measurements differ from the standard as multiples of 7 by the addition of 1 u.; instead of the expected distance of 154 u. (= 22 u. × 7), the width was actually laid out as 155 u. This change from 154 u. to 155 u. can only be explained, *in our opinion*, as a simple rounding off so that in written specifications the dimensions to be laid out could be expressed concisely and without risk of error in a simple verbal instruction as "1 × 1½ *plethra* [1 *plethron* = 100 feet], both distances increased by 5 feet." (Fig. 5).

At another point, too, one notes deviation from the predicted standard. In the Central Building the depth of the East Hall is not exactly half that of the West Hall which would yield the simple proportions 28 u. : 56 u. (i.e. 1 : 2) (Fig. 6). Instead, the screen wall has been moved ¾ u. to the west, yielding measurements of 55¼ u. : 28¾ u. This slight shift can be explained only by the desire to apply the regular interaxial spacing of 12 u. of the West Hall's Ionic colonnade to the distance of the elements located at either end of the colonnade, that is the screen wall on the east and the Doric columns of the west façade.

If the architect had not deviated in this way from his original sketch concerning the depth of the Pinakotheke and the shift of the screen wall, the first phase of the design would have been much clearer. In the initial stage of the design (Fig. 6) the Pinakotheke and the West Hall had the same depth (56 u.), while the East Hall and the Southwest Wing would similarly have been identical in depth (28 u.). If we have recovered here the first stage of planning, Dörpfeld's hypothesis that Mnesikles originally planned the wings to be symmetrical but was thwarted by the priests of the adjacent sanctuaries in the south

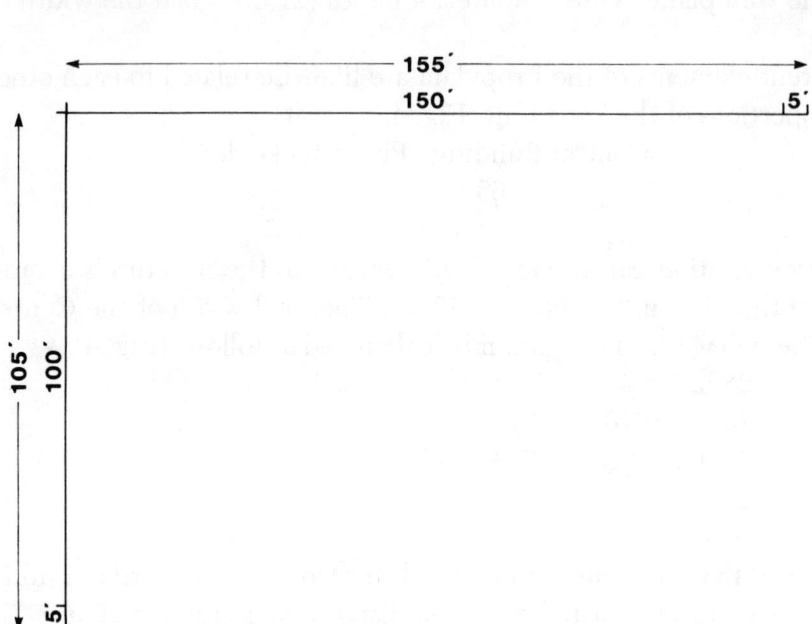

FIG. 5. Plotting out the width and depth of the Propylaia. Drawing Peterse.

is utterly unwarranted. Any such change would have taken place in a period before the initial planning of the Propylaia had begun.

Dörpfeld was definitely mistaken concerning the measurements of the unexecuted East Halls. Although never built and thus hypothetical, they could never have found a place on the Akropolis rock if planned according to the measurements proposed by Dörpfeld and later by Dinsmoor, because there is no room there for structures of that size (Pl. 39b, Fig. 2). It seems more likely indeed that proportions in multiples of 7 would have been applied in this case too. If one assumes two halls both 70 u. wide on either side of the Central Building, the total width of the Propylaia measured along the east would have been 210 u. (= 3×70 u.). It is more than fortuitous that the overall depth of this structure (105 u.) would have been half its width (210 u.).

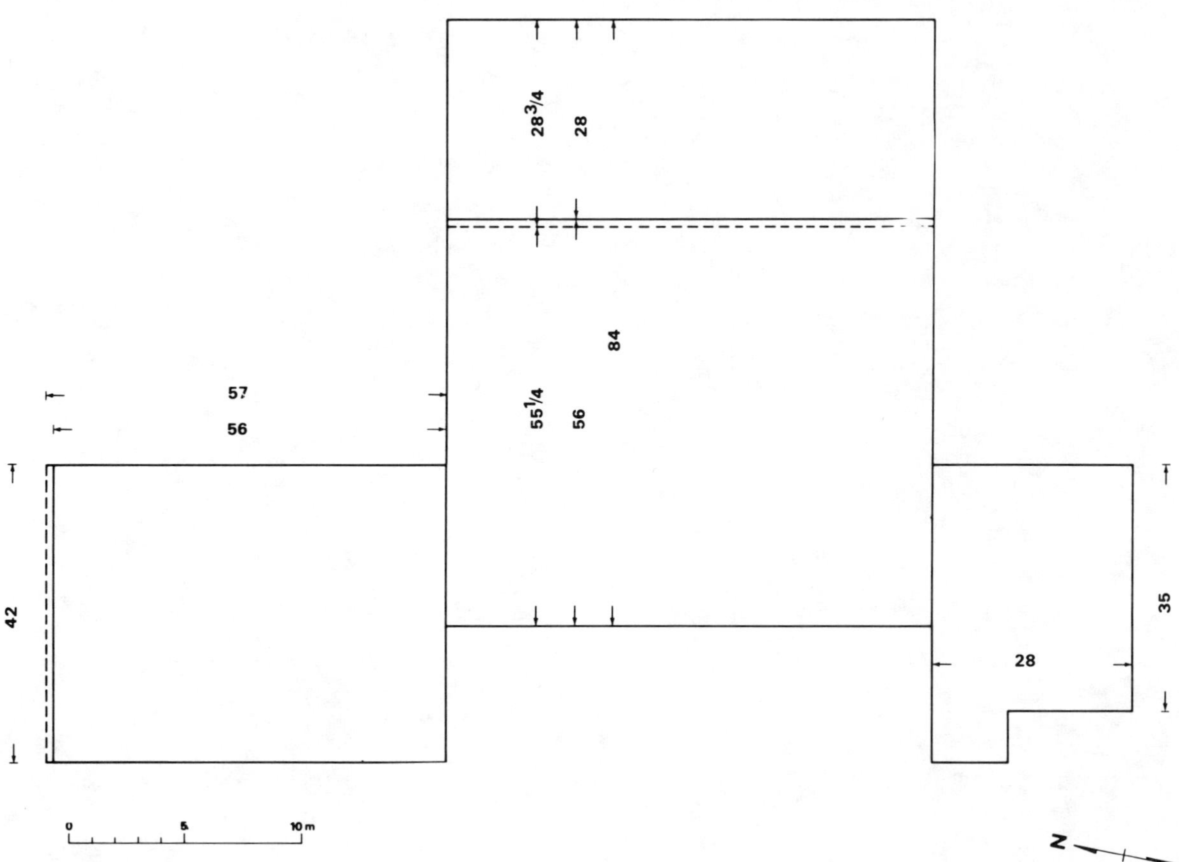

Fig. 6. The design of the Propylaia. The broken lines indicate the executed measurements. Drawing Peterse.

Although we have not been able to discuss all problems here, this analysis reveals the essentials of Mnesikles' method in the only building that has come down to us under his name. Such an analysis can only be undertaken, once the measurements taken in meters are converted into the architect's unit. If (as Boerhaave states) "simplicity is the mark of truth," then we are dealing with an architect of true genius. Even from such a brief exposition it might be suggested that we have discovered the brilliant plan by which a building consisting of disparate elements was forged into a unified architectural whole. I hope also to have proven with this example that we have developed a valid method for the analysis of ancient architecture, one which brings to light clearly the ideas and working methods of the ancient architect.

PORPHYRY'S *AD MARCELLAM*: MARRIAGE AND THE PRACTICE OF PHILOSOPHY

Kathleen O'Brien Wicker

I

Those of you familiar with the reputation of Porphyry,[1] the third century Neoplatonist, as the most formidable opponent of Christianity in antiquity, may think it inappropriate to mention him in the same breath with that dedicated champion of orthodox Catholicism, Raymond V. Schoder, S.J., whom we honor in this volume. But it is not unreasonable to suppose that each man would have respected that passionate commitment to the truth so clearly reflected in the life of the other, despite the fact that the one espoused the very truth the other sought to discredit. These two men also have other things in common: a solid grounding in the study of the Classics, an abiding interest in the writings of Homer, a lifelong commitment to the education of students, and a choice to live an ascetic life in a community of idealists. Unfortunately, the lives of both men were cut short soon after their seventieth birthdays.

II

When Porphyry was close to seventy years of age, however, he surprised everyone by marrying a woman named Marcella,[2] the widow of a friend, who had seven children. The *Ad Marcellam* is a fascinating epistle that the philosopher wrote to his wife of ten months, following his departure for an indefinite duration on a divinely sanctioned trip occasioned by "the needs of the Greeks." It functions as a gift to sustain Marcella in his absence and as an exhortation to continue her efforts to live the philosophic life.[3]

[1] The ancient authorities for Porphyry's life are: Porph. *Plot.* 1, *passim*; Eunapius *VS* 455–58; Eusebius *Hist. Eccl.* 6.19; Socrates *Hist. Eccl.* 7.2.27–28.

Modern discussions of Porphyry's life and work are found in J. Bidez, *Vie de Porphyre* (Leipzig: Teubner 1913; reprint Hildesheim: Olms 1964); R. Beutler, "Porphyrios," *RE* 22 (1953) cols. 271–313, esp. 292–93; W. Pötscher, "Porphyrios," *Die Kleine Pauly* 4 (Munich: Druckenmuller 1972) cols. 1064–69; A.H. Armstrong, *The Cambridge History of Late Greek and Early Medieval Philosophy* (Cambridge: University Press 1967) 272–325; H.D. Betz, "Gottmensch II," *Reallexikon für Antike und Christentum* (Stuttgart: Anton Hiersemann 1982) cols. 275–77.

The generally accepted date of Porphyry's birth is 232–234 A.D. The date of his death is uncertain; Pötscher (supra) col. 1064, says between 301 and 304/305 A.D. J. M. Rist, "Basil's 'Neoplatonism': Its Background and Nature," *Basil of Caesarea: Christian, Humanist, Ascetic*, P.J. Fedwick ed. (Toronto: Pontifical Biblical Institute of Medieval Studies 1981) 151, suggests a date as late as 310 A.D.

This research has been supported by the Scripps College Faculty Research Fund and the John Anson Kittredge Educational Fund.

[2] The ancient sources that refer to Marcella in addition to Euanpius (infra n. 5), are Cyril of Alexandria *Adv. Iul.* 6.209B (Migne PG 76, col. 819) and Aristocritus *Fragmente greichischer Theosophien*, H. Erbse ed. (Hamburg: Hanslacher Gildenverlag 1941) 201, *θ*.85.

[3] See the Introduction to Kathleen O'Brien Wicker, *Porphyry the Philosopher to Marcella* (Decatur, Ga.: Scholars Press 1987) for a full discussion of the purpose and rhetorical strategies of the *Ad Marcellam*.

The *Ad Marcellam*, a philosophical epistle, is a short text of sixteen folio pages with a fragmentary ending.[4] The manuscript of the epistle has had an elusive history. Porphyry's biographer Eunapius knew of its existence,[5] but there are no other ancient attestations of it. Somehow, the text survived through the centuries to be copied in the fifteenth century. It was this fifteenth century copy which Cardinal Angelo Mai discovered in the early nineteenth century in the Ambrosian Library in Milan where he was looking for manuscripts of Dionysius of Halicarnassus. He recognized what he had found and promptly published the text with a Latin translation in 1816.[6] Since then, other editions of the text have been published and several translations have appeared in English, French, German and Italian.[7]

III

In chapters 1–4 of the *Ad Marcellam* Porphyry reminds Marcella of the reasons he married her. He denies that he acted out of such self-interested motives as a desire for children, economic security, companionship, or to have someone to care for him in his declining years. Rather, he stresses, the marriage has imposed a number of burdens upon him, including the care of Marcella's children and the overt hostility of her relatives. (1)

Porphyry offers two positive motivations for his marriage. The first, that he must appease the gods of generation before his death, may be a bit of sophisticated humor at the expense of the traditionally pious.(2) The second reason seems to express his primary motivation: a concern to continue the philosophic education of his friend's widow.(3)

Porphyry acknowledges that the ten months of their marriage have been a special time for Marcella. But he vindicates his decision to respond to "the needs of the Greeks"

[4] Ae. Martini and D. Bassi, *Catalogus codicum graecorum bibliothecae Ambrosianae* II (Milan 1906) 747–51, contains a detailed description of the manuscript.

[5] Eunapius, *VS* 457.

[6] A. Mai, *Porphyrii philosophi ad Marcellam in Porphyrii, Philonis et Eusebii Pamphili fragmenta* (Milan: Regiis typis 1816). The codex (Ambrosianus Q13 sup. part. fol. 214vo.—222ro.) is dated to about 1500A.D. by Walter Pötscher, *Porphyrios* ΠΡΟΣ ΜΑΡΚΕΛΛΑΝ (Leiden: Brill 1969) 1–3. I have had access to a photocopy of the codex through the courtesy of the Ambrosian Library in Milan and the Center for the Study of Ancient Biblical Manuscripts in Claremont, California.

[7] I am aware of the following texts and translations of the *Ad Marcellam*: A. Mai (supra n. 6); Joh. von Orelli, *Opuscula Graecorum veterum sententiosa et moralia* (Leipzig 1819); A. Mai, *Classicorum auctorum e Vaticanis codicibus editorum* IV (1931); A. Nauck, *Porphyrii philosophi platonici opuscula tria* (Leipzig: Teubner 1860); M.-N. Bouillet, *Porphyre, son rôle dans l'école neoplatonicienne. Sa lettre à Marcella, traduite pour la première fois en français* (Paris: Donnaud 1864); A. Nauck, *Porphyrii philosophi Platonici opuscula selecta* (Leipzig: Teubner 1886); A. Zimmern, *Porphyry the Philosopher to His Wife Marcella* (London: George Redway 1896; 2nd ed. London; Priory Press 1910; reprint with Introduction by D. Fideler (Grand Rapids: Phanes Press 1986); K. Gass, *Porphyrius in epistula ad Marcellam* (Diss., Bonn 1927); A.J. Festugière, *Trois devots païens* II (Paris: La Colombe 1944); G. Faggin, *Porfirio Lettera ad Anebo, lettera a Marcella* (Florence: Sansone 1954); W. Pötscher (supra n. 6); E. des Places, *Vie de Pythagore; lettre à Marcella* (Paris: Les Belles Lettres 1982). My text and translation, from which are taken all translations of the *Ad Marcellam* in this paper, is cited supra n. 3. Citations are by traditional chapter divisions.

by asserting that the trip was divinely sanctioned.[8] And, though Marcella wished to accompany him, he argues that her responsibility to her children, her daughters in particular, requires her presence at home. But he promises to return and "to resume [her] instruction again as soon as possible." (4)

Chapters 5–10 begin the discussion of the theory and the practice of the philosophic life.[9] Porphyry empathizes with Marcella's situation, saying that she must feel she is being abandoned, like Philoctetes, but he assures her that the gods will not abandon her as the Greeks did that hero. (5) He urges her to "hold fast to philosophy, [her] only unfailing lifeline." She can practice the philosophic life by using adverse circumstances to obtain possession of "the true goods." (5) Reason can be a consolation to her as well, since she knows that a "life of ease" is appropriate for the gods, but not for humans who must ascend with difficulty from their fallen state to the gods. (6)

He reminds her, through the use of an *exemplum*, that good things can be enslaving without our being aware of it, and thus their loss "often contributes to an extraordinary distress." Nevertheless, "it is not by men who have lived for pleasure that ascents to God are made, but rather by those who have learned to bear nobly the greatest difficulties." (7)

Recognizing that she may fear his departure will cause her to "be bereft of the path to salvation and its master", Porphyry tells Marcella that his true reality is not material and tangible but rather spiritual and comprehensible by thought alone. (8) Further he recalls her belief that she has an inner guide who is her true leader and guide to all true goods. (9)

Finally, Porphyry promises Marcella that she will be able to encounter him "in complete purity as one both present and united to [her] night and day in a pure and most beautiful form of union and not as one likely to be separated from [her]" if she can "ascend into [herself]", attempt to recollect the intelligibles, to ponder them, and to practice what she has learned, even in the midst of difficulties. (10)

Chapters 11–24 demonstrate how traditional piety and ethics, properly understood and practiced, embody the ideals of the philosophic life. The divine, says Porphyry, is present everywhere, but its most fitting abode is in the intelligence of the wise man. The wise man, because he exists in close relationship with the divine, is enabled to do good. (11) Evil, however, is the result of one's own choice. (12) It is through the practice of virtue, not external acts of piety, that the wise man honors God, and indeed becomes

[8] Porphyry (4) says elliptically: "But the needs of the Greeks summoned me and the gods joined in their request." H. Chadwick, *The Sentences of Sextus* (Cambridge: University Press 1959) 142, suggests that this statement "may mean that he had been invited to attend the confidential deliberations which preceded the launching of the persecution of the Church under Diocletian in 303. (Porphyry would be a natural person to consult about such a project, as the author of several formidable books against the Christians.)" Zimmern 1896 (supra n. 7) 36, thinks there may be some justification for this view but Bidez (supra n. 1) 112, n. 2 and 116, and Festugière (supra n. 7) 8, are sceptical of this interpretation. I share their scepticism.

[9] A. Smith, *Porphyry's Place in the Neoplatonic Tradition* (The Hague: Nijhoff 1974) provides a comprehensive assessment of Porphyry's philosophical views and their place within the Neoplatonic tradition.

God's temple. (14, 16, 17) The wise man, who recognizes that God exists and governs the universe, should practice four virtues in relation to God: faith, truth, love, hope.

> For it is necessary to have faith that conversion to God is the only salvation; and for the faithful to be as eager as possible to know the truth about Him; and for the knower to love the one who is known; and for the lover to nourish his soul throughout life on good hopes. For by good hopes the good prevail over the wicked.(24)

In the discussion of law in chapters 25–34, Porphyry distinguishes between divine, natural, and positive law.(25) He quickly dismisses positive law from consideration. Divine law he describes as absolute, strong, and unalterable. It can be comprehended only by intellect which finds it stamped upon itself. The divine Intelligence thus

> becomes the very teacher and savior and nurse and guardian and guide to the ascent. By speaking in silence, and by allowing truth to unfold its divine law through its insight into it, the intellect comes to recognize in its investigations into it that the divine law has been stamped upon the soul from eternity.(26)

Through the divine law, one comes to recognize that the body "is not part of a man but exists in order for him to be born in the womb." (32) Thus

> the more an individual has turned toward the mortal element, the more he makes his heart unsuitable for the sublimity of immortality. But the more he holds aloof from passionate attachment to the body, the more he draws near to the divine. (32)

In order to insure the soul's attachment to the divine, the divine law has also established the law of nature. The law of nature dictates self-sufficiency (27), "remaining pure by abstinence from food and sex" (28), avoidance of excess and control of the passions (29), and imperturbability. (30) In fact, the pure soul which recognizes its tenuous connection to the body can imprison the passions of the body rather than becoming their prisoner. (33) One should be willing to do anything, even to amputate the whole body, in order to save the soul. (34)

The *Ad Marcellam* seems to have concluded with a paraenetic section. (35) The text in its present fragmentary state[10] contains only an admonition to Marcella on how to deal with her slaves and an exhortation to manual labor. It concludes: "regard the foundation of piety as love of mankind." Additional injunctions on the care of her children, dealings with her relatives, and remaining faithful to the philosophic life were probably also part of the original conclusion.

[10] A. Harnack, "Greek and Christian Piety at the End of the Third Century," *Hibbert Journal* 10 (1911) 78 n. 1, cites the suggestion of Nauck that the following sentences ascribed to Pythagoras in the *Florilegium* of Stobaeus actually belong to this letter:

51. We should strive to have such a spouse and such children and friends as may remain to us even after death.
52. Rather seek to be strong in soul than in body.
53. Know that nothing is in thy possession unless it belongs to thine inner self.
54. Seek to be the parent of such children as shall—not cherish the body in old age, but—nourish the soul with food eternal.
55. Do not attempt to hide thy sins behind words, but by full exposure to heal them.

IV

Opinions were divided in antiquity on the desirability of marriage for the philosopher and on the practice of philosophy by women. Socrates in Plato's *Republic* rejected conventional traditions of marriage, family life, and education for all members of his ideal state. He proposed instead the replacement of the family by a community of wives, children, and goods, and a new system of equal education for both sexes.[11] The views of the Platonic Socrates were not adopted except in a few utopian communities, however.[12]

Socrates' companion Aristippus married and had a daughter, Arete of Cyrene, who was his disciple and who trained her son Aristippus, the founder of the Cyrenaic school, in philosophy.[13] Xenophon[14] and Aristotle[15] both justified traditional marriage and familial relationships, and did not encourage wives in the formal study of philosophy. Theophrastus, Aristotle's successor, reflected the Peripatetic perspective on women when he theorized that education would turn them into lazy dilettantes.[16]

The Cynic tradition offers the example of Crates, the pupil of Diogenes, who married one of his pupils, Hipparchia of Maroneia. The letters of Crates to Hipparchia indicate that they eschewed traditional marital roles and family life.[17] In the Garden, women and men were welcome as disciples, but Epicurus discouraged the practice of marriage and childbearing except under special circumstances. He regarded these social relationships and obligations as constituting a threat to the imperturbability of the wise man.[18]

Pythagoras had accepted women pupils; in fact, Diogenes Laertius reports that many men sent their wives to study with him.[19] Later Neopythagorean texts addressed to women encouraged them to practice traditional domestic virtues.[20] Some of these texts

[11] Pl. *Resp.* 450A–480A. D. Wender, "Plato: Misogynist, Paedophile, and Feminist," *Arethusa* 6 (1973) 75–90, discusses Plato's attitudes toward women and marriage.

[12] The utopian ideal was advocated by the Stoics Zeno and Chrysippus, and by Diogenes the Cynic, according to Diogenes Laertius 7.131. What the actual status of women was in these utopias is unclear. See Sarah B. Pomeroy, "ΤΕΧΝΙΚΑΙ ΚΑΙ ΜΟΥΣΙΚΑΙ. The Education of Women in the Fourth Century and in the Hellenistic Period," *American Journal of Ancient History* 2 (1977) 58.

[13] Diogenes Laertius 2.86. See also the epistle of Aristippus to his daughter Arete, Ep. 27, *The Cynic Epistles*, A. J. Malherbe ed. (Society of Biblical Literature Sources for Biblical Study 12; Missoula: Scholars Press 1977) 282–85.

[14] Xen. *Oec.* 7.29–30. See also Plato, *Meno* 71E–72A.

[15] Arist. *Eth. Nic.* 8.7.1–2; *Pol.* 1.2.12, 1.5.1–9. See also D. K. Modrak, "Philosophy and Women in Antiquity," *Rice University Studies* 6/1 (1973) 1–11.

[16] Theophr. in *Stobaeus* 4, 193, no. 31 (Meineke). For an ancient refutation of this stereotype, see Musonius Rufus, "That Women Too Should Study Philosophy," (frag. 3) *Musonius Rufus. The Roman Socrates*, trans. A. D. Lutz, *YCS* 10 (1947) 38–43. See also S. G. Cole, "Could Greek Women Read and Write?" *Reflections of Women in Antiquity*, H. P. Foley ed. (New York: Gordon and Breach 1981) 219–45, esp. 228–29.

[17] Crates, Eps. 29–33 (Malherbe, supra n. 13).

[18] Diogenes Laertius 10.4–7, 119. Pomeroy (supra n. 12) 58, suggests that since Epicurus did not enjoy a good reputation in antiquity, identifying some of his pupils as courtesans may have been an attempt to discredit both him and them.

[19] Diog. Laert. 8.41–42.

[20] *The Pythagorean Texts of the Hellenistic Period*, H. Thesleff ed., *ActaAbo*, Ser. A. Humaniora 30/1 (1965) 51, 115–16, 123–24, 142–46, 188–89, 193–201. See also M. Meunier, *Femmes pythagoriennes:*

were attributed to the Neopythagorean women Theano and Myia (third century B.C.) and Melissa and Perictione (first century B.C.).[21]

Plutarch, in his *Coniugalia praecepta*, encouraged husbands to train their wives in philosophy. He viewed the husband-wife relationship as one of superior to subordinate, but he insisted that each spouse show appropriate respect, consideration, and love for the other.[22]

The Stoics generally supported equal training and education for men and women,[23] but by this they did not necessarily suggest that the sexes were equal either in nature or in opportunity.[24] Musonius Rufus, for example, argued against those who feared that the study of philosophy would make women arrogant, presumptuous, and negligent. He countered that "the teachings of philosophy exhort the woman to be content with her lot and to work with her own hands" and to practice modesty, self-restraint, and temperance.[25]

While the Stoics assumed that the household was the only valid sphere for women, they debated whether marriage was desirable for all men. In one place Musonius argued that even the philosopher should marry, since to repudiate marriage was to destroy "the home, the city, and the whole human race."[26] The Stoic Antipater had supported this view earlier.[27] In another place, however, Musonius questioned whether marriage was, in practice, appropriate for every man,[28] a view also espoused by the later Stoics Epictetus[29] and Hierocles.[30]

Plotinus, Porphyry's teacher, lived a celibate life, but Porphyry tells us in the *Vita Plotini* that Plotinus had among his disciples two women named Gemina and another called Amphiclea, whom he described as having a strong devotion to philosophy. Further, a widow named Chione and her children lived with Plotinus as did orphans for whom he had been named guardian. It appears that Plotinus had "spiritual marriages" with at least two of these women, the elder Gemina and Chione. "Spiritual marriage," a practice found

Fragments et lettres de Theano, Perictione, Phintys, Melissa et Myia (Paris: L'Artisan du livre 1932) and A. Städele, *Die Briefe des Pythagoras und der Pythagoreer* (Meisenheim am Glan: Hain 1980).

[21] H. Thesleff, *An Introduction to the Pythagorean Writings of the Hellenistic Period*, *ActaAbo*, Humaniora 24/3 (1961) 99, 113–16. S. B. Pomeroy, *Goddesses, Whores, Wives and Slaves* (New York: Schocken 1975) 134–36, contains an English translation of Perictione, "On the Harmonious Woman."

[22] Plut. *Coniugalia praecepta*, *Mor.* 139D, 140A, 140EF, 142DE, 145BC. See also K. O'B. Wicker, "First Century Marriage Ethics: A Comparative Study of the Household Codes and Plutarch's Conjugal Precepts," in *No Famine in the Land. Studies in Honor of John L. McKenzie*, J.W. Flanagan and A.W. Robinson eds. (Missoula: Scholars Press 1975) 141–53.

[23] Musonius Rufus, frag. 3, 4 (pp. 38–43, 43–49 ed. Lutz).

[24] C.E. Manning, "Seneca and the Stoics on the Equality of the Sexes," *Mnemosyne* 26 (1973) 170–77; D. L. Balch, *Let Wives Be Submissive: The Domestic Code in I Peter* (Society of Biblical Literature Monograph Series 26; Chico: Scholars Press 1981) 143–49 and idem, "I Cor, 7:32–35 and Stoic Debates about Marriage, Anxiety, and Distraction," *JBL* 102/3 (1983) 437 and n. 31.

[25] Musonius Rufus, frag. 3 (p. 43 ed. Lutz).

[26] Musonius Rufus, frag. 14 (p. 93 ed. Lutz).

[27] See Balch ("I Cor. 7:32-35," supra n. 24) 432–33.

[28] Musonius Rufus, frag. 13A (p. 89 ed. Lutz).

[29] Epict. *Ench.* 3.22.67–76.

[30] Balch ("I Cor. 7:32–35," supra n. 24) 434, cites the evidence.

also among certain Christians, allowed a man and a women to live together in an exclusive celibate relationship for mutual support in the pursuit of perfection.[31]

V

If the example of a lifetime is any indication, then one would expect Porphyry to advocate celibacy rather than marriage as the most advantageous state for the practice of philosophy. His decision to marry Marcella is intelligible only in the context of "spiritual marriage," for which he also had the example of Plotinus. Several passages in the *Ad Marcellam* suggest that Porphyry regarded traditional marriage as a potential threat to the practice of the philosophic life. He says that women who have heavy gold shackles are very reluctant to regard them as enchaining, whereas women who have iron shackles of the same weight seek to be rid of them.(7) This *exemplum*, used in the context of the difficulty Porphyry's departure has caused Marcella, suggests that detachment is a very difficult state to attain, yet it is absolutely necessary for the ascent. Even a good spouse may distract from the pursuit of the absolute good.

Porphyry further reminds Marcella that his true reality is not material but spiritual, and it is this kind of union they should aspire to attain, through their mutual practice of the philosophic life.(8) Finally, he tells her that she does not need him as her guide to the philosophic life, since she has already recognized the presence of the inner guide who is her true leader and guide to all true goods, the most perfect of which is mystical union with the divine.(9)

This perspective can be compared with the views expressed by Father Schoder in 1971 in a short pamphlet "Celibacy: A Glory of the Priesthood"[32] where he argues that priestly celibacy enhances the "total dedication to supernatural and time-transcending goals of life."[33] "No man," he states, "reaches true human fulfillment in this life on earth, even in a happy and holy Christian marriage."[34] However, he claims, celibacy is not a loveless state. The priest's

> commitment to give his heart to no one human being, and his body to none, gives a special security to his even human love. Since there is no question of sexual intention or exclusive giving of himself, the love that a priest shows various people should be above suspicion; it is not on the same level as romantic love, it is not competing against others' rights, it has no designs on its recipients' integrity. What it necessarily lacks in intensity and intimacy, it makes up for with its freedom, unselfishness, and purity.[35]

[31] Porph., *Plot*. 9. On "spiritual marriage," see K. O'B. Wicker, "'The Politics of Paradise' Reconsidered: John Chrysostom and Porphyry," Festschrift in Honor of J.M. Robinson (Bonner MT: Polebridge Press, in press).

[32] R. V. Schoder, S.J., "Celibacy: A Glory of the Priesthood" (St. Louis: Missouri Knights of Columbus [1971]; 24 pp.).

[33] Ibid. 1–2.

[34] Ibid. 8.

[35] Ibid. 17. A number of people have been the recipients of this kind of celibate love from Father Schoder, and it is a privilege for me, on behalf of all, to thank him for it.

Rather than regarding Porphyry's marriage as part of his philosophical commitment, some have considered it to be a last desperate effort to overcome his sense of desolation at the triumph of Christianity over the culture for which he was so eloquent an advocate, and to give his existence more human warmth and a concrete sense of responsibility.[36] But this does not appear to be a legitimate interpretation of Porphyry's marriage.

Arguments in support of the claim that Porphyry and Marcella had a celibate marriage are based on several passages in the *Ad Marcellam*. Porphyry tells Marcella: "I summoned you to my own way of life, sharing philosophy and pointing out a doctrine consistent with that life." (3) The "way of life" to which he refers is the philosophical life which embraces sexual asceticism. In addition he asserts that he does not want to have children, (1) that "even the gods have prescribed remaining pure by abstinence from food and sex" (28) and that sexuality is not a significant category in their relationship. He exhorts her:

> do not be overly concerned about whether your body is male or female; do not regard yourself as a woman, Marcella, for I did not devote myself to you as such. Flee from every effeminate element of the soul as if you were clothed in a male body. For the most blessed offspring come from a virginal soul and unmated Intelligence. For the incorrupt come from the incorruptible, while what the body begets is considered contaminated by all the gods.(33)

While Porphyry's desire not to beget children physically is not, in itself, sufficient reason for assuming a celibate marriage, and while his statement on abstinence suggests that control of the appetites, rather than their total renunciation, was intended, the final statement does provide a strong argument for this conclusion. This text is a classic rejection of the bodily, material world symbolized by human sexuality. It is an affirmation of a higher, spiritual dualism, not between the body and the soul, but between the soul and the mind. Things that are pure, physically and spiritually, are produced by the immortal part of one's nature. By contrast, physical procreation, the shadow of this reality, produces "contaminated offspring."

If the assumption that Porphyry and Marcella had a celibate marriage is correct, why did they elect to marry? If Porphyry is to be taken at his word, he was motivated in his decision by a sense of duty. He states that he "did not think it fitting, after [Marcella was] bereft of [her] husband, who was a friend of [his], to leave [her] abandoned without a partner and protector wise and suited to [her] character." (3) Marcella apparently needed protection from the pressure exerted upon her by those Porphyry described as her fellow-citizens. Porphyry protests that "because of the foolishness of [her] fellow-citizens and in their jealousy of [them]" he "encountered many slanderous remarks, and, contrary to every expectation, [he] ran the risk of death at their hands because of [Marcella] and her children." (1) He also boasts that he "endured their unreasonable outrages and bore their acts of treachery with composure." (3)

[36] Faggin (supra n. 7) 30, 140.

Why did Porphyry feel the need to rescue Marcella from her fellow-citizens and why did they respond to Porphyry with such hostility? The hostility of the fellow-citizens was probably based on the assumption that Porphyry had taken advantage of a vulnerable widow. At the time of their marriage Porphyry was close to seventy, while Marcella, "mother to five daughters and two sons (some of them still young children, some now waiting to attain puberty)"[37] was probably half his age. Porphyry, in turn, accused them of being "bent on mistreating [Marcella] under false pretenses." (3) But the real concern of the relatives was most likely less altruistic, to gain guardianship of the children and thus also the family inheritance.[38] Though they did not succeed, their hostility probably accounts for Porphyry's grave concern about Marcella's accompanying him on his trip, an act which would have necessitated leaving her daughters behind at the mercy of scoundrels. Further, it may explain Porphyry's comment that they entered their marriage "not for [themselves] but for others." (2)

VI

Recognizing the difficulties which this marriage created for both Porphyry and Marcella, what can be concluded about the relationship between their marriage and the practice of philosophy? For Porphyry, it was a commitment to a friend which imposed great burdens on him, particularly with regard to the care of the children. There was the satisfaction of seeing a person with potential adopt the philosophic life through a bold strategy which provided her this opportunity. It was, finally, a carefully calculated means to an end, and not an end in itself. For Marcella the marriage made possible continued training in philosophy, in its contemplative and active, intellectual and moral

[37] *Ad Marcellam* 1. For a similar situation, see Apuleius *Apol.* 73–74, *The Apologia and Florida of Apuleius of Madaura*, H.E. Butler ed. (Oxford: Clarendon 1909) 118–21. Epictetus *Ench.* 1.10 also discusses Epictetus' late marriage in order to provide a home for an unwanted child.

[38] Porphyry has so carefully concealed the identity of the people who exerted pressure on Marcella, threatened his life and reputation, and appeared to be a danger to Marcella's children, that, in the final analysis, we cannot know for certain who they were. We can assume, however, that they did not have legal authority over Marcella. It is most probable that Marcella had been married to her first husband *sine manu*, consistent with the practice of the period (see W. W. Buckland, *A Text-Book of Roman Law from Augustus to Justinian* [Cambridge: University Press 1932] 101). That she was able to proceed with her marriage to Porphyry, despite opposition, suggests that she was at the time *sui iuris* (see A.S. Gratwick, "Free or Not so Free? Wives and Daughters in the Late Roman Republic" in E. M. Craik ed., *Marriage and Property* [Aberdeen: University Press 1984] 41). As a mother of seven children, she was also exempt from *tutela* by the *ius liberorum* (see Buckland, supra 167).

Upon the death of their father, Marcella's children would have come under her guardianship unless he had designated another *tutor* in his will (see E. Sachers, "Tutela," *RE* II [1948] VII A, 2, cols. 1529–30). But her husband's agnate relatives may have been concerned about the estates of the children, particularly in view of a remarriage of which they did not approve, and also about the estate which Marcella herself may have inherited from her deceased husband (see M. Humbert, *Le Remarriage à Rome. Étude d'histoire juridique et social* [Milan: Guiffre 1972]). They are probably the scoundrels who caused Porphyry and Marcella so much difficulty at the beginning of their marriage. Their jealous behavior, slanderous remarks, and attempts on Porphyry's life (1.18–20) imply that they had no legal basis to exert pressure on the couple.

dimensions, which made her independent, theoretically and practically, within the structure of the οἶκος. But even more importantly, it provided her training in the asceticism necessary for the contemplative ascent to the divine, the ultimate goal of human existence. In this regard, Porphyry's absence may have been as important for Marcella now as his presence was for her earlier.

Porphyry and Marcella's marriage also served as a paradigm of the philosophic life. Porphyry's divinely sanctioned trip, which necessitated his absence from home (4), modeled the soul's descent into the body at the command of god. His subsequent efforts to return he likened to the effort the soul must make to return to its true home. (6, 7, 8, 9, 10, 25, 26, 33) In comparing Marcella to the wounded Philoctetes, Porphyry acknowledged that Marcella's wound was not physical but consisted in the recognition of the nature and extent of the fall of the soul in the process of coming-to-be. But unlike Philoctetes, who could not count on his gods to rescue him, Marcella had the hope of salvation from the gods. (5)

Porphyry claimed initially that he did not marry Marcella for wealth, comfort or honor (9, 34); subsequently he denounced wealth as detrimental to the ascent of the soul (14, 27), comfort and ease as antithetical to the ascent (5, 6, 12), and honor as due to God, not man.(23) The plots, hostilities, and physical dangers he faced at the hands of Marcella's kin were paralleled by the coercive power of physical nature and the emotions upon the soul. (6, 7, 33) And his efforts to free Marcella from every attempt to dominate her (3) mirrored the effort the individual must make to free the soul from the captivity of the passions through the practice of philosophy. (9, 34)

Porphyry called Marcella his σύνοικος. (1, 3, 4)[39] Later he used the same term to describe the relationship of God to the pure soul (20), as well as of the evil daimons to the wicked soul. (21) He also paralleled himself as Marcella's father, husband, teacher, and kin (6) to the Intelligence, her teacher and savior, nurse, guardian, and leader in the spiritual realm. (26) He carefully admonished her not to regard his presence as essential to her attempt to live the philosophical life, however, since the indwelling Intelligence makes her self-sufficient and independent of all other external goods. (5, 8, 9, 28, 30)

Thus, the marriage of Porphyry and Marcella had the important positive benefit of helping them, experientially, to reflect on the paradigm of human existence provided in the Neoplatonic tradition, and it renewed, rather than weakened, their commitment to the pursuit of that vision of the divine which was its ultimate goal. The *Ad Marcellam* is Porphyry's carefully constructed effort to persuade Marcella, despite his absence, to remain true to the goal of their marriage, the pursuit of the philosophic life.

[39] For the use of this term and its cognates for "spiritual marriage," see K. O'B. Wicker, "'The Politics of Paradise' Reconsidered" (supra n. 31).

PAUL WROTE FROM THE HEART

Philippians & Galatians

A New Translation in Straightforward English

Raymond V. Schoder, S.J.

Original Greek Text with apparatus criticus • Facing new English translation.
New explanatory notes • References to parallel passages in NT and OT

ISBN 0-86516-181-X Cloth $24.50 ISBN 0-86516-194-1 Paper $12.00

From the Translator's Preface:

This *new English translation* attempts to be in "full color," conveying in the language all the myriad facets of the author's statement — not just its intellectual content. Otherwise it will be inadequate, no better than a black-and-white photo of a sunset, where all the facts are imagined but not the splendor and impact of the original.

Paul wrote from the heart. . . We want to hear Paul in *full stereo*, to get his complete message and share his reactions to it. Paul in Greek has great impact. Paul in English should stir us too. But it has to be Paul who speaks: straight out, excited, sublime, gently human, "high" on Christ.

The Greek Text is reprinted from *The Greek New Testament*, edited by Aland, Black, Martini, Metzger, and Wickgren, third edition.

From the Publisher:

This new translation had been originally prepared for inclusion in the revision of the New Testament of the New American Bible. Because of editorial differences, Schoder withdrew his translation. It was a courageous and highly principled act to give up voluntarily being published by such a prestigious and official organ of the Catholic Church. Bolchazy-Carducci Publishers, in the interest of philology, published Schoder's translation intact (facing the original Greek) because its editor and readers believed it represented a superior degree of fidelity to and understanding of Paul's Greek; the mythological world-view of his times; his social, economic, religious, political, and philosophic milieu; and Paul's passionate addiction to Christ. Schoder knew these various "textual" languages, and he also knew the geography and topography of Paul's world. Thus he had the resources to try to capture Paul in "full color" and in "full stereo."

Tolle, Lege, et Confer.

ANCIENT GREECE FROM THE AIR

AN OLYMPIC VIEW

The Story Behind Schoder's Slides

Standing at the open door of an aging DC3 is not exactly Father Raymond Schoder's idea of fun, but it was the only way the Jesuit classicist could get the aerial shots he wanted of Greece's major archaeological sites.

Of the 2,000 photos he took, 175 — the cream of the crop — are now available as slides for purchase, including 140 which are published in his book, *Wings Over Hellas*.

Schoder dedicated these slides to the officers and pilots of the Hellenic Air Force, "whose friendly and effective cooperation made this book possible." All of the 175 slides were taken during 13 flights in Greek Air Force planes made between 1962 and 1968.

For each trip, Father Schoder would tie himself to the inside floor of the plane with a six-foot strap adjusted to allow him to stand or kneel at the edge of the open door of the plane. He used a small hand-held 35mm camera with several lenses — no professional or special air photo equipment. Most of the views were taken at an oblique angle, not directly down as in air mapping.

"This allows much better results for my purpose, which is not a ground plan but a meaningful perspective of a whole site from on high," explains Father Schoder. As Father Schoder puts it in the introduction to the book, this enables the reader to see Greece as the ancient gods did on their way down from Mt. Olympus.

The theatre at Epidaurus.

"The aim of these 175 slides," says Father Schoder, "is to present all important excavated sites of ancient Greece, both mainland and islands, from Minoan to Roman times, from the advantageous aerial point of view as a new aid to archaeology and to historical studies as well as to visitors at the sites. This air photo approach should bring a new perspective towards understanding ancient Greece."

Students, travelers, all who love Hellas and any who cannot resist handsome, clarifying images of famous places will find delight in these slides. Little has escaped the author.

—Scientific American

SCHODER'S SLIDES
Ancient Greece from the Air
WINGS OVER HELLAS
Are Now Available

FROM

BOLCHAZY-CARDUCCI PUBLISHERS

Duplicate slides of all the widely-admired and unique air photos of Greek archaeological sites published by Raymond V. Schoder, S.J. in his book, *WINGS OVER HELLAS: ANCIENT GREECE FROM THE AIR* (Thames & Hudson/Oxford, 1974), are now available. Also *35 new views not in the book* — additional sites or different perspectives on sites in the book. (This book is also available at $10.00 *only* with the purchase of these slides.)

These 35mm color slides are made directly from the originals by a Kodak authorized lab on SLIDE DUPLICATING FILM (#5071) — giving better quality and color fidelity than the plates in the book. And they will not soon fade or turn red or brown, like less expensive copies.

A numbered list of all the 175 slides is below. Corresponding numbers are on the slide mounts for identification of each site. Numbers 1-140 are also correlated with the book, *ANCIENT GREECE FROM THE AIR (AGFA)*.

Use of these slides in publication is restricted by copyright, 1987, to those who obtain a prior license from Bolchazy-Carducci Publishers.

CATALOGUE
COLOR SLIDES: ANCIENT GREECE FROM THE AIR (AGFA)

Set A
(Pages Refer to AGFA)

1. AEGINA: Aphaia Temple (p. 17)
2. AIGOSTHENA: (p. 18)
3. HAGHIA TRIADA: And Context (p. 20)
4. HAGHIA TRIADA: Close Up Detail (p. 21)
5. AMPHIAREION: (p. 23)
6. AMPHIPOLIS: from N (p. 24)
7. ARGOS: City (p. 26)
8. ARGOS: Aspis (p. 27)
9. ATHENS: General (p. 29)
10. ATHENS: Acropolis, from SW (p. 33 top)
11. ATHENS: Acropolis, from SE (p. 33 bottom)
12. ATHENS: Agora (p. 35)
13. ATHENS: Roman Agora (p. 37 top)
14. ATHENS: Olympieion (p. 37 bottom)
15. ATHENS: Stadium (p. 39)
16. ATHENS: Kerameikos (p. 41)
17. ABDERA: (p. 43)
18. AULIS: Harbors (p. 44)
19. DELPHI: Setting (p. 46)
20. DELPHI: Sanctuary General (p. 49)
21. DELPHI: Stadium, to Itea (p. 51)
22. DELPHI: Marmaria (p. 52)
23. DELOS: All, from High (p. 55 top)
24. DELOS: Center, from SE (p. 55 bottom)
25. DELOS: Center, from W (p. 57)
26. DELOS: Center, from E (p. 59)
27. DONONA: Theater, Temples (p. 61)
28. ELEUSIS: from SW (p. 63)
29. EPIDAUROS: All, from N (p. 65)
30. EPIDAUROS: Theater, Oblique View (p. 67)
31. EPIDAUROS: Theater, Straight Down (p. 69)
32. ERETRIA: General, from E (p. 70)
33. PHAISTOS: General, from SE (p. 73 top)
34. PHAISTOS: Palace Close, from N (p. 73 bottom)
35. PHYLE: Fort, from N (p. 74)

Set B
(Pages Refer to AGFA)

36. PHILIPPI: General, from SE (p. 76 top)
37. PHILIPPI: Center Close, from NW (p. 77 bottom)
38. GLA: General, from SW (p. 79)
39. GLA: Palace Close, from NE (p. 80)
40. GORTYN: Odeion, Agora, from E (p. 81)
41. GORTYN: Other Ruins, from E (p. 82)
42. GOURNIA: General, from N (p. 85)
43. HALIEIS: General, from SW (p. 87)
44. HALIEIS: Submerged Shore Structures, from S (p. 88)
45. CHALCIS: Site and Euripus Strait (p. 91)
46. ARGIVE HERAION: Temples, Detail, from NE (p. 93 top)
47. ARGIVE HERAION: Temples, Detail, from SW (p. 93 bottom)
48. CHAERONEA: Acropolis, Theater, from NE (p. 95)
49. CHAERONEA: Lion Monument (p. 96)
50. ISTHMIA: General, from W (p. 99 top)
51. ISTHMIA: Theater, Temple Close (p. 99 bottom)
52. ITHACA: Polis Bay (p. 101)
53. ITHACA: Upper Half of Island, from S (p. 102)
54. KABEIRION: Near Thebes, from N (p. 105)
55. KALYDON: Temples, from W (p. 107 top)
56. KALYDON: Heroon, etc., from W (p. 107 bottom)
57. KEA: Haghia Irini and Bay, from W (p. 109)
58. KEA: Haghia Irini Close (p. 111)
59. KENCHREAI: Harbor Ruins under Water, from S (p. 113)
60. CORFU: Palaiokastritsa, from NW (p. 114)
61. KNOSSOS: Context with Valley and Sea (p. 116)
62. KNOSSOS: Palace Close, from NE (p. 119)
63. CORINTH: Central Area, from NW (p. 121)
64. CORINTH: Demeter Sanctuary (p. 123 top)
65. CORINTH: Gymnasium Area, from NE (p. 123 bottom)
66. COS: Agora and Harbor Area, from SW (p. 125)
67. COS: Asklepeion, from NW (p. 126)
68. LERNA: and Bay, from E (p. 128)
69. LINDOS: Acropolis, from NW (p. 131 top)
70. LINDOS: Acropolis and Cliff, from SE (p. 131 bottom)

Set C
(Pages Refer to AGFA)

71. MALLIA: Context, from SE (p. 133 top)
72. MALLIA: Palace, from NW (p. 133 bottom)
73. MANTINEIA: Wall, from NE (p. 135)
74. MANTINEIA: Agora, Temples, Theater, from N (p. 136)
75. MARATHON: From Coast to Mountains, from SE (p. 139)
76. MAGALOPOLIS: Theater, Thersilion, from N (p. 141)
77. MESSENE: Sebasteion, Temple Court, from SE (p. 143)
78. MESSENE: Temple Area, from NE (p. 144)
79. MYCENAE: Citadel, from NW (p. 147 top)
80. MYCENAE: Citadel, from SW (p. 147 bottom)
81. NAXOS: Strongyle Islet, Temple, from W (p. 149)
82. NAXOS: Harbor Area, from SW (p. 150)
83. NEMEA: Temple, etc., from E (p. 153 top)
84. NEMEA: Temple Close, from SE (p. 153 bottom)
85. NIKOPOLIS: Stadium, Theater, from NW (p. 155)
86. NIKOPOLIS: Byzantine Area, Wall, from N (p. 157)
87. OLYMPIA: Context, from W (p. 159 top)
88. OLYMPIA: Altis, Kronion, from SE (p. 159 bottom)
89. OLYMPIA: Sanctuary Close, from SE (p. 161)
90. OLYMPUS: Summit, from N (p. 163)
91. OLYMPUS: Summit and Mavrolonghos Gorge, from E (p. 164)
92. OLYNTHOS: North Hill, from S (p. 167)
93. OLYNTHOS: Both Hills, from S (p. 168)
94. PELLA: Context, from SW (p. 171 top)
95. PELLA: Houses, from SE (p. 171 bottom)
96. PERACHORA: General, from S (p. 172)
97. PYLOS: Setting, from NE (p. 174 top)
98. PYLOS: Palace, from SW (p. 175 bottom)
99. PIRAEUS: From SE (p. 177)
100. PLATAEA: From SW (p. 179)
101. RHAMNOUS: From W (p. 180)
102. RHODES CITY: Harbor, Knights' Enclosure, from SE (p. 183 top)
103. RHODES CITY: Temple, Odeion, etc., from NE (p. 183 bottom)
104. SALAMIS: Bays, from NE (p. 185)
105. SALAMIS: Bays, from W (p. 186)

Set D
(Pages Refer to AGFA)

106. SAMOS: City, from E (p. 189 top)
107. SAMOS, City, Wall, Harbor, from NW (p. 189 bottom)
108. SAMOS: Heraion, from NW (p. 191)
109. SAMOTHRACE: Center, from SW (p. 193 top)
110. SAMOTHRACE: Center, Close, from E (p. 193 bottom)
111. SPHACTERIA: Bay, from W (p. 195 top)
112. SPHACTERIA: Voidokilia, Island, from N (p. 195 bottom)
113. SICYON: Theater, Temples, from NE (p. 197)
114. SOUNIUM: Promontory Tip, from SW (p. 199)
115. SOUNIUM: Temple, from NW (p. 200)
116. SPARTA: Acropolis, from NW (p. 202)
117. SPARTA: Artemis Orthia Area, from N (p. 203)
118. STRATOS: Temple, from NW (p. 205)
119. TEGEA: Temple, from S (p. 207)
120. THASOS: Port, Agora, from W (p. 209)
121. THASOS: Agora, from W (p. 211)
122. THERMON: From W (p. 212)
123. THERMOPYLAE: Middle Pass, from NW (p. 214)
124. THESSALONIKE: Forum Area, Odeion, from SW (p. 216)
125. THERA: All from High, from W (p. 218)
126. THERA: City Site, from NW (p. 219)
127. THEBES: Ismenion, Apollo Temple, from NW (p. 221)
128. THEBES: Acropolis, from N (p. 223)
129. THORIKOS: Theater, from SW (p. 224)
130. TYLISSOS: From E (p. 226)
131. TENOS: Xombourgos, from SE (p. 227)
132. TENOS: Poseidon/Amphitrite Sactuary, from SE (p. 228)

Set D (continued)

133. TIRYNS: Citadel, from W (p. 230)
134. TROIZEN: Hippolytus, Asclepius Shrines, from W (p. 231)
135. BASSAE: Setting (p. 233 top)
136. BASSAE: Temple Close, from SE (p. 233 bottom)
137. BRAURON: Sanctuary, from N (p. 235)
138. XERXES' CANAL: From SW (p. 237)
139. KATO ZAKROS: Bay, from SE (p. 239 top)
140. KATO ZAKROS: Palace, from SE (p. 239 bottom)

Set E
(Sites Not in Book, or Different Angle Than in Book)

141. AMPHIPOLIS: Close View, from S, of Acropolis, Strymond Bend, Thracian Plain
142. ATHENS: Acropolis, from SE, showing its steep elevation above Pnyx and Agora, which are also seen well
143. ATHENS: Acropolis, from SSE, Close; Good view of Theater, Odeion, Stoa, etc.
144. ATHENS: Close Detailed View of Hadrian's Library and Roman Agora
145. ATHENS: Agora, from NW, with Hephaisteion, Acropolis, Part of Areopagus
146. ATHENS: From SE, High View of Stadium, Olympieion, Zappeion to Syntagma, Acropolis, Agora
147. ATHOS: South Tip of Peninsula (where Persian Wreck), from SE
148. AULIS: From SE, Both Bays, to Chalcis
149. CORINTH: From N, Close of Whole Excavated Area—Temples, Agora, Theater, etc.
150. ACROCORINTH: From W, Byz./Venetian/Turkish Wall (on ancient foundations), with Close View of Great West Gate
151. COS: Ancient City Ruins near Harbor
152. COS: Roman Area Close; Odeion
153. DELPHI: Close View, from S, of Sanctuary, Stadium, Phaidriades, Part of Deep Ravine Below
154. DEMETRIAS: Temple on Hill, from SSW, side view of Theater at foot
155. DEMETRIAS: Close View of Wall, Fort on Acropolis
156. EPIDAUROS: Apollo Maleatas Sanctuary on Knyortion above Theater
157. ELEUSIS: From NE, Close, Ruins, Sea Beyond
158. ELEUTHERAI/PANAKTON: From N, Fortification Wall on Hill above Road Athens-Thebes
159. GLA/ARNE: General View from W far, showing context in Copaic Basin (now drained)
160. ISTHMIA: From E, Close of Theater, Temple Area
161. ITHACA: Vathy Bay and Town, from over Gulf of Molos (NW)
162. LECHAION: From N, of Harbor Area, Christian Basilica
163. LESBOS: Mytilene Acropolis, Fort, City
164. MARATHON: From W, Mound Clear, Plain to Coast
165. MESSENE: NW Corner of Wall, Arcadia Gate
166. MONEMVASIA: Whole Island (ancient Minoa), with Byzantine Ruins, from E
167. NAUPACTUS: General View from S over Gulf of City, Fort on Steep Hill Behind
168. PATMOS: Monastery, Bays Close
169. PELLA: General View of Whole Site: Areas II (1), III (Stoa), I, IV; Baths, Edge of Modern Palaia Pella Town, N. Road
170. SALAMIS: From E, of Strait, Psittalia, Kynosoura, St. George, Perama
171. SICYON: From N, White Cliff below Site; Theater, Temple, Agora, Museum
172. Sounion: Temple Close, from SW
173. TEMPE: Valley and Stream at S. Foot of Olympus
174. THASOS: Athena Poliouchos Temple on Hill above Theater, Close View from E
175. OLYMPIA: From S, Altis, Kronios, Kladeos, Museum

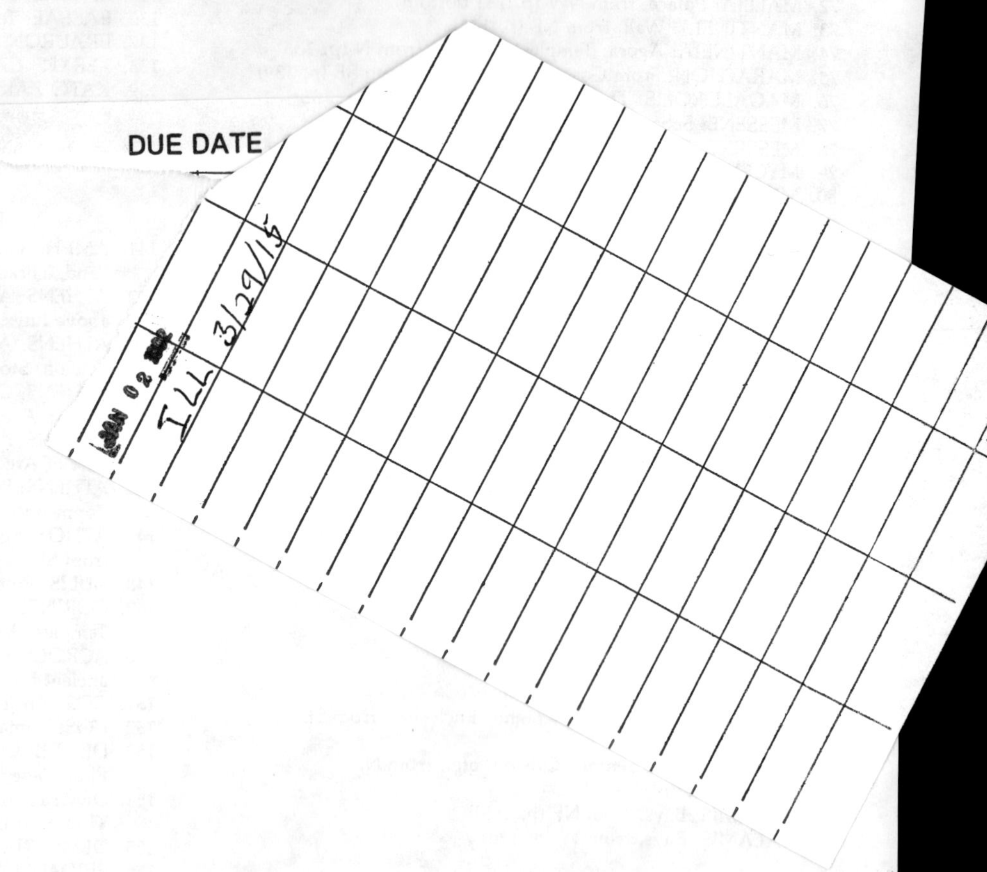